Orderly and Humane

Orderly and Humane

The Expulsion of the Germans after the Second World War

R. M. Douglas

Yale
UNIVERSITY
PRESS
New Haven & London

Published with assistance from the Louis Stern Memorial Fund.

Copyright © 2012 by. R. M. Douglas.
All rights reserved.

This book may not be reproduced, in whole or in part, including illustrations, in any form (beyond that copying permitted by Sections 107 and 108 of the U.S. Copyright Law and except by reviewers for the public press), without written permission from the publishers.

Yale University Press books may be purchased in quantity for educational, business, or promotional use. For information, please e-mail sales.press@yale.edu (U.S. office) or sales@yaleup.co.uk (U.K. office).

Set in Postscript Electra and Trajan types by Tseng Information Systems, Inc.
Printed in the United States of America.

Library of Congress Cataloging-in-Publication Data

Douglas, R. M., 1963–
Orderly and humane : the expulsion of the Germans after the Second World War / R. M. Douglas.
p. cm.
Includes bibliographical references and index.
ISBN 978-0-300-16660-6 (cloth : alk. paper) 1. Population transfers—Germans—History—20th century. 2. Forced migration—Czech Republic—History—20th century. 3. Germans—Czech Republic—Sudentenland—History—20th century. 4. Czechoslovakia—Politics and government—1945–1992. 5. Czechoslovakia—Ethnic relations—History—20th century. 6. World War, 1939–1945—Forced repatriation. I. Title.
D820.P72G426 2012
940.53′14508931—dc23
2011045449

A catalogue record for this book is available from the British Library.

This paper meets the requirements of ANSI/NISO Z39.48-1992 (Permanence of Paper).

10 9 8 7 6 5 4 3 2 1

To my beloved wife, Elizabeth

Contents

Acknowledgments ix

List of Abbreviations xi

Introduction 1

ONE The Planner 7

TWO The *Volksdeutsche* in Wartime 39

THREE The Scheme 65

FOUR The "Wild Expulsions" 93

FIVE The Camps 130

SIX The "Organized Expulsions" 158

SEVEN The Numbers Game 194

EIGHT The Children 229

NINE The Wild West 254

TEN The International Reaction 284

ELEVEN The Resettlement 301

TWELVE The Law 326

THIRTEEN Meaning and Memory 346

Conclusion 363

Notes 375

Bibliography 441

Index 469

Acknowledgments

Considerations of space preclude me from acknowledging more than a handful of the many people who assisted me in the course of a research project that consumed more years than I would have dared to contemplate when commencing it. That this book exists at all is due to three people without whom it certainly would never have seen the light of day. Jane Pinchin, Colgate University's president, was the person whose justifiable impatience with my endlessly reiterated complaints that a work of this kind did not exist led her to insist that I cease grousing and do something about it myself. And the assurance of Sam Stoloff, my magnificent agent at Frances Goldin Literary Agency, that it would find its way into print at a time when I despaired of its ever attracting the attention of anyone other than my family and increasingly put-upon circle of friends — a promise on which he then proceeded in the face of considerable obstacles to make good — boosted my morale at a time when it was running at a low ebb. Above all my wife Elizabeth, my partner in this academic enterprise and much more than that in life, knows how much the appearance of this book owes to her. Its dedication to her is an inadequate form of recompense.

I should also like to express my thanks to some of those who went far out of their way to assist me without thought of reciprocation. I received especially invaluable assistance from Martina Čermáková and Michaela (Misha) Raisová of Charles University in Prague, and from Karolina Papros of the University of Warsaw. The incomparable Fabrizio Bensi and Daniele Palmieri of the Archives du Comité International de la Croix Rouge in Geneva were unfailingly helpful, as was Fania Khan Mohammad of the CICR Library. Mrs. Vlasta Měšťánkova of the National Archives of the Czech Republic provided me with the same unstinting and expert assistance as she does to all who work in this field; and Colonel

Josef Žikeš and his staff at the Military Central Archives in Prague exerted themselves mightily in tracking down relevant material. So too did Amy K. Schmidt, the *Volksdeutsche* specialist at the National Archives and Records Administration in the United States, as well as Paola Casini and Romain Ledauphin of the United Nations Archives, New York City. My former Colgate colleagues Dr. Jim Bjork (now of King's College, London) and Prof. Jonathan Wiesen (Southern Illinois University) read parts of the manuscript in draft, as did Prof. Timothy Waters of the Maurer School of Law at Indiana University; Dr. Kevin White of the University of Portsmouth; Prof. Rob Nemes of Colgate; and Mic Moroney of Dublin. I am deeply grateful to all of them for their expertise, advice, and guidance. I would also like to mention my particular appreciation of the contribution made by Gavin Lewis, whose detailed knowledge and keen editorial skills rescued me from an embarrassing number of mistakes and greatly improved the final product. Lastly, the Colgate University Research Council, through whom I obtained a Mellon Sabbatical Improvement Grant in 2007, ensured that the financial resources necessary to the completion of the book would be forthcoming. I stand indebted to them all, as well as to many others not mentioned here.

ABBREVIATIONS

AAN	Central Archives of Modern Records, Warsaw
ACC	Allied Control Council
ACC (H)	Allied Control Commission (Hungary)
BAK	Bundesarchiv Koblenz
CAB	Cabinet records (Great Britain), in PRO
CAME	Committee Against Mass Expulsions (United States)
CCG (BE)	Control Commission for Germany (British Element)
CICR	Comité International de la Croix Rouge et du Croissant Rouge; Archives du CICR, Geneva
COGA	Control Office for Germany and Austria
CRX	Combined Repatriation Executive
FO	Foreign Office records (Great Britain), in PRO
FRUS	U.S. State Department, *Foreign Relations of the United States* series
HS	Special Operations Executive records (Great Britain), in PRO
IRO	International Refugee Organization
KPD	Communist Party of Germany
LAB	Ministry of Labour records (Great Britain), PRO
MNO	Ministry of National Defense (Czechoslovakia); MNO records, in VÚA
MZO	Ministry for the Recovered Territories (Poland); MZO records, in AAN
MV-NR	Ministry of the Interior (Czechoslovakia), New Registers, in NAČR

NAČR	National Archives of the Czech Republic, Prague
NARA	National Archives and Records Agency, College Park, Maryland
OMG	Office of Military Government
OMGB	Office of Military Government, Bavaria
OMGUS	U.S. Office of Military Government for Germany
PREM	Prime Minister's Private Office records (Great Britain), in PRO
PRO	Public Record Office (Great Britain), Kew, UK
PUR	State Repatriation Office (Poland); PUR records, in AAN
PW & DP	Prisoners of War and Displaced Persons Division
RKFDV	Reich Commissariat for the Strengthening of Germandom
SdP	Sudeten German Party
SNB	Committee of National Security (Czechoslovak secret police)
SOA, Plzeň	State District Archives, Plzeň, Czech Republic
UB	Office of Security (Polish secret police)
UNHCR	Archives of the United Nations High Commission for Refugees, Geneva
UNRRA	United Nations Relief and Rehabilitation Administration
ÚPV	Office of the Prime Minister (Czechoslovakia) records, in NAČR
ÚPV-T	Office of the Prime Minister (Czechoslovakia), confidential records, in NAČR
VoMi	Nazi German *Volksdeutsche Mittelstelle* (Ethnic German Liaison Agency)
VÚA	Military Central Archives, Prague

Introduction

Immediately after the Second World War, the victorious Allies carried out the largest forced population transfer—and perhaps the greatest single movement of peoples—in human history. With the assistance of the British, Soviet, and U.S. governments, millions of German-speaking civilians living in Czechoslovakia, Hungary, and the parts of eastern Germany assigned to Poland were driven out of their homes and deposited amid the ruins of the Reich, to fend for themselves as best they could. Millions more, who had fled the advancing Red Army in the final months of the war, were prevented from returning to their places of origin, and became lifelong exiles. Others again were forcibly removed from Yugoslavia and Romania, although the Allies had never sanctioned deportations from those countries. Altogether, the expulsion operation permanently displaced at least 12 million people, and perhaps as many as 14 million. Most of these were women and children under the age of sixteen; the smallest cohort of those affected were adult males. These expulsions were accomplished with and accompanied by great violence. Tens and possibly hundreds of thousands lost their lives through ill-treatment, starvation, and disease while detained in camps before their departure—often, like Auschwitz I, the same concentration camps used by the Germans during the Second World War. Many more perished on expulsion trains, locked in freight wagons without food, water, or heating during journeys to Germany that sometimes took weeks; or died by the roadside while being driven on foot to the borders. The death rate continued to mount in Germany itself, as homeless expellees succumbed to hypothermia, malnutrition, and other effects of their ordeal. Calculating the scale of the mortality remains a source of great controversy today, but estimates of 500,000 deaths at the lower end of the spectrum, and as many as 1.5 million at the higher, are consistent with the evidence as it exists at present. Much more research will have to be carried out before this range can be narrowed to a figure that can be cited with reasonable confidence.

On the most optimistic interpretation, nonetheless, the expulsions were an immense manmade catastrophe, on a scale to put the suffering that occurred as a result of the "ethnic cleansings" in the former Yugoslavia in the 1990s in the shade. They took place without any attempt at concealment, under the eyes of tens of thousands of journalists, diplomats, relief workers, and other observers with access to modern communications, in the middle of the world's most crowded continent. Yet they aroused little attention at the time. Today, outside Germany, they are almost completely unknown. In most English-language histories of the period they are at best a footnote, and usually not even that. The most recent (2009) edition of Mary Fulbrook's excellent *History of Germany 1918–2008* disposes of the episode in a single uninformative paragraph; the antics of the tiny ultraleftist Red Army Faction in the 1970s and 1980s, in comparison, rate four. The *Cambridge Illustrated History of Germany* is typical in not according the expulsions even a single mention. What is true of German history textbooks is also the case with those dealing with the history of Europe as a whole, and even of the central European states most directly concerned. Joseph Rothschild and Nancy Wingfield's fine survey of the region in the postwar era, *Return to Diversity*—by far the most accessible and reliable one-volume treatment of the subject—takes a cumulative total of less than a page to explain the means by which Poland and Czechoslovakia, until 1939 among the most heterogeneous and multicultural countries in Europe, had just ten years later become ethnic monoliths. It is, then, entirely understandable why so many of my splendid and learned colleagues on the Colgate faculty should have expressed their confusion to me after reading in the newspapers in October 2009 that the president of the Czech Republic, Václav Klaus, had demanded that the other members of the European Union legally indemnify his country against compensation claims by ethnic German expellees, as the price of his country's ratification of the Lisbon Treaty. None had been aware that anything had occurred after the war in respect of which the Czech Republic might require to be indemnified.

It would be incorrect, however, to attribute this pervasive ignorance of the expulsions, their context, and their consequences to any conspiracy of silence. What has occurred in the postwar era is something less calculated in nature, but more insidious in effect: the phenomenon of a historical episode of great significance that is hidden in plain sight. Certainly information, albeit of highly variable quality, on the expulsions is available—for those who possess the requisite language competence and are prepared to go looking for it. A 1989 bibliography lists almost five thousand works dealing with them to some degree in the German language alone. Even today, some sixty-five years later, living expellees are not hard to find; it has been calculated that a quarter of the current German population are expellees or their immediate descendants.[1] What is denied, then, is not the fact of the expulsions but their significance. Relegated in textbooks to a single passing mention in a vaguely phrased sentence referring to the "chaos" existing in Germany in the immediate postwar era, or simply passed over in silence, the impression is effectively conveyed that they occupy a less important place in modern European history than the cultural meanings of football hooliganism or the relevance of the Trabant automobile as a metaphor for East German society.

Why this should be so is not difficult to understand, because any discussion of the expulsions immediately brings to the fore a host of deeply uncomfortable and—still—highly contentious and divisive questions. For Germans themselves it invites debate over the dubious wartime record of the ethnic German minorities living outside the Reich—the so-called *Volksdeutsche*—and the degree to which they can be considered to have drawn their eventual fate upon themselves. For Poles, Czechs, Slovaks, and citizens of other expelling countries, it complicates and undermines a series of national narratives, supported by overwhelming consensus, of Germans exclusively as perpetrators and their own peoples exclusively as victims, as well as raising concerns about the durability of the legal arrangements through which ex-German properties came into the possession of their current owners. For citizens of the Allied countries, and especially those of the United States and Britain, it invites scrutiny of the complicity of their leaders and peoples in one of the largest episodes of mass human rights abuse in modern history, which bore a disturbing resemblance in some respects at least to Nazi Germany's wartime effort to reconfigure the demographic contours of the continent by similar means. The history of the expulsions is one from which few if any of those directly involved emerge in a creditable light. It is not surprising, then, that there should be a great deal of reluctance to try to integrate a messy, complex, morally compromised, and socially disruptive episode that remains to this day a political hot potato into the history of what most people still rightly consider a justified crusade—or, as Americans put it, a "Good War"—against one of the most monstrous regimes of modern times.

In the long run, however, this refusal to engage with the expulsions and their meaning not just for European history but for our contemporary world is unwise as well as unsustainable. For one thing, to do so is in effect to concede the field to individuals like Holocaust "revisionists" who, seeking to equate the expulsions with the extermination of the European Jews as "war crimes" that counterbalance each other, do not scruple to pervert the historical record for their own ends. For another, from a scholarly perspective it ignores the revolution in central European historiography that has been under way since the collapse of the Communist empire in 1989. With the opening of official archives in Poland, the Czech Republic, Slovakia, Hungary, and some at least of the Yugoslav successor states, polemical and ahistorical treatments of the subject have begun to be supplanted by well-researched empirical studies of the policies and processes of expulsion. Although an immense amount of investigation remains to be done in this field, the pioneering studies of scholars like Tomáš Staněk for the Czech lands, Bernadetta Nitschke and Bernard Linek for Poland, Soňa Gabzdilová and Milan Olejník for Slovakia, Vladimir Geiger and Zoran Janjetović for the former Yugoslavia, as well as many others, are accomplishing a transformation in our understanding of the immediate postwar history of central and southeastern Europe. Their work has been broadened and supplemented by an unusually talented cohort of younger Western scholars of the region, among whom the names of Chad Bryant, David Curp, Benjamin Frommer, David Gerlach, Eagle Glassheim, Padraic Kenney, Jeremy King, Andrea Orzoff, and Tara Zahra figure prominently. For all of them, the expulsions and their effects are pivotal factors in explaining what these countries became after the Second World War, and what, despite the fall of Communism, in many respects they remain today. German historians too, working alongside and in cooperation with their counterparts in the countries that were the scene of the expulsions, have made contributions of great importance in this area during the past fifteen years, although paradoxically the justifiable concern of many of them to ensure that discussion of the expulsions does not become the basis for a self-pitying "victim" mentality, in which questions of culpability for Nazi crimes are pushed to the background, has given the debate in that country a sharper tone than elsewhere.

What is lacking at present, however, is a study of the expulsions that examines the episode in the round—from the time of its earliest origins and in all of the countries affected—and that carries the story forward to the present day where it continues to cast a long shadow across European and world events. That is what this book attempts to do. It goes without saying that no single work can hope to encompass the vast range of themes and topics that are involved in such a wide-ranging and multifaceted aspect of European history. In what follows, I have chosen to emphasize certain elements that appeared to me to call for particular attention: among them the mechanics of mass expulsion; the archipelago of "concentration," "internment," and "assembly" camps for ethnic German civilians that sprang up across central Europe after the war; the implications of the expulsions for the development of international law; and the underappreciated part played by the Western Allies in the operation, something that went far beyond mere acquiescence. But I make no pretension here to anything in the nature of an encyclopedic treatment of the subject, even assuming that such a thing were possible in a one-volume survey. Some pieces of the puzzle are still missing, and must await the opening of the relevant archives: in this category especially belongs the full story of the part played by the Soviet Union, as well as events in Romania and the former Yugoslavia. Others, for reasons of time and space, will not receive the detailed scrutiny which some readers may legitimately consider they deserve. Nevertheless, a start must be made somewhere. If, in attempting to come to grips with the complexities of the subject, I can do no more than erect a temporary and somewhat rickety edifice that other historians will (as I hope) supersede with taller, stronger, and more durable constructions of their own, it will have served its purpose.

It is appropriate at the outset to state explicitly that no legitimate comparison can be drawn between the postwar expulsions and the appalling record of German offenses against Jews and other innocent victims between 1939 and 1945. The extent of Nazi criminality and barbarity in central and eastern Europe is on a scale and of a degree that is almost impossible to overstate. In the entire span of human history, nothing can be found to surpass it, nor, with the possible exception of recent revelations about Mao's China, to equal it. Germany's neighbors suffered most grievously and unjustifiably at her hands, and were profoundly traumatized as a result. Whatever occurred after the war cannot possibly be equated to the atrocities perpetrated by Germans during it, and suggestions to the contrary—including those made by expellees themselves—are both deeply offensive and historically illiterate. Nothing I have written in the book should be taken to suggest otherwise.

But it is a long way from there to conclude that the expulsion of the Germans was inevitable, necessary, or justified. The expelling countries, needless to say, maintained that it was all of those things. Both at the time and to the present day, commentators from outside the region, for wholly understandable reasons, have been reluctant to challenge the judgment of peoples who suffered so greatly under German occupation. When we examine closely the record of the largest forcible population transfer in human history, however, we find that the result is a tragic and largely destructive episode that never fulfilled its professed aspirations—even in the extreme circumstances of postwar Europe when, if anything could ever have justified the use of such an expedient, this situation would.

In what follows, I have made relatively little use of first-person testimonies of expellees themselves, of the kind published in the massive German Federal Government *Dokumentation der Vertreibung der Deutschen aus Ost-Mitteleuropa* in the 1950s and 1960s, and the almost equally voluminous compilations by organizations like the *Donauschwäbische Kulturstiftung* in recent times. This is intentional on my part. While it might at first sight seem perverse not to place the voices of those most directly affected by the expulsions to the foreground, the fact that this remains so contentious and emotive a subject for so many people suggested the need for an unusual degree of attention to the matter of verifiability of sources. In the 1950s and 1960s, one of the most common strategies used to dismiss the veracity of events described in works like the *Dokumentation der Vertreibung* was to challenge the credibility of the witnesses. German expellees, it was alleged, had a vested interest in playing up the wrongs done to them as a means of playing down the atrocities for which they shared culpability. The reasoning of Czechoslovak President Edvard Beneš in 1945, that "all German stories should not, of course, be believed, for Germans always exaggerated and were the first to whine and to try to enlist outside sympathy," has been persuasive to many others also. I have therefore made it a rule to exclude direct expellee testimony that is not supported by independent sources. As my research continued, I found that I lost little in doing so, because the broad picture depicted in the *Dokumentation der Vertreibung* was confirmed, and in some cases amplified, by the accounts of humanitarian agencies like the Red Cross; other nongovernmental organizations; Western diplomats and officials; foreign journalists; and, most importantly of all, the archival records of the expelling countries themselves.

1

THE PLANNER

A week after the Munich Conference of September 1938, the Czechoslovak president, Edvard Beneš, composed his letter of resignation. After a quarter of a century at the heart of political life in Czechoslovakia, and almost three years as its unchallenged leader, he had become in the space of seven days a political irrelevance. While the great powers haggled over the future of his country at Munich—Czechoslovakia had not even been invited to send a delegation to the conference—Beneš was made to stand by helplessly, watching his life's work crash in ruins. Two decades previously, as the foreign minister of the Provisional Czechoslovak Government and right-hand man of the Republic's "Father-Liberator," Tomáš Garrigue Masaryk, Beneš had argued, lobbied, and negotiated behind the scenes at the Paris Peace Conference to brilliant effect, securing the great powers' agreement to a larger expanse of territory for the new Czechoslovak state than the most optimistic of his countrymen had dared to imagine. Now he looked on as the same powers accepted Adolf Hitler's demand that the Czechoslovakia he had worked so unsparingly to create and to preserve must be dismembered. More than a quarter of Czechoslovakia's territory—the German-speaking Sudetenland, extending in a broad band along three sides of the country's frontier—and a similar proportion of its population were to be turned over to its aggressive northern neighbor as the price of staving off a new world war. Within a fortnight of the Munich accord, the Czechoslovak government had completely evacuated the Sudetenland, which was immediately divided into *Gaue* (districts) and integrated into the Nazi Reich. What remained of the country, abandoned by its French and British allies, was left to make the best deal it could with Hitler. Having been vilified for six straight months in the Goebbels-controlled Nazi press as Germany's principal external enemy, Beneš knew that he was not the man to undertake that task. He preferred to go into exile, accepting a teaching position at the University of Chicago as his mentor Masaryk, a onetime philosophy professor, had done in the years before the Great War.

Although world opinion sympathized with Beneš over the manner in which he had been driven from office, a general consensus held that, as the London *Times* put it, the transfer of territory to Germany had been "both necessary and fundamentally just."[1] The people of the Sudetenland—like the Czechs and Slovaks, citizens of the Austro-Hungarian Empire until its collapse in 1918—had never been consulted as to whether they wanted to be part of Czechoslovakia. If they had been, their overwhelming preference would have been to join their fellow German-speakers in the postwar Austrian state. Even in 1919, Allied diplomats had worried that giving the Sudetenland to Czechoslovakia—making the Germans the second largest nationality within the Republic and relegating the Slovaks to a distant third place—would be to strain the assimilative capacity of the infant state too far. Harold Nicolson, a member of the British delegation at the Paris Peace Conference, recorded his anxiety "about the future political complexion of the Czech State if they have to digest solid enemy electorates, plus an Irish Party in Slovakia, plus a Red Party in Ruthenia, to say nothing of their own extreme socialists."[2] But Beneš and Masaryk had carried the day over these objections. While Czechoslovak troops created "facts on the ground" by forcibly suppressing the provisional governments established in each of Bohemia and Moravia's four German provinces at the end of 1918, the two leaders persuaded the Allies that only a strong Czechoslovakia could check the revival of German hegemony in central Europe. The Sudetenland with its vibrant export-oriented industries, they argued, was vital to Czechoslovakia's economic prosperity. Without it the country would be strategically indefensible, vulnerable to attack from the north, west, and south. Somewhat against their better judgment, and in contradiction of Woodrow Wilson's professed commitment to the principle of self-determination, the Allies assented, as the British prime minister David Lloyd George would ruefully recall, to the incorporation in the new state of "hundreds of thousands of protesting Magyars and some millions of angry Germans."[3] Beneš, for his part, promised the Allies that independent Czechoslovakia would become a model multinational state. The rights of the *Sudetendeutsch* minority would benefit from the most comprehensive system of protection in domestic and international law in Europe. German, he declared, would become "the second language of the country," and in public affairs would stand "on equal footing with Czech." Sudeten rights would be safeguarded by a nationality law based on the principles of the Swiss constitution. Proportional representation would prevent the Germans from being subjected to the tyranny of the Czech majority.

In the event, the record of the First Republic never lived up to these lofty aspirations. Although Czechoslovakia's constitution declared the equality of all citizens "without consideration of race, language or religion," in reality an ever-present tension existed between "the ideal of building up a State on a modern, democratic basis . . . and the psychologically comprehensible but in practice self-destructive tendency to transform that State into an instrument of Czech and Slovak nationalism."[4] Little was done to make good on Beneš's undertaking to the Allies at Paris to convert Czechoslovakia into "a sort of Switzerland." And indeed, to have done so would have required a degree of generosity and far-sightedness of which few Czechs—not even Beneš himself—fully recognized the necessity. It would also have made the Republic into a very different kind of country from the one of which Czech nationalists had dreamed. Under the Austro-Hungarian Empire, Czech and—to an even greater degree—Slovak speakers had received scant consideration at the hands of the dominant German and Magyar linguistic groups. Now the boot was on the other foot, and the temptation to reply in kind was almost irresistible. Even the popular and conciliatory Tomáš Masaryk, himself the son of a Czech-German mother and who grew up speaking German more fluently than Czech, had sometimes displayed a degree of triumphalism, in his inaugural address referring infelicitously to his *Sudetendeutsch* fellow-citizens as "immigrants and colonists."[5] Many Czechoslovaks, less diplomatic than he, made no secret of their conviction that German-speakers, the human residue of an alien and oppressive culture, had no place in their new Republic. If the Germans were a minority within Czechoslovakia, moreover, the Czech people never forgot that they were a small linguistic island in a larger Germanic sea extending across central Europe in which they were outnumbered by more than ten to one. The concept of "Czechoslovakia" was itself a fragile structure, to which even a large proportion of Slovaks were not fully reconciled. To try to accommodate the cultural idiosyncrasies of yet another people might sow the seeds of separatism, and eventually of national disintegration.

After the Munich conference, Czechoslovakia's many Western defenders unanimously asserted, in the words of one of their number, that "these German-Bohemians were the best-treated minority in Europe."[6] The truth was more complicated. Certainly the Sudeten Germans were never the targets of a systematic government-directed persecution, though physical attacks on *Sudetendeutsche* and their institutions and symbols were far from uncommon during the Republic's early years. But neither were they treated on anything like terms of equality.[7]

By a variety of means, the state from above and Czech nationalists from below tried to eliminate manifestations of German culture, especially by using administrative expedients to drive down the number of officially registered "Germans" in each district below the critical 20 percent threshold that, under Czechoslovak law, entitled minority populations to formal recognition. Thus, as Tara Zahra notes, "Thousands of citizens who professed to be Germans on the census of 1921 were subject to interrogations, fines, and imprisonment for illegally declaring a 'false' nationality." The fines involved were usually modest, typically a week's salary for an ordinary worker, and the periods of imprisonment brief. Nevertheless, "in all the cases in which individuals were fined or imprisoned for declaring a false nationality, self-declared Germans were changed into Czechs."[8] When the next census was taken in 1930, ethnic manipulation occurred on an even larger scale. One investigation by the Ministry of the Interior found that enumerators in Brno had forged 1,145 signatures and reclassified another 2,377 individuals so as to reduce the town's German population to a whisker below the 20 percent threshold. The central government in Prague, for its part, attempted to dilute the ethnic composition of the Sudetenland by posting Czech civil servants and their families there; dismissing tens of thousands of German public servants either for their inability to pass newly required examinations in Czech language and culture or in response to denunciations (which were officially encouraged and received on a massive scale), and replacing them with Czech functionaries; and selectively closing German schools. Lastly, a controversial land reform program benefited Czech and Slovak farmers at the expense of their German- and Magyar-speaking counterparts: "a social policy in its original intention," in Zbyněk Zeman's summation, "became, in its execution, a national policy."[9] Between the wars, Zahra concludes, "Czech nationalists finally enjoyed the opportunity to realize nationalist fantasies unchecked by the moderating influence of a neutral state."[10]

In spite of this unpromising beginning, as the new Republic began to stabilize a real possibility existed that Czechs and Germans, given enough time, would reach a mutually satisfactory modus vivendi in their new country. Tomáš Masaryk, one of the few members of the majority population to recognize the dangers of driving the *Sudetendeutsche* into a corner, dedicated himself as president to diminishing Czechoslovak chauvinism and German separatism alike. By the mid-1920s, these efforts had begun to bear fruit. In the 1925 elections, the "rejectionists" among the *Sudetendeutsch* population, who denied the legitimacy of the state and vowed to take no part in it, were decisively outnumbered by the "activists," who aimed at striking the best possible deal for the German population within the framework of the Republic. The "activists" were strengthened by the support they received from Berlin. Unlike the German territories lost to Poland under the Treaty of Versailles, the Sudetenland had never formed part of the Reich. The Weimar Republic's leaders were therefore relatively undisturbed by its inclusion in Czechoslovakia. Some of the more far-sighted among them, like Gustav Stresemann, could perceive definite advantages in having a substantial pro-German element represented in the Prague government, which would serve Berlin's interests in central Europe far better than the addition of a few million more German-speakers to Austria's population. Consequently, the German government encouraged *Sudetendeutsch* leaders to play a full part in the political life of Czechoslovakia. Relations between the two communities underwent a definite thaw, assisted by the fact that many Sudeten Germans recognized that their own conditions compared favorably to those of their co-linguists in inflation-ridden, war-debt-burdened and politically unstable Germany. In 1926 Franz Spina, a Sudeten German parliamentarian who served twice as a minister in the Czechoslovak government, told a French newspaper, "We have lived with the Czechs for a thousand years, and through economic, social, cultural and even racial ties, we are so closely connected with them that we form one people. To use a homely metaphor: we form different strands of the same carpet."[11]

Unfortunately this positive momentum was not sustained. When the ailing and elderly Masaryk stepped down from the presidency in 1935, he carried away much of the *Sudetendeutsch* community's goodwill with him. In contrast to the charismatic Father-Liberator, Edvard Beneš, his long-time heir apparent, seemed a colorless and uninspiring replacement. Across the political spectrum, Czechoslovaks paid tribute to Beneš's intelligence, diligence, and efficiency. In administrative ability he stood head and shoulders above his peers. But if his talents were those of the skilled bureaucrat, so too were his flaws. Thin-skinned, intensely self-righteous, cold, and prone to bearing grudges, he was to prove an unfortunate choice as Masaryk's successor. His own secretary, Jaromír Smutný, acknowledged that although a "brilliant master of tactics and strategy, the greatest Machiavelli of our time . . . he is unable to awaken the enthusiasm of the masses. . . . People leave him persuaded, but not feeling entirely with him, full of confidence but without affection."[12] Beneš also had a tendency toward political *idées fixes* that would twice prove disastrous for his country. An ardent Francophile, between the wars he placed his complete trust in the relationship between Prague and Paris, only to be abandoned by the French at Munich. A similar disillusionment lay in his future, after he transferred his unquestioning and unrequited confidence to the Soviet Union. The Sudeten German population's attitude to Beneš, hence, was at best one of reserve. It was suspicious of his efficient public relations network that ceaselessly reiterated to Western Europeans what they wanted to hear about Czechoslovakia's and its president's exemplary liberal and democratic credentials—an image it knew to be more than a little rose-colored.[13] It recognized him as a committed Czech nationalist, whose regard for minority rights owed more to pragmatism than conviction. And it had little confidence that in any situation in which Czechoslovak and *Sudetendeutsch* interests were in conflict, Beneš would treat the two communities even-handedly and impartially. When the resolution to confirm Beneš in the presidency was put before the Prague parliament in 1935, not a single *Sudetendeutsch* deputy voted in favor.

The differential impact of the Great Depression on Czech and German communities intensified the Sudetenland's sense of alienation. As one of the most export-dependent parts of the country, the Sudetenland was hard hit by the contraction in international trade. But the Prague government added greatly to the region's distress by its practice of preferring Czechs for public-sector jobs, dismissing thousands of *Sudetendeutsch* workers in the process. Germans, more than 23 percent of the population in the 1930 census, five years later made up only 2 percent of the civil servants in ministerial positions, 5 percent of the officer corps in the army, and 10 percent of the employees of the state railways.[14] Not a single ethnic German was to be found in Beneš's own Foreign Ministry.[15] State contracts, even for projects in the German-speaking districts, were steered toward Czechoslovak firms. By 1936, more than 60 percent of all Czechoslovak unemployment was concentrated in the Sudetenland.[16] No less injurious to German sensibilities was Prague's dismissive response to their complaints of discrimination. It was unreasonable, Czech leaders argued, for the *Sudetendeutsche* to complain about their exclusion from public-sector employment while they remained equivocal in their loyalty to the very state that they expected to pay their wages. Germans, on the other hand, recalled that Czechoslovakia had come into existence as a result of Czech and Slovak soldiers deserting from the Austro-Hungarian army during the Great War and forming a Czechoslovak Legion to join the conflict on the Allied side against their former comrades in arms. For Beneš and his followers, with their record of disloyalty to the Hapsburg Empire at a moment when it was fighting for its life, to preach to anyone else about minority nationalities' duty of fidelity to countries to which they had been unwillingly attached seemed to most *Sudetendeutsche* the epitome of hypocrisy.

In 1933 a new factor emerged to complicate Czechoslovakia's internal politics: the accession to power of Adolf Hitler's Nazi regime in Germany. In the same year, Konrad Henlein founded a new party in the Sudetenland, the *Sudetendeutsche Heimatfront*. Militant, populist, and openly hostile to Prague, Henlein's movement grew steadily more assertive and confrontational in response to the rise of its powerful patron in Berlin. To this day, historians remain divided over whether the *Heimatfront*—soon to rename itself the *Sudetendeutsche Partei* (SdP) and to claim to speak on behalf of all Sudeten Germans—was from the outset a Nazi front organization or merely attached itself to Hitler's bandwagon for pragmatic reasons.[17] Most authorities share the view of Mark Cornwall that at least until 1937, the SdP "drew its strengths and weaknesses from being a broad church, encompassing diverse elements of the German community and a range of political outlooks."[18] However that may be, Henlein's party quickly became the principal vehicle for the expression of Sudeten Germans' discontent with the existing dispensation in Czechoslovakia. In the 1935 elections—the same ones that brought Beneš to power—it won two-thirds of the vote in German districts, aided by large subventions from Berlin, and became the single largest party in the Republic. Equally, there is no question that after the *Anschluss* between Germany and Austria in the spring of 1938, Henlein, and his still more unsavory deputy Karl Hermann Frank, were anything other than Nazi puppets, nor that most Sudeten Germans by then favored the inclusion of their region within the Reich. Such views, to be sure, were no means universal. Social Democracy was strong within the industrial Sudetenland, and many workers were only too conscious of what would befall their trade union rights if they fell into the hands of Adolf Hitler. Partly for that reason, one of the most prominent Sudeten German Social Democrats, Wenzel Jaksch, twice visited London in 1937 on behalf of the Prague government to counter Henlein's claims that there was no place for Germans in a Czechoslovak-dominated state. In March of the following year, Jaksch assumed the leadership of the SdP's principal left-wing opponent, the *Sudetendeutsche Sozialdemokratische Partei*. But it is a measure of how much ground it had already lost to Henlein that Jaksch's party was forced to drop its previous demand for Germans to receive their own autonomous region within the Czechoslovak Republic for fear that, if granted, this would have the effect of delivering the Sudetenland over to the Reich.

Ultimately, though, Czechoslovakia's fate would be decided by outsiders. From the moment of his assumption of leadership over the infant National Socialist party in 1920, Adolf Hitler had never ceased to highlight the incompatibility of the territorial provisions of the Treaty of Versailles with the aims for which the Allies had professed to fight the Great War. The existence of Czechoslovakia in its current form, he insisted, was unanswerable proof of the victors' hypocrisy. While preaching the virtues of democracy and of the rights of small nations to determine their own future, the Allies had sanctioned the creation of a state that held millions of unwilling subjects under its control by sheer force. To be sure, the leaders at the Paris Peace Conference had not needed a Hitler to remind them of the imperfect fit between Czechoslovakia's frontiers and Wilsonian principles, but "because the existence of a Slav state bang in the middle of ethnic German territory was central to the Franco-British vision of how postwar Central Europe should be reorganized, everyone was at first willing to overlook the contradictions."[19]

By 1938 these were harder to ignore. Nazi Germany's absorption of Austria in March—another exercise of "self-determination"—placed Czechoslovakia in grave peril. No longer did it share a single short border with Germany to its northwest and west, but now was virtually encircled by a greater German Reich extending along approximately half the length of its northern and southern frontiers also. Estranged from its other immediate neighbors, Poland and Hungary, by ethnic antagonisms similar to those involving the *Sudetendeutsche*—neither Warsaw nor Budapest had forgiven or forgotten the cultural and economic discrimination to which the Magyar-speaking population in southern Slovakia and the Polish minority in the Teschen [Těšín] district were subject—Czechoslovakia found itself lacking friends at a moment when it needed them most. Even its allies considered it had a weak case. Though France and Czechoslovakia had had a treaty of mutual assistance since 1924, Édouard Daladier, the prime minister, did not believe that most French citizens would understand why, as the law professor and commentator Joseph Barthélemy put it, there must be a general European war "to maintain three million Germans under Czech sovereignty." The Soviet Union, which had concluded a mutual defense treaty with Prague in 1935 safe in the knowledge that the two countries did not share a common border, sat on its hands throughout the Munich crisis; no evidence has ever emerged to substantiate the Czechoslovak Communist Party leader's self-serving and incredible claim ten years later that Stalin undertook to go to war with Germany to defend Czechoslovakia even if France did not do so.[20] As for Great Britain, "appeasers" and "anti-appeasers" alike agreed that the Sudeten Germans' claim to determine their own allegiance was justified, differing only as to how it should be given effect. Even Winston Churchill told Hubert Ripka, one of Beneš's closest associates, in the summer of 1938 that if he had been prime minister he would have acted as Neville Chamberlain had done, and after Munich carefully avoided suggesting that the *Sudetendeutsche* should not have had the right to choose to which country to belong, but instead maintained that any lines of demarcation ought to have been drawn by the League of Nations rather than Adolf Hitler.[21]

For that reason, although international public opinion lavished praise upon Edvard Beneš as he prepared to go into exile—the former French prime minister Léon Blum, the novelist H. G. Wells, and even the League of Nations all nominated him for the 1939 Nobel Peace Prize—few doubted that his decision was the correct one. Lord Halifax, the British foreign secretary, declared in the House of Lords that even if negotiations at Munich had broken down and a war had resulted, "no body of statesmen drawing the boundaries of a new Czechoslovakia would have redrawn them as they were left by the Treaty of Versailles."[22] Gallup polls revealed popular majorities in Britain and France, and a still larger one in the United States, in favor of the Munich Pact. Little notice was taken of the true victims of the agreement, Czechoslovak Jews and anti-Nazi *Sudetendeutsche*. Both now faced persecution, not only from the Nazis but from their own countrymen who, as Beneš passed from the scene, set up the short-lived Second Republic under the presidency of the ineffectual Emil Hácha. Though it lasted only for six months, Mary Heimann warns against ignoring the Second Republic's history, which was "a crucially important period in turning Czechoslovakia from an imperfectly democratic to a frankly authoritarian state, one whose central and autonomous governments ruled by decree, promoted racism, neutralized political opponents, rigged elections, set up forced labor camps, and persecuted Jews and Gypsies, all before any of this could plausibly be blamed on Nazi Germany."[23] While unable to take a line opposed to that of Berlin in foreign or economic policy, Hácha's regime was far from a Nazi puppet. Rather, it was in part an expression of forces latent in Czechoslovak society that until then had lacked the opportunity to reach their mature form. It was Hácha's troops and police, not Hitler's, that rounded up approximately twenty thousand *Sudetendeutsch* anti-Nazis, most of them Social Democrats, and deported them to Germany where they disappeared into concentration camps. (Wenzel Jaksch, leader of the *Sudetendeutsch* Social Democrats, would have joined them had he not fled to London in the spring of 1939.) It was the Slovak government in Bratislava, whose demand for autonomy was backed by Germany as a reward for the Slovaks' anti-Czech stance during the Munich crisis, that first ethnically cleansed the territory under its control, expropriating Jews and Czechs and dumping them into Moravia. And it was the Prague parliament, just before Hitler put an end to the Czechoslovak state on March 15, 1939 by declaring a "protectorate" over Bohemia and Moravia and militarily occupying both provinces, that passed a law providing for the dispatch of all unemployed males over eighteen years of age to forced labor camps. This affinity for extreme solutions to social and economic problems, clearly visible in Czechoslovakia before the war, would manifest itself afterward in new and still more disturbing forms.

The eclipse of the Second Republic in the spring of 1939, and the simultaneous establishment of a nominally independent Republic of Slovakia that, in contrast to its counterpart in Prague, was indeed a German lapdog, gave the exiled Edvard Beneš his opportunity for a comeback. Possessing behind a façade of modesty an absolute and lifelong belief in his own indispensability to Czechoslovak politics, he had departed his homeland for the United States with three firm convictions. The first was that there would soon be a world war, "perhaps next year or perhaps in two or three years' time," that would both put an end to Nazi Germany and justify his own policy at Munich.[24] The second was that as a result, the Soviet Union would become the leading factor in European affairs; in consequence, it was important that Czechoslovakia and the USSR not only maintain the closest possible relationship but that the two countries share a common border.[25] The third was that the political and economic changes the war would inevitably bring in its train would provide a once-in-a-lifetime opportunity to complete the Czechoslovak national project, and that the solution of the minority problem though mass expulsions constituted the only possible means to that end.[26] Beneš would set his political course by these three beliefs, but especially the last, for the remainder of his life.

It was typical of his unwavering self-confidence—or, in the eyes of his critics, arrogance—that he should soon persuade himself that he had not, after all, ceased to be Czechoslovakia's president. As long as the Second Republic remained in existence, there was no possibility of arguing that his resignation in October 1938 had been made under duress and was thus invalid. The Western countries had already recognized Hácha's government and established diplomatic relations with it. Even though juridically the Hácha regime continued to exist after the German occupation of March 1939, however, the de facto extinction of the Second Republic was seen by a majority of Czechoslovaks as a vindication of Beneš's stance at Munich. As it appeared to prove, there had after all been no possibility of inducing the democracies to honor their commitments to Czechoslovakia's territorial integrity; Beneš's decision not to lead his people into a suicidal war but rather to live to fight another day had been the correct one. The ex-president could also count on the assistance of many supporters who remained in influential positions in the Czech bureaucracy, and with whom he remained in frequent contact through back channels. Even the unheroic Hácha, who for all his instinctive authoritarianism was neither a pro-Nazi nor an antipatriot, kept in touch with his predecessor with the help of intermediaries.

When the Second World War commenced, then, Beneš was well placed to resume his self-appointed role as the embodiment of the Czechoslovak national will. His plan of campaign was broadly the same as it had been during the Great War. With a network of émigré organizations, an army in exile, and an underground resistance movement in Czechoslovakia itself at his command, he would seek to exchange material assistance to the Allies for recognition as the country's true leader. Taking advantage of his unrivaled network of personal contacts with

Western politicians and opinion-formers, he would contrive, as he had done in 1918 and 1919, to make the eventual peace settlement as favorable as possible to Czechoslovakia's interests. After his restoration to power in Prague, he would secure the country from future external threats by forging an alliance with a powerful neighbor with similar strategic aims—no longer equivocal and unreliable France, but a Soviet Union that, he was confident, was rapidly outgrowing its truculent Communist phase and was as anxious as he to see Czechoslovakia emerge as the principal conduit of a postwar "convergence" between East and West.

Beneš would live just long enough to see this vision, which in naïveté rivaled that of the conservative German politicians who elevated Adolf Hitler to power in 1933 in the belief that they could control him, collapse in ruins for the second time in his ill-starred public career. At the outset, though, the auguries were promising. Through the good offices of his friend Hamilton Fish Armstrong, editor of the influential American journal *Foreign Affairs*, he obtained a private meeting with Franklin D. Roosevelt at Hyde Park in May 1939 and obtained from the president's own lips a declaration that so far as the U.S. administration was concerned, "Munich does not exist." A Czechoslovak National Council was formed in Paris in October, consciously evoking the similarly named body established by Masaryk in the same city in 1916. Initially ignored by the Allies, for whom Czechoslovakia's entire recent history was an embarrassment of which they did not wish to be reminded, the council became more important after the fall of France as one of the few lines of communication Britain still possessed to anti-Nazi movements in occupied Europe. Winston Churchill's administration acknowledged the council as the provisional Czechoslovak government in exile in July 1940; and although the path to complete recognition was far from straightforward, by mid-1941 Britain, the USSR, and the still neutral United States had entered into full diplomatic relations with the Czechoslovak regime in London and accorded Beneš the status appropriate to a friendly head of state. The final mark of his complete restoration in the eyes of the world as Czechoslovakia's sole legitimate leader came a year later when, in response to countless hours of patient lobbying, the presentation of Czechoslovakia's case in every conceivable venue, and unabashed recourse to emotional blackmail, the Big Three in separate declarations stated that they no longer considered themselves bound by the Munich Treaty. It was a moment of personal triumph for Beneš, who made haste to proclaim that Czechoslovakia's unity and territorial integrity had at last been restored. But so too had the Sudeten German problem.

The question of what to do with the *Sudetendeutsche* had not gone overlooked by the British who, as the occasionally somewhat exasperated hosts of the Czechoslovak government in exile, were most immediately concerned with trying to conform Beneš's initiatives to Allied war aims. Philip Nichols, a Foreign Office diplomat appointed in 1942 as British ambassador to—and to a still greater extent, minder of—the London Czechoslovaks, repeatedly made clear to Beneš that the denunciation of the Munich Pact did not necessarily commit the Allies to restore the Czechoslovak borders of September 1938, or indeed any particular borders at all. Throughout the war, the official British stance was that all territorial questions must await the eventual peace conference, when such matters would be examined from a comprehensive perspective and the outline of the new world order would finally be determined. No piecemeal commitments could be entered into in the meantime, especially one that would open the door to a host of similar claims from Poles, Yugoslavs, Danes, and others. Needless to say, this "wait and see" policy was wholly unsatisfactory to Beneš, who had not labored so long and endured so much only to see Czechoslovakia emerge from the war with a less favorable territorial status than it had enjoyed before falling victim to Hitler's aggressions. Even if the 1938 borders were re-created, moreover, the problem of national minorities within Czechoslovakia would still have to be dealt with.

When Beneš had pleaded Czechoslovakia's case before the Allies at Paris in 1919, the idea that the country should embrace the Sudetenland but not the *Sudetendeutsche* had never been seriously considered. Like many of his generation, Tomáš Masaryk reposed great faith in the assimilative capacity of nation-states; he himself had undergone a teenage conversion from a partly Germanic upbringing to a keen Czech cultural nationalism. Economically, the Republic could not have hoped in any reasonable time-frame to make good the loss of the productive capacities of a fourth of its population. In any event, the entire question was rendered moot by the certainty that the Allies would never agree to it. By the late 1930s, though, such things were no longer unthinkable. The exchange of populations between Turkey and Greece under the Treaty of Lausanne in 1922–23 had shown that large-scale movements of peoples were at least possible. Beneš had had the Lausanne example in mind when, in a secret initiative that would have had explosive ramifications had it ever been made public, he offered Hitler on September 15, 1938, some six thousand square kilometers of Czechoslovak territory if the Führer would admit between 1.5 and 2 million *Sudetendeutsche* in a compulsory population transfer as part of the bargain.[27] More concerned with his meeting with Chamberlain at Berchtesgaden the same day, Hitler had not troubled to respond.

Yet Beneš was far from the only Czechoslovak to be thinking along those lines. His chief publicist, Hubert Ripka, was if anything even more determined that the

Sudetendeutsche be removed, predicting that if left unmolested after the war they would shelter within Czechoslovakia just long enough to gain immunity from demands to pay reparations, and then immediately restart separatist agitation.[28] A report from Prague that reached the president a month after Nazi Germany's occupation of Bohemia and Moravia described the popular mood with respect to the *Sudetendeutsche* as "very radical. . . . A thorough reduction in their numbers seems to be a general demand at present."[29] This was, in all likelihood, an exaggeration. ÚVOD, the central council of the Czechoslovak resistance movement, consistently took a more extreme position on postwar matters than the majority of ordinary citizens, a reflection of the predominance of military officers among its membership.[30] Because most of the information he received about domestic public opinion reached him through an ÚVOD filter, however, Beneš was led to believe that his compatriots demanded a harsher line than was probably the case. An example of this tendency came in 1940, when Beneš began to explore the possibility of deporting about a million "young, incorrigible Nazis" and concentrating the remainder of the *Sudetendeutsch* population in three homogeneous Swiss-style cantons. When he floated this idea to the resistance, an infuriated Lieutenant-Colonel Josef Balabán of ÚVOD responded sardonically in a coded radio message, "We look forward to bidding farewell to the dear Hitlerites. We will beat them so hard that the three damned cantons you thought up and for which people here would tear you to pieces will be somewhere near Berlin."[31]

Yet it would be a mistake to see Beneš's stance on the Sudeten German question as being influenced entirely, or even mainly, by pressure from home. Temperamentally he was highly resistant to being pushed by subordinates in directions he did not wish to go, and he did not hesitate to reprove ÚVOD for its naïveté in supposing that "we can simply destroy or wipe out three million Germans . . ."[32] He was also conscious of the indispensability of Allied backing for whatever arrangements would ultimately be made, and in the early stages of the war he knew that a policy that recognized no distinction between "guilty" and "innocent" Germans was unacceptable to them. After the Dunkirk debacle, when the prospect of a conventional military victory over Germany had all but disappeared, one of the few possibilities that encouraged the British government to continue the fight was the hope that Hitler might be overthrown by an anti-Nazi revolution as the economic strain of the war began to tell on ordinary German civilians.[33] Punitive war aims stood in the way of such a scenario, playing into Goebbels's hands by suggesting that the British sought not an end to Nazism but the destruction of the German nation. It was for this reason that Churchill's government had hesitated in 1940 to grant full recognition to Beneš's government in exile, which did not contain a single representative of the

Sudeten German democratic movement in London headed by Wenzel Jaksch. As a sop to the British, Beneš indicated his willingness eventually to offer the *Sudetendeutsch* Social Democrats six seats on the Czechoslovak State Council, a forty-member advisory body; the government in exile itself, though, remained a Czech and Slovak monopoly. For the same reason, he specifically, and mendaciously, denied in meetings with the *Sudetendeutsch* refugees that the rumors flying around London that he and his government were considering mass expulsions of the German population had any foundation.[34]

The entry of the Soviet Union and the United States into the war in 1941, however, changed the equation dramatically, as did the intensifying antagonisms the conflict itself was generating on all sides. By the end of the year the defeat of the Axis on the battlefield was once again a realistic prospect, while it had become clear that hopes of an anti-Nazi revolution breaking out in Germany were so much wishful thinking. The marked hardening at this time of Beneš's rhetoric, both private and public, on the future of the *Sudetendeutsche* was not coincidental. In a radio message to ÚVOD leaders in September 1941, he assured them that he was sympathetic to the objective of expelling all Sudeten Germans at the end of the war, though for diplomatic reasons he might have to assent to a less radical program.[35] His exchanges with Wenzel Jaksch also took on a new and much more uncompromising tone. A year previously, the two had agreed that Beneš's suggestion that the Sudeten German problem be solved by a process of internal transfer to ethnically homogeneous cantons that would enjoy a significant measure of autonomy offered a realistic basis for talks over the shape of the postwar Czechoslovakia. The president's insistence that this be accompanied by a partial expulsion of the *Sudetendeutsche*, though, had stalled the negotiations; and in the event Beneš proved unable to sell the canton idea even to his own government in exile. It is hard not to conclude that by the end of 1941 he had abandoned the idea of—or no longer saw the necessity for—an agreed solution with the Sudeten Social Democrats. Jaksch began to fear, with much justification, that "Beneš hoped to gain a commitment from the British Government to restore the previous frontiers of Czechoslovakia after which he would be in a position to claim that the Sudeten question was purely an internal Czechoslovak matter."[36]

That Jaksch had read the tealeaves correctly was shown by the fact that Beneš now felt sufficiently confident to reveal in public the way in which his mind was working. Cautious as ever, he commenced with a series of trial balloons. In September 1941, for the first time, he publicly indicated his support for "the principle of the transfer of populations" in the context of a "New Order in Europe."[37] Two months later, in a pair of speeches at Edinburgh and Glasgow Universities, he expressed the opinion that "Germans, good and bad, European-minded and Nazi-minded, must learn . . . that war does not pay." There was, he maintained, "no way other than the way of suffering of educating a social and political community and there never was any other way."[38] Emboldened by the lack of Allied disagreement with these arguments, in an article in Hamilton Fish Armstrong's *Foreign Affairs* in January 1942 Beneš proceeded from the general to the particular. "National minorities," he declared, "are always—and in Central Europe especially—a real thorn in the side of individual nations. This is especially true if they are German minorities." Before speaking of minority rights, it was necessary to "define the rights of majorities and the obligations of minorities." Indeed, in light of wartime experience, whether it was necessary or desirable for national minorities as such to continue in existence was an open question.

> Hitler himself has transferred German minorities from the Baltic and from Bessarabia. Germany, therefore, cannot *a priori* regard it as an injury to her if other states adopt the same methods with regard to German minorities. . . . It will be necessary after this war to carry out a transfer of populations on a very much larger scale than after the last war. This must be done in as humane a manner as possible, internationally organized and internationally financed.[39]

Beneš conceded that the victors had a moral obligation to "design measures for the protection of loyal minorities, for guaranteeing them their political and cultural rights, on the basis of absolute mutuality." But there could no longer be any doubt that the Czechoslovak government in exile was now openly committed to the removal of all or most of its *Sudetendeutsch* population after the war. In separate meetings with Jaksch and the British foreign secretary, Anthony Eden, in the month his *Foreign Affairs* article appeared, Beneš confirmed that this was his intention. He was willing, he indicated, to adjust Czechoslovakia's frontiers so as to give up some small tracts of exclusively *Sudetendeutsch*-inhabited territory to Germany, provided he received suitable compensation elsewhere. But no more than 600,000 to 700,000 Sudeten Germans, or a fifth of the prewar population, would be allowed to remain. Eden gave Beneš a noncommittal response, which angered him greatly. The Foreign Office's lack of enthusiasm, he complained to Philip Nichols, was yet another British betrayal of Czechoslovakia, reminding the Ambassador that the "issue of our Germans is for me the issue of *Munich in general.*"[40]

Once again wider wartime developments worked in Beneš's favor. On May 27, 1942, acting on the Czechoslovak president's instructions, a pair of Czech agents with the Special Operations Executive ambushed and killed Reinhard Heydrich, Himmler's genocidal deputy, as he drove through a suburb of Prague. The previous September, Heydrich had been appointed "Protector" of Bohemia and Moravia, the Nazis' Orwellian title for the colonial governor of the Czech lands. So successful had he been in pacifying the area through a combination of carrot-and-stick measures—Czech munitions workers, for example, received higher rations than even their German counterparts, and the Czechoslovak economy as a whole "obediently produced roughly 10 percent of the Nazi Reich's industrial output in exchange for handsome salaries"[41]—that an alarmed Beneš ordered his assassination for fear that the Allies might conclude that Czechoslovakia had reconciled itself to Nazi occupation.[42] If his intention was to provoke a reaction from the Germans, the mission achieved its purpose. Responding with their customary lack of restraint, the Nazis razed the villages of Lidice and Ležáky to the ground as a reprisal, massacring the men and sending the women to concentration camps. More than a thousand Czechoslovak Gentiles died in the repression that followed; a thousand more Czech Jews were sent to Mauthausen camp, never to return. Worse still from Beneš's point of view, the German dragnet hauled in practically the entire membership of ÚVOD, leaving Czechoslovakia without a functioning resistance organization and depriving the government in exile of any means of reliable communication with the homeland.

If the assassination failed abysmally in its objective of sparking greater militancy on the part of the Czech people—for the remainder of the war, the Germans found that fewer than two thousand officials were all that were required to keep tabs on a Czechoslovak administration employing more than 350,000 people—it nonetheless succeeded admirably in polarizing opinion at home and abroad. The *Sudetendeutsche* were infuriated by Heydrich's killing to so great a degree that "the German authorities had to intervene to prevent lynchings of Czechs in ethnically mixed areas. Party organizations in the Sudetenland and in Vienna demanded mass expulsion of Czechs from their respective territories."[43] Some commentators have implied that Beneš foresaw just such a reaction, counting on it to ensure that the legacy of bitterness would be so great as to preclude any possibility of Czechoslovaks and Sudeten Germans ever living together again once the war was over.[44] Certainly some of the more injudicious statements by the president and his ministers might be thought to lend support to such a theory. A silver lining to the destruction of Lidice, Beneš later remarked, was that "under no circumstances can doubts be cast any more upon Czechoslovakia's national integrity." His political secretary and party colleague Prokop Drtina, the minister of justice in the postwar government, expressed himself still more unfortunately when he proclaimed that "The response to the assassination and Lidice in Allied opinion was so enormous that it equalled for us a victorious battle." Without the sacrifice of those who had carried out the operation, "we would never have achieved the purification of the Czech lands from the German settlements."[45] To conclude, however, that the assassination was carried out for the purpose of setting the ethnic communities in Czechoslovakia at each other's throats is altogether too cynical an interpretation. A much more likely explanation is that Beneš, dismayed and embarrassed in his interactions with the British by the lack of overt resistance in his homeland, felt the need to demonstrate that he and his government were still relevant, and accepted the inevitable Nazi backlash that would result as a price that must be paid in wartime.

Whatever his motives, the martyrdom of Lidice strengthened Beneš's hand immensely when dealing with the Allies. Although countless Polish, Soviet, and Yugoslav villages and towns had already suffered a similar fate, none received any publicity in the West. Lidice, however, quickly became a household name, thanks in part to the highly developed public relations network of the Czechoslovak Ministry of Information in London and also to the fortuitous decision of the leading U.S. propaganda agency, the Office of War Information, to make the massacre "the one cap-stone incident of the Axis terror and barbarism, which will fire the United Nations to smash the Nazi beasts."[46] (Ležáky, being smaller than Lidice and, still more importantly, with a name that was far more difficult for Westerners to pronounce, was almost immediately forgotten.) Under intense pressure from the Czechoslovaks and others to respond with reprisal air raids against Germany, an idea the British government opposed for fear that a cessation of Nazi atrocities against civilians might result in demands that the RAF respond by discontinuing its strategic bombing campaign, Eden looked again at the possibility of giving ground over the expulsion of the *Sudetendeutsche*.[47] In a meeting with Stalin in Moscow in December 1941, he had learned that the Soviet leader considered the removal of the population of German lands that would be given to Poland after the war to be an important element of the eventual settlement.[48] A February 1942 study by the Foreign Office's research wing had pronounced large-scale forced population transfers a feasible method of dealing with the European minorities problem.[49] Five weeks after Lidice, then, Eden brought forward a paper in the War Cabinet in which he stated his belief that "it would probably be impossible to avoid some measures of this kind in post-war Europe" and warned that "if they are not carried out in an orderly and peaceful manner it is only too likely that the Czech and Polish populations will forcibly expel the German minorities from their midst. The question is whether we should now commit ourselves to the principle of such transfers, and let both Dr Beneš and the Sudeten German representatives know that this is our view." At the beginning of July 1942 Eden obtained his colleagues' approval of "the general principle of the transfer to Germany of German minorities in Central and South-Eastern Europe after the war in cases where this seems necessary and desirable, and authority to let this decision be known in appropriate cases."[50]

Where the Czechoslovaks had led, the Polish government-in-exile was eventually to follow. In the early stages of the war, it is true, the London-based administration of Władysław Sikorski had been much more concerned with ensuring that Poland's prewar borders be restored, and in particular that the Soviet Union should evacuate the Polish territories it had invaded and absorbed in September 1939. Though some Poles cast covetous eyes on East Prussia, the idea of territorial acquisitions in the west was of much less importance to them. They reacted cautiously to Czechoslovak suggestions in the winter of 1939–40 of an expulsion of German minorities as a preparatory step toward a postwar confederation between the two countries.[51] As it became increasingly clear that at least some of the eastern lands they had lost to the Soviet Union would never be returned to them, however, Poles of all political stripes began to look much more seriously at the prospects of expanding at Germany's expense in the west—an idea that had already been promoted between the wars by Roman Dmowski's ultranationalist and anti-Semitic National Democratic movement. In a December 1942 session, the Polish Parliament in London adopted a resolution advocating that the Polish-German frontier be "straightened and shortened" in the interests of Poland's future security. What this meant in practice was clarified by Sikorski four days later, when he informed Roosevelt that Poland wished to annex East Prussia and German Silesia as far as the line of the Oder and the eastern Neisse rivers.[52] The removal of Germans, however, was not the most important demographic question pressing on Sikorski's mind. At the beginning of the year, he had told Anthony Eden that it would be "quite impossible . . . for Poland to continue to maintain 3.5 million Jews after the war. Room must be found for them elsewhere."[53] The Nazis would solve that problem for the Allies, although Sikorski, who died in an air crash in July 1943, would not live to see it.

Initially, the Poles were inhibited from pressing their claim for even greater territorial acquisitions at Germany's expense by their belief that Allied public opinion would never accept the massive transfer of Germans that so extravagant a demand would necessitate.[54] They had also by no means abandoned hopes of securing the return of most, if not all, of their lost eastern territories, and rightly suspected Stalin of encouraging them to expand in the west as a way of placing further obstacles in their path. Nevertheless, the temptation was too difficult to resist, especially after Beneš's success showed that so far as the Big Three were concerned, they were pushing at an open door. Clearly the population of the German lands in question could not be allowed to remain without saddling Poland with a German minority proportionately as large as, and in absolute numbers far greater than, the one in Czechoslovakia. Expulsion consequently became almost as important an element of the Polish government in exile's postwar planning as it had been for the Czechoslovaks, and they greeted Eden's conversion to the principle with approval. By September 1944, the London Poles had determined that those Germans "who do not leave Polish territory after the war will have to be removed from it. This applies equally to the area of the Polish state in 1939, and the territories whose incorporation into Poland will be demanded as a result of the present war."[55] Plans to carry out the operation and to confiscate the property of those who would be forced to leave were already in preparation.[56]

Credible rumors that the British government had thrown its weight behind postwar population transfers came as a bombshell to the Sudeten German refugees in Britain and their leader, Wenzel Jaksch. An estimable and in many respects a tragic figure, Jaksch had been fighting not one but several rearguard actions since his arrival in Britain after Munich. His own exile community was divided between those who wanted to work for a restoration of Czechoslovakia in its pre-1938 borders and others who, while committed to the struggle against Hitler, believed that the Sudetenland should remain attached to a democratic postwar Germany. He was also aware that members of the Czechoslovak government in exile were trying hard to split the *Sudetendeutsch* émigrés so as to weaken their claim to Allied protection and undermine his own status as their spokesman. As Beneš had done in 1938, Jaksch decided that his best hope of persuading the British to reverse course was to maintain his own and his community's dignity, avoid responding to provocations or polemics, and remind the Allies of the importance of remaining true to their own public undertakings. His reward for this principled stance was to be the same as the Czechoslovak president's at Munich. Yet it is unlikely that any other course would have yielded a different result.

The provocations were not long in coming. Since May 1941, Jaksch had made numerous broadcasts to his fellow *Sudetendeutsche* on the BBC German service, reminding them of their duty to the Czechoslovak state and appealing to them to resist the Nazis. The Czech historian Francis Raška, who has made a study of these talks, is unable to detect in them "even the slightest hint of any disloyalty to Czechoslovakia."[57] Nonetheless they provoked Beneš and his publicist, Ripka, to fury. By advocating Sudeten autonomy within a decentralized Czechoslovakia, they complained, Jaksch was traversing the same ground as had Konrad Henlein in the 1930s and was paving the way for the ultimate breakup of the Czechoslovak state. Such a person had no right to be heard on the radio, or anywhere else. Summarizing their protests in a sentence, Frank Roberts of the Foreign Office wryly remarked that they supposed that "His Majesty's Government is building up another Sudeten Führer."[58] British officials did not take these fulminations seriously. Both Beneš and Jaksch were well known to them, and if anything they had a higher opinion of the latter than the former. Ever since Versailles, the Foreign Office had considered Beneš prone to double-dealing and duplicity. When in 1925 he had put his name forward as a future secretary general of the League of Nations, Alexander Cadogan had minuted: "If the League is destroyed, it will be by the appointment of an unfit man to the post . . . Dr Beneš would be an admirable candidate for anyone who desired that result."[59] So far from being a crypto-Nazi, on the other hand, Jaksch was plainly an old-fashioned socialist internationalist of a type that two world wars had rendered all but extinct. British officials recalled his visits to London before Munich at Beneš's request to try to gain support for Czechoslovakia's stance against German aggression, and his ongoing wartime work on behalf of Special Operations Executive, the British anti-Nazi sabotage organization in occupied Europe.[60] Still more awkwardly for the Czechoslovak president, Philip Noel-Baker, a Labour Party parliamentarian and junior minister in the Churchill coalition government, had already recounted in another BBC broadcast how he had joined Jaksch in Czechoslovakia during the summer of 1938 to rally *Sudetendeutsch* opposition to Hitler and Henlein.

> [N]ight by night I drove from town to town with their gallant leader, Wenzel Jaksch, to speak with him to great meetings of his followers. . . . I can still hear the deep, fierce cheers resounding through the hall when Jaksch declared they would rather fight and die for liberty than yield.
> And I remember how President Beneš, in his lovely palace on the hill at Prague, told me that these German Social Democrats were nothing less than heroes; that they had shown us all what resolution, what nobility of mind, the fight for human freedom could evoke.[61]

Whatever shape a postwar Czechoslovakia took, however, Jaksch clearly would have no part to play in Anglo-Czechoslovak relations. Beneš and Ripka would. Inasmuch as there was little evidence to indicate that his broadcasts were making an impact on Sudeten German opinion in any event, from London's point of view there seemed no point in having an unnecessary row with the future Prague government over them. Jaksch was taken off the air in the summer of 1942. It would not be the last time he, and other German opponents of Nazism, were to be sacrificed to Allied *raison d'état*.

Support for ejecting the Sudeten Germans quickly followed from the USSR as well. Sensibly, Beneš wasted little time negotiating with the Czechoslovak Communist Party, the KSČ, whose absurd contortions in its effort to keep up with the twists and turns of Moscow's line had already proven that it possessed no independent decision-making capacity. Since its launch in the early 1920s, the KSČ had staunchly supported minority rights, condemning Czech internal colonialism as an instrument of bourgeois exploitation and upholding the right of the *Sudetendeutsche* and other ethnic groups to "national self-determination," even to the point of secession from the Republic. That stance had lasted until the conclusion of the Czechoslovak-Soviet Treaty of Mutual Assistance in 1935, when nothing further was heard about self-determination for minorities. Instead, during the Munich crisis the party had called on Sudeten "antifascists" to "follow the orders of the [Czechoslovak] democratic institutions."[62] When the Nazi-Soviet Pact was announced, "national self-determination" was once again back on the Communist menu, and party leaflets circulating in the Protectorate warned against "the dangers of [Czech] chauvinism." It was clear, then, that the KSČ would invariably follow where Moscow led, notwithstanding the significant proportion of Sudeten Germans in its own ranks. In June 1943, the Soviet ambassador to London advised the Czechoslovak government in exile of the USSR's agreement with the expulsion of the Germans; Beneš heard the same from Stalin's own lips when he traveled to Moscow at the end of the year.[63] When he met with the exiled leaders of the KSČ there shortly afterwards, it was to notify them of his expectations of them rather than to solicit their agreement.

In the summer of 1943 Beneš obtained the final endorsement required for the success of his scheme. During a lunch meeting with Churchill in March he had ensured that the prime minister was still firmly committed to the idea of transfer. According to Jan Masaryk, Churchill went further than that. When the war eventually ended, he told Beneš, "Many [Sudeten] Germans will be killed in your country as well—it cannot be helped and I agree with it. After a few months we'll say 'that's enough,' and we shall start on the work of peace: try the guilty men who stayed alive."[64] Whether Churchill's remark was accurately recorded—and throughout his life he did have a penchant for bellicose overstatement—he is likely to have been speaking of the meting-out of summary justice to high-level collaborators like Henlein and the *Sudetendeutsch* second in command in Bohemia and Moravia, Karl Hermann Frank, rather than offering the Czechoslovaks an open-ended mandate for massacre. Beneš felt confident enough in the prime minister's backing for transfers, nonetheless, to bring it up in Churchill's presence during a visit to the White House in May 1943 for his first, and only, wartime meeting with Franklin D. Roosevelt. Again, no official record exists of what was said there. On his return to London, though, he euphorically reported to his colleagues that after learning of the British and Soviet support that had already been promised, the U.S. president too had assented to the postwar expulsion of the entire Sudeten German population.

In this instance also, though State Department officials would later hotly deny that Roosevelt had said any such thing, it seems improbable that Beneš's version was manufactured out of whole cloth. To obtain American approval of the eviction of the *Sudetendeutsche* was why he had traveled to Washington in the first place, and there is no reason to doubt that he raised it at the meeting. In its aftermath he would hardly have broadcast Roosevelt's concurrence so widely had he been given no encouragement to do so; the story would have been too easy to contradict. On the other hand, Beneš's later claim that the president agreed to a complete clearance of the Sudetenland has less of the ring of credibility about it. In his previous dealings with London and Moscow, he had been studiously vague about the precise number of Germans he intended to expel, and it is most improbable that he would have opted for the high-risk strategy of trying to make Roosevelt accept his maximum demand in their very first discussion of the matter. This interpretation is strengthened by Anthony Eden's action in instructing the British minister in Washington to repudiate Czechoslovak reports that the United States had endorsed a clean sweep of the *Sudetendeutsche*, and to point out that the Allies had committed themselves only to agreement in principle on the question of postwar population transfers.[65]

By the end of 1943, nevertheless, the expulsion project had taken on a momentum that only a decision of the Big Three could have reversed. Not only on the part of policymakers, but among important sections of Anglo-American public opinion as well, population transfers briefly became what C. A. Macartney, an expert adviser to the Foreign Office on international relations, characterized as a "fashionable panacea for all difficulties connected with national minorities."[66] Thus the former U.S. president, Herbert Hoover, called for consideration of what he described as "the heroic remedy of transfer of population" as a means of preventing future European conflict.[67] Sumner Welles, previously second in command at the State Department and a man who until recently had been Roosevelt's closest collaborator in foreign affairs, likewise would abandon his belief that after the war "no element in any nation will be forced to atone vicariously for crimes for which it is not responsible," and that it was unacceptable that whole peoples should be "transferred, like cattle, from one sovereignty to another." Instead, he was coming round to the idea that "we should avail ourselves of this moment of world upheaval to effect transfers of population where these are necessary to prevent new conflicts, and thus enable peoples to live under the government they desire, free from racial discriminations."[68] Endorsing Beneš's expulsion scheme, the Oxford historian A. J. P. Taylor declared that the Czechoslovak state could only be resurrected using the same "ruthlessness" and inflicting "as much suffering" as the Germans had employed in destroying it.[69] In the House of Lords, Robert Vansittart, a former Foreign Office mandarin who in the 1930s had been for appeasement before he was against it and who was now the loudest British voice in favor of a Carthaginian peace for Germany, applauded Stalin's robust indifference to questions of guilt or innocence, when driving the Soviet Union's German-speaking population from their homes in 1941, as a model for the Allies to follow. "He was a thousand times right; five hundred thousand times right. . . . I say, these [deportees] were not Hitlerite Germans. They had a quarter of a century's training in the doctrines of Communism. . . . Nevertheless they were held to be Germans and unreliable."[70] Even Lord Robert Cecil, president of the League of Nations Union and an impassioned defender of the rights of minorities between the wars, now agreed that the *Sudetendeutsche* at least would "have to be removed," and that their fate should be of no concern to anyone but the Czechoslovak government.[71]

While expulsionist sentiment transcended partisan lines in Britain, it was the Labour Party which greeted the idea most enthusiastically. Between the wars, Labour had been the strongest advocates of internationalist principles in foreign policy, with the ultimate aim of seeing the League of Nations evolve into an embryonic world government. Little of this idealism remained by 1942. The collapse of Wilsonianism in the face of Axis aggression generated a sharp reaction on the left wing of British politics in the direction of national exceptionalism and a great power–dominated new world order. To the extent that minority populations stood in the way of this agenda, Labour policymakers contended, they were to be eliminated, through complete assimilation or forced migration. Philip Noel-Baker and John Parker, both of whom would hold ministerial office after 1945, individually advocated systematic population transfers as a necessary condition of the postwar peace; influential Labour intellectuals like Harold Laski spoke in the same vein.[72] In a widely publicized 1944 statement on the foreign policy a Labour government would follow after the war, these views became official party doctrine. Labour warned ethnic Germans who failed to cooperate with their own removal that they would have no valid grounds for complaint if they forfeited their lives as a result.

> '[N]ational minorities' in Central Europe, left outside the boundaries of their own nation, should be encouraged to rejoin it. In particular, all Germans left outside the post-War German frontiers, unless they are willing to become loyal subjects of the State in which they find themselves, should go back to Germany. Indeed, they will be well advised to do so in their own interests, for,

in the early post-War years at any rate, there will be a depth of hatred against Germans in the occupied countries, which it is impossible either for us or for Americans to realise.

Germans in many of those areas may have to face the choice between migration and massacre.[73]

That this green light by one of Britain's governing parties to the use of mass terror to displace ethnic German populations after the war was not intended to be taken lightly was indicated by a speech at its annual conference a fortnight after V-E Day by Denis Healey, soon to become the Labour Party's international secretary and, in that capacity, a key contact between ministers in the Attlee administration and the socialist parties of central Europe. British leftists, he acknowledged, would probably regard as "extremist" some of the actions Continental left-wing leaders were already taking to settle postwar accounts. But "if the Labour Movement in Europe finds it necessary to introduce . . . more immediate and drastic punishment for their opponents than we in this country would be prepared to tolerate, we must be prepared to understand their point of view."[74] The appeal of population transfers to Labour, however, went beyond revanchism alone. By the mid-1940s, they were increasingly being regarded on the left as a means of accomplishing not just social but socialist engineering. Inasmuch as movements on such a scale would by definition overturn the socio-economic *status quo* in the countries in which they occurred, they could be a vital tool in breaking the power of entrenched capitalist interests and paving the way for a once-for-all transition to a planned economy that might take decades to accomplish by other means. Beneš himself was thinking in these terms, pointing out to the leader of the Czechoslovak Communist Party, Klement Gottwald, in December 1943 that the expulsions would be accompanied by a state-controlled confiscation and redistribution of all German property. "This will be a national revolution," Beneš promised, "combined with a social revolution. By means of measures taken against German wealth as well as German national characteristics, the way will be opened to radical economic intervention and social change in the Bohemian lands."[75]

In the most extravagant formulations of its partisans, population transfer appeared as a cure-all for the difficulties that had ensued as a result of the divergent historical evolution of "nations" and "states." According to this view, a major cause of world discord was the lack of correspondence between the two, with members of a given nation residing on the territory of a state that was not their own. After the Great War, an attempt had been made to shift the boundaries of states to accommodate the geographical distribution of nations. This had proven a failure. Ethnic intermixing, the existence of linguistic enclaves and islands, and a lack of goodwill on all sides had defeated the best attempts of experts at the Paris Peace Conference to make the "nation" and the "state" synonymous terms. The situation that resulted was unsatisfactory for everyone. The presence of "foreign" elements on their soil provoked postwar governments to adopt coercive policies of national homogenization and forced assimilation that only alienated their minority populations further. Likewise, the plight of persecuted co-nationals in a neighboring state was a standing temptation to the "mother country" to wage aggressive wars for the purpose of—or, as in Hitler's case, under the pretext of—rescuing them from foreign domination. Population transfers offered a way of cutting this Gordian knot, by making nations accommodate themselves to the existing boundaries of states. Once the operation had been completed, the new international order would start life with the advantage, never enjoyed by its predecessor, of not having to defend itself against peoples bent on its revision in the name of "national self-determination." But the window of opportunity to bring about this once-for-all reversal of centuries of European settlement patterns was small indeed. As the British Labour Party declared, it was vital to strike while the iron was hot. Only after a major war were such vast changes possible. If the moment was lost, the existing distribution of population would crystallize and become immovable.

> The organised transfer of population, in the immediate post-War period, may, indeed, be one of the foundations of better international relations in a later phase. Nor would this be a new departure. Between the Wars the transfer of population between Turkey and Greece was an undoubted success.
>
> In any case, there will be a vast problem of repatriation and resettlement in Europe, when tens of millions of refugees, slave labourers, and prisoners of war return to freedom and their own homes. Compared with this, the transfer even of substantial national minorities, German and other, to the right side of the post-War frontiers, will be a small affair. However, just when so much is fluid, there will be a unique opportunity, which will not recur, to make a permanent settlement of this vexed question.[76]

This does not mean that a consensus in the democracies on the necessity of mass population transfers ever emerged. Even within the British Labour Party, a strong minority found the reasoning behind them impossible to understand. The journal *Socialist Commentary* called attention to the incongruity of trying to preserve in aspic the often artificially defined European frontiers of 1939, the product of centuries of dynastic squabbling and historical accident, for all time. More than that, "Once the frontiers have been settled, all discussion is then to be discouraged as to whether they were the right ones after all." It would have been more fitting, it pointed out, for a party that professed to be both democratic and internationalist "to bring justice and freedom to the national minorities wherever they choose to live, and not to continue the odious Nazi method of shifting people about like cattle."[77] The member of Parliament and future minister George Strauss, although himself Jewish, asked the 1944 party conference to repudiate population transfers that would, in his view, "punish the innocent with the guilty, damage the whole economy of Europe, lead to the reappearance of Fascism and involve us in another world war."[78] For their part, members of the political Right, in keeping with their ideological tendency to regard with caution grandiose state-driven projects aimed at eliminating complicated problems at a stroke, responded coolly to the first public indications that expulsions were being seriously considered. The London-based *Economist* warned in the same month that Beneš's *Foreign Affairs* article appeared that punishment of Germans after the war "must fall on those who are guilty in a moral and not in a racial sense. The Nazis have made racial scapegoats; the Allies must not fall into exactly the same error."[79] The following year, as signs of Czechoslovakia's and Poland's intentions became clearer, the journal spoke out in more forceful tones. If, notwithstanding the Allies' stated principles, "dismemberment, mass transfers of population, massacre, the permanent oppression of minorities are to be part of the settlement this time, let it be plain from the start that neither Britain nor America will in ten years from the signing of the peace raise a finger to maintain it."[80]

Probably the most perceptive critique offered of the expulsion project was published in 1943 by Allan Fisher, a New Zealand economist, and David Mitrany, a brilliant young Anglo-Romanian political scientist who had served as an adviser on international questions to both the Foreign Office and the Labour Party. To claim that this practice was now justified because of the Nazi government's previous recourse to it, they argued, seemed a curious way of reeducating the German people "at a time when they are being urged to abjure Hitler and all his works." In any event, it was futile to suppose that attempts to create nationally homogeneous states by expelling alien populations could be sustained over the long term except by hermetically sealing those countries from all outside movements in the future.

> [I]t is clearly not enough merely to create such "pure" states. Like race, they must also be kept pure. Therefore, whatever the criterion of purity for the time being, if it is to achieve the ends for which it is advocated the policy of transfer

must have as its corollary a *continuous* policy of segregation. Migration or any free movement of people would have to be prohibited lest it should lead to the gradual creation of new unwanted and irritating minorities. The habitual natural adjustments of population, to fit economic conditions, would thereby be checked; and the "New [postwar] World" would be inaugurated by the suppression of an old freedom.

Presciently, Fisher and Mitrany warned that Western advocates of expulsion should not delude themselves that the same tactic would not be used against them in their turn. In Africa, Asia, and the Middle East white minority communities were also to be found. "Their presence and interests have always been used to justify intervention on their behalf by the home states. Therefore the 'solution' adopted in Europe for ending the trouble with minorities would very soon come to be used for 'transferring' European minorities . . . back to their home countries."[81]

For all the cogency of their arguments, though, the opponents of expulsions had little hope of being able to reverse a policy decision that had already been taken at the highest level. From this point onward, as he later acknowledged in his memoirs, Beneš himself saw no reason to conceal his intentions any further. In what would prove to be his final meetings with Wenzel Jaksch and the other *Sudetendeutsch* refugee leaders, at the end of 1942, he informed them frankly that he regarded the overwhelming majority of Sudeten Germans as at the least *"passive war criminals"* and that the only solution acceptable to him was *"our complete separation."*[82] When one of Jaksch's colleagues, Eugen de Witte, protested that this stance meant that "If Hitler wins the war, we Sudeten Germans are lost and if the Czechs win it, we are lost too," Beneš replied that their fate was indeed tragic but nonetheless unchangeable. But the president would also ominously note that in resisting his plans, Jaksch and other anti-Nazi *Sudetendeutsche* may not have "clearly realise[d] that by so doing they automatically took full responsibility for what the Germans were doing to us as a Nation in the war . . ."[83] A month later, in January 1943, Beneš sent Jaksch a lengthy memorandum in which he accused the *Sudetendeutsch* Social Democrats of going behind his back to the British; displaying their disloyalty to Czechoslovakia by continuing to claim the right of self-determination; and refusing to accept that the will of the majority in the postwar Republic ought to prevail in determining all questions relating to Czechoslovakia's future, including any putative transfer of Germans.[84] For Jaksch, however, this last demand placed his people in a Catch-22. If they rejected it they marked themselves out, at least according to the government in exile's terms, as traitors to the Czechoslovak state, and hence liable to transfer. Should they accept it, on the other hand, they acknowledged the right of the Czech majority to legislate their denationalization as "passive war criminals," leading to precisely the same end result.

By the beginning of 1943, therefore, the possibility of finding a middle ground had disappeared. As he had already told Philip Nichols he would do if Jaksch rejected his scheme, Beneš broke off all further contact with the anti-Nazi *Sudetendeutsche*. Thereafter, the government in exile pursued an increasingly vitriolic and, in the end, obsessive public relations campaign against Jaksch and his colleagues, declaring them to be "pan-Germans" seeking precisely the same objective as Konrad Henlein and, indeed, Hitler himself—the breakup of Czechoslovakia. The justification offered for this startling contention was a crude syllogism: Jaksch favored an autonomous Sudetenland within the context of a postwar European federation; a European federation would inevitably be dominated by its largest member, Germany; hence Jaksch favored German domination of the Sudetenland. In a typically venomous specimen of what would become a tidal wave of ad hominem literature directed against the *Sudetendeutsch* leader, at the end of 1943 Hubert Ripka denounced Jaksch, formerly "a good friend of his,"[85] as not only a fifth columnist but a social reactionary.

> It has been the deplorable lot of this German Socialist to bring to a climax the work of destruction which was begun and continued by Henlein, the Nazi. . . . There is no difference between Henlein's proceedings then and those of Jaksch now. . . . There is, of course, a difference between Henlein, the Nazi, and Jaksch, the Socialist: the former desires German domination in a Nazi régime, the latter in a Socialist régime, but both are pursuing the same final purpose, Pan-German domination of other peoples. Henlein and his followers are adherents of Hitler's European "New Order," while Jaksch is an advocate of a European socialistic federation, but a federation organized in such a way that socialistic Germany would be the strongest element in it and for all practical purposes would have the decisive word and hold sway over all the others. It is not surprising that this socialistic Pan-German can scarcely conceal his distaste for the Soviet Union and his disapproval of the Czechoslovak-Soviet alliance.[86]

Ironically, after the Communist coup of 1948 Ripka—who rarely permitted himself to think or say things that Edvard Beneš had not thought or said first— upon fleeing Czechoslovakia once more and setting up yet another government in exile would himself advocate "the rebirth of a free Czechoslovakia 'within the framework of the future European federation.'"[87] In 1944, though, he indicated that such ideas were grounds for an eventual treason prosecution, declaring in the State Council that "from the Czechoslovak point of view, the activity of

Jaksch is anti-State, and that it must be judged as such with all the consequences which it involves."[88]

As the war began to draw to a close, then, Jaksch was left with fewer and fewer cards to play, beyond appeals to international public opinion that were unlikely to succeed. His protest to Beneš over the stance the government in exile was taking "against old allies who stood at the Czech Nation's side when it was abandoned by all its friends" at the time of Munich was ignored.[89] A pamphlet published in English in July 1943, pointing out that anti-Nazis in the Sudetenland would hardly be motivated to rise against Hitler when nightly BBC broadcasts to Czechoslovakia reminded them that "victory over Nazism will be followed by new disasters of evacuation and transfer,"[90] merely drew attention to the fact that if overt resistance to the German occupation in the Czech lands was minimal, in the Sudetenland it simply did not exist. Recognizing this, at the beginning of 1945 Jaksch approached one of his contacts at the Foreign Office, Frank Roberts, for permission to broadcast to his homeland on the BBC one last time. Though there was not more than a "tiny chance," he acknowledged, that his attempt to warn the people of the Sudetenland of the fate that awaited them would succeed, it might still be possible to prevent the worst after the war "if the anti-Nazi element in the Sudeten districts . . . could, in a decisive hour, act simultaneously with the masses in the Czech interior." In August 1944, after all, Slovak insurgents had rebelled against the Nazis, following five years of enthusiastic collaboration with Berlin in the course of which Slovak forces had participated in the invasions of both Poland and the USSR, to say nothing of assisting in the deportation of most of the country's Jewish population to Hitler's extermination camps. Though the rising had been a failure, it was sufficient to insulate Slovakia against the threat of a systematic campaign of postwar retribution. By early 1945, the only faint hope for the *Sudetendeutsche* seemed to be a similar demonstration, however belated, of their willingness to identify themselves with the Allied cause. In the text of his address to the Germanophone population of his homeland, Jaksch did not mince words about the peril in which they stood if they failed to do so.

> Only a general refusal of obedience, from Asch [Aš] to Jägerndorf [Krnov], can avert from you the impending doom. The fate of our people and our homeland hangs on a last thin thread. In your name have Henlein, K. H. Frank, Krebs, May and their accomplices heaped crime upon crime. . . . You have only the choice between standing before the tribunal of the peoples for the atrocities of a K. H. Frank in Prague and of an Ernst Kundt in Poland, and breaking away from them at the last hour. We entreat all decent Sudeten Germans, and above

all the men in the *Volkssturm* battalions, that they should not for anything allow themselves to be used as tools to suppress a Czech popular rising. Should you be ordered to shoot at Czech fighters for liberty, reverse your rifles.... You, the Germans in the Protectorate, have to make many amends. Any further support of the Nazi régime spells certain disaster.[91]

The Foreign Office's fear about such a broadcast was the opposite to Jaksch's: not that his appeal might fail, but that it might succeed. The Czechoslovak government in exile's settled policy, a British official reminded his colleagues, was to eject most of the *Sudetendeutsche* from the country. If in response to exhortations from Britain they were to rise against the Nazis, London would thereby be accepting "responsibilities for these Sudetens who responded to this appeal. This responsibility we should not be able to accept..."[92] Jaksch's request for broadcast facilities was consequently denied. By the time the war ended, he was unable to point to a single concrete example of Sudeten German assistance—or even attempted assistance—to the Allied campaign.

Edvard Beneš returned to Czechoslovakia on April 3, 1945, accompanied by members of his government, and set up a temporary administration in the recently liberated Slovak city of Košice. Despite the terrific strain of the previous six years that had taken a severe toll on his health, he could look back with satisfaction on what he had achieved since the beginning of his exile. With the exception of the small eastern territory of Carpatho-Ruthenia, which he had had to promise to the USSR as the tribute for Stalin's patronage, Czechoslovakia was to be restored in its 1938 frontiers. Though he remained for the moment the head of an unelected government, he faced no immediate challenge to his domestic leadership. Most importantly, the minorities problem that had bedeviled Czechoslovakia since the moment of its creation was on the point of being resolved once and for all. Certainly some difficulties remained. Although the Allies had agreed to the expulsion of the *Sudetendeutsche*, they had as yet made no commitments as to when, how, or to where the population would be removed. They had turned a deaf ear to his frequent requests that the 700,000-strong Hungarian minority in Czechoslovakia be treated likewise. Nonetheless, the prospect of a Czechoslovakia the overwhelming majority of whose people would be Czechs and Slovaks was clearly in sight. And most of this had been Beneš's doing. To be sure, he had not done it alone. The Allies had not adopted a policy of population transfers to gratify an exiled central European politician in respect of whom they harbored a bad conscience, but because it suited their interests. Nor did he force the idea onto an unwilling Czechoslovak population. A great many contingencies, furthermore, had to occur to make such an outcome possible. Had the war been shorter, or longer; had it been Patton's Third U.S. Army that liberated most of Czechoslovakia rather than the Red Army; had there been a significant Sudeten German anti-Nazi resistance movement, the expulsions might never have taken place, notwithstanding all Beneš's efforts. But it had been he, as Chad Bryant correctly says, who "forced the issue at every moment, and in the end he did everything in his power to see that the Germans were expelled from Czechoslovakia. Without him, the expulsions would not have happened as they did, if at all."[93]

Wenzel Jaksch's exile, in contrast, would never end. As one of its earliest acts, Beneš's new government introduced the so-called "Great Decree," providing for the punishment of "Nazi criminals, traitors, and their accomplices." Its fourth clause made punishable, by a prison sentence of up to twenty years, any act by a Czechoslovak citizen living abroad that "subverted the movement to liberate the Czechoslovak Republic in its pre-Munich constitutional form and unity, or who otherwise consciously harmed the interests of the Czechoslovak Republic . . ." This section, Benjamin Frommer notes, "above all . . . threatened Wenzel Jaksch," and was intended to deny the *Sudetendeutsche* "a strong advocate who could have credibly advanced the position that not all his people were Nazis and that retribution must be individual, not collective."[94] Jaksch knew well what awaited him should he return home, having already publicly been declared guilty by Hubert Ripka, who now became a minister in the Czechoslovak government and as one of his first official acts dispatched a formal note to the U.S. chargé d'affaires warning that the new regime "cannot regard as a loyal citizen any of those who, though residing in freedom abroad, did not act in a manner becoming a Czechoslovak citizen. I am thinking mainly of the group of so-called Sudetic Germans headed by W. Jaksch."[95] His own future uncertain, Jaksch remained in London, campaigning and writing energetically but with increasing desperation against a tragedy he was powerless to avert.

Yet just as the expulsion scheme was not the work of one man acting alone, neither was the failure to prevent it. Undoubtedly some of Jaksch's decisions during the war can be second-guessed. His advice to Sudeten German refugees to join the British forces rather than the "Free Czechoslovak" army so long as the future of the Sudetenland remained unsettled made him no friends among the government in exile and was a definite tactical error, although one that probably made little difference in the long run. He was mistaken, as Beneš triumphantly reminded him, to think that the British would come to his assistance. Lastly, he failed to foresee how long and bitter the war would be, and how small a part traditional concepts of national self-determination would play in the postwar world order.

It would be a mistake, though, to view what had occurred as a duel between

Beneš and Jaksch, in which the former outplayed the latter. In the final analysis, the Allies listened to Beneš and ignored Jaksch because one had influence over the people for whom he spoke and the other did not. Until the end of the war, the *Sudetendeutsche*, whether enthusiastic Hitlerites or passive anti-Nazis, continued to serve the Greater Germany of which they considered themselves a part. In this they did not differ from any of the other ethnic German—or *Volksdeutsch*—communities in Poland, Hungary, Yugoslavia, the Baltic states, and elsewhere who, regardless of their individual political leanings, either aligned themselves with the Reich or did nothing to oppose it.

Both at the time and until the present day, defenders of the postwar expulsions have seen in this fact a complete justification for the policy of population transfer. In Czechoslovakia and everywhere else, when the test came, the *Volksdeutsche* had proven more loyal to their ethnic community—even in its monstrous Hitlerite form—than to the states of which they were nominally citizens. It was hardly unreasonable, therefore, that after the war they should be made to accept the logical consequences of that choice. Even if this resulted in unfairness and suffering to those whose guilt was less than others, Germany's neighbors could not be expected to tolerate forever the presence of a permanent fifth column in their midst. And because it would be necessary to reverse the Nazi state's wartime displacement of peoples in any event, there was no reason not to make a thorough job of it for fear of causing disruption to communities who had no claim to the Allies' consideration.

There is no question that the postwar expulsions cannot be separated from the wartime experience that preceded them. Yet each of these arguments for transferring the *Volksdeutsch* populations—questions of ethics or legality aside—is based on flawed premises. While it is going too far to depict ethnic Germans as hapless victims of fate, as in the case of Czechoslovakia the overall picture is far more ambiguous than the conventional rationales offered in favor of the expulsion scheme would suggest. The proposed population transfers were not simply an undoing of Nazi deportations, but a demographic experiment on a scale unprecedented in human history. And whether the *Volksdeutsche* ought to be regarded as Hitlerite auxiliaries or as something less or more—whether, indeed, in many cases they can meaningfully be considered even as "German"—is a question that can only be answered through a detailed examination of their wartime history.

2

The *Volksdeutsche* in Wartime

In one respect it is misleading to speak of "the postwar expulsions." From the very beginning of the Second World War, the European totalitarian powers engaged in ethnic cleansing on a scale never before seen in history. For Adolf Hitler, a continent from which "undesirable" peoples—Jews, Slavs, Roma, and others—had been displaced to make room for incoming German colonists lay at the very heart of his nightmarish racial vision. Even the Holocaust, when it had finally been decided upon, was but a means to this larger end. But his fellow dictator Josef Stalin also had grand ambitions to redraw the ethnographic map of the continent. During the two years of their uneasy partnership under the Nazi-Soviet Pact, both men found it convenient to work together.

Neither was a newcomer to the task. Stalin especially had a notable record of moving potentially troublesome national minorities around his empire, both as a form of collective punishment and to ensure that vulnerable borderlands were inhabited by ethnic groups—principally Russians and Georgians—in whose loyalty he considered he could repose greater confidence. To be sure, the internal transfer of smaller nations falling within the Russian orbit already had a long and dishonorable history by the time Stalin assumed control. Tsar Alexander II, the ironically named "Tsar-Liberator," displaced nearly half a million natives of the western Caucasus in 1863–64 to enhance the security of the border. His grandson, Nicholas II, would follow his example in the first months of the Great War, removing to the Russian interior the ethnic Germans of central Poland along with an even greater number of Polish Jews. With the front beginning to collapse in the face of Hindenburg's counterattacks in January 1915, Army General Headquarters stepped up this purge of potentially disloyal German, Austro-Hungarian, and Turkish subjects, by the simple expedient of giving the expellees a short period to collect what goods they could and then setting fire to their houses and crops. As the displaced people fled east, without food or any semblance of an evacuation system in operation, they began to die in large numbers.[1] In the central Asian regions and the Far East of the Russian Empire, Chinese, Korean, and Moslem populations were removed for similar reasons.[2] But it was only after the Bolshevik Revolution that internal deportations of entire peoples became a regular instrument of state policy.

A youthful Stalin cut his teeth as an architect of forced removals when as "Commissar for Nationalities" he assisted his fellow Georgian, Sergo Ordzhonikidze, to clear out the Terek Cossacks from the northern Caucasus in 1920.[3] In the second half of the 1930s, movements of this kind reached unprecedented levels. "Between 1935 and 1938," as Terry Martin notes, "at least nine Soviet nationalities—Poles, Germans, Finns, Estonians, Latvians, Koreans, Chinese, Kurds, Iranians—were all subjected to ethnic cleansing."[4] Most of these movements were connected to the Soviet leader's paranoia over "spies" and "wreckers" within the country. In 1937, for example, 11,868 ethnic Germans living in the USSR were arrested as suspected Nazi agents; the following year no fewer than 27,432 were detained on similar charges.[5] The number of Soviet Poles held for espionage was greater still. The majority of these detainees were executed; the peoples to which they belonged were internally exiled by police and NKVD units. During the years of Stalin's "Great Terror," a total of approximately 800,000 members of national minorities were victims of execution, arrest, or deportation—generally to the Central Asian republics of Kazakhstan and Uzbekistan, which began to rival Siberia as convenient dumping grounds for peoples the government viewed with disfavor.

Although Hitler had less scope than his Soviet counterpart for large-scale transfers of population, he too worked energetically to convert Germany into an ethnically and racially homogeneous state even before the war. The persecution of the Jews since 1933 had the explicit intention of compelling them to leave the country: in its crudest form, this consisted of physically pushing those who held dual citizenship across the borders into the territory of neighboring countries.[6] A further wave of coerced migrations, this time under international auspices, ensued as a result of the Munich Agreement, which provided a six-month window of opportunity for ethnic Czechs and Slovaks to move out of the Sudetenland (and Germans elsewhere in Czechoslovakia to transfer in) and established a German-Czechoslovak commission to "consider ways of facilitating the transfer of population."[7] In the spring of 1939, Germany browbeat neighboring Lithuania into ceding the largely German Memelland to the Reich, though tens of thousands of *Volksdeutsche* were left in the areas remaining under Lithuanian control. Lastly, at Mussolini's behest, Heinrich Himmler opened negotiations with Italy in May 1939 to secure the removal of the 200,000 ethnic Germans of the Alto Adige region in the Italian Alps. Notwithstanding his "Pact of Steel" with Hitler concluded in the same month, the Duce had not been oblivious to the recent fate of countries bordering on the Reich that harbored German minority populations. After the Nazi state's absorption of Austria in the *Anschluss* of 1938, Mussolini considered it wise to remove temptation, and his ethnic Germans, from his new partner's field of vision. By July, an agreement in principle had been reached for the "voluntary" departure of the German-speaking population, though no decision was taken as to their ultimate destination. Although the pact supposedly required the ratification of the ethnic Germans themselves in a plebiscite, an affirmative vote was ensured by declaring that any who elected to remain ipso facto consented to be resettled anywhere within the Italian domains that Mussolini chose to send them. According to rumors deliberately spread to make certain that voters saw the matter in the correct light, this was to be Abyssinia.[8]

Only the war itself, though, would provide the opportunity for creating the ethnically and racially "pure" spaces that were Nazism's ultimate objective. In its most grandiose and unhinged expression, the *Generalplan Ost* (General Plan East) drawn up by the SS in 1939–40, up to fifty million people in central and eastern Europe were to be killed or expelled over a period of some thirty years to make room for settlement colonies of Germans and other "Germanizable" peoples like Czechs and Aryanized Ukrainians.[9] The first steps toward this goal were taken in the secret protocol attached to the Nazi-Soviet Pact. In the cynical horse trade signed by Hitler's foreign minister Joachim von Ribbentrop in Moscow on August 23, 1939, it was agreed that Stalin would be allocated a "sphere of influence" extending over the eastern half of Poland, as far as the line defined by the Vistula, Narev, and San Rivers. German hegemony was confirmed over the western portion. The Soviets also demanded, and received, a similar sphere of influence over the Bessarabia and northern Bukovina regions of Romania and the Baltic states of Latvia and Estonia. Lithuania would remain a German concern. Left unmentioned, though hardly forgotten, was the question of each country's national minorities in the other's sphere. Eastern Poland was of little immediate moment to Hitler—only about 128,000 ethnic Germans lived there, in comparison to the 500,000 or more inhabiting the western districts—but there were centuries-old German-speaking communities in the Baltic. Alfred Rosenberg, the Estonian-born chief Nazi ideologue and editor of the NSDAP daily newspaper, the *Völkischer Beobachter*, was only one of many leading party members to hail from this region. Obviously the Baltic Germans could not be allowed to remain where they were. Stalin, as noted above, already considered the existing ethnic German settlements of the USSR to be hotbeds of anti-Soviet espionage, and would hardly shrink from taking what he saw as the necessary murderous steps to neutralize threats from that quarter. For his part, Hitler, about to go to war with Poland on the pretext of protecting the *Volksdeutsche* of that country, would not be able to stand by with folded hands as his new ally consigned his racial comrades to the Gulag or the grave.

For the moment, however, the Nazis had bigger fish to fry. On the morning of September 1, 1939, German armies swept into Poland. Ostensibly their mission was to rescue the ethnic German population of that country from oppression. For the previous three weeks, the Nazi press had worked itself into an officially inspired frenzy over the supposed sufferings of the German minority, in conformity with a directive by the propaganda minister, Joseph Goebbels, on August 11 that "as of now, the first page should contain news and comments on Polish offenses against *Volksdeutsche* and all kinds of incidents showing the Poles' hatred of everything that is German."[10] Not every one of these stories was manufactured out of whole cloth, though most were exaggerated out of all recognition. Between the wars, Poland's record of respecting the rights of its Jewish, German, and Ukrainian minorities had been a thoroughly undistinguished one. Some eight thousand Germans were interned in a former prisoner of war camp for several months in 1919; most ethnic German state employees lost their jobs; boycotts of German businesses were common; and German schools, associations, and newspapers were frequently shut down by the state, often acting in response to pressure from nationalist organizations eager to complete the Polonization of the country by repressive means.[11] In September 1934, the authoritarian regime of Field-Marshal Józef Piłsudski announced that it would no longer regard itself as bound by the minority protection treaties it had concluded in 1919 with the League of Nations.[12] As Nazi policy toward Poland became more bellicose and menacing in the winter of 1938–39, moreover, the government in Warsaw cracked down hard on what it was coming to regard as the snakes in Poland's bosom. The use of the German language in newspapers published in Poznań-Pomorze was banned in February 1939; German cultural festivals were suppressed; and up to seventy thousand *Volksdeutsche*, their homes and farms subject to attacks by the majority population, were forced to flee across the border.[13] The true objective of the German invasion, though, had been set out by Hitler himself in his "Second Book," the unpublished sequel to *Mein Kampf*, as early as 1928: "[A Nazi Germany] must under no conditions annex Poles with the intention of wanting to make Germans out of them someday. On the contrary, it must muster the determination either to seal off these alien racial elements . . . or it must without further ado remove them and hand over the vacated territory to its own national comrades."[14]

The point, then, was never to "rescue" *Volksdeutsche* under Polish administration. Making up no more than 3 percent of the prewar population of Poland, from the very beginning they were cast as no more than bit players in the larger drama of building a racial empire in the Nazi *Lebensraum* to the east. Within a few years of the conquest, it was envisaged, they would be reduced to numerical insignificance by millions of colonists arriving from elsewhere. Typical of the ad hoc improvisation and lack of planning that characterized the Nazi regime's operations, however, Hitler had given practically no thought since his seizure of power to the question of what was to be done with the conquered territories, beyond pushing their Polish Gentile and Jewish populations out of them.[15] Still less attention was devoted to deciding from where the new German colonists were to come, how they were to be transported to their future destinations, or what kind of logistical preparations would be required to induce them to remain there.

Ironically, the German invasion of September 1, 1939 itself led, in some cases, to the kind of atrocities against the *Volksdeutsch* population that the Goebbels-directed press had been assiduously fabricating or, at the least, embellishing. Like other countries menaced by German invasion in 1939–40, Poland in the first chaotic days of the war gave way to a fifth column panic of considerable proportions. The same rumors that were to become familiar in the Netherlands, Belgium, France, and Great Britain—of ethnic German saboteurs cunningly disguised as Polish servicemen or nuns, of farmers who pointed out targets to Luftwaffe bombers by plowing or mowing their fields in the shape of an arrow, of *francs-tireurs* who fired on troops from bedrooms or cut telegraph wires—received their first public airing in the "September Campaign" of 1939.[16] As in those other countries, nearly all such stories were unfounded. It is certainly true that there were pro-Nazi organizations of long standing among the German minority in Poland. In February 1936, for example, around a hundred members of a shadowy group with links to the Nazi government, the *Nationalsozialistische Arbeitsbewegung*, were tried for subversion in Katowice and received sentences of between six and ten years. Members of another German political group, the *Wanderbund*, from Tarnowiskie Góry received lesser sentences in the same year. Some evidence exists, moreover, to suggest that Himmler's intelligence organization, the *Sicherheitsdienst*, had been recruiting members of the German minority for service in underground militia units up to a year prior to the outbreak of war.[17] But there is little to suggest that the *Volksdeutsche* in Poland as a body were let into the secret of the German invasion or—with the exception of a coordinated assault by saboteurs on Polish forces in the city of Katowice—played any significant role in facilitating the Wehrmacht's advance.[18] Neither the Polish authorities nor ordinary Poles, though, had any way of knowing this, and their reaction, while understandable, was excessive. As soon as the war began, some fifteen thousand *Volksdeutsch* suspects were rounded up and forced to march to internment camps in the interior. One of the deportees, Fr. Hilarius Breitinger, an assistant to the auxiliary bishop of Gniezno and Poznań, Dr. Walenty Dymek, kept a record of his experiences on what the historian Michael Phayer describes as "a three-week, death-threatening ordeal."

> Breitinger, along with other mostly lay Volksdeutschers, were led endless miles around the countryside by Polish vigilantes. Poles heaped abuse on them, stoned them, threw garbage and horse droppings at them and beat them with whatever was at hand. Breitinger was struck in the head by a brick which, he thought, would have killed him had it not struck the arm of his glasses. This treatment continued day and night without the captives having much to eat or to drink. The elderly, physically unable to keep pace, were murdered. "It was clear to us what the purpose of all this was," Breitinger later wrote, "we were open game."[19]

In the western town of Bydgoszcz (Bromberg), events took a still more tragic turn. Three days after the invasion, a retreating Polish military unit, believing itself to have come under attack from a German-owned house, commenced a massacre of elements of the civilian population. Similar episodes occurred elsewhere in the town. The number of *Volksdeutsche* killed over the next two days in the course of what the Nazis described as "Bromberg Bloody Sunday" is still a matter of fierce dispute between German and Polish historians, as is the question of whether the Polish soldiers' belief that they had been fired upon was well founded.[20] There is no doubt, though, that many German civilians were killed after mistakenly being taken for fifth columnists, at Bydgoszcz and other places. Perhaps a hundred *Volksdeutsche* died in the course of a forced march to Kutno; thirty-four others were executed in Toruń on suspicion of having signaled to German aircraft flying overhead.[21] Similar, though generally smaller-scale, excesses occurred elsewhere, often directed against other minorities, like Ukrainians, Byelorussians, and Jews, whose loyalty to the Polish state was also regarded as doubtful.[22] Altogether, a German Criminal Police investigation in 1940 calculated that 5,437 civilian members of the German minority had been killed by the Poles during the five-week-long "September Campaign"—although, typically, Goebbels inflated that figure more than tenfold in the version he released for public consumption.[23] More recent scholarship suggests a death toll of 4,500 is nearer the mark.[24]

Nevertheless, the attacks on ethnic Germans provided the invading forces with a convenient ex post facto justification for their onslaught against Poland. During the weeks to come, both they and the *Volksdeutsche* themselves would take their revenge on the Poles in a manner that vastly exceeded whatever provocation they had suffered. In Bydgoszcz itself, ethnic Germans would accompany Wehrmacht and SS units, identifying alleged perpetrators who were shot out of hand. Under Hitler's direct order, about five hundred Poles from the town were executed. The Security Police also carried out a search of the Schwedenhöhe suburb for suspects, in the course of which approximately two hundred more people were killed.[25] The pattern was repeated in other occupied towns and cities. In the weeks immediately following the invasion, moreover, *Volksdeutsch* males aged between seventeen and forty-five flocked to join so-called *Selbstschutz* or "self-defense" militias to assist the German police battalions that assumed responsibility for security in German-occupied Poland. These quickly took on a much more sinister complexion when, in October 1939, they were placed under SS control. By then, there were more than seventeen thousand volunteers serving in *Selbstschutz* units in the region of West Prussia alone. There and elsewhere they played an important role in fingering Polish suspects and Jews to the police and SS; they guarded internment and forced labor camps in which the detainees were held, often in atrocious conditions; and, before long, they were assisting the murderous *Einsatzgruppen*, the SS bands charged with liquidating political and racial enemies in the occupied lands, to carry out large-scale massacres of Polish Jews and Gentiles.[26] The Danzig *Selbstschutz* took a prominent role in the murder of three thousand patients in Polish mental asylums; many more were killed in hastily erected detention camps. In total, the "self-defense units" may have been responsible for as many as twenty thousand killings in the twelve months following the German invasion; they also assisted in the removal of another ten thousand to the new concentration camp at Stutthof. Their career, though, was short-lived. As the Polish "pacification" campaign drew to a close, Himmler decided that such amateur bodies had served their purpose and, with all danger of further Polish resistance eliminated, directed in August 1940 that they be wound up.[27]

By that point the Nazis had turned their attention to the much more ambitious task of reshaping the ethnographic character of their freshly conquered territories. The matter became more urgent after the Soviet Union, in accordance with the secret protocol to the Nazi-Soviet Pact, invaded Poland from the east on September 17—ironically, using precisely the same pretext as Germany, the only difference being that the minorities Stalin accused Warsaw of mistreating were in this case Byelorussians and Ukrainians. As the USSR proceeded forcibly to expel a quarter of a million ethnic Poles from what would become the western provinces of the Ukrainian and Byelorussian Soviet Socialist Republics,[28] the Germans arrived at a similar solution. After weighing and then abandoning the idea of leaving a much-truncated Polish state as a sop to appeasement-minded Westerners, Hitler resolved to bisect the part of Poland under German occupation. Approximately half would be incorporated directly into the Reich as two new *Gaue*, or districts, named Danzig–West Prussia and the Warthegau respectively. The remainder—a forty-thousand-square-mile tract of central Poland, including the cities of Warsaw and Kraków, named by the Nazis the *Generalgouvernement* (General Government)—was to become a demographic dustbin for inhabitants of the annexed districts found unsuitable for Germanization.

The acquisition of the Incorporated Eastern Territories, as the new *Reichsgaue* became known, and the problem of *Volksdeutsch* populations within the Soviet orbit were intimately linked. A week after the USSR's attack on Poland, Stalin notified Hitler that he intended to claim his reward in Latvia and Estonia. On September 28, the day Warsaw fell, Berlin and Moscow concluded a further secret agreement, transferring Lithuania with its substantial German minority to the Soviet sphere in exchange for the addition to the German portion of the districts of Lublin and eastern Warsaw, originally assigned to the USSR the previous month. For Hitler, the removal of the German population of the Baltic had become a matter of urgency, as Stalin had intimated he was in no mood to be patient. The availability of the Incorporated Eastern Territories enabled him to kill two birds with one stone. Jews and racially unassimilable Poles would be forcibly transferred to the *Generalgouvernement*. Their houses, farms, and businesses would be assigned to the Baltic Germans, for whom persuasion to move to the newly conquered lands would hardly be necessary. Fear of the Soviets would see to that. The solution was of the kind that appealed most to Hitler, being simple, symmetrical, and brutal.

It did not, on the other hand, appeal to many *Volksdeutsche*. In a keynote address to the Reichstag to mark the end of the Polish campaign, Hitler announced on October 6, 1939 a "new order of ethnographic conditions" to be accomplished by a "resettlement of nationalities in such a manner . . . as to remove at least part of the material for European conflict." Germany and the USSR, he intimated, had already agreed on such a transfer. What would be called the *Heim ins Reich* (Back to the Reich) program was thus revealed to the world. The prospect horrified many ethnic Germans, much of whose enthusiasm for Nazism had been predicated on the expectation that the boundaries of the Reich would, as in the cases of Austria, the Sudetenland, and Danzig, extend to embrace them. The prospect of being uprooted from their homes to face an uncertain future not even in Germany proper, but in the considerably less salubrious environment of western Poland, was much less attractive. So far from rallying enthusiastically to the Führer's call, therefore, many *Volksdeutsche* greeted the declaration of the *Heim ins Reich* initiative with a deep sense of betrayal.

Their disillusionment would have been all the greater had they known how few preparations had been made for what was to be to that point the second largest population transfer in history after that between Turkey and Greece—and one, moreover, that was to be completed in a matter of weeks rather than years. Not until the morning after Hitler's Reichstag speech was Himmler commissioned with the task of overseeing the "return" of ethnic Germans from overseas, "eliminating harmful alien elements" in the conquered territories, and accomplishing their colonization. Establishing an agency for the purpose to which he gave the grandiose title of Reich Commissariat for the Strengthening of Germandom (RKFDV), Himmler worked quickly to bring the Nazi Party's competing liaison agency for ethnic Germans, the *Volksdeutsche Mittelstelle* (VoMi) under his control. From then on, the SS would take the lead in reconfiguring the distribution of population in central and eastern Europe so as to make the region into what Hitler would optimistically describe as an Aryan "Garden of Eden."

From the very beginning, things started to go wrong. As daunting as the challenges would have been under normal conditions, it immediately became evident that neither Himmler nor anyone else concerned had the least idea how to address them in the midst of a world war. Slapdash improvisation was the order of the day, with the Nazis largely unable to cope with any problem associated with the resettlement for which mass murder, summary expulsion, or recourse to fanciful racial theories did not provide a solution.

These difficulties came to the fore with the first wave of movements from the Baltic states. Scant respect was accorded to the sensibilities of the governments concerned; the agreement governing transfers of the sixteen thousand *Volksdeutsche* from Estonia was signed on October 15, a week after removals began. Similarly, the first ship to commence the transport of fifty thousand Latvian Germans docked on October 9, three weeks before the conclusion of negotiations with the Riga government. The Baltic states took their revenge for these slights by driving exceptionally hard economic bargains with Berlin. Taking full advantage of the minimal period allocated for the transfer—the Estonian protocol specified that the operation was to be completed by December 15—the two Baltic states snapped up German properties for a fraction of their true value. Estonian Germans were permitted to take with them only the equivalent of twenty dollars in local currency, together with household furniture and tools; all remaining assets, including real property, were to be assigned to a German Resettlement Trust in

Tallinn which would oversee their liquidation and the application of the funds thus realized to the settling of the *Deutschbalten* in their new homes. Disputes concerning ownership or valuations were to be settled by a bilateral commission. In the end, official Estonian intransigence compelled the Resettlement Trust to sell off German-owned lands to the government at fire sale prices. The Latvian government took a still more avaricious stance. No more than ten dollars in Latvian currency could be taken out of the country; the export of precious metals or jewelry was prohibited; and all productive equipment larger than hand tools had to be left behind. The Latvian state moved to acquire German-owned lands and settle Latvian citizens on them in exchange for the promise to supply commodities to Germany, and to a still greater degree than their Estonian cousins lowballed the former owners on a massive scale.[29] Cynics declared the initials of the UTAG, the Latvian equivalent of the Resettlement Trust, to stand for *Untergang Tausender Arischer Geschlechter*, or "Ruination of Thousands of Aryan Descent." Joseph Schechtman has estimated that the Estonian and Latvian governments paid a mere $16 million in 1939 values for the German assets they acquired.[30] The Nazis, though, were not disposed to quibble over pennies. Any sums realized from these transactions, however meager, were regarded as a bonus in light of the certainty that Stalin would soon take over in both countries and nullify all previous agreements made by their governments—as he duly proceeded to do in June 1940.

A similar process of horse trading took place, this time directly between the two principals in Berlin and Moscow, over the "return" of the 128,000 *Volksdeutsche* living in the Polish areas assigned to the USSR under the Nazi-Soviet Pact, most of them Volhynian and Galician Germans from the districts on the border with Ukraine. Their property, valued at $1.6 billion, was made over to the Soviets in exchange for a like amount in oil and foodstuffs to be delivered to the Reich. Meanwhile, after the conclusion of the Alto Adige "plebiscite," Himmler reached a final settlement with Mussolini providing for the removal of the Germans there by December 31, 1942. He had already set aside for them a part of the Beskid mountain range in southern Poland, whose geographic and climatic conditions were thought to be equivalent to those they were leaving.

The process of moving all these peoples in wartime was at best haphazard. With great difficulty, fifty thousand *Deutschbalten* were evacuated on *Kraft durch Freude* cruise ships before November 15, 1939. Even so, thirty-five hundred Estonian and more than twelve thousand Latvian Germans—many of them partners in mixed marriages—stayed behind, their places being taken by individuals who had no connection whatever to Germany but who, by dint of bribery or connections, had fraudulently obtained the certificates testifying to their Germanness that would enable them to escape Stalin's clutches. Though a large number of "returnees" were brought by train, many of the Volhynians, Galicians, and others arriving from central and eastern Poland were left to transport themselves and their possessions on horse carts, their livestock being driven along beside them. Their trek westward in the depths of winter was grueling, with many appalled and angered by the lack of assistance and organization from Reich authorities. "Usually nothing went smoothly," one disgruntled settler recalled.[31] Throughout the journey, the caravans were not allowed to rest for more than two hours at a time, for fear of frostbite and hypothermia.[32] Nonetheless, the *Volksdeutsch* exodus was mythologized by a tidal wave of Himmler-inspired *Heim ins Reich* propaganda depicting the emigrants as hardy pioneers striking out for a new life in the frontier lands of the West. As one breathless chronicler of the movement put it, the settlers were the modern analogue of the Germanic tribes who, in the fourth and fifth centuries A.D., had dealt the ailing and corrupt Roman Empire its final death blow. The agents of this latter-day *Völkerwanderung* were "in the midst of their new mission posed to them by the Reich, finally to settle the German east as a German area."[33]

That turned out to be precisely the problem. The Nazi state's ability to move large numbers of people, willingly or unwillingly, from one place to another at short notice vastly exceeded its skill at accomplishing the rehousing and resettlement of those thus moved. An early portent was provided when patients in psychiatric hospitals in Gdynia, Stettin, and Swinemünde were murdered under the Nazi "T-4" euthanasia program to enable the facilities to be used as temporary accommodation for some of the incoming *Deutschbalten*. Altogether, some ten thousand Poles were gassed or shot in connection with the transport. This combination of hasty, slapdash measures and unbridled savagery would become characteristic of the *Volksdeutsche* colonization scheme over the following years. In the RKFDV's early imaginings, scarcely less simplistic than those of Hitler himself, "resettlement" involved nothing more complex than the driving out or murder of Poles and Jews and the reassignment of their property—less a suitable consideration for administration costs—to the newcomers. The reality was to be infinitely more challenging.

Expropriating the *Untermenschen*, a process set in hand by Goering who established the *Haupttreuhandstelle Ost* (Main Trusteeship Office East) to confiscate Jewish and Polish assets in the conquered territories and redistribute them to colonists, was a far bigger task than anticipated. An unforeseen complication was that there were fewer properties to go around than once believed. Of the 102,800 square kilometers of land annexed by Germany for the Incorporated Territories, three-quarters had been German before 1914. The conquest was thus followed by a flood of claims by former owners whose properties had been acquired compulsorily for minimal compensation by the interwar Polish state, and who now wanted them back with interest.[34]

The main obstacle, though, was the toxic brew of bureaucratic infighting, institutional confusion, last-minute changes of plan, and clashing objectives that stultified almost every major initiative undertaken by the Nazi state. Initially, Himmler and the RKFDV—aided by two lieutenants, Reinhard Heydrich and Adolf Eichmann, who would later achieve global notoriety in the context of a still more ambitious and deranged demographic engineering program—set about the task of clearing the two new *Gaue* of the Incorporated Eastern Territories of their "excess" Polish and Jewish populations. The operation quickly fell behind schedule, however, firstly because of the unexpectedly slow pace of the confiscation bureaucracy, and secondly because of the unhelpfulness of the two *Gauleiter* concerned, Arthur Greiser of the Warthegau and Albert Forster of Danzig–West Prussia. Each cordially detested the other; both were determined to be first to complete the Germanization of their respective *Gaue*. The very different ways in which they pursued this objective proved equally subversive to the *Volksdeutsch* reception program. Greiser, an unbending Himmler loyalist, SS-*Obergruppenführer*, and race crank, proposed to tackle the problem by the book, calling in the specialists of the SS Race and Settlement Main Office to conduct a person-by-person racial screening to determine who was fitted to remain and who would be forced into the *Generalgouvernement*. (Jews, being unassimilable by definition, were not subject to screening, but summarily expropriated and deported.) Only a few hundred racial investigators were available, however, and the scale of the task soon overwhelmed their efforts. Albert Forster, a quintessential organization man whose roots lay in the Nazi Party and whose relations with Himmler and the SS grew more poisonous by the day, sought a less cumbersome solution. Convinced as he was that most inhabitants of his *Gau* were individuals of at least part-German blood who had been led astray before 1939 by "Polonizers," Forster sent his officials into the midst of the population to sign up erstwhile Poles as "ethnic Germans." Since the alternative was deportation to the *Generalgouvernement*, he did not lack for takers. Inability to speak German was no obstacle, nor were many questions asked to verify respondents' claims of distant German descent. As the *Gauleiter* ingenuously explained, "We would not be National Socialists if we did not possess the unshakable belief that we will succeed in making men with German blood into enthusiastic Germans through our leadership and education."[35] Apart from its simplicity, the advantage of the bureaucratic approach to the task of Germanization—and probably its chief attraction to Forster—was that it offered no opportunity to the SS and its retinue of race monitors to interfere in Danzig–West Prussia's affairs. From the point of view of the agencies charged with overseeing *Volksdeutsch* resettlement, however, neither *Gau's* handling of the problem was in the least satisfactory. Greiser's method of meticulous racial examination meant that Poles would be removed to the east, freeing up space for incoming colonists, only with agonizing slowness; Forster's, of converting Poles to Germans at the stroke of a pen, meant that they would not be removed at all.

The consequences were predictable. In the winter of 1939–40 a large backlog of colonists for whom no space in the Incorporated Eastern Territories was yet available built up, compelling the RKFDV to house 150,000 of them in improvised camps in the Sudetenland, Saxony, Pomerania, and the Warthegau. Belated efforts to create additional space led only to further confusion. Early in November, for example, the Polish city of Łódź was detached from the *Generalgouvernement* and assigned to the Warthegau to provide a suitable home for the highly urbanized *Deutschbalten*. Łódź, however, had a large Jewish population, and the immediate effect was vastly to increase the number of people who had to be deported to the *Generalgouvernement*, placing additional strain on already overburdened transport facilities. Hence, although Heydrich appointed Eichmann in December as his special officer for clearances in the annexed provinces, the program fell further and further behind schedule. Only 87,838 Poles and Jews had been transported to the east by December 17, when the operation had to be suspended so that the rolling stock could be used to bring Volhynian and Galician Germans in from Soviet-occupied Poland. Large-scale removals were not restarted until April 1940; even then, only 133,000 of a planned 600,000 were removed by early 1941, when the logistical requirements of Operation Barbarossa once again brought clearances to a halt.

Nor did this do anything to reduce the backlog. To the contrary, the number of spaces that needed to be made available to accommodate new participants in the *Heim ins Reich* program took a sharp turn upward in the summer of 1940. The Soviet Union's absorption of the three Baltic states in June compelled another hasty exodus of some 12,000 remaining ethnic Germans from Estonia and Latvia and 48,000 more from Lithuania.[36] Under the terms of the Second Vienna Award two months later, in which Hitler forced Romania to cede northern Transylvania to Hungary, by now a Nazi client state, the 95,000 ethnic Germans living there were given the right to join the *Heim ins Reich* scheme rather than be compelled to transfer their allegiance from Bucharest to Budapest. Some 77,000 availed themselves of the opportunity by the end of the year. Stalin, too, had had his eye on Romania, and sent its government an ultimatum demanding the cession of the part-Ukrainian northern Bukovina region, together with Romanian Bessarabia, in June 1940. The Romanians meekly complied. About 137,000 *Volksdeutsche* lived in the transferred territories; under yet another Nazi-Soviet accord, they were transported to Germany in the autumn. All told, according to Götz Aly's calculations, about a quarter of a million ethnic Germans were transferred from southeastern Europe in 1940, a larger number than had by that time arrived from the Baltic states and eastern Poland combined.[37]

Once again, the racial engineers of the Third Reich had nowhere to put them, and the camp population ballooned. Of the absurdly ambitious target set by Nazi population organizers of 5.3 million deportations from the Incorporated Eastern Territories for the winter of 1940–41, just 408,000 had been carried out by March 1941. To add to the difficulty, an ever-increasing proportion of colonizable land was set aside by the SS to be distributed as rewards to demobilized soldiers at the end of the war; by March 1942, half of the Warthegau had been designated for this purpose.[38] Lastly, the poverty of many of the Polish and Jewish deportees meant that a single confiscated property was rarely considered adequate for the needs of the colonists. As Himmler explained to a campfull of impatient and disgruntled Volhynians at Kirchberg (Wiśniowa Góra) in May 1940, "You must understand that you have to wait. Before you get your farm, a Polack must first be thrown out. Often they are such holes that we first have to put the buildings in order or combine two farms."[39] In practice, the actual "multiplier" effect was higher still. Himmler's insistence that the minimum size of a *Volksdeutsch* farm was to be 25 hectares (62.5 acres) meant that on average, three Polish farms had to be amalgamated to provide a holding for a single *Volksdeutsch* family.[40]

The confiscations, moreover, rarely went to plan. According to a protocol laid down by Wilhelm Koppe, head of the SS and police in the Warthegau, areas targeted for clearance should be raided without notice in the predawn hours to prevent the inhabitants from hiding or destroying their goods. The expellees should be taken immediately to an evacuation camp, pending their relocation to the *Generalgouvernement*. The new *Volksdeutsch* colonists should be standing by, but care was to be taken to ensure that they did not witness the distressing scene. Often, female "settlement advisers"—typically, middle-class young women from Germany performing their obligatory six months' labor service—would be brought along to give the confiscated properties a quick spruce-up. "On resettlement days they ensured that the evicted Poles did not take everything with them, but left the necessary items behind for the settlers." They were also supposed to clean the houses and provide a hot meal for the new arrivals "so that the settlers would quickly feel at ease in their new home."[41] In most cases, these operations took place in a far more chaotic fashion. Sometimes it was left to the Nazi women to carry out expulsions by themselves; one of them, Melita Maschmann, later recalled her fury when she and the girls of the Labor Service camp she headed were detailed in 1942 by the local SS-men to remove the Polish inhabitants of a Warthegau village, armed only with a wooden coat hanger.[42] Local *Volksdeutsche* possessing advance knowledge of planned clearances frequently leaked the information to Poles selected for deportation in the hope of being able to buy their goods at knockdown prices. The reliance of German resettlement agencies on Polish ancillary workers also meant that secrecy was hard to maintain. In the summer of 1940, consequently, only about 40 percent of the Poles selected for deportation from the Warthegau were falling into the authorities' hands. The remainder had gone to live with relatives, disappeared in the cities, or taken to the forests.[43]

The recipients of the confiscated properties, for their part, often found it impossible to maintain that comfortable distance from the squalid reality of the process to which Koppe attached such value. Irma Eigi, the seventeen-year-old daughter of an Estonian hotelier, was disturbed to find herself surrounded, in the flat assigned to her family by the housing office in Posen (Poznań) in December 1939, by evidence of the sudden catastrophe that had overtaken the previous owners. "Some of the cupboards stood open. The drawers were open. On the table were the remains of food. And then the unmade beds, messed up."[44] Shaken by the spectacle, her father asked to be transferred to a slightly less visibly morally compromised dwelling, but to no avail. Herr Eigi did, however, accept the invitation of the local resettlement agency to tour the Polish-owned restaurants of the town and find one he liked, following which a deed of ownership to his selected business was issued to him. Sylvia Bannister, the English wife of a German obstetrician sent to Bydgoszcz in October 1939, was similarly disconcerted on her arrival in the town to be handed a list of confiscated houses to view. At one of them she found the wife of a Pole who had been shot in a reprisal action the same morning still in residence; the woman was equally ignorant of her husband's murder and her own impending eviction. Bannister too, though, saw little point in crying over spilt milk, or blood. "How could we ever live happily in one of these homes haunted by the misery of our predecessors? But what alternative had we? Kurt [her husband] had to carry on with his work and we had to live somewhere near."[45] Before long she was agreeably situated in an attractive residence previously owned by a Polish architect, whose entire family, conveniently, was nowhere to be seen.

At all levels of German society, scruples over profiting from the displaced Poles' and Jews' misery were rapidly overcome. *Volksdeutsch* colonists brought in from outside the Incorporated Territories fought vigorous turf battles with those already there, who pressed the authorities—often successfully—for compensation for their losses at the hands of the Polish state during the interwar years. Both found themselves competing with hundreds of thousands of predatory *Reichsdeutsche*, the citizens of the "old Reich," who flooded into the conquered districts with an eye to the main chance. (One of them was Hitler's favorite tank commander, General Heinz Guderian, who trawled the Warthegau in search of an estate befitting his elevated status. When an aghast Field Marshal von Manstein asked him what had become of the Polish owners of the manor he eventually selected, "Guderian said that he did not know, when he had taken over his estate the Poles had gone and he had no idea what had become of them.")[46] Tensions among all three groups, and among different ethnicities within the *Volksdeutsch* "family," frequently ran high:

> Settlement advisers depicted Bessarabian German children fighting local *Volksdeutsche* children. Native ethnic Germans were portrayed complaining that everything was done for the incoming settlers but nothing for them, and murmuring that if the settlers hadn't come, they would have got all the confiscated Polish land for themselves. One settlement adviser reported that the local ethnic Germans called the settlers from Bukovina "gypsies." Bukovina Germans hit back by calling the local ethnic Germans "Poles." . . . Settlement advisers were also quick to criticize fellow Reich Germans, usually men, for arrogance towards the *Volksdeutsche*. One told the story of a settler's wife from Bukovina who forgot to wear the badge showing she was German and was thrown out of the post office, where she was trying to post parcels to her son at the front, by a Reich German man who hit her in the face.[47]

Trying in just a few years to concoct a cohesive Germanic whole from a *Volksdeutsch* melting pot that constantly threatened to boil over was thus a forlorn hope. For many colonists, the dream of an idyllic life in the Incorporated Territories ended even sooner. The *Volksdeutsch* holding camps proved irresistibly attractive as reservoirs of available personnel to military recruiters and to businesses struggling to maintain production in the face of Germany's increasingly acute labor shortage. Inmates, facing an open-ended sojourn in ramshackle facilities whose commandants were prone to imposing upon them "a militarized regimen, separating them by sex and treating the newcomers as children, if not prisoners," were susceptible to such overtures.[48] Sometimes even Himmler yielded to the temptation, ordering in December 1940 that the Bessarabian Germans, who had not fulfilled his expectations as potential colonists, be conscripted instead into labor battalions. On other occasions it was the *Volksdeutsche* themselves who threw in the towel. Some colonists from Galicia, disappointed with the farms assigned to them in the Warthegau, abandoned them in the autumn of 1940 and sought readmission to their holding camp in Łódź; another group was arrested for rejecting the properties they were offered and holding a demonstration against the authorities.[49] And sometimes the mismatch between colonist and colony was so great that no amount of official intervention could make Germanic silk purses out of sociological sow's ears. The genteel Estonian and Latvian *Volksdeutsche* proved a particular disappointment as settlers, looking askance at the notion that they should become agrarian pioneers in the agoraphobia-inducing Polish steppes. "Either they were large landowners, who were not prepared to accept the conditions of peasant settlements (which would be like suggesting to Thomas Jefferson or 'Turnip' Townshend that they take on three acres and a cow) or they were urban dwellers. . . . Soon planning officials were calling on the evacuation staff not to send them any more Balts."[50]

The sheer diversity among the *Volksdeutsche*, indeed, was probably the biggest single impediment to the success of the colonization program. Other than their regional accents, some were indistinguishable from their *Reichsdeutsch* counterparts. Arthur Greiser, born in Poznań province, was himself *Volksdeutsch*. But the claims of others were far more tenuous, if not completely fictional. Poles and Jews often observed with bemusement that many members of the *Selbstschutz* militias that sprang up to assist the Germans were, as one woman put it "people from our town, Poles," who as soon as the Nazis arrived "suddenly heard the call of their German blood! Mostly they were scum: ex-jailbirds, card-sharps, thieves, petty (and not so petty!) crooks."[51] The ease with which yesterday's Pole, Ukrainian, or Czech could become today's German was not lost on the *Reichsdeutsche*, who began to describe their supposed co-racials as *Beutegermane* or "booty Germans" who had attached themselves to the *Volk* solely for the purpose of grabbing as much loot as they could. Nor was the SS unaware of or indifferent to the phenomenon of "piggybacking" on German ethnic identity. In October 1939, Arthur Greiser ordered the compilation in his *Gau* of a racial census, the *Deutsche Volksliste*, to separate the authentically German from the pretenders. The *Volksliste* classification scheme, however, was not itself a German invention. It was modeled on the lettered gradations used by the French to determine the expellability of Germans from Alsace in the early 1920s.[52] By Himmler's order, the scheme was extended to the whole of the Incorporated Territories in March 1941.

As with its French predecessor, four gradations of Germanness were specified by the *Volksliste* in its mature form. Persons in category I were those who had given proof of their national loyalty by participation in German organizations before September 1939; undisputed Germans who had taken no part in the "ethnic struggle" between the wars were registered in category II. In practice, few if any distinctions were observed between the two classes; members of each automatically received German nationality and carried the same identity card. For all intents and purposes, then, the only meaningful categories on the *Volksliste* were the third, for individuals of German racial heritage who had "abandoned" their national allegiance, e.g. by speaking Polish normally or exclusively at home; and the fourth, who notwithstanding possessing German racial characteristics had actively opposed Germanization in their respective countries between the wars. Individuals assigned to these categories were liable to be sent to the "old Reich" for Germanization; if eventually found suitable for German citizenship, they would be required to serve a lengthy probationary period. At the very bottom of the German ethnic pyramid were the *Deutschstämmige*, persons of more or less nebulous "German heritage." The significance of this category could vary widely—from nil in some instances to a fast track to inclusion on the *Volksliste* in others, especially when military recruitment drives or labor shortages made it convenient for the authorities to have to hand a pool of "potential Germans" that could be expanded at will.

Initially the Nazis invested a great deal of energy in compiling and policing the *Volksliste*, local versions of which were extended later in the war to Bohemia and Moravia—where Heydrich hoped to "Germanize" half the Czech population—Yugoslavia, and the western districts of European Russia. In theory, all *Volksdeutsche* were subject to screening, and purges of the lists were occasionally carried out when Himmler feared that the definitions of Germanness were becoming excessively elastic. With the passage of time, though, the process of selection for the *Volksliste* degenerated into farce. Local administrators, facing a variety of pressures from various higher authorities, reached decisions that were so arbitrary as to be practically meaningless, but that nearly always erred on the side of inclusion. "If the *Volksdeutschen* had not existed," Doris Bergen observes, "Nazi ideologues might have invented them. And in some very significant ways, they did precisely that."[53] In truth, they had little choice but to do so. Proving German ancestry by documentary means was difficult enough within the "old Reich," but virtually impossible outside it. Members of ethnic communities long separated from the homeland spoke German badly, or in dialects incomprehensible to the *Reichsdeutsche*, or not at all. In the Czech lands, as Chad Bryant notes, "Many 'new Germans' spoke only Czech."[54] Lacking any objective means of determining—or even defining—Germanness, the "ethnocrats" of the RKFDV applied whatever criteria tended to yield the desired result, "ranging from elaborate orange cards with questions about the shape of individuals' eyelids and chins, to designating entire villages as ethnic German settlements, to tests of political reliability."[55] By mid-1942, however, the emphasis had swung decisively on the side of signing up as many "Germans" as possible. With the war against the USSR turning into a quagmire, cannon fodder was urgently required and the supply of conscriptible *Reichsdeutsche* was running low. Only "Aryans" could be drafted into the German armed forces in Hitler's Reich, so "Aryans" the previously despised Poles, Ukrainians, Bessarabians, and Byelorussians in many cases had to become. Himmler, who had once tried to impose a cap of a million names on the *Volksliste* in the Incorporated Territories, now made refusal to enroll by a person declared eligible an offense punishable by detention in a concentration camp. In many areas, individuals were placed on the *Volksliste*, or "promoted" to a higher grade that would render them liable to military service, without their consent or even, in some cases, their knowledge.[56] As Anna Bramwell wryly concludes, "The *Volksliste* became a sifting procedure to procure potential citizens of the New Order: loyal, healthy, and possessed of five fingers on each hand."[57]

The effect of this policy of forced Germanization was witnessed by Zygmunt Klukowski, a doctor and hospital administrator from Szczebrzeszyn in the Zamość district of the *Generalgouvernement*. In 1942 this district was chosen as the first outside the Incorporated Territories to be opened up for German colonization. Soon afterward, his hospital was visited:

> Yesterday morning two soldiers from *Sonderdienst* came into the local pharmacy with new registration forms. On special forms they registered all the employees and then ordered them to sign. Some people signed without checking the forms. Among the physicians, Dr. Spoz was first. He looked at the form and realized that it was a request for identification papers for people claiming German nationality. At first he refused to sign, but after being pressured he did. Very shortly thereafter he came to the hospital, very nervous and informed me of what had happened, and he asked how he could get his form back. I called all the physicians together to discuss the matter. As I found out, all physicians, pharmacists, veterinarians, dentists, and nurses must fill out the registration forms. During the meeting it was decided that everyone had to make their own decision, whether or not to sign the form or refuse. . . .
>
> I learned that many people in Zamość signed this questionnaire without any reservations. This was stated also in the underground press. Now we ask ourselves what kind, if any, repressions we will face.[58]

The struggle that ensued between the Polish underground Home Army and the Germans over *Volksliste* registration became a microcosm of the larger conflict. Tens if not hundreds of thousands of ordinary Poles of both sexes found themselves in a Catch-22 situation, menaced with beatings, imprisonment, or deportation if they did not subscribe to the *Volksliste*, and arson, pillage, or assassination at the hands of the Home Army if they did. Even members of the same family could find themselves on opposite sides: the *Volksdeutsch* Mayor of Urzędów, Kazimierz Łoziński, was shot in 1943 on the orders of the Home Army, of which his two sons were members.[59] So common were Resistance attacks on settlers in the *Generalgouvernement*, as well as savage Nazi reprisals—as Dr. Klukowski recorded, in December 1942 some 160 Poles were executed in retaliation for an arson attack in the hamlet of Nawóz in which five *Volksdeutsch* houses were burned down—that the ethnic German *Selbstschutz* militias were revived in Poland, as well as in Ukraine, Estonia, and Yugoslavia.[60] In general these were units of limited military effectiveness, known more for their indiscipline and their readiness to assist the Germans in rounding up and massacring Jews than for their ability to protect their fellow colonists. The Nazis, too, reposed little confidence in them, conscripting the most capable into the army or *Waffen-SS* and often withholding even small arms from the remainder.

The "ethnic struggle" was not everywhere waged so fiercely, though even in the much quieter atmosphere of Bohemia and Moravia, ethnic Germans who offended their neighbors by taking out Reich nationality stood in danger of somewhat melodramatically named "'Czech terror'—being ignored in Czech shops, insulted, and sometimes even beaten up."[61] In fact, a greater problem for the Nazis was to prevent *Volksdeutsch* colonists from "going native" and making common cause with the indigenous population—with whom, objectively, they often shared closer bonds of culture, religion, lifestyle, and even language than their nominal *Volksgenossen* (racial comrades). Endless complaints were received from "settlement advisers," VoMi officials, and SS racial monitors of the failure of the *Volksdeutsche* to exhibit that "necessary consciousness of superiority which we need to be able to maintain our rights as a colonial state and nation."[62] Colonists "found it difficult to recognize their German heritage and get over their friendliness to the Poles."[63] The same deficiencies extended to lifestyle. While official propaganda represented ethnic Germans as "paragons of Aryan purity and National Socialist loyalty,"

> Reich authorities of all kinds griped about *Volksdeutschen* whom they said lacked proper German qualities: diligence, cleanliness, sexual self-control, and the ability to speak German.... As soon as their husbands were out of the picture, one reporter carped, the women took up with Ukrainians and Poles. The men, the account continued, were no better; they slept with Polish women and assumed the cultural habits of Poles, while the youth were lazy and promiscuous.[64]

Nazi officials had, of course, many tools of coercion at their disposal to enforce ethnic separation. As early as September 1940, Greiser issued a directive threatening with "protective custody" (i.e. detention in a concentration camp) those persons "belonging to the German community who maintain relations with Poles which go beyond those deriving from the performance of services or economic considerations.... In all cases the maintenance of repeated friendly contacts with Poles must be regarded as failure to observe the prescribed distance."[65] Ethnic Germans could be punished for "having a history of siding with the Poles" by being stripped of their farms and sent back to the settler camps; others were downgraded in or struck off the *Volksliste* for similar offenses; others again were sent to join labor battalions in the "old Reich."[66] The sins of the fathers could even be visited on their children, and *vice versa:* Doris Bergen tells the story of an aged woman from Kulm (Chełmno) who "lost her German status and was sent as a Pole to a concentration camp when her grandson deserted" from the German army.[67] But as with peoples everywhere throughout Nazi-occupied Europe, many *Volksdeutsche* became adept at negotiating the conflicting demands of the state and of their indigenous neighbors, keeping their heads down and avoiding taking sides. Gestapo officers noted many cases, especially after the defeat at Stalingrad in early 1943 (though in the case of some far-sighted individuals, as early as Pearl Harbor in December 1941) of *Volksdeutsche* prudently insuring their future by returning goods to the Poles they had displaced.[68] With the *Volksliste* becoming ever more elastic, moreover, few if any objective differences could in many cases be perceived between the two peoples. As one young German woman assigned to a village in Danzig–West Prussia reported in 1942, "those belonging to group 3 [of the *Volksliste*] do not stand out in any way from the Poles and speak just as much or as little German as the Poles. One could even say that those of more valuable [racial] character have stayed Polish."[69] A Nazi Party official in Czechoslovakia formed the same impression, advising Heydrich that in his view "the children of these fanatical Czechs of the past 20 years are much more valuable subjects for Germanization than these unprincipled scoundrels who change their views from day to day."[70]

Whether the *Volksdeutsche* are to be regarded as "perpetrators," "victims," or "bystanders" in relation to Nazism and its crimes—to invoke Raul Hilberg's famous three-part classification—is thus a question without an obvious answer. For half a century the equation of *Volksdeutsche* and "fifth column" was virtually axiomatic, even in the scholarly literature. Certainly those seeking examples of collaboration by ethnic Germans in some of Nazism's most horrific atrocities do not have to look far for evidence. In the Baltic States, Poland, and Romania, *Volksdeutsch* vigilantes participated directly, alongside police, army, and SS units, in extermination actions against Jews. Women as well as men joined in the killing: a female *Volksdeutsch* translator in the Ukraine, for example, personally shot Jewish children in the clearance of the Khmil'nyk district in 1942.[71] Among SS units with the most appalling reputations were some, like the infamous Yugoslav *Prinz Eugen* division, composed almost entirely of *Volksdeutsche*. Though only a minority of ethnic Germans during the Second World War were transferred from their homes and settled in other countries, those who did so evinced few conscientious qualms over the fate of the people they had—however unwillingly in some cases—displaced. While many were conscripted into the German armed forces, many more who might have avoided doing so volunteered their services out of ideological conviction, the hope of proving their "Germanness" to their professed co-racials, or the expectation of future reward. And while a small number of *Volksdeutsche* aligned themselves with the opponents of Nazism—Ludwika von Kleist, the moving spirit behind the Polish underground in Wilkołaz, was a relative of the German field marshal of the same name—the great majority either supported the German cause which, as they saw it, had delivered them from the oppression of their previous rulers or the threat of Bolshevism, or circumspectly said and did nothing to dissociate themselves from it.

In this, though, they differed little if at all from other Germans. And indeed they differed less from the inhabitants of the occupied countries under German rule than is generally acknowledged. It is often forgotten, for example, that more than twice as many Dutch citizens volunteered to fight with the *Waffen*-SS during the war than joined the Free Netherlands forces.[72] The idea that the *Volksdeutsche* constituted a Nazi fifth column in neighboring countries, awaiting orders from Berlin to stab their own countries in the back before heading off to play their part in extending the New Order in the East, is not one that survives detailed examination. Even if they had had aspirations in that direction, Nazi policy would have doomed them to disappointment.[73] In the end, the wave of German-orchestrated population transfers in 1939–41, undertaken above all to avoid premature conflict with the USSR, was a signal failure. Only about half a million *Volksdeutsche*, of the 20 million envisaged by the *Generalplan Ost*, were ever placed in new homes. Hundreds of thousands more would-be "settlers" never reached the new colonies, instead spending much of the war in a network of more than fifteen hundred so-called "observation camps."[74] As early as December 1940, Himmler had to row back on his resettlement mania, promising in a speech to disgruntled *Gauleiter* that he would discontinue further *Heim ins Reich* propaganda and seek to relocate only the smaller and more scattered German populations in other countries, leaving the larger and more homogeneous ones where they were.[75] Hence, although ethnic Germans normally enjoyed a privileged minority status freeing them in many respects from the control of local administrations—the outstanding exception being the three million *Sudetendeutsche*, nearly all of whom had Reich citizenship conferred upon them after Munich—the *Volksdeutsche* of Slovakia, Hungary, Romania, and Yugoslavia "were expected to cooperate and remain loyal to their states, rather than serve the Reich as disloyal 'fifth columnists' working for their destruction."[76] Some qualification of this general rule, Valdis Lumans reminds us, is necessary in the case of Yugoslavia, where after the German invasion of April 1941 the state was dissolved into smaller puppet administrations. There, a not inconsiderable number of *Volksdeutsche* had indeed played the part of fifth columnists, heeding German calls to evade military service in the royal army and serving the Wehrmacht as informers, translators, or guides. Even in this instance, though, they were expected after the conquest to get along with the new "Serbo-Banat" and Croatian regimes of the areas in which they lived in the interest of lightening Berlin's administrative burdens.

As the tide of battle turned in 1944 and 1945 and the Red Army began to menace not just the occupied territories in the east but the German homeland itself, the process of colonization was put into reverse. *Volksdeutsche* who had freely subscribed to the *Volksliste* began to think of their future; those who had done so under duress assembled evidence that they had not willingly betrayed their country. (Dr Klukowski and his staff, after being forced to sign, placed an affidavit formally disavowing their applications for German nationality in a bottle and buried it in the hospital garden.) Some colonists labored under the delusion that they would at last be able to return to their countries of origin, which they had never wanted to leave. The more realistic understood that their only genuine hope of survival lay in withdrawing to the west as the Wehrmacht retreated. But the majority of *Volksdeutsche* who had remained in situ throughout the war—the Sudeten and Hungarian Germans, the German-speaking indigenes of the Incorporated Territories, and the Balkan Germans—faced a final agonizing decision about their true allegiance.

Throughout the war, relations between *Reichsdeutsche* and *Volksdeutsche* had always been strained. At mealtimes in Germany itself, according to the VoMi, "people tried to relegate the Germans from the southeast (i.e. Yugoslavia and Romania) to the table with the alien workers and the prisoners of war."[77] Elsewhere, *Volksdeutsche* resented the *Reichsdeutsch* monopoly over the best jobs and the choicest spoils: "in the small towns, even the tennis-club membership was split down the middle between *Volksdeutsche* and *Reichsdeutsche*."[78] Now, mutual mistrust rose to the surface. Germans from the "old Reich" often regarded their ethnic German counterparts as a craven rabble indifferent to the fate of the

Fatherland and concerned only with saving their own skins; *Volksdeutsche* took note of the elaborate evacuation procedures prepared by the Wehrmacht for "real" Germans, and suspected their better-connected co-nationals of planning to fight to the last *Volksdeutsch*. In such an atmosphere of paranoia, the decision of not just whether, but when to flee was fraught with danger. To leave too soon was to risk condign punishment for "desertion" or "spreading defeatism"; to wait too long opened one to accusations from the German authorities of being an "amphibian," scheming to betray the *Volk* and resume one's former non-German nationality as soon as the Wehrmacht retreated from the scene. Dr. Klukowski witnessed both elements of this dilemma in Zamość, where in February 1944 he recorded that "Our 'own' . . . *Volksdeutsche* are just waiting to move out, but so far German authorities are trying to force them to stay. They are under constant surveillance. They cannot leave their homes without written permission." Three months later, he observed, "the Gestapo began interviewing *Volksdeutsche* to learn why they are still in town. Some were beaten, such as the barber Gortner."[79]

The evacuation and flight of the German population in the eastern part of the Reich, when it finally began in earnest in January 1945, is one of the few episodes of the Second World War whose public discussion was not surrounded by taboos — mainly because it was one of the few not to be disfigured by a lengthy list of Nazi atrocities. In the postwar years, the experience of *die Flucht* was memorialized and mythologized, becoming one of the founding tropes of the Federal Republic in 1949: a new democratic Germany, born in victimhood and suffering, standing as a beacon of hope and a haven for those seeking refuge from the Bolshevik hordes. Unquestionably, for the millions who fled the Soviet offensive, and the millions more who, after days or weeks on the roads of East Prussia and German Silesia in subfreezing temperatures, were overwhelmed by the Red Army's shockingly rapid advance, the withdrawal was a grim ordeal. Large numbers did reach relative safety, thanks in part to the greatest seaborne evacuation in history in which more than two million refugees were transported from the collapsing northeastern provinces by the German Navy. From the insignificant Baltic port of Pillau (Baltiysk) alone, a larger number of people were evacuated than had been rescued at Dunkirk five years previously. But the death toll among the refugees was on no less dramatic a scale, certainly reaching the hundreds of thousands. Almost entirely ignored in this narrative, however, is the fact that large-scale evacuations of the *Volksdeutsche* had begun a year and a half previously. As early as June 1943, as the Soviets pressed forward into the Black Sea region, the first ethnic German communities were moved to the north and west; in a repeat of earlier history that was in equal parts tragic and ironic, the following spring Poles were driven out of the Warthegau to make room for them.[80] The first withdrawals in Ukraine commenced at the end of 1943, and were followed six months later by the dismantling of *Volksdeutsch* villages in the *Generalgouvernement*. By the autumn of 1944, the process was in full swing, with 160,000 following the *Wehrmacht* out of the Banat and Bačka in Romania and Yugoslavia, and more than 100,000 from Slovenia. In a pattern that would be repeated in the future, most of the evacuees were women and children, a large proportion of the adult men having already departed to Germany as members of the armed forces or war workers.

Obtaining reliable figures on the numbers of ethnic Germans who fled, as opposed to those who remained, is difficult even more than sixty years later. Nearly all of those living in the *Generalgouvernement*, and around half of the *Volksdeutsche* who had resided in the Incorporated Territories before the war, were withdrawn to the "old Reich." The Yugoslav *Volksdeutsch* population was similarly reduced by perhaps a third in 1944–45. In contrast, few departed from Hungary. The *Wehrmacht* briefly considered forcing them to leave, but gave the idea up as impracticable; during the closing weeks of the war, about 50,000, or one in ten of the prewar German community, decamped on their own initiative. The single largest ethnic German population, the *Sudetendeutsche*, with minor exceptions did not have the option of withdrawal: not until the war's last days did the area fall to General George Patton's Third U.S. Army advancing from the west and Marshal Ivan Konev's First Ukrainian Front coming from the east, making any large-scale evacuation impossible.

Many did not see the necessity to leave. Taking comfort from the good relations they possessed—or imagined themselves to possess—with their non-German neighbors, their lack of Nazi Party membership, or Allied disavowals from the early part of the war of "territorial changes that do not accord with the freely expressed wishes of the peoples concerned," they assumed that at worst their situation would revert to what it had been between the wars. They entirely failed to understand how profoundly the experience of living for years in an environment of unbridled terror, in which any non-German had been liable to imprisonment, deportation, torture, or execution for any reason and at any time, had traumatized and radicalized the societies of which they were a part. Themselves the beneficiaries of a *Herrenvolk* status that even in the midst of war surrounded them in a cocoon of relative privilege, they were unaware of how much resentment their taken-for-granted advantages—better food, housing, and employment; the right to sweep to the head of the queue at shops and post offices; the marking in most towns of theaters, cinemas, park benches, and even street pavements as *nur für Deutsche* ("Germans only")—generated among those they had usurped.[81] They did not recognize how hollowly Wilsonian rhetoric about self-determination now rang in the ears of Nazism's victims, or why it seemed illogical that the victorious Allies should continue to bind themselves to apply to Germany a principle that Germany itself—with the seeming approval of its people—invariably honored only in the breach. This failure of imagination and of empathy, which with rare exceptions would continue to be the most distinctive psychological trait of the "expellee generation," was to have fateful and tragic consequences in the months and years to come.

In the last analysis, though, the fate of the ethnic Germans, and of Germans in general, would be determined not by their immediate neighbors but by the great powers. It was they, not Poland or Czechoslovakia, that had defeated the Axis; their armies of liberation or of occupation would dictate the strategic, political, and demographic future of the European continent. While each of them found it convenient from time to time to depict their choice of action as having been dictated by popular feeling on the ground, in reality no initiative was undertaken—or was allowed to continue for very long—in the areas under their control that did not conform to their wishes. It is at the level of Allied high policy, therefore, that explanations for the decision to repeat at the end of the war a policy that Adolf Hitler had already shown to be a disastrous failure during it must be sought.

3

THE SCHEME

The expulsion of the ethnic Germans was not only to be by any measure the greatest forced migration in human history, but may well constitute the greatest single movement of population.[1] No precedent—not even Hitler's or Stalin's—existed for rounding up, transporting, and resettling so massive a number of people in such a short time. Nor did recent experience of the totalitarian states' smaller-scale attempts to displace and transplant the indigenous populations of a given region augur well for the operation that was now being contemplated.

Among the most remarkable aspects of the expulsion was the deliberate refusal of those who carried it out either to seek to learn the lessons of those previous examples or to make any preparations, of however rudimentary a character, for an enterprise whose disruption to the normal life of central Europe was second only to that caused by the war itself. Although the Allies could not even guess at how many people might need to be removed—that would depend on the number of ethnic Germans who would be killed, or flee to the west, before the war came to an end—it was clear from the outset that many millions would remain for deportation. Quite apart from any ethical considerations, the scale of the logistical effort involved was immense. The Allies would require to arrive at some definition of who was a "German," in one of the most ethnically diverse parts of the continent—a process that, whatever criteria might be imposed, would inevitably leave hundreds of thousands of families divided by nationality. The expellees would have to be concentrated in some fashion so as to facilitate their deportation and ensure that they did not go underground among the majority population. Decisions would have to be taken as to how much of their property, if any, they were to be allowed to take with them, and what would happen to the houses, businesses, and farms they left behind. They would need to be moved along a European transportation network that the Allies had attempted during the previous five years, with considerable success, to disable or destroy. They would have to be rehoused in that part of Germany that the Allies, with still greater success, had worked assiduously to bomb flat. In the longer term, jobs would have to be found for masses of expellees who, coming as they did from the largely agrarian east, would require retraining to take up whatever positions might become available in the predominantly industrial west. Postwar German society too would have to adapt as best it could to the influx of a huge number of outsiders the majority of whom were unproductive and a significant proportion of whom spoke German poorly or not at all. Lastly, some means would need to be found, for at least a generation and perhaps for several, to prevent these millions of uprooted, embittered people, possessing no stake in the status quo and every reason to wish to see its destruction, once again from setting whatever German polity would ultimately emerge along the path toward revising the postwar settlement and regaining the country's lost eastern territories by force.

In light of these facts, one might conclude that never before in European history did those responsible embark upon so ambitious a program in such an insouciant, even reckless, frame of mind. This would, however, be to misread the mood of the times. The Big Three were under no illusions as to how much chaos the expulsion would, even under the best of circumstances, involve. They refrained from setting up international machinery to oversee the transfers and minimize the suffering of the deportees principally because they attached no great importance to that goal. To the contrary, indeed, they considered the anguish the displaced population would undergo to be a salutary form of reeducation, bringing home to the mass of ordinary Germans the personal risks involved in lending support to extremist regimes and wars of aggression. They fully recognized that to impose even a semblance of order on the population transfers would, as expert opinion unanimously advised them, require a vast and expensive international machinery—one they had no intention of creating. In a period of great scarcity, they firmly believed, resources dedicated to relief and resettlement should be applied to the victims of Germany rather than to Germans themselves. Any international organizations that might be created to conduct or supervise the transfers, moreover, would almost inevitably become lobbies in favor of adjusting governments' utopian ends to available means as soon as serious economic or humanitarian problems arose, as they were certain to do. The leaders of the Big Three knew that the immediate postwar period offered them an all-too-brief window of opportunity to redraw the political and ethnographic map of central Europe, and in the process to achieve a social as well as a political revolution in the region. Though their respective visions of the forms those revolutions ought to take profoundly differed, each saw the expulsion project as a vital component of the changes they desired to achieve, and was willing to accept the risks involved in the pursuit of their goals.

The driving out of unwanted peoples, to be sure, is a practice almost as old as recorded history. The Old Testament tells the story of numerous forced migrations carried out by the Israelites and their neighbors against each other, the Babylonian Captivity being the most celebrated. Philip II of Macedonia was renowned for the scale of his population transfers in the fourth century B.C., a precedent that his son, Alexander the Great, appears to have intended to follow on a far more massive scale.[2] The colonial era witnessed many more forced displacements, often accompanied or initiated by massacre. Some of these bore a distinctly "modern" tinge. The Act of Resettlement that followed Oliver Cromwell's conquest of Ireland, for example, ordered Irish property owners in three-quarters of the island to remove themselves to the impoverished western province of Connacht by May 1, 1654, to make room for incoming English and Scottish colonists; those remaining east of the River Shannon after that date were to be killed wherever found. "The human misery involved," in the judgment of Marcus Tanner, "probably equaled anything inflicted on Russia or Poland in the 1940s by Nazi Germany."[3] On a smaller scale, but proportionately just as lethal, was the United States' forced relocation of part of the Cherokee nation from Tennessee, Georgia, and Alabama to eastern Oklahoma along the so-called "Trail of Tears" in 1838; perhaps a quarter of the fifteen thousand men, women, and children who were driven out perished, most of them while detained in assembly camps. Extensive forced migrations occurred in Africa and Asia also. In what is today Nigeria the Sokoto Caliphate, the largest independent state in nineteenth-century Africa, practiced slavery on a massive scale—by 1860 it possessed at least as many slaves as the United States—as an instrument of forced migration, the purpose being to increase the security of disputed border areas. "Enforced population displacement . . . was supposed to strengthen the Islamic state, which was achieved through demographic concentration."[4] On the western borderlands of China, the Qing Empire in the seventeenth and eighteenth centuries "used deportations and mass kidnappings to build a human resource base."[5]

Contemporary scholars agree, though, that the twentieth century has been the heyday of forcible population transfers. The rise of the nation-state, in place of the dynastic multinational empires of the earlier period, was both cause and effect of the ideological claim that political and ethnographic boundaries ought to be identical. The Industrial Revolution and the quantum leap in military technology produced by it created an insurmountable imbalance between the ability of the state to impose its will and that of ordinary people to resist, rendering the most extravagant visions of nation and empire builders not merely possible, but relatively easily achievable. This combination of totalizing ideologies and technological capability, Richard Bessel and Claudia Haake argue, has in the modern age given "this dreadful phenomenon a qualitatively and quantitatively new character."[6] Whereas in the past unwanted minority populations had, in many cases, been able to fly beneath the radar of the governments that persecuted them—either by an outward show of compliance or, for those living in disputed borderland regions, by assuming an "amphibian" identity—the modern bureaucratic state with its elaborate systems of classification, surveillance, and control made this impossible. And because the twentieth century was incomparably the most violent in human history, featuring more and bloodier wars than ever before, motive and opportunity for displacing minorities were joined to means. It is no accident that few modern wars, from the former Yugoslavia to Darfur, from Iraq to the Caucasus, are now unaccompanied by overt attempts to alter the demographic character of the contested areas by forcibly driving out some or all of their peoples.

In many ways, the Great War of 1914–18 was a dress rehearsal for the gross displacements of population that would take place later in the century. Three-quarters of a million ethnic Germans were expelled into the Russian interior by the tsarist armies during the first months of the conflict; before it was over, Jews, Poles, Latvians, Lithuanians, Chinese, Koreans, and Caucasian Muslims would be added to the list of peoples the Russian Empire would find it expedient to displace. Tens of thousands of Serbs suffered a similar fate at the hands of the Austro-Hungarian Empire.[7] The Kaiser's forces deported elements of the Belgian, French, and Lithuanian populations for strategic reasons, clearing territories for use as specially prepared killing zones that Allied troops would be compelled to cross. Most notoriously of all, between September 1915 and February 1916 the Ottoman Empire drove out perhaps a million Armenians into the Syrian and Iraqi deserts in what would become a template for future genocidal operations: the ejection of peoples accompanied by, and as a means of accomplishing, mass murder. The death rate among the expellees, who were not intended to survive the transfer, may have been of the order of 50 percent; hundreds of thousands of others were done to death by more conventional methods. There is, nonetheless, much justice in Donald Bloxham's observation that the year 1914 was not some great watershed that disrupted a previously peaceful international scene. Ever since the mid-1880s, southeastern Europe had been the scene of "coercive population movement as well as great violence directed at civilians as well as soldiers. . . . These were all ethnic wars, and their lineage of ethnicized violence was perpetuated into the First World War and beyond, and provides a continuum upon which the civil conflicts unleashed by Nazi rule in Eastern Europe are best viewed."[8]

Even after the return of peace, national governments would pioneer methods of displacing unwanted minorities that would be applied on a much larger scale twenty years later. A case in point was France's "cleansing" (*épuration*) of the border provinces of Alsace and Lorraine between 1918 and 1921, in what Mark Mazower describes as "a blatantly racist assault on the civil rights of German-speakers" in the region.[9] After his victory in the Franco-Prussian War of 1870, Bismarck had ill-advisedly annexed the ethnically mixed provinces to the Reich, creating a permanent antagonism between the two countries. When France reconquered Alsace-Lorraine in 1918, it immediately set out to eliminate any basis for future disputes about the provinces' political complexion by purging them of those who might be thought to favor their reincorporation into Germany. To facilitate the process, the population was divided into four categories by the end of December 1918. Residents whose French loyalties were unquestioned were given identity cards marked with the letter "A," signifying that they had been citizens of France before the Franco-Prussian War. Those who had at least one pre-1870 French parent received "B" cards. Citizens of Allied and neutral countries were placed in the "C" category; the remainder—a total of 513,000 "enemy" nationals and their children, including those who had been born in Alsace-Lorraine—became members of the "D" class. As we have seen, Heinrich Himmler's racial gurus would use this system as a model when devising the *Deutsche Volksliste* in occupied Poland two decades later.

Like the *Volksliste*, the French classification scheme could readily be applied for the purpose of discrimination as well as expulsion. Category "A" card-holders, for example, could exchange Reichsmarks for francs at a much more favorable exchange rate than members of the other classes. Holders of "B" cards were often turned down for public-sector jobs on the ground of their mixed parentage. The most stringent disabilities, needless to say, applied to the "D" class, whose members among other restrictions were not permitted to travel. Petty persecution, however, soon gave way to deportation. The first to be removed were German-speaking civil servants; later, those marked for expulsion included factory owners and the unemployed. Their fate was determined by *commissions de triage* that held meetings in camera to assess the French patriotism of the persons concerned, often on the basis of denunciations solicited by local officials from individuals waging personal vendettas. Those who failed this examination were pushed across the frontier into Germany. They were permitted to take thirty kilograms of baggage with them and a maximum of two thousand Reichsmarks, all their remaining property being forfeited to the French state. But an even larger number were induced to opt for "voluntary repatriation" on the same terms. They did so because they expected to be removed eventually; because life in the "D" category had become intolerable; because, although not personally removable, their spouses or children were "D" card-holders; or, in some cases, because they feared physical attack by members of the majority population. Altogether, nearly 100,000 expellees and "voluntary repatriates" were transferred to Germany before the system was discontinued in July 1921.[10]

Following its genocidal debut in Armenia, Turkey, too, would play a leading role after the war in what would be the largest population transfer in history to that point. After the defeat of the Central Powers in 1918, the Allies punished the Ottoman Empire for its decision to throw in its lot with Germany by stripping it of its Middle Eastern provinces; compensating the Armenians with their own independent republic; and demilitarizing Turkey to an even greater extent than the Treaty of Versailles had done to Germany. All told, the Ottoman Empire lost 72 percent of its prewar land area. The most controversial element of the Treaty of Sèvres, which imposed these terms, however, was the concession of eastern Thrace—the hinterland of Constantinople—and the granting of a provisional administration over western Anatolia and its principal port, Smyrna (today's Izmir), to the Kingdom of Greece. The Allies' intention had been to use the Greeks as proxies to enforce the partition of the Ottoman Empire, but the idea backfired disastrously. Ethnic antagonisms between the two countries had been so intense for so long that there was no possibility of the Turks ever reconciling themselves to what in any event was a heavy-handed Greek occupation. Nor could 5 million Greeks constitute an effective counterweight against a Turkish population that was almost twice as large. By 1922 a new and highly effective Turkish army under Mustafa Kemal had forced the Greeks out of Anatolia and Thrace; sacked Smyrna, in the process killing up to 100,000 Greeks and Armenians in one of the most horrific but least-known massacres of the twentieth century; and replaced the ineffectual Sultanate with a Republic of Turkey under the leadership of Kemal, now styled "Atatürk." As with almost every other Greco-Turkish conflict of the previous hundred years, the conflict was accompanied by ethnic cleansing of towns and villages on both sides. Having lost the war as badly as they did, though, the Greeks got very much the worst of it. Nearly a million fled before the Turkish armies to Greece proper before an uneasy truce was concluded in October 1922. The following summer, the Treaty of Lausanne, undoing most of Sèvres and settling the boundaries of Greece and Turkey, was concluded largely as a result of the diplomacy of the British foreign secretary, George Nathaniel Curzon. One of its key components was a convention providing for a compulsory population exchange between the two countries.

In view of the frequency with which Lausanne was invoked by the western Allies during and after the Second World War as a successful example of mass transfer of peoples, it is remarkable how ignorant they remained of its actual consequences. The first point to be noted about the Lausanne exchange was that it did little more than ratify a state of affairs that already existed. Of the 1.2 million ethnic Greeks affected by the convention, all but 190,000 had taken refuge in Greece before the fighting concluded. The number of Turks living in lands under Greek administration was only about 350,000. The physical removals, therefore, involved only about half a million people, a far cry from the numbers that would require to be moved after the Second World War. The fact that religion could be used as a marker of identity, additionally, greatly simplified the logistics of the operation. Because the number of Greek Muslims and Turkish Christians was negligible, as were mixed marriages, disentangling the two peoples presented few difficulties. The transfer was to take place under international auspices and with international assistance. A Refugee Settlement Commission was established to oversee the operation and settle any points of dispute; the League of Nations provided a loan of £20 million to enable Greece to cope with the task of resettling about a quarter of its population. The expellees were allowed to take all their moveable property with them, and given help in transporting themselves and their goods to their new homes. Lastly, sufficient time was provided to enable the operation to be completed with a minimum of hardship.

Despite all these favorable circumstances, the Lausanne transfer was in many respects a fiasco. The immediate consequences for Turkey were comparatively limited: finding new homes for the expellees from Greece, a mere 4 percent of the total population, presented few real challenges. In the longer term, more serious problems arose, with parts of Anatolia remaining virtually depopulated to the present day and the economy burdened by the loss of a significant component of its entrepreneurial class. While the transfer of Christians, Gareth Jenkins believes, "made it easier to create a nation, it also set back the economic development of the Turkish state by at least a generation."[11] For the Greeks, though, Lausanne had a long-lasting and almost uniformly negative impact. The pressure of the incoming population forced an extensive though mismanaged land redistribution program, as well as the construction of more than a thousand new villages to accommodate the newcomers. Even this was not sufficient. Large numbers of deportees took refuge in shanties in the vicinity of Athens and other large towns, becoming a marginalized element looked down upon by the indigenes as having been tainted with foreign and Turkish habits. The destabilization of Greek society was accompanied by the undermining of the economy. Notwithstanding international assistance, the cost of servicing the debt incurred in rehousing the expellees and building roads, bridges, and schools in the new settlements was high. Between 1922 and 1932, more than 40 percent of the Greek budget was being spent on resettlement activities.[12] Worst of all, perhaps, were the political ramifications. Uprooted, impoverished, and unwelcome, the expellees became a natural constituency for extremist political movements, especially the hitherto insignificant Communist Party of Greece. Though the bitter and bloody Greek civil war that erupted in 1946 had more complex roots than merely the social divide between expellees and the settled population, the radicalization of Greek politics that resulted from the transfer did a great deal to make it possible.[13]

The notion that the Lausanne transfers represented any kind of success story thus flew in the face of abundant contrary evidence. Curzon himself was the first to recognize the fact. Although he had reluctantly acquiesced in Ankara's insistence that the population movements be compulsory, in the face of Atatürk's threat that otherwise Turkey would proceed to the systematic extermination of the Greek minority, he warned presciently that the driving out of peoples was "a thoroughly bad and vicious solution, for which the world will pay a heavy penalty for a hundred years to come."[14] The supposition that the displacements prevented further conflict between Greece and Turkey took a heavy blow in 1974 with the Turkish invasion of Cyprus, which was followed three weeks later by a demand from Ankara for a fresh population transfer to complete the work left undone half a century earlier. It is unsurprising, then, that the *New English Weekly* should have marveled in January 1945 that Lausanne was regarded as "an achievement of 'peacemaking' upon which the League of Nations preened itself notably at the time, and is being upheld as an example to be followed in several cases, in which the consequences are not likely to be less incendiary."[15]

For these reasons, population transfers did not commend themselves to political leaders in the West between the wars. When they were discussed at all, they tended to be counsels of last resort. A similar forced exchange between Arabs and Jews in Palestine, recommended by the Peel Commission in 1936, was dropped in the face of League of Nations criticism the following year.[16] Both the British and the French governments floated the idea of a population exchange between Germany and Poland during the last week of peace in 1939; the British ambassador, Sir Nevile Henderson, formally proposed it to Hitler on August 25.[17] This, though, was exceptional. In the early years of the war, the foremost opponent of the kind of demographic engineering in which Hitler and Stalin had been engaged had been Winston Churchill himself. Explaining to the Australian prime minister, John Curtin, on Christmas Day 1941 why he could not accept Stalin's absorption of Poland east of the Curzon line and the clearance of much of its population to the USSR, he said that "the forcible transfer of large populations against their will into the Communist sphere" would "vitiate the fundamental principles of freedom which are the main impulse of our Cause."[18] Despite its own history of forced internal displacements of the aboriginal population, the United States too officially opposed population transfers, often citing its own success in "Americanizing" immigrant ethnic groups.[19]

As we have seen in chapter 1, though, under the stress of total war this principled stance rapidly eroded. The United States carried through a major forced migration of its own after Pearl Harbor, transferring some 112,000 ethnic Japanese from the coastal areas to the interior and lodging them in misnamed "concentration camps" (objectionable though the principle of internment on ethnic grounds may have been, a third of the camps' population was granted permission during the war to leave, for education or employment). With the United States and the Soviet Union participating in the war, moreover, it was no longer necessary for Britain to point quite so frequently to Hitler's inhumane population transfers as a point of distinction between the British Empire's war aims and those of Nazi Germany.

To change one's mind about what constituted a "war crime" was one thing. To determine how to carry out a mass expulsion of ethnic Germans was quite another. The United States conducted no inquiries into this question, considering it a European responsibility. Preliminary British investigations, though, made clear that it would be a formidable undertaking. The first outline study was carried out by the Foreign Office's private think tank, the Oxford-based Foreign Research and Press Service (later the Foreign Office Research Department) in February 1942. In typically idiosyncratic style the job of drafting this report was assigned to John Mabbott, a metaphysician at St John's College best known for works like "The Place of God in Berkeley's Philosophy." Nonetheless, Mabbott justified his appointment by producing a lucid, logical, and realistic appraisal of the problem. Unlike previous population exchanges, he pointed out, one of the parties in this case would have no incentive to see it succeed. Responsibility for implementing the transfer would therefore fall entirely on the Allies. If a repetition of the debacle into which the Lausanne exchange had descended, in which the Anatolian Greeks "mostly carried out a 'Dunkirk evacuation' at Smyrna," was to be avoided, both the areas to be cleared and those into which the expellees were to be sent would need to be under the direct control of an international agency. Should this not happen, widespread abuse of the German population by the Poles and Czechoslovaks, and their sending into Germany with "little but the light summer clothes on their backs," could be expected. If the Allies did not wish to see central

Europe's road and rail network congested with expellees, moreover, a timescale of five to ten years for the completion of the operation would be required. "The estimate of ten years is likely to be nearer the truth if the evacuation of each area is to wait until adequate reception or settlement plans are organized at the other end of the journey." Because in practice it was unlikely that the expelling states would wait that long, "the surviving Germans would have to be herded into concentration camps in Germany.... Such temporary measures had to be adopted in Greece [after Lausanne], where many refugees spent long periods (frequently several years) in schools, theatres, markets and primitive hovels which tended to become permanent slums."[20]

While Mabbott carefully avoided going beyond his brief by volunteering any opinion as to the wisdom or otherwise of compulsory transfers, he offered enough food for thought to make clear that a demographic reshuffle of Europe on the scale Allied policymakers were contemplating would present far greater logistical challenges than anybody had yet considered. Once the Big Three decided regardless to proceed in 1942–43, the obvious next step was a detailed study of the practical aspects of a mass expulsion of ethnic Germans from central Europe. Remarkably, it was not until November 1943 that the British government commissioned such a survey; neither of the other principal Allies is known to have addressed the problem at all. The British investigation was carried out by high-ranking civil servants representing the Foreign Office, the Cabinet Office, the Treasury, the Ministry of Economic Warfare, the War Office, and the Dominions Office, and was chaired by a senior official of the Foreign Office's German Department, Jack Troutbeck. After six months' study this "Inter-Departmental Committee on the Transfer of German Populations" presented its report, which ran to fifty-one printed pages, to the Armistice and Post-War Committee, a group of cabinet ministers charged with making plans for the postwar world. The report's significance lies not so much in the action taken on its recommendations as in the fact that it represented the only attempt ever made by any of the countries involved to consider what in concrete terms the requirements and consequences of the expulsion project might be.

The Inter-Departmental Committee's work was made more difficult by the fact that at the time of its creation, no decision had been made as to how the postwar frontiers of Germany were to be redrawn and, consequently, how many Germans it might prove necessary to remove. In the summer of 1943, the Cabinet's Military Sub-Committee had suggested that approximately 4.5 million Germans be expelled from the area to be given to Poland after the war. Anthony Eden was disquieted by the scale of the proposed transfer, and recommended to the War Cabinet that Poland receive a smaller tranche of German territory with fewer removable inhabitants. Churchill, however, seemed to be pushing in the opposite direction, making an informal commitment to transfer an undefined number of Germans to benefit the Poles at the Tehran Conference in November 1943. This first wartime meeting of the Big Three nearly broke down over Stalin's truculent and insulting treatment of the British prime minister, and Roosevelt's unwise decision openly to demonstrate his sympathy for Soviet geopolitical aims in Europe. In an impulsive attempt to regain the initiative and, perhaps, prove his continued relevance, Churchill held a private meeting with Stalin and, using three matchsticks as visual aids, outlined a scenario in which the USSR would be allowed to keep its conquered Polish territories of 1939 in exchange for which the Poles would gain an equivalent amount of territory from Germany in the west. Although the question of transferring the German population was not discussed in detail, the clear implication was that Poland was not to be burdened with a substantial alien minority. If the London government in exile did not agree, the prime minister declared, he would wash his hands of them. Stalin was delighted with Churchill's concession, and the conference closed in a much more cordial atmosphere than when it had begun. The Soviet dictator showed how much importance he attached to Britain's sacrifice of Polish, German, and British interests by sending Edvard Beneš in hot pursuit of the homeward-bound Churchill, bearing "a map of Poland personally marked by Stalin" as confirmation of the deal. The Czechoslovak president, who had his own motives for wishing the Poles to be able to displace as many Germans as possible, was eager to undertake this rather demeaning task for his new patron.[21]

The Inter-Departmental Committee drew up its report, then, in circumstances under which the scale of the expulsions it had been requested to take into account was expanding, as a result of political decisions at the highest level, almost by the day. Although there was necessarily a large element of guesswork in its approach, the rapid advance of the Red Army in the spring and early summer of 1944 raised the possibility that the war might come to an end leaving the whole of the area in question in the Soviet Union's sphere. If this should prove to be the case, then no direct British participation in the expulsions might be necessary at all. "Large-scale transfers, however carefully organized, would be bound to cause immense suffering and dislocation and to give rise to widespread criticism. His Majesty's Government might therefore prefer to wash their hands as far as possible of any active participation in their execution." The committee was not certain, though, that this Pilate-like stance would in reality be possible, inasmuch as the British government would share responsibility for the policy decision to remove the Germans and "might be unable, even if they wished, to disclaim responsibility for the human suffering and economic dislocation involved, which their active participation might tend to lessen."[22]

The number of potential expellees, the committee acknowledged, would dwarf "the Greek-Turkish or Greek-Bulgarian exchanges which followed the last war, or in the various would-be permanent transfers carried out by the Germans in the course of, or just before, this one."[23] Little historical guidance, therefore, would be available to those charged with executing the transfer. According to the most optimistic scenario, some 5,340,000 Germans would be removable if Danzig, East Prussia, and Upper Silesia were given to Poland after the war; if the new frontier ran along the line of the Oder River to the north, assigning Breslau and Stettin to the Polish zone, an additional 3,300,000 would have to leave. While the answers Beneš gave to questions about the number of *Sudetendeutsche* he proposed to deport fluctuated constantly, the Czechoslovaks for their part were believed to want to be rid of approximately half, or 1.5 million, of their ethnic Germans. The committee thus counted on a total, "at the worst," of 10,140,000 people to be transferred.

It was clear to the committee that the overwhelming majority could go nowhere other than to whatever postwar German state or states would eventually come into being. While Austria's absorptive capacity was thought to be proportionately greater than that of Germany itself, the number of expellees who might be resettled there could not be significantly higher than 100,000. Taking up a point previously made by Sir Orme Sargent of the Foreign Office, who had suggested that "the future of these [expelled] people is much less likely to attract attention and give rise to political agitation if they disappear into Siberia," the committee noted that "The problem of resettlement in Germany would be considerably eased if, at the period when transfers were taking place, some millions of active Germans should happen to be engaged as organised labour forces in devastated areas outside Germany, e.g. in the Union of Soviet Socialist Republics."[24] But there was little prospect, it added, of any substantial proportion of the ethnic German population finding a long-term home in Stalin's Gulag, noting ruefully that "Siberia must be ruled out for the present." While some Latin American countries like Argentina might be willing to admit substantial numbers of Germans, the United States would hardly look kindly on the idea of a large and compact ex-enemy colony in its hemisphere. The same consideration was still more true for the British themselves. "As regards the Empire, the objection to flooding the Colonial Empire with immigrants from Germany is too obvious to need discussion."[25]

Economically, the committee saw the first few postwar years as the period of maximum danger. Its conclusions about the magnitude of the risks involved were sobering. In the short term, it warned,

> the transfers would create economic problems of the gravest character, severe both in Germany and the expelling countries, but more severe by far in Germany. It is not too much to say that the addition of the heavy extra economic burden on Germany which transfers would impose, over and above the grave dislocations following on the loss of the war, the devastation caused by it and the general demands of the United Nations, might create an economic problem which would prove insoluble and lead to a complete German collapse.[26]

Even in the unlikely event of the Allies foregoing any reparations payments or contributions from Germany for their own occupation requirements, the domestic economy would probably be unequal to the task of providing houses, jobs, and food in the necessary quantities for the expellees. If the number arriving in Germany proved to be at the very bottom of the committee's range, the Allied authorities would still have to reckon with the entry of "some 6 million persons—say, 1 1/2 million families—into a country already short of well over 4 million dwellings. The new houses which the building industry, working at maximum output, could provide would hardly touch the fringe of this problem."[27] Before the war, German contractors had built 300,000 houses annually. Even if that number could somehow be boosted by 50 percent in the first year of peace and by 100 percent in each subsequent year—a wholly unrealistic prospect—a decade would pass before all the expellees could find accommodation. Assigning the 300,000 peasant families needing to be resettled on new farms created by breaking up large estates would take at least thirty years. As for jobs, only a third of the expellees could expect to find work in their previous fields of employment, with the rest becoming unskilled and probably unemployed labor. For their part, the expelling countries as well as Germany would be hit by the dislocation of production that would result from the loss of so many skilled workers for whom no replacements were readily available, a deficiency that "might have serious repercussions, since it would occur at a time of general agricultural shortage."[28]

To minimize the grave difficulties that a population transfer would carry in its train, the committee recommended that an international Population Transfer Commission be established. Representing the Big Three, Poland, and Czechoslovakia, the Transfer Commission's function would be to coordinate and regulate the scheduling and conditions of the expulsions, subject to the overriding control of the Supreme Allied Authority in Germany. Three Regional Commissions—with responsibility for the Sudetenland, East Prussia-Danzig, and Upper

Silesia, respectively—should also be created to supervise the logistical aspects of the removals. The committee insisted, though, that responsibility for resettling the expellees should fall on the shoulders of neither the Transfer Commission nor the United Nations Relief and Rehabilitation Administration (UNRRA), the recently launched agency whose function it would be to provide welfare services for the peoples of liberated Europe. Rather the costs of resettlement should be borne by the Germans themselves. Nor should the Transfer Commission attempt to grapple with the problem of who was, and was not, a German, a question to which no satisfactory answer existed. Unlike the Lausanne population transfers, religion on this occasion would provide no satisfactory marker of nationality. But neither would "race or language" offer any guidance as to how to deal with the many people who were bilingual, partners in or offspring of mixed marriages, possessed of non-German surnames, or had accepted German nationality under coercion. "The Committee has reached the conclusion that the difficulties of selecting by any objective criterion are so great as probably to be beyond the powers of any international authority."[29] It therefore proposed that, as Beneš had suggested, any person regarded as German under Nazi nationality law should be considered removable, but that the expelling governments should possess the power to retain any person whose services were considered economically necessary.

Lastly, the committee thought it vital that the Transfer Commission have exclusive authority to determine the timing and circumstances of the expulsions. The Poles and Czechoslovaks would no doubt wish to force the pace, to a degree that might well propel Germany into economic collapse at a time when the Allies would bear responsibility for its fate. But the precise definition of the parts of Germany to be transferred to its neighbors was unlikely to occur for a long time. It was, moreover, improbable that sufficient transport would become available to enable the operation to proceed for at least a year after V-E Day. The expelling governments would be adequately compensated for the costs of the removals, which they would have to bear, by confiscating the whole of the Germans' moveable and immoveable property. But the Allies would have to reconcile themselves to the fact that to pursue the expulsion project would mean that there would be little or nothing left over for reparations. If it went ahead, Germany's standard of living even under the best-case scenario would be reduced to "the lowest point considered safe, just or practicable for the first few years after the war. There will be no margin to play with."[30]

The committee's terms of reference explicitly precluded it from discussing the wisdom of the idea of mass population transfers, a policy decision that had already been taken by the Allied governments. Considered in the abstract, it agreed that the removals were "*prima facie* desirable," and that if they were to proceed it was important to carry them out as thoroughly as possible. "We do not want to expel enough Germans to create grave problems and bitter feelings in Germany and at the same time leave enough behind to create a standing political problem in the Succession States and a permanent temptation to Germany to intervene." It is a measure of the anxieties that the study of the problems involved aroused in its members, however, that they took the unusual step of effectively asking the Cabinet to think again.

> [T]he committee desires to draw attention to certain political aspects of the problem. In the first place the human suffering involved would inevitably be very great. Secondly, the actual physical problem of uprooting compact blocks of German population (amounting to some 6 million persons and possibly to as many as 10 million) from their long-established homes and transporting them across the frontiers could not fail to be the main problem of the Succession States during their reconstruction period, just as the resettlement of these Germans in Germany would be one of the main problems for that country. Having arrived in Germany, the migrants would be impoverished and embittered, and would for a long time represent a distinct and undigested element in the population of Germany as a whole. Nor has it yet been proved that the mere process of removing persons of a particular nation from territory long settled by them diminishes the sentiment of that nation for the lost territory or its determination to regain it.

Foreboding as the committee's conclusions were, as the actual history of the transfers was to show it had erred in many significant respects on the side of optimism. The possibility existed, it considered, that almost the entire population of the territories to be handed over to Poland might flee the advancing Red Army of its own accord, leaving only 750,000 people to be removed after V-E Day. It assumed that slightly more than half of the Sudeten Germans would be allowed to remain in Czechoslovakia. It took into account the transfer of Germans from Poland and Czechoslovakia only, ignoring the possibility that other countries in the region might seize the opportunity, with or without the assent of the Big Three, to disencumber themselves of their *Volksdeutsch* populations. Lastly, it counted on there being no more than 10 million expellees in total. None of these assumptions would be borne out in practice.

Nevertheless, the report proved far too gloomy for the politicians who had commissioned it. When the members of the Armistice and Post-War Committee met to discuss it in July 1944, the general response was one of disbelief and anger. Sir James Grigg, the war secretary, complained that "some of the statements in it were much too lenient from the War Office point of view." The minister of labor, Ernest Bevin—who the following year would assume overall responsibility for British expulsion policy as foreign secretary in the postwar government—at first confused ethnic Germans and those from the Reich, and then farcically claimed that "breaking up the great German landed estates—on which the strength of Prussian militarism was largely based" would create farms for three million expellee families.[31] After a detailed study of the question pointed out that many of the estates to which Bevin referred were in the same eastern German territories from which the occupants were about to be expelled and that, if all publicly as well as privately owned holdings elsewhere were to be redistributed, a maximum of only 110,000 farms could be found, the minister of labor continued in the teeth of the evidence to insist that the problem could be resolved by dispossessing the remaining Junkers of Prussia.[32] Clement Attlee, the deputy prime minister who chaired the Armistice and Post-War Committee, received the Inter-Departmental Committee's report even more critically. For the previous year, Attlee had been insisting that Germans in the mass must be made to suffer as a matter of policy and a salutary form of reeducation. While reluctantly conceding that considerations of humanity could not be "left entirely out of account," he had also argued: "the criterion that should properly be applied in these matters is, I suggest, not how hardly will a particular course of action bear upon Germany, but how far can we go in the direction of achieving our desiderata in Germany without serious embarrassment or injury to ourselves. . . . everything that brings home to the Germans the completeness and irrevocability of their defeat is worthwhile in the end."[33] He now underlined this punitive stance, taking, as Troutbeck recorded, "a very stern line about any thought of giving undue consideration to German feelings or interests in this matter."[34]

Lacking a sponsor in Cabinet, the report was shelved. No further discussion of the document took place after January 1945, nor were any of its recommendations ever implemented. That no minister other than Bevin had been willing even to dispute the committee's findings was an indication that for the British government the expulsion project had become an end in itself, one that it was determined to carry through regardless of the cost.

Ignoring the unpleasant facts to which the committee had drawn attention, though, did not make those facts go away. For a while British ministers and officials took refuge in wishful thinking, attempting to persuade themselves that the problem might either resolve itself or be taken care of by others. Arnold Toynbee, head of the Royal Institute of International Affairs, who had been appointed an expert adviser to the Foreign Office in the Great War on the strength of his encyclopedic knowledge of the literature of ancient Greece, typified this attitude of ostrich optimism. "It looks," he wrote at the end of January, "as though the clearance of the German civilian population of all categories from territories east of the Oder–Western Neisse line and south of the frontier of Czechoslovakia may well be a *fait accompli* by the time hostilities cease.... The question, after the end of hostilities, will then be, not whether a German population, so far undisturbed, is to be uprooted in cold blood, but whether a German population already uprooted and transferred into the post-war German area is to be moved again and re-transferred to its previous domiciles."[35] The Political Warfare Executive and the U.S. Office of Strategic Services—the precursor of the CIA—were no less cocksure, advising in an intelligence summary of the same day that 4.5 million Germans had already fled the advancing Soviet armies from the eastern territories, including the million-strong population of the Warthegau.[36] The Foreign Office warned in response that these cheerful reports were not to be relied upon. As Con O'Neill of the German Department dubiously replied, "It seems to me inconceivable that 4 1/2 million civilians could have extricated themselves from the path of the astonishingly rapid Russian advances of the last fortnight, even if they had wished to."[37]

The British and American political leadership, however, were reluctant to abandon the beguiling vision of a land that would have spontaneously cleared itself of its own population. Stalin, for his part, was only too happy to play on these illusions when he met again with Churchill at Moscow in October 1944, and with both the British and U.S. leaders for what would prove to be the last wartime Big Three conference at Yalta four months later. Although Churchill had already reconciled himself to the inevitability that the Polish lands absorbed by the USSR as its share of the spoils from the Nazi-Soviet Pact would never be returned, he was torn between his sense of responsibility to Poland and his apprehension over the consequences of delivering large portions of Germany over to it in compensation. An additional complication was the fact that by now there were two entities claiming to be the legitimate government of Poland: the London-based government-in-exile headed by Stanisław Mikołajczyk, and a Soviet puppet regime, the "Polish Committee of National Liberation," based in the recently liberated eastern city of Lublin.

From the moment of its creation, the Lublin regime, in contrast to the vacillating attitude taken by its London counterpart, had declared itself in favor of extensive annexations of German lands in the west. This was Stalin's objective also. The further that postwar Poland encroached into eastern Germany, the further Soviet influence too would extend, for Stalin had no intention of tolerating anything but the most subservient of Polish neighbors. Both the annexation and the transfer of population, moreover, were certain to create a permanent enmity between Poland and Germany. So long as this remained the case, Poland would have no option but to turn to the USSR to help defend its new frontiers against a Germany whose population would be more than twice as large as its own. The Soviet leader intended to extract a high price for this service. To be sure, there were limits to the extent to which the USSR wished to see even a communist Poland grow; nobody in the Kremlin had forgotten the historic antagonism existing between the two peoples.[38] But however unrepresentative the Lublin regime might be, it would need to demonstrate some concern for Polish national interests. Expanding to the west would enable it to do so without clashing with Soviet objectives.

In a series of secret meetings with the Lublin Poles during the midsummer of 1944, then, Stalin laid down the line that he and they were to pursue in their discussions with the western Allies. Not only would Poland be obliged formally to renounce the eastern territories seized by the USSR and agree to the compulsory transfer of their population, but the German seaport of Königsberg and its hinterland in East Prussia, which both the London and Lublin Poles had long expected would be allotted to their portion, would become a Soviet possession also. But as compensation, Stalin assured the Lublin element, the USSR would support Poland's claim not only to the German port of Stettin but to the line defined by the rivers Oder and the western Neisse, one of the two relatively small tributaries of that name. Although some mention of the "Oder-Neisse line" had already been made as a possible frontier between Poland and Germany, the supposition had been that the river in question was the eastern Neisse, which had at least some ethnographic logic in separating the two countries. The western Neisse lay 120 miles further to the west. "This move," R. C. Raack notes, "would at least double the number of Germans who would have to be forcibly evacuated from their homelands and housed and fed in whatever remained of occupied Germany after the war."[39] Stalin sardonically assured the Lublin Poles that Churchill would never notice the difference.

For the next six months, indeed, both Moscow and Lublin maintained a studied ambiguity when speaking of the "Oder-Neisse line," being careful never to specify which of the two tributaries they meant. But to ensure that the Lublin Poles did not waver, Stalin proceeded, even while the fighting was still under way, to implement the population transfer from eastern Poland to which he had compelled them to agree. Beginning in the autumn of 1944, more than two million Poles living east of the river Bug were removed, in the brutal and chaotic manner which had by now become a hallmark of both Stalin and Hitler's style of rule, and deposited in the devastated and freshly reconquered former *Generalgouvernement*. The prospect of having them remain there, an alienated, rootless and dangerous population, would provide more than sufficient incentive for the Lublin regime to press for the shifting of Poland's boundary with Germany as far as possible to the west, regardless of the difficulties involved. The same consideration, according to Władysław Gomułka, head of the Polish Communist Party and deputy prime minister in the Lublin Polish regime, made necessary the wholesale removal of the Germans. In the first place, he reminded the party's congress in May 1945, clearing the new western territories of its inhabitants would provide land for redistribution by the new people's government and thereby "bind the nation to the system." In the second, "We have to expel [the Germans], because all countries are built on the principle of nationality rather than [multi-]ethnicity."[40] As members of a party owing whatever influence it possessed to the Soviet Union's patronage, it was especially important for Polish Communists not to allow themselves to be outflanked by their rivals to the right on the "national question."

The Western Allies, however, remained ignorant both of the Polish-Soviet population transfer and Stalin's behind-the-scenes deal with the Lublin Poles, and as a result their ideas on postwar expulsions from this point became increasingly decoupled from reality. The United States' thinking on the subject was particularly naïve. A State Department study in August 1943 expressed the unreasonably optimistic view that Poland's territorial ambitions could be confined to East Prussia and Danzig alone, and that "not all the Germans need be evacuated" from the two districts.[41] In several subsequent appreciations, U.S. policymakers continued to delude themselves that, as Secretary of State Cordell Hull advised Roosevelt at the end of August 1944, a middle ground could be found of opposing "the mass transfer to the Reich of Germanic people from neighboring countries" but sanctioning "the removal of individuals and groups who constitute an especially difficult problem . . ." The supposition that at such a late date a formula of this kind might find favor with Edvard Beneš, much less Stalin, was nonsensical, and indicated above all the almost complete lack of attention the Americans had devoted to the question. The British, for their part, bore some measure of responsibility for the simplistic nature of U.S. thinking, having decided not to furnish Washington with a copy of the Inter-Departmental Committee's report out of anxiety that learning about the difficulties involved in the scheme might turn the Roosevelt administration off the idea of population transfers altogether.[42]

Nonetheless, by the time the Moscow Conference convened in October 1944, the Western Allies belatedly began to grasp that they were in danger of being presented with a fait accompli in central Europe. In preparations for the conference, Anthony Eden and the U.S. ambassador to the Soviet Union, Averell

Harriman, attempted to stiffen the backbones of their respective bosses, warning that too extravagant a cession of German lands to the Poles risked creating a state of chaos within Germany itself with which the occupying powers would have to deal. Their representations, though, fell on deaf ears. Both at the conference itself and afterwards, for all his growing suspicions of Stalin's true intentions, Churchill made it clear that the maintenance of the alliance with the USSR was an overriding priority. That being the case, paying off the Poles with German territories was the only means he had left to avoid exposing himself to the charge that the ostensible reason Britain had entered the Second World War—the defense of Poland's territorial integrity from external aggression—had not been and never would be achieved. Thus it was "understood," Churchill reported to Roosevelt after the conference, "that Germans in [the] said regions shall be repatriated to Germany . . ."[43] While the prime minister was neither unaware of nor indifferent to the problems that a big population transfer might cause, those were of less importance than preventing the rise of a new antagonism between East and West.

Though he was less willing to say so in so many words, that was Roosevelt's position also. A month after the Moscow Conference, he wrote to Mikołajczyk to say that if the postwar Polish government and people should "desire in connection with the new frontiers of the Polish State to bring about the transfer to and from the territory of Poland of national minorities, the United States Government will raise no objections and as far as practicable will facilitate such transfer."[44] An astute politician, Mikołajczyk was able to read between the lines of this message that the United States, and no doubt Britain also, would try to throw the primary responsibility for expulsions, and any international odium that would arise as a result, onto the Poles' shoulders. Deeply suspicious of the Allied leaders' eagerness to write blank checks that postwar Poland would be obliged to try to force the Germans to make good, he was nonetheless willing to show some flexibility over the Polish-Soviet frontier. When his colleagues in the London government in exile made clear that they were not, he staged a tactical retreat, stepping down as prime minister on November 24. Yet he continued to believe that the gross population movements the Anglo-Americans were considering in the west would prove not merely misguided but unworkable. In December he told Rudolf Schoenfeld, U.S. chargé d'affaires to the London government in exile, that the British people if not the British government were "conscious of the immense transfer problems that the proposed frontier arrangements would involve." The right course, he said, was to make the USSR disgorge at least some of its ill-gotten gains in the east. Mikołajczyk went on to ask Schoenfeld why the Western Allies should "make the transfer question harder than necessary, and . . . expressed his belief that the Prime Minister with all his popularity would not succeed in making so drastic a plan acceptable to British and American opinion."[45]

Churchill was aware of this danger also. To avert it, he made a major speech on the future of Poland in the House of Commons on December 15, 1944. Until this moment, the public position of the British government had been that no discussion of boundary changes or population transfers could be made in advance of the peace conference. As recently as August, when Eden had been challenged by several MPs to confirm or repudiate the rumors swirling around London that Britain had approved large-scale expulsions from Poland and Czechoslovakia after the war, he had maintained that even to discuss such things was "premature."[46] Now, just four months later, Churchill spelled out in words of one syllable that expulsions on a larger scale than had previously even been imagined would be not just a component, but one of the basic foundations, of the postwar European order.

> The Poles are free, so far as Russia and Great Britain are concerned, to extend their territory, at the expense of Germany, to the West.... It would, of course, have to be accompanied by the disentanglement of populations.... The transference of several millions of people would have to be effected from the East [of Poland] to the West or North, as well as the expulsion of the Germans—because that is what is proposed: the total expulsion of the Germans—from the area to be acquired by Poland in the West and the North. For expulsion is the method which, so far as we have been able to see, will be the most satisfactory and lasting. There will be no mixture of populations to cause endless trouble, as has been the case in Alsace-Lorraine. A clean sweep will be made. I am not alarmed by the prospect of the disentanglement of populations, nor even by these large transferences, which are more possible in modern conditions than they ever were before.
>
> The disentanglement of populations which took place between Greece and Turkey after the last war . . . was in many ways a success, and has produced friendly relations between Greece and Turkey ever since.[47]

The prime minister had little to say to a House that listened to his address, as another speaker in the same debate pointed out, in "a sort of awful, ugly, apprehensive, cold silence," about how this "disentanglement" was to be accomplished.[48] His sole reference to the practicalities of the operation was to promise that there would be ample room in the truncated postwar Germany for the expellees. "After all, 6,000,000 or 7,000,000 Germans have been killed already.... Moreover, we must expect that many more Germans will be killed in the fighting in the spring and summer...."[49] The response of the Labour elder statesman,

Frederick Pethick-Lawrence, was much more in tune with the mood of the House. Even if the Germans had forfeited the moral right to protest expulsions, Pethick-Lawrence replied, "[t]hat is not to say that we can play about with territories . . . and that we can move about not hundreds of thousands but millions of people. . . . we are creating a situation for the future that will not make for the peace either of Poland or of the world."[50] The reaction of some London Poles was also unenthusiastic. Tomasz Arciszewski, Mikołajczyk's replacement as prime minister, rejected Churchill's offer of German territory *ad libitum* the same evening. "Poland does not desire to annex Breslau and Stettin," he told the press; at most it wanted East Prussia, cleared of its Germans.[51] The most acid commentary of all came from George Orwell, writing in the staunchly antiexpulsionist left-wing journal *Tribune*.

> This is equivalent to transplanting the entire population of Australia, or the combined populations of Scotland and Ireland. I am no expert on transport or housing, and I would like to hear from somebody better qualified a rough estimate (a) of how many wagons and locomotives, running for how long, would be involved in transporting those seven million people, plus their livestock, farm machinery and household goods; or, alternatively, (b) of how many of them are going to die of starvation and exposure if they are actually shipped off without their livestock, etc.
>
> I fancy the answer to (a) would show that this enormous crime cannot actually be carried through, though it might be started, with confusion, suffering and the sowing of irreconcilable hatreds as the result. Meanwhile, the British people should be made to understand, with as much concrete detail as possible, what kind of policies their statesmen are committing them to.[52]

If the response to Churchill's revelations was uneasy in London, however, they generated a full-blown furor in Washington. Outraged Republican senators demanded to be informed when the Atlantic Charter of August 1941, an Anglo-American statement of war aims that declared the two countries' opposition to "territorial changes that do not accord with the freely expressed wishes of the peoples concerned," had been abrogated. The Polish-American community, which only weeks previously had helped return Roosevelt to a fourth presidential term, scoffed at the notion that territorial gains in the west could compensate Poland for its losses in the east. In an effort to diminish the storm of criticism that erupted, the newly appointed Secretary of State, Ed Stettinius, publicly revealed Roosevelt's pledge to Mikołajczyk promising U.S. aid to Poland to remove Germans from the western lands to be given to her. This maneuver had little impact either.[53]

Churchill's attempt to "sell" mass population transfers to the general public was thus a failure. Yet the basic terms of the equation had not changed. The United States' and Britain's most important aim was to preserve the alliance of the Big Three into the postwar era. That this aspiration, laudable in itself, would even be possible was based largely on the belief, for which no credible evidence existed, that Stalin and the Soviet system had undergone a Damascene conversion after the Nazi invasion of June 1941; had renounced both the objectives and the methods for which they had become notorious prior to that date; and were now committed to a future of peaceful coexistence with the West. While Roosevelt has been the target of much deserved posthumous criticism for giving way to wishful thinking on such a heroic scale, it is clear that Churchill too for a time indulged the same fantasy.[54] Ironically, their stance with respect to Stalin closely paralleled that of the appeasers with respect to Hitler in the 1930s. In both instances, Western leaders substituted an evidence-based appraisal of the totalitarian dictators with whom they had to deal with a more pleasing image of their own making, largely because the alternative—and the deeply unappealing choices they would then be compelled to make—were too disturbing to contemplate. So long as the Anglo-Americans pursued the mirage of a close postwar relationship with the USSR, however, the German card, along with whatever population adjustments might prove necessary to make it work, was the only one they had to play.

In one respect, though, their task was made a little simpler. In the winter of 1944–45, as the Allies prepared for the Yalta Conference, it became increasingly clear that there was little future for the London Polish regime. Stalin had already severed relations with it when it refused to accept his patently false claim that the USSR was not responsible for the massacre at the Katyn Forest of almost twenty-two thousand Polish Army officers who had been taken prisoner by the Red Army after the Soviet invasion of 1939. The more "pragmatic" among the London Poles, like Mikołajczyk himself, were indicating their willingness to abandon the exile administration and join a Soviet-dominated "government of national unity." Most important of all, the Red Army, not Western forces, was driving the Germans out of Poland and would be in a position to determine what happened there afterwards. The need for "sweeteners" in the west to induce Poland to swallow the bitter pill of the new frontier in the east, therefore, no longer existed. As Eden reminded the War Cabinet, "Since the Lublin Poles are ready to accept the Curzon Line anyhow, there is no longer any need for His Majesty's Government to support more extensive transfers of German territory than we think convenient and proper on other grounds."[55] Accordingly, Churchill at least went to Yalta resolved to scale back the extent of the German territories to be given to Poland as much as possible.

Here too he failed. Part of the difficulty was the lack of support he received from the visibly ailing Roosevelt, who was in the final weeks of his life and, like Woodrow Wilson, was looking to an international organization—in FDR's case, the United Nations—to resolve the numerous problems that the peace settlement would leave unaddressed. A UN without the Soviet Union was futile, and the president was willing to give way on almost every other point to secure its participation. Hence he ignored Stettinius's advice that the United States at the conference should "oppose, so far as possible, indiscriminate mass transfer of minorities with neighboring states."[56] In the discussion of the matter on February 7, Churchill tried to persuade Stalin that while he himself saw no objection to displacing very large numbers of Germans, public opinion in Britain was unlikely to view the matter in the same light. While transferring 6 million people from East Prussia and Silesia should prove "manageable," any removals beyond that number should be geared to Poland's ability to colonize the cleared areas. "It would be a great pity to stuff the Polish goose so full of German food that it died of indigestion."[57] Stalin replied that the problem was solving itself, "for when our troops come in the Germans run away and no Germans are left."[58] Though Churchill was unpersuaded by this assurance, he chose not to contradict it. The conference ended without any decision having been reached as to how much German territory Poland was to receive, the official communiqué speaking only of "substantial accessions of territory in the north and west."[59] Throughout, Roosevelt had made virtually no contribution to the discussion on Poland's western frontiers.

Choosing not to make a decision, however, was a decision in itself. By the time the Yalta Conference opened, the Red Army had already reached the Oder. The only remaining question was whether the Western Allies were willing to risk a confrontation with the USSR over recognition of Poland's western frontiers—and, it followed, over their willingness to cooperate in the expulsion of the German population—or whether conciliating Stalin and the Lublin Poles was still the most important consideration. To senior British policymakers, this question answered itself. Oliver Harvey, the staunchly Germanophobe assistant under-secretary at the Foreign Office, who had Eden's ear, set the tone at the end of March: "I am afraid I regard the possibility of an orderly transfer of population from Eastern Germany on old-fashioned League of Nations lines as so improbable that I do not believe that it is even worth trying, at the price of incurring enmity both in Czechoslovakia and Soviet Russia. Nor do I believe that the arrival of these refugees will necessarily be so catastrophic if it is carried out once and for all and immediately."[60] The deputy prime minister Clement Attlee backed him up two weeks later, when he formally vetoed the Foreign Office's renewed proposal to establish a Transfer Commission to organize the expulsions. "I cannot really see that there is any need for us," he wrote, "to take the initiative in this matter. The outflow of Germans, whether from Poland or Czechoslovakia, will go first into the Soviet and American zones. We are the last to be affected."[61]

When the Big Three assembled for their last-ever summit at Potsdam on the outskirts of Berlin in mid-July 1945, therefore, they did so less to take decisions on Poland's future than, in the case of the Anglo-Americans, to reconcile themselves to—or rationalize to themselves—the decisions they had already taken. Fifteen miles to the northeast, as they conferred, spectacularly overloaded trains from the German territories under Polish administration were disgorging cargoes of the dead, the dying, the diseased, and the destitute onto the platforms of Berlin's main line railway stations. Hundreds of thousands more were arriving in the city, in no better condition, on foot. To the south, similar ragged columns were being driven across the Bohemian and Moravian frontiers by Czechoslovak troops and militia. Reading about one of these "wild expulsions" in a London daily newspaper shortly after the Potsdam Conference opened, Churchill expressed his alarm at what was unfolding. On July 21, he brought the matter up at a plenary session with his fellow heads of government, complaining about the "wholly disproportionate number of Germans" who would have to be accommodated in "a greatly reduced Germany" if Poland's full claims to the line of the Oder and western Neisse were to be admitted. Up to 9 million Germans, he reminded his Soviet and American opposite numbers, would be removed to make room for well under half that number coming from what had previously been eastern Poland. When Stalin repeated his incredible Yalta assertion that "Not a single German . . . remained in the area from which it was suggested that Poland should get her accessions of territory," the prime minister pointed out that even if true, this hardly addressed the problem.

> If the Germans had run away from the territory in question, they should be allowed to go back. The Poles had no right to pursue a policy which might well involve a catastrophe in the feeding of Germany. . . . We did not want to be left with a vast German population on our hands deprived of the sources of supply on which they had previously depended for food. . . . If enough food could not be found to feed this population, we should be faced with conditions in our zone of occupation such as had existed in the German concentration camps, only on a scale a thousand times greater.[62]

These were cogent arguments. Yet they had been no less cogent when the Inter-Departmental Committee had made them more than a year previously, only to be summarily dismissed by Churchill's own ministers. It is difficult to see what purpose he thought was served by raising them now, other than affording him an opportunity to disclaim responsibility for a policy he himself had been advocating for nearly two years. Such action on his part would not have been unprecedented. In January 1945, he had repeatedly demanded to be told why "large cities in eastern Germany should not now be considered especially attractive targets" for heavy area bombing attacks.[63] When the Royal Air Force responded to the prime minister's urgings with a devastating raid on Dresden two weeks later that aroused widespread international concern, Churchill ran for cover. In a minute to the Chiefs of Staff on March 28, he described the Dresden operation as "a serious query against the conduct of Allied bombing" and reminded them of "the need for more precise concentration upon military objectives . . . rather than on mere acts of terror and wanton destruction, however impressive."[64] On that occasion, the outrage of his military advisers had compelled the quick withdrawal of this attempt at revisionist history.

When the Big Three returned to the matter in subsequent meetings, therefore, Stalin reminded Churchill, and Roosevelt's successor Harry S. Truman, that so far from being "averse to making additional difficulties for the Germans," it was already settled Allied policy "to make difficulties for them and to make it impossible for them to aggress again." He declared it was now "too late to consider this question." In the end, the Soviet leader unbent so far as to agree to a pair of compromise formulae presented by the U.S. and British delegations respectively, to enable the Allied leaders to cover their blushes. In the first of these, the Poles were assigned a provisional administration over "the territory in the eastern part of pre-war Germany to which they were laying claim," rather than a de jure outright transfer. This at least kept open the theoretical possibility that a future peace conference might return some of these lands to Germany, and enabled the Western leaders to maintain for a little longer the fiction that the western boundaries of the new Polish state were yet to be determined. The second concession, drafted by a subcommittee of the three foreign ministers, was included as Article XIII of the final Potsdam Agreement.

> The three Governments having considered the question in all its aspects, recognize that the transfer to Germany of German populations, or elements thereof, remaining in Poland, Czechoslovakia and Hungary, will have to be undertaken. They agree that any transfers that take place should be effected in an orderly and humane manner.
>
> Since the influx of a large number of Germans into Germany would increase the burden already resting on the occupying authorities, they consider that the Allied Control Council in Germany should in the first instance ex-

amine the problem with special regard to the question of the equitable distribution of these Germans among the several zones of occupation....

The Czechoslovak Government, the Polish Provisional Government and the Control Council in Hungary are at the same time being informed of the above and are being requested meanwhile to suspend further expulsions pending the examination by the Governments concerned of the report from their representatives on the Control Council.[65]

The Western Allies attached greater importance to the second of these provisions than the first. As Churchill had already pointed out at the conference, the declaration that the handing over of the German lands east of the Oder-Neisse line to Poland was "provisional" was a meaningless formula. Once assigned this region, the Poles "would be digging themselves in and making themselves masters."[66] It was futile to suppose that anything short of military force would make them relinquish it. On the other hand, the Big Three's appeal to Czechoslovakia, Poland, and Hungary to put an end to additional "wild expulsions" was not mere window dressing. Soviet military commanders in Germany, as well as their Western counterparts, were facing immense difficulties as a result of the chaotic arrival of masses of expellees in their occupation zone. The prospect of a breathing space was welcome to them.

The remaining provisions of Article XIII, however, reflected little credit on their drafters. To assert publicly that population transfers should be "orderly and humane," when the governments concerned had already rejected the idea of setting up machinery for that purpose, implied either cynicism or self-deception on a breathtaking scale. The fact that they would continue to insist that nothing of the kind could be contemplated suggests that the former was the true explanation. The question, though, is largely moot. Even if the Allies had resolved to set up an International Transfer Commission in the summer of 1945, it was already too late to prevent a humanitarian crisis. Significantly, too, the Potsdam Agreement had nothing to say about *Volksdeutsch* populations in countries other than Czechoslovakia, Poland, and Hungary—some of which, as in Yugoslavia, were in a still more vulnerable situation. The implications of this silence were ominous.

As "wild expellees" continued to flood into Germany notwithstanding the Potsdam Agreement's call for a suspension, the Western Allies began to consider where the responsibility lay for the fact that, as a British government minister put it, the expulsions were "completely disorderly and carried out without any regard to humanitarian considerations, the Germans simply being bundled out without warning or preparation."[67] The blame for this state of affairs, which had led to "high" casualties and "appalling" suffering, lay in their view with the expelling states and with the Soviet Union alone. This was, and remains, a wholly self-serving interpretation. While the expelling countries were undoubtedly guilty of wholesale violations of human rights, the Western democracies were equally implicated in the catastrophe that was unfolding before them. Over a three-year period, they had not just ignored, but consciously and after mature consideration rejected, the unanimous advice of experts who had predicted with great accuracy the state of affairs their policies would produce. They had knowingly opted to pursue a course that would cause greater rather than less suffering, so as to generate what they regarded as an "educational" effect upon the defeated German population. They had dismissed as irrelevant distinctions between the innocent and the guilty, far less any effort to distinguish between degrees of guilt. They had encouraged their allies to carry out, and promised their cooperation in accomplishing, deeds for which they would later prosecute their enemies as war crimes. The suggestion that the Western Allies were somehow surprised by, or unable to prevent, the wave of state-sponsored violence that washed across central and southeastern Europe in the immediate postwar years is therefore not to be taken seriously. When making the choices they did, they went in with their eyes open.

4

The "Wild Expulsions"

In calling for "orderly and humane" population transfers, the Potsdam Agreement was attempting to close the door upon a horse that was already halfway out of the stable. For more than three months, German civilians had been displaced from what the Polish government was now calling the "Recovered Territories"—a reference to the fact that Poland had once ruled Silesia and Pomerania under the Piast dynasty some six hundred years previously. Czechoslovakia had been following the Polish example since mid-May. Further to the south, although Yugoslavia had neither asked nor received permission from the Allies to expel its *Volksdeutsch* population, large-scale deportations would soon begin from that country. Though never issuing a formal expulsion order against its ethnic Germans, Romania too would find effective means of compelling them to depart. Disorganized and crude as these operations were, they were neither spontaneous nor accidental. Instead they were carried out according to a premeditated strategy—if also an inefficient and in many respects counterproductive one—devised by each of the governments concerned well before the war had come to an end.

For Poland and Czechoslovakia, the "wild expulsions" were a way to hedge their bets. While it was true that the Big Three had stated their support for a wholesale eviction of German minorities, the Czechoslovaks and Poles knew from bitter prewar experience how much trust was to be reposed in the "solemn undertakings" of the great powers. There was no guarantee that the leaders of one or more might not renege on previous commitments to the central Europeans, nor any doubt that they would not hesitate to do so if it appeared to be in their national interest. The Western Allies were also in a state of political flux. The untested and almost anonymous Harry Truman had succeeded Franklin D. Roosevelt in April 1945; while his views on the future of Europe were an unknown quantity, there was no reason to suppose he would prove as accommodating in the matter of expulsions as his predecessor had been. A general election was due in Great Britain which Winston Churchill might very well lose—as indeed, in July 1945, he did. Lastly, even if the Western leaders remained true to their word, British and American public opinion might recoil from the suffering that was an inescapable element of mass population transfers and exert irresistible pressure on both governments to allow international humanitarian agencies to play a part in their supervision, a prospect that threatened to derail the entire operation. The safest course, then, seemed to be to take the decision out of the great powers' hands by creating "facts on the ground" before the eventual peace conference convened and presenting them with a fait accompli.

Ironically, however, the Polish and Czechoslovak governments had given scarcely more thought to planning the removal of the Germans than did the Big Three. They may have been misled by their recent harsh experience under Nazism to overestimate the efficacy of force alone: their constant invocation of Hitler's deportations and forced migrations as justifications for the actions they now proposed to take perhaps blinded them to the abysmal failure of those wartime precedents even to come close to their stated objectives. At all events, with the exception of some outline schemes drafted by a "Secret Study Group" of the Czechoslovak military in exile—most of which assumed frontier adjustments that would not, in the event, occur—nothing in the nature of a coherent plan for identifying, assembling, and transporting millions of people at short notice was ever put together by any of the expelling states.[1] Instead, most relied almost exclusively on the use of terror to try to stampede the German minority across the frontiers. So chaotic was this process that foreign observers, and even many people in the expelling countries themselves, mistook the violent events of the late spring and summer of 1945 as a spontaneous process from below, in which members of the majority communities rose up to purge their towns and villages of the Germans in their midst—a process that has been given the name of "wild expulsions." It bears emphasizing that this is almost entirely incorrect. Except in a very few instances, deportations as a result of mob action did not feature in the Europe of 1945. Rather, the so-called "wild expulsions" were in almost every case carried out by troops, police, and militia, acting under orders and more often than not executing policies laid down at the highest levels. The notion that true "wild expulsions" were taking place, nonetheless, amply suited the interests of the expelling governments, which were more than happy to allow the myth to grow. It enabled them to disclaim responsibility for the atrocities that were essential components of the operation; supplied fictitious but plausible evidence for the proposition that the German minorities must be removed or face immediate massacre at the hands of their neighbors; and strengthened the argument that the only humane alternative to "wild expulsions" was a program of "organized transfers" to be carried out by the Allies themselves.

One of the factors that made the scenario of spontaneous "wild expulsions" more credible was the brief but intense outbreak of revenge-taking that occurred across Czechoslovakia in May 1945. Emotions were raised to fever pitch, especially in Prague, by the determination of German forces to continue fighting up to, and even after, V-E Day. On May 5, having misjudged the proximity of American and Soviet forces and mindful that Karl Hermann Frank had already ordered a partial German evacuation of the city, Czechoslovak resistance forces launched a rebellion the aim of which was largely demonstrative. Although the war was in its final hours, units of the *Waffen-SS* declined to withdraw, instead mounting a ferocious counterattack—including the use of civilians as human shields—against the lightly armed and poorly trained Czechs. Only the providential intervention of a pro-Axis Russian force, the so-called "Vlasov Army," that belatedly turned its coat and came to the rescue of the insurgents, prevented a bloodbath; as it was, the Czech fighters were compelled to negotiate a ceasefire on unfavorable terms on May 8. The fact that fighting nevertheless continued in some parts of Prague until the following day, and that isolated German units in western Bohemia were still engaging in combat as late as May 11, aroused intense public anger. That Czechoslovak citizens were still dying violently at German hands while the rest of the continent was celebrating the end of the war seemed an especially bitter coda to an occupation that had already lasted longer than in any other country in Europe.

It was, then, unsurprising that the "revolutionary days" in Prague and elsewhere that followed the final German capitulation should have been marked with violence and revenge-seeking. Even so, foreign observers and some Czechs themselves were shocked by the scale, the intensity, and above all the lack of discrimination of the reprisals.

> Retaliation was blind. An old woman was defenestrated; a member of a visiting German orchestra was beaten to death in the street because he could not speak Czech; others, not all of them Gestapo members, were hanged, doused with gas and lit, as living torches. Enraged mobs roamed through hospitals to find easy victims there. One [of those murdered] was a Czech patient, who happened to be the father of the writer Michael Mareš, but his papers listed a Sudeten birthplace.[2]

Colonel Harold Perkins, a Czech-speaking British intelligence officer and no Germanophile, was nonetheless appalled by the scenes of violence he witnessed in Prague, including the spectacle of two German women who had been beaten by a large crowd until they were "one mass of blood from head to foot."[3] Marjorie Quinn, another Briton living in the town of Trutnov near the Polish border, wrote to her sister that although the local Czechs, in contrast to the Red Army, "seldom murder or rape," they had "developed plundering and torturing to a fine art. . . . The English prisoners of war here have made themselves very unpopular among the Czechs by protecting German women and children as far as they could; they too are horrified at what is happening here."[4]

As a general rule, though, the worst atrocities during the so-called "May days" (which, in reality, ran well into June in many cases) were perpetrated not by mobs but by troops, police, and others acting under color of authority. Some of the earliest internment camps for German civilians functioned less as detention centers and more as temporary holding pens from which their inmates could be taken out and put to death. At the most notorious of these, a pheasant-raising plant converted into an improvised compound at Postoloprty in northern Bohemia, parties of up to 250 Germans at a time were removed and shot by Czechoslovak soldiers on June 5 and 6. The precise number who were killed remains unknown; estimates range from a low of 763 (the number of bodies unearthed in 1947) to a high of 2,000. In a similar category was Kaunitz College in Brno, where a subsequent Czechoslovak investigation found that at least 300—a number that is almost certainly an underestimate—died as a result of torture, shooting, or hanging in May and June 1945.[5] In a single incident, 265 *Sudetendeutsche*, including 120 women and 74 children, were killed on June 18 by Czechoslovak troops who removed them from a train at Horní Moštěnice near Přerov, shot them in the back of the neck, and buried them in a mass grave that they had first been forced to dig beside the railway station.[6] By no means were all official "repressions" carried out in secret. At Lanškroun, the head of the National Revolutionary Committee, a prominent member of Beneš's party named Josef Hrabáček, presided over a two-day "People's Tribunal" in front of the municipal hall in which at least twenty people were shot; two hanged; others tortured; and others again drowned in the town's fire pool. Still more ghastly was the "cleansing operation" conducted by Staff Captain Karel Prášil in the city of Chomutov in which, following a roundup of several thousand German inhabitants, up to a dozen were tortured to death on the Jahnturnplatz sports field on the morning of June 9 in full view of sickened Czech passersby. Although no one was brave enough to intervene, one anonymous Czech correspondent wrote to the prime minister's office to express disgust at the spectacle: "Even the brutal Germans did not get rid of their enemies in such a manner, instead concealing their sadism behind the gates of concentration camps." Similar killing, raping, and looting sprees, perpetrated by soldiers, "partisans," and "Revolutionary Guards" acting for no more cogent reasons than avarice and the gratification of sadistic or sexual impulses, occurred on a greater or lesser scale at hundreds of other locations throughout the Czech lands.[7]

In spite of their resolve to drive the German population out of the country, some Czechoslovak leaders expressed alarm at both the scale of the violence and the publicity it was attracting. As early as May 12, the prime minister, Zdeněk Fierlinger, proposed to his colleagues that the government make a nationwide radio broadcast calling on Czechoslovaks to desist from their attacks upon "innocent" Germans. Fierlinger found himself, however, in a minority of one, and no appeal was ever made.[8] But if Czechoslovak policymakers responded to the moral aspects of the "repressions" with relative indifference, they were aware of the damage it was doing to the country's reputation in the West. Former pro-Czechoslovak figures like the longtime diplomatic correspondent of the *Manchester Guardian*, F. A. Voigt, for example, began publishing unattributed, but broadly accurate, accounts of what was happening to the *Sudetendeutsch* population. The Czechs, he wrote, were themselves adopting "a racial doctrine akin to Hitler's . . . and methods that are hardly distinguishable from those of Fascism. They have, in fact, become Slav National Socialists."[9] Responding to similar complaints, especially those raised by the International Committee of the Red Cross (CICR), the Communist interior minister, Václav Nosek, underwent a change of heart at a Cabinet meeting on May 23. It was now important, he said, that "the cleansing (*čištění*) of the Republic . . . be accomplished according to a central plan," so as to prevent "wrongdoing and chaos."[10] The chief of staff of the Czechoslovak Army, General Bohumil Boček, had already informed subordinate commanders the previous day of his knowledge that "the arrest of undesirable elements (Nazi criminals) in the ČSR has in some places been carried out with unnecessary brutality" and warned them as to their future conduct of these operations.[11]

Yet beyond oft-repeated and universally ignored tut-tuttings of this kind, the Czechoslovak government never seriously attempted to rein in the agencies over which it exercised control. Its reluctance was due in part to the fact that it was a mutually suspicious coalition that included all five legal parties in the state, each of which was looking ahead to the 1946 elections and determined not to let its opponents paint it as "soft" on the German question. But the government was also conscious of the very real limits to its authority. Most local administration throughout the country was in the hands of a network of 156 District National Committees ("National Committee" being the Czechoslovak term for government authorities below the state-wide level), in which Communists exercised disproportionate influence and which answered to few higher authorities for actions taken within their own bailiwicks. The Ministry of National Defense, headed by the philo-Soviet General Ludvík Svoboda, controlled the armed forces and was largely a law unto itself. The civil ministries, of which Interior and Foreign Affairs were the most prominent, feuded constantly. Theoretically President Beneš, who until the restoration of Parliament at the end of October 1945 had the power to rule by decree, could give orders to all of them. But his effectiveness was limited by the need to maintain his perceived position as standing "above parties," as well as by the fact that two foreign armies—Soviet and American—continued to occupy much of his country. Lastly, nothing but the application of force on a massive scale could rid Czechoslovakia of its German population. Too much terror might result at worst in temporary embarrassment abroad; too little would defeat the entire purpose of the operation. Beneš himself acknowledged as much when he declared in a speech broadcast on Radio Prague, "We are accused of simply imitating the Nazis and their cruel and uncivilized methods. Even if these reproaches should be true in individual cases, I state quite categorically: Our Germans must go to the Reich and they will go there in any circumstances."[12]

In light of the euphemistically styled "excesses" of May and June, it was reasonable for outsiders to assume that a similar dynamic underlay the "wild expulsions." Yet in most districts pogrom-like actions were conspicuous by their absence. One of the rare exceptions was the so-called "Brno Death March" of May 30, 1945. While much German expellee literature has depicted the events at Brno as a template of the "wild expulsions" in general, the differences are far more significant than the similarities. As an industrial city with a strong Communist trade union movement and an acute housing crisis, Brno was especially vulnerable to pressure exerted from demagogic elements. Throughout the second half of May, a series of incendiary public demands for a radical solution to the German problem were made by local Communist organizations, which threatened a citywide strike if a harder line were not taken. At the least, it was urged, the unproductive sections of the German population should be transferred elsewhere, to enable their houses and flats to be redistributed to Czechs. On May 30, a trade union deputation, headed by the Communist activist Josef Kapoun, descended upon the city hall to threaten the local authorities that if they did not take immediate action against the Germans, he and the munitions workers of Brno would. Faced with this ultimatum, the mayor agreed that an expulsion action would begin the same evening, a decision ratified by Interior Minister Nosek on condition that the expellees not be forced out of Czechoslovak territory. Women, children, and those over the age of sixty were to present themselves at 21:00 hours at the city's thirteen police stations, which were designated as the assembly points, carrying hand baggage and food for three days. Working-age men were not to be expelled for the time being, but "concentrated" elsewhere. The sick and pregnant, German-speaking Jews and spouses in mixed marriages, and officially recognized "antifascists" were exempted. Shortly before midnight, the first column of expellees was marched off in the general direction of the Austrian frontier. A second, composed of *Sudetendeutsche* rounded up from neighboring villages and towns, followed them a few hours later. Local Red Army commanders were notified and promised not to intervene. Upon reaching the frontier, some twenty miles away, an attempt was made in defiance of Nosek's instructions to push the expellees, who by now numbered some twenty-eight thousand, into Austria. They were, however, denied permission to cross by the Allied occupation authorities. The Brno activists responsible for the expulsion had made no preparations against such an eventuality. Rather than allow the Germans to return home, they confined them in a collection of impromptu camps in the border village of Pohořelice. Lacking food, water, or sanitary facilities, the oldest, youngest, and weakest detainees died there in their hundreds, chiefly of infectious diseases.[13]

Marie Ranzenhoferová, a young mother of Czech and Hungarian parentage from Modřice on the southern outskirts of Brno, had been forced to join the exodus by a militiaman seeking revenge for her refusal to sleep with him. While elements of the column were supervised by men liberated from German concentration camps, who protected the expellees as best they could from abuse by the factory workers, she recalled, the treatment she observed of women and children during the night she spent at Pohořelice was far worse than on the march itself. On the march "people were beaten, and they tore their earrings off and took their rings; some people died; but in the camp, it was like a slaughterhouse. The next morning, at around 4 A.M., I got up and wanted to continue walking, and I saw they were loading the trucks with corpses." The following day Ranzenhoferová and her baby son succeeded in fleeing the column and obtaining the protection of the authorities at Milukov, where she continues to live to the present day.[14] The *Sudetendeutsche* left behind were not so fortunate. Those who were successfully pushed across the border into Austria in the following days and weeks found themselves in camps in which conditions were little better than at Pohořelice and where another 1,062 would perish. Estimates of the number who died in the course of this clearance operation vary widely. Eagle Glassheim has calculated that the total death toll exceeded 1,700—though even this figure does not include those who may have lost their lives during the course of the march itself.[15]

Harrowing though it was, the Brno episode was a most unusual occurrence in

May 1945: firstly for having taken place at all, and secondly because the prime movers were local civilians, albeit highly politicized ones. Few of the misnamed "wild expulsions" that took place later during the summer followed this pattern. To the contrary, Czechoslovak Army units repeatedly complained, in the words of one report, that National Committees in the border areas were dragging their feet and forbidding "strict action against the Germans." A memorandum of the Ministry of National Defense in mid-June remarked wryly that "it is necessary to support the initiative of national action committees. It would not be detrimental if this initiative got some momentum."[16] Business interests in particular proved resolute opponents of wholesale expulsions, causing impatient military officers to complain that economic experts considered half the German population to fall within the category of "essential workers."[17] One army major, frustrated by the failure of local officials in the municipality of Posevsko to move against their Germans with the necessary ferocity, threatened to make the town "a second Lidice" unless it changed its ways.[18] Accordingly, the security forces began to force the pace. A paramilitary police force, the SNB or National Security Corps, was formed to assist with expulsions; satisfy Communist demands for "popular" participation in the operation; and soak up the pool of undisciplined armed groups like the self-styled "Revolutionary Guards" that were responsible for much of the chaos in the borderlands.

Early in June, as a "test," some 1,300 Germans were rounded up by Czechoslovak Army units from the vicinity of the town of Děčín, transported to the border, and successfully ejected into the Soviet zone despite the attempts of town police to impede the deportation by occupying the railway station. Thereafter the removals accelerated rapidly. On June 20, for example, soldiers participated in a combined operation with local security corps to march several thousand Germans from the border town of Krnov, northwest of Opava, to Poland. Turned back on this occasion by Polish forces, the column of Germans was led along back roads to Králíky, forty miles to the west, and successfully pushed across the frontier there.[19] As the number of expulsions increased, the pattern became stereotyped. *Sudetendeutsch* expellees would be rounded up, normally at an hour's notice; permitted to gather together some hand baggage; searched for contraband; and then marched on foot either to the border or to a holding camp. Some of these forced processions were conducted at a ferocious pace, with groups being hustled along the roads by their armed escorts at a rate of twenty-five miles per day for a week or more; made to sleep in factories or barns; and receiving no food or water other than what they could beg from the inhabitants of the villages through which they passed en route. When the passage of these disheveled columns into Germany was refused by the occupying forces, as often happened, the expellees were in many cases returned by the same means to their starting points. Marches of this kind resulted in particularly high numbers of deaths among young children, whose lower physical stamina was unequal to the stresses placed upon them, and especially among babies whose mothers, after several days of extreme physical effort without nutrition, were no longer able to produce milk. The not infrequent protests of District National Committees that these indiscriminate and often futile clearances were unnecessarily disrupting the local economies were brushed aside, sometimes forcibly.

The process of selection for expulsion during this period was to a great degree arbitrary. In Czechoslovakia, until the reestablishment of the National Assembly on October 28, 1945 (the country's national day), President Beneš was empowered to issue decrees having the force of law. One of the first of these confiscated the property of Germans, Hungarians, traitors, and collaborators; a second that went into force—probably not coincidentally—on the final day of the Potsdam Conference stripped all those who had declared themselves of German or Hungarian ethnicity in any census after 1929 of Czechoslovak nationality. Those affected by the decrees could, however, apply for restoration of their property and citizenship if they could prove that they had actively resisted the Nazis, or had suffered persecution at German hands because of their loyalty to the Republic. As critics pointed out, this formula contained many flaws. Ethnic Czechs and Slovaks who had merely kept their heads down during the era of the Protectorate were unaffected by the law; ethnic Germans who did precisely the same became liable to expropriation and removal. Jews—even concentration-camp survivors—who were German-speakers acquired no immunity on account of their oppression unless they had been part of a resistance movement. In all cases, those wishing to claim immunity as "antifascists" had to petition "verification" committees, whose standards and procedures differed widely, to prove their case.

Those antifascists who did so faced high obstacles. The man who would become the most celebrated *Sudetendeutsch* antifascist of all—Oskar Schindler, rescuer of Jews from Gross-Rosen and Auschwitz, who was born in Svitavy in 1908 and himself narrowly escaped internment by fleeing from Czechoslovakia into Germany disguised in the uniform of a concentration camp inmate during the chaotic first days of peace—never submitted an application, considering that as a onetime Abwehr agent and Nazi Party member he had no chance of succeeding.[20] The experience of other, lesser Schindlers bore out the accuracy of his belief. In September 1945, for example, forty-two British former prisoners of war from Stalag IV C near Teplice petitioned the Ministry of the Interior in Prague and the Foreign Office in London on behalf of H. and J. Kunert, owners of a textile factory in Varnsdorf. During the war the Kunerts had protected the British POWs working in the factory from German mistreatment, provided them with food, and enabled them to listen to the BBC. On several occasions the pair had narrowly escaped imprisonment for their unpatriotic solicitousness for the welfare of the British workers. During the "May days," the liberated POWs had taken it upon themselves to guard the factory from violent Czech mobs. Despite these unsolicited testimonials, however, the government in Prague saw no reason to intervene. After the Czech workers in the factory threatened to strike unless their "German" bosses were removed, the Kunerts were imprisoned in Varnsdorf; their property confiscated; and following their eventual release they were forced to go to Germany.[21]

Cases of this kind were not unusual. The minister of defense and future president of Czechoslovakia, General Ludvík Svoboda, took a typically robust stance in a speech calling for "the complete expulsion from Czechoslovakia of all Germans, even those so-called anti-Fascists, to safeguard us from the formation of a new fifth column."[22] Verification committees typically suited the action to the minister's word; those that did not, as in Ostrava, were dissolved and replaced by more pliable ones.[23] The names of applicants were publicly displayed, so that any citizen might voice his or her objection—anonymously, if desired. By the end of June 1945, of some four thousand applications submitted in České Budějovice, only thirty-four were accepted.[24] To be successful, applicants normally required affidavits from ethnic Czechs or Slovaks attesting to their loyalty; those who provided them faced public ostracism, or worse. A "spontaneous" demonstration by Communist women in Žižkov, a working-class district of Prague, was one of many that condemned Czechoslovak nationals who provided positive testimonials for Germans.[25] In Nýřany near Plzeň, another "spontaneous" women's initiative prevailed upon the District National Committee to have the names of those who had vouched for antifascist Germans publicly displayed outside the town hall. "So today everyone has the opportunity to read the names of these 'patriots.'"[26] Often, political tests were applied. At first only Communists and Social Democrats qualified for antifascist status; later, in a very few cases, members of nonleftist parties might also pass muster after meticulous scrutiny. Some commissions interpreted the criterion of "resistance" to Nazism literally, requiring a record of armed partisan activity as the sole acceptable measure of antifascist status. Others issued certificates of exemption, but withdrew them in the face of pressures from above or below.[27] Poland, too, saw little reason to exert itself in trying to distinguish between "innocent" and "guilty" Germans. Stanisław Mikołajczyk, now deputy prime minister in the Communist-dominated coalition government, urged in 1946 that no exceptions be made for Germans who had worked with the resistance movement during the war. "If someone is a German, then his place is in Germany, and not in our country."[28]

In these circumstances, luck and connections counted as much as anything else in determining who was to stay and who to go. Colonel František Havel of the Ministry of National Defense reported, with some understatement, that members of District National Committees in border regions were not "always completely reliable and unbiased" when compiling lists of Germans for transfer. Often the lists included the names of their own estranged relatives, or acquaintances against whom they harbored some grievance.[29] At the other end of the spectrum, Colonel František Dastich discovered that numerous National Committees were actively hiding Germans to prevent their removal, and that agencies of the state were routinely exempting *Sudetendeutsche* who had joined the Communist Party after the end of the war.[30] Enough complaints of this kind were made to state authorities to undermine the official contention that all Germans had to be removed to prevent them from being lynched by their neighbors. In spite of a decree by the Ministry of the Interior making it a criminal offense for anyone to harbor, conceal, feed, clothe, or provide overnight accommodation to Germans, many newspaper articles subsequently upbraided "unpatriotic" Czechoslovaks who continued to hide or protect them from the authorities, as well as lamenting "the increasing number of cases, in border areas, of benevolent people succoring German workers and prisoners of war escaping from internment camps in our area."[31]

Not all the cross-border traffic was in a single direction. At the end of the war, many hundreds of thousands of Germans from what would become the Recovered Territories who had fled the Red Army's advance to the west now returned to their homes. Gunter Lange, a twelve-year-old boy expelled in June 1945 from Neumarkt (Środa Śląska), west of Wrocław, encountered "thousands of refugees" at Görlitz heading in the opposite direction to their places of origin in the east. "They did not believe that we had had to leave there. They could not understand that there was not going to be a return home."[32] The alarming spectacle of the population of "New Poland" actually increasing in the weeks after V-E Day was one of the factors spurring local authorities to proceed with "wild expulsions" as quickly as possible, and to reinforce their precautions against further unwanted arrivals.[33] At Frankfurt an der Oder, a city bisected by the river bearing its name, Polish soldiers routinely opened fire from the east bank at Germans approaching the western shores to fish.[34] Emilie Melina, a thirty-seven-year-old woman who found herself on the wrong side of the river Neisse when the war ended, had an even more distressing experience when she tried to get back to her mother and sisters at Rakau (Raków). She and two other young women were arrested as they made their way across the border near Kohlfurt and placed in a cell with sixteen other illicit frontier crossers of both sexes. Although the women were not abused, they were traumatized by the spectacle of their male cellmates repeatedly being beaten by the prison officers for thirty-minute stretches in front of them. Melina's terror was so great that she could not raise her eyes from the floor at her feet. To her consternation, an attempt was then made to compel her and the other women to hit the men with clubs. Though the Polish guards were displeased with the few half-hearted blows they delivered, shouting "We stuck it out in your concentration camps for six years, but you can't stand even one week with us!" Melina and the other women were not further mistreated. After four days in custody, they were marched back to the Neisse and reexpelled into Germany.[35]

Hazards like these did not deter many others from trying to return to their homelands, in the hope of reaching separated family members, retrieving hidden property, or being able to live there undetected. Like the expellee population in general, most of these would-be returners were female. By November 1945, so many of them were finding their way back into Czechoslovakia that Major Otakar Fischer of the Ministry of National Defense recommended that they be given short-term residence permits, valid for a year. The majority, he wrote, were young women of the manual working class who posed no political threat and were readily finding work in Czechoslovakia because of the depleted labor pool.[36] Fischer's proposal, however, was not adopted. Instead, returners were typically given prison sentences of a few months and then reexpelled to Germany. In Poland the Ministry of the Recovered Territories gave up the unequal struggle of trying to deter illicit border-crossers through prison sentences, ruling that they should not be detained but instead escorted back to Germany immediately upon apprehension.[37]

Although nearly all "wild expulsions" were carried out under color of authority, some were "wilder" than others. Impatient local agencies or security forces, responding to pressure from below, often decided to solve their problems on their own without involving, or even informing, the central government. In some cases this involved conducting their own "foreign policy." Thus the National Security Office in Jablonec nad Nisou, assailed by "increasingly radical voices" in the town demanding that something be done about the Germans and anxious about the apparent insouciance of the local *Sudetendeutsche*, visited the local Red Army commander, General Samokhvalov, and obtained his blessing for a thousand expellees to be marched to the border east of Polubný, about four miles away. The Jablonec National Security Office carried out the operation in mid-

June without notifying the military authorities, a tactic that almost went awry when a Polish army officer, pointing out that the area into which the Germans were being driven was now part of the Recovered Territories, refused to let them enter. While the officer was diverted by being engaged in day-long negotiations, the Germans were put across the border elsewhere.[38] Although the Ministry of National Defense was unamused by this usurpation of its authority, similar cases were common. The Děčín-based newspaper *Severočeská Mladá fronta* lauded the local authorities of the area for their effectiveness in this regard. "How many journeys to Dresden and how many successful actions have we carried out thus far in this matter, without having to wait upon the permission of any higher expulsion authority!"[39]

For every Jablonec or Děčín, however, there were a dozen localities that got in badly over their heads when they tried to seize the initiative in this fashion. A revealing analysis of the difficulties typically associated with "wild expulsions," based on its own experiences in the Svitavy district of Moravia, was provided by the Regional National Committee of Moravská Třebová to the Ministry of the Interior at the end of August 1945. The report is notable for its frankness; the story it tells could apply equally well to dozens of other districts. On May 12, Svitavy had a population of 34,000 Germans and only 115 Czechs. Some 8,000 of the former quickly left of their own volition or were taken away by the Red Army, but it was far from clear what to do with the remaining 26,000. The authorities in Moravská Třebová—according to their own account, at least—initially held out against pressure from below for precipitate action. Only 291 German suspects were rounded up, on information laid by the few Czechs and German antifascists in the area, and 40 of these were soon released. The position of the National Committee, though, was undercut at the end of May by news arriving of the removal of the Germans at Brno, and of a lethal "wild expulsion" carried out by the Czechoslovak Army in Litomyšl and its environs, ten miles away.[40] Members of the public expressed great bitterness that while the new citizens of Svitavy had been instructed to refrain from driving out the local *Sudetendeutsch* population by force and instead to wait patiently upon the central government, the people of neighboring districts had been allowed to solve their German problem employing as much violence as they pleased. "Radical elements" arriving in the area who sought only to enrich themselves, along with the first of 2,500 Czech "colonists" dispatched from the interior, helped turn this simmering resentment into a feeding frenzy. Under their influence, young people clamored for immediate action against the Germans; other would-be property seekers attempted to go over the National Committee's head, sending deputations to lobby ministers in

Prague and Brno. These demagogic appeals, the authorities considered, were aimed at causing the maximum degree of chaos so that the self-interested parties behind them could obtain for themselves as much German booty as possible.

After it had become clear that the ever-growing number of settlers would not contain themselves in patience for the "organized expulsion" at which the authorities were aiming, the National Committee at the beginning of June tried to defuse the situation by conducting large-scale roundups of Germans into camps, thereby making possible a swift interim redistribution of their property. Four makeshift detention centers were opened in Svitavy; another was established in Březová nad Svitavou; and part of an adjacent municipality was cordoned off and used as an overflow facility. The National Committee acknowledged that the roundup had been shambolic, and conditions in the camps were grim. Because of the haste with which the detentions had been carried out, entire families were taken into custody, along with proven antifascists and essential workers in industry. As the local medical officer, Dr. Votava, recorded, epidemics of typhus and dysentery soon broke out among the internees. To reduce overcrowding in the camps, parties of two hundred detainees at a time had been quietly taken out and pushed across the border into occupied Germany; these expulsions were always carried out before six o'clock in the morning in the hope of avoiding detection by the American or Soviet authorities. By these means, the number of Germans in Svitavy was reduced by almost half by mid-August. This did not, however, succeed in satisfying the "radicals." Because "every Czech wanted a house or a villa," those Germans who possessed the choicest properties were proceeded against first, defeating the National Committee's efforts to carry out an orderly transfer. Members of the subcommittee charged with expropriating the expellees included "many individuals . . . who acted in their own interest." They were abetted by the Czechoslovak Army, against whom many serious and credible allegations—of torture, hangings, beatings, and robbery of Germans—had been lodged. These had reached such a scale that even the Red Army had intervened, tearing off the white armlets which the National Committee had obliged Germans to wear and which marked them out for maltreatment. Once again, though, pressure from "radicals" and from the Czechoslovak Army led the Germans to be relabeled with a letter "N" (for *Němec*, "German") on a white square, worn on the breast.

The disruption caused by these events, the National Committee recorded, was so great that in the end it proved necessary to call a temporary halt to the operation. Further "concentration" of Germans was suspended until proper lists of detainees could be drawn up. In conformity with guidelines received from the Ministry of the Interior, young children and their mothers were taken out of the internment camps—although, to appease public sentiment, it was decided not to release them into the community, as the regulations stipulated. Instead they remained confined to a "ghetto." A "control committee" had been established which, it hoped, would assist the authorities in fending off further pressure from below and avoiding similar "errors" in the future. No fewer than 15,500 of the original German population of 26,000, though, still remained to be expelled, and the National Committee left the government in no doubt that more trouble awaited unless these could be removed quickly.[41]

Even the rather less shambolic expulsions conducted by the Czechoslovak Army ran into increasing difficulties with the advent of midsummer. One of the most serious was a shortage of suitable border crossings. At first some of the U.S. forces occupying western Bohemia had been willing to help. Lieutenant Colonel V. Drozda reported on June 19, 1945 that in his district the Americans were cooperating with the Czechoslovak authorities in the latter's roundup of "the local nationally unreliable population" and that U.S. military police were involved in the majority of these operations.[42] According to an American journalist on the scene, Edward Angly, the U.S. role in the "wild expulsions" had gone further even than this. Assisted with "an occasional well-planted kick to hurry them along," he reported, expellees were "being herded into the custody of the United States Third Army . . . since they came here, troops of the Fifth Corps have removed an average of 1,000 Germans a day out of Czechoslovakia in trucks."[43] It is probable, though, that such unofficial U.S. participation in expulsion operations was not continued after the announcement of the Potsdam moratorium. With the passage of time, American commanders became steadily more uneasy about the methods being used by the Czechoslovaks to rid themselves of the *Sudetendeutsche*, so that by October Major General Ernie Harmon of XXII Corps, headquartered in Plzeň, was advising the U.S. ambassador that "I do not feel that the American Army can be a party to this."[44] Consequently, by midautumn 1945 the U.S. Army was placing so many obstacles in the way of movements of expellees through western Bohemia that they had become almost impossible. On the other side of the country, the absorption by Poland of the Recovered Territories had shrunk the northern Czechoslovak-German frontier by about half, seriously impeding operations there. To the south, Austria's absorptive capacity was much lower than Germany's, and Soviet military commanders there were particularly unsympathetic to Prague's difficulties. As a result, Czechoslovakia found its expulsion actions being channeled into a comparatively narrow frontier strip between Jáchymov and Liberec, with the town of Děčín at its epicenter. Even here, the Soviet military authorities in the adjacent German districts became ever more demanding in their requirements. The Red Army's 13th Division, for example, specified that large columns must be accompanied by Czechoslovak troops for twenty kilometers beyond the border; they were to carry food for several days; the expellees were not to have their possessions and rations pillaged; the very old and very young were to travel on wagons; and the center of the town of Zittau was to be circumnavigated. Other commanders imposed a weekly limit of two parties of 250 each at the frontier post at Boží Dar; demanded that no expellee be admitted who did not possess at least twenty-five kilograms of baggage and personal documentation; or required forty-eight hours' prior notice for all movements. A Czechoslovak Army memorandum noted, however, that gifts of alcohol had a most helpful effect in eliciting a flexible attitude respecting these criteria among the Soviet border guards.[45]

Curiously, bearing in mind the infinitely more savage and inhumane nature of the German occupation of Poland, the initial occupation of the Recovered Territories was not marked by the kind of violent reprisals seen in Czechoslovakia—though this would soon change. Removals of Germans from Danzig began as early as mid-April 1945, and were voluntary rather than coerced. Those willing to depart by themselves were issued certificates requesting the civil and military authorities to facilitate the bearers' travel to Germany, valid for a month from the date of issue. These were usually accepted on trains in lieu of tickets. The mood turned darker in early June, however, when the first of a series of military directives requiring the immediate expulsion of the German population was issued. General Karol Świerczewski, commander of the Second Army Corps, referred specifically in an order he issued on June 24 to the Czechoslovaks' success in driving out their Germans, and urged his troops to do likewise. "One must perform one's tasks in such a harsh and decisive manner," he told them, "that the Germanic vermin do not hide in their houses but rather will flee from us of their own volition and then in their own land will thank God that they were lucky enough to save their heads."[46] Little more detailed advice was offered as to how the mission was to be accomplished, leading, as in Czechoslovakia, to many local variations. In the area covered by the Fifth Infantry Division, expellees were allowed to carry twenty kilograms of baggage consisting of clothing and food only. The commander of the Eleventh Division, for his part, sanctioned the use by Germans of horses and ox-drawn carts, though these needed to be turned over to the Polish authorities upon reaching the border. On the whole, though, the expulsions were attended with an extraordinarily high degree of violence; in the view of Bernadetta Nitschke, the methods used by the Polish Army "were far from humane, and often no different from those of Hitler."[47] Civil authorities often protested the expulsions, citing the impact on the economy and above all the fact that they were occurring as the harvest was approaching. The Red Army, too, sometimes interfered, leading General Świerczewski to remind his subordinates of the importance of avoiding discussions with Soviet commanders and instead presenting them with faits accomplis.

By mid-June, the roads between the Recovered Territories and the river Oder were thronged with parties of Germans, ranging in size from twos and threes to hundreds, who had been forced out of their homes with little or no notice and pointed westwards. Lacking food or shelter, and with journeys of hundreds of miles on foot in front of them, their survival depended on what they could beg or steal en route. Nor were they left unmolested while on the road. The experience of Johanna Janisch, a twenty-five-year-old mother of three small children, can stand for thousands of others. Evicted in the middle of the night from a village near Świebodzin (Schwiebus), Janisch was already suffering from gonorrhea contracted as a result of having been raped some twenty times by Red Army soldiers. (The Polish police of the village, she testified, had shielded her and her sister from still further assaults by pretending to the Soviets that the German women were their wives.)

> At Schwiebus, the fugitives from many surrounding villages met and formed a great trek which now started on its way towards Frankfurt an der Oder. We spent the first night in the open; later we found barns or sheds to protect us against the weather during the nights. . . . During the walk of five weeks on the road we lived only by eating potatoes and fruits from the fields which we digged ourselves. . . . Many weak and sick people, old folks and children had to be left on the road dead. It was a lamentable procession of utmost misery. We had all lost much weight and many of us looked like skeletons. Heaven only knows how often we were plundered by Poles or Russians and how many times the women were [sexually] assaulted again and again.[48]

However great the hazards and miseries of life on the road may have been—in a report to Bishop Stanisław Adamski, the vicar general of Wrocław diocese called them "indescribable"—they were to be preferred in most cases to the expulsion trains that the Polish authorities now began to operate. Taking up to two weeks, and sometimes longer, to reach Berlin, the focal point of most of these transports, the trains were usually unprovisioned and lacking the most basic of amenities. Unsurprisingly, the death rate soared.

> In our freight wagon there were about ninety-eight people, and it is no exaggeration to say that we were squeezed against each other like sardines in a can. When we reached Allenstein people started to die, and had to be deposited along the side of the rails. One or more dead bodies greeted us every morning

of our journey after that; they just had to be abandoned on the embankments. There must have been many, many bodies left lying along the track . . .

The train spent more time stopping than moving. It took us more than fourteen days to reach the Russian occupation zone. We rarely traveled at night. . . . We had no idea where we were, because the names of the stations were now all in Polish. For a long time we were afraid that we were being taken to the interior of Poland to be left somewhere to die of hunger. But in the end we realized we were traveling in a westerly direction. After a few days we had no more to eat. Sometimes, by begging the Polish driver, we were able to get a little warm water drawn from the engine. . . . The nights were unbearable because of the overcrowding. We could neither keep upright nor sit down, much less lie down. We were so tightly squeezed together that it was impossible not to jostle each other occasionally. Recriminations and quarrels erupted, even attempts to exchange blows in the middle of this human scrum. The very sick suffered the worst. Typhus was widespread throughout the entire transport and the number of deaths grew with each passing day. You can well imagine the state of hygiene that prevailed in the wagon.[49]

For the two smallest expelling countries, Yugoslavia and Romania, all removals of Germans were by definition "wild expulsions" inasmuch as the Allies never undertook to accept their minorities into occupied Germany or Austria. Tito's government did belatedly, on January 16, 1946, submit a formal request for authority to carry out an organized transfer of its German population. "For ten years before the Second World War," it alleged, "the destruction of Yugoslavia was systematically planned and prepared by the German minority"; according to a postwar Yugoslav state commission of inquiry, "only one thousand . . . remained neutral during the occupation." The Germans thus constituted "a pernicious enclave within the national blood of the Yugoslav peoples," and the menace they posed to international peace and security was so immediate that their removal should receive priority over all other such transfers.[50] If the request was approved, Belgrade proposed to expel all 130,388 Yugoslav *Volksdeutsche* in a fifteen-day operation.[51] Although the Foreign Office in London supported the idea, reasoning that "it would be difficult to refuse to the Yugoslavs what we have granted to the Poles, Czechs and Hungarians,"[52] others were skeptical of the remarkably low—and suspiciously precise—figure given by Belgrade for its German minority. This, it was recalled, had been stated as being more than 600,000 strong in prewar censuses. It therefore seemed likely that "the Yugoslavs are deliberately quoting a low figure to us now, in order that we may agree the more easily to the transfer, and will later, after we have agreed, discover that there are in fact two or three times as many Germans left as they first informed us."⁵³ Even though massacres of *Volksdeutsche* were known to have taken place on a massive scale, with the British military mission reporting in January 1945 a typical reprisal action in which "150 *Volksdeutsch* in the Vojvodina were shot for the murder of a Russian soldier by a local woman," it seemed unlikely that these alone could account for the missing half-million.⁵⁴ By the time the Yugoslav request was taken up by the Allied Control Council in Berlin, moreover, the occupying powers were struggling to cope with the influx of Germans from the three "Potsdam countries" of Poland, Czechoslovakia, and Hungary. All feared that to grant Tito's request would set an unfortunate precedent that would greatly add to their troubles. "It is known that there are German minorities in Bulgaria, Rumania, Iran, Turkey and other countries, and it is therefore not unlikely that requests for the transfer of these minorities into Germany will be received."⁵⁵ General Vasily Sokolovsky, Red Army commander in chief in the Soviet occupation zone, had already rejected a back-channel approach by Belgrade to accept expellees in the area under his administration.⁵⁶ In a rare display of four-power unity, therefore, the Allies supported a Soviet proposal to shelve the Yugoslav application indefinitely. Though this did not deter Tito from driving out his *Volksdeutsch* population regardless, it did at least have the effect of stretching out the process and thereby reducing to a degree the difficulties of resettlement.

A similar pattern can be seen in the removal of the *Volksdeutsche* from Romania. Uniquely, the Bucharest government neither formally demanded their expulsion, nor issued an expulsion decree against them. Indeed, Bucharest formally protested the first move made in this direction by the Soviet military authorities. In January 1945, General Vladislav Vinogradov required the Romanian government to round up all ethnic German males between the ages of eighteen and forty-five, and females between eighteen and thirty, for transportation to the USSR as forced laborers. The coalition government of Nicolae Rădescu appealed this directive, pointing out that among the 500,000 *Volksdeutsche* of Romania there were many "of a very remote German origin or simply bearing names of German consonance . . . [who had] constantly performed their military duties in the Roumanian Army and accomplished faithfully their civic obligations. Their mobilization and removal will be all the more unjust and unfounded."⁵⁷ Some Western officials also took a dim view of the Soviet initiative, less on account of its indiscriminate nature than because they considered the use of forced labor to be a form of "reparations in kind," which could properly be decided only by an Allied council appointed to share out German assets rather than by unilateral action. Sir Orme Sargent at the Foreign Office, however, declared that "we and the Americans will have to get used to these mass deportations, which the Russians are certainly going to carry out when they get into Germany."⁵⁸ He was backed up by Winston Churchill, who recalled that in his notorious "percentages" agreement with Stalin at Moscow in October 1944, the latter had been assigned 90 percent of the influence in postwar Romania.[59] In a pair of splenetic minutes to Foreign Secretary Eden, the prime minister now demanded to know "Why are we making a fuss about the Russian deportations in Roumania of Saxons [ethnic Germans] and others? It was understood that the Russians were to work their will in this sphere. Anyhow we cannot prevent them."[60]

The deportations from Romania were carried out in as chaotic a manner as those that would later take place in Czechoslovakia and Poland. Combined Soviet and Romanian patrols began roundups in the predawn hours of January 11, 1945, requiring deportees to be ready with clothing and sufficient food for ten days within fifteen minutes. The British ambassador recorded, and General Vinogradov admitted, that in many cases "Roumanian police [were] taking bribes from Germans for release, their place being taken by some casual passer-by picked up by Roumanian police. Naturally these are Roumanians."[61] Up to seventy-five thousand *Volksdeutsche*, nonetheless, were removed from the country by these means. Others were taken up into internment camps, to facilitate the redistribution of their property.

Although most ethnic Germans from Romania were not formally deported, both they and the survivors among the forced laborers in the USSR, who were progressively released between December 1945 and 1949, were confronted with conditions that made it impossible for many of them to remain. After the Soviets engineered the fall of Rădescu's government in March 1945 and replaced it with a pliant Communist administration, a pair of decrees forfeited ethnic Germans' real property to the state and stripped many of them of Romanian citizenship. Both the remaining *Volksdeutsch* population and returning deportees, therefore, found that ethnic Romanians were living in their former homes and that they themselves were officially classified as illegal immigrants. The new Bucharest government denied the Red Cross the right to extend charitable assistance to the *Volksdeutsche* "on the ground that these people had lost Romanian nationality." Their situation, consequently, was pitiable. The returning deportees, the CICR found, "generally camp out in the open air or in cellars and sometimes they have nothing to eat but what they can find growing in the fields." Those who had escaped deportation were not much better off: "they have literally been put out into the street. . . . Usually, their houses were given to Gypsies who, often, employ the former owners as domestic servants."[62] Deprived of the means of existence, Romanian *Volksdeutsche* were in the position of having been "constructively expelled." Significant numbers began making their way to Germany and

The "Wild Expulsions"

Austria; by August 1945, some twenty-one thousand were in the latter country, most having arrived in a very poor state of health.[63]

Greatly to the surprise of many observers, the Germans in each of the expelling countries put up little or no resistance to their removal. The demographic profile of the expellees no doubt had something to do with that—women, children, and the elderly are rarely in the forefront of popular insurgencies. But the quiescence with which the German populations greeted their fate was positively unnerving to the Polish and Czechoslovak governments, which expected to encounter fierce opposition from "stay-behind" German guerrilla units—the so-called Werewolves. Though it is now clear that no organized activity of this kind ever took place,[64] the authorities in the borderlands of both countries did their best to imagine a Werewolf conspiracy into existence. This was especially true of Czechoslovakia, where a sabotage panic of considerable proportions was constructed on a foundation of "sweeping statements, half-truths and sometimes outright inventions" in the summer of 1945.[65] Just as the Nazis during the occupation had exaggerated the scale of Czechoslovak resistance and categorized accidents as examples of sabotage, so now any unexplained occurrence resulting in death or injury tended to be attributed to Werewolf activity.[66] In mid-July, for example, nine *Sudetendeutsch* civilians were summarily executed in Rudoltice, northwest of Olomouc, in reprisal for a gunshot wound inflicted upon a Czechoslovak soldier that upon further investigation turned out to have been caused by the man carelessly discharging his own weapon. Werewolves were also blamed for an altercation in which U.S. forces and Revolutionary Guards blundered into each other in the dark near Aš on the night of June 30–July 1 and began exchanging fire, wounding three. Such minor incidents often had large-scale ramifications. When an SNB officer accidentally blew himself up in Bruntál while handling a grenade, Colonel V. Janko of the notoriously trigger-happy 1st Czechoslovak Armored Brigade jumped to the conclusion that the explosion had been caused by a radio-controlled bomb; his subordinate, Captain I. Gaš, retaliated by shooting twenty local *Sudetendeutsche* on July 5; interning hundreds of others; driving 4,300 over the border on July 10 and 11; and sending some 750 more for labor service in the interior. Again, after members of the brigade began shooting at a unit of the Financial Police near Javorník on the outskirts of Svitavy on the night of July 9–10 after mistaking them for Werewolves and triggering a full-scale firefight, the commanding officer of the brigade covered up the debacle by blaming "saboteurs" and ordering as a punishment the expulsion of the entire unproductive *Sudetendeutsch* population of the district. Forty-eight hours later, the men and childless women were rounded up into camps; 340 elderly people, mothers, and children were driven into a makeshift ghetto in the village of Vápenná. In a similar vein was an explosion on July 9 at the Körber munitions factory in Hrádek nad Nisou, two miles from the border opposite Zittau, in which seven Czech soldiers and seven German workers were killed. The evidence pointed to mishandling of detonators as they were being loaded on trucks; the authorities, however, preferred to believe that one of the dead Germans had carried out a suicide-bombing operation. A collective fine of more than one hundred thousand Reichsmarks was imposed on the local German community, who were then driven across the border a week later. The Hrádek incident became an oft-quoted piece of evidence by Czech officialdom to prove the reality of an organized resistance movement.[67]

The most infamous incident attributed to Werewolf activity was the explosion of an ammunition dump in the border town of Ústí nad Labem (Aussig) in northwestern Bohemia on the afternoon of July 31. Twenty-eight people were killed. Although most of the victims turned out to be *Sudetendeutsche*, the rumor that sabotage was responsible quickly spread, and within an hour of the explosion Germans, easily recognizable by their colored armbands, were being hunted through the streets by workers, Czechoslovak Army units, Revolutionary Guards, Soviet troops, and members of the SNB. Many were beaten to death where they were found; others were hurled from the bridge over the River Labe (Elbe) connecting the two sides of the town and shot as they floundered in the water. In an incident recalled by nearly all observers at the scene, at least one baby carriage with a baby inside was also thrown into the river. Estimates of the number killed vary widely—from several hundred to several thousand—though recent scholarship has tended to coalesce around a figure of 100–150 deaths.

The Ústí massacre quickly turned into a bitter point of contention between the Czechoslovak government and the *Sudetendeutsch* Social Democrats in London. The Cabinet in Prague, already rattled by reports arriving from low-ranking officers who were anxious to parade their vigilance by depicting every find of discarded weapons or discovery of a German civilian in possession of a pair of binoculars as evidence of a "Werewolf cell," immediately put two and two together and made five. Even though the army stated that the cause of the explosion had not yet been determined, the Cabinet concluded that it was undoubtedly the fruit of a "planned sabotage action." Unverified rumors were supplied to—and uncritically published by—the national and international press as confirmed fact, including a story that a Werewolf aircraft had flown low over Ústí and might have dropped a bomb on the ammunition dump at the time of the explosion.[68] (Six weeks later, Wenzel Jaksch's Social Democrats mockingly inquired of Prague why nothing had been heard since then from "the powerful

Werewolf conspiracy, its radio stations, its grey airplanes, its centres in Belgrade, Paris and Argentine.")[69] For their part, Sudeten Germans aired their suspicions that the explosion had been the Czechoslovak version of the Reichstag fire of 1933, pointing to what seemed the remarkable coincidence that the Potsdam Conference was taking place at the same time. Rumors circulated in the *Sudetendeutsch* camp that printed notices imposing a curfew on Ústí to quell the disturbances had begun to be posted up on walls even before the explosion took place, and that the massacre had been deliberately staged to impress on the Big Three at Potsdam what would happen on a far larger scale if they did not give final approval to the expulsions. Neither the government's nor the Sudeten Germans' rival conspiracy theories, however, need be taken very seriously. The truth was almost certainly, as a pair of British-born residents in Ústí who had witnessed the killings reported to Ambassador Nichols, that a tragic accident had been followed by "a spontaneous outburst by Czech hooligans" in and out of uniform.[70]

In the immediate aftermath of the massacre, public as well as official paranoia over Werewolf activity escalated considerably, with ludicrous claims like "hundreds of Werewolves have been destroyed and disposed of every day" and "our entire border is now a combat zone, where the hidden enemy launches attacks against the Czech people" appearing regularly in the popular press.[71] The precise reason remains unclear. It may be that in the wake of the Potsdam Conference's call for a temporary suspension of expulsions, Czechoslovak authorities felt themselves under pressure to generate the evidence that would prove the presence of the Germans to be an ongoing threat to the country's national security and strengthen the argument for their removal. Tomáš Staněk also points out that the Communist-dominated Ministry of Information had a vested interest in generating a steady stream of stories about Werewolves and spies seeking to undermine the "People's Democratic State."[72] At all events, from early August an atmosphere reminiscent of the seventeenth-century Salem witch trials prevailed in the Czech borderlands, in which numerous Germans were tortured to persuade them to reveal the names of members of Werewolf cells, who would themselves be subjected to equally rigorous interrogation to elicit still more names. As Staněk notes, a high proportion of the "confessions" thus obtained bear an uncomfortable resemblance to those extracted using identical methods from "counterrevolutionaries" and "capitalist spies" after the Communist coup of February 1948.[73]

The fact nonetheless remained that proven cases of opposition to forced removals were somewhat nowhere to be found. The uniform, almost eerie, meekness of the German population was recorded in report after report in both Czechoslovakia and Poland. The month before the Ústí explosion, the commander of the gendarmerie declared the area to be entirely peaceful; and although the local SNB headquarters three weeks later complained of shootings and robberies occurring on a daily basis, it placed the blame for these on Czechoslovak military and Red Army elements.[74] Elsewhere, even after the massacre, police and army accounts spoke overwhelmingly of the "passivity and servility" of the Germans; of their evident appearance of being "frightened" and "depressed"; and of the security forces' confidence that any truly dangerous elements among them had already either been removed from the country or were safely in custody.[75] Newspapers likewise testified to the Germans behaving with the "servility to which the Czechoslovaks ha[d] become accustomed."[76] Much the same was true of Poland. With the exception of isolated incidents like a standoff in Prudnik, when looted Germans laid siege to a militia barracks suspected of holding the officers who had robbed them, overt resistance was conspicuous by its absence.[77] A Polish observer who traveled from Poznań to Szczecin and back again at the end of August dismissed as propaganda government claims of Werewolf activity, testifying instead to the "nauseating obsequiousness" and "cowardly" demeanor of the ill-fed Germans he encountered on the trip.[78] In Wrocław only twenty-five cases of oppositional behavior, nineteen of which involved the distribution of leaflets protesting the actions of the authorities, were attributed to Germans by the security forces in 1945. For the whole of 1946 the number of recorded cases, all consisting of leaflet distribution, had fallen to a mere nine.[79] In Olsztyn province, too, as Claudia Kraft has found, "The source materials are full of references to the Germans' utter passivity."[80]

Neither the Polish nor the Czechoslovak governments expected that the period of "wild" expulsions would last for ever. Their aim had been, through the strategic use of terror, to cause the remaining German populations to flee by themselves, preferably before the Potsdam Conference and certainly before the eventual Peace Conference. "Organized expulsions" would come into play only if this attempt to create facts on the ground proved insufficient. This may not have been true of Yugoslavia. According to Vice President Milovan Djilas, while the decision to drive out the *Volksdeutsche* of that country had been taken in principle, "we might have changed our minds had not the Russians, Poles, and Czechs already decided for, and partially carried out, the expulsion of their Germans. We adopted this stand without any discussion, as something which the German atrocities made understandable and justifiable."[81] Klejda Mulaj, on the other hand, considers that Tito's regime used extermination as a catalyst for expulsion as early as the autumn of 1944, engaging in mass killings of German civilians in a "well-planned and systematic" operation for that purpose.[82]

For the Czechoslovaks and Poles, though, despite all their efforts the operation was proceeding much too slowly. Notwithstanding the violence, few ethnic Germans voluntarily left their homes—a fact that came as no surprise to Wenzel Jaksch, who recalled that a decade previously only 10 percent of the *Sudetendeutsch* Social Democrats, despite facing the real possibility of arrest and punishment by the Gestapo, had fled to the Czechoslovak interior after the Munich Pact.[83] At the midsummer peak, some 5,350 Germans were being forcibly removed from Czechoslovakia, and probably a somewhat larger number from the Recovered Territories, each day.[84] Even if such a rate could be sustained through the winter season, which was highly unlikely in light of the fact that freight wagons sent to Germany often never returned, the clearances would take at least two years to complete. In view of the near certainty of a backlash by the Big Three long before then, this was even more unrealistic a proposition.

The backlash, indeed, was not long in coming. Throughout the summer of 1945, trains of expellees continued to pour into Berlin and other German and Austrian cities, becoming the earliest and most enduring symbol of the operation. Despite their understandably Germanophobic inclinations, the Western journalists who had flocked to Berlin to cover the Potsdam Conference found themselves aghast at the scenes they encountered at the main line stations in the summer of 1945, with dead and dying littering the platforms. Charles Bray, German correspondent of the London *Daily Herald*, described finding four corpses on a visit to the Stettin Station, with "another five or six . . . lying alongside them, given up as hopeless by the doctor, and just being allowed to die." Others in the same condition were in what his colleague Norman Clark of the *News Chronicle* called a "cattle truck mortuary,"[85] which was cleared each night to make room for the next day's dead. Bray discovered to his chagrin that the spectacle of German suffering "gave me no satisfaction, although for years I have hoped that the Germans would reap from the seeds they had sown."[86] A *Times* reporter found at a Berlin hospital the following month another sixty women and children who had been "summarily evicted" from a hospital and orphanage in Gdańsk. They had been transported in cattle trucks without food or water: by the time of their arrival in Berlin twenty were dead.[87] Major Stephen Terrell of the Parachute Regiment, outraged at the spectacle of "entire populations dying by the thousands on the roads from starvation, dysentery and exhaustion," broke the chain of command by sending an eyewitness report, via Bray, to the Foreign Office. "Even a cursory visit to the hospitals in Berlin, where some of these people have dragged themselves, is an experience which would make the sights in the Concentration Camps appear normal."[88] A British military doctor, Adrian Kanaar, working in another Berlin medical facility, did likewise, reporting on an expellee train from Poland in which seventy-five had died on the journey due to overcrowding.[89] Although Kanaar had just completed a stint as a medical officer at the Belsen concentration camp, what he witnessed of the expellees' plight so scandalized him that he declared his readiness to face a court martial if necessary for making the facts known to the press. He had not, he declared, "spent six years in the army to see a tyranny established which is as bad as the Nazis."[90] The same comparison suggested itself to Gerald Gardiner, later to become Lord Chancellor of Great Britain. A member of a volunteer ambulance unit working with concentration camp survivors, Gardiner was on hand in the late summer and autumn of 1945 to witness the arrival of expellee trains from the Recovered Territories that had taken up to fourteen days to complete their journeys. "The removal of the dead in carts from the railway stations," he recorded, "was a grim reminder of what I saw in early days in Belsen."[91]

This perception was not confined to journalists and members of humanitarian agencies alone. Robert Murphy, a career diplomat who had served as General Eisenhower's political adviser and was now the State Department's senior representative in Germany with the rank of ambassador, became so uneasy about the expulsions and his government's part in facilitating them that in October he sent a combined report and protest to his friend Harrison Freeman ("Doc") Matthews, Director of the Office of European Affairs at the State Department. Like Freeman, Murphy had been a member of the U.S. delegation at the Potsdam Conference and had raised no objection there to the expulsion scheme. Indeed he had "hesitated" before sending his memorandum, he told Freeman, because "even mentioning the matter exposes one to the charge of 'softness' to the Germans." In the end, however, he found himself "not so much concerned regarding what is happening to the German population as I am regarding our own standard of conduct, because I feel that if we are willing to compromise on certain principles in respect of the Germans or any other people, progressively it may become too easy for us to sacrifice those same principles in regard to our own people."[92]

> In viewing the distress and despair of these wretches, in smelling the odor of their filthy condition, the mind reverts instantly to Dachau and Buchenwald. Here is retribution on a large scale, but practiced not on the *Parteibonzen* [Party bigwigs], but on women and children, the poor, the infirm. The vast majority are women and children. . . .
>
> Our psychology adjusts itself somehow to the idea that suffering is part of the soldier's contract . . . That psychology loses some of its elasticity, however, in viewing the stupid tragedy now befalling thousands of innocent children, and women and old people. . . . The mind reverts to other recent mass deporta-

The "Wild Expulsions"

tions which horrified the world and brought upon the Nazis the odium which they so deserved. Those mass deportations engineered by the Nazis provided part of the moral basis on which we waged the war and which gave strength to our cause.

Now the situation is reversed. We find ourselves in the invidious position of being partners in this German enterprise and as partners inevitably sharing the responsibility.[93]

By the time the Potsdam Conference issued its call for a suspension of further "wild expulsions," Berlin had become the epicenter of an accelerating humanitarian crisis. Most expellees from Poland, and a significant number from Czechoslovakia, were converging on the city "chiefly because rail traffic was possible and with the hope . . . of finding some central organisation which would deal with them. . . . In many cases the sick and the aged were left behind and many spoke of thousands of children separated from their families."[94] Despite an alarmed Marshal Zhukov first putting up posters warning expellees to stay away and then declaring the city closed to new arrivals at the end of July, a month during which 550,000 people had entered, another 262,000 came in the first half of August, showing that the prohibition had had no measurable effect on the influx. Proportionately, smaller German cities and towns were in even worse straits. By mid-August about 50,000 Germans displaced from Opava and České Budějovice had accumulated in Zittau, trebling the town's normal population; more than 100,000 were swamping Görlitz.

Although the Soviet ambassador to Czechoslovakia, Valerian Zorin, had told Prime Minister Fierlinger after Potsdam that his government would turn a blind eye to further discreet expulsions, Red Army commanders on the ground, who enjoyed considerable autonomy, took a far less accommodating stance. As early as mid-June, local units attempted to close the Zittau-Görlitz corridor, the main entry point for "wild expulsions" from Czechoslovakia to the Soviet zone, and in some cases physically forced back those already admitted, citing an outbreak of typhus and a lack of food in the border regions.[95] At the end of August, when the head of the Czechoslovak military mission in Berlin, General František Hrabčík, pressed Zhukov to admit another 200,000 expellees immediately, he was met with a flat refusal in light of the masses of new arrivals from the Recovered Territories with whom the Soviet occupation authorities already had to deal.[96]

When attempted "wild expulsions" failed, the consequences could be lethal, for army and militia units were sometimes determined not to take "no" for an answer. On June 28, 1945, a party of twenty-one Germans was conducted from Teplice nad Metují (Wekelsdorf) to the nearby Polish border. After the Poles refused to admit them, the expellees, most of whom were children and elderly women, were taken by the leader of the military escort, Captain V. Svoboda, into the forest at Buky in what is now the Krkonoše National Park and executed there. The bodies were exhumed in 1947, when a Czech witness wrote of the scene: "the sight of a baby in swaddling clothes was terrible, its face crushed beyond recognition, obviously by the butt of a rifle."[97] In many cases, however, guards considered their duty to have been discharged once the expellees had been conducted to the border, whether the occupying powers admitted them or not. Thus two "wild expulsions," each of more than a thousand Germans from Ostrava, on June 13 and July 2, were rejected by the Poles and Soviets respectively. Although many expellees had died in the course of their journeys to the frontier, the survivors were abandoned there by their escorts and instructed to fend for themselves. Some found refuge in neighboring villages; others were left to wander in the forests before eventually finding their way back to Ostrava to await their roundup for another transport.[98]

Balked to the north and east, the Czechoslovak authorities in the late summer and autumn of 1945 turned once again to the west. Though "wild expulsions" were becoming increasingly difficult, with only a comparative trickle being accepted by the Soviets through a narrow corridor between the Elbe and the hamlet of Boží Dar near Jáchymov, the Allies were still admitting convoys of "voluntary emigrants" into Germany.[99] According to the regulations in force, ethnic Germans wishing to leave Czechoslovakia of their own accord were supposed to obtain a release certificate from their local District National Committee and confirmation from the occupation authorities in Germany that no objection would be raised to their entry. In reality the number of genuine voluntary emigrants was small: by the end of 1945 a total of just eleven thousand had entered the Soviet zone, in what was sometimes referred to as *Aktion Zhukov*.[100] Insubordinate local authorities, however, seized upon this category to continue "wild expulsions" by another name, especially in south Moravia and western Bohemia.

In many cases their subterfuges were even more elaborate. A typical example is provided by a pair of transports organized by the local authorities of Stříbro, a town in northwestern Bohemia under U.S. military occupation. Three weeks after the announcement of the Potsdam moratorium on expulsions, Dr. Josef Hrdlička, head of the Stříbro District National Committee, issued an order requiring 1,236 German residents of the town to assemble at the railway station two days later "under threat of severe punishment." Simultaneously, the District National Committee applied to the American military authorities for permission to send the Stříbroites to the Soviet occupation zone as compulsory labor for the beet harvest, stating that they would return in three or four weeks. Smelling a rat, the U.S. authorities examined the "agricultural workers" and found that at least half were incapable of work, including amputees lacking artificial limbs, cripples, pregnant women, babies, blind people, and "many elderly persons in need of medical attention." Undaunted by the Americans' refusal to permit the expellees to cross the zonal boundary, the District National Committee entrained them on August 29 and tried to pass through, only to be turned back at the checkpoint at Rokycany. Dr. Hrdlička then sought and obtained approval for the train to go to Blatná, south of Stříbro and still in the U.S. zone. Instead it reappeared at the U.S.-Soviet zonal boundary at Čáslav in central Bohemia the following day. The Americans directed that it be returned to Stříbro. Hrdlička, however, insisted that "there would not be a German removed from the train and, if necessary, he would use Czech soldiers [against American forces] to prevent it." The passengers remained on a siding at the village of Chrást near Plzeň for thirty-six hours, without food or water, until the Ministry of Foreign Affairs in Prague prevailed upon the U.S. authorities to allow it to pass through. Encouraged by its success, the Stříbro National Committee tried the same tactic four weeks later. On this occasion, the Americans insisted that 167 *Sudetendeutsch* forced laborers of a batch of 1,299 rounded up at thirty minutes' notice in Dobřany be exempted for medical reasons and sent back to Stříbro. The District National Committee kept the rejects in four boxcars for eleven days and, on October 13, attempted to transport them, unsuccessfully, to Blovice. Two days later the train was sent out a second time to try its luck at the boundary. Once more the Americans refused to let it through and a three days' standoff ensued during which the expellees were again left without food or water. Finally, on October 18, the 167 passengers were given K rations by troops of the 94th Division and returned to Stříbro. After sixteen continuous days in the boxcars, nearly half required medical treatment on arrival; twenty-two of the patients were children under ten years of age.[101]

Though the Soviet authorities were usually more accommodating than the Americans, they too had their limits. The hapless Regional National Committee of Moravská Třebová discovered these when, in another of its ad hoc initiatives aimed at reducing the *Sudetendeutsch* population of the town of Svitavy and without notification to any higher authority, it organized a "voluntary transfer" of seven hundred Germans on October 12. Like many such "voluntary" transports, the expellees involved had simply been rounded up at random and "had no idea how they got there." After a journey of some 200 miles, the train arrived at Löbau, west of Görlitz, in the Soviet zone. The Red Army refused to accept the transport and ordered its immediate return to Czechoslovakia, without allowing the passengers to get out. The train made the short journey back to the border town of Hrádek nad Nisou, from whence it made another attempt at crossing into Germany on October 16. On this occasion it got as far as Zittau in Germany, where the Soviets once again stopped it and allowed three corpses to be unloaded. Finally it was returned once again to Hrádek, where the Czechoslovak Army found it on October 17 and permitted the expellees to be disembarked. By now a further eighteen had died. The survivors were incarcerated in Hrádek concentration camp, while the army sought further instructions.[102]

As a result of fiascos like these, the Czechoslovak government itself was becoming disillusioned with "voluntary transfers" by the end of 1945. Regional National Committees, the Ministry of National Defense reported, were misusing this category to sweep entire areas clean of Germans on their own initiative, decanting the expellees into trains, and sending them off to the Soviet zones in Germany and Austria without notice. The USSR authorities were no longer accepting these transports, but returning them, accompanied by cascades of outraged protests, to their Czechoslovak counterparts. The wasted journeys were placing an unnecessary burden on the barely functioning railway system. Moreover, Czechoslovak Railways refused to acknowledge any responsibility for transporting the Germans on the return trip, for which the company received no payment, and were simply dumping the expellees on the side of the rails as soon as the trains crossed back into Czechoslovak territory. Most of them were taking two or three days to straggle back on foot to the nearest camps, and had nothing to eat during that time. The ethnic Czech population in the border regions was becoming alarmed by the presence of these starving returnees, some of whom were burglarizing houses in search of food, and was loudly demanding better frontier security.[103]

For these reasons the government in Prague at last began to assert its authority, cracking down on further misuse of the "voluntary emigration" category. As the year 1945 drew to a close, unauthorized transports from Czechoslovakia gradually ceased. No sooner had they begun to do so, though, than "wild expulsions" from Yugoslavia came to fill the vacuum. From September, using methods pioneered by the Czechoslovaks, Tito's regime sent large parties of *Volksdeutsch* expellees into Austria, either directly across the border from Slovenia in northern Yugoslavia or, with the cooperation of the Budapest authorities, along a circuitous route to the northeast via Hungary. The Yugoslav expulsions differed from their Polish and Czechoslovak counterparts in being entirely illicit, apart from the transit facilities granted by the Hungarians. Not even the Soviets at this time had any desire to see the *Volksdeutsch* population in their zones of Austria or Germany increase. In defying them, therefore, Tito was risking alienating his ideological allies as well as his opponents.

The Yugoslavs became particularly adept at finding soft spots in the border across which parties of expellees could be spirited. In some cases, whole trains and their passengers were simply abandoned once they had crossed the frontier. The Reuters news agency reported the fate of a cattle-truck train containing 650 *Volksdeutsch* women and children from Maribor in Slovenia which had been sent northward at the end of September 1945. Its passengers received no food other than what they had brought themselves. After reaching Vienna the train was turned away by the authorities. Sixteen days later, it remained "in a siding at Wilfersdorf, forlorn and unattended, while children die and women insane."[104] More often, however, the finding of a remote location where expellees could be "pushed in" to Austria was a torturous process taking days or even weeks. In December 1945, partisan soldiers descended during the night on the town of Tržič (Neumarktl) in northern Slovenia, rounded up the ethnic German inhabitants, and took them to camps. Nine days later the troops conveyed the detainees by train to Rateče (Ratschach) on the Italo-Austrian border, where an initial attempt to cross ended in failure. The villagers were returned to the train and transported eastward to the opposite side of Slovenia. After a lengthy forced march on New Year's Day, during which "there were repeated threats that those who could not keep up will be shot," the escort tried again to push the party across the Austrian-Hungarian border at Szentgotthárd, only to be intercepted by Soviet troops. Following another detour, the Yugoslav troops finally found an unguarded point opposite the Lower Styrian town of Fehring. "Before they left us they took away everything we had with us, clothes, underwear and valuables and said: 'This is the frontier. Get across it. Anyone who comes back will be shot.'"[105]

That such warnings were not to be taken lightly was indicated by a discovery made in March 1946 by Jean Pfeiffer, a Swiss Red Cross official working at Hof in Bavaria. For several weeks previously, the Soviets had been preventing unauthorized *Sudetendeutsch* expellee trains from crossing into their occupation zone in Austria. As a result, the persons responsible for the transports had been disembarking the expellees at the frontier and pushing some three or four hundred across each night. While walking in the woods near the Austrian border town of Lichtenberg, one of the principal crossing points, Pfeiffer had discovered the bodies of a man, a woman, and a little girl of about six years of age. All had been shot—whether by the Soviets attempting to prevent them from entering, or by the Czechoslovaks attempting to prevent them from returning, was not known.[106]

The Potsdam Conference's appeal for a suspension of "wild expulsions" had least effect upon the Poles. They too attempted to work the "voluntary emigration" trick, sometimes with the assistance of the German Communist Party (KPD) in the Soviet occupation zone. The KPD played an active part in organizing westbound transport from the Recovered Territories, in what some of its supporters with unconscious irony described as a *Heim ins Reich* program. With the cooperation of the Soviet authorities, KPD officials laid on freight trains in the autumn of 1945 upon which would-be "resettlers" could ride as far as the new border towns of Küstrin and Frankfurt an der Oder, leaving them to continue their westward journey on foot.[107] Polish soldiers and militia bands continued forcibly to remove Germans from their homes and farms, although in deference to the Potsdam decision they no longer conveyed those displaced under guard to the border. In some cases this defeated the purpose. The inhabitants of one village, for example, were transported "some 11 miles to the nearest station—from which no trains were running. However, since there was no one to prevent them from going back, they dispersed again into the countryside."[108] For most such expellees, however, the operation of hunger and homelessness would provide sufficient incentive for them to leave the country by their own efforts. A pair of British diplomats touring Lower Silesia in September found that "There is very little doubt that the Poles will in the future endeavour to use economic pressure to induce even larger numbers of the German public to leave voluntarily if they cannot get rid of them in any other way and the *Starost* [district administrator] at one place we went to told us so in so many words."[109]

"Excesses" like these nonetheless served a useful purpose. As Beneš and his ministers ceaselessly reiterated to the Western Allies, the only alternative to continued abuse of the German minorities was the replacement of "wild" with "organized" expulsions, conducted under the auspices of the Allies themselves. The deluge of German cities with hundreds of thousands of starving, destitute, and unproductive expellees in the summer and autumn of 1945 proved an even more effective means of holding the great powers' feet to the fire. Negotiations to decide when, how many, and to which destinations expellees would be removed were thus opened between the representatives of the countries concerned at the meetings of the Allied Co-ordinating Committee in Berlin during the late autumn of 1945. These finally bore fruit in an outline scheme devised by the Polish and Czechoslovak governments in collaboration with the representatives of the United States, the USSR, France, and Britain, which was speedily approved by the Allied Control Council, the occupying countries' temporary governing body for Germany, on November 20.

The so-called "ACC agreement," a skeletal accord less than two pages in length, did not mean, as Lord Jowitt, the British lord chancellor, explained to Parliament, that there was to be any "international machinery for carrying out transfers or for supervising their execution. The arrangements are left to be worked out directly between the Government of the expelling country and the authorities of the zone in Germany to which the immigrants are to be expelled."[110] Rather, the deal specified the approximate timing of the deportations, and the proportions to be sent to each zone of occupation. Of an estimated 6,650,000 ethnic Germans still living in Poland, Czechoslovakia, Hungary, and Austria, the Soviets undertook to admit 2,750,000 from the first two countries. The United States would take 2,250,000 from Czechoslovakia and Hungary. Britain would accept in its zone 1,500,000 expellees from the Polish Recovered Territories, as soon as a "head-for-head" program ("Operation Honeybee") under which the British and Soviets had already agreed to transfer within Germany those expellees and evacuees with families in the other's zone had been completed. France, having rejected an initial Czechoslovak appeal to admit 500,000 *Sudetendeutsche*, would assume responsibility for the remaining 150,000, then temporarily in Austria.[111] The expulsions would commence in December 1945, during which month 10 percent of the total were to be transported. Five percent would be removed in each of the months of January and February 1946; 15 percent per month in March and April; 20 percent per month in May and June; and the remaining 10 percent in July 1946, by which time the operation was to be completed. The Paris government successfully sought a rider that removals to the French occupation zone were not to commence until April 15, 1946; London stipulated that the beginning of its acceptance of expellees from Poland would be a matter for negotiation between British and Soviet officials in the quadripartite German administration.[112]

International public opinion, while generally relieved by the announcement that the Allies were at last proposing to assume control of the expulsion process, was taken aback by the numbers it was proposed to transfer in such a short time. Nothing of the kind had previously been attempted in human history. A *New York Times* editorial put the scale of the operation into perspective by noting that the number of Germans who were to be removed from their homes in seven months was "roughly equal to the total number of immigrants arriving in the United States during the last forty years."[113] In truth, in its specific details the ACC agreement was an almost meaningless document, as well-informed observers recognized from the outset. The idea that "organized expulsions" could begin within ten days of its signing in the midst of winter and without any kind of prior arrangements was hopelessly unrealistic, as was the supposition that more than 6 million people could be moved from one part of the continent to another in half a year without paralyzing what remained of the European transport network. The proposed distribution of expellees between the various zones, likewise, made no provision for the hundreds of thousands who could be expected to travel to their own preferred destinations without waiting to be formally expelled, nor those who would, equally illicitly, gravitate from one zone to another.

All the elements that a serious attempt to come to grips with the problem might be expected to include—the appointment of an executive body to conduct and oversee the operation; a description of the means to be used; the assignment of responsibility for making the necessary preparations for assembly, embarkation, reception, and assimilation of this colossal number of people—were absent from the ACC agreement. It would be a mistake, though, to judge the accord mainly from this perspective. Its real objectives were much more limited: to contrive that the number of uprooted Germans arriving in each power's respective occupation zone would be as low as possible, and, by reassuring an increasingly anxious public that the Allies were finally addressing the problem, to deflect further media criticism.

Viewed in this light, the ACC agreement satisfied the requirements of those who drafted it. One of its immediate effects was to torpedo Robert Murphy's attempts to generate an official U.S. protest over the means by which the Poles in particular had been clearing the Recovered Territories of their German population. The memorandum he composed the previous month had received an unusually positive response at the State Department, whose opposition to the principle of population transfers was of long standing. David Harris, a Stanford University historian recruited as an expert on central European affairs, concurred that the United States' effort to reconstruct Germany on a democratic basis would not achieve "any useful and lasting results if we lend ourselves to the indecencies and the obscenities which we have been fighting." A formal protest, on the other hand, might exercise "some moral influence on the restitution of European decency."[114] Benjamin Cohen, special assistant to Secretary of State James F. Byrnes and another leading member of the U.S delegation at the Potsdam Conference, also recommended that Washington make a formal statement to the various Allied Control Commissions for the ex-Axis countries as well as to the expelling governments "to make clear that we are not a party to these inhumane and terrible things."[115] Accordingly, the State Department prepared a message to be conveyed in the first instance to the Polish government by the U.S. ambassador in Warsaw, Arthur Bliss Lane. The most trenchant condemnation of the expulsions ever drafted by any governmental agency in the West, the State Department's proposed demarche did not hesitate to draw pointed comparisons between the conduct of the Poles and the transfer operations conducted by the Nazis during the war.

> [The] vast bulk of the people arriving in Germany from areas east of Oder-Neisse line are women, children and old people who arrive in all states of exhaustion and disease. Their plight is such as to give the impression they have

been treated with utmost ruthlessness and disregard for humanitarian principles.

US Gov[ernmen]t understands Polish Provisional Gov[ernment] takes [the] position [that] exodus of most of these Germans across frontier is "voluntary" on their part. It is doubted that so many would be crossing frontiers under these appalling conditions unless virtually forced to do so by expulsions and other forms of economic pressure. . . .

American people were horrified by mass deportation perpetrated by Nazis and by Nazis' utter disregard for human life which they exhibited in Poland and elsewhere. This deep seated aversion to Nazi practices and ideology gave American people part of moral basis for their war against Nazi Germany. American people still hold firmly to principles on basis of which they engaged in that war.[116]

The conclusion of the ACC agreement, however, cut the ground out from under the feet of those in the U.S. government who desired retrospectively to disclaim American responsibility for the more unsavory aspects of the expulsions. Arguably it was as well that it did so, for Washington—as Murphy indicated in his memorandum—had been fully implicated in the decision to proceed with them. The logic of the State Department's equation of "mass deportation" with "Nazi practices and ideology" was that the principle of forced population transfer was no less unacceptable to the United States than the manner in which it was being carried out. Any attempt to pursue this line, though, would have drawn an immediate rejoinder that the Americans were hypocritically seeking to cast aspersions on their wartime allies for pursuing a policy they themselves had adopted at Potsdam only three months previously. It would also have unleashed a firestorm of criticism directed against the United States by the expelling countries themselves, as Ambassador Lane at the Warsaw embassy hastened to inform Byrnes. Lane had already made it a point of pride to assure his Polish hosts that he fully appreciated the necessity of a policy of "greatest severity" toward the Germans. As he had recounted proudly to a Polish newspaper only a few weeks previously, when confronted with some *Volksdeutsche* in the Silesian town of Zabrze, "I told them that I cannot understand their complaints about Poles ill-treating the German population. Who started the war; who established concentration camps and Auschwitz? People who are guilty of all these atrocities may not, today, blame anybody but themselves."[117]

The ACC agreement, then, provided the secretary of state with an opportunity he eagerly seized to retreat from the exposed position in which his officials had temporarily placed him. Once informed of the deal, the State Department abandoned the uncompromising draft protest with which it had been working.[118] In its place was substituted a watered-down remonstrance two weeks later that made no mention of Washington's second thoughts about the expulsions as such. Instead, the document Byrnes directed to be sent the Poles merely informed them that the U.S. government was "seriously perturbed" by the condition in which expellees from east of the Oder-Neisse line were continuing to arrive in Germany.[119] Even this was rejected by Ambassador Lane, who advised Byrnes that he was "not convinced that Germans have been subjected to any widespread harsh treatment" and that many of the reports to the contrary "came from Germans themselves who, in keeping with their characteristic of whining after losing [a] war, make the picture as black as possible." Lane added that his views were shared by General Eisenhower, who had recently told him that "the view held by others that Germans from Poland were being ill treated" was incorrect, and appealed for "a reconsideration of the instructions given me."[120] The result was that the year ended without any formal U.S. protest over the manner in which the "wild expulsions" had been conducted, Ambassador Lane being directed merely to convey orally to the Polish government the "substance" of American concerns whenever a suitable opportunity arose.

The number of Germans displaced by the "wild expulsions" remains unclear. According to the Red Army's figures, 775,000 had been transferred from Czechoslovakia to the Soviet occupation zone of Germany alone by December 12, 1945.[121] Although these figures do not agree with Czechoslovak data, Tomáš Staněk and Adrian von Arburg point out that official reports often contain "suspiciously precise figures" that may well have been inflated to "increase the prestige of the responsible commanders."[122] Based in part on a study of the number of ration cards issued to Germans, itself an imprecise measure, they believe that between 800,000 and 1 million were forced out of Czechoslovakia by the end of 1945. Seeking hard data for the numbers removed from the Recovered Territories during the same period is probably an exercise in futility. For the two-month period of June and July alone, estimates by Polish historians range from a low of 200,000 to a high of 1.2 million—an indication of the reliance that can be placed on the available documentation. For the whole of 1945 a figure of 1 million deportations from Poland would probably err considerably on the side of conservatism. Bernadetta Nitschke reminds us, however, that there is evidence to suggest that Germans displaced from the Recovered Territories during this first wave of expulsions often returned; that throughout the year refugees who had fled to the west in early 1945 continued to drift back to their homes; and that a significant number of Germans resident in the country districts went underground in the cities for a time before returning to their places of origin.

What remains beyond dispute is that the seven-month-long period of the "wild expulsions" witnessed the eruption of a massive state-sponsored carnival of violence, resulting in a death toll that on the most conservative of estimates must have reached six figures. As such it is unique in the peacetime history of twentieth-century Europe. Yet it was an episode that escaped the notice of most Europeans, and practically all Americans, other than those physically present on the scene. Now the Allies would try their hand at administering the same task of mass deportation, this time by the "orderly and humane" methods that the Potsdam Agreement had specified. In the circumstances, it hardly seemed possible that they would not, at any rate, perform better in this respect than the authors of the "wild expulsions." Yet as we will see, their actual record was so ambiguous in its results that even this may be open to question.

5

The Camps

Wenzel Hrneček was, in the view of those who knew him before the war, a thoroughly unremarkable young man. Like all Czechs of his generation he had been born a subject of the Austro-Hungarian Empire, an entity that had collapsed before he was halfway through his teens. He spent the years of his early adulthood as a citizen of the Czechoslovak Republic in the ethnically mixed city of České Budějovice in southern Bohemia, a municipality that under its German name of Budweis had gained a worldwide reputation for the Budweiser beer produced there in vast quantities. Fluent in Czech and German, Hrneček joined the town police force in 1928. His work record was good though not outstanding: by the time the Second World War began eleven years later, he had not gained a single promotion. After the Nazi takeover of the Sudetenland in September 1938, Hrneček served the third regime he had known in his short lifetime with the same efficiency as he had the previous ones. Catastrophe struck, however, in 1940, when he was falsely accused with other Czechs of possessing an illegal radio transmitter. Although the charges were eventually dismissed, Hrneček, like thousands of others who had aroused German suspicions for one reason or another, was placed under "protective custody" in the Theresienstadt concentration camp north of Prague. He would spend the rest of the war being shuttled from one camp to another in Czechoslovakia, Poland, and Germany, including Sachsenhausen and Gross-Rosen, before eventually winding up in Dachau. Here he was appointed *Stubenältester*, the lowest rank among the category of *Kapos*, or camp trusties, selected by the Germans to control their fellow prisoners and whose brutality often equaled that of the SS guards. As his fellow prisoners testified, though, Hrneček defied his captors' efforts to make him complicit in their crimes, doing everything he could to shield the Czech detainees for whom he

Map 1. Principal detention camps for ethnic Germans.

was responsible from the worst rigors of concentration camp life.[1] After being liberated by the U.S. Army in April 1945, he spent three weeks recuperating from his ordeal before returning to České Budějovice and reporting for duty at his old police barracks. He was immediately appointed deputy commandant of the Linzervorstadt internment camp for *Sudetendeutsche*, four kilometers outside the city, in which many of the ethnic German inhabitants of the area had already been corralled. His nominal boss was Staff Captain Alois Veselý; the day-to-day operations of the camp remained in the hands of Hrneček himself.

Linzervorstadt was a typical specimen of the thousands of improvised detention centers for ethnic Germans that sprang up across central Europe in the days or weeks after the retreat of the *Wehrmacht*. Used during the war as accommodation for itinerant workers of the German Labor Front, it consisted of five residential barracks with an administration block, kitchen, and infirmary.[2] Even with two prisoners assigned to each bunk, its capacity of two thousand was quickly filled. Whereas one *Sudetendeutsch* prisoner sent to Linzervorstadt on May 10, 1945—forty-eight hours after V-E Day—received the camp number 682, the number assigned to a retired hairdresser detained in late July was 2212.[3] Some of the camp's administrators and guards, recruited personally by Hrneček, were themselves recently released inmates of German concentration camps; others were "young lads of 15 to 18 years of age who we [prisoners] called 'partisans.'"[4] They immediately proceeded to turn the camp into a Dachau on a smaller scale, establishing a regime for the local German civilian population modeled as precisely as possible on their own recent experiences at the Nazis' hands. In place of the SS motto *Arbeit macht Frei*, the Biblical verse *Oko za Oko, Zub za Zub* ("Eye for eye, tooth for tooth") was inscribed on the camp gate. Newly admitted inmates—often scooped off the streets of České Budějovice by Hrneček himself, who roamed the area in a police car in search of potential detainees—were stripped and examined for SS tattoos; forced while still naked to run a gauntlet of guards who "initiated" them into camp life by beating them with rubber truncheons, canes, and clubs; shorn of all their hair; and issued with a convict uniform bearing colored markings (some inmates recalled these as being triangular in shape, others remembered stripes) according to their assigned status as "party members," "collaborators," or ordinary civilians. Punishments for such trivial offenses as forgetting to remove one's cap in the presence of a camp "supervisor" or failing at all times to run at the double were frequent and severe, including such characteristic features of the Nazi concentration camp regime as pole-hanging (being suspended from a pole by one's bound wrists tied behind one's back), flogging with steel-cored whips, physical exercises while carrying heavy stones or bricks, and all-night *Appelle* or parades in which the prisoners were made to stand at attention from evening until the following morning.[5] Josef Neubauer, a Catholic priest who was detained at Linzervorstadt until his expulsion from Czechoslovakia in November 1945, later testified about a flogging he received for breaching camp rules by administering the last rites to dying inmates in the infirmary:

> On June 27, 1945, I was suddenly ordered to the guard-room. There I was made to strip completely naked and was beaten with sticks and fists. As a result, one of my ribs was broken and my teeth were knocked out. I then received at the hands of my two tormenters another 50 strokes with a length of steel cable, the thickness of my thumb, on my stomach, back, chest and buttocks. I was made to count the blows myself. At the end of this beating, my entire body was bleeding. I told my tormentors that I forgave them and that God should not count it as a sin against them. They were baffled by this statement of mine and from that moment onward left me in peace.[6]

Much of the violence inflicted upon detainees involved private score-settling. Hrneček personally took revenge on his former captain in the České Budějovice police force by pole-hanging the man for four to five hours while having him "beaten with cow-hide horsewhips" until he fainted, and resuscitating him by pouring water over him.[7] An inmate recorded how "supervisors" would inspect the barracks and their inhabitants for cleanliness each night, and take to the washrooms for beatings "those persons . . . toward whom, originating from earlier times, they nourished hatred. . . . Often you could—after a person had been picked up—from the yard also hear a short salvo from a machine-gun." Another recalled that "the tortures usually took place in the evening between 21:00 and 22:00 hours. But the roaring of the tortured persons always continued until midnight." Hrneček acknowledged that each evening "former political refugees and prisoners [from the town] were permitted to go into the camp to find out persons who had worked against the Czechs" and that "seriously ill-treated [inmates] were often found who had been beaten by these persons."[8] Suicides among the prisoners as a means of escaping further torture, as well as killings by the guards and *Kapos*, he conceded, were common occurrences. Some prisoners hanged themselves; others put an end to their lives by throwing themselves upon the barbed wire that surrounded the camp and being shot by the guards as a result. Hrneček did not deny, though, that many of these so-called suicides may have been faked. "It was always reported to me that during the night the prisoner . . . had committed suicide by hanging. Whether the man had actually committed suicide or whether he had been hanged by the supervisors, I cannot state. But I do not want to deny this possibility."[9]

Again like its German inspirations, Linzervorstadt featured a network of subcamps, including a compound for female detainees at Zámostí near Hluboká nad Vltavou—to which Hrneček and his subordinates would also periodically make visits for the purpose of administering corporal punishment to the inmates or, in Veselý's case, raping the underage girls—and a labor colony at the nearby Mydlovary coalmine. In conformity with a Czechoslovak government decree of September 1945, all *Sudetendeutsch* prisoners of both sexes were liable to compulsory labor, the men typically being employed on construction projects and the women in the camp cookhouse or laundry. Although work outside the wire sometimes provided opportunities for escape, absconding was no less dangerous for the other members of the work crew, who were liable to receive the same punishment as recaptured fugitives. As was common at Linzervorstadt, and indeed at other camps, the beatings or floggings were often administered by fellow detainees. Hrneček recalled an episode in which "three or four internees received their corporal punishments simultaneously. These persons had run away, but were caught again. Then a little team was composed who performed the corporal punishment on those who had been caught."

Conditions at Linzervorstadt were by no means exceptional. Similar tales were recorded, by former inmates and international observers alike, of dozens if not hundreds of the camps for ethnic Germans established in Czechoslovakia, Poland, Yugoslavia, Hungary, and Romania in the closing months of the war. The first such detention facility, Târgu Jiu in Romania, was opened in September 1944; others were created in the vicinity of Bucharest and the Bačka region of northern Yugoslavia in October and November.[10] Many ex-Nazi concentration camps like Majdanek or Theresienstadt—and even the camp at Auschwitz—never went out of business, but were retained in operation as detention facilities for ethnic Germans for years after the war. At Oświęcim (Auschwitz), the liberation of the last surviving Jewish inmates of the main camp (Auschwitz I) and the arrival of the first ethnic Germans was separated by less than a fortnight. The number of these establishments, and of their inmates, is impossible accurately to estimate,[11] but it was certainly very large.[12] Many left no documentary trace behind them—in Poland, for example, the complete prison register of only a single camp, Łambinowice, is known to have survived—and in some cases central government remained unaware of their existence. The Polish state repatriation agency and the Szczecin provincial government each learned of a camp in Koszalin holding more than a thousand ethnic Germans only after a typhus epidemic broke out there in March 1947.[13] Likewise the Prague Provincial National Committee, supposedly responsible for the day-to-day administration of detention facilities for Germans in the capital region, complained that it did not always know where and by whom camps had been set up.[14] The head of the International Committee of the Red Cross (CICR) delegation in Czechoslovakia reported in February 1946 that his wife, while making a social call, had accidentally stumbled across an impromptu camp for *Sudetendeutsche* set up in a wing of a girls' school in Bohemia. "This is just another example of the 'hidden' camps . . . we only discover their existence by chance or when in search of a particular case, and there is therefore no way of knowing the exact number of internees in the country."[15]

In most cases, though, the detention of the Germans was centrally directed. The Polish Committee of National Liberation issued a decree on November 4, 1944 ordering all *Volksdeutsche* above the age of thirteen years living within the *Generalgouvernement* to be placed immediately in camps and subjected to forced labor.[16] The measure was extended three months later to those from all parts of the country whose names appeared in the second category of the *Deutsche Volksliste*. However, large numbers of Germans living in the Recovered Territories were also detained in similar fashion, under decrees issued by local governors.[17] More than forty thousand additional *Volksdeutsche* from Poland were deported to forced labor camps in the USSR in the spring of 1945.[18] Though these detention decrees were occasionally countermanded by individual Red Army officers—in April 1945 the Soviet military commander in Tczew (Dirschau) ordered that all Germans in the county's labor camps were to return to their homes; resume their normal work; and take off the swastika armbands and identification numbers the Polish authorities had compelled them to wear—the USSR authorities normally adopted a policy of noninterference in such matters so long as their own interests were not affected.

In the Czech lands, Decree no. 16 of June 19, 1945 ratified the internment of Sudeten German craftsmen, businessmen, and professionals whose services were considered unnecessary; those representing "superfluous educated people"; and "excess personnel" of industry and commerce, together with their families.[19] District National Committees on the ground, however, often took a much more broadly encompassing view of the propriety of detention: a legal interpretation in Plzeň that authorized the roundup of Germans "regardless of whether they were covered by the German provisions of Presidential Decree No. 16 of June 19, 1945 or not" was copied in many other places across the Czech lands.[20] In mid-June, too, the Slovak National Council had charged the Ministry of National Security with the establishment, organization, management, and maintenance of camps for the German and Hungarian minorities there, though local roundups had taken place earlier still.[21] According to incomplete Czech records, around 152,000 detainees, 93 percent of whom were ethnic Germans, were in custody in November 1945, with at least another 7,000 in various prisons and lockups in Bohemia alone. Up to 40,000 more were in custody in Slovakia. These figures do not, however, include those detained in camps run by the Ministry of National Defense.[22] The impression gained by a U.S. officer who visited Prague in January 1946 to coordinate the expulsions and was advised that "there are about 250,000 now collected and concentrated in camps" may, therefore, not be very far from the truth.[23]

A similar edict of the Tito regime in November 1944 provided for the internment of all Yugoslav *Volksdeutsche* except those who had played an active part in the struggle against Nazi occupation. Although the Allies would ultimately refuse to sanction the expulsion of *Volksdeutsche* from that country, the existence of ninety-six separate Yugoslav camps was known to the Red Cross in 1947.[24] At least 170,000 ethnic Germans, apart from those who had already been "randomly shot en mass [sic]," had already been taken into custody by mid-1945; "the majority of the internees," the Extraordinary Review Commission of Vojvodina reported to Belgrade in May, were "old people, women, and children."[25] Though plans by the Budapest government to establish a network of twenty-two "assembly camps" for German expellees never came to fruition, a large camp was established for ethnic Germans in Hungary at Debrecen, where conditions were reported as being "difficult";[26] another outside Bonyhád, said to hold some twenty thousand internees from the southern county of Baranya near the Croatian border, was reported by American diplomats in June 1945.[27] The Târgu Jiu camp in Romania was soon followed by others, after the Soviet-backed government ordered the internment of the entire adult German and Hungarian minority populations above the age of sixteen in the case of males, and eighteen in the case of females, in December 1944.[28] Whereas the population of the German concentration camp system had grown from 21,000 at the outbreak of the war to reach a recorded peak of 700,000 at the beginning of 1945,[29] it is possible that the number of persons incarcerated across Europe in similar establishments by the end of that year might have been even higher.

Second only to the scale of the postwar camp system was its variety. At the end of the war, the same pattern of haphazard local improvisation that had marked the establishment of the German concentration camp system in the early 1930s was much in evidence in central and southeastern Europe also.[30] Complementing the "wild expulsions" of the summer of 1945, many of these first detention centers were "wild" camps created by local government agencies, elements of the Czechoslovak SNB and Polish *Milicja Obywatelska* ("People's Militia"), or self-appointed "citizens' committees" without explicit instructions from—or even notification to—any higher authority.[31] As noted above, existing facilities, including former concentration camps, prisoner of war compounds, prisons for ordinary criminals, and Labor Front workers' barracks were immediately reconstituted as civilian internment camps. But a wide assortment of temporary establishments, ranging from sports stadia and abandoned factories to churches and private houses, were also pressed into service. At Prague at least 10,000 detainees were corralled under the open skies in the Strahovský football ground until September 1945 under conditions described by the Red Cross as atrocious, before being transferred to other camps; the Workers' Sports Ground at Popovice (Pfaffendorf) near Děčín served a similar purpose.[32] The makeshift camp at Patrónka airfield near Bratislava held 2,449 internees, almost three-quarters of whom were women and children, when the Red Cross visited it in July 1945.[33] Though Patrónka was by no means the largest such establishment—some of which, like Rudolfsgnad (Knićanin) in Yugoslavia, had populations well in excess of twenty thousand—the tiny Svidník camp in eastern Slovakia, which housed a mere fifteen men of the German-speaking Zipser minority, may well have been the smallest, consisting of "a cave, damp, with one small window giving hardly any light . . . [Inmates] sleep on the ground with some straw; on account of the smoke no fire can be lit."[34] Svidník detainees were employed in land mine clearance operations; ten of them had been killed on this work within a two-month period prior to the CICR's visit. Koszalin camp in central Poland crammed 1,090 expellees into two center-city residences that lacked any toilet or cooking facilities, and only one of which possessed a source of water: by March 1947 dysentery and typhus had broken out among the inmates.[35] In Yugoslavia the largest "camps" took the form of entire villages into which German-speakers were corralled behind barbed-wire perimeters, although the death rate as a result of overcrowding, malnutrition, infectious diseases, and beatings in the worst of these, like Gakowa and Kruševlje in the Bačka, rivaled mortality levels in any barracks camp.[36]

While it is impossible to say how large the total camp population may have been—though undoubtedly the majority of ethnic Germans were not interned before their expulsion—few differences are observable between the cohort taken to the camps and those spared detention. Regulations exempting the young, the old, pregnant women, or the disabled were routinely ignored: as was true of the expellee population in general, the majority of inmates in many camps were women and children. Additional evidence tending to the same conclusion is the indiscriminate nature of the roundups, which made no distinction in practice between those who had welcomed and those who opposed the German occupation. In numerous cases the net even drew in the Nazi regime's victims. Some two to three thousand inmates of the Czechoslovak camps were Jews who had attempted to reduce their exposure to anti-Semitic attacks by registering as "German" in the 1930 census. Although a few succeeded, after considerable effort, in gaining their release, others were "forced to wear the white armbands that designated Germans; were given smaller rations"; and were ultimately expelled to the very country that had sought their extermination.[37] (The interior minister, Václav Nosek, created a minor international furor in February 1946 when he declared that the mere fact that certain Jews had "suffered somewhat" at the Nazis' hands did not mean that they had not been complicit in "Germanization" during the First Republic.)[38] The same was true of surviving German-speaking Jews in Yugoslavia, as well as of the ethnic German relatives of soldiers of the Yugoslav army who had been killed fighting the Nazi invaders in 1941.[39] Others again were political prisoners who had spent part or all of the war in German concentration camps, only to be reincarcerated as ethnic Germans after returning home following their liberation.[40] An anti-Nazi Sudeten German émigré who served in the Royal Air Force during the war reported that his Social Democratic party comrades around his home town of Podmokly (Bodenbach) had been rounded up into four improvised camps by the SNB, whom he described caustically as "young men in uniforms resembling those of the SS and in similar boots."[41] Foreigners too were swept into the camps. The Czech Ministry of the Interior complained in June 1945 that Swiss nationals were being detained after having been overheard speaking German in public.[42] Similar indiscriminate detentions occurred in the Katowice district of Poland, including a fourteen-year-old boy from the Netherlands whose blond hair and blue eyes sufficed to prove his "German" nationality to the satisfaction of the militia who arrested him at Gliwice. Genuine Dutch people, his captors assured him before incarcerating him in Świętochłowice-Zgoda (Schwientochlowitz), a former subcamp of Auschwitz III (Monowitz), all had dark hair and spoke French.[43]

Conditions in the camps, though almost always harsh, exhibited distinct variations. Sometimes no effort was made to segregate ethnic Germans from other categories of detainee. The Autopark camp in the Smíchov district of Prague held German prisoners of war as well as women and children (ironically, camps dedicated exclusively to POWs, whose inmates were protected by the Geneva Convention, featured living standards that were markedly superior to those of the typical civilian internee establishment). Potulice—formerly the German Potulitz concentration camp—near Bydgoszcz contained not just POWs in addition to German expellees, but "politically unreliable" Poles including former Home Army members and soldiers who had fought under British command during the war.[44] Jaworzno, previously a subcamp of Auschwitz, was home to a substantial population of ethnic Ukrainian as well as ethnic German minorities, the former detained under still more rigorous conditions. Although family groups were frequently separated, the younger children sometimes being transferred to orphanages or children's homes for adoption by local families, many camps housed detainees of both sexes and all ages. There were, however, a number of specialized children's camps: the former *Konzentrationslager* of Bolesławiec (Bunzlau), a subcamp of Gross-Rosen in Poland, held approximately twelve hundred boys aged between twelve and fifteen, who were used as forced labor on road-building projects.[45] Of the ninety-five inmates of the children's camp at České Křídlovice in Czechoslovakia during the month of July 1947, a third were under six years of age.[46]

The question of how these detention centers are to be categorized is a complex one.[47] At one end of the spectrum, the term "concentration camp" is appropriate—not merely because it was at first unapologetically employed by the Czechoslovak and Polish governments that operated them,[48] but also because some camps, like Wenzel Hrneček's Linzervorstadt, were purposefully organized so as to replicate, as faithfully as possible, the conditions that had prevailed in their German predecessors. Few distinctions could be observed between these and many "internment camps," the stated purpose of which was sometimes claimed to be to hold persons suspected of collaboration with the Nazis pending their investigation.[49] Given the presumption of guilt that usually prevailed, the regime in such establishments was harsh. Conditions in "labor camps" were typically more variable. Some inmates were serving lengthy sentences for real or fancied offenses; others were technicians and specialists whose skills were considered essential and who enjoyed greater privileges, especially food rations, than many unincarcerated *Volksdeutsche*. The majority, though, were ordinary civilians who were hired out to local employers at cut-price rates, the revenue thus generated being used to defray camp expenses. In principle, detention in "assembly" or "displacement" camps near railheads in which inmates were intended to spend only a short period before their embarkation carried the fewest risks, if only because of the brevity of the average stay.[50] Due to congestion, though, expellees might be obliged to wait many weeks or months at assembly camps. The infrastructure of these establishments was more rudimentary than at many internment or labor camps, with the result that death rates from infectious diseases and the effects of malnutrition and exposure to the elements could, especially in winter, exceed those in even the more rigorously conducted internment camps.

In a great many instances, nonetheless, differences in official designations attached to various kinds of camp were more theoretical than real. A typical illustration can be found in the Mirošov detention facility near Plzeň, which was opened on May 12, 1945. Until the following August its official designation was "Mirošov Concentration Camp" (*Koncentrační tábor Mirošov*), with rubber stamps on camp documents bearing this title. Thereafter it was renamed "Mirošov Assembly Camp," though the Ministry of the Interior considered it an "internment camp." During its lifetime, however, Mirošov's purpose remained the same: as a holding facility for civilian *Sudetendeutsche* from the locality, who were put out to forced labor pending their expulsion unless—as was often the case with elderly detainees—they died from hunger or disease before their removal from the country. While it was still officially a "concentration camp," every seventh prisoner at Mirošov was younger than fourteen years of age; forty-five of them were below the age of six.[51]

Throughout central Europe, those interned at any time during 1945 ran by far the highest risk of execution, torture at the hands of the camp staff, or death through starvation and preventable infectious diseases, in comparison to later detainees. This in turn was in part the result of the abdication or ineffectiveness of any kind of central control over the camps, and the turning over of their administration to what the British ambassador in Prague accurately described as a class of "young thugs."[52] The Świętochłowice-Zgoda establishment, whose Jewish inmate population was replaced almost overnight by a German one in February 1945, provided one of the worst examples of the consequences of this practice. Its twenty-year-old commandant, a Polish secret police officer named Aleksy Krut, assisted by a camp staff whose ages typically ranged from seventeen to twenty-three,[53] presided over a system of organized and ferocious maltreatment of internees, with the stated intention of completing in five months what the Nazis had failed to accomplish at the camp in five years. When Krut was succeeded in May by his deputy Salomon Morel, only six years his senior, that aspiration came closer to being realized. Through physical abuse on a massive scale—in addition to torture by guards and *Kapos*, prisoners were forced by camp staff to beat each other—the denial of food, overwork, and an outbreak of typhus among the detainees which Morel may have acted deliberately to aggravate, well over a third of Świętochłowice-Zgoda's inmate population of five thousand, according to camp records, had died by the time the Office of Public Security in Katowice closed it down in November 1945.[54]

The death rate at Świętochłowice may have been high, but it was by no means unprecedented. Mysłowice, west of Jaworzno, acknowledged 2,227 deaths between March 6, 1945 and the end of the year, under the administration of its hapless twenty-year-old commandant, Tadeusz Skowyra. As Wacław Dubiański cautions, this figure is likely to be an underestimate inasmuch as it does not include those for whom death certificates were not issued, or the inmates who died at Mysłowice's many subcamps.[55] Two hundred sixty-five recorded deaths occurred at the Zimne Wody (Kaltwasser) camp during a ten-day period between late March and early April 1945; by December, the Civil Registry Office in Bydgoszcz had ordered that records of deaths at Zimne Wody be omitted from the register on the ground that the revelation of their causes might attract unwelcome international attention and depict Polish camps "in a negative light."[56] At Łambinowice, whose commandant, Czesław Gęborski, was twenty-one years of age at the time of his appointment, between forty and fifty inmates were killed by shooting in a single day in October of the same year, and a total of nearly sixty-five hundred died before the camp's dissolution in 1946.[57]

A notable element of the postwar camp system was the prevalence of sexual assault as well as ritualized sexual humiliation and punishment suffered by female inmates. Women survivors of German concentration camps have recalled that, notwithstanding the unrestrained brutality that pervaded most other aspects of daily life, rape or other forms of sexual maltreatment at the hands of their guards was an extremely rare occurrence, and severely punished by the authorities if detected.[58] After the war, in contrast, the Red Cross recorded that the sexual abuse of female detainees by their captors was pervasive and systematic. This verdict was confirmed by Czechoslovak and Polish witnesses themselves.[59] A foreign observer of two Czech camps in August 1945 noted that women in the first were "treated like animals. Russian and Czech soldiers come in search of women for purposes which can be imagined. Conditions there for women are definitely more unfavorable than in the German concentration camps, where cases of rape were rare." In the second, nightly parties were organized in which "fifteen or so young girls would await the arrival of visitors"; Czech and Soviet soldiers would "take away the prettiest girls, who would often disappear without trace."[60] Jean Duchosal, secretary general of the CICR, reported that girls were often raped at the Matejovce camp in Slovakia when he visited it in November 1945, and that beatings were daily occurrences.[61] The same was true of Patrónka.[62] The British Army received several independent reports of the guards at Riđica labor camp, a subcamp of Sombor in the Bačka region of Yugoslavia, freely admitting "soldiers and any other person wishing to 'enjoy' himself" for similar purposes.[63]

Sexual exploitation was no less prevalent in Poland. Jaworzno, as a pair of official inspections in May and August 1945 revealed, functioned as a sexual supermarket for its 170-strong militia guard contingent, whose practice, Antoni Białecki of the local Office of Public Security reported, was to "take *Volksdeutsch* women at gunpoint home at night and rape them."[64] At Potulice, one of the largest Polish camps for German internees, the sexual humiliation of female prisoners had become an institutional practice by the end of 1945. New inmates of both sexes were shaved of all body and head hair upon arrival, supposedly as a hygienic measure. "The women had for that purpose to lie on two stools and to spread their legs wide apart so that their body hairs could be removed. The shaving was done by men, and the whole procedure was watched by the Polish officials and militia men." Beatings during the nightly room inspections, or "controls," were administered "if possible on the naked body. If a woman was suffering badly during her days [menstrual periods] and asked not to be beaten so hard this time, the men asked her to prove it, and there was nothing left to her but to show it, if she didn't want to get a worse beating." In the penal gangs, male detainees were occasionally forced to simulate sexual intercourse with the females for the amusement of camp guards.[65] Some of the punishments could result in horrific injuries. A male inmate of Potulice witnessed one procedure in which the victim was forced to perch in a sitting position on the leg of an upturned stool in such a way that the full weight of her body fell upon her perineum. Serious physical harm, including genital and anal lacerations, often resulted.[66] In Czechoslovakia, too, a Prague police report of June 1945 mentioned that Revolutionary Guards were in the habit of "exposing women's body parts and burning them with lighted cigarettes."[67]

Sexual abuse or torture of male detainees was by no means unknown—in some cases, they too were compelled to perform sexual acts upon each other. As a rule, though, credible accounts of sexual assaults of males described an escalating crescendo of violence that often ended in the death of the victim rather than the kind of ongoing and systematized exploitation to which female detainees were in many cases subjected. Kicks and blows (including with sharp instruments) directed at the genitals of male prisoners were, however, so common as almost to go unremarked upon. It is not necessary to resort to Freudian interpretations to see in all of these sexualized forms of abuse a desire on the part of the young male perpetrators to exorcise, by such displays of pathologically distorted hypermasculinity, the emasculating and humiliating experience of German occupation during the war.

At most camps, of whatever official classification, inmates were expected to defray the costs of their incarceration either through forced labor or, in numerous cases, by means of ransom payments, especially from detainees with relatives already in Germany or Austria. British military observers learned in 1947 of "a very definite organisation" created by the Yugoslav authorities "for leading people out of the camp and into Hungary against payment. . . . It is obvious that the Jug[o-slav]s approve of this method of ridding themselves of their *Volksdeutsche*, and probably find it very lucrative."[68] More typically, however, camp administrators relied on the revenue generated by the labor services of inmates. In both Poland

and Czechoslovakia, indeed, the German detainee population became an important component of the transitional postwar economy, with prisoners being hired out at peppercorn rates to local authorities and private-sector employers. In most cases the terms were laid down in standard contracts, of which an agreement in October 1945 between the *Starost* of Wyrzyk and the camp authorities of Potulice was typical. According to its terms, the employer obtained the services of twenty-five male Germans for a two-month period, at a rate of 1.50 zlotys (a little under three cents) per person per day, plus a 15 percent administrative charge. The hirer assumed responsibility for the feeding, housing, and guarding of the prisoners, as well as the costs of any accident insurance or medical care; transport to and from the camp; and losses through escapes. The camp reserved the right to recall the prisoners, and to carry out snap inspections at any time. Regulations for those obtaining labor from Mirošov camp in Czechoslovakia were remarkably similar. At this establishment, workers could be obtained at either an hourly (Kčs 3.60 [seven cents] for males, Kčs 3.00 for females) or a daily (Kčs 11 for males, Kčs 8.20 for females) rate. The hirer was obliged to promise that the work-week would not exceed ninety-eight hours and was responsible for delivering the detainee back to the camp after use. The contract specified that no private arrangements between employer and detainee — e.g., subcontracting the detainee to other employers, or granting him or her free time or other benefits — could be entered into without the permission of the camp authorities.[69] Central government also benefited from these labor contracts, the Ministry of the Interior ordering that 20 percent of the gross receipts were to be remitted to the Treasury.[70] Frequently, however, employers withheld payment on the ground that the workers provided to them were too elderly, sick, or malnourished to be productive; wrangles in court sometimes resulted.[71]

Living and working conditions for detainees put out to labor varied immensely. Some prisoners were marched to their workplaces each morning and back again at night, using the camp only for sleeping and the twice-daily parades. Others went to their jobs in workshops attached to the premises. Agricultural laborers could spend months or years with a single private employer, being treated almost as members of the family and sometimes attracting denunciations from neighbors or officials for excessive leniency. In August 1945, for example, Bohumil Pechman of the Terešov District National Committee complained to the local SNB about two employers who were feeding detainees on what he considered to be too lavish a scale, and two more who permitted their workers to travel the roads without supervision.[72] But workers seconded to state-owned enterprises, especially mines or farms, could fare much worse. Ignacy Cedrowski, the camp physician at Potulice between 1945 and 1948, was not noted for his solicitousness for the welfare of his charges—an understandable attitude, in light of the fact that he was himself a survivor of Auschwitz whose entire family had been killed in the Holocaust. Even he, however, was taken aback by the often lethally exploitative regime to which German workers were subjected on state farms in the Pomerania voivodeship (province) in 1946 and 1947. In some cases, he reported, the administrators hid diseased Germans from quarantine inspectors, fearing that they would be deprived of valuable workers. Up to two hundred prisoners were herded together in these establishments in a single dwelling space.

> These prisoners live in unsuitable rooms, sleeping on the ground on matted foul-smelling straw, having neither soap nor laundry soda with which to do washing, working from early morning until night-time without any days off, leaving them no time to put their lodgings in order, or to wash their dirty laundry or their own persons. Their level of lice infestation reached a point of up to 60 percent and in some places 100 percent. They lack medical and hygienic care. The prisoners suffer from itching to an unbelievable degree.[73]

Conditions at all camps were not uniformly so harsh, and international observers as well as prisoners noted cases in which individual commandants or guards made energetic efforts within the limited means at their disposal to treat their detainees humanely, often at some risk to their own careers.[74] A common feature of life in most camps regardless of the country in which they were located, however, was the provision of so little food as to make not merely malnutrition but actual starvation largely a function of the length of incarceration. The Red Cross, which investigated this matter in some detail, found that in Czechoslovakia published regulations regarding the dietary allotment to internees were almost invariably ignored, with the open connivance if not at the insistence of the very authorities that had issued those regulations.[75] Against the daily minimum of 2,000 calories required for adult humans not engaged in manual labor to sustain their body weight, Pierre W. Mock, head of the CICR delegation in Bratislava, calculated the calorific intake of prisoners at the Petržalka I camp at 664 per person during the third week of October 1945; when he returned in the last week of December it had declined to 512. The daily ration to which this corresponded—an issue of ersatz coffee in the morning with a calorific value of zero; a watery vegetable soup accompanied by 100 grams of bread at midday; and additional coffee in lieu of dinner in the evening—was not atypical for other detention centers also. As Mock noted, Petržalka I was comparatively speaking not a very bad camp. At Nováky, a former German concentration camp with a population of more than five thousand, 250 babies, 33 invalids, and 13 pregnant and nursing women shared 18 liters of milk, and the 100-gram bread ration was distributed only two or three times a week. The nominal ration of 100 grams of bread issued at Trnavská Cesta (Bratislava), when Mock weighed it, was found in reality to be 45 grams; the soup the Red Cross inspectors viewed "had the appearance of a slop of tepid, dirty water, without definition and without anything in it."[76] The regime at the hospital camp of Selmovska for German detainees suffering from infectious diseases was somewhat better, with a daily ration of 800 calories; even so, a CICR medical official observed that most of the patients exhibited cachexia—a condition in which the body consumes the long muscles of the arms and legs in a last-ditch effort to maintain life, resulting in the stereotypical skeletal appearance of camp inmates—and that their typical weight had fallen to 30–40 kilograms (70–90 pounds).[77] In the Jaworzno camp in Poland, too, the soup issued to inmates was described as "pure water" by an inspector of the provincial office for public security, who found that large quantities of food was being withheld on "the Commandant's orders." The death rate, he noted, was running at a rate of "about 50 people per month as a result of the cutbacks in food rations."[78] At Oświęcim (Auschwitz I), an official report recorded shortly after its reopening as a *Volksdeutsch* detention center that "Prisoners do not receive any food, and hunger is steadily increasing. They sustain themselves with food sent from their homes."[79]

Worst of all were the camps in Yugoslavia. The British embassy in Belgrade, which succeeded in securing the release of a Canadian woman with dual nationality in the summer of 1946, reported that the ration at the Riđica labor camp at which she was first detained "consisted of watery soup, and 200 grammes of maize bread, of so rock-like a consistency that it had to be soaked in water to be edible.... At the end of January, [she] was transferred to the internment camp at Kruševlje, where work was not compulsory and where consequently the food consisted of two wooden spoonfuls of maize porridge a day and nothing else. In this camp there was a mortality rate, especially among children, as high as 200 a day." The embassy noted that this account was consistent with reports it had received about other Yugoslav establishments for *Volksdeutsche* from various sources.[80]

When protests were made to the governments administering these camps by charitable bodies and nongovernmental organizations, the invariable response was that the food situation was exceptionally difficult all round, and that prisoners received no worse rations than those provided to the indigenous civilian population.[81] While even the first of these assertions was of questionable accuracy so far as Poland and Czechoslovakia were concerned and was often contradicted by official statements in other quarters,[82] there was no truth to the second. To the contrary, at least in 1945 and 1946 the detaining governments as a matter of policy contrived to ensure that there would be no improvement in the rations provided to ethnic German civilian internees, regardless of the availability of food. A social worker attempting to ameliorate the worst elements of the Czechoslovak camp system confidentially advised the British Foreign Office in February 1946 that there was no point in organizing relief supplies from abroad even for *Sudetendeutsch* women and children only, as his government would not permit them to be distributed to their intended beneficiaries.[83] The Red Cross found this assessment to be justified when it learned that none of the 4.5 tonnes of food it had delivered shortly before Christmas 1945 to the Hagibor camp, at which malnutrition-related deaths were occurring at a rate of three per day, had been issued to the inmates.[84] (The same was true of medical supplies, which, according to Dr. Novák of the Ministry of the Interior, were being prevented from reaching the camps by "chauvinistic elements" within his own government.)[85] Starvation was also a common occurrence at Mirošov, where cachexia appeared as a cause of death on more than half of the 145 death certificates issued during the five-month period between May and October 1945; and at the Hradištko camp near Prague, where the guard in charge of the distribution of food informed a Red Cross visitor that the inadequate ration issued by him to internees was fixed by law and unchangeable and that the few Czech children there "receive[d] twice as much as the Germans."[86] Likewise in Yugoslavia, a Red Cross observer concluded that the ration at the four internment camps of Bački Jarak, Filipovo, Gakowa-Kruševlje, and Sekić (Lovćenac), to which detainees from other establishments who were no longer capable of working were sent, had been fixed at so low a level as to have no other purpose than to bring about the death, by "natural" causes, of the inmates confined there.[87]

Almost from the beginning it became apparent to observers in both the detaining countries themselves and in the West that, in the words of John Colville, formerly Winston Churchill's private secretary and now a senior Foreign Office official in London, "concentration camps and all they stand for did not come to an end with the defeat of Germany."[88] As had been the case in the 1930s, however, a combination of policy considerations and a perception that the inmates of the camps had largely brought their sufferings upon themselves militated against any effective response.

Despite the fact that in the immediate aftermath of the war, for wholly understandable reasons few Europeans were disposed to shed tears over the fate of any "Germans," regardless of age, sex, or nationality, it was not the case, as the Czechoslovak and Polish governments often maintained, that the strength of popular feeling tied the hands of responsible officials in those countries. Some individuals, like the Communist publicist Zdeněk Novák—himself a survivor of Buchenwald—did indeed express grim satisfaction at what he saw as poetic justice for the German population. "How long was it that we sat helplessly behind barbed wire? And now—go home, and the concentration camps are full of Germans."[89] But in many other cases, local sentiment viewed the maltreatment of the German minority with disapproval and dismay. Philip Nichols reported in June 1945 that he and his American counterpart were receiving numerous letters "all complaining bitterly of the way the Germans are being treated . . . [and] that the Czechs are treating the Germans just as harshly as the Germans treated the Czechs and that this ill accords with the achievements and intentions of the Founder-Liberator Masaryk."[90] Colonel John Fye, deputy chief of staff of the U.S. XXII Corps headquartered at Plzeň, also reported that "many kind hearted Czechs were constantly reporting incidents of mistreatment of every conceivable nature to the XXII Corps."[91] In Slovakia, the Kežmarok District National Committee requested permission of the government in Prague to transfer its internees to the Czech lands, on the ground that the local population had "sympathy with the Germans."[92] A remarkable series of readers' letters appearing in the Czech journal *Obzory* ("Horizons"), organ of the Catholic People's Party, in November 1945 corroborates these testimonies.[93] In a previous issue, the journal had published a guarded exposé of conditions in an internment camp for ethnic Germans near Prague. Although *Obzory* acquitted camp authorities of any vindictive intent and credited the government with wishing "to do away as quickly as possible and as honorably as possible with its concentration camps," the response from readers revealed that Czechoslovak citizens were under few illusions as to the true state of affairs in the camps—and were prepared to say so openly.[94] A Prague lawyer reported his personal observations in terms that might have been taken verbatim from a CICR inspection report:

> I have seen several assembly camps and I have gained credible information from others. . . . In a room measuring 4m by 6m 50 men are housed, without coverings or overcoats (these are confiscated from them upon their entrance to the camp). . . . Everything is infested with lice. . . . The food is notoriously inadequate for workers, and much more so for men engaged in heavy labor. Black coffee without sugar is provided in the mornings and evenings; at midday, a watery soup, made from the remnants of vegetables and potato peelings. . . . Typhus is in evidence. Guarding the prisoners is assigned to teams of SNB-men. While 20 weak and emaciated prisoners are on the way to work they are escorted by 8 to 10 SNB, strong young men, of course armed with automatic

weapons. In contrast, if a peasant woman comes to hire some workers, she is given two prisoners whom she brings home by herself, unarmed.[95]

Several correspondents did not hesitate to draw uncomfortable comparisons between their own reaction to the existence of such camps and that of ordinary Germans during the Nazi era. A student wrote: "None of us can pretend that we don't know what is going on behind the gates of prisons and in the assembly camps; however, hardly anyone will say out loud that the Czech nation cannot put up with these shameful scenes any longer. We keep silent; we keep silent; just as the German nation kept silent."[96] A survivor of Auschwitz recalled "how, in the face of the worst brutalities committed by the Germans, we used to console ourselves by saying 'only the Germans are capable of such things.' For all the world I would not have it that anyone could speak in the same terms of us."[97] The response of a Prague resident typified the mixture of exasperation and alarm felt by many Czechoslovaks:

Devil take the Germans! During the war, they decimated our nation and now, because of them, along comes a fresh scandal. . . .
Let nobody fall back on the excuse that the Germans have done the same things. Either we are qualified to stand as their judges, in which case we cannot conduct ourselves as they do, or we are no different from them, and give up the right to judge them.[98]

If the detaining governments could not credibly invoke the pressure of public opinion for the treatment accorded to internees, however, it remains the case that the principle of detention, as opposed to elements of its operation, was loudly applauded by the populations of these countries. In both Poland and Czechoslovakia, many hundreds of rallies were held by political parties demanding the total removal of Germans from society; one, in the Polish county of Kępno, called for all *Volksdeutsche* to be imprisoned "regardless of their behavior during the occupation."[99] Leszek Olejnik points out that this stance was driven by more than anti-German animus alone. Because there could be no redistribution of German property until its owners had been taken into custody, members of the majority populations, many of whom had lost everything in the war, regarded a comprehensive roundup as a necessary step toward making good their own losses.

By autumn 1945 Western governments had received so many reports of human rights abuses in the camps as to cause apprehension that public opinion might demand the suspension or even the abandonment of the entire expulsion project. Such concerns were probably groundless: an exposé of camp conditions in Czechoslovakia by the British journalist Eric Gedye, in the governing Labour

Party's *Daily Herald* newspaper, was exceptional for attracting any public attention at all.[100] Nonetheless, American and British representatives on the scene warned that misplaced expressions of humanitarian concern might produce an eruption of popular feeling in central Europe against the Western powers in light of what they perceived as a massive local consensus in favor of the detention of ethnic Germans. Laurence Steinhardt, the U.S. ambassador in Prague, feared that any appearance "of favoring the German population as against our Czech allies may in the course of time have serious political consequences in Czechoslovakia, particularly in the struggle between the Communists and the moderates for control of the country."[101] When Philip Nichols, concerned about reports he was receiving on conditions in the camps, took it upon himself to remind Beneš that it was "important that our public opinion, which was, I am sure, at present strongly in favour of a radical solution of the minorities question, should not have the issue clouded for them by stories of Czech cruelty, etc.," Sir Orme Sargent at the Foreign Office cautioned him that "this line can easily be overdone with the Czechs and we must be careful not to get the reputation of being unnecessarily soft-hearted with the Germans."[102]

The firm resolve of the Western powers to "see no evil"—in October 1946 British Ambassador Victor Cavendish-Bentinck declined an invitation while visiting Szczecin to speak with German detainees, remarking to his Polish hosts that "he is convinced that as usual they will complain"[103]—proved increasingly difficult to sustain. Since the end of the war, the International Committee of the Red Cross had been making determined efforts to gain access to the camps. Although a proposed Geneva Convention extending the CICR's remit to civilian victims of conflict had not yet been adopted when the Second World War began, both the German, Italian, and Western Allied governments had agreed that civilian internees should receive conditions similar to those enjoyed by prisoners of war. No such consensus prevailed after the war. Romania's government, which initially permitted Red Cross inspections of its *Volksdeutsch* civil internment camps, prohibited further visits in March 1945.[104] Its counterpart in Prague, where a well-established CICR delegation had been present throughout the war years, promised in late May 1945 that the organization would be permitted to visit all *Sudetendeutsch* detention centers, an undertaking on which it too promptly reneged.[105] Only in Slovakia, where the President of the Slovak National Council provided the local CICR delegate with a *laissez-passer* authorizing him to enter any camp unannounced, was the Red Cross able to carry out its mission. In the Czech lands, the organization was permitted to make visits only in the presence of the senior official of the Ministry of the Interior responsible for camp administration, to whom prior notice of each intended inspection had to be given. In May 1946 even this limited facility was withdrawn. The Yugoslav Red Cross, one of several national affiliates whose primary allegiance lay with its own government rather than the organization of which it was a part, assured the CICR in Geneva that the eleven "labor colonies" in the country to whose existence it admitted were so perfectly conducted by the People's Federative Republic that no improvement, far less inspection, of the facilities could possibly be envisaged.[106] The Polish authorities from the beginning responded with a blanket refusal to all applications from the CICR or from Western journalists to see the camps; and although the Polish Red Cross was more impartial in the matter of the German detainees than its Yugoslav counterpart, it had "hardly any influence in certain regions, notably in Lower Silesia."[107] Most of its resources, moreover, were already devoted to caring for colonists displaced from the lost eastern lands who were arriving, often in a pitiably debilitated condition, to take up residence in the Recovered Territories, as well as for Polish survivors of Nazi concentration camps.[108] Even if the will to succor the German inmates of the internment camps had been present, the means were not.

In spite of all these rebuffs, and notwithstanding the reservations of some of its own leaders,[109] the CICR continued to exert pressure on detaining governments about the state of the camps. Walter Menzel, head of the CICR delegation in Prague, warned Foreign Minister Jan Masaryk in February 1946 that "it would go against my conscience for me to continue keeping silent about the conditions prevailing in the camps in Czechoslovakia."[110] Several months previously, Menzel had leaked information to the British ambassador about "the disgraceful condition of the camps for German civilians in Slovakia." As had been its practice during the Second World War, however—a stance for which it was later to be much criticized[111]—the CICR rarely shared its knowledge with third parties. Fearing that its reports might be used as propaganda fodder in the intensifying war of words between East and West, the Red Cross typically kept to itself the particulars it gathered of human rights violations, especially if it considered that a possibility existed of being able to modify the conduct of the government concerned through "quiet diplomacy."[112]

For the same reason, as the Cold War intensified and the prospect of any meaningful Western influence in central and southeastern Europe receded, British and American governments evinced a new sympathy with persons they had previously denounced as collaborators and fifth columnists. That sympathy did not, however, extend so far as to offer asylum for the internees in the Western occupation zones of Germany or Austria, already staggering under the weight of a vast influx of malnourished, penniless, frequently diseased, and predominantly unproductive *Volksdeutsche*. When the British Embassy in Belgrade pointed out that "we feel that those now in the [Yugoslav] concentration camps cannot all be guilty of great crimes, particularly the women and children," and suggested that the Allies, notwithstanding the noninclusion of the Yugoslav *Volksdeutsche* in the Potsdam scheme, should attempt to save their lives by "encourag[ing] the Jugoslavs to deport them to Germany," the German Department of the Foreign Office warned against "any tendency to put ourselves too much in the forefront over this. With the present food difficulties it is almost certain that we shall not want to have any extra Germans in our zones, and we do not want to give anyone the impression that we are ready to do so."[113] While humanitarian considerations continued to be raised from time to time, the British Embassy in Belgrade protesting in the summer of 1946 that the "indiscriminate annihilation and starvation" of the Yugoslav *Volksdeutsche* "must surely be considered an offence to humanity" and warning that "if they have to undergo another winter here, very few will be left," the Foreign Office devoted its efforts instead to prevailing upon the Yugoslav authorities to take measures to stop any further influx of *Volksdeutsche* into the Western occupation zones.[114]

In default of any more tangible form of assistance, some British officials pinned their hopes on a publicity campaign. "Conditions in which Germans in Yugoslavia exist," the Belgrade embassy reported in 1946 in a dispatch that was circulated to Attlee's cabinet, "seem well down to Dachau standards."[115] There was little to be lost by placing these facts before the public, embassy staff added, "as it will hardly be possible for the position of those that are left in camps to deteriorate thereby."[116] In London, too, the idea of "naming and shaming" the Yugoslavs found some support. No immediate action was taken, however, and the proposal was eventually dropped in the face of the U.S. State Department's fear of worsening relations with Tito; the opposition of British occupation authorities in Austria; and the perceived indifference of the Western press to atrocity stories of any kind.

As events were to show, a well-directed publicity campaign against the European camp system might well have had some impact, if not in Yugoslavia, then at least in Czechslovakia and Poland. In September 1946 the prominent British member of Parliament and future minister in the Attlee government, Richard Stokes, made a visit to Czechoslovakia and succeeded in briefly gaining access to the camps at Most, Ústí nad Labem, Hagibor, and Litoměřice. Upon his return, he published a lengthy letter in the *Manchester Guardian* detailing his findings, including the disturbing fact that "many of the Sudeten German Social Democrats who were put in concentration camps by the Germans for being anti-Nazi when liberation came were transferred to Czech labor camps merely because they were of German origin." The daily food ration at Hagibor he calculated to be "750 calories a day, which is below the Belsen level."[117] Stokes had also, to the chagrin of the camp authorities, witnessed the daily selection of prisoners for labor details. "Around 6 A.M. the employers started to arrive in cars and lorries to select and transport their slaves for the day.... Three or four hundred slaves were then let in from the camp end and the visitors made their selection, giving a receipt for the persons carried off, returning them at the end of the day." At Ústí he had interrupted the camp commandant "in his shirt sleeves rifling the belongings of an old man of 65 whilst other officials stood by, one of whom was helping himself to what looked like a silver snuff box, empty silver match box and a cigarette lighter from one of the other elderly prisoners near by." With what may have been studied naïveté—for he had first discussed his discoveries with local representatives of the CICR, who had presented their complaints about the camps in person to the Czechoslovak president on five separate occasions between May 1945 and April 1946—Stokes wondered "whether Dr Beneš knows that these dreadful happenings are going on."[118]

The Stokes report, in marked contrast to the revelations by the *Daily Herald* a year previously, created a minor sensation in Britain and was deeply embarrassing to the Czechoslovak government. Unwisely relying on a briefing document filled with unblushing fictions that had been prepared for him by the Ministry of the Interior, Prime Minister Fierlinger asserted at a press conference that "Czechoslovakia had no concentration camps" but rather nine "internment camps" with a total population of just two thousand, all of whom were awaiting trial for various offenses. Inmates in these camps received the same food rations as the rest of the Czechoslovak population.[119] The Ministry of the Interior issued an equally mendacious point-by-point rebuttal of Stokes's charges, in the course of which it asserted that—by a series of improbable coincidences—every one of the individual prisoners named by him had independently been found suitable for release by the Prague authorities, and that the Hagibor camp had already been scheduled for immediate closure.[120] The Czechoslovak authorities publicly called upon the CICR to inspect its places of detention to verify the truth of these assertions.

The pressure of international public opinion thus achieved what the Red Cross, by its own unaided exertions, could not. At the end of January 1947, the Ministry of the Interior granted the CICR a *laissez-passer* authorizing it to visit all camps in Bohemia, Moravia, and Silesia under ministry control during the month of February, with the sole proviso that any report resulting therefrom first be submitted to Prague.[121] The impact was immediate. One of the longest-serving detainees at Linzervorstadt, a man whose camp number was 83, recalled that "After each visit [from the CICR] conditions improved considerably." The number of guards was decreased; inmates were permitted to walk unescorted to their work details outside the camp; Sunday labor ceased; and forced laborers even received small sums of pocket money in respect of their work.[122] While progress in other countries was on a less dramatic scale, CICR relief supplies had begun to reach inmates in Polish internment camps from June 1947 onward, and some limited inspections of assembly camps in that country were sanctioned at the end of 1948.[123]

For most detainees, however, the only effective amelioration of their condition would come as a result of their eventual expulsion to Germany or Austria. By mid-1947, so many had already been removed as to make it possible for the detaining governments to scale down the camp networks. Romania, the first country to intern German-speaking civilians, declared to the Red Cross in June 1946 that all of its camps had been closed.[124] Czechoslovakia, having already expelled most of its *Sudetendeutsche* by December 1946, was next to follow suit, dissolving some camps and consolidating others. According to the Prague government, only nineteen detention centers remained on May 31, 1947.[125] The expulsion action in Poland was also nearing completion by the same time, making it possible to close many of the smaller camps like Oświęcim in the spring of 1947.[126] By early 1948, according to Polish Ministry of Public Security data, the total camp population in Poland had fallen to forty-seven thousand of all nationalities; only half that number, the majority of them "old and feeble persons," remained in custody a year later.[127] Yugoslavia, which had already had to dissolve several camps—notably Bački Jarak, Sekić, and Filipovo—because the mortality in them was on so excessive a scale as to render them no longer viable, also took initial steps to wind down internment operations early in 1947, in the process realizing from its remaining camp population whatever sums the market would bear. According to British intelligence officers, inmates could either buy their way out using the services of human-trafficking networks which would pay off the camp authorities, or, for the higher price of one thousand dinars[128] per person, deal directly with the camp staff, who would conduct groups of about sixty inmates at night to the border. "The advantage of leaving the camp under official arrangements is that, if the party is turned back by the Hungarian Frontier police ... they are then taken again to the frontier on the following night without having to pay another 1,000 dinars. If, however, an unofficial party is caught the leader and the entire group are arrested by the Jugoslav authorities who presumably object to their cut-price competitors."[129] In the summer of 1947, thanks to the operation of these networks and to instances of Yugoslav camp commandants throwing open the gates of their establishments and inviting their more impecunious detainees to depart for the frontier without further ado, the number of Yugoslav *Volksdeutsche* illegally crossing into Austria via Hungary more than doubled. Rudolfsgnad, the last remaining camp for ethnic Germans in Yugoslavia, closed in March 1948, although many former inmates remained liable thereafter to forced labor in state "enterprises" or farms.

Inspired by such developments as the Communist coup in Czechoslovakia of February 1948, the Berlin crisis in the summer of that year, and the establishment of the Federal Republic of Germany the following spring, Western governments came to view the relatively small number of *Volksdeutsche* remaining behind the Iron Curtain, and especially those still detained in camps, in an entirely new light. With relations between the two superpower blocs having irretrievably broken down, Western governments could occasionally use the camps as a propaganda foil with which to attack their Communist counterparts. Christopher Mayhew, minister of state at the Foreign Office, for example, publicly upbraided Czechoslovakia at the UN in February 1949 for maintaining concentration camps for *Sudetendeutsche* and subjecting 170,000 of them to forced labor.[130] (With this figure, however, Mayhew appears to have confused the number of Sudeten Germans performing compulsory labor with the number said to be remaining in Czechoslovakia.) Nonetheless, Western leaders, with rare exceptions, adhered to the principle of "least said, soonest mended" with regard both to the past incarceration of *Volksdeutsch* civilians and to the fact that a few camps containing ethnic German detainees, like Jaworzno, continued in operation well into the 1950s.

Except in the rarest of instances, the government officials, commandants, and guards of the Central European camps never faced trial for the abuses they had perpetrated. One of the unlucky exceptions was Wenzel Hrneček. Although he had risen rapidly as Linzervorstadt's de facto chief, arriving as a corporal and finishing as a first lieutenant, after the Communist coup of February 1948 Hrneček incurred the disfavor of the new regime in Prague. According to his own account, he was arrested and charged with "high treason for collaboration with the United States of America"; former internees spoke of his having been accused of misappropriating large quantities of expellee property instead of turning it over to the state. Fleeing across the border to Bavaria in 1949, he adopted the persona of "Johann Richter," a *Sudetendeutsch* expellee, and found work with the U.S. Army in Munich. His decision to remain in southern Germany was unwise, inasmuch as many of his former prisoners were now living there. Soon reports that Hrneček had been seen on the streets of Munich were circulating in the expellee press. It was not until July 1952, though, that he was arrested after a desperate struggle outside the Munich telegraph office. At the time of his detention he was found to be in possession of passports in four different names; his car contained a loaded Walther PPK, a nine-millimeter Belgian FN handgun, and a starting pistol. Placed on trial by the U.S. authorities—the scene of his crimes having been under American military administration in 1945—he was charged with forty offenses ranging from simple assault to manslaughter. Hrneček was convicted on eighteen of these and sentenced to eight years' imprisonment, three of which were suspended. After he had served six months, the balance of his sentence was remitted on condition that he leave the Federal Republic of Germany within forty-eight hours.

A tiny handful of other perpetrators also faced prosecution, though few spent much time in prison unless, like Hrneček, they were so foolish as to go to Germany or, if they remained in Czechoslovakia or Poland, were German themselves. Jan Kouřil, a guard at the gruesome Kaunitz College camp in Brno who was later promoted to be deputy commandant at the typhus-ridden Kleidovka detention facility on the edge of town, was tried at Karlsruhe in 1951—reportedly after having tried to sell to a dentist a bagful of gold fillings harvested from former detainees—and received a fifteen-year sentence.[131] Kurt Landrock, an ethnic German *Kapo* at Theresienstadt, was somewhat hypocritically tried by the Czechoslovak authorities for his part in the deaths of some thirty prisoners under his control and sentenced to twenty years in 1947. Lieutenant Karol Pazúr, author of the Přerov massacre who had rationalized his decision to kill children by arguing "What am I supposed to do with them, now that I've shot their parents?" was one of the few ethnic Czechs or Slovaks to answer for his crimes, however inadequately. In January 1949 he was sentenced to a twelve-year term at a court martial at Bratislava, but was freed in an amnesty three years later.[132]

Efforts to bring perpetrators in Poland to justice were still less successful. Czesław Gęborski, the youthful commandant of Łambinowice, was removed from his post in October 1945 after an atrocity in which he ordered guards to shoot ethnic German inmates attempting to flee a camp barracks that had caught fire. He was quickly restored to the Polish regime's good graces, however, and was promoted to the rank of captain in the secret police. The investigation against him was reopened by Władysław Gomułka's government in 1956, but once again dropped. Following the fall of communism, Gęborski was at last arraigned by Polish prosecutors in the year 2000 on charges of murder, torture, and rape of prisoners. Though a vast amount of evidence was collected, no trial had taken place by the time Gęborski died in 2006. The price paid by Salomon Morel, commandant of Świętochłowice-Zgoda, was smaller yet. So notorious did the abuses for which he was responsible become that the director of the Department of Prisons and Camps, Colonel Teodor Duda, punished Morel with three days' house arrest and a reduction in pay in the autumn of 1945. Like Gęborski, nevertheless, he quickly resumed his upward career trajectory, retiring in 1968 as a colonel. The Commission for the Investigation of Crimes Against the Polish Nation began an investigation in 1990 of Morel's tenure at Świętochłowice-Zgoda, prompting him to emigrate to Israel. Attempts by the Polish authorities in 1998 and 2003 to have him extradited were rejected by the Israeli Ministry of Justice, which asserted that it considered there to be "no basis to charge Mr. Morel with serious crimes, let alone crimes of 'genocide' or 'crimes against the Polish nation.'"[133] His prosecution, the former director of the World Jewish Congress (WJC) Elan Steinberg asserted, was part of a politically motivated effort by Holocaust deniers and neo-Nazis to "relativize" Germany's crimes against the Jews. Morel died of natural causes in Tel Aviv in 2007.[134]

Leaving to one side the question of Morel's guilt—the evidence for which is overwhelming and incontrovertible—the WJC director had a point about the willingness of some Germans to proffer equations between the camp experience of Jews and other victims of Nazi Germany during the war and that of ethnic Germans afterwards. The far right *Deutsche Volksunion* includes Gęborski, Morel, Ignacy Cedrowski, and Jana Dragojlović (head of the women's and children's camp at Bački Jarek in Yugoslavia) alongside such figures as Sir Arthur Harris and Dwight Eisenhower in a rogue's gallery of "the 100 terrible armchair perpetrators and executors of the war of extermination against Germany."[135] Maria Tenz, a former inmate of Rudolfsgnad, describes it as an "extermination camp" in her published memoirs.[136] However forgivable rhetoric of this kind may be on the part of former inmates—and Tenz was one of those who could justifiably consider themselves fortunate to have escaped with their lives—no such excuse can be found for others. In reality, there is no valid parallel between even the worst of the postwar camps and their wartime predecessors. With the possible exception of the Yugoslav detention centers in 1945 and 1946, in which a policy chillingly reminiscent of the Nazis' *Vernichtung durch Arbeit* ("extermination through labor") did indeed for a time prevail, the inmates of camps for *Volksdeutsche* were the victims of maltreatment, abuse, and malign neglect, not a systematic program of mass murder. The great majority, even in Yugoslavia, survived their incarceration; eventually all the central and southeastern European countries would voluntarily release their captives. None of this can be said of the camp system operated by Nazi Germany during the war.

This is an important distinction. Nonetheless, the threshold for acknowledging mass human rights abuses for what they are cannot be the unprecedented barbarities of the Hitler regime. With the exception of the war years themselves, Europe west of the USSR had never seen, nor would it again see, so vast a complex of arbitrary detention—one in which tens of thousands, including many children, would lose their lives. That it largely escaped the attention of contemporaries elsewhere in Europe, and the notice of historians today, is a chilling commentary on the ease with which great evils in plain sight may go overlooked when they present a spectacle that international public opinion prefers not to see.

6

The "Organized Expulsions"

Major Frederick Boothby, commander of the British Liaison Team at Kaławsk (today's Węgliniec), a railhead seven miles east of the new Polish-German frontier, eyed expellee train No. 165, as it pulled up to the platform on the evening of May 18, 1946, with considerable suspicion. The first curious thing he noticed was the unusually large quantity of personal effects, including "everything from commodes to double beds," that the expellees had been permitted to take with them. In contrast to most Germans arriving from Poland, they were without exception well nourished and adequately clothed. Furthermore, practically all of them appeared to be Jewish. Lacking the facilities to examine the documents of all 1,572 people on board, he sent the train onward to its destination with a request that the authorities at the point of arrival check it and its passengers carefully.[1] The British Army contingent at the Marienthal transit camp in Lower Saxony, who did so, found that Major Boothby's reservations were amply justified. By the time it reached Marienthal the train had acquired an additional 456 passengers, presumably placed on board somewhere between Kaławsk and the frontier. The supposed expellees were accompanied by a thirty-four-year-old man named Günther Sternberg from Wrocław, who wore a homemade UNRRA armband and whose identity papers, purporting to have been issued by a "Captain Baker, Royal Signals, U.S. Army," gave the camp authorities still more reason to question his bona fides. Field Security officers promptly placed Sternberg under arrest, but persuading the "expellees" to leave the train proved a far more difficult matter. All of them appeared "surprised to learn on arrival that they were going to be treated as refugees" and refused to cooperate. In the end, for the first time in Marienthal's history it was necessary to call out a company of the Yorkshire and Lancashire Regiment to induce them to obey orders. The soldiers had a great deal of trouble disinfecting and registering the passengers, a process that took nine hours and revealed that only 56 of the more than 2,000 persons screened were genuine expellees. Sternberg, under interrogation, acknowledged having forged identity papers for 180 of his charges, and having sold them seats on the train in Warsaw at a rate of five to six hundred dollars per head. The final piece of the puzzle fell into place the following morning when a Dr. Sanek of the American Jewish Joint Distribution Committee, a New York–based relief and emigration agency, put in an appearance. He explained that he had made arrangements with the American authorities for the passengers, Polish Jews, to proceed southward to Oberammergau in the U.S. zone and thence to Palestine. A freight ticket was produced showing that the train had been chartered in Poland for a fee of RM 26,152 ($2,600), which also had paid for its complement of Polish Army guards. Unable or unwilling to pursue the matter further with thousands of additional expellees following hot on train No. 165's heels, the Marienthal officers passed the émigrés along the line and released Sternberg to continue his journey to the U.S. zone.[2] Nine weeks later, the American authorities reported that they knew nothing of the train or its passengers, and had granted them no facilities to travel to the U.S. zone or anywhere else.[3]

This intersection of expulsion and entrepreneurialism was in no respect extraordinary. Indeed, just seven weeks later, another "train No. 165"—a number seemingly particularly favored by people-smugglers—arrived at Marienthal. This transport contained seventeen hundred passengers, all of whom carried documents identifying them as expellee German Jews from the Recovered Territories and visas authorizing them to travel onward from Le Havre in France to the United States. Once again, British suspicions were raised. Major-General G. W. E. J. (Bobby) Erskine of the Office of the Deputy Military Governor had already received reports that Polish authorities, whose anti-Semitism remained unaffected by the Holocaust, were solving their remaining Jewish problem by providing Polish Jews with papers describing their nationality as German, as an inducement to leave the country for good. The camp staff at Marienthal interviewed a cross-section of the passengers and found that "practically everyone had paid the sum of 30 U.S. dollars for the passage on this train." Once again, however, the new arrivals were sent onward for processing "as nothing could be proved that they were not genuine German [expellees] although there is good reason to believe that many of the papers were forged."[4]

As episodes like these indicated, from the outset the optimistically named "organized expulsions" of 1946–47 defied the efforts of the countries involved to impose any kind of order on the process. Given the minimal resources dedicated to the operation, the breakneck pace at which it was conducted, and the expelling countries' ambivalence over whether the efficient removal of the deportees should take precedence over their collective punishment or vice versa, it could hardly have been otherwise. Thus the eighteen-month-long period during which "organized expulsions" took place rapidly degenerated into a macabre race against time, as expelling governments sought to rid themselves of as many unwanted minorities as possible before a combination of a sufficiently large number of deaths en route, and the chaos into which the reception areas in occupied Germany were rapidly descending, should impel the great powers to call a halt to further transfers. That such a point would sooner or later be reached was recognized by policymakers on both sides even before the first "organized" removal took place. Rather than reexamine the wisdom of the operation in light of that fact, however, authorities in the expelling and receiving countries alike embarked upon a course that they fully recognized would result in the immediate impoverishment of both; divert vital transport resources away from reconstruction and relief to a wholly unproductive purpose; and leave a trail of human misery in its wake. Their persistence in such a profoundly self-defeating enterprise raises questions about what lessons, if any, the victors had learned from the unhinged Hitlerian effort to reshape the demographics of the European continent during the Second World War.

The adoption of the Allied Control Council expulsion agreement of November 20, 1945 was followed by the creation of a skeletal logistical and administrative apparatus to oversee the execution of the operation. In view of the fact that mass expulsions were scheduled to begin just six weeks later, this machinery could take only the most rudimentary form. Its most important component was the Combined Repatriation Executive (CRX), an agency set up by the ACC on October 1, 1945 to cope with the enormous transport challenges the expulsions would involve. The remit of CRX was to coordinate and regulate any organized movement of ten or more persons into or out of Germany, or between the four Allied occupation zones. In addition to the expulsions, CRX was responsible for overseeing the transport of almost 2 million Allied displaced persons, most of them forced laborers press-ganged by the Nazis from central Europe, back to their homelands, as well as the repatriation of hundreds of thousands of German prisoners of war in captivity in other lands. The possibility thus existed of using the same trains to carry returning Poles, Czechoslovaks, and Hungarians as well as ethnic Germans, gaining maximum benefit from scarce transport resources. It was quickly realized that representatives of the expelling countries, if added to CRX, could play a vital role in smoothing out the difficulties that would inevitably arise. By the end of 1945, the Executive had acquired a definite structure, with fewer than a dozen "repatriation officers," from all seven countries involved, assisted by a tiny secretarial staff, attempting by themselves to resolve the logistical problems associated with the operation.[5] To the degree that any international apparatus existed to impose order upon the process of expulsion, CRX came closest to fitting the bill; and in view of the low priority attached by the Allies to its work—none of its members held a higher rank than lieutenant colonel—and the scale of the task confronting it, its achievements were remarkable.

That is not to say that CRX's proceedings were always harmonious. To the contrary, an atmosphere of tension set in from the moment its members tried to agree on norms and procedures for transporting and accepting expellees. The negotiations were long and difficult, reflecting the justified suspicion that the receiving powers harbored both of the expelling governments and of each other. The requirements of the Polish State Repatriation Office (*Państwowy Urząd Repatriacyjny*, or PUR), headed by Dr. Władysław Wolski, deputy minister for repatriation, were greatest of all, posing a particular challenge to CRX. The Poles needed to coordinate the simultaneous transfer not just of the Germans but of the displaced Poles from east of the River Bug. As Norman Davies and Roger Moorhouse point out, "The movement of about six million human beings from the USSR to Poland and from Poland to Germany required administrative expertise of the sort attributed to Adolf Eichmann, and logistical planning on a scale at least twice as large as anything attempted during the Holocaust."[6]

The first questions to be decided through the medium of CRX were start dates for the organized expulsions, and the minimum welfare standards to be maintained throughout the operation. In both respects the interests of expelling and receiving countries diverged, with the former seeking to begin the transfer as quickly as possible while retaining as much ex-German property as possible. During preliminary conversations in Berlin at the beginning of 1946, Wolski demanded of both the British and Soviet governments that they not only accept large numbers of expellees immediately but provide the locomotives and rolling stock with which to remove them from Poland. More than a million displaced Poles from east of the Curzon line, together with 170,000 cows, 100,000 horses, 120,000 pigs, and 180,000 sheep, he said, were already on their way to the Recovered Territories. "On the very day of our discussion," Wolski told one of the British negotiators, "the Minister had 38 trains on his hands loaded with individuals bound for the west." Unless these colonists and their livestock could be settled on farms in the Recovered Territories in time for the spring sowing, there would be "famine to face the incoming population." It was pointless, he contended, for the British authorities to agree to accept 1.5 million expellees unless they were prepared to fetch them. Neither the British nor the Soviets, however, allowed themselves to be stampeded into premature action by "this pretty hard-faced demand." The military commander in the Soviet zone, Marshal Georgy Zhukov, was not inclined to be helpful, having already complained to Wolski that German expellees from Poland were arriving at their destinations in a state of destitution, compelling the authorities to provide them with necessities like blankets, clothing, knives, and forks from local resources. The British reminded Wolski that he had been allocated 2,000 covered railway wagons exclusively for the Polish part of the expulsion operation, whereas the total available to British transport officers to disperse the new arrivals in their zone was 750. As an indication of good faith, they offered to accept four thousand expellees a day if the Polish or Soviet governments provided suitable transport. The Soviets, for their part, gave staunch support to the British in resisting the demands of the importunate Wolski. Indicating their suspicion of their wartime ally as well as of the Polish government, however, they went on to insist that British liaison missions whose task it would be officially to accept transports from Poland should be established at the point of embarkation rather than at the new Polish-German frontier, fearing that any expellees rejected by the British would be unceremoniously dumped by the Poles in the Soviet zone.[7]

At first sight it might appear that the receiving powers had the upper hand in these negotiations, for they could simply close their borders and refuse to accept expellees altogether unless their conditions were met. It is certainly true that the British were in no hurry to see the discussions arrive at a conclusion. By the end of January they had reached an agreement in principle with their Polish and Soviet counterparts governing the routes over which expellees were to be transported and the minimum standards of welfare to be assured. They were much slower, however, to translate this understanding into action on the ground. As the ACC expulsion timetable had specified, they wanted to see the "head-for-head" exchanges with the Soviet zone come to a conclusion before launching into a much larger and more difficult round of population transfers. They also hoped that by drawing the talks out until the worst of the winter had passed, the number of deaths through hypothermia that would inevitably occur in transit might be reduced. But there was a limit to these temporizing tactics, one which a British minister's injudicious revelation of the motives behind them to Parliament at the end of January 1946 probably brought closer.[8] By mid-February the British CRX representatives warned that the Poles were becoming exceptionally agitated over the Western powers' failure to set a firm date for the start of mass transfers, which had already fallen more than two months behind schedule. Unless the British made a commitment within the following forty-eight hours to begin accepting expellees forthwith, they feared that the Polish authorities "will despatch trains from starting points without our agreement."[9]

As it turned out, these concerns were exaggerated. The USSR, whose own occupation zone was swamped with destitute Germans from the Recovered Territories and the Sudetenland, was in no greater a hurry than the British to see the organized expulsions commence. Believing, though, that no advantage could be gained by further prevarication, the British CRX representative signed a final agreement with his Polish counterpart the following day. Under its terms, a thousand expellees were to be transported daily by sea across the Baltic from Szczecin to Lübeck, from whence they would be taken by truck to the transit camp at Pöppendorf. A rail route from Szczecin to Bad Segeberg, fifteen miles west of Lübeck, would carry another 1,520 expellees a day in a single train. A second route from Kaławsk via Helmstedt to Marienthal or the adjoining railhead at Alversdorf would receive two trains daily, with a maximum combined capacity of 3,000. The third planned rail route, from Kaławsk to Friedland near Göttingen, was to carry 2,500 expellees each day; for logistical reasons this never came into operation. Expulsions along the Szczecin-Segeberg and Kaławsk-Marienthal-Alversdorf lines were to commence on February 20; the starting dates for the commencement of the other routes were to be decided later. Although it was not expected that the total throughput of 56,000 expellees per week would be attained immediately, the British declared their willingness to admit at least 45,000 per week by March 1, 1946.[10]

The Anglo-Polish agreement also laid down detailed norms for the conditions under which expellees were to be transported. The British undertook to accept the Germans at the embarkation points, and—as the Soviets had demanded—to establish six-man liaison teams at Kaławsk and Szczecin for that purpose. After these squads had inspected and approved the transports, they would proceed without further interference to their final destinations in the British zone. All locomotives and rolling stock were to be provided by the Poles, or, where applicable, the Soviets; the Poles also undertook to provide a guard of ten soldiers for each transport who would be accommodated overnight at the British reception centers. The expellees were to be dusted with DDT at the embarkation points. Each was allowed to take as much baggage as he or she could carry by hand, and no more than five hundred Reichsmarks in paper currency. Families were not to be divided, nor were pregnant women to travel within six weeks before and after their predicted or actual date of confinement. On the first two routes, the Poles were to provide sufficient rations for a two days' journey to be carried on the transport, with a further day's rations held in reserve. On the second pair of routes, three days' rations, along with the one-day reserve, were required. The physically and mentally ill, orphans, and criminals were not to be removed until the very end of the operation. Lastly, a nominal roll—or list of names—of the expellees and a medical certificate attesting that all those traveling were free of communicable disease were to accompany each transport.[11]

Other agreements between the expelling and receiving authorities followed a similar pattern. The Soviet authorities in Germany drove an even harder bargain with the Czechoslovak government, requiring that the 600,000 expellees from that country receive a baggage allowance of fifty kilograms per person and that each arrive with not less than five hundred Reichsmarks or occupation marks—if necessary to be furnished by the Czechoslovaks themselves. Two medical certificates, signed by both a Czechoslovak and a German doctor, were to confirm the fitness to travel of the expellees, and two German nurses were to travel in each train. Separate coaches were to be provided for those requiring medical treatment and the mentally ill. No more than thirty expellees were to be loaded into each of the forty-two or forty-three closed wagons attached to the trains, making for a maximum of approximately twelve hundred persons per transport. In return, the Soviets agreed to accept with effect from July 10, 1946 three daily trains, six days a week, on the short Podmokly (Bodenbach)–Bad Schandau route, and three more originating from Tršnice and terminating in Gera or Altenburg in Thuringia. A strict arrival timetable would be adhered to so that the trains could return to Czechoslovakia by the same evening. During the summer months, river barges of expellees would also be received at Wittenberg in Saxony and Wittenberge in Brandenburg. The agreement between the USSR and Poland, on the other hand, reflecting the Soviet Union's strategic interest in clearing the Recovered Territories of Germans as expeditiously as possible, was much more rudimentary. The USSR promised to admit trains at Forst and Görlitz, each with a complement of fifteen to seventeen hundred expellees, and to require no more elaborate documentation than a dispatch order and a sanitary certificate for each transport, along with the expellees' own personal identification.[12]

The most stringent conditions of all were imposed by the U.S. zonal commanders, who were required under the ACC plan to accept expellees from both Czechoslovakia and Hungary. The Americans had learned a hard lesson when they allowed themselves to be talked into agreeing on a premature beginning to the organized expulsions, without seeking any written standards for the operation. At the end of November Colonel John H. Fye, the former deputy chief of staff of the U.S. Army's XXII Corps, was appointed liaison officer for expulsion affairs with the Czechoslovak General Staff. The "unit" he headed consisted of himself, a local interpreter, a clerk, and a driver. "Throughout the entire operation the section was an orphan." Ill-advisedly, Fye agreed with his hosts that transports could commence to the U.S. zone just two weeks later. The results were disastrous. The first trains, which embarked on December 13, 1945, "brought a loud protest from OMG Bavaria" on account of "the stripped conditions of the expellees" arriving in Germany. A train reaching Hof on December 16, 1945 contained 650 expellees who had traveled while the external temperature was minus nine degrees centigrade. When the doors were opened at the destination, representatives of the Red Cross awaiting the transport found that ninety-four of the passengers, including twenty-two children, were dead.[13] Complaints by the U.S. forces over the conditions of these transports were rejected by the Ministry of National Defense, which pointed out that "there was no prescribed allowance for expellees other than 'minimum essential clothing and bedding.' This did not necessarily mean too much in the way of clothing and a blanket could be considered minimum essential bedding." Due to a combination of American protest and Czechoslovak lack of preparation, however, further transports were suspended on December 29, pending negotiations with a team of U.S. officers from Munich and representatives of the Czechoslovak civil and military authorities the following week.[14]

According to the written protocol agreed at this meeting, *Sudetendeutsche* were to receive from the local authorities at least forty-eight hours' notice of their deportation. They were then to be assembled at a transit camp for medical examination and documentation. Once this procedure had been completed, they would be entrained at a maximum rate of fifty expellees per freight wagon. The American authorities would become involved only when the train reached the boundary of the U.S. zone. There they would inspect the train; check the nominal roll and ensure that no expellee was being removed unaccompanied by his or her family; and either accept the train, direct that unauthorized persons be removed, or reject the entire transport. Once admitted by the Americans, expellees would be given a hot meal, disinfected, and passed on to the German *Land* authorities who would see to their further resettlement.[15] In contrast to the British, who provided the expellees with documentation upon arrival, the U.S. authorities insisted that each *Sudetendeutsch* be furnished with an identity card in Czech, German, and English before embarkation. The printing of these papers alone, the Czechoslovak authorities complained, would set back the resumption of the operation by several weeks.[16] Initially, one train per day, containing twelve hundred expellees, was to be accepted at Fürth im Wald. The dispatch rate doubled after a month, when Wiesau, east of Bayreuth, was brought into service as a second reception point. By May 1, seventy-two hundred expellees were entering the U.S. zone daily at the two stations, with smaller numbers continuing to travel by road or cross the border on foot. A Czechoslovak General Staff proposal to use ships on the Danube to bring additional *Sudetendeutsche* from Slovakia to Passau was rejected by the Americans for logistical reasons.[17]

Reflecting the fact that Hungary was an ex-enemy state, the Allied Control Commission for Hungary (ACC [H]) did not engage in discussions with the interim Budapest government, but rather issued directives to it. In practice, the U.S. authorities, to whose zone ethnic Germans from Hungary, the so-called "Swabians," would go, were given a free hand to dictate their requirements to Béla Miklós's provisional administration. The Americans ordered that expulsions would begin on December 15, 1945, with a single train of forty heated cars or wagons, carrying a total of one thousand passengers, who were to be medically examined and provided with the necessary documents before embarkation. Each expellee, including children, would receive a baggage allowance of one hundred kilograms. An inspectorate composed of representatives from the three occupying powers would ensure that conditions in the "concentration areas" and on the trains were appropriately humane, though Marshal Voroshilov pointed out to his colleagues on the ACC (H) that "the word 'humane' could only be considered relatively, having regard to the conditions of the whole move."[18]

In all three "Potsdam" countries, foreign diplomats and representatives of the world's press were invited to witness the model conditions of the initial "organized expulsions." Predictably, the Czechoslovak government was the most successful in arranging a suitably reassuring spectacle for the observers. The British consul at Karlovy Vary, Oswald Bamborough, formerly a journalist for the state-owned Czechoslovak Broadcasting Corporation, attended the first "official" transport of *Sudetendeutsch* expellees from Mariánské Lázně on January 25, 1946. Like the other invitees, the U.S. ambassador, Steinhardt, who was present together with various other foreign dignitaries, marveled at the evident pains to which the Czechoslovak authorities had gone to ensure that the deportees should have no legitimate grounds for complaint. Almost 1,000 women and children, and 240 men, had first been assembled in a former U.S. Army barracks capable of accommodating at least six times that number. A week's ration of food was immediately issued to each expellee, with an additional three days' supply held in reserve. The train supplied to remove them to Bavaria included a "Red Cross" compartment, staffed by German nurses, and all passengers were first medically examined by a German doctor. The Czech commandant overseeing the proceedings confirmed that none of the expellees' possessions had been confiscated, and that so far as the fifty-kilogram baggage allowance was concerned, "his instructions were to exercise benevolence in this matter." Indeed, those who arrived lacking adequate clothing were provided with what they needed by the

Czechoslovaks themselves. A *March of Time* film crew, brought there for the occasion, recorded footage of smiling, neatly dressed *Sudetendeutsch* women and their babies queuing to receive a last hot meal from the camp commissary before their embarkation.[19] Bamborough was moved by the spectacle, and in his official dispatch testified to "the deep impression the conduct of the Czech officials made on me; I am convinced that they are determined to implement the words frequently uttered by their spokesmen, that the transfer of Germans should be carried out humanely."[20] A British journalist, invited by the authorities to witness another staged transport near Karlovy Vary, found the scene "more like the end of a village garden-party than part of a great transfer of population." Like many of the foreign observers, he expressed gratification over the poetic justice that had overtaken the *Sudetendeutsche*. "As their train bumps on towards the Reich, the Sudetens will perhaps recall the happy days when the Jewish shop-windows went flying into smithereens and the fires in the trade-union buildings were starting up, and the folk, the ordinary folk, were running about looking for somebody to take a smack at, and shouting, 'We want to be home in the Reich!' Soon they will get their wish."[21]

Similar attempts at Potemkin expulsions organized by other Potsdam countries were markedly less successful. British and U.S. military observers and a correspondent of the Reuters news agency, invited to witness the first group of deportees leave Hungary, found that contrary to the government's undertakings, those rounded up had in some cases been given no more than ten minutes' notice of their removal. Many took the opportunity provided by the general chaos surrounding the operation to flee into the countryside; of the thousand *Volksdeutsche* from the small town of Budaörs, eight miles outside Budapest, who were to travel on the first expulsion train on January 19, 1946, only seven hundred—not all of whom were Germans—could be found when they were counted at the station. The system of predeparture medical screening quickly broke down and was abandoned, and the train, when it eventually got under way, proceeded so slowly—taking nearly three days to cover the 160 miles between Budapest and its initial stop at Vienna—that passengers were seriously affected by hunger. Contrary to the expulsion protocol, no food had been provided for the journey, and the inspectors who met the train as it entered the U.S. zone at Freilassing concluded that taking all the various breaches into account, the conditions under which the transport had taken place constituted "inhumane treatment."[22] The story was similar in the case of a Polish "Red Cross" train intended to show the special care taken by the authorities with sick and elderly expellees from the Recovered Territories. On its first, well-publicized trip from Wrocław to Aurich, west of Wilhelmshaven, the desired effect was undermined by the fact that "rather a number" of the passengers were Alzheimer's patients who "did not realise even during the journey what was going on with them," and by the inadequacy of the food ration—less than 150 grams of bread per person per day. Five of the expellees died en route, and another two shortly after arrival.[23]

Notwithstanding the general disorganization, some Allied military officials considered that the Hungarian government at the outset was at least trying, however ineffectually, to meet the ACC (H)'s requirements. The same was not at all true, though, of the expulsions from the Recovered Territories to the British zone of Germany, which had been given the designation of "Operation Swallow." The correspondent of the *Manchester Guardian*, who met the first transport from Szczecin to Lübeck on March 3, 1946, found that 250 of the expellees were so seriously ill as to require immediate hospitalization; a child of eighteen months and a seventy-three-year-old man were dead on arrival. "In later transports the figures have been higher." The expellee convoys bore a distinctly geriatric aspect, most of those removed being over fifty with "many in their eighties." A considerable proportion had had no food for up to a week, in transit or while detained at the Szczecin-Gumieńce assembly camp before their embarkation. However, the most disquieting aspect was the marks they bore of systematic maltreatment over a long period, with the scars of physical and sexual abuse much in evidence. "Most of the women," it was established by the examining British medical officers, "had been violated, among them a girl of 10 and another of 16."[24]

After only a few weeks of the "organized expulsions," it became clear to the occupation authorities in Germany that the Swallow removals, rather than the stage-managed deportations, would be the template for the operation as a whole. From all sides, reports began to flood in from reception centers of the immense strain exerted upon them by attempting to cope with the consequences of systematic maltreatment of the new arrivals. The first three Swallow trains received at the Pöppendorf transit camp in the British zone contained a "large percentage of old people, most of them in very bad condition with a good many almost on the verge of death with bruises and other marks of having been beaten up." Of the 4,100 expellees on these three transports, 524 were admitted directly to hospital on arrival.[25] Once again, the camp commandant reported to his superiors that most of the women in these transports were multiple rape victims, as were some of the children.[26] A British Army colonel meeting an expellee train at Bielefeld in April was struck by the "remarkable and terrifying fact" that nearly all the passengers had been "severely ill-treated" in the recent past, exhibiting "deep scars in the skull bone, fingers crippled by ill-treatment, fractures of the ribs which were more or less healed, and partly large [*sic*] bloodshot spots on their backs and their legs. The latter was also seen with women."[27] There too a "high percentage" of expellees was being sent straight to hospital upon arrival.[28]

A detailed report on the first Swallow train received at Detmold in Westphalia paints a typical picture of "organized expulsions" from the Recovered Territories at this time. Of the 1,507 expellees on board, 516 were children, many of whom were barefoot. The passengers had been awakened from their beds during the night of February 20, 1946, and told to be ready to leave at ten minutes' notice, which proved insufficient for many of the parents to be able to find their children's shoes. The Germans were brought to a camp, where the men were taken away; nothing more was known of them. The women and children were then marched to a railway station, their baggage being taken from them and some beaten along the way. They were then placed on a train, which did not arrive in Detmold until March 3. "Passing through the Soviet zone the Reds had given some of them coffee, about a pound of bread and some sugar, which was all the food they had for the ten days of their journey."[29] Surprisingly few deaths had occurred in the course of this evacuation.

Virtually every report remarked upon the extraordinarily high proportion of elderly persons included in the transports. Two British reception officers, meeting a Swallow train of fourteen hundred expellees at Bad Segeberg in April 1946, found a scene that "resembled an Emmett drawing in *Punch*. . . . Very many old men and women, with only a few months to live. Some of these could hardly walk; most of them needed to be lifted down from the train. . . . We saw only 2 fit young men and we walked the whole length of the train."[30] At the other end of the age spectrum, military observers noted an "alarming absence of young babies under 2 years of age," a consequence of high infant mortality caused by starvation of the expellee population in the Recovered Territories.[31] A series of statistical investigations in March and April made clear that the Polish authorities were taking the opportunity to rid themselves of the unproductive element of the German population, retaining employable males for compulsory labor. Only about 8 percent of the expellees entering the British zone from the Recovered Territories were fit men; the proportion in the same category arriving in the Soviet zone at the same time was estimated by a Red Army officer at 10 percent.[32]

Of no less concern to the British was the shambolic manner in which Operation Swallow was being administered on the Polish side of the frontier. The Warsaw authorities persistently failed to provide rations for the expellees during their journey or for the day of their arrival in Germany, as their agreement with CRX obliged them to do; even when the British offered to supply the food themselves, the Poles often refused to accept it. As one investigation found, to feed

37,000 freshly arrived expellees for a day at Alversdorf camp the Poles had sent along 198 loaves, 180 kilograms of meat, 10 kilograms of ersatz coffee, and 4 kilograms of onions.[33] Sometimes the Polish train guards themselves were not provided for, and were obliged "to beg for rations on arrival." Nor were the guards able to prevent the Soviets from taking advantage of the passage of Swallow trains through their occupation zone to dump into the British zone persons of whom, for one reason or another, they wanted to be rid. In one instance reported by the Polish authorities, the Red Army stopped the train at Völpke in Saxony-Anhalt and forced 70 Germans, not from the Recovered Territories, on board.[34] In another, a standoff at Wittenberg between Soviet forces attempting to place additional passengers aboard an expulsion train and the Polish guards ended tragically when in the course of a heated argument a Red Army soldier accidentally shot a German child.[35] The same problem was noted at Pöppendorf, where a random check of 4,000 new arrivals found 195 persons whose names did not appear on the nominal rolls accompanying them, while 100 others listed had gone missing.[36]

More vexatious still was the train guards' general trigger-happiness. The crossing points in the British zone were perennial flashpoints, as departing Germans took the opportunity to "heap insults on the heads of the guards" as soon as they passed beyond Polish jurisdiction. It was, however, unwise to yield to such temptations. Many train guards were as quick to respond to any provocation in the British or Soviet zones as in the Recovered Territories themselves.[37] By no means, moreover, were Germans the only targets of Polish ire. As a result of these incidents, the commandant at Kaławsk noted, "the Polish Guards, who detrain here, return [from the British zone] very angry and this places members of this unit in no small danger."[38] In April the British submitted a formal complaint to Warsaw that guards on trains departing Marienthal were in the habit of "opening fire with sub machine guns. This has happened on numerous occasions since [the] start of Swallow."[39] In another incident two months later, an intoxicated train guard at Szczecin opened fire with his machine-pistol as Germans were being marshaled for departure, killing a female expellee.[40] It was hardly surprising, then, that British officers should have concluded that "the train guards appear to be worthless and utterly undisciplined," and recommended that they be ordered to stand down whenever an expulsion train halted at a station in the British zone.[41] At the end of June, Major Boothby made a direct appeal to Wolski to stop assigning train guard duties to members of the militia, which, he undiplomatically observed, was "composed of youths who have neither military discipline nor military training," and to reserve the job instead for "disciplined soldiers."[42]

Although the logistics of transfer from Poland to the Soviet zone were less complicated, in view of the shorter distance to be traveled, the USSR's experience of dealing with the Poles—as evidenced by the litany of formal complaints with which the Red Army began to bombard the Ministry for the Recovered Territories (MZO)—did not differ greatly from what the British had already encountered. Though large-scale removals would not begin until midsummer, army commanders in the Soviet zone did try to accommodate their Polish counterparts by accepting a modest number of transports before then. They soon came to regret their helpfulness. Thus in early March the Soviet Military Administration in Germany demanded to know why a train had arrived with 379 fewer passengers than shown on the nominal roll, and how it was that the train guards had apparently done nothing to prevent them from absconding en route. Three days later, the Soviets protested the Poles' action in rounding up some 350 Germans from the town of Toruń and, without notice, transporting them to Frankfurt an der Oder, and unceremoniously dumping them in the city center.[43] The inadequacy of food provided to expellees featured prominently in the Soviet list of grievances also.[44] Consequently, British expulsion officials on the ground were surprised to find that their Soviet counterparts, confronting many of the same problems with the Polish authorities, were uncharacteristically helpful and cooperative. In some cases, Red Army officers even took it upon themselves to conduct medical inspections of trains bound for the West and, when necessary, to give the British liaison teams "a friendly warning that, in their opinion, conditions were not satisfactory."[45]

Only two months after the beginning of the Polish "organized expulsions," then, the operation had already degenerated into such a state of near chaos that officials in the reception areas had begun to press for its immediate suspension. The British mood was not improved by the tenor of the statements about the transfers emanating from the Polish official media. At the end of March, Radio Warsaw unwisely reassured listeners that they need not be concerned about the economic effect of the expulsions because the persons transferred thus far "were mostly nonworkers." The same broadcast claimed that the departing Germans were always given ample notice and "allowed to take all the belongings they could carry. In practice they have been taking a great deal more." The expellees were leaving "in distinctly cheerful mood, amid laughter and jokes.... Not infrequently Germans have expressed eloquent thanks to the Polish authorities. This should be noted by certain foreign circles which cannot find words strong enough to commiserate with the Germans." Radio Warsaw went on to chide the British for impeding the pace of transfers by refusing to allow the Poles to squeeze a greater number of expellees into each railway wagon than was specified in the CRX agreement. "[T]his change would require the consent of the British authorities who so far, have shown more concern for the Germans' comfort than for our facilities."[46]

Contradicting his formerly unsympathetic attitude to the sufferings of Germans, Jack Troutbeck of the Foreign Office responded to the many reports of Polish failures to live up to their agreements by suggesting that the British "might take a leaf out of the American book" and require the Polish authorities to ensure that minimal standards respecting the conduct of the expulsions were observed. In default of compliance, "we should cut off transport and close down transfer routes."[47] Bevin concurred with this hardline approach, and Ambassador Cavendish-Bentinck at the Warsaw Embassy was told on April 10 to threaten the Poles with suspension of Operation Swallow and to inform them that "as we control the transport, we have no intention of continuing to accept immigrants in the conditions which have hitherto prevailed."[48] The ambassador was aghast at this uncompromising instruction, which threatened to undermine the rapport he believed he had established with the Polish government. In a flurry of telegrams to London, he pleaded Warsaw's case. It was inappropriate, he argued, to apply Western concepts of human rights to Slavs. "Whilst the conditions under which the Polish are expelling Germans may seem to us inhumane, the Polish—like the Russians—have different standards from ourselves."[49] The following day, he made a special visit to an assembly camp at Szczecin to view the expulsion facilities. What he saw there persuaded him, he reported to London, that "the Poles are not to blame" for any difficulties that had arisen. Deaths and births in transit were the result of sick people and pregnant women concealing their condition so as to avoid being separated from their families. The reason that women, children, and the elderly constituted the overwhelming majority of expellees, he believed, was that "there are very few able-bodied male Germans" left in the Recovered Territories. Cavendish-Bentinck also enlisted the support of Frank Savery, onetime British consul general in Warsaw, who advised the Foreign Office that "it looks as if British public opinion had been led up the garden-path by the German propaganda."[50]

Officials in London did not find these defenses of the Poles especially persuasive. The deplorable condition in which expellees were arriving was not a figment of German propaganda, but an observable fact with whose all too tangible consequences the overstretched British authorities in the reception areas were struggling to cope. Polish radio had already confirmed that a definite policy existed of holding back employable males for compulsory labor, and that expulsions in cities like Wrocław had been halted altogether as a result.[51] As for the notion that a different definition of humanitarianism applied to Eastern Europe, one British official commented sourly, "We are always being told what an essentially Christian people the Poles are. Could they not for once behave like Christians?"[52] But the Ambassador's questioning of his instructions did give hardliners in London a breathing-space in which to coordinate their response. Denis Allen of the Foreign Office, who had counseled against "being grandmotherly" during the Czechoslovak "wild expulsions" of the previous year, strongly backed Cavendish-Bentinck. "He has repeatedly warned us that the charge of undue tenderness towards the Germans is virtually the only item of the current anti-British propaganda campaign which never fails to evoke a response from almost all sections of Polish opinion."[53] British representatives in the Control Commission for Germany also recommended taking a more understanding approach with the Poles, who, they pointed out, had confessed on April 29 that they had indeed been guilty of holding back fit men and promised to modify this practice in the near future.[54] In the end, *raison d'état* triumphed over the complaints of Military Government in the British zone. Bevin sent a countermanding order to Cavendish-Bentinck on May 7, asking him merely to "emphasise informally" to Warsaw that "both we and they are likely to come under strong criticism from world opinion about these transfers" unless conditions improved.[55] In the meantime, the British liaison teams at Kałwask and Szczecin were instructed to refuse onward clearance to any train not in compliance with the CRX criteria agreed with the Poles three months previously.[56]

In reality, as both the British and the Poles fully understood, this was an empty threat. So immense was the tidal wave of humanity bearing down upon the two embarkation points each day that any attempt to exclude all but a handful of the most vulnerable expellees quickly resulted in a backlog of terrifying proportions. As Lieutenant Colonel Growse, Boothby's predecessor as head of the liaison team at Kałwask, explained, "Once let there be a residue left on the station after the departure of the second train [each day] and this will go on increasing daily until eventually the whole town is flooded by a multitude of homeless and half-starved Germans."[57] This had in fact already occurred in Szczecin. One of the city's two assembly camps, a disused sugar factory in the western suburb of Gumieńce (Stettin-Scheune), lacked windows, doors, furniture, or floor covering; robberies or rapes of the inhabitants at the hands of the People's Militia were frequent occurrences. Gumieńce had been intended to accommodate expellees for between twenty-four and forty-eight hours. By early April, trains were taking so long to return from the British zone that the camp population ballooned to more than eight thousand, nearly three times its stated capacity, and the supply of food ran out.[58] So bad were the conditions in this camp that the Soviets demanded in 1946 that the Polish authorities refurbish the buildings and take action to prevent the spread of disease by isolating sick expellees in hospital. The Poles refused, advising Soviet officials that "most of the Germans were reaching Szczecin completely exhausted and weakened, and that if all of them were to be hospitalized, Szczecin would become a hospital town."[59]

The problem of overcrowding—of the camps, the trains and ships, and the reception areas—was to bedevil Operation Swallow throughout its year-long existence. It was, however, to a significant degree a problem of Britain's own making. After the idea of making a formal protest to Warsaw was abandoned, the British representatives on CRX turned to the opposite strategy. Instead of seeking to restrict the intake to a level that could be accommodated—a policy that would, admittedly, have prolonged the transfer operation into the indefinite future—CRX officials agreed to a Polish request at the end of April to increase the daily rate of acceptances from five thousand to eight thousand. While this was still fewer than the ten thousand who, according to the original plan, were to be expelled each day once Swallow reached its summertime peak, the hope was that an all-out effort, in spite of the difficulties, might enable the program to be completed before the onset of another winter. Defensible though the reasoning behind it may have been, this decision meant that any prospect of imposing a degree of control over the conditions under which expulsions took place evaporated. Already burdened beyond its capacity, the machinery of mass expulsion in the Recovered Territories was reduced to its crudest and most basic form: the cramming of as many bodies into railway wagons as could physically be wrestled inside. In a perpetual crisis atmosphere, with the equivalent of the population of a small- to medium-sized town descending upon the railheads every day, there was neither time nor resources for anything more elaborate. Increased suffering and higher mortality among the expellees was the inevitable result. The British expulsion administrators, however, consoled themselves with the reflection that an even greater number might die, of starvation or abuse, if they stayed very much longer in Poland.

If the British and Soviets struggled to cope with the logistical problems with which the mass expulsion program confronted them, their difficulties were as dust in the balance compared with the challenges faced by the Polish repatriation agency PUR. Its records testify to the almost incredible disorganization, low morale, and, in many cases, physical danger with which its underpaid and unappreciated employees had to deal each day. In principle, the process of expulsion ought to have proceeded according to an orderly plan. According to MZO circulars drawn up for the use of local officials, nonincarcerated Germans were to be left in situ until the category to which they belonged was called up for removal. In order of priority, those scheduled for deportation were the unemployed and unproductive; "disruptive elements"; agricultural laborers on Polish-owned farms; employees of private businesses; unskilled workers; dispossessed peasants; and all remaining Germans. Following notification by the MZO, Germans from one of these categories in a given district would either be ordered to report at an assembly point at a stated time, usually by posters placed on walls twenty-four hours in advance, or be rounded up by militia or army units. In either case, they would be taken to an internment camp or railway station, when they would turn over the keys to their houses or apartments and any savings deposit books, stock certificates, or insurance policies in their names. They would also be searched on arrival for excess baggage or contraband, both of which would likewise be forfeited to the state. (The definition of "contraband" was normally elastic; as a female doctor testified, on her departure "the custom-house officers even took the women's knickers [underpants].")[60] They would then be transported to an assembly camp close to one of the main embarkation points—most often Kaławsk or Szczecin for transfers to the British zone, Tuplice (Lubusz) or Kaławsk for those to the Soviet zone—and, after a stay of a day or two, be placed on board the train or ship that would carry them to their destination in Germany. A "car leader" in each wagon, and a "transport leader" in each train, chosen by the expellees themselves, would be appointed to help maintain good order and discipline throughout the journey, and to make any necessary representations on behalf of their fellows to the officials in charge of the operation. Any robberies or violations of the expellees' human rights in the course of the process, the regulations stated, were to be immediately notified to the proper authorities.[61]

As MZO and PUR officials reported, however, hardly any expulsions from Poland followed this orderly pattern. The first complications arose with the round-ups. Soviet and Polish employers of cheap or free German labor were highly reluctant to be deprived of it. "The Poles . . . are exploiting these people and are very loath to see them go. They realise that the Germans are good workers, their demands to-day are nil and their upkeep negligible."[62] Giving advance notice of planned deportation actions merely provided an opportunity for these elements to hide their workers until the danger had passed. The Soviets, according to Polish authorities, treated the edicts of the Warsaw government with particular disdain. Registers of German labor supposedly employed by them bore "no relationship to reality."[63] Red Army officers stashed their favorite Germans in barracks, cars, or other places inaccessible to the Polish authorities whenever PUR representatives were in the vicinity. Cases were recorded of Red Army troops opening fire on Polish officials coming to confiscate "their" Germans.[64] Potential expellees concealed themselves, or their property, in the cities or took to the forests until the clearance operations had concluded. In one sweep in Szczecin province that had been intended to round up 900 expellees, only 232 were found. Polish enterprises, too, were discovered to be busily falsifying their records in the hope of retaining their Germans' services. Some were maintained "off the books"; in other cases inessential workers—sweepers, nightwatchmen, or hairdressers—were classified as "specialist labor."[65] And individual Poles, sympathetic to the Germans' plight, sometimes tried to shield them from expulsion, "even going so far as hiding them in their own apartments."[66]

More commonly still, the problem was not too few Germans to deport, but too many. The continuing prevalence of "wild expulsions," and of Germans lacking any means of support presenting themselves at the assembly camps or embarkation points for expulsion or simply in hope of a meal, could also wreck the PUR's already shambolic arrangements. Often keyed up to a fever pitch of nationalist fervor by "All Germans Out Now" demonstrations—the Recovered Territories Department of the Polish Socialist Party organized manifestations in fifty-four cities and towns across the country in December 1946 alone—local authorities or militia units were prone to take matters into their own hands, clearing their own districts of Germans of all categories and either depositing them at the nearest assembly camp or organizing unofficial removals to the zonal frontier. The numbers affected by these ongoing "wild expulsions" were significant: in the month of June 1946 alone, 4,447 Germans from Gdańsk voivodeship, 4,268 from Western Pomerania, and 3,694 from the central Polish voivodeships were disposed of in this way.[67] The Soviets, too, while continuing to hold Germans back for their own purposes, had an unfortunate tendency abruptly to disgorge those whose services they no longer required onto the streets adjacent to expulsion facilities, whether or not the Poles were ready to accept responsibility for the cast-offs. Even after the internment camp at Koszalin closed in April 1947, Red Army trucks continued to deposit surplus German laborers, like unwanted puppies, on the outskirts of the town.[68] But even these clearances were dwarfed by the hordes of Germans who, in defiance of regulations requiring them to remain at their places of origin until called up for expulsion, descended upon the assembly camps or points of embarkation on their own initiative. Frequently they did so because—having been compelled to leave their homes by force or intimidation, lacking ration cards or means of support—swift expulsion or, at the least, admission to an assembly camp was the only alternative to starvation. Just as often, though, Germans who had already resigned themselves to the inevitable reasoned that the sooner they began their new life in postwar Germany the better. These individuals, a British officer thought, were usually from "what, in England, would be described as the Middle Classes."[69] Many were undeterred by the penalties specified for those who sought to jump the expulsion queues, recognizing that local authorities were often willing to turn a blind eye to Germans prepared to collaborate in the process of their own removal. In some cases, those same local authorities earned considerable sums by selling "official" passes to expellees permitting them to leave the country as quickly as they pleased.

These "out of turn" expellees, though, caused immense headaches for MZO personnel and receiving powers alike. By May 1946, the number of "unofficials" at the embarkation points designated for transports to the British zone had built up to such an extent that the complements of "grossly overcrowded" trains were threatening to cause "a breakdown of camp staff . . . and probable mortality" at the Marienthal and Alversdorf reception centers in the British zone.[70] The beleaguered Major Boothby, in response, pointed out that the problem was more acute still at his end. A thousand "unofficial" expellees were descending upon Kałavsk every day. Fifteen hundred were camping out at the railway station, often for days at a time. The Poles disclaimed all responsibility for feeding or accommodating them, and "cases of collapse" from hunger and illness were everyday occurrences.[71] Although he made formal protests to the civil authorities, Boothby did not believe that they were making the slightest effort to check the influx.[72] "Rather to the contrary, in fact, as it saves a lot of work in conveying people to recognised assembly points and entraining them there."[73] In the circumstances, the British liaison teams considered that they had no alternative but to fill the trains to bursting point, and beyond, so as to prevent an immediate public health catastrophe. "Legally," Boothby conceded, "the 'extras' can be refused and turned back. In fact, no Englishman could do such a thing."[74]

Understandable as the liaison teams' willingness to wink at breaches of the CRX agreement on humane conditions of transfer may have been, this permissive policy gave the Polish authorities every opportunity to continue ignoring its requirements, of which they proceeded to take full advantage. Paradoxically, the best rolling stock was usually reserved for expulsions to the Soviet zone, although the journey times involved were much shorter. This was largely due to the fact that the Soviets did not hesitate to refuse admission to any train that did not conform to the standards they had laid down for acceptance. The difference was evidenced by the trains themselves. The normal allocation for each transport of 1,500–1,750 expellees to East Germany was fifty-five wagons.[75] By contrast, the trains provided by Warsaw for removals to the British zone typically consisted of just thirty wagons, and in some cases as few as seventeen—frequently lacking doors or, on occasion, roofs.[76] "This subject has been taken to the Polish Officials but they reply that . . . the Russians are supposed to supply transport, so we are compelled to overcrowd every train."[77] While the British liaison teams attempted to hold the number of expellees on each transport to 1,750, they acknowledged that they usually failed to do so. Instead, complements of 2,000–2,200 on each train were the norm, with still higher loads—in excess of 80 persons per wagon—far from unusual. The inevitable consequence was much needless suffering at best, and at worst deaths through heat exhaustion or suffocation.

Whether they made their own way to the assembly and embarkation points or were sent there by the Polish authorities, expellees faced hazards at every stage of their journey. Tens of thousands of them spent weeks or months shuttling through one assembly camp after another, as the authorities engaged in a game of "pass the parcel" to relieve local overcrowding. The greatest perils existed during these intercamp transfers within Poland, with militia bands, who sometimes operated in collusion with the train guards, preying on the transports en route. Most commonly the bandits' objectives were robbery or rape, but the lawlessness of the Recovered Territories also provided ample opportunity to run lucrative protection rackets. On one transport from Świdwin in Pomerania to Szczecin, the guards solicited and obtained a "voluntary contribution" from expellees to ensure their safety.[78] On another, a band of would-be plunderers from the Red Army ambushed a train late at night as it stood at the Świdnica station and tried to break into the wagons with crowbars. The guards, resentful of this Soviet incursion upon what they considered ought to remain a wholly Polish enterprise, began shooting at the raiders, and a full-scale firefight ensued. After the Soviets had been driven off, the Polish noncommissioned officer warned the German transport leader that "there would be incidents until Kohlfurt." He added that the train would stop overnight at Chojnów "in a completely evacuated area. If the refugees preferred to be in safety they [would] have to make financial sacrifices to the Polish guard." The transport leader gave the NCO fourteen hundred Reichsmarks and his wedding ring to insure against further incursions, though this did not prevent the demand for money being repeated once the train reached Kaławsk.[79]

The assembly camps themselves were no safe havens. Originally intended to accommodate expellees for a day or two before their departure, by the autumn of 1946 each was housing thousands of people, often put out to forced labor during the daytime, for weeks or months. The British ambassador, who viewed Szczecin's two assembly camps in April and considered them adequate for a short stay, was dismayed by how far conditions had deteriorated when he revisited one of them in October. "Since I have been promoted to be Ambassador I have smelt many nasty smells, but nothing to equal the immense and over-powering stench of this camp." The commandant confessed to Cavendish-Bentinck that he was unable to feed the long-stay inmates, and that he had been releasing them to try to find work with local employers in exchange for food. The normally Germanophobe ambassador advised Wolski that the camp should be closed down, fumigated, and repaired.[80] In the event this was never done, and the assembly camps continued to be centers of hunger and disease. The resulting mortality was on a significant scale. At the Gumieńce camp in Sczcecin, fifty-two inmates died, "mainly through undernourishment but [in] one or two cases . . . also through frost-bite" in the month of January 1947 alone.[81] Its twin on the northern side of the city, Golęcino (Frauendorf), had to be temporarily closed due to a pair of typhoid fever outbreaks in February and March.[82] Other assembly camps were still worse. Ninety-five inmates died of disease in the month of February at the Dantesque facility at Świdwin, which lacked water, heat, bedding, intact roofs, and medical supplies; as the local PUR medical officer of health reported, "the grounds of the entire camp are atrociously polluted with waste of various kinds, e.g. human excrement." Nearly thirty-five hundred cases of illness were reported from the camp in the same month.[83]

Many MZO and PUR officials on the ground were no more satisfied with the conditions of the assembly camps than the foreign dignitaries and journalists. Captain Edmund Kinsner, a roving MZO camp inspector, discovered massive levels of overcrowding at Wrocław, a facility that he thought was to all appearances being run for the sole benefit of the corrupt camp administration. On the day of his visit in July 1946, there were 4,213 Germans in residence; another 1,778 were admitted before his departure that night. A further 800 expellees were turned away because there was no room for them and told to return to their places of origin, notwithstanding the fact that their homes had already been allocated to Poles. Still another 1,300 were scheduled to arrive the following day. Those admitted, Kinsner reported, were being systematically robbed by representatives of the state Tax Office, who conducted individual searches of the expellees in defiance of MZO regulations.[84] At Świdwin, about 1,000 of the expellees admitted in December 1946 were still there when two MZO officials conducted an inspection the following May.[85] Kazimierz Kuźmicki, Deputy Commissar for German Repatriation Affairs in Wrocław, found that the story was the same in the Lower Silesian assembly camps of Legnica, Jawor, and Świdnica, the population of the last of which grew by more than 500 during the six hours he spent there.[86] Virtually no administration at all, corrupt or otherwise, could, according to Kuźmicki, be discerned at Ząbkowice Śląskie (Frankenstein), a camp with 1,500 inmates. The militia commander theoretically in charge was rarely if ever to be seen; and although his subordinates were conducting an illicit traffic in Reichsmarks confiscated from the expellees, their invariable state of dipsomania rendered them so ungovernable that nothing could be expected of them other than hooliganism and indiscipline.[87]

Lastly, the embarkation points at which the expellees were entrained presented the same general picture of mismanagement, hunger, disease, and ill-treatment The British liaison team at Kaławsk made numerous protests to their Polish counterparts over abuses they had discovered: pregnant women who had been beaten with rubber truncheons by their guards while working as forced laborers laying railway tracks; rapes of female expellees by militiamen; and failure to provide food for those awaiting transport. Although the Inspection Department of the MZO rolled its eyes at these and similar representations by the two British liaison teams, marveling over their insistence on "the most minute details" of the expulsion protocol and their seeming anxiety to take the Germans "under their solicitous protection, to the extent of frequently threatening to withdraw and thereby disrupt the evacuation," Polish officials on the ground conceded the general accuracy of these criticisms.[88] The commandant at Kaławsk compiled a similar list of the problems with which he had to deal for a meeting with the Commissar of German Repatriation Affairs. The militia supposedly providing security were undisciplined, trafficking in currency with or stealing from the Germans. The trains lacked adequate rations and were habitually late and overcrowded. Necessary documents were not provided (both the British and the Poles agreed that trains coming from Wrocław were the worst organized in the whole of Silesia). The infirmary lacked medicines, and officials were often absent from their posts. It was unsurprising, then, that the MZO should have reported with some alarm in August that a "pretty substantial number of deaths of German repatriates" was occurring at Kaławsk, and requested that more careful measures be taken to prevent a possible epidemic there.[89]

Confronted with conditions like these and their inability to do much to alleviate them, morale among the more conscientious expulsion administrators underwent a visible decline. Inspector Kinsner was especially angered by the undisguised contempt for his authority displayed by staff at the assembly camps. Because so many items confiscated from expellees at a facility in Wrocław never featured on the returns submitted to the ministry, he decided to compile his own inventory during an inspection in November 1946. Even as he added items to his list, he reported furiously to his superiors, the camp staff did not hesitate to filch others from under his very nose: in the most blatant example, an electric oven beside which he was standing "grew legs and disappeared" as he gave dictation to his assistant.[90] Inspector Józef Lipiński of the MZO simply turned in his resignation, tired of being robbed on the job by those he was attempting to supervise.[91] The camp staffs, too, had their own grounds for complaint. Militiamen and soldiers at loose ends and lacking money in their pockets quickly discovered that the assembly camps contained unlimited reservoirs of free labor that could be hired out to farmers and other local employers at cut-price rates. Accordingly, they developed a profitable sideline in "sticking up" the camp staff, temporarily kidnapping a few dozen of their inmates, putting them out to manual labor, and drinking the proceeds. In one such incident, two carloads of militiamen swooped upon the Glubczyce camp on the Polish-Czechoslovak border. The raiders in the first vehicle sought out Adam Targosz, the PUR officer in charge, and held him at gunpoint. Their accomplices in the second carried off between forty and fifty of his Germans in trucks and hired them out for work in the fields.[92]

In such an atmosphere of general lawlessness, all kinds of moneymaking schemes and scams proliferated. Inspector Lipiński collected for his own records a "sheaf" of improper *laissez-passers* issued, usually for fat fees, by local officials authorizing their German bearers to proceed independently to railheads at the border.[93] Some camps levied admission charges upon expellees; those who failed to pay up were left to fend for themselves without food or shelter and denied access to transports.[94] At other camps, boxes, carts, or stoves were sold to inmates; confiscated from them hours or days later; and resold to their newly arriving successors.[95] An officer at one of the assembly camps in Wrocław displayed a price list on the wall offering such services as expulsion out of turn, transport in sanitarium cars, and the opportunity to circumvent the mandatory baggage inspection for 500 zlotys all-inclusive. For the more impecunious à la carte expellee, sanitarium car berths alone could be had for 100 zlotys.[96] Less fortunate Germans scheduled for expulsion could find themselves removed from the transports and returned to assembly camps to make room for others who had paid PUR officials to place them at the head of the queue.[97] (This was the principal explanation behind repeated British and Soviet complaints that nominal lists provided with transports failed to tally with the names given by arriving expellees.) Train crews sold, rather than issued, the rations provided for the journey to passengers; on one transport to the Soviet zone, mothers of hungry children were charged up to 120 Reichsmarks ($12) per slice of bread.[98] Polish soldiers extracted payoffs by stopping trains after their departure and threatening to load so many additional Germans into the wagons that the expellees already aboard would be compelled to stand for the entire duration of a journey that could last a week or more, unless they were paid off by the existing passengers.[99] Others persuaded Germans arriving at the camps to turn over any sums of money they still had concealed about their persons by issuing receipts for the currency which, they were promised, could be redeemed at any German bank on arrival. The receipts, needless to say, were worthless.[100]

For venal expulsion officials, however, the most profitable opportunities were to be found in collaborating with Zionist organizations working to circumvent the restrictions imposed by the British authorities on emigration from Europe to Palestine. Despite the virtual annihilation of the Jewish population of central Europe, anti-Semitism remained after the war at pathologically high levels. Nowhere was this more evident than in Poland, where even Ambassador Cavendish-Bentinck appreciatively remarked in September 1945 that "The slaughter of Jews in this country has made the towns a good deal cleaner and has certainly decreased the number of middle-men."[101] Once the war was over, large numbers of Holocaust survivors, facing continued pogroms like the ones at Kielce and Kraków, became convinced that they could never again hope to live in safety in Europe.[102] They therefore sought by every possible means to flee to the Holy Land. The British government, which had administered Palestine under a League of Nations mandate since 1919, was no less determined to prevent them. Fearing a renewal of the violent Arab backlash against further new arrivals that had led to widespread rioting in the 1930s, the British imposed a rigid quota of fifteen hundred Jewish immigrants entering Palestine per month, far below the number who wanted to settle there.

For European and United States–based Zionist bodies alike, the beginning of organized expulsions offered a golden opportunity to transfer the nearly 200,000 surviving Polish Jews to Germany, from whence they could be transported via Italy to Palestine. A Viennese-based underground Jewish agency, the *Bricha*, had already been active in providing money and documents enabling would-be emigrants to pass themselves off as Greek citizens. With the collaboration and financial backing of the American Jewish Joint Distribution Committee, it now began operations on a much larger scale. In Vienna, *Bricha* officials like the future Nazi hunter Simon Wiesenthal recruited collaborators among the occupying forces, humanitarian agencies like UNRRA, and even among the German expellee population themselves, whose local knowledge of the border regions could be put to good use.[103] A Polish *Bricha* leader negotiated a secret agreement with the deputy defense minister in Warsaw, General Marian Spychalski, under which Jews would be allowed to leave the country without exit permits from July 30, 1946.[104] In the three months that followed, more than sixty-six thousand Jews left Poland with the *Bricha*'s assistance. About half were allowed to transit openly through Czechoslovakia, with the connivance of ministers Gottwald and Masaryk, to the U.S. occupation zone of Germany; many of the remainder entered the British zone as bogus "Swallow" expellees.

The possibility that the mass expulsions might be exploited for this purpose had been foreseen by the Western Allies. As early as December 1945, Ernest Bevin had inquired whether Jews had been arriving with the *Sudetendeutsch* expellees entering Austria.[105] Around the same time, Robin Hankey of the British

Embassy in Warsaw recommended threatening the Polish government with a postponement of Swallow unless it took effective action to prevent Jewish "infiltration."[106] The problem, though, did not seem urgent; and it was not until the second half of May 1946, after the Polish prime minister, Edward Osóbka-Morawki, publicly declared that the government would place no obstacles in the way of Jews seeking to leave the country, that the exodus commenced in appreciable numbers. On May 26 the British vice consul in Szczecin reported widespread "consternation" among Polish colonists in the town at the number of Jews arriving from the lands east of the Bug.[107] The Gentile settlers' dismay was held in check, however, by the belief that the Jews would quickly leave for the west. This expectation was justified, and within a matter of weeks the British liaison teams began reporting the arrival of spurious expellees on a large scale. As a Military Government officer complained,

> this detachment has been placed in an embarrassing position by the arrival of Jews from Poland bearing certificates signed by the so-called Jewish Committee of Breslau certifying that these Poles are Germans.... Some of the Jews sent here by this Committee can hardly speak German yet they carry papers signed by this Jewish Committee stating that they are Germans and, in some cases, that they left Germany because of Hitler's attitude to the Jews.
>
> It is significant that, whereas practically all Germans entering the British Zone have been denuded of their valuables and new or almost new clothing, these Jews arrive in a state of comparative opulence. This present batch of 30 Jews who travelled in one wagon from New Poland had very extensive wardrobes composed of absolutely new materials. The men were carrying an average of one dozen new shirts each in addition to silk pyjamas, silk underwear and silk handkerchiefs. The women were equally well catered for with silk underwear, silk stockings, etc. All were absolutely firm in their statements that they had passed through the Polish customs at Kaławsk and that no item of finery had been taken from them.[108]

Not all Jewish would-be emigrants were in so fortunate a condition. Major Boothby ejected 252 Jews from one train at Kaławsk with considerable reluctance, noting that "their sufferings over the past years were only too apparent."[109] These persons, though, had attempted to cross without credentials identifying them as Germans, and were easily detected. It was a mistake the *Bricha* did not repeat. Later parties of supposed expellees were supplied with "forged papers on a vast scale"—so many, indeed, that the embarrassment of documentary riches occasionally had unfortunate results. "When I turned 40 Viennese Jews off a train a Polish-Jewish Officer came to me and said that they had only showed

Austrian papers because they thought they would get better treatment that way. Might they now show me their German papers? They remained Austrians."[110]

For every party turned back, though, dozens more were able to proceed without interference. A British officer investigating the influx considered that the "organisation of parties is a masterpiece in an almost completely disrupted country like Poland." Payment on a lavish scale, in sterling and dollars, smoothed the emigrants' path out of the country and across states of transit like Czechoslovakia and Hungary. So efficient, indeed, was the Jewish network that "many Polish Gentiles of a normally considered good type of citizen . . . [who] cannot obtain visas in the normal way . . . have been known to get them and leave the country by applying under Jewish names!"[111] Although the numbers of "infiltrators" escaping Poland by these means were comparatively modest when set against the total number of Swallow expellees—probably fewer than fifty thousand in total—the realization that nearly all were likely to end up in Palestine caused the British authorities to expend a great deal of energy in trying to check the influx. It did not take them long to confirm the existence of an elaborate and well-funded organization behind the sudden upsurge in Jews masquerading as Germans. Servicemen in the Polish, Czechoslovak, British, and U.S. armies, as well as UNRRA and Red Cross officials, were discreetly scrutinized for indications that they were recipients of *Bricha* largesse. Military intelligence cast suspicion on the commanding officer of the British liaison team at Szczecin on account of his Jewishness. But the authorities found it more difficult to convert suspicions into proof. All efforts to obtain definite information, the chief of the British Army's Intelligence Division in Germany fulminated in July 1946, had failed because "the moment an investigation comes into non-Aryan [*sic*] hands a blank wall is reached."[112]

Even if inquiries had proven more successful, cutting off the flow would have been far from easy. When the problem was first addressed in the winter of 1945–46, Sir George Rendel of the Foreign Office Refugee Department, who feared that if Warsaw was allowed to get away with sending fake Jewish expellees to Germany, it and other central European governments would rapidly unleash a tidal wave of "undesirables" on the British zone, had advocated a hard line. Should eastern European Jews succeed in reaching Germany as expellees, he said, they should be treated as such and held in transit camps alongside the *Volksdeutsche*. It was true that this would have the unfortunate consequence of detaining them alongside "people who had persecuted them in the past," but such measures might prove "the most effective deterrent to further unauthorised movement."[113] As other officials pointed out, though, quite apart from its impracticality—in July 1946 there were already almost two thousand ex-Swallow Jewish residents of the Hohne (Bergen-Belsen) displaced persons camp alone, who could hardly be made to leave other than by arresting them—the idea of according Holocaust survivors "treatment no more favourable than that accorded to the defeated enemy" would infallibly set off a firestorm of international criticism.[114]

An indication of the sensitivity of the Jewish question was provided by a series of cloak-and-dagger meetings between British and U.S. officers in the summer of 1946 to exchange information about the involvement of Allied and UNRRA personnel overseeing the expulsions in people smuggling. The American colonel participating in the discussions said that "the U.S. Authorities considered the subject so delicate that he was not allowed to put anything on paper." Lieutenant General Sir Brian Robertson, deputy military governor of the British zone, found that this apprehensiveness extended to the highest level when he gave his American counterpart, General Lucius D. Clay, the name of a U.S. Army officer believed by British intelligence to be working for the *Bricha*. A nervous Clay confirmed that the name of the officer concerned was known to him and promised to do what he could to prevent infiltration via expulsion trains, but "emphasized throughout that his instructions precluded any drastic action on his part towards Jewish refugees."[115] The British were unimpressed by what they saw as American pusillanimity in the face of Zionist pressure—Colonel Ralph Thicknesse, a senior officer administering Operation Swallow, had already placed on record his belief that the U.S. authorities' stance in the matter was "ostensibly directed by the principles of protectors of the oppressed but in fact more probably by the power of their own Jewish-controlled newspapers"—but ultimately thought that the only solution was a complete end to organized expulsions.

Officials in the U.S. zone, for their part, were independently coming to the same conclusion. According to conventional wisdom, transfers from Czechoslovakia were the best-organized of the three major expulsion operations from the "Potsdam" countries. The shortness of the distance to be traversed simplified the process, and meant that some of the worst consequences associated with crowding masses of expellees without food or water into carriages for journeys in adverse weather conditions that might last for weeks were avoided. By and large this is correct. In a significant number of cases, however, reports from U.S. and Czechoslovak officers on the ground tell a story that in some respects was not materially different from what had already been seen with Operation Swallow.

The principal obstacle to a streamlined expulsion process in Czechoslovakia was the extraordinary degree of bureaucratic infighting and interagency conflict that marked the operation. At the outset, the Ministry of the Interior claimed precedence in organizing the expulsions, setting up a special section for the purpose headed by Dr. Antonín Kučera, counselor of the ministry. It was to oversee the selection of the Germans; assemble them in camps; and see that the necessary documentation, medical inspection, and personal baggage for each expellee required by the U.S. and Soviet authorities was in order. The Ministry of National Defense, represented by Colonel František Dastich, would be responsible for shipment across the border and for coordinating transports with the principal liaison officers for expulsions to the U.S. and Soviet zones, Colonel Fye and General S. N. Gorochov respectively. In practice, it proved impossible to prevent almost every ministry of the Czech government from demanding a say in the conduct of the expulsions. The young, energetic, and highly ambitious Communist head of the Settlement Office of the Czech Lands, Miroslav Kreysa, responsible for overseeing the colonization of the vacated Sudetenland, had his own ideas about the order in which removals of Germans should proceed, independent of the Interior Ministry of which his office was nominally a part.[116] The Ministry of Agriculture was concerned both with the timing of German transfers, so as not to interrupt the crop-growing cycle, and the process of redistributing farmland to incoming colonists. The Ministry of Social Welfare and Labor Protection was often at odds with the Ministries of the Interior and National Defense, which it accused of taking an unnecessarily hard line with regard to especially vulnerable expellees and thereby damaging Czechoslovakia's image abroad. The Ministry of Health was concerned about the possibility of epidemics spreading from camps and ghettoes crowded with diseased Germans, and the disruption caused to the health sector by the loss of so many highly trained German doctors and nurses. The Ministry of Justice opposed the expulsion of suspected war criminals, or persons who might be called as witnesses in trials. The economic ministries— Finance, Industry, Internal Trade, and Foreign Trade—fretted about disruption caused to Czechoslovakia's precarious postwar recovery. The Office of the Prime Minister considered itself entitled to give instructions to all the other agencies. And at the bottom of the Czechoslovak administrative pyramid, Provincial, District, and Municipal National Committees attempted to comply with, ignored, or openly subverted the torrent of directives—often mutually contradictory— that cascaded upon them from above.

Compounding these difficulties was the fact that, as previously mentioned, the actual expulsion protocols with the U.S. and Soviet authorities were not concluded until just before the movements into the two zones were to begin, in January and June 1946, respectively. As a result, a great deal of the early planning was wasted, as it was based on scenarios that failed to materialize. The location of some assembly camps, for example, was decided at a time when some elements of the Ministry of National Defense were thinking in terms of an expulsion operation that would be completed in thirty to forty days, along routes the U.S. and Soviet authorities would not ultimately use.[117] Logistical difficulties also compelled last-minute changes of plan. Due to a shortage of covered wagons, the Czechoslovaks were forced during the early summer to set down expellees at Pirna and Plauen in the Soviet zone, only six to ten miles across the border, rather than carry them to the originally agreed disembarkation point at Gera, forty miles further on.[118] OMGUS officials, on the other hand, found a different solution to the problem of obtaining sufficient rolling stock. Because a very high proportion of Czechoslovakia's own freight wagons were being used by the Soviets to carry German booty back to the USSR or to transport units of the Red Army, the Americans turned to the only significant remaining source: the freight trains employed by UNRRA to carry aid supplies into Czechoslovakia. In the spring of 1946, these were pressed into service to transport the expellees to the U.S. zone. Not only did this diversion of UNRRA resources from the humanitarian purpose for which they had been provided contravene the organization's charter, which limited its activities to "the administration of measures for the relief of victims of war," but the logistical tangles affecting the expulsion program soon ensnared UNRRA as well. By early April, according to U.S. figures, no fewer than six thousand UNRRA freight cars were stranded in Czechoslovakia.[119]

As in Poland, the process of removal was also impeded from below, especially by the expansive interpretation Czechoslovak employers often gave to the definition of "essential worker." Examples included a sixty-five-year-old man with bilateral hernias employed as a "miner"; doormen, maids, and chauffeurs classified as "indispensable labor"; and workers in a knife factory in Mikulášovice whose services were said to be vital to the Czechoslovak economy.[120] The manufacturing sector, Dr. Kučera alleged in June 1946, was deliberately trying to obstruct or delay the transfers.[121] *Rudé právo* too claimed that numerous cases still existed of Czechoslovaks concealing Germans from the authorities.[122] Often enough, though, the government griped about the opposite problem: the carelessness of overzealous army units or District National Committees which indiscriminately threw out all the Germans of a particular locality without sparing a thought for the impact on production.

On the whole, the number of expellee deaths occurring in transit was much lower in Czechoslovakia than in the Recovered Territories. This was not only the result of shorter distances to travel, but also of the fact that the operation began in the relatively mild winter of 1945–46 and was largely completed before the far harsher conditions of 1946–47 set in. Nonetheless, the very fact that so many transports were trying to pass along a very few rail routes led to enormous bottlenecks. When expulsions to the Soviet zone commenced in June, trains were taking four days to complete the eighty-mile round trip from Tršnice to Plauen or Pirna, most of which was spent waiting to be allowed to cross the border.[123] Congestion on the routes to the U.S. zone grew so severe that a shuttle service was established in May using fifty cars to transport *Sudetendeutsch* antifascists by road and deposit them on the far side of the zonal boundary.[124] With few undamaged railway lines available, the Ministry of National Defense was forced to bring ever more circuitous routes, like the 220-mile Cheb-to-Bebra link which transited the Soviet occupation zone, into operation to meet their daily targets. Though this made for increasingly long journey times, transports taking more than a couple of days were comparative rarities during the "organized expulsions" of 1946, a marked contrast to the weeks-long odysseys that had often occurred the previous year.

This does not mean that the expulsions from Czechoslovakia came close to satisfying the criteria laid down in the Potsdam Agreement, or those of the protocols concluded with the U.S. and Soviet authorities. As a rule they did not. A retrospective assessment by General Karel Klapálek in December 1946 of the transfer to the Soviet zone identified many shortcomings that had never been overcome (predictably, Klapálek blamed all of these on the deficiencies of the Ministry of the Interior). A very large number of *Sudetendeutsche* had been transported while suffering from infectious diseases contracted in the camps: at the Meziměstí assembly camp in eastern Moravia, up to five inmates were dying of disease each week in January 1946.[125] Trains were persistently dispatched with insufficient rations for the journey, something of which the Red Army complained repeatedly. Endless difficulties had arisen with the composition of trains, with unusable, incompatible, or obsolete wagons being supplied. This had often made it impossible to transport expellees' baggage, eliciting another flood of protests from the Soviet authorities.[126] Other official reports spoke of systematic pillage of expellees by both military and civilian personnel; of ethnic Czechs and Slovaks being included in the transports; and of continued unauthorized expulsions by local authorities under the guise of "voluntary transfers."

OMGUS officials had their own lengthy list of grievances to present. The Expulsion Officer at Furth im Wald, Captain H. W. Lambert, gained a particularly comprehensive insight into the many ingenious methods particular District National Committees, as well as the Czechoslovak government and army, used to conceal their violations of the protocols. Like the British, U.S. observers were immediately struck by the high percentage of unemployables arriving in the transports from Czechoslovakia. A preliminary survey in June 1946 found that "not more than 15% were men of 15 years or over and capable of work"; by the time the operation was concluded, the number of able-bodied and skilled workers who had been included in the expulsions was described as "ridiculously low."[127] The conclusion that productive individuals were being held back in violation of the requirement that families not be separated was obvious; according to U.S. estimates, this was happening in up to a third of all cases. One of the principal loopholes Czechoslovak authorities exploited was the provision in the agreement that any German sentenced to prison sentences of more than a year for war crimes was not to be considered as having been "held back"; instead, the rest of the family would be admitted to the U.S. zone on production of a certificate from the court attesting to the conviction of the missing family member. Captain Lambert remarked upon the curious fact that trains from districts like Bruntál always contained an exceptionally high proportion of such families, and that "in the majority of cases the men were skilled workers who were sentenced just before the families were expelled. Stranger still, they continued to work at their trades in their same positions while serving the prison terms." In some cases the District National Committees did not even bother to provide a copy of the court record, merely supplying a note promising that the missing individual would be convicted at some point in the future. U.S. officials found that rejecting such families for admission was pointless, as they "would be shipped again with the next train and with the proper papers, thus mainly working a hardship on the expellees. The Czech authorities always went to some length to point this out."[128]

Even more frequently, expellees were coached to lie about the reason for separated family members' absence, on pain of severe punishment if they failed to convince the U.S. inspectors. In May 1946, for example, U.S. officials refused to accept Anna Laner and her daughter Maria, expellees from Olomouc, because records showed that a teenage son, Ludwig, had been kept in Czechoslovakia presumably for labor services. Two weeks later, the two Laner women were again presented at the border post. On this occasion they pleaded not to be returned because "they had been threatened by the Czech officials and told that if they insisted upon having the son evacuated with them disciplinary action would be taken."[129] On another occasion Lambert interrupted a Czechoslovak army officer, Staff Captain Meitner, in the act of instructing German car leaders "to tell any separated families in their cars that if questioned they were to state that the retained member was either dead or missing."[130] As Colonel Fye reported, expellees were reminded at such briefings that "If any complaints were made it would go hard with the car leader."[131]

Similar too were the tales of venality and corruption associated with the operation. A Czech expulsion officer discovered two Prague lawyers to be selling entry permits with which expellees could enter the U.S. zone independently for fifteen hundred crowns each; the permits themselves appeared to have been provided by an equally shady American partner.[132] The commandant of the main camp at Liberec, one of the very worst Czechoslovak detention centers, worked out an ingenious scheme for enriching himself by forbidding expellees to take any baggage on their journey, instead requiring them to use a commercial shipping agency in the town and pay "customs charges" on the property. The shipments were never made; when the agency was pursued for two trainloads of expellee baggage, it said that it had dispatched them to the border, where they had all been confiscated by the SNB. The agency produced a "receipt" to that effect, declaring that it considered itself to have fulfilled its part of the contract. The same misfortune occurred to other shipments using the same firm.[133] On the other hand, valuables that ought not to have been on expellee trains sometimes were there — as when the U.S. authorities discovered, through intercepted telephone calls, that the transports were being used by an international currency smuggling ring to move laundered money across the border.[134]

The composition of "expellee" transports had an all too familiar ring. Indeed, an even more heterogeneous cross-section of the central and southeastern European population was to be found on the Czechoslovak trains than on the Polish or Hungarian ones. Lieutenant Colonel Edgar Jordan of the Office of Military Government in Bavaria conducted a check at the Freilassing border crossing of train no. 7315-A, said to contain 1,265 *Sudetendeutsche*. In reality fewer than half were from the Sudetenland; the train also carried 256 Yugoslav *Volksdeutsche*, 126 Germans from the Recovered Territories, 70 Swabians from Romania, 20 Soviet *Volksdeutsche*, and 94 assorted *Reichsdeutsche* bound for zones other than the American. Train no. 7527-A, spot-checked at the same place nine days later, featured an even more exotic cross-section of humanity, with genuine *Sudetendeutsche* representing fewer than one in four of the persons on board.[135] In view of the fact that at least half the complements of Czechoslovak expellee trains destined for Soviet-occupied Germany absconded while transiting the U.S. zone, the American CRX representative lugubriously concluded that a situation of virtual open borders prevailed, making a nonsense of any attempt to achieve demographic balance between the districts controlled by the four occupying powers.[136]

Once again, though, the factor that gave rise to the greatest tensions between expelling and receiving states was the condition in which the deportees were reaching their destination. Though fewer new arrivals in the U.S. zone died or had to be sent to hospital because of the rigors of the journey, the gain to American military authorities was small if, through systematic abuse or long detention in internment camps, they needed emergency medical treatment on arrival in any event. A transport from Jablonec to Furth im Wald in April 1946, the Americans recorded, consisted of expellees in a "terrible" condition, some having been reduced to mere "skeletons." As a consequence of their stay in one of the Liberec camps, where they had nothing to drink but stagnant water from pools on the ground, 70 percent of these *Sudetendeutsche* arrived suffering from severe diarrhea and some were expected to die of the consequences of starvation in the near future.[137] Even with immediate medical attention, such deaths were far from unusual. A Red Cross medical report, for example, noted that two weeks of hospital treatment had not been sufficient to prevent the death from starvation of a forty-five-year-old male expellee from one of the early Czechoslovak transports who had spent the previous ten months in an internment camp.[138]

One category of expellee, the so-called "antifascists," did benefit from preferential treatment. Although opponents of Nazism were theoretically exempted from removal, the difficulty was easily overcome by making their willingness "voluntarily" to be transferred to Germany, "on the ground that they are needed there to reeducate the people," the test of their antifascist credentials.[139] In view of the fact that the Czechoslovak Ministry of National Defense had ruled as early as July 28, 1945 that all inquiries to determine Germans' antifascist record were to be discontinued, and of the discovery by groups like the Wrocław antifascist committee that "the Poles wanted them out of town, plain and simple, and were not interested in the Germans' help in rebuilding an antifascist Poland," there was little point in seeking to remain.[140] Instead, by submitting to the inevitable, "antifascists" could at least qualify for more favorable conditions of removal. In Slovakia, proven "antifascists" might be exempted from internment in the camps and allowed to proceed directly to the railway stations on the day of departure.[141] Czechoslovak "antifascist" transports normally carried just three hundred expellees on each train, rather than the twelve to fifteen hundred that was the typical complement. Occasionally "antifascists" were allowed to organize their own transport. An enterprising Wrocław German, Paul Eggers, operated in cooperation with the Commissariat for Repatriation Affairs for Lower Silesia an "enormously popular" coach service from the city center to the border crossing at Zgorzelec. For a fare of fifteen hundred zlotys, passengers could travel in relative comfort, benefiting from a baggage allowance of two suitcases and a backpack and protected by an escort of three soldiers or militiamen. The service came to an end at Christmas 1945, however, when the Soviet authorities suspended admissions to their zone for the winter.[142]

There were, though, definite limits to the indulgence of the expelling and receiving countries alike. The Czechoslovaks, for example, used the "antifascist" transports as a means of recycling the five-hundred-Reichsmark allowance without which expellees would not be permitted to enter the U.S. zone. Passengers were warned before departure that if they did not agree to give back the cash, they would be returned to an internment camp and eventually expelled on a "normal" transport under much less favorable conditions. Once the train had cleared the U.S. inspection point and had entered Germany, a designated person would retrieve the money from his fellow passengers and deliver it to the offices of the Social Democratic Party in Munich, from whence it would be transferred to the Antifascist Central Office in Prague to secure the admission of a fresh trainload of expellees.[143] Not only were the benefits of "antifascist" status less favorable than they appeared, then, but those receiving this designation were regarded on all sides with particular suspicion. The "preferential treatment, such as unlimited baggage allowance," they received aroused "resentment toward them on the part of ordinary expellees," who speculated darkly about how far the extent of their cooperation with the expelling governments might have gone.[144] In the reception areas, "antifascists" were also viewed as being especially untrustworthy, although for opposite reasons. Colonel John Fye warned his superiors that "among them were Communists who will try to undermine and destroy all western influence in U.S. occupied Germany." The authorities in East Berlin, contrariwise, regarded them as "voluntary" migrants who deserved no special privileges. Thus the Wrocław "antifascists," after experiencing a "difficult and humiliating" transport to the Soviet zone, experienced a frosty welcome from local KPD officials and "subsequent confinement in the former Buchenwald concentration camp" before eventually being resettled in Weimar and Halle.[145]

As 1946, the year of "organized expulsions," began drawing to a close, each of the Big Three was feeling the strain. "At present," Colonel Thicknesse warned, "we tend to regard occupied Germany as a waste-paper basket with a limitless capacity for the unwanted waste of the world. We are not convinced that this attitude is correct, either economically or politically."[146] According to figures reported to CRX, by November the Soviet zone had admitted more than 1.8 million expellees from Poland and Czechoslovakia; the U.S. zone approximately 1.7 million from Czechoslovakia and Hungary (including 160,000 who had arrived via Austria); and the British zone more than 1.3 million from the Recovered Territories: a cumulative total of almost five million people. To this figure could be added a number which could not be precisely calculated—but certainly one in the hundreds of thousands for each occupation zone—of *Volksdeutsche* who had made their way under duress out of their countries of origin, but entered Germany as unregistered "infiltrees." All were arriving in a country whose urban centers the Western Allies had gone to immense trouble and expense during the previous five years to level to the ground, an endeavor in which they had enjoyed considerable success and which had left Germany with "a worse housing problem than has ever before existed in any area of comparable size and population."[147] Even after every available camp, military base, school, church, barn, air raid shelter, and, in some cases, cave had been filled with expellees, the onrushing human tide continued to overwhelm the best efforts of the rudimentary German administration upon whose shoulders the occupying forces thrust the responsibility. As a rule, according to reception officers in all three occupation zones, the expellees were arriving in possession of little more than the—usually insufficient—clothing in which they stood. The overwhelming majority were women and children. Few could make any meaningful contribution in the short term to their own support. Hundreds of thousands needed immediate care, in hospitals, old-age homes, orphanages, or residential centers for the disabled, though the shortage of resources meant that a great many would not receive it.

This was not at all how the Allies had envisaged the population transfers when they had been sold on the idea during the war. Then the stated rationale had been to remove a cohort of "dangerous" Germans—above all, fit men of military age—who might threaten the security of the countries in which they lived. Instead, it had been the least dangerous Germans who had been deported, while the fit men were being held back for forced labor, and in many cases pressured to take out Polish or Czechoslovak nationality against their will. The occupying powers thus found themselves presented with a first-class social, economic, and humanitarian crisis that threatened to undo whatever plans they had made for German reconstruction, as well as to disrupt the economies of the expelling states for years to come. Predictably, each of the Big Three with the benefit of experience discovered its enthusiasm for this novel method of "stabilizing" the European continent shrinking to the vanishing point. After coping—or failing to cope—with the "wild expulsions" of 1945, and finding the "organized expulsions" of 1946 from their perspective to be less satisfactory yet, each of the Allied powers entered 1947 with the same overriding objective: to put an end to what was proving an intolerable burden to it as quickly as possible.

7

THE NUMBERS GAME

The screams that alerted Dr. Loch, formerly the chief medical officer of St Joseph's Hospital in Wrocław, that his services were required at the other end of the pitch-black cattle car provided his only means of locating his patient. As a skilled worker the doctor was not supposed to have been on the train, as it jolted across the darkened Polish countryside on the night of December 20, 1946 en route to the Marienthal reception center in the British occupation zone. His sick wife, however, had been scheduled for deportation, and rather than waiting his turn and being separated from her, he had elected to become a "wild repatriant" and smuggled himself on board the transport.[1] As he clambered over fellow expellees, piles of baggage, and buckets that were being used in lieu of toilets, his path was blocked by an old woman who ignored his request to move out of the way. On closer examination, the doctor found that she had frozen to death. Having no time to spare on her, he struggled onward until he eventually reached his patient, a pregnant woman who had gone into premature labor.

> She was bleeding a great deal. When I tried to get her into a more comfortable position, I discovered that she was frozen to the floor with her own blood. Someone still had a little spirit-lamp. With its help we prepared some hot water from pieces of ice. After sprinkling hot water for some time I managed to get the unfortunate woman free. With the exception of a hypodermic syringe and some blood-stanching preparation that happened to be at hand, I had nothing of what was necessary for such an operation, not even cotton-wool. By means of an injection I managed to stop the bleeding. That was all I could do. During the task my own feet all but froze.
>
> Whether the woman lived, I do not know. In view of the tremendous amount [of work] that fell upon we doctors, I lost sight of her.[2]

Most of Dr. Loch's fellow passengers were scarcely less vulnerable. Of the 1,543 expellees from Poznań and Łódź crammed into the train, 600 were over sixty years of age. Many more were babies in arms aged between three and twelve months; twenty-two were children from an orphanage in Leszno. They had boarded the train five days previously, when the temperature was already minus fifteen degrees centigrade, to find that the cattle trucks into which they were herded contained neither any form of heating nor straw to cover the floor. During the four and a half days it took to complete the 240-mile journey to Marienthal, each passenger received a daily ration consisting of three ounces of bread, two-fifths of an ounce of barley, one-fifth of an ounce of sugar, a twelfth of an ounce of coffee, and a fifteenth of an ounce of salt. A single herring was to be shared between each group of twenty-five. The intense cold meant that there was no liquid water to drink; mothers placed vessels filled with ice between their thighs in an attempt to thaw the contents and assuage their children's thirst. Rations on such a scale provided little nutrition to ward off hypothermia and, as the temperature fell further, the very old and the very young began to die. As one woman recalled:

> Up to 40 people were packed into one truck. It got colder and colder. In the mornings our luggage, hair and the whole truck were covered with a thick layer of frost. Our breath froze in the air.
> The truck leader was an old man. He was always trying to cheer us up. After we had passed Sagan, we were still singing Christmas carols with him in the evening. The next morning the truck leader was dead. Nobody had noticed how he died. So I became truck leader. I could not possibly do anything.

When the train finally reached Marienthal on the evening of December 21, the bodies of sixteen people who had died of the cold were removed. There had been three live births and two miscarriages en route.[3] Fifty-three passengers required immediate hospitalization for frostbite, with six emergency amputations being performed. Major E. M. Tobin, the commanding officer at Marienthal, thought that the passengers seemed "to have been living an existence of cowed servitude and gave more the impression of whipped curs than human beings." Even in comparison to earlier transports, the train carried "a remarkably high percentage of old people and cripples. The degree of infirmity of these cripples was also very high."[4] Marienthal, however, possessed no accommodation of its own, and after disinfecting the expellees and giving them a hot meal the British military authorities returned them to the cattle cars for onward transport to their ultimate destinations. Sixteen more would die by the time the train reached Hameln, with another 130 taken to hospital. At Runteln 27 additional passengers were removed for medical treatment. When the train arrived at its terminus at

Bückeburg in Lower Saxony on December 23, a week after its departure, 141 of the remainder were immediately hospitalized. Before the end of February, a further 26 passengers had succumbed to the after-effects of their ordeal. Among the dead was the wife of Dr. Loch.

It can hardly be said that the Wrocław train was an accident waiting to happen, because in the previous weeks, a series of transports had passed through Marienthal in little better condition. On December 7 and 8, for example, a party of 1,853 Swallow expellees from Lubań in Silesia, including 459 children, had been ordered by the Polish authorities to assemble at Ujazd near the border town of Zgorzelec for transport to Germany. The train that was to take them there, however, failed to show up until December 11, with the expellees being forced to wait for it in an open field for up to four days and nights. It had rained for much of the time, and upon boarding all were soaked to the skin. The temperature then fell well below the freezing point. Three days later on the morning of the fourteenth, Major Tobin received word that an expellee train was stranded on a siding at Eilsleben in the Soviet zone, lacking an engine. He gave instructions that if it proved to be the missing Zgorzelec transport it should be brought to Marienthal without further delay. By 1700 hours, having heard nothing further, he sent his staff, who had been standing by since 0630, home. Three hours later Tobin was informed that the train was about to enter the British zone. With no staff to hand, Tobin ordered that it be halted at Barmke overnight until the reception center reopened. The train arrived at Marienthal the next morning at 0900 hours, having taken four days to cover the 230 miles from Zgorzelec. One hundred nine of the passengers were frostbitten—the youngest a five-month-old girl—resulting in fifteen emergency amputations. Major Tobin personally inspected two frostbitten babies, who had been healthy at Zgorzelec where their mothers had wrapped them in blankets, "but they had been caught in the rain and on the train journey the moisture in the blankets had turned to ice." On this occasion too, the Marienthal camp staff had admitted the twelve worst cases to the hospital at nearby Helmstedt and placed the remainder back on the train for another day's journey to their ultimate destinations, reasoning that an additional twenty-four hours would do the passengers no further harm and that there was no room for more patients at Helmstedt in any event.[5] Again, Tobin spoke with some of the expellees on the platform. "Their morale was at the lowest possible point and one man confessed that he had not even the energy to commit suicide." Nonetheless, because his only options were "to eject them *in situ* or to return them to the freezing wilderness from which they had come," Tobin believed that he had "no real alternative but to accept trains once they had been despatched."[6]

The suffering of the expellees on the Marienthal transports, which was publicized extensively in the German and British press, gave administrators in London and Lübbecke what they had been long seeking—an opportunity to shut down Operation Swallow for good. The truculent attitude taken by the Polish authorities, which issued an official statement claiming that "records signed by the British liaison teams confirmed the receipt of the transport in good order" and disclaiming "any responsibility whatever for transports" once they had been approved by the British, reinforced them in their determination to do so.[7] It would not be correct, though, to conclude that the conscience of the authorities had suddenly been awakened by these ugly scenes. While the privations experienced by expellees traveling from Poland may have been distressing to contemplate, they were no worse than their predecessors in the early spring of 1946 had already undergone. Nor were they worse than what Germans being transferred to the Soviet zone were simultaneously enduring, out of sight of the Western media. On December 16, for example, a expellee train left the Gumieńce assembly camp in Szczecin, bound for Stendal west of Berlin, about 160 miles away. Most of the passengers, after their stay in Polish camps, were emaciated to the point of starvation, covered in lice, and suffering from a variety of infectious diseases. During their five-day ordeal, their misery was exacerbated by third-degree frostbite. By the time the train reached Wriezen just across the German border, eighteen were already dead. Twenty-one more frozen corpses were offloaded when the train finally reached its destination, and a total of 248 seriously ill people were admitted to hospital, most at Stendal, by December 21.[8]

What had changed by the end of 1946, then, was not the degree of suffering caused to the expellees, but the enthusiasm of British administrators and politicians for a project that was creating an accelerating, open-ended, and ruinously expensive social crisis in their occupation zone, for which taxpayers at home would have to pick up the bill. Ever since the summer of 1946, British Military Government officers had been casting about for a suitable pretext that would enable them to put an end to Operation Swallow. The few dozen deaths that occurred in the Marienthal transports of December 1946—a drop in the ocean compared to the number that had already occurred as a result of the entire expulsion process over the previous eighteen months—finally permitted them to do so.

When the idea of terminating Swallow first began to be seriously discussed in July 1946, officials in the British occupation zone made no bones about the fact that the administrative and financial burdens the expulsions were placing upon them, rather than humanitarian concerns over the fate of the expellees, were uppermost in their minds. From all sides within the zone, alarming reports had been streaming in about the "impossible situation" Military Government officers were confronting in trying to deal with the influx from Poland. As soon as the ACC agreement was signed, the French delegation had warned that by the summer of 1946, expulsions from the three "Potsdam" countries of Poland, Czechoslovakia, and Hungary would require the diversion of eighteen hundred trains a month to the operation. It wondered whether "the use of so considerable a quantity of additional trains is not apt to handicap seriously other essential transport in Germany and even in Europe."[9] The British now found these predictions to be coming true before their eyes. Not only were desperately needed transport resources going to waste in shuttling expellees across international borders, but once arrived in Germany the rolling stock was being tied up for extended periods by dispersal trains having to make "long circuits dropping small numbers of expellees in different *Kreise* [counties]." The need for these was occasioned by the acute shortage of accommodation—which, ironically, was worsened by the refusal of Polish displaced persons in Germany to go home. Even where houses existed, the inadequacy of water or drainage facilities appropriate to the excessive number of occupants now being accommodated in them was giving rise to the "grave danger" of epidemics.[10] Because of the high proportion of sick, abused, or infirm expellees, "all asylums and hospitals in the Zone [were] full to overflowing."[11] Of more than a million expellees that had arrived in 1946 from Poland by official or unofficial means, only seventy-seven thousand were adult men capable of work.[12] For their part, the American authorities were experiencing similar difficulties with the simultaneous transfers from Czechoslovakia. As early as April 1946, the U.S. representative in the Manpower Directorate of the ACC officially complained that the Prague government had "refused to allow German miners and other skilled workers to leave Czechoslovakia with the rest of the expelled German population." By midsummer the problem of the Czechoslovaks sending "exclusively non-productive" expellees to the U.S. zone had become so acute that the Americans demanded that a minimum of one able-bodied person be included in every family group destined for removal.[13] These appeals were unanswered. Instead, Colonel John Fye, the U.S. liaison officer for expulsions in Prague, found that "the majority of the Czech field force, the local National Committees, the SNB, the assembly camp commanders and supervisors, simply ignored the numerous directives and strong letters issued by the Czech Expellee Section demanding that the conditions of the Czech-OMGUS agreements be carefully adhered to in the handling of the Sudeten shipments." Not only were "flagrant violations of the transfer agreement" occurring, but OMG officers had found "deliberate attempts to deceive the American authorities and threats to the expellees by the commissioners of certain districts if they complained while in Czechoslovakia."[14]

The idea of calling a halt to Swallow in the summer of 1946 was seriously considered at the highest levels of the British Government. At the end of July John Hynd, the chancellor of the Duchy of Lancaster whose responsibilities included the British occupation zone in Germany, presented a paper to the Cabinet's Overseas Reconstruction Committee pointing out that the situation in the British zone was "gradually reaching a condition of over-crowding such as has never been experienced before" in an urban and industrial society. The time, he thought, had "now come when stronger measures should be considered."[15] Although the minister was unaware of it, they already had been. A short time previously, British Military Government officers learned that their counterparts in the United States zone had negotiated a reduced rate of inflow of *Sudetendeutsch* expellees, from 7,200 to 4,800 daily with effect from July 15.[16] Encouraged by this example, British administrators in the occupation zone resolved that it was preferable to ask for forgiveness than permission. On July 26 they imposed a unilateral reduction in the number of expellees accepted from Poland, from 8,000 to 5,000 a day. At the same time, British liaison teams were instructed that "under no circumstances are they to accept for the British zone any expellees from institutions, bedridden inmates, parties of lunatics, orphans etc., non German Jews."[17] When a startled Lieutenant Colonel Ford of CRX queried this instruction, pointing out that it appeared to contravene the Anglo-Polish agreement on population transfers of the previous February, he was sharply told, "Your refusals must be outright, firm and frank. Humanity must not enter into the question."[18] A similar answer was given to Major Boothby at Kaławsk, who was worried that the Kielce pogrom, in which many Holocaust survivors had been shot and beaten to death by Polish civilians and security personnel the previous month, might be the prelude to a nationwide massacre of Polish Jews. Boothby asked for instructions as to what to do if a trainload of Jewish refugees should turn up seeking to flee the country via the expulsion routes. He too was ordered, if that situation arose, "to make every endeavour to stop the train and have it returned to Poland."[19]

In light of what seemed a state of near-panic among British administrators in Germany, officials in London ignored the slight to their authority and allowed the cutbacks to stand. But they were unwilling to close down Swallow altogether, in spite of importunate pleas from Military Government personnel to do just that. The Germans from the Recovered Territories, occupation zone administrators argued, could not make "any contribution to their own upkeep or to any reconstruction of Germany by reason of their deplorable physical and economic conditions." As a result, "we are carrying out a scheme exceptionally disadvantageous to the British Zone and which has now become an intolerable burden."[20] This was the view of some Foreign Office officials also. As Andrew Franklin of the German Department bluntly put it, "the population transferred was largely human wreckage" that would become a permanent burden on the British taxpayer.[21] But in spite of these remonstrances on the ground in Germany, the final verdict was that the acceptance of expellees must continue, even if on a much reduced scale. In the first place, the transfer of Germans was "the only point on which all parties in Poland are united," and Britain would gain instant unpopularity "if we cannot give irrefutable reasons to make clear why we cannot do what we undertook in November last." In the second place, London was determined that whichever zone wound up being saddled with Yugoslav and other non-Potsdam *Volksdeutsche* arriving in Austria, it should not be the British. In quadripartite negotiations, Britain had adhered to the principle that it and the Soviet Union should assume responsibility for receiving expellees from northern Europe, while the United States and France should do the same for the south. To renege on these existing commitments might expose Britain to demands to accept a new flood of Germans from the Balkans. Lastly, there were the 166,000 East Prussian Germans still being held in Danish camps, who could no longer go home. London hoped to strike a deal with the USSR, in which these Germans would be taken across the border into the British zone, in exchange for a credit of 166,000 Swallow expellees to be accepted by the Soviets. "Such an arrangement would clearly be of great benefit to us since we should get better fed Germans and we should hope to get Danish help with food and hutments."[22]

Nonetheless, though the transfers continued on the reduced scale, the prospect of finally being rid of the obligations of Operation Swallow proved too beguiling to ignore. From this point onward officials in Britain as well as Germany began to cast about for a rationale that would allow them to claim that they had fulfilled their commitment to the Poles and bury Swallow once and for all. One possible argument was that while the British were loyally discharging their obligations, the Soviets were not. From mid-1946, the Foreign Office became increasingly convinced that the Poles and Soviets were conspiring to channel all expellees from the Recovered Territories in the direction of the British zone, industriously cooking the books along the way. Sir Orme Sargent in particular had always been highly suspicious of the Polish population figures. In December 1945 he had said that "Just as we were deceived at Potsdam by the Russians saying that there were only 1 1/2 million Germans left east of the Oder and Neisse, so we shall now, I suspect, find that there are still considerably more than the 3 1/2 million budgeted by the [Allied] Control Commission . . ."[23] His subordinate Robin Hankey, formerly of the Warsaw embassy but now working at Whitehall, arrived at the same conclusion from opposite premises. He was, he announced in July 1946, unable to avoid "a suspicion that we are being deceived over the Berlin agreement. I have never believed there were 3 1/2 million Germans in Poland when it was concluded. I suspect the Soviets are taking none, or only those capable of work." Five days later, he reiterated his conviction to Con O'Neill that "the Soviets are crooking us over this." Andrew Franklin was another who believed that Britain had "been taken for a ride on 'Operation Swallow.'"[24] As a result, the Foreign Office began almost obsessively to collect evidence that would tend to show that the Soviet zone had not been taking its fair share. A Radio Warsaw broadcast stating that 900,000 Germans had been removed from the Recovered Territories as of July 17, 1946 was seen as a key admission: inasmuch as 700,000 expellees had already been admitted to the British zone under Operation Swallow, clearly the Soviets had taken much fewer—perhaps even none at all.[25] Soviet housing figures were pored over to show that the population density in East Germany was lower than it ought to have been: if two million expellees had indeed arrived there, average dwelling space per person ought to be no more than 6 square meters, rather than the 14.4 square meters the USSR was claiming.[26] A chance comment by an officer at the Polish military mission in Berlin to the effect that the Soviets had diverted two trains from Operation Swallow to clear their own territory in the Memelland of Germans was seized upon as evidence of their lack of commitment to the task at hand.[27]

In truth, there was a good deal of justification for British skepticism about the number of Germans arriving in the Soviet zone. No statistical expertise was required to appreciate that the data of movements supplied by the USSR to CRX, at least for the first half of 1946, were nonsensical on their face. If the Soviets were to be believed, no fewer than 209,000 Germans had been extracted from Poland in the ten days immediately following the signature of the November 1945 ACC agreement—more than the British had succeeded in moving, by rail and sea, during the first two months of Operation Swallow. Another 341,000 supposedly had traveled in December 1945, in the depths of winter. By contrast, the number of expellees allegedly transported by the Soviets in the first half of June 1946 was a mere 938. Altogether, the USSR claimed to have taken 748,373 Germans from the Recovered Territories up to June 15, 1946, a figure duly certified by the Polish CRX representative, Lieutenant Colonel Konarski.[28] When challenged as to how these numbers could possibly be accurate, the Soviets and Poles claimed that they included foot traffic between the two countries as well as an alleged "mass migration over the frozen Oder" during the winter of 1945–

46—explanations that the British understandably greeted with loud guffaws of incredulity.[29]

From the end of August, consequently, proceedings in the monthly meetings of the four-power directorate responsible for expulsion movements were enlivened by mutual denunciations by the Soviet and British representatives of the veracity of each other's expulsion figures. The British poured scorn on Soviet assertions that 100,000 expellees from the Recovered Territories had illegally made their way from the British to the Soviet zone. The Soviets dismissed British counterclaims that 188,800 more had traveled in the opposite direction. Each accused the other of clandestinely dumping unwanted Germans across the zonal frontier. According to one report, the Poles had introduced into the British zone some 80,000 expellees not counted in the official tally by running unauthorized trains from Szczecin to Schwerin, northwest of Berlin, depositing the Germans there, and leaving them to find their own way by foot into the British sector of the city.[30] In an effort to obtain credible figures and ratchet back the war of words, Brigadier Kenchington proposed the creation of a joint Soviet-British audit office, operating with the assistance of CRX, to conduct inspections of the records of transit camps, dispersal centers, and housing authorities. The Soviets, though, ultimately rejected the proposal, arguing that to abandon the self-reporting system "would constitute an act of mistrust towards the recorded data submitted by the delegations concerned."[31] The British side took this as final confirmation of its belief that the USSR habitually fabricated "entirely unacceptable and unverifiable figures to show that all balances [of expellees] are in their favour."[32]

While there was every excuse for the British looking on the Soviet data with a jaundiced eye, they were mistaken in their explanation for Moscow's all too obvious exercise in creative accounting. In reality, the Soviets were not seeking to wriggle out of their obligations under the ACC agreement. Like the British themselves, they were simply swamped. Having borne the brunt of the "wild expulsions" from both Czechoslovakia and Poland in 1945, during which nearly a million and a half newcomers had been disgorged, often without warning, into an area that was predominantly agricultural and rural, the Soviet zone's absorptive capacities were strained to the utmost. According to the USSR's own internal figures, at least another 248,000 had arrived in 1945 as "wild repatriants." An early attempt to accept organized transports from the Gdańsk and Poznań regions in late November 1945 had had to be abandoned after a few weeks due not only to the inclement weather but to the strains it imposed on the transport system.[33] As the harried and short-fused General Kvashnin, chief of the Transport Administration in the Soviet zone, had told his Czechoslovak counterpart in March 1946, even providing transit facilities for the British in the early stages of Operation Swallow was overloading the eastern German railway network.[34] The Soviet authorities' chief priority in 1946, therefore, was to delay the restart of the transfer from Poland as long as possible, especially while they were attempting to cope with the prospect of another 750,000 expellees from Czechoslovakia. Hence an agreement specifying the conditions of the transfer was not signed with Poland until May 5, and large-scale removals only began on June 17. At all times, nevertheless, the USSR reassured Warsaw that it would fully discharge its commitments; in the late summer of 1947, it even undertook to admit to its zone as many Germans as remained in Poland, without limit of number. Why, then, the Soviets should have been so anxious to conceal their difficulties from the Western Allies must remain a matter of speculation. The most likely explanation is that both they and the Poles feared that any admission on their part that the schedule in the ACC agreement was not being strictly followed would be seized upon by the Americans and British as a pretext for going back on their own promises.

If the Western powers were not yet willing to go that far, at all events they were determined not to admit a single expellee more than they were contractually obliged to receive. Their nightmare scenario was a situation in which, having accepted their full complement according to the ACC agreement, they would then find themselves the unwilling hosts of an endless stream of additional Germans entering illegally across the "green frontier" (unguarded places along the zonal boundary)—supplemented by large numbers of political and economic refugees fleeing the Soviet zone. As a result, they began pressing for all arrivals from Czechoslovakia and Poland, including "wild repatriants," to be counted against their respective quotas. Some ingenious British administrators even suggested that the estimated 550,000 Germans from the Recovered Territories who had entered the British zone in 1945 prior to the conclusion of the ACC agreement should be deducted from the total of 1.5 million expellees to be accepted, which would make it possible to declare Operation Swallow as having been completed by July 27, 1946. They were persuaded not to press this argument by the reminder that—as a Soviet official had half-seriously maintained the previous April—nearly 3 million Germans from the Recovered Territories and another 800,000 *Sudetendeutsche* had already entered the Soviet zone. If these arrivals were also to be taken into account, the USSR could claim to have fulfilled the entirety of its commitments before the first train of the "organized expulsion" had ever departed.[35] But the British and Americans insisted that at least those "wild repatriants" who had been processed in transit camps in the Western occupation zones since November 20, 1945 should be credited to their accounts. By early

August the British were claiming to be accommodating 184,182 of these from Poland, the equivalent of one trainload of "wild repatriants" for every five trainloads of expellees accepted through official channels. There were also in the U.S. zone 100,000 Germans whose homes were in the Recovered Territories; rather than send them back to Poland only to have them reexpelled to the British zone in considerably worse condition, London had agreed to admit them directly and count them against the Swallow quota. The United States used a different basis of calculation for their own claimed figures, adding to their total those entrants to the American zone who had arrived from Czechoslovakia prior to the signing of the ACC agreement. Nonetheless, as of March 31, 1947, U.S. authorities were demanding credit for 325,439 *Sudetendeutsche* who had arrived in their zone by unofficial means, together with another 118,574 who had fled or been driven into Austria but of whom the government in Vienna wanted to be rid.[36]

In the end, though, both governments decided against taking their stand against further admissions of Germans on the basis of what promised to be an unprofitable wrangle over numbers. Instead, they decided to invoke the Potsdam Treaty's declaration that expulsions be conducted in an "orderly and humane" manner as a basic law governing all previous or subsequent accords, including the ACC agreement. As British Military Government officers in Berlin pointed out in August, due to the complete saturation of all available or potential accommodation; acute food shortages; the spread of infectious diseases like tuberculosis and typhus; and a demographic balance that was now tilted heavily toward the unproductive cohorts of the population, "a situation has been reached when a further importation of refugees is indefensible on humanitarian grounds."[37] As a result, the British informed the Polish government that, having regard to "the danger to public health arising from the extreme shortage of housing and of food," it would be necessary to reduce the rate of acceptances in the British zone to two trains a week with effect from September 5, 1946. The note to the Polish Government also announced that the British would seek the formal review of the functioning of the expulsion operation provided for in the Four-Power Agreement of November 17, 1945.[38]

The British initiative produced an anguished response from both the Poles and Ambassador Cavendish-Bentinck who, in the face of much contrary evidence, had succeeded in persuading himself that the key to good relations between Warsaw and London lay in Britain's maintenance of an understanding stance on the German question. Communicating Minister Wolski's urgent request that the decision be reconsidered and that the British commit to accepting a minimum of seven trains a week, Cavendish-Bentinck warned that the government's action would cause "a considerable shock to Polish public opinion which is very sensitive on this subject."[39] British officials, though, had heard too many variations from the ambassador on this theme, and had waited too long for the gratitude of the Polish government to materialize, to be impressed by these arguments now. Nor were they moved by the broadside launched by Lieutenant Colonel Jakub Prawin of the Polish Military Mission against the new cutbacks. Reminding the British that they must have been satisfied they had sufficient resources to accommodate 1.5 million incoming Germans when they signed up to the ACC agreement the previous November, Prawin insisted that Poland could not be held responsible for Britain's failure to earmark enough housing for the incomers, nor should it be penalized for demonstrating flexibility when, according to the ACC agreement, Operation Swallow ought to have been completed by July 1946. British claims of concern over orderly and humane conditions, he observed, rang hollow in light of the fact that large numbers of Polish colonists from the east would now have to be put in transit camps over the winter instead of being settled in the ex-German properties promised to them, creating no less serious a humanitarian crisis. As for the appeal to the Potsdam Agreement as an overriding law, Prawin argued that Article 13 imposed "an international obligation on the Occupying Powers concerned, which by no means can be construed in such a way as to make the principle inefficient." Until such time as the quadripartite review of expulsions for which the British had called actually took place and made its recommendations, the Anglo-Polish agreement of February 1946 remained operative and "can NOT be declared void by onesided declarations."[40]

Suiting the action to Prawin's word, the Polish authorities sent six trainloads to the crossing points on September 6. Reasoning that the transports might have made a good-faith effort to reach the British zone before the imposition of the previous day's deadline, Sir Brian Robertson, the deputy military governor, allowed them to enter. But he also made contingency plans against any repetition. After ordering that no further trains be accepted before September 12, and only two per week thereafter, he stationed detachments of the South Staffordshire Regiment at Helmstedt and Lübeck to counter any attempt by the Poles or Soviets to force expellees across the frontier. The troops were, however, instructed that if it should prove "necessary to use force of arms, only firing over heads is permitted."[41] In the event, a confrontation was avoided. Although five more trains appeared at the border on September 9, all were turned back without incident.

The British, for their part, made clear to the Poles their determination not to yield. As Andrew Franklin contended, it was "essential to take a firm line even if this means a bit of a row."[42] Replying to Prawin in uncompromising terms, General "Bobby" Erskine made clear that he was fully prepared for one. The

Potsdam Agreement, he maintained, unambiguously stated the will of the Big Three that any transfers "should be effected in an orderly and humane manner." This could not be superseded by any decision of the ACC, a subordinate body. The schedule providing for the removal of all Germans from Poland, Czechoslovakia, and Hungary by July 1946, moreover, was a mere plan, not any kind of binding commitment to have completed the operation by then. "According to my information," Erskine pointed out, "none of the Occupying Powers has in fact found it possible to accept Germans at those rates." Indicating exactly where he thought responsibility for the problem lay, Erskine assured Prawin that "The British authorities are fully aware of the importance which the Polish Provisional Government attach to the movement from Poland of the German population, but for which they might well have reduced the rate of acceptance sooner in view of the deplorable condition in which many of the expelled persons have been arriving in the British Zone and the extremely low proportion of able-bodied persons included among them."[43]

Later Polish appeals were greeted with the same curt dismissiveness. Wolski's lament to the British Embassy in Warsaw that the Soviet authorities were "being more helpful" by accepting fifteen trains a week into their zone cut little ice with officials in the British zone. "If this is being quoted to us as an example to follow, it leaves our withers unwrung, since through the summer months we were moving 30 to 40 trains per week."[44] The British were equally unmoved when Warsaw, having discovered that attempts to arouse their sympathies over the plight of Polish colonists got them nowhere, tried to see whether they were more sensitive to hints that German expellees would be made to suffer in Poland if not quickly removed. At the end of September the Ministry of Foreign Affairs advised the embassy that "The greater part of the German population in Poland ... is at present housed in transit camps. Those Germans would have to remain in those camps throughout the autumn and winter periods in conditions which it is easy to understand would be hard. The British order would therefore affect painfully this population as well." To this veiled threat, Duncan Wilson of the Foreign Office acerbically commented, "The Poles might some time be reminded of what their champion, Stalin, said at Potsdam—that there were neither 7 nor 3 nor 1 million but no Germans in the area taken over by the Poles. But better not now."[45]

Although surprisingly little discussion took place between the two English-speaking democracies about expulsion matters, OMGUS in Germany by the early summer of 1946 was independently dissolving into much the same exhausted and angst-ridden state as was its British counterpart. The U.S. military governor, General Clay, calculated in May 1946 that there were already nearly

2.9 million expellees living in the U.S. zone, at a time when only 375,000 of the expected 1.75 million *Sudetendeutsche* and 75,000 of the 500,000 Germans from Hungary had been admitted.[46] While OMGUS reluctantly accepted that it was obliged to make good on its commitment to Czechoslovakia, the same was not at all true of Hungary. In view of the fact that the Budapest government was all too plainly a Soviet puppet, little or no advantage was to be gained from accommodating its wishes over the German question.

Because Hungary was an ex-enemy state, no agreement had ever been required, or sought, with the provisional government in Budapest over the procedure for removing the Germans. Instead, the Potsdam conference had made the Allied Control Commission for Hungary (ACC [H]), composed as in Germany of military commanders from the USSR, the United States, France, and Britain, responsible for overseeing expulsions from that country. That does not imply that the Hungarian government was opposed to the idea of driving out the German populations, but rather that the planners could not count on the groundswell of popular anti-Germanism that facilitated removals in Poland and Czechoslovakia. During the war, the half a million or so Germanophones of Hungary had greeted Nazi Germany's initial victories with the same enthusiasm as did *Volksdeutsche* elsewhere in central Europe. Some forty-six thousand had volunteered for service with the German forces, even though by doing so they forfeited their Hungarian citizenship. When the tide of war turned after the Battle of Stalingrad, though, the supply of additional recruits quickly dried up. Under heavy pressure from Berlin, the Hungarian government agreed in April 1944 that the *Volksdeutsch* population could be drafted into the German army. Unwilling to become cannon fodder in a losing cause, the German minority quickly rediscovered their Hungarianness, attempting to enlist in the Hungarian army and publicly demonstrating against their conscription into "the army of a foreign state." This had little effect, and it is estimated that some 100,000 Hungarian *Volksdeutsche* became unwilling wearers of German uniform by the end of the war.[47] Nevertheless, the dilemma of divided loyalties that the *Volksdeutsche* faced was appreciated by some elements at least of the majority population. Many Magyars were sympathetic to the argument that it was by order of their own government in Budapest, in fulfillment of its accord with Nazi Germany, that the *Volksdeutsche* had been compelled to enlist in the German armed forces. The postwar regime, for its part, while never questioning the desirability of forced migrations, was ambivalent about their scope. The most determinedly expulsionist group in the four-party coalition was the National Peasant Party, whose motives were frankly confiscatory. Speaking on behalf of the country's small farmers, who hoped to benefit from the expropriation of the *Volksdeutsche*, the party's leader, Imre Kovács, insisted that they "should leave the country as they had come, with a single bundle."[48] The Communist Party of Mátyás Rákosi, too, launched a press campaign in the spring of 1945 demanding the de-Germanization of the country. The Smallholder Party, on the other hand, represented by Ferenc Nagy, speaker of the National Assembly, and János Gyöngyösi, the foreign minister, pointed out that it was at least injudicious to seek to drive out the whole of Hungary's German population at the precise moment that Budapest was trying to prevail upon the Big Three to prevent Czechoslovakia from expelling its 500,000 Magyars.[49] The remaining party in the coalition, the Social Democrats, took little active part in the discussion beyond attempting, by various largely specious expedients, to have its German-speaking activists reclassified as "Magyars" or "antifascists." As in September 1938, then, when it had joined enthusiastically in Hitler's intimidation of Czechoslovakia and been rewarded with a slice of Czech-administered territory in Ruthenia for its services, Hungary in 1945 was a "vulture state," for which material rather than ideological considerations came uppermost. In general, Hungarians after the war were torn between their desire to profit from the expropriation and removal of a prosperous but temporarily powerless minority, and anxiety over setting a precedent that might later rebound upon themselves.

The Budapest government attempted to resolve the difficulty by seeking to throw the entire responsibility for the expulsions upon the Big Three, of which it depicted itself as merely the reluctant instrument. In reality its part in removing the German minority had been considerably more active. When the Red Army cleared the last Wehrmacht units from Hungary in December 1944, it promptly announced the conscription of all *Volksdeutsch* males aged between seventeen and forty-five, and females aged between eighteen and thirty, for forced labor in the Soviet Union. Far from seeking to impede or resist this roundup of Hungarian citizens, the new interior minister in Budapest, Ferenc Erdei, issued decrees providing for the enumeration and processing of the potential deportees. Up to sixty-five thousand Hungarian Germanophones were removed from Hungarian soil by February 1945 of whom, it is estimated, a third died in Soviet camps. Many of the survivors were never allowed to return to their homeland, being transferred directly from the trains bringing them back from the USSR to others bound for the U.S. occupation zone of Germany.[50] Those who did return typically found that their homes had been expropriated and their families deported to Germany in their absence.[51] A series of further Hungarian decrees created tribunals to try as war criminals all those who had served in the German armed forces or police (a later ruling by the prime minister, Béla Miklós, specified that no distinction was to be drawn between volunteers and conscripts); made all German citizens—a category expanded in practice to include members of the *Volksbund der Deutschen in Ungarn*, the ethnic Germans' prewar representative body—liable to internment; and finally, on May 14, 1945, authorized the rounding-up of detainees' family members as well.

Long before the ACC (H) took up the question, then, an expulsionist dynamic in Hungary was well under way. Indeed it was the Budapest Ministry of Foreign Affairs that first approached A. D. F. Gascoigne, the British diplomatic representative in Budapest, a week after V-E Day to inquire semiofficially about the possibility of expelling 200,000 *Volksdeutsche* to Germany, a request it repeated at the same time to Moscow and Washington.[52] Joseph Grew, acting secretary of state, replied that the State Department had "no desire to be solicitous on behalf of a group probably largely made up of Nazis," although the U.S. government's general reservations about the principle of mass expulsions still applied.[53] London greeted the suggestion with great disfavor in light of the enormous numbers of expellees expected to arrive from Poland and Czechoslovakia. Notwithstanding a British request at the end of May 1945 to drop the idea, however, Budapest replied that it had already proceeded to round up its *Volksdeutsche* as a preliminary to deportation. The purpose, as Gyöngyösi explained to Gascoigne, was both as a punitive measure and to make room for ethnic Magyars who had been, or would be, evicted from neighboring countries, especially Czechoslovakia.[54] Indicating where its true priorities lay, Budapest proceeded first to expropriation rather than expulsion. A decree of July 1, 1945, set up district committees to enquire into the wartime loyalties of the German-speaking population aged sixteen years or more. Those found to have been leaders of the *Volksbund*, or members who had taken a definitely collaborationist stance during the war, would be interned forthwith and their property confiscated by the state. Four days later, the Hungarian government addressed a note to the ACC (H) formally requesting its cooperation in deporting the *Volksdeutsche* from the country.

The precise number to be expelled, though, proved controversial. In his early overtures to the British and U.S. representatives, Gyöngyosi had spoken of removing between 200,000 and 340,000 of the German-speaking population. Shortly after the Potsdam Conference, the Soviet representative on the ACC (H), Lieutenant General Vladimir Sviridov, requested Miklós to draw up a plan of action to deport up to 450,000 *Volksdeutsche* as quickly as possible. His motives for doing so remain a matter of dispute. The French historian Jean-Léon Muller considers that the reason for this urgency was to reduce the number of anti-Communist voters in advance of the upcoming elections; to smooth the process of land confiscation and redistribution; and, perhaps, to destabilize the Western Allies by dumping an additional half-million pauperized Germans in their zones. Some Hungarian historians, on the other hand, have seen the malign hand of Prague behind this request, suggesting that the Beneš government pressed for the largest possible number of *Volksdeutsche* to be removed so as to deprive Budapest of any pretext for refusing to accept a like number of Magyars expelled from Czechoslovakia.[55] Wherever the truth may lie, the Soviet initiative produced divisions within the government between those who wished to make a clean sweep of the *Volksdeutsche* and more moderate voices who feared that this would play into Prague's hands. A compromise was ultimately reached under which those who had recorded themselves in the 1941 census as both Germanophone and of German nationality would be expelled: some 303,000 in all.

The Hungarian Communist Party's failure to make the gains it had expected in the November 1945 elections, however, led it to adopt a more radical stance on the German question. Making clear that it spoke for the Soviet occupying authorities, it successfully prevailed upon the Cabinet to reopen the debate. Imre Nagy, the new Communist minister of the interior who, a decade later, would lead Hungary's doomed attempt to break free from the USSR's grasp, took an especially hard line, describing the purification of the country from German influence as "our national duty" and pressing for everyone who had declared themselves as German-speaking in the 1941 census to be transferred. The new, harsher stance was reflected in the draft scheme finally presented to the ACC (H) by the Budapest government in December 1945. This proposed the expulsion of all 510,000 *Volksdeutsche*, in an operation that would necessitate the employment of nine army battalions, seven thousand railway wagons per month, and twenty-two transit camps. The southwestern county of Tolna as well as Budapest and its hinterland would be cleared first, followed by the county of Baranya on the border with Croatia and finally the rest of Hungary. The principal dangers foreseen were the flight of the Germans and the destruction, concealment, or loss of their property. To guard against this, six of the nine battalions would be employed in sequestering and compiling an inventory of the assets of the *Volksdeutsche*, who were to be confined to their houses under martial law until taken to the camps. The entire transfer was to be completed by July 1946.[56]

In practice, though, relatively little of this plan ever got off the drawing-board. Major A. D. Spottswood, an expulsion officer attached to the U.S. element of the ACC (H), accurately described the Hungarians as having created "only a paper organization for operations." The promised transit camps were never built; instead, villages were cordoned off and designated as assembly areas from which deportees could be sent. Once the "organized expulsions" began, as Spottswood had predicted, disorganization reigned. Not only were trains routinely dispatched without food for the passengers, but no notice of any kind had been provided of two-thirds of the transports in early May before their appearance at Freilassing and Passau in the U.S. zone. Only fifteen trains, composed of wagons pilfered from the Allies or lent by the Soviets, were available for the operation. Some of these were found to be in "deplorable condition." According to General Clay, "a majority of Swabians arriving in the U.S. Zone are for all intents and purposes destitute and penniless."[57] The American authorities thus had numerous grounds for charging that the deportations from Hungary fell far short of the "orderly and humane" requirements stipulated by the Potsdam Agreement.

The Hungarian people themselves seemed ambivalent about whether or not they wished to be rid of the entire German population. In January 1946, Miksa Fenyö, a Jewish ex-member of Parliament and prominent literary figure, and György Parragi, a survivor of the Mauthausen concentration camp, issued a manifesto on behalf of Hungarian intellectuals denouncing the expulsion of those Germans who "did not commit criminal acts and were only part of a mass hysteria, or those who were indifferent." Many Hungarians, they pointedly observed, could themselves have been placed in both categories during the war.[58] The Catholic Primate of Hungary, Jószef Cardinal Mindszenty, and his brother bishops were also outspoken in their condemnation of what they saw as an act of injustice against the German minority (though cynics observed that few of them had dared to speak out against the deportation of Hungarian Jews two years previously). There seemed little reason to fear that a suspension of the transfers would result in an anti-American backlash from Hungarian public opinion. On June 4, 1946, therefore, having accepted 118,474 Germans from Hungary, OMGUS announced that it was imposing an open-ended suspension of further transports. Its stated reasons for doing so were "abuses observed in shipping out the Swabian trains, the disorderly manner in which the program was executed, and the inhumaneness consequent to burdening German welfare agencies with penniless and destitute people."[59] In reality, there was no evidence to suggest that the Hungarian expulsions were any worse than the transports the Americans continued to accept from Czechoslovakia. Nine weeks earlier, Con O'Neill of the Foreign Office had written that "if one had to award marks out of a hundred for good order and humanity, I should give Hungary 40, Czechoslovakia 30 and Poland 5."[60] The U.S. decision to halt admissions from one country and not the other, then, had less to do with the objective circumstances than with the fact that while Budapest could easily be pushed around, Prague could not.

The Hungarian government was completely wrong-footed by OMGUS's abrupt action. As Mátyás Rákosi later ruefully admitted to Molotov, the authorities had "started the process of eviction assuming that we would be able to resettle 100,000 [more] Swabians in the American zone."[61] Having failed to build an extensive camp network, as in Poland or Czechoslovakia, to intern the Germans and being unable to depend on the support and assistance of the public while they created one, ministers in Budapest had little alternative but to accept any terms for further expulsions the Americans might be willing to offer. After a series of one-sided talks in the summer of 1946, the two governments concluded a revised expulsion protocol on August 22. Budapest was now obliged to give a minimum of ten days' notice to expellees before attempting to round them up. Expellee trains would consist of thirty-five passenger wagons, five baggage wagons, a kitchen wagon, and a medical wagon; at least one doctor, two nurses, and a guard would accompany every transport. The maximum number of passengers would be eleven hundred. Each trainload of expellees would elect a committee of five who, in cooperation with the train guards, would prevent robberies from occurring. In addition to the hundred-kilogram baggage allowance, each passenger would be furnished with a minimum of five hundred Reichsmarks (fifty dollars) in cash, and allowed to retain wedding rings or watches. The Budapest government was required not to hold back some expellees, nor prioritize the removal of others, on the basis of "present political affiliations, wealth, age, sex [or] physical condition." ACC (H) or OMGUS inspectors were authorized to carry out spot checks on the trains at the points of departure, arrival, or anywhere in between. Expulsions would be suspended during periods of unfavorable weather or in case of outbreaks of epidemic disease. If each of these conditions was satisfied, the United States undertook to resume admissions on September 1, 1946, and to continue at the rate of twenty trains per month until April 1, 1947, by which date an upper limit of 90,000 Germans would be accepted. If OMGUS was satisfied with the Hungarians' record of compliance, it would then allow a further 100,000 to enter the U.S. zone under the same terms until December 1, 1947, when the operation would be deemed to have been completed. Budapest was warned that a system of "slots" for the dispatch of trains would be strictly adhered to. Each expulsion train was to provide the American authorities with a month's notice of its expected arrival at the U.S. zonal boundary. If it failed to show up on the specified day, that "slot" would be permanently forfeited and the Hungarians would not be permitted to send the day's quota of expellees by a subsequent transport.[62]

The revised stipulations imposed by OMGUS on the Hungarians were by far the most stringent ever required by any of the countries of reception throughout the expulsion process. Their announcement drew a chagrined reaction from the British, firstly because they showed that it was possible to demand and obtain from the expelling countries standards of conduct that were "much stiffer than anything we insisted on with the Poles," and secondly because "we are just stopping 'Operation Swallow,' and it would have been all to the good if we could have pointed out that the Americans had also on a unilateral basis stopped their intake from Hungary."[63] As experience would show, London need not have been concerned on either count. In Hungary as elsewhere, the organizers of mass transfers faced an inescapable choice between humanity and practicality. As soon as they were obliged by the United States to make the first of these a priority, the second proved beyond their capabilities. According to the revised schedule, in the three months following the resumption of the operation in September 1946 57,200 Germans should have been transferred to the U.S. zone. In fact, only six trainloads, containing a total of 6,090 people, did so, in a two-week period beginning on November 10. Though the Americans declared themselves satisfied with the manner in which Budapest was complying with the agreement, on December 1 they again shut the operation down until the following March, citing adverse winter weather and a buildup of more than 100,000 unhoused expellees in reception camps in the U.S. zone.[64] Simultaneously, they declared that the Hungarians' failure to take up their assigned "slots" for sixty expulsion trains between September and the first half of November—the result, Budapest pleaded, of an insufficient supply of Reichsmarks to give to each expellee—meant that the number of Germans to be accepted by the U.S. zone would now permanently be reduced by 66,000.

This second suspension caused Hungarian and Soviet tempers finally to boil over. In a formal protest, Dr. Gyula Fischer of the Ministry of the Interior demanded to know what would have happened had the Hungarian government been in a position to fill all its "slots" from the beginning of September. "After resettling 5,000 persons, would expatriation have [had] to be stopped owing to lack of accommodation in the camps?" At a meeting of the ACC (H) on December 6, General Sviridov accused the U.S. side of trying to sabotage the process by manufacturing a fresh set of contrived requirements every time Budapest complied with the previous ones. As an example, he cited "a new condition whereby every train was to carry 50 tons of coal without which it would not be allowed to enter Germany." Even General Oliver Edgcumbe, the British ACC (H) representative, backed up his Soviet colleague, expressing his incomprehension "that the agreement between the U.S. authorities and the Hungarian Government would permit Schwabians to remain in Hungary simply because the timing of the programme had not been adhered to."[65]

The man assigned the task of defending this new American policy, Brigadier General George ("Pappy") Weems, was one of the more exotic personalities involved in the expulsion operation. Assigned to replace the hard-charging General William Key as U.S. representative on the ACC (H) in the summer of 1946, the former horse cavalryman Weems could hardly be considered an improvement over his predecessor. According to one of his subordinates, Lieutenant Colonel William Karp, Weems's behavior was so erratic that it was widely believed among his staff that he had recently suffered an undiagnosed stroke. In addition to memory lapses, confusion, impaired gait, and a tendency to fly into rages if interrupted, "[h]e was obsessed with the idea that there was some sort of international conspiracy to steal typewriters and any case involving the theft of a typewriter had to be brought to his attention."[66] The appointment of such a man to oversee the expulsions from Hungary is probably an accurate reflection of the extent of Washington's commitment to the completion of the operation. And at least in carrying out his assigned task of erecting every possible obstruction to its resumption, Weems did not disappoint. For several months, he had complained officially about Budapest's habit, in the words of his colleague General Edgcumbe, of trying to "make it appear that the deportations are taking place as a result of Allied pressure, and not at the request of the Hungarian Government."[67] Weems now called the Hungarians' bluff. The ACC agreement of November 1945, he argued, "permitted the Hungarian Government to deport those they wished but did not require them to deport to the U.S. Zone any specific number." At the beginning of March, when the winter hiatus was due to expire, Weems told Budapest that the program for 1947 would not be resumed unless the Hungarian government sent a delegate to Berlin for discussions about additional conditions to be satisfied before movements would be allowed to resume. When the administration of Ferenc Nagy, Miklós's successor, acquiesced even in this, Weems once again reverted to wrecking tactics, informing the ACC (H) that the American authorities in Germany could not contemplate new admissions from Hungary unless the social and economic environment in the U.S. zone became more favorable. "It is not anticipated by U.S. authorities in Germany that any substantial improvement in resettlement conditions within the U.S. Zone will occur within a minimum of twelve months."[68]

In the face of this renewed suspension—which General Clay privately made clear was, from his point of view, a permanent cessation—Tildy's government dropped all further pretense that it was doing no more than obediently carrying out the ACC (H)'s instructions. The removal of the remaining Germans, Budapest now protested, was an urgent national priority. Some twenty-five thousand had already been "processed" for expulsion; should the Americans continue their intransigent attitude, the result would be chaos.

> The property of these individuals was blocked and the family was either moved into a house with another Schwabian family or a Hungarian settler was moved into the house with the Schwabian. The property then came under the

joint control of the new settler and the Schwabian owner, and the population of the villages therefore became mixed. The Hungarian authorities report that fights and quarrels break out daily between the Schwab[ian]s and the Hungarian settlers, and that several murders have occurred.... It is reported that the Schwabians openly state that the Americans are supporting their resistance to expatriation, and have stopped the programme as a means of protecting them....

As a result of the stoppage of the Schwabian expellations [sic], considerable pressure has been exerted by groups desiring the expulsion of all Schwab[ian]s, and some embarrassment has resulted from the inability of the government to meet its commitments in this respect.[69]

The Hungarian government's complaints about a rise in the number of clashes as a result of the transfer were certainly grounded in fact, even if most of these incidents were of Budapest's own making. Hungary, indeed, was the only country in which expellees felt confident enough to display more than negligible resistance to their expropriation and removal. "In Baranya county, Swabians were reported as dubbing the immigrants [ethnic Hungarian settlers] 'gypsies' and sometimes physically assaulting them in broad daylight."[70] Often whipped up by Communist and Peasant Party officials, settlers responded by developing a "lynch mob mentality" in which they vented their frustrations over the slowness with which former German property was being redistributed, sometimes with fatal results. But just as disturbing to the authorities were manifestations of sympathy for the expellees, as in the county of Tolna where eighty members of the Magyar majority were arrested for coming to the aid of an expellee convoy and providing them with food for their voyage.[71] In desperation over what appeared to be the program's imminent breakdown, Rákosi approached Molotov seeking permission to send the Germans rejected by the Americans into the Soviet zone, promising that the expellees' terror of Bolshevism would surely cause them to infiltrate into Bavaria via the "green frontier." The skeptical Soviet foreign minister, less convinced than the Hungarians that the Soviet zone would serve as a "scarecrow" in this manner, rejected the request.[72] As a gesture to help the Hungarian Communist Party out of its troubles, however, the USSR agreed in an exchange of notes with Budapest in July 1947 to accept fifty thousand Germans directly into the Soviet zone, at a rate of three trains per week.[73]

This last round of expulsions from Hungary degenerated into a tragicomic parody of Budapest's original scheme. Previous removal efforts had focused especially on those regarded as the "guiltiest" Germans: families whose menfolk during the war had joined the *Volksbund* or the *Waffen*-SS. These, however, had generally been people at the bottom of the social scale, forced into the armed services less through ideological conviction than as a result of legal coercion or "economic conscription." The spectacle of poor peasants and workers being deported from Hungary while the better-off German "kulaks," many of whom had successfully evaded military service during the war, were left undisturbed sat ill with the Hungarian Communist Party. To ensure that class enemies alone should be transferred, the criteria for expulsion were amended in 1947, providing that only those deemed by the authorities to have been "voluntary" adherents to the *Volksbund* or SS should be marked for removal. Industrial workers, miners, agricultural laborers, and essential workers were to be exempt, in most cases irrespective of their wartime record in the German armed forces. As Michael Mevius dryly remarks, "Dodging the SS draft now seemed more of a crime than fighting with the SS."[74]

The Soviets proved far more accommodating than the Americans when it came to minimum standards of welfare for Hungarian expellees. As British military observers found, these were conspicuous largely by their absence. A week-long operation to clear the neighboring small towns of Dunabogdány, Visegrád, and Nagymaros north of Budapest in August 1947 affords an example of the methods with which the removals to the Soviet zone were accomplished. At Dunabogdány, rather more than half of whose population of three thousand were ethnic Germans, Major M. Hanley of the British Military Mission noted that "the Swabians were given at most 2 hours notice and in some cases less." Some fourteen hundred persons were transported by truck to the railway station at Nagymaros. "Empty space on the lorry seems to have been filled up somewhat at random and there are reports that one or two Hungarians were taken (but more evidence is required here)."[75] The scene at Nagymaros was more chaotic still. Corporal C. Sassie, who had been refused access to the Visegrád roundup, nonetheless succeeded in observing Hungarian police in the midst of herding seven hundred Germans toward Nagymaros railway station. Locals to whom he spoke considered that the lowest-ranking constables involved in the operation were "orderly, helpful, sympathetic," but that "the officers were pigs." That was Sassie's conclusion as well. "Bullying attitude, shouting, appeared to be under the influence of drink. 3 were accompanied by civilian female police or girl friends." The Hungarian policemen cordoning off the town, with whom he spoke, told him that they had turned a blind eye as some Germans fled to the hills; that three elderly expellees had already died during the roundup; that the officers in command of the operation had been observed confiscating property from expellees and loading it into their own cars; and that, contrary to the Hungarian Communist Party's hopes, "Lots of wealthy Swabians had bought the right to stay [by] bribing the police. . . . Nearly all the expatriates were the poorer class. Lots of ex-Volksbundists and S.S. had bought their way out."

Equal disorder prevailed at Sassie's next stop, the railway station. There he found

> 20 cattle wagons, some covered, some with no roof, each to hold 35 people and luggage which appeared to be mostly bedding. No sanitary arrangements at the station. No kitchen cars, no ambulance car. No general supply of food, all had to be provided by individuals. . . .
>
> Everybody appeared to be crying. Scene was very much like a prisoners' transit point. Saw one mother imploring guards for her child who was left behind with the eldest daughter. . . . Saw an old man hurrying towards the station and was told he was lying in hospital when he heard that his wife was already at assembly point, whereupon he proceeded to join her.[76]

Despite the arbitrariness and disorganization of the expulsions to the Soviet zone, they were relatively short-lived. After the 50,000 *Volksdeutsche* had been removed, a process that was completed by August 1948, no further transfers from Hungary took place. There is no doubt that the go-slow mounted by the U.S. authorities almost from the beginning of the "organized expulsions" saved many Germans of Hungary from being driven out of their homeland. Of the 25,000 to have been deported in the month of January 1946, only 3,866 were removed; the number had reached just 41,500 by the end of April, out of a planned total of 250,000.[77] All told, 126,843 Hungarian *Volksdeutsche* were forced to leave for the U.S. zone, and 50,000 to the Soviet zone, instead of the 447,000 originally marked for deportation by the Budapest government. The Hungarian case, therefore, is a vivid illustration of the truth that expulsions that could not be carried out immediately could not be carried out at all. As an unsympathetic Molotov told Rákosi in 1948, "You missed the favourable moment."[78]

The fact that the United States had simply declared an end to further admissions from Hungary and made it stick also served as an inspiration to British policymakers, who dearly wished the same to happen to Operation Swallow. After the debacle of the Marienthal transports of December 1946, CCG officials had suspended further acceptances for two weeks in the first instance. Sir William Strang, political adviser to the commander in chief of the British occupation zone, thought that in addition, the Poles should be warned against "accumulating refugees at the starting points where they appear to be kept under even worse conditions than in the trains," and that "any disposition on their part to resist this measure will be met by full publicity for the conditions in which they have been carrying out repatriations in recent weeks."[79] Just ten days after the suspension, however, the Polish authorities tested British resolve by sending another trainload of expellees to Marienthal. Because this train contained straw as floor covering, was heated, and arrived with only seven dead passengers, it was admitted to the British zone. But the liaison team at Szczecin finally balked at the train provided by the Poles to carry a transport of Germans to Lübeck, 220 miles away, on January 6, 1947. By the time it appeared, two days behind schedule, the expellees, 693 of whom were children, had already been waiting in the open in a temperature of minus twenty-one degrees centigrade for nearly six hours. The train, which the British Liaison Team considered "unfit for cattle let alone human beings," consisted of nine passenger cars, all without windows, and twenty-three freight wagons, half of whose doors could not be closed. With expulsion trains along the route typically making no more than forty or fifty miles per day, it was obvious that there would be many deaths if it were allowed to proceed. For the first time on record, consequently, the British refused to allow the expellees to be entrained and lodged a strong protest with the Polish railway authorities.[80]

Polish warnings—or threats—that this would do nothing to diminish the suffering of the expellees were soon borne out in practice. By the beginning of February, more than four thousand Germans were piled up at Kaławsk, with their numbers daily increasing, in spite of the fact that there was no accommodation for them.[81] Thousands more—"mainly women, old people and children," according to the Polish Red Cross—were being decanted by the authorities outside Szczecin-Golęcino assembly camp, which had been temporarily closed because of a typhoid outbreak. These were squatting in ruined buildings surrounding the camp, "in indescribably bad sanitary conditions and lacking any social services or welfare." The local Red Cross officer sourly reported that "the delegate of the American Red Cross, Mr. Slendziński, desired during his last stay to visit the . . . Camp. . . . With some difficulty I managed to dissuade him, as I knew well that his report in this matter would be extremely unfavorable and would have caused us international embarrassment."[82] An even worse state of affairs existed in Gdańsk, where Marta Dobrzyńska, the voivodeship Plenipotentiary for Settlement Affairs, reported that the condition of the remaining German population had deteriorated precipitously after the suspension of expulsions:

> In the Gdańsk Voivodeship there are 34,500 Germans. The vast majority are women, children, and old people.
> The death rate among the Germans is frightening—between January 1, 1947 and April 1, 1947 5.7% of the Germans have died.
> Causes: hunger and lack of medical care in cases of disease.[83]

Military Government officers in Germany, though, took a sanguine view of the situation. "We feel," one wrote, "that this is a good opportunity for stopping Swallow."[84] While some senior officials in London had difficulty seeing why such a fuss should be made over what they regarded as a comparatively trivial matter—one drew attention to a newspaper report that thirty-seven people in Hamburg had frozen to death in the month of January 1947, adding in a notation: "To restore a sense of proportion on Swallow"—British administrators in both countries saw to it that Polish failure to comply with agreed conditions for expulsions should receive full publicity. Unusually, censors permitted the German press to publish detailed and highly critical accounts of the manner in which transports to the British zone in late December and early January had been conducted. Questions were asked in the House of Commons, where John Hynd stated bluntly that "the Polish authorities have not carried out the movement of these Germans in a humane and orderly manner, as was required by the Potsdam Agreement."[85] The choice that British policymakers now faced was whether to resume accepting expellees under much more stringent conditions, with Military Government officers given "a free hand from London to stop *forever* the movement immediately any single clause of our agreement is broken," or, like the Americans, unilaterally to declare without further ado that the period of "organized expulsions" had come to an end.[86]

After debating the matter through the spring of 1947, London opted for the second alternative. Though the decision immediately "produced a pathetic appeal from H[is] M[ajesty's] A[mbassador] Warsaw as was to be expected," both the Foreign Office and the Military Government ignored it and turned their attention to the mechanics of closing down Swallow.[87] The first step was to withdraw the British liaison teams at Kalawsk and Szczecin. "Experience has shown," a Berlin-based administrator wrote, "that they are powerless to prevent Germans from being transferred under inhumane conditions and their presence only serves as an excuse for the Poles to claim that the British authorities have approved the conditions under which the Germans have been expelled."[88] The second step was to concoct a suitable rationale for the termination of the program. To this end, Military Government engaged in a little creative accounting of its own. According to figures it presented at CRX, 1,134,000 Germans had been received from Poland through official channels by the end of November 1946, together with another 184,000 unofficial expellees from the Recovered Territories who had presented themselves at British reception camps. Additionally, 100,000 Germans from the Recovered Territories had found their way, by one means or another, to the U.S. zone. The British were bound to accept these also in an interzonal transfer. Altogether, then, the British zone had admitted or would shortly admit rather more than 1,400,000 Recovered Territories Germans. Because "unofficials" were continuing to arrive at a rate of two thousand per week, Britain's quota of 1,500,000 million admissions from Poland under the ACC agreement would be fulfilled sometime around the end of July 1947.[89] No need existed, therefore, for any further "organized transfers," and none would be accepted.

Predictably, Colonel Prawin, backed up by Soviet representatives in the four-power administration of Germany, vigorously disputed the British calculations. Prawin disagreed that any "unofficial" expellees ought to be counted against the quota. There was no telling when, or how, these had arrived in Germany, but in light of the fact that the British zone did not share a frontier with Poland, they had clearly not done so directly. According to Polish figures, only 1,156,000 Germans had been transferred to the British zone. Another 334,000 thus remained to be admitted. As the British remained obdurate, Prawin softened his position. His government, he told the British, was "not so much interested in the full amount being received into the [British] Zone as in the fact that British Authorities do not reject the principle of receiving any transferees from Poland altogether."[90] If London were prepared to accept, say, another 150,000 Germans, Warsaw might be willing to call it a day.[91] Dangling a still more tempting carrot before the British, Prawin added that "the percentage of able-bodied men among prospective transferees is high, embracing qualified workers in industry and mining who may be usefully employed in your Zone. Under [the] circumstances I strongly feel that British agreement to resume transports into the British Zone would be of real advantage to the economy of your Zone and would certainly be highly appreciated by the Polish Government." In a face-to-face meeting with Bevin at the end of April 1947, the Polish foreign minister, Zygmunt Modzelewski, intimated he would be satisfied if the British took just 50,000 more expellees. If this were agreed, he promised, "much would have been done to improve Anglo-Polish relations."[92]

British officials remained unimpressed. After two years of increasingly acrimonious exchanges between the two countries over everything from the fate of the London Poles to the future of Polish displaced persons still in Germany, they no longer considered that the prospect of better relations with Warsaw was worth paying even the bargain-basement price Modzelewski declared himself willing to accept. The ever-credulous Cavendish-Bentinck aside, they were more skeptical still of Prawin's offer of skilled workers. Several months previously, the Poles had suggested that the pace of expulsions be doubled before the onset of the worst winter weather, hinting that if the British agreed, they would be rewarded by being sent a large number of German miners—the most valuable category of skilled labor in postwar Europe. The offer was rejected, firstly because the British were convinced "we should not get these miners and it would give the Poles another chance to cheat," and secondly because if, having insisted that there was no more room in Germany for additional newcomers, Military Government was to find housing and food for especially valuable workers, "the arguments we used when reducing Swallow would look foolish not to say dishonest."[93] In any event, officials saw Prawin's tacit acknowledgment that the Poles had indeed been holding back fit men while dumping the Recovered Territories' unemployables upon the British zone as further confirmation, if any were needed, that Warsaw could not be trusted.

The British responded even more forcefully to Soviet accusations that they were engaging in deceptive practices to wriggle out of full compliance with the ACC agreement. To include "unofficial expellees" in the overall tally, the Soviets argued, meant that a German officially transferred from the Recovered Territories to east Germany who then made his way into the British zone would be counted twice, to Poland's disadvantage. Furthermore, British claims that their occupation zone was full were belied by the presence in displaced persons camps of 260,000 anti-Soviet Poles, and tens of thousands of anticommunist Balts, Yugoslavs, and others to whom the authorities were giving asylum. Let these elements be forcibly returned home, Soviet delegates proclaimed, and there would be plenty of room in the west for the remaining Germans of the Recovered Territories.[94] To these arguments Military Government officials responded with spluttering fury. As one officer fumed, "We don't care a damn whether these [unofficial expellees] have been counted twice (once over Soviet border, once over ours)—the fact is we have them and they are eating here and living here." After insisting that its own occupation zone could accept no more expellees, moreover, the USSR was in no position to cast aspersions at others in light of its recent unilateral decision to admit fifty thousand more from Hungary to spare the blushes of its protégés in Budapest. "This is a breach of faith and also an excellent reason for [the Soviets] keeping their mouths shut about our Chetniks and Yugoslavs."[95]

On July 28, 1947, consequently, the British Government officially announced the termination of Operation Swallow. Its end went unmourned in the West, especially among those humanitarian organizations whose resources had been stretched beyond the breaking point in trying to mitigate the suffering it had caused. A great deal of this distress never found its way into official statistics. In this context "Operation Swallow," Father Edward Swanstrom of the U.S. Catholic Church's War Relief Services remarked, had been "as callous a bit of human engineering as the post-war west can boast." In a single makeshift geriatric infirmary that he visited at the former Salzgitter concentration camp southeast of Hanover, "more than 400 old people, weakened by the deportation and the consequent hunger and lack of care, had died while Swallow was in progress."[96] Human consequences like these, no mention of which is to be found in the Foreign Office files, should be borne in mind in light of recent assertions that Operation Swallow was accomplished "with very little loss of life . . ."[97]

The process by which the U.S. authorities cast off the burden of further "organized transfers" from Czechoslovakia was almost identical to the method used by the British, though there is nothing to suggest coordinated action between the two Western powers. In April 1946, Colonel Fye had obtained a private interview with President Beneš and "told him quite frankly of the difficulties we were having as a result of the 'little people' in his machine, who either through willfulness or indifference, were ignoring the terms of the transfer." Fye was struck by the president's "complete familiarity with the expulsion movement as far as the technical details were concerned," but noted that Beneš offered "no commitment or promise of corrective action."[98] Accordingly, the U.S. authorities had proceeded to unilateral action. As noted above, admissions were curtailed from six daily trains to four on July 15. On October 4, OMGUS informed the Czechoslovaks that no trains at all would be accepted from eight named districts, in light of their persistent lack of compliance with the transfer agreement. Twelve days later, the daily flow was reduced to three trains, and from November 1, to just three ordinary trains and five "antifascist" trains—each carrying just three hundred especially privileged Socialist or Communist German expellees, with their luggage—per week. Finally, after admitting about 1,340,000 *Sudetendeutsche* through official channels—a figure the Czechoslovaks disputed, claiming that only 1,222,000 had been transferred—OMGUS declared an open-ended suspension of further acceptances on December 1, 1946, citing unfavorable weather conditions and "the desperate economic and housing conditions prevailing in the [U.S.] Zone."[99]

Like the British, the Americans saw no good reason not to make the "temporary" hiatus a permanent one, by adding to their count another 118,000 *Sudetendeutsche* who had arrived in their zone via Austria, and a further 325,000 entering between the conclusion of the ACC agreement and the beginning of organized expulsions two months later or by illegal means. Combining all these figures, together with those expelled Germans who properly belonged to the Soviet or British zones but were unlikely to be removable, the U.S. embassy in Prague calculated that the Americans had already overfulfilled their quota by about 30 percent.[100] Major General Frank Keating, Clay's deputy, privately confirmed in April 1947 that so far as OMGUS was concerned, expulsions from both Czechoslovakia and Hungary to the U.S. zone had concluded and would never be resumed.[101] The U.S. authorities did not announce their decision, though, until the following August, eliciting "a howl from the Czechs who said that the Americans were going back on their word, breaking the Potsdam Agreement and so forth . . ."[102] Trying the same tactics that had already been used by the Poles, Interior Minister Václav Nosek denied in back-channel representations to the American authorities that more than 230,000 unofficial expellees could possibly be in the U.S. zone. OMGUS, according to Czechoslovak calculations, was liable to admit nearly 400,000 more *Sudetendeutsche*. However, in the interest of a quick resolution of the matter, Prague volunteered to waive all further claims if the Americans would take just 100,000 additional Germans.[103] This offer made as negligible an impression on OMGUS as did Colonel Prawin's similar overture to the Foreign Office. As an American official pointed out to Eric Mayer of the CICR, the admission of each additional expellee burdened U.S. taxpayers with more than a hundred dollars per year in enhanced occupation costs, which the American government was no longer prepared to pay.[104] Like their British counterparts, then, by the end of 1946 the United States authorities were no longer in the expulsion business.

That left the USSR as the last remaining power that still was. Shortly after the Anglo-Americans had suspended movements into their zones at the end of 1946, the Soviets took the opportunity to do likewise. With previous experience in mind, they were in no hurry to resume them. Negotiations with the Poles proceeded at a deliberate pace, and were not concluded until April 12, 1947. This time, in return for removing the 520,000 Germans that Wolski estimated still remained in the Recovered Territories, the Soviet authorities in Germany insisted on a protocol considerably more favorable to them—and, hence, to the expellees—than its 1946 predecessor. Under its terms, Prawin was obliged to lift all limits on the quantity of baggage and German currency expellees were permitted to carry with them; to enforce the rules concerning medical certification (the previous year the Soviets had repeatedly complained about the "poor sanitary conditions in which the sick were transported"); to ensure that each expellee carried his or her own personal identity document; and to provide all necessary food for the journey with a three days' reserve.[105] In return, the Soviets agreed to accept two trains on weekdays, each of no more than 1,500 Germans, at the Kałaswk or Tuplice entry points.

Some evidence suggests that the Soviets did try harder than in previous years to maintain these standards. Once again, though, the overriding necessity of transporting a large number of people in a short period of time made any kind of systematic enforcement impossible. Soon after the trains began running again on April 18, the same complaints about overcrowded wagons, malnourished and diseased Germans, the separation of families, and illegal confiscations and robberies began to resurface. Within less than a week, the Soviet Military Mission had presented its Polish counterparts with a comprehensive laundry list of grievances: the provision of unsanitary cattle cars without floor covering; insufficient food for the journeys; medical certificates that were dirty, written in pencil, and illegible; inaccurate nominal lists; ambulance cars that were unhygienic or missing; and many similar deficiencies. Part of the problem, the official who forwarded these representations to the PUR director in Wrocław reminded him, was that his personnel had received no wages for the previous month.[106]

At least twice during the 1947 expulsion season, the Soviet authorities imposed partial suspensions of transports due to outbreaks of typhus among the expellees.[107] As the PUR office at the Kaławsk transit point splenetically reported, a "violent breakdown" of the repatriation action had occurred even before the second of these shutdowns as a result of mismanagement, ignorance of duty, poor communication of instructions, and alcohol abuse on the part of the Polish personnel. While the hiatus lasted, Kaławsk—lacking as it did adequate accommodation, toilets, and delousing facilities—had degenerated into a shocking state of dung-covered filth. "One would have supposed that the railway authorities, the train dispatcher, the medical officer on duty, etc., were working with all their strength to furnish the representatives of first the British and then the Soviet Missions with arguments to discredit contemporary Poland." The PUR demanded that the head of the transfer point be given the powers of a "repatriation dictator" over all other officials, who were "graciously condescend[ing]" to comply with requests that they follow regulations only when they could be bothered to do so.[108] No action, however, was taken to address these shortcomings. A CICR delegate who revisited Kaławsk in August found much with which he was dissatisfied, including an elderly couple who had been beaten up and robbed by the People's Militia. (When he complained to the Polish commandant, the latter initially claimed that this was the first such incident that had ever occurred—as the CICR man dryly observed, "a rather strange coincidence" with his own visit—and then explained that "this act had undoubtedly been perpetrated by bandits disguised as Militia.")[109] Theft from and abuse of Germans continued, to such a degree that an MZO inspector based in Olsztyn recommended that nighttime expulsions be discontinued so as to reduce the vulnerability of the deportees to the bands that preyed upon them.[110] The Soviets, it is true, did crack down on the practice of separating families, on one occasion sending an entire transport back to Potulice camp because family members had been removed en route.[111] As Bernadetta Nitschke points out, though, the reduced number of deaths occurring in the course of the 1947 transports had as much to do with the fact that they avoided the winter months as with any supposed improvement in organization.[112]

While on a much reduced scale compared with the mass deportations of the previous year, the 1947 population transfers from Poland still posed a significant administrative burden in the Soviet zone. As the autumn approached, and despite their earlier promises to take as many Germans as the Poles were prepared to send, the Soviet authorities in Germany began dropping increasingly heavy hints that the time to draw a line under the operation would have arrived when the number of acceptances reached the figure of 520,000 that Wolski had mentioned earlier in the year. In the event, that target was overshot slightly. The last official transports accepted were those already on their way to the Tuplice crossing point by November 1; others arriving later were turned back. Nonetheless, according to MZO figures a total of 593,120 Germans were removed from Poland in 1947; when unofficial departures are included, the average weekly rate of deportations during the thirty weeks of the year in which organized expulsions had taken place exceeded 20,000. By the time they came to an end, the number of Germans remaining in "New Poland" was insignificant, consisting of a few hundred thousand skilled workers, detainees in labor camps, unreleased prisoners of war, spouses (usually wives) in mixed marriages, and children whose relatives could not be traced. With the main phase of the expulsion program completed, the Polish state's concern increasingly swung round in the direction of trying to retain and Polonize its remaining Germans, in the face of their desire not to remain as members of a shrinking and discriminated-against minority.

Even so, small-scale aftershocks of the mass expulsions persisted into 1948 and 1949. Between October 1947 and October 1948, around 100,000 Germans were deported by the Red Army from the East Prussian territory around Kaliningrad (Königsberg) annexed by the USSR to the Soviet occupation zone. Each family was allowed to bring three hundred kilograms of personal possessions, in an operation that earned praise from expellees for the efficiency with which it was conducted.[113] In a bilateral accord concluded with Warsaw in May 1948, the Soviets promised to accept up to 30,000 additional Germans, dispatched in twenty trains via Tuplice during the summer and early autumn, in exchange for Poland's guarantee that the deportation would be accompanied by 3,000 German miners (70 percent of whom, the Soviets prudently specified, were to be under the age of forty-five years) and their families.[114] The final organized transports occurred in the summer of 1949, when another Polish-Soviet agreement provided for the dissolution of the remaining labor camps for Germans in Poland and the removal of their inmates, a total of 24,000 persons, to East Germany.

Under the terms of this arrangement, every individual transport was to carry a specified minimum percentage of fit workers, the precise number to be determined by the age distribution of the expellees concerned. The operation was completed between April and August 1949.[115] Of all the transfers that had taken place since the war, these came closest to satisfying the Potsdam Agreement's demand for "orderly and humane" conditions. The reason was less the result of any steps taken by the Warsaw government—the assembly camp at Głubczyce, for example, remained a black spot in which far too many expellees were crowded in unsanitary conditions for many days—than the final exhaustion of the Soviet authorities' patience with Polish breaches of the agreement.[116] From the summer of 1948 onward, the Red Army liaison team at Tuplice developed a hair-trigger mentality, rejecting any train that was not in full compliance with the minimum standards specified.[117] This, in turn, obliged the Poles to pay greater attention to the fulfillment of their commitments. Thus when Jerzy Szczepanik of the PUR found that a train of 1,528 expellees from Gorzów Wielkopolski in June 1948 was predominantly composed of paralyzed and disabled people, invalids, mothers of small children, nuns, and individuals with no experience of agricultural work—and that none was in possession of identification papers—he insisted that it be returned to its place of origin and the process of assembling the transport be started again from scratch, in view of the near-certainty that the Soviets would refuse to admit it.[118]

In this final phase of mass expulsions, about seventy-seven thousand Germans were deported from their birthplaces. A comparative trickle would continue to be removed in subsequent years, with a total of approximately thirty thousand former *Volksdeutsche* from Poland being transported to the DDR, with the agreement of the East Berlin government, in the years 1950 and 1951.[119] Long before then, the expelling countries began a series of public celebrations, both local and national, to mark the "cleansing" of their territories. In Lower Silesia, for example, a bonus pool of 300,000 zlotys was established for PUR staff in recognition of the expulsion of the 500,000th German from the province.[120] The passage of the half-millionth expellee through the Kaławsk border point was also the occasion of festive events. The German concerned, a small child, was given a bar of chocolate by the PUR in recognition of the milestone; the Polish expulsion staff celebrated with a banquet the same evening.[121] In Czechoslovakia, too, a series of commemorative functions was organized to mark the last official transfer of Germans. The Prague government had tried hard to complete the operation by October 28, 1946, the country's Independence Day. Although that deadline was missed, with eight transports to the U.S. zone continuing each week until December 1, elaborate ceremonies were held in numerous towns across the country at the close of 1946, to which foreign dignitaries were invited and decorations awarded to those who had distinguished themselves by their zeal in the de-Germanization campaign.[122] Particularly helpful Allied officers were also honored: Colonel John Fye, for example, was awarded the Order of the White Lion, the country's highest decoration for foreigners, in recognition of his services, as *Rudé právo* put it, "in expelling Germans from Czechoslovakia."[123] In his Christmas Eve broadcast, Edvard Beneš invited his compatriots to rejoice over the fact that "this was Czechoslovakia's first Christmas without the Germans."[124]

This sense of satisfaction, though, would not last for long. For one thing, the expelling countries could never be sure that their German populations had gone for good. Because no peace treaty was concluded at the end of the war, the frontiers of the postwar Germany—and those of its neighbors—remained provisional. There was no guarantee that the Allies might not decide after all that it was too dangerous to have a divided Germany filled with rootless, embittered people in the middle of the European continent, and at some point in the future return at least some of its lost territories to it. Nor could the fear that Germany might one day rise again, and seek revenge for what had occurred during the expulsions, entirely be dispelled. In consequence, Poles and Czechoslovaks were never able to stop looking over their shoulders. To this day some continue to do so.

A second sobering consideration was the extent of the self-inflicted damage done to the demographic and economic fabrics of the expelling societies. Already severely disrupted by the war, they were ill prepared for another round of profound upheavals—especially when these were conducted from the top down by politicians and bureaucrats whose ideological idées fixes insulated them from reality. The belief of all the expelling states that eager colonists would flock into the districts newly purged of Germans was quickly disappointed. For decades to come, these borderland regions would remain the most sparsely populated and undeveloped parts of the countries to which they belonged.

Probably the most damaging consequences of the expulsions, though, were the aspects that could not be quantified. In each of the expelling countries, the removal of the Germans had made necessary the suspension of any concept of human rights and the rule of law. Arbitrary decrees had proclaimed entire categories of people to be, as a group of American critics put it, "men without the Rights of Man." By administrative fiat, individuals were deprived of property, bodily integrity, liberty, and life itself. The exercise of "surplus cruelty" in the accomplishment of the goal of national cleansing—even against the most helpless or unresisting of victims—was deemed a positive good, a demonstration of patriotic commitment, or a necessary catharsis. Knowledge of these abuses was concealed or denied, not just by the state but by ordinary citizens, who in this way assumed a degree of complicity, however remote, in what was being done in their names. The culture of the lie, as a means of assuaging or deadening individual consciences no less than as an instrument of official policy, was allowed to prevail. And even after the supposed defeat of the totalitarian heresy epitomized by the Nazis, entire societies continued to be reinforced in the belief that immensely complex political and social problems, developed over centuries, could be banished at a stroke by the adoption of radical solutions involving massive amounts of violence. The supposition that all these things could be directed against a single group of perceived enemies and then never again resorted to for any other purpose, that afterwards it would be possible to return to a peaceful, ordered existence in which individual rights would once more be upheld and respected, would prove to be the most delusional aspect of this entire tragic episode.

Figure 1. Edvard Beneš.

Figure 2. Wenzel Jaksch. ČTK Photo FO00460325.

Figure 3. Column of prisoners at Jaworzno camp. PRO FO 371/100718. © HMSO

Figure 4. A Polish colonist is shown the location of the confiscated German farm he is to receive. Shaw Jones, UNRRA 2416, UN Archives, New York.

Figure 5. A Czech "organized expulsion" in progress at Nový Jičín. Margaret Fait Papers, box 4/16, Hoover Institution Archives.

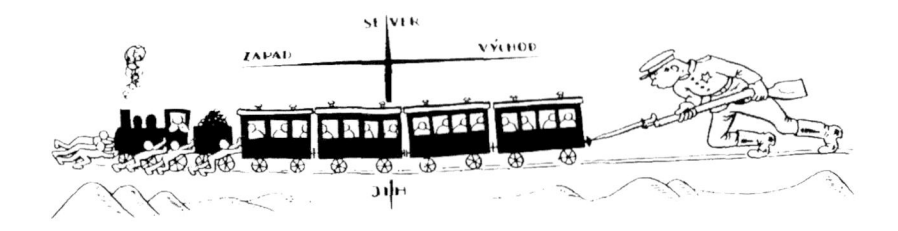

Figure 6. One Czech cartoonist's view of the expulsions: a Soviet soldier pushes the *Sudetendeutsche* across the country's western frontier, obstructed by the Anglo-Americans.

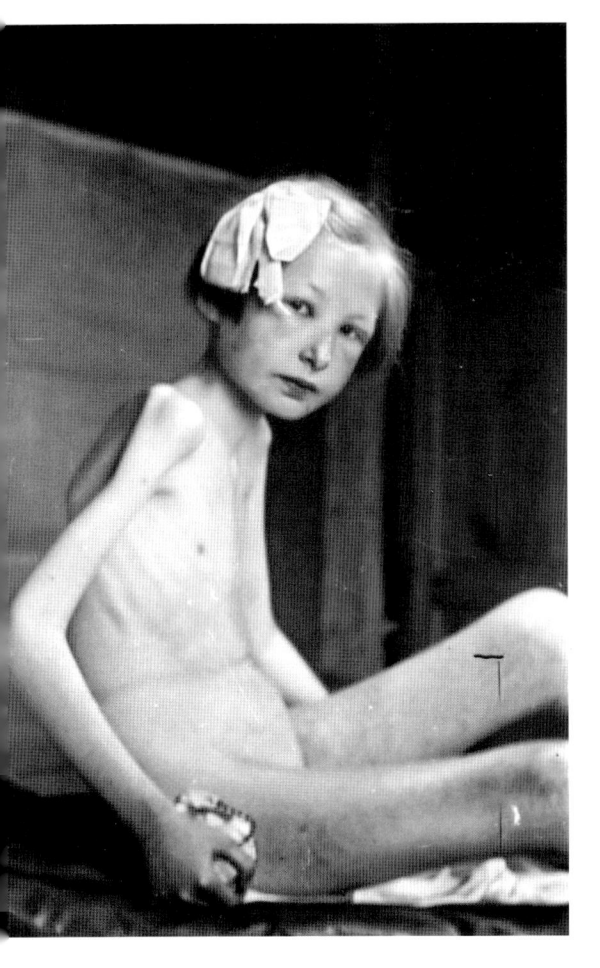

Figure 7. Operation Swallow: An expellee from the Recovered Territories, her lower limbs swollen from hunger edema. Christopher Emmet Papers, box 29, Hoover Institution Archives.

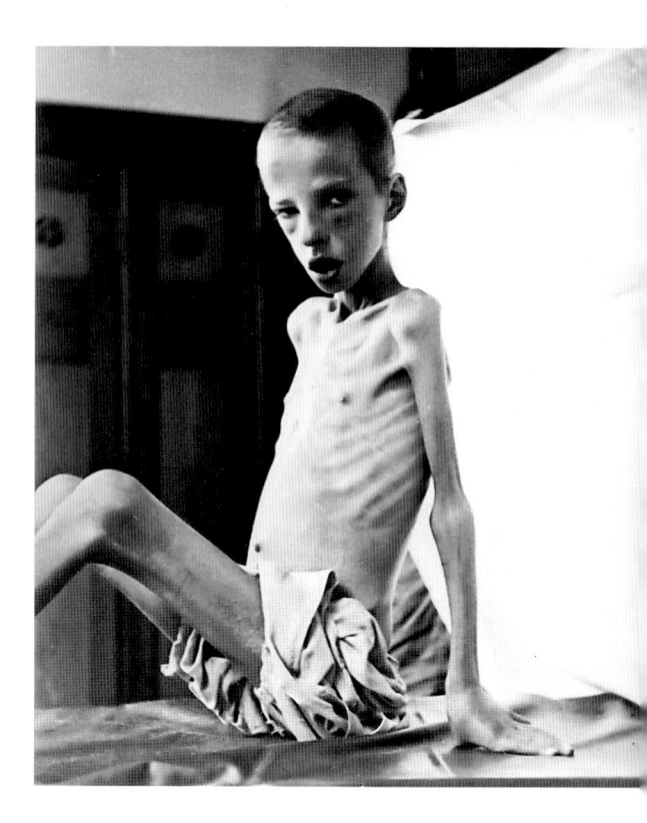

Figure 8. Operation Swallow: A shaven-headed eleven-year-old girl from the Recovered Territories, weighing only thirty-one pounds at the time of her expulsion. Christopher Emmet Papers, box 29, Hoover Institution Archives.

Figure 9. Operation Swallow: Elderly expellees assisted onto German soil at Travemünde near Lübeck, under the supervision of a British soldier. Christopher Emmet Papers, box 29, Hoover Institution Archives.

Figure 10. An ethnic German child, transported from Eastern Europe, waits beside sacks of provisions. ICRC V-P-HIST-03226–22.

Figure 11. Václav Hrneček, deputy commandant of Linzervorstadt camp, arriving for his trial in 1953.

Figure 12. A West German postage stamp commemorates the tenth anniversary of the expulsions.

8

The Children

In April 1946 Willy Montandon, a member of the CICR delegation in Czechoslovakia, called at the Modřany internment camp in the southern suburbs of Prague. He had brought a doctor with him in the hope of providing medical attention to an elderly female *Sudetendeutsch* inmate who was soon to be expelled, but was allowed to proceed no further than the camp commandant's office. There he was shown an order of the minister of the interior, issued two weeks previously, that "formally prohibited any person whatever from entering the camp and speaking with the internees who did not possess a written authorization by the said ministry—the representatives of the International Red Cross and UNRRA included." On his way out of the compound, Montandon was stopped by a young detainee, Emma Duda, who asked for his help. Duda, a Prague resident, told him that her two little daughters—Inge and Ilse, aged five and three respectively—had been taken from her by the Czech authorities at the time of her arrest during the May 1945 "revolution." She had heard nothing of them since then.

> To our question as to whether she could give us any details, any indications that might facilitate fresh inquiries, she remained silent for a moment, then resumed in that same almost inaudible, quiet, even-toned voice: "Yes, they were both so very pretty and very well-behaved . . ." That was all. The sight of this mother, indifferent to anything apart from her missing little girls; this almost instinctual grief; this total obliviousness to everything that surrounded her; this perfect unconcern for her own circumstances; the contrast between this steady voice and these drawn, almost hard features, at once calm and tragic, had something unbearable in it that left me, accustomed to such things as I

am, speechless. I was unable to do anything except silently grip that unresponsive hand of hers and quickly signal to the driver to move on.[1]

Such cases were neither unusual nor accidental. According to an estimate by Monsignor Edward Swanstrom, who spearheaded the U.S. National Catholic Welfare Conference's relief effort in Europe after the war, between 160,000 and 180,000 of the children who became separated from their parents in the course of the transfer operation had not been reunited with them by 1950.[2] Many of these separations, as he pointed out, were the inevitable consequences of "snap" expulsions, as exemplified by the story of "a young boy who had walked to a nearby town to go to the store, and before he returned his whole family was forcibly loaded on to a truck and taken to a detention camp for expulsion."[3] Others occurred as a result of the equally common practice of separating families during the expulsion process itself, when "men and women, if they were healthy and able to work, were fetched out of the train . . . and the children were left alone travelling in that train."[4] But in innumerable cases the sins of the parents were knowingly visited on German children, both within and without the internment camps. And many others, like the Duda daughters, were treated as war booty, being kept behind after the removal of their parents to make good wartime losses of population, or in conformity with quasi-racial theories of the proportion of Czechoslovak or Polish "blood" carried in their veins.

Like so many other aspects of the expulsion program, the precedent was set by Nazi Germany in its plans for occupied Poland. Under the *Generalplan Ost*, the Germans' master plan for the ethnic cleansing of central and eastern Europe, the Race and Settlement Main Office, an agency of the SS, was made responsible for identifying and removing from their parents "racially valuable" Polish children under the age of eight to ten years. Heinrich Himmler, who visited Poland after the September campaign of 1939, had been impressed by the number of blond-haired and blue-eyed children he found there. Many supposed "Poles," he believed, were racial Aryans who had undergone "Polonization" and who, if they were young enough, could be reeducated to become part of the German nation. In the following years, teams of women (the so-called "Brown Sisters") from the *Nationalsozialistische Volkswohlfahrtsamt* or National Socialist People's Welfare Office scoured occupied Poland in cooperation with SS racial investigators, abducting "potentially Nordic" children from orphanages, schools, and sometimes public streets. These children were subjected to a battery of physical and psychological tests. The many failures—some 90 percent—were returned home, taken as forced labor to Germany, or, in some cases, sent to death camps for immediate extermination. Children satisfying the racial criteria would be placed in *Lebens-*

born institutions; if older, they might be adopted by German families charged with the task of reversing the "Polonization" they had undergone since their birth.[5] Most records of the Nazi racial kidnapping scheme were destroyed before the war's end; estimates of the number of Polish children swept up in it range from 20,000 to 200,000.[6] Whatever the true figure may have been, it is thought that no more than 15 percent of the abductees were ever reunited with their parents.[7] In like manner, smaller numbers of "racially valuable" children, whose parents had been killed by the Germans as partisans or in the course of reprisals—as in the case of the massacre at Lidice—were removed from the occupied Soviet Union, Czechoslovakia, and Yugoslavia and sent to the Reich for Germanization.[8] A further rationale behind the operation, as Himmler explained, was not merely to ensure that reservoirs of desirable genetic material should not be lost, but to weaken the racial stock of Germany's eastern enemies by diminishing the quotient of "Nordic blood" in the Polish or Ukrainian gene pools.

After the war, Czechoslovak and Polish discourses on the fate of children in the expulsion program sometimes bore an uncomfortably close resemblance to those of their Nazi predecessors. The already vexed question of "who is a German?" presented itself in the case of the offspring of mixed marriages in an especially acute form. The debate often revolved around the supposed "strength" of the respective racial influences: whether "Aryan" or "Slavic" tendencies—which in the postwar era had the values the Nazis had attached to them simply inverted— would gain the upper hand once the child reached adulthood. The answer to this question frequently determined whether the children of mixed marriages would be expelled along with their German parent for possessing "tainted" blood or be permitted to stay with their "Slavic" one. However unsavory such Social Darwinian categories might have been, they nonetheless implied that these children would remain in the custody of at least one of their natural parents. Those officials who maintained that "nurture" was more powerful than "nature," on the other hand, raised a more ominous scenario yet: that the children of mixed marriages, or even those of purely German descent, could be reeducated as good Czechoslovaks or Poles by removing them altogether from the corrupting influence of their German relatives.

Before the Second World War, heated disputes over the national identity of children had been a regular feature of Czechoslovak life in the First Republic. Schools in particular were seen as key battlegrounds in the quest to de-Germanize the country. As Tara Zahra notes, in the early years of Czechoslovak independence "local Czech nationalist associations flooded the government with petitions urging the state to eliminate German schools . . . in the name of protecting both Czech ethnicity and democracy."[9] Sudeten Germans responded by vandalizing Czech-language schools, a practice that had been a popular pastime for Czechs and Germans alike before the Great War when both linguistic groups were subjects of the Austro-Hungarian Empire.[10] Under the First Republic, the tendency of some Czech parents to send their children to German-language schools, believing that they would receive a better education there and that the language would be more useful to them, caused particular anxiety to the majority population. Members of the local gendarmerie often intervened in such cases to seize the children and enroll them compulsorily in Czech schools; sometimes German schools were closed by the state for admitting children of the "wrong" ethnicity. Where ethnic German parents sent their children to the better-funded Czech schools, on the other hand, the fact was taken by census authorities as evidence for reclassifying them as ethnically Czech. The result was to sharpen the self-segregation of the two communities, as ethnic Germans found themselves compelled to enroll their children in German institutions and associations in an attempt to provide the "objective" markers of national identity that might hold sway with a Czechoslovak court. "In its determination to prevent the Germanization of Czech children," Zahra concludes, "the Czechoslovak state imagined [into existence] extraordinary social and cultural boundaries between the German and Czech populations in the Bohemian Lands."[11]

During the war years, although the tables between the two ethnic groups were turned, the underlying equation was not. Nazi occupiers and Czech nationalists continued to try to police the national identities of the Protectorate's children, and enjoyed little more success in this endeavor than their prewar counterparts. Upwardly mobile Czech families had additional incentives to place their children in German schools or to enroll them in German-language courses; on the other side of the ethnic divide, a surprising number of *Sudetendeutsche* resisted what they saw as the obtrusive Germanization policies of the occupiers, even to the point of refusing to apply for the German citizenship for themselves and their children to which, under Nazi law, they were entitled.[12] In general the children of mixed marriages were automatically classified as possessing German nationality. Nonetheless, the comparatively light hand with which the Germans governed the Protectorate—such a qualification, needless to say, having only a relative meaning in the Nazi spectrum of brutality—as well as the degree of respect accorded by the occupiers to "German-loyal" Czech culture; the noninterference of the Germans in the educational policy of the collaborationist Tiso regime in Slovakia; and the brevity of the occupation meant that the war years witnessed fewer attempts to conscript Gentile Czechoslovak children of all ethnicities into the Nazi new order than might have been expected.

Poland's experience was very different. Between the wars, attempts by the

Polish state to eradicate "Germanism" within the republic, again especially within the schools, had been pursued even more vigorously and coercively than in Czechoslovakia. Aided by lavish subventions from Berlin, the German minority vigorously resisted these efforts, hiring itinerant German teachers to provide home schooling to children who otherwise would have been obliged to attend a Polish institution.[13] Both sides' paranoia over "Germanization" and "Polonization" of each other's children was fueled by a sense of vulnerability. From the earliest days of the Polish Second Republic, the Warsaw government remained keenly conscious of the tenuousness of the Polish nation-building enterprise. The state contained within its borders more than a dozen ethnic minorities, from Ukrainians in the east to Lithuanians in the northwest. Less than two-thirds of the republic's population at the moment of its creation was Polish. The dominance of the Catholic Church over the Polish education system also gave rise to constant tensions with the country's *Volksdeutsche*, the majority of whom were Protestants. By 1939, in response to Hitler's increasingly menacing stance vis-à-vis his Polish neighbor, the Warsaw government was actively targeting members of the German minority who sent their children to private German-language schools.[14] If the grievances of the German population had been greater than in Czechoslovakia, however, the revenge taken by Poland's German conquerors after 1939 was disproportionate in the extreme. Other than the compulsorily Germanized youth of the Incorporated Eastern Territories and the "racially valuable" component of the juvenile population elsewhere in Poland, the Nazis regarded Polish children, like the Polish people in general, as suitable only for satisfying the manual labor requirements of the Reich. All Polish schools above the elementary level were closed, their teachers often being murdered as part of a deliberate strategy to deprive the Polish nation of an intellectual class; children were made liable to eviction from their homes or to compulsory labor service in the German war economy; and some were subjected to medical experiments in the camps.

After the Nazis' defeat, the new regimes of central and eastern Europe were in no humor to try to distinguish between culpable and innocent Germans. This uncompromising attitude extended to German children, for whom in practice few exceptions were made. One example of the prevailing mood was the satisfaction expressed by the Prague newspaper *Mladá Fronta* over the British government's rejection of proposals to provide a temporary haven for ten thousand starving German children during the winter of 1945–46, against which it had been running a ferocious campaign: its headline, when an announcement was made that the scheme would not after all go ahead, read: "British Will Not Feed Little Hitlerites: Our Initiative Crowned With Success."[15] Another example was the official scale of food rations laid down by the Czech government, which made even the youngest *Sudetendeutsch* children answerable for the misdeeds of their parents. From August 1945, German children under the age of six were allocated only half the allowance of milk, and rather less than half the allowance of barley, specified for their Czech counterparts. German children were to receive no meat, eggs, jam, or fruit syrup at all, these being reserved for the infants of the majority.[16] In the Recovered Territories, on the other hand, such considerations did not arise: as ration cards were progressively withdrawn from the German population, like their parents German children found themselves entitled to no rations at all. Thus the head of the Szczecin-Stołczyn Commissariat indignantly contradicted the allegation of a local newspaper that Germans in his district had been receiving daily supplies of milk; since the end of November 1945, he proudly reported, even German children under the age of two had had their milk allocation withdrawn from them.[17] Likewise, the age at which children were counted as "adults" for the purpose of compulsory labor was largely at the whim of local administrators. Normally, Germans in Czechoslovakia were liable to become forced laborers on their fourteenth birthday (sometimes, in the case of girls, their fifteenth). In some districts, though, labor services were required of all those aged ten or above.[18] Children of ten years of age and above were also routinely used as forced laborers in Yugoslavia.[19]

By far the worst conditions were experienced by children in the detention centers. As the first improvised internment camps were thrown up—some forty of these, housing between twenty and twenty-five thousand ethnic German detainees, had been established in Prague alone by the end of May 1945[20]—babies and children were swept inside along with their parents. Their undeveloped immune systems and lack of physical reserves left them particularly vulnerable to the ravages of hunger and disease. The terrifying speed which the condition of the very young deteriorated in the camps was recorded by a social worker from Prague, Přemysl Pitter, in the summer of 1945. A quietly heroic figure, Pitter had been converted to a profound Christian pacifism by his experiences as a soldier in the Austro-Hungarian army during the Great War. Between the wars he had directed a shelter for vulnerable children; his courageous efforts to shield his Jewish charges from the Nazis throughout the occupation would later be recognized by his designation as one of the Righteous Among the Nations at the Yad Vashem memorial in Jerusalem. After V-E Day, he reopened his shelter at a derelict castle in Lojovice to succor Jewish children who had survived imprisonment in Nazi camps. As he visited the new Czechoslovak regime's detention centers, however, he quickly found that the overwhelming majority of those who needed his aid were ethnic Germans. At the K. V. Rais school, a makeshift internment camp in the Vinohrady district of Prague, for example, Pitter and his handful of helpers discovered at the end of July 1945 "a hell of which passers-by hadn't the faintest notion." More than a thousand German detainees, the great majority women and children, were "crowded together in an indescribable tangle. As we brought emaciated and apathetic children out and laid them on the grass, I believed that few would survive. Our physician, Dr. E. Vogl, himself a Jew who had gone though the hell of Auschwitz and Mauthausen, almost wept when he saw these little bodies. 'And here we Czechs have done this in two and a half months!' he exclaimed."[21] Conditions at the other Prague camps, Red Cross officials found, were no better. The CICR informed the interior minister, Václav Nosek, at the beginning of July that the fifty-one ethnic German children interned in another improvised detention center, a house at U Půjčovny near the Masarykovo railway station, had received so little food that in the previous week two had died of malnutrition. Nosek was advised that the same situation prevailed in other such detention facilities.[22] Outside the city, conditions were still worse. 508 children, 74 of whom were under two years of age, were prisoners in the harsh Suchdol nad Odrou camp in late August 1945; by the end of the camp's first three weeks of operation, thirteen had died.[23]

The response of the authorities to appeals on behalf of these incarcerated children, in Czechoslovakia and elsewhere, was almost without exception to ignore them. It is true that the first edicts providing for the detention of the Germans in camps usually had exempted younger children, as well as their mothers, from arrest. In practice no such distinction was observed. Precisely because the majority of *Volksdeutsche* were women and children, to have granted immunity from arrest to both would have been to accept that most of the ethnic German population could not be interned. Nor could the adults alone have been sent to camps without throwing the burden of caring for millions of young people on the detaining governments. The result, therefore, was that—as in the case of similar "exemptions" for antifascists—the Czech, Slovak, Polish, and Romanian governments contented themselves with issuing and, in the face of external protests, repeating regulations that they had no intention of enforcing. Nosek, for example, reiterated in August 1945 that internment camps throughout the Republic were to release immediately all children under the age of fourteen, with the exception of those whose parents desired them to remain pending deportation. Youths aged between fourteen and eighteen would remain interned, but in dedicated camps separate from their families.[24] No action, though, had been taken to give effect to this instruction by the time Philip Nichols asked Prime Minister Fierlinger in late October to release women and children from the camps. Although the prime minister once again promised to do so, Nichols prudently advised Ernest

Bevin that "this was in casual conversation, and I find it difficult to believe that the Czechoslovak Government will in fact be able to follow this policy, at least for some time."[25] Thus according to the CICR, on April 1, 1946, there were approximately 2,000 children under the age of six, almost 3,300 aged between six and sixteen, and more than 1,200 youths between sixteen and twenty confined in camps in Slovakia alone.[26] In like fashion, a directive of the Polish Ministry of Public Security issued in April 1945 specifying that nobody under the age of thirteen was to be detained was accorded precisely the same level of compliance as were similar regulations prohibiting physical abuse of inmates.[27] More than two years later, the Ministry of Labor and Social Welfare was complaining that the regulations against imprisoning children in camps continued to be "completely ignored."[28] As late as January 1949, an interministerial commission ordered the immediate release of 128 German children for whom no legal basis for internment existed, while another inspectorate discovered the following August not only that 171 children continued to be held in the Gronowo camp, but that any contact between them and their incarcerated parents in the same facility was prohibited.[29]

The camp regime for child detainees varied as widely as it did for adults. With certain exceptions, there is little evidence to suggest that the authorities exerted themselves to shield children from the harsher aspects of camp life. Some detention centers required labor services of children below the age of fourteen.[30] (An extreme case was Mirošov, where the local definition of "adult" consisted of all inmates above six years of age.)[31] In the immediate postwar period, indeed, incarceration could have no less lethal consequences for children than for their elders. At the Postoloprty camp in northern Bohemia, five *Sudetendeutsch* children were flogged on the orders of a police officer, Bohuslav Marek, in June 1945 as a punishment for attempting to abscond. As he acknowledged before a Czechoslovak parliamentary commission two years later, however, the army officer overseeing the camp, Major Vojtěch Černý, disapproved of what he regarded as Marek's unwarranted leniency and had the five executed the same day by firing squad.[32] Often justified—as in this instance—by the claim that victims were members of the Hitler Youth and hence were liable to the same treatment as those belonging to other Nazi organizations, extrajudicial executions of children were covered by the same culture of impunity that applied to similar excesses directed against adults. Indeed, the widely held, though inaccurate, belief that under Nazism children had been indoctrinated to become "unquestioning automata" and "fanatical little devotees of the Führer" who robotically obeyed their leaders and routinely "blackmailed their parents by threatening to denounce them to the Party for lack of zeal" could lead them to be perceived as being even more dangerous than adults.³³ It was all of a piece, therefore, that the 1947 commission investigating the Postoloptry massacres should have found, notwithstanding Černý's forthright admission of his actions, that there was no case to answer.³⁴

Occasionally, specialized children's camps were established in which inmates, some of whom were orphaned or had become separated from their parents in the course of the expulsion, were treated humanely. The British member of Parliament Richard Stokes was generally impressed by the standard of care provided at the children's camp at Litoměřice when he visited it in September 1946, although he cautioned that he had been able to spend very little time there.³⁵ The CICR also recognized the efforts made by the camp authorities at Brno-Jundrov and České Křídlovice. Even though the children lacked adequate clothing and footwear and were forbidden to speak German, the Red Cross was favorably impressed when it viewed the camps in the summer of 1947 by the evident attention being paid to their welfare.³⁶ In both cases, though, the inspections were made at a time when the great majority of the *Sudetendeutsche* had already been expelled.

Elsewhere, however, the general picture at children's camps was far bleaker. Two fifteen-year-old German boys who escaped from the vermin-ridden Bolesławiec camp in Polish Lower Silesia in the summer of 1948 reported that the twelve to thirteen hundred children detained there were being put out to work on building projects. In December 1947 a thousand of the boys had been deported to the Soviet Union; nothing more was known about what had happened to them.³⁷ Children's camps, staffed by female *Volksdeutsch* internees, had also been set up for a brief period in 1946 in Yugoslavia to house children whose parents had died in institutions like Gakovo or Kruševlje. After three months the children were taken away by the authorities and the camps dissolved. Again, the Red Cross could obtain no further information about their fate.³⁸

However poor conditions in even the worst children's camps like Bolesławiec may have been, they were nonetheless preferable to many of the facilities in which children and adults alike were detained. To be sure, the care that parents could provide was a definite survival advantage in some facilities. The British officers who visited the squalid Turnu Măgurele camp for *Volksdeutsch* internees in southern Romania in September 1945 and recommended that the children under twelve years of age incarcerated there be set free only "where there is no political objection to the mother or father being released" no doubt feared that these young people would fare still worse if left to fend for themselves outside the camp.³⁹ But in other detention centers, juvenile inmates shared all the hardships to which their elders were subject, with the predictable consequences. The

CICR complained to Nosek in September 1945 that in the Czechoslovak camps, the young male guards treated detainees with "the utmost cruelty" and that beatings of children as well as adults were widespread.[40] Physical violence was compounded by psychological abuse of children, some of whom were compelled—as at Kruševlje in Yugoslavia—to witness their parents' torture or execution at the hands of camp guards.[41]

By far the largest number of child deaths, however, occurred as a result of starvation and its attendant diseases rather than overt maltreatment. Again, the very youngest were the most vulnerable. A credible and detailed account by a female detainee at Potulice recorded that of 110 children born in the camp between the beginning of 1945 and her eventual expulsion in December 1946, only 11 were still alive by the latter date.[42] Investigations by the CICR found high rates of infant mortality attributable to malnutrition to be no less widespread in Czechoslovakia, where a few Western journalists like Eric Gedye had also managed to see inside the camps.

> The most shocking sight was that of the babies with which most huts were filled.
>
> One woman sat with a medicine bottle full of mothers' milk—there is no other milk in the camp—trying to moisten the lips of something which she called her baby.
>
> Two months old, it was smaller than a healthy newborn baby. It had a wizened, monkey-like face, dark brown skin stretched taut over the bones, arms like matchsticks—a starving baby.
>
> Near her stood another mother holding a shrunken bundle of skin and bones, smaller than a normal two-month-old baby. I stared incredulously when she told me it was 14 months old.[43]

That Gedye had not exaggerated conditions at Hagibor, the camp to which he gained access in October 1945 by passing himself off as a Red Cross official, was confirmed when a genuine CICR delegation visited the facility three months later. The Czechoslovak commissary officer, "who gave us the impression of being a pretty hard and hypocritical individual," informed the delegation that pregnant women were not entitled to any nutritional supplement. Nursing mothers, he claimed, received 750 milliliters of milk a day, a statement contradicted by inmates. The "man of confidence" elected by the detainees to speak for them told the CICR that deaths in the camp were running at a rate of three per day, nearly all of whom were infants or the very old.[44]

The same story was received from camp after camp. A journalist from *Obzory*, who visited one of the Prague detention centers in the company of a five-year veteran of Hitler's concentration camps in the autumn of 1945, acknowledged that "mortality has increased to a horrifying degree" among the children, due to the complete absence of infant formula and the fact that the majority of nursing mothers were too emaciated to breastfeed their newborns.[45] At Nováky in Slovakia, where the guards often prevented mothers from washing their babies' linens, inmates of all ages "have their daily ration diminished if they cannot work whatever the reason. Accordingly, a mother who is taken ill will send her children to work, even if they are under 12." This camp, a perennial black spot, saw an average of one child under the age of three die each day in July 1945 as a result of malnutrition and inadequate sanitation.[46] Petržalka I contained 1,279 women and children when the CICR visited in November 1945; the thirty to fifty nursing mothers then under detention were theoretically entitled to a ration of eighteen liters of milk to be shared among them, to supplement a daily regime estimated by the camp medical staff of between 430 and 520 calories. In practice even this meager allotment was often withheld. The CICR noted that among the list of those who had died in Petržalka "the great number of children is truly striking," and the clothing of surviving children was "in a piteous, terrible state."[47] So prevalent was "malnutrition, leading to many deaths" at the Hradišt'ko prison east of Prague, where a commissary guard ill-advisedly revealed to CICR visitors that "Czech children"—presumably the offspring of mixed marriages—in the prison "receive[d] twice as much as the Germans," that embarrassed officials of the Interior Ministry who had brought the Red Cross there to display the humane conditions of the *Sudetendeutsch* camps in the Czech lands ostentatiously dismissed the commandant on the spot.[48] Still worse was the Slovakian facility at Trnavská Cesta in Bratislava, where at the end of 1945 the CICR found that every one of the emaciated infants and children was "suffering from hideous skin eruptions," and at which conditions were "in general so desperate that it is difficult to find words" with which to comfort the detainees.[49]

An additional reason for the high rate of child mortality was the difficulty, and in some cases the impossibility, of obtaining medical care for sick children. Though Tomáš Staněk notes that as a rule, German detainees in need of hospital treatment were able to receive it, numerous cases nonetheless existed of children being denied care on the ground of their ethnicity. A British national detained at the Rupa internment camp in Prague during the summer of 1945 recorded that even the commandant's personal intervention had not been sufficient to persuade local hospitals to admit the sick child of a Norwegian fellow inmate, the wife of a German. Not a day passed during the period of her detention, she testified, without the death of a child in the camp occurring; once three of them had perished.[50] The commandant of Suchdol nad Odrou justified his refusal to do anything about the appallingly high child mortality rate in his camp by alleging that mothers deliberately made their children ill in the hope of gaining their release. A guard in this camp offered the same explanation; in his view, however, the objective of the mothers in poisoning their children was "to generate propaganda aimed at people from abroad."[51]

Many appalled local people did what they could to alleviate the suffering experienced by *Volksdeutsch* child detainees. The Potulice inmate quoted above testified that "kind farmers" had rescued some of the children of the camp as they were being transported to Bydgoszcz and brought them into their own homes. Some members of the majority populations pinned their hopes on the Western media, to which they appealed to bring the pressure of international public opinion to bear against their own governments. A guard at Hagibor confessed to Eric Gedye: "I have a baby of my own at home. Cannot someone do something, at least about the horrors these children here suffer? Sometimes I feel I cannot stand it here another day."[52] The CICR, for its part, attempted to follow up some of the many tip-offs it received—both anonymously and "on the record"—from ordinary citizens, but because of the inadequacy of the information provided was often unable to help. In January 1946, for example, the Prague delegation received a letter from a Czech woman informing them that the inmates in a camp for little girls in Veltrusy near the capital were suffering most severely from neglect. A party of Red Cross officials spent a day searching the area, but was unable to find the camp from the information provided. Later they learned that about fifty inmates were interned there. All had been detained on V-E Day in Prague and transferred to Veltrusy a month later. Six of the children had died since then from malnutrition.[53]

Any hopes that the governments or peoples of the Western Allies would intervene to assist at any rate the children behind barbed wire were quickly to be dashed. While sympathy for and outrage over their plight was expressed by a vocal minority of nongovernmental organizations and lower-ranking politicians— sometimes in the most vehement terms—Western opinion in general was not ready to deviate from the established narrative of Germans as perpetrators, regardless of the age or exact ethnic status of the "Germans" concerned. Although both the expelling countries and the Western Allies had subscribed in 1926 to the International Declaration on the Rights of the Child, which stipulated that children were to "be the first to receive relief in times of distress" without taking into account "considerations of race, nationality or creed," this remained a dead letter throughout. Like their parents, *Volksdeutsch* children were denied aid from international relief bodies like UNRRA and the International Refugee Organization (IRO) as a matter of policy. In a typical ruling of January 1948, the chief of IRO's Eligibility Division in Austria declared nine children "ineligible for any kind of assistance due to the fact that they are of German ethnic origin . . ."[54] Even the UN International Children's Emergency Fund (UNICEF) maintained a discriminatory stance, assigning priority in the provision of aid to the children of "victims of aggression" and relegating those of German background to the end of the queue.[55]

In the face of such a mentality, attempts by concerned citizens both inside and outside the expelling countries to ameliorate conditions for child detainees were uniformly unsuccessful. A letter writer in the London *Daily Herald* spoke for many of his fellow Britons when he wrote: "Enemies remain enemies in spite of the cessation of the activities of their respective armed forces, and anything done by us to alleviate their well-earned misery is against British interests."[56] In a Commons debate in October 1945, the minister of state at the Foreign Office, Hector McNeil, refused to admit any distinction between *Volksdeutsch* babies and their parents, or to "accept the suggestion that these are comparatively innocent people."[57] The German people as a whole, he declared, shared collective responsibility for the misdeeds of their political leaders. The former Minister of Food in the Churchill coalition, Lord Llewellin, took a similarly robust stance: "I remember that at the end of the last war appeals were made on the basis that the youth of Germany were suffering from malnutrition and rickets and that we ought to do something to save them from the dreadful conditions under which they had to live. Good gracious me! Those were the people who became Hitler's S.S. men twenty-five years later. Do not let us run into that kind of stupidity again this time."[58] Llewellin's Conservative colleague, Lord Mountevans, strongly agreed, expressing outrage at the damage to British prestige that humanitarian pleas on behalf of ethnic German children were doing abroad. "We are asking Europe, in fact we are asking the whole world, to laugh at us. . . . Why all this sloppy sentiment?"[59] In vain did Michael Foot, a newly elected Labour backbencher, remind Parliament of the passage of St. Luke's Gospel containing Jesus' warning that "whomsoever should offend against one of these little ones, it were better that a millstone be fastened around his neck and he be drowned in the depths of the sea." Foot disconsolately noted that "If these infamies are to be allowed to continue there will be a shortage of millstones to set beside the other shortages in Europe."[60] The left-wing publisher Victor Gollancz likewise demanded to know why McNeil, an "unusually decent and humane" man, should feel compelled "the moment he becomes a Minister, to talk like a Nazi?"

> At what age does a child become "guilty" or "responsible"? At twelve? At six? At the moment of conception? Before conception? A hair-splitting question, I

suppose: they are all guilty, says Mr McNeil, in their own persons or "through their rulers"—because "they are Germans."

This is the pure milk of the Hitlerite word.[61]

Přemsyl Pitter, for his part, concluded by early 1946 that moral appeals directed at his own government to spare *Sudetendeutsch* children were pointless. The previous summer, in an effort by the authorities in Prague to deflect persistent CICR complaints about the conditions of the camps, he had been appointed adviser to the Social Commission of the Central People's Committee, with special responsibility for women and children. In this capacity he had visited several internment camps in and around Prague accompanied by a representative of the Federation of Czech Youth, compiling evidence of homicides, flogging of pregnant *Sudetendeutsch* women, torture, and theft of food intended for inmates. His career as an official whistleblower was soon brought to a halt by Ladislav Kopřiva, the future minister of national security, who dismissed him from his position in the autumn.[62] As the highest-profile advocate of human rights for *Sudetendeutsche* in Czechoslovakia, however, Pitter continued to receive information from fellow citizens aghast at the scenes they were witnessing—as well, to be sure, as an even larger number of letters and newspaper denunciations accusing him of betrayal of the Czech nation and demanding that he be expelled to Germany along with his young charges.[63] He was also supported behind the scenes by elements of the Ministry of Social Welfare, who were fighting a determined rearguard campaign against their colleagues in the Ministry of the Interior and against the District National Committees that bore much of the responsibility for the day-to-day administration of the camps. He and they now concurred that the only chance of saving the lives of *Sudetendeutsch* children lay in getting them, and their mothers, out of Czechoslovakia as rapidly as possible. Instead of trying to halt the expulsions, these should be speeded up, and the most vulnerable given priority. Even a transit camp in a devastated Germany on the brink of famine offered its inmates a better prospect of survival than continued incarceration at home.

Encouraged by officials of the British Red Cross and by Foreign Minister Jan Masaryk, who provided him with a letter of introduction to the Foreign Office, Pitter traveled to London in February 1946 to try to persuade the British and U.S. governments to accept ten thousand children and mothers detained in the worst of the camps in central Bohemia. It is unclear why Masaryk should have lent his back-channel assistance to this mission. He may have been overtaken by a belated fit of conscience, after more than half a year of assuring the CICR that conditions in the camps would soon improve; a more likely explanation is that the foreign minister hoped that the removal of these *Sudetendeutsche* might be made a precedent for the expedited deportation of others whose situation could also be represented to the Allies as especially precarious.

In reality, Pitter's mission was doomed before it began. Five months previously, the Foreign and Home Offices in London had considered an application to provide a temporary home in Britain for some of the most vulnerable Sudeten German children to enable them to survive the winter. The Foreign Office was vigorously opposed to the idea. "We feel it would be better to do nothing than to do so little. . . . If we took a few of these people in we should only be pressed to take more; we should have no equitable basis for selecting them; and we should create a host of awkward precedents." Even if eligibility for temporary asylum was to be limited to the doubly persecuted *Sudetendeutsch* Jews, "this would not alter our view, as we feel that we can scarcely continue at this stage to rescue Jews from a Europe supposed to have been made fit again for them to live in."[64] It was, therefore, unsurprising that Pitter—whose British hosts erroneously supposed him to be the Czechoslovak Minister of Social Welfare—should have made no more progress in London than he had done in Prague. Conditions in the central Bohemian camps, he explained to officials in London, "were extremely bad, and infant mortality was 100%."[65] Nor would it be possible "for political reasons, to provide help for them in Czechoslovakia, even from outside sources."[66] British ministers, however, remained unmoved by this appeal also. John Hynd flatly refused to accept any more expellees than those contracted for in the Allied Control Council agreement of November 1945. Czechoslovakia, he pointed out, was already in receipt of large quantities of food aid from UNRRA, and there was no reason why some of this should not be used to feed the *Sudetendeutsch* detainees. "The idea that they should be forced out of an U.N.R.R.A. country into Germany, where prospects of widespread starvation are already appearing and no U.N.R.R.A. supplies [are] allowed, seems monstrous."[67] A reflection of the urgency Whitehall attached to the plight of the *Sudetendeutsch* children was provided by the fact that Ambassador Nichols in Prague did not offer his views on Pitter's appeal until the beginning of April 1946, two months after this visit to London. For "various reasons," he advised, "it is difficult for the Czechs much to improve the conditions in these camps." Little could or should be done by the British, he thought, though he optimistically predicted that "with the advent of spring . . . conditions in the camps will automatically improve to some extent."[68]

By then, however, even those children who had thus far escaped being taken into camps were often in dire straits. The expropriation of German religious and charitable organizations, in particular, caused occupants of orphanages and facilities for physically and mentally handicapped children to lose their homes.

These residences, many of which were located in imposing buildings with spacious grounds, proved especially attractive to officials of the postwar regimes seeking accommodation appropriate to their new status. In the Polish town of Kladsko, as British diplomats recorded, "two members of the P.P.R. (Communist Party) arrived with a document making over the land of a Children's Home to them personally."[69] By April 1946 the condition of German orphanages in the Recovered Territories, British expulsion officers advised the voivode (governor) of Lower Silesia, was reported as "desperate."[70]

Even for children who were fortunate enough to have a roof over their heads, schooling in both Poland and Czechoslovakia was generally unavailable. The Czechoslovak government ordered all schools providing instruction through the medium of German to close in June 1945.[71] Regulations later issued by the Ministry of Education dictated that the pupils enrolled in them during the war would be allowed to attend Czech schools only in "exceptional cases, and if the children are of Czech nationality and can prove that they attended German schools owing to German pressure. . . . Applications . . . should be accompanied by a certificate issued by the District National Committee confirming the national reliability of the pupil and his parents."[72] Similar provisions applied in Poland — where, nonetheless, some "underground" schools were able to continue for a time, usually under Soviet protection — and in Yugoslavia.[73]

In the long run the only hope for these children, as Přemsyl Pitter correctly discerned, lay in their most expeditious possible removal to Germany. Significant numbers, however — how many cannot at present be determined — were never allowed to leave. Some were orphans or the products of mixed marriages; others, of "pure" Slavic antecedents, were simply taken from their parents inside the camps to make good demographic deficiencies caused by wartime losses and by the expulsions themselves.

The problem of "half-German" children was a vexed one for all the expelling countries. Before the war, legal intermarriage between *Volksdeutsche* and "Slavic" partners had been common. Benjamin Frommer estimates that in Czechoslovakia alone, at least 90,000 mixed couples and 150,000 children of such partnerships existed in 1945.[74] Though the majority of these marriages had been contracted before the war, their number continued to grow, albeit at a slower rate: during the first year of the conflict, one in five *Sudetendeutsch* marriages involved a Czech spouse. More stringent racial criteria adopted in 1941, requiring the Czech partner inter alia to submit a nude photograph of him- or herself to the authorities for evaluation, caused this number to diminish, as did the tendency of many Czechoslovaks during the occupation to regard mixed marriages, especially those entered into by women, as a form of "horizontal collaboration" with the enemy. In Poland, the number of mixed marriages that had been solemnized in the prewar years, especially in the Catholic district of Upper Silesia, may have been even greater, though further unions between Germans or *Volksdeutsche* and Poles were made virtually impossible after the 1939 September campaign and were outlawed altogether in 1943. Under Nazi rule, the status of the Polish spouse in preexisting marriages was in the majority of cases regularized by his or her inclusion as a "German" of some category or another in the *Volksliste*. Where the non-German spouse refused, or was denied, "Germanization," the marriage was normally dissolved, with custody of any children going to the German parent. In both countries, though exceptions existed, the children of mixed marriages were usually categorized as German under Nazi nationality law.[75] As Tara Zahra notes, however, such tidy classifications were frequently defeated by the failure of "families that were bilingual, flexible about their national loyalties, or altogether indifferent to nationality" to conform to them. A vivid illustration can be found in the fact that in the Přerov branch of the Hitler Youth in eastern Moravia, "80 percent of the members reportedly spoke Czech, and the leader there was forced to give commands in Czech out of necessity. The Hitler Youth in Bat'ha/Bata was also composed mostly of children of mixed marriages who spoke only Czech."[76]

After the war, the legal status of "hybrid" children was particularly complicated. Prewar nationality laws provided little guidance, yielding different answers according to whether the child was legitimate or illegitimate, the "German" parent was the mother or the father, or the date of birth had fallen before or after the beginning of the Nazi occupation. In a few countries, ex post facto laws ratified the wholesale deportation of children carrying "tainted" blood. Thus a postwar statute in Norway declared that Norwegian women who married German men after April 9, 1940, the date of the Wehrmacht's invasion of Scandinavia, were deemed to have forfeited their citizenship by virtue of that act (predictably, the law remained silent about those Norwegian men who married German women). A considerable proportion of these women, together with their Norwegian-born children, were interned in camps and later expelled to Germany; not until 1989 was this statute rescinded. A similar law in Denmark, on the other hand, went largely unenforced, although strident voices like that of the underground newspaper *De Frie Danskere* agitated for "dragons' spawn," as it termed the children of mixed marriages, to be forcibly transferred to Germany after the war.[77] At the other end of the spectrum, at least in theory, both the Hungarian expulsion decree of December 1945 and Yugoslav government regulations issued six months earlier excluded all children of mixed marriages, as well as their Germanophone parent, from forcible transfer—although, as will be seen below, a wide gulf separated precept and practice.[78]

More commonly, however, the expelling countries took the same view, mutatis mutandis, of the children of mixed marriages as had the Germans: that those possessing "Slavic blood" must be reeducated and reclaimed for the nation. In some cases, this amounted to no more than attempts to reverse the impact of Nazi racial and settlement policy. The Polish Red Cross in Wrocław, for example, alerted the Ministry for the Recovered Territories in June 1946 that the offspring of many mixed marriages had been placed during the war by the Nazi authorities with German families for the purpose of Germanization. A great danger existed that these children, few of whom spoke Polish or had any awareness of their Polish lineage, would be expelled along with their German adoptive families, to the detriment of Poland's demographic future. The Polish Red Cross urged that measures be taken to guard against this possibility, and that in particular the birth certificates of such children be carefully scrutinized by the repatriation authorities.[79]

The same principle ought to apply, many Czechoslovak and Polish authorities held, to the offspring of mixed marriages who remained in the custody of their parents. The fewest complications arose in those cases where the German spouse had died or disappeared, especially if that spouse was the husband. The Office of the Plenipotentiary for Lower Silesia pleaded the case in February 1946 of Polish women whose German husbands could no longer be accounted for. Under existing nationality law, there was no means by which these women could regain their prewar citizenship. To expel them, on the other hand, would result in their children being "Germanized and lost forever to Polishness."[80] Similar representations were made from a wide variety of quarters in Czechoslovakia. Edvard Beneš's expulsion decree No. 33 of August 1945, which stripped "Czechoslovak state citizens of German or Magyar race" of their nationality, had instructed District National Committees to treat applications from the German wives of Czechoslovak men and from their children "considerately. Such applicants shall be regarded as Czechoslovak citizens until their applications are decided upon."[81] As Benjamin Frommer notes of the sexually discriminatory character of this provision, "The government and the public apparently viewed German women as far less threatening to the state than their male counterparts."[82] This relatively liberal stance, though, was contradicted by other regulations that defined marriage with a German spouse after the creation of the Protectorate of Bohemia and Moravia (or, in some more rigorous versions, after the partial Czechoslovak military mobilization in the early days of the Sudeten crisis on

May 21, 1938) as a punishable act of collaboration. Under the so-called "small decree" of October 27, 1945, social or sexual relations with *Sudetendeutsche*, whether or not legitimized by marriage, were commonly treated as "improper behavior... causing offense to the national sentiments of the Czech or Slovak peoples" and punished by up to twelve months' imprisonment and heavy fines. As we have seen, moreover, the government's recommendation that "consideration" be exercised with respect to German women and their children did not prevent District National Committees from sending tens of thousands to the camps and eventually deporting them.

If appeals for more generous treatment of *Sudetendeutsch* women largely fell on deaf ears, the plight of Czechoslovak wives and their children did, over time, begin to arouse some popular sympathies. Reports of these former members of the national community being detained in squalid and brutal camps, forced to wear armbands identifying them as German, and undergoing the death-by-inches punishment of "German rations" troubled an increasing number of Czechoslovak consciences. The newspaper *Nová doba*, for example, carried a series of articles in the summer of 1946 devoted to the plight of ethnic Czechs who were "condemned by Czechs and the Czech Republic for taking their German partner at a time when that was no treason." As one embittered Czech man rhetorically inquired, "Are we now supposed to leave our German women and spit on our children?"[83] Relatives and friends took action to ensure that anomalies like these were not forgotten by politicians and the public. A particularly large quantity of journalistic ink was spilled over the frequent spectacle of hundreds of Czech-monoglot children being transported, with their Czechoslovak mothers and *Sudetendeutsch* fathers, to the only country against which Czechoslovakia would in future find it necessary to defend itself. *Obzory* argued that so inhumane and short-sighted a policy would leave a legacy of bitterness with which the next generation of Czechoslovaks would have to deal. "It is in the republic's interest to keep these children within the State and within the nation inasmuch as they are—or at the very least half of them are—Czech children who, once expelled from the land of their birth, will detest it with all their strength for the manner in which their mothers were treated!"[84] Appealing still more directly to *raison d'état*, the Ministry of the Interior warned the following year, "Many hundreds of children are being gratuitously delivered, thoughtlessly or maliciously, to certain Germanization and are thereby being consciously consigned to the ranks of the greatest enemies of the Czech nation—for these children will be turned into German janissaries. While impoverishing our own nation, we are enriching a foreign nation inimical to us."[85]

The authorities in Prague, however, were to find that even when it came to children the expulsion process had a momentum of its own, being easier to initiate than to restrain. On December 31, 1945, as the Allied-sanctioned mass expulsions were about to commence, the Ministry of the Interior issued regulations extending the indulgence previously granted to *Sudetendeutsch* wives of Czechoslovak citizens to German husbands also, provided that the marriage had been solemnized before the mobilization of May 21, 1938. Prevailing upon District National Committees to recognize this exemption, on the other hand, proved to be another matter entirely. Six months later, the ministry complained that notwithstanding its instructions, an expulsion train had carried off hundreds of Czech children and their Czech mothers to southern Germany. "The Czech language predominated throughout the entire transport—as if it were a transport of Czechs not Germans—because in the transport were mainly mixed marriages, Czech women with their German husbands." Similar scenes were being reported as late as the following September, as the Czechoslovak phase of the mass expulsions began to draw to a close.[86] Material rather than ideological considerations, Frommer suggests, best accounts for the insubordination of the national committees in this matter. To exempt mixed-marriage families from expulsion was to forego the opportunity to seize and redistribute their property. However concerned they may have been in the abstract about the nation's demographic future, few local authorities were capable of the level of self-denial adherence to this policy would have demanded of them.

A more ruthless method of resolving the problems posed by the existence of ethnically mixed families was simply to remove the offending parent from the equation. During the occupation, the Nazis had exerted intense pressure on Czechoslovak Gentiles married to Jews to divorce their spouses and thereby escape the range of discriminatory measures to which members of "non-Aryan" families were subject. After V-E Day, National Committees attempted to induce Czechoslovak partners to do likewise, holding out the possibility of the restoration of normal rations, the right to attend public venues or to travel, and the removal of curfew restrictions. These inducements were successful in some cases, the legal scholar Josef Frydruch sardonically observing in 1945 that the boom in divorces by Czechoslovak "Aryans" from their Jewish mates during the war "now has its analogue in the . . . divorce litigation between spouses, where one is Czech and the other is a German citizen."[87] But others were made of sterner stuff, though it is likely that few displayed the commitment that one Czech man from Šumperk did when he attempted to pass himself off as an expellee and gain admission to a camp so as not to be separated from his German spouse.[88] To encourage the dissolution of mixed marriages, the revision of Polish family law that immediately followed the war provided a specific ground for divorce in one of the partners "having declared allegiance to the German nation" or being designated for expulsion, though the strength of Catholicism in that country stood in the way of state-sponsored dissolution of marriage as a general solution to the German problem.[89]

If numerous obstacles made it difficult to remove the parents from their children, administrators in Poland, Czechoslovakia, Hungary, and Yugoslavia found it a great deal easier to separate the children from the parents, as the Germans had done during the war. As the story of Emma Duda and her daughters illustrates, the abduction of *Volksdeutsch* children began as soon as the German armed forces withdrew. Sometimes, as in Duda's case, the children were taken away at the time of the parents' arrest. At other times, a policy of selecting parents for transfer led to the abandonment of their children. Cardinal József Mindszenty complained in a letter to the Hungarian prime minister—to which no reply was ever received—that local transfer commissions were illegally detaining and sending to Germany both partners in mixed marriages, leaving behind "children whom no one dared to protect for fear of political consequences."[90]

More typically, especially in Poland, periodic visits were made by social workers to detention camps, enabling them to make a more leisurely selection of the most desirable candidates in an environment occasionally resembling a Roman slave market. In the majority of cases, the removals were carried out on the spot, offering no opportunity for parents and children to make their goodbyes. At the Potulice camp, the first children's transport in the summer of 1945 "was carried out so quickly that the mothers did not even have time to tie a name plate on the children. Many of the small children did not know their names yet."[91] Martha Kent, an American neuropsychologist who as a seven-year-old was confined in the children's barracks at Potulice (and whose autobiography is a classic of expellee literature that regrettably has not yet been published in English) has described the pressure to which older children were subjected, and to which her sister, a fellow internee, almost succumbed, to "opt" to remain in Poland after their parents' expulsion, with better food and living conditions being held out as inducements.[92]

When the "organized expulsions" commenced in 1946, consequently, the Allied authorities began to be inundated with pleas from distraught parents arriving in Germany after having had their children taken away at the camps. A Frau Bauer of Łódź, interned since April 1945, saw her four-year-old son Gerd removed from her in November, the camp authorities telling her that "her child would remain in Łódź and be educated as a Pole." She was expelled to the British zone of Germany six weeks later, and had heard nothing by the time the authorities took note of the matter in September 1946.[93] Twenty-three-year-old Lydia

Hauk, interned at Jaworzno, was separated from her younger brother Robert in May 1946 by the Polish militia, who assured her that "her brother being only 13 years old would certainly become a good Pole." Josefa Arndt, her husband, and five children were also detained at Jaworzno, where the Kraków police took away the three youngest—aged fourteen, nine, and eight years—for adoption. Ida Hartmann of Matzhausen and her two sons, aged sixteen and nine, were arrested at the end of the war, detained in the notoriously harsh Sikawa camp near Łódź and put out to forced labor; on February 6, 1946, Polish soldiers took the nine-year-old away and expelled the other two to Germany. The same happened to Magdalena Martin, another Sikawa detainee who lost the two youngest of her four children, a boy aged twelve and a girl of nine. Lisbeth Fladda of Szczytno (Ortelsburg) in East Prussia was detained in a variety of Polish detention facilities with her mother, fifteen-year-old daughter, and eleven-year-old son. Her mother starved to death while in custody. Fladda's son was taken to Skierniewice prison upon her expulsion and afterwards given to a Polish woman living at Strzyboga near Skierniewice to rear as her own.[94] Similar cases were reported from Czechoslovakia. A *Sudetendeutsch* prisoner of war in British custody, for example, sought to enlist the assistance of the CICR after learning that his children, aged two years and six months respectively, had been removed from the custody of his wife, a detainee in an improvised Prague camp, by the Czechoslovak police who proposed to place them in a home in Ústí nad Labem "so as to be able to bring them up as Czechoslovakians and incorporate them into the Cz[echo-] Sl[ovak] nation."[95]

By the summer of 1946, the British occupation authorities had concluded that there was a definite movement underway "to recruit by force manpower for the future by turning young Germans into 'good Poles.' Eight to fifteen appears to be the age needed."[96] The Polish government also extended its reach to younger children, and those outside the camps. Max Runge, an official instructed by the U.S. military commander at Aš (Asch) to oversee the return of fifty-four *Sudetendeutsch* babies and toddlers who had been evacuated from their homes in Kłodzko (Glatz) to escape the fighting in the last days of the war, found the Poles in possession of the disputed town when he arrived there and that the children's parents had already been expelled. The head of the Polish Western Association refused him permission to take his charges to Germany to be reunited with their families. "She intended to send to the Reich [*sic*] only those children, whose parents reported [in person in Kłodzko], and to make the others Polish subjects. As her endeavours to obtain Polish nuns or other Polish nursing personnel remained unsuccessful (no salary, insufficient food), she declared [herself] prepared to give the children to Polish families."[97]

Disputes over the nationality and custody of children would continue to cause difficulties between the expelling countries and the Allies for years into the future. Some mothers "repeatedly tried to reach the Polish Occupation Zone in order to fetch their children."[98] While these efforts were nearly always unsuccessful, the unresolved question of "stolen children" was an obstacle to any normalization of relations between East and West. Ugly "tug-of-love" scenes also ensued as a result of the unplanned separation of parents and children during the course of the expulsions. Under Czechoslovak law, "unclaimed" children whose parents had disappeared would be put out for permanent adoption after twelve months. Often, ethnic Germans had been swept into the camps and held incommunicado, or expelled with the customary fifteen minutes' notice, while their children were away from home. By the time of their eventual release or discovery of their children's whereabouts, many had already been placed with Czechoslovak families and formed strong attachments to their adoptive parents, who in turn refused to give them up. Unseemly wrangles between the respective governments frequently ensued.[99]

The immediate future of these children was an unenviable one. Whether permitted to remain in their homelands with their parents or transferred to the custody of families belonging to the majority nationality, ethnic German children were placed under enormous pressure to expunge every trace of their former identity. Carrying the stigma of having been "born guilty" and penalized whenever they manifested Germanness through their language, accent, or even their names, these young people, as they grew up, learned to keep their German antecedents a dark, shameful secret. In Poland, the possession of a German-sounding name proved a considerable social handicap. "So a Helmut would become a Kazimierz; and a Hilda, a Halina. Surnames were sometimes changed too. Polonization was being pushed into the most intimate corners of identity."[100] For this generation, concealment became a habit of life and social mobility a comparative rarity. The pattern continues to the present day, with Karl Cordell and Stefan Wolff noting that even the younger generation of ethnic Germans in the Czech Republic do not "register their children as German at school and rarely profess to German culture and traditions, partly because of fears of being disadvantaged if they do so." In Poland, though the remaining German population is larger and better organized, "it is extremely rare to find a member of the German minority born before 1980 who has received a university education."[101]

No less traumatic was the experience of expellee children who arrived in postwar Germany or Austria without their parents. The Irish journalist Dorothy Macardle reported that the suffering they had undergone was "indescribable," and that "there were all sorts of diseases among them . . . they were in need of careful dieting, but very little could be given to them except gruel and oatmeal soup."[102] Aleta Brownlee, chief of the International Refugee Organization's Child Welfare Branch in Austria, likewise found that the separated and orphaned children from Yugoslavia that she encountered all had the same story to tell:

> [T]hey were interned in Volkesdeutsche [sic] camps operated by the Jugoslav government; their fathers had been in the German army and were either Jugoslav or Russian prisoners of war if they were still living. The women and children had gone to the camps; the women worked as long as they were able; when they became ill, or were too old to work, they slowly starved to death. There were sometimes people to help the children; the guards apparently did not always care whether they escaped or not; they crawled out under the fence and came by a tortuous route usually through Hungary and then to Austria.[103]

Under the IRO's regulations Brownlee could do little for these expellee children, to her increasing and oft-expressed frustration. Finally, in September 1948, she lost patience and on her own authority instructed her subordinates that the mark of Cain represented by a *Volksdeutsch* classification—which rendered a person ineligible for aid from any international organization—was to be applied to no more ethnic German children arriving in Austria. In future, she ordered, they were to be "classified by the country of their birth or presumed citizenship or, in cases of doubt, as of undetermined nationality."[104]

In Germany itself, various improvised solutions to deal with the problem of orphaned or separated expellee children were adopted. Colonel Wilfred Byford-Jones of British Military Government was present in Berlin when a "Lost Baby Show" was organized by the Soviet authorities, at which "people could attend to see the children, who were presumed orphans, and to adopt them. The attendance far exceeded expectations, and after a few hours some wit among the organizers erected outside the building where the event was staged the notice 'Ausverkauft' (sold out)."[105] So many lost children were scattered throughout Germany, though, that expedients like these made little impact. For years after the war, both the Western and the Soviet occupation zones resembled nothing so much as a massive milk carton, with separated parents and children trying desperately to trace each other. As Father Swanstrom reported:

> Public searches conducted by posters, by advertisements and by thousands upon thousands of radio-broadcasts, have given a tone of tragedy to everyday life in Germany. There are special radio programs for those children who know their names and the former addresses of their parents. There are also special radio programs for parents who still believe that their children who were sepa-

rated from them during the deportation can be located somewhere in Germany or in the neighboring lands. Day after day, one can hear these heartbreaking announcements of parents who still hope to find their children three or four years after the separation.[106]

Even for these children the situation was not always hopeless. The astonishingly efficient Red Cross tracing service, based in Hamburg, was still successfully reuniting parents and children well into the 1950s. The majority of expellee children whose families remained intact, moreover, proved more resilient than even the most optimistic had dared to predict. Fears that the "expellee generation" might succumb to widespread juvenile delinquency, sexual promiscuity, or educational underperformance were not borne out by events. Whether these young people would settle down in their new surroundings or whether, as they grew to adulthood, they would seek revenge for their childhood traumatization and demand the right to return to the lands of their birth, however, remained an open question for far longer. On how it was answered would depend the fate of the two Germanies, as well as the future peace of Europe.

9

The Wild West

Kazimierz Trzciński was one of hundreds of thousands of eager colonists from central Poland who flocked to the Recovered Territories in 1947 in search of fortune. A demobilized soldier, he was just the kind of warrior-colonist the Polish government was most anxious to attract to the western borderlands—a man who knew how to fight and would not hesitate to defend his property, with armed force if necessary, should the Germans or, more likely, the peace conference attempt to take it away from him. Some of his actions, however, offered hints that he might not be the model settler he first appeared to be. One of them was his request to the mayor of Jelenia Góra (Hirschberg), the pleasant small city in the foothills of the Krkonoše mountains to which he first went, that he be given a confiscated German property opulent enough to support him without his having to work for a living. Any such estates having already been assigned to persons far higher in the pecking order of the Polish *nomenklatura* than Trzciński, he was instead offered his choice of four small farms, each of which he rejected. Trzciński's eye then fell on the Jelonka Hotel and Restaurant in the nearby ski resort of Szklarska Poręba, a business which he considered far more appropriate to his status as a brave soldier who deserved well of the Republic than a peasant smallholding would have been. Unfortunately this property was already occupied by a Mrs. Pudlo, who showed no inclination to relinquish it. Although the municipal authorities of Jelenia Góra briefly considered forcing the pair to share the Jelonka, they eventually prevailed upon Trzciński to accept an adjacent corner shop instead. The life of a retailer did not appeal to him and his new venture was not a success, though his pronounced alcoholism may have been the main reason for its underperformance. When another settler opened a competing establishment across the street, Trzciński seized the excuse to abandon the shop and renew his claim, with greater importunity than ever, to the Jelonka. So persistent was he that local officials investigated Mrs. Pudlo's ownership of the hotel and discovered to their surprise that she had no better a title to it than he did. Upon her arrival in Szklarska Poręba she had been assigned an ex-German villa, but had done nothing more with it than to strip it of every item of its furniture to fit out the Jelonka, in which she had installed herself without authority and restarted in her own name as a going concern. Equipped with these new facts, the municipal council issued an eviction order to Mrs. Pudlo and presented Trzciński with the title to the property. When he arrived to take possession she kept him waiting for a considerable time; eventually opened up the hotel; and then proceeded methodically to smash it to pieces around him as he cringed in the lobby. There being no militia or police in the vicinity, Trzciński turned tail and fled for his life, followed down the street by Pudlo's curses and threats. After this traumatic experience, the town fathers found it easier to persuade him to content himself with yet another confiscated property in Rokossovski Street—which itself had a complicated history, having passed through several sets of hands since it was first expropriated from its German owners—and leave the terrifying Pudlo in undisputed possession of the Jelonka.[1]

Trivial though it may have been, this dispute illustrates in microcosm many of the problems associated with "recolonization" of the lands from which the German population had been driven. The removal of the ethnic Germans was not just an enormous logistical undertaking. It was also the source of a highly disruptive economic and social transformation of the affected areas, one whose impact remains to the present day. In much the same way that the wartime cooperation of ordinary Germans (and, indeed, Poles, Ukrainians, and other nationalities) in the persecution and removal of Jews had been obtained by the opportunity it provided to appropriate Holocaust victims' property, Czechoslovak, Polish, and Hungarian citizens' enthusiasm for the expulsions owed a great deal to the prospect that they would profit from the confiscation of their German neighbors' wealth. The new borderlands, however, proved to be no Eldorado, and the new economic and social realities that were produced under abnormal circumstances brought a fresh set of unforeseen complications in their train.

To a substantial degree, the scramble for booty dictated the breakneck pace of the expulsions, as local authorities, militia bands, or politically connected individuals rushed to grab the most desirable German properties for themselves before others, or the central government, got in ahead of them. The lion's share of the loot, nonetheless, wound up in the state's hands, where it became an important instrument of communization. Before the Second World War, Communist parties had been negligible influences throughout central and eastern Europe.

The Nazi-Soviet Pact; Stalin's treacherous attack on Poland's eastern frontier when the country was fighting desperately for its life; the expulsions and massacres that had followed, at the Katyn Forest and elsewhere; and the Red Army's cynical abandonment of the Polish Home Army to the Nazis in the Warsaw Rising of August 1944 did nothing to persuade ordinary Poles that the Russian leopard had changed its spots. Though the USSR's standing in Czechoslovakia was higher—thanks in large measure to the perception that Moscow, in contrast to the appeasement-minded Western powers, had been ready to assist Prague militarily before the Munich Conference—there was little enthusiasm for state socialism on the Soviet pattern. Because Communists controlled the Ministries of the Interior and of Agriculture in both countries after the war, however, they were also in a position to decide the redistribution of confiscated German property. They took full advantage of the rich sources of patronage this provided to buy, if not the support, then at least the acquiescence of citizens in their continued rule. The expulsions, then, provided the material basis that enabled the governments of the Soviet satellites to solidify their domestic standing at the moment of their greatest vulnerability.

As the dispute over the Jelonka Hotel demonstrated, though, property redistribution could be an instrument of social disruption as well as social cohesion. Disputes over the true ownership of a confiscated house or farm, in a situation in which the premises might have changed hands several times over the card table in a single weekend, would clog up the court systems of the expelling countries for years into the future. Overnight, the borderland areas were stripped not just of population but of agencies of government: when a German town was cleared of its residents, its local council, police force, municipal administrators, and providers of essential services like waste removal or water supplies usually went with them. Even in those relatively rare cases when replacement officials from the majority population could be found to take their place, Soviet military commanders, preferring to concentrate the skeins of power in their own hands, often prevented them from taking up their positions. In a literal and not merely a metaphorical sense, then, many of these districts became lawless areas—as the hapless Kazimierz Trzciński had discovered when he tried to take possession of his hotel. For several years after the change in jurisdiction, a vacuum of state authority existed and the rule of the gun prevailed. It was hardly surprising, then, that fewer people than resettlement authorities hoped were willing to put down permanent roots in such areas; or that a disproportionate number of those who did, like Trzciński himself, turned out to conform poorly to the image of the sturdy, self-reliant pioneer depicted in Communist propaganda. The name that both Poles and Czechoslovaks gave to their frontier regions after the war—the

"Wild West"—reflected their awareness that even after the Germans' departure, these were places that remained alien in many respects from the countries of which they were nominally a part.

When the expulsion schemes were first conceived, few of these difficulties were foreseen. Their authors were enthusiastic about the opportunities the colonization and redistribution programs would offer not just to create new social and economic realities in the borderlands, but to use them as templates to reshape society in the heartland as well. On his visit to Moscow in December 1943 to obtain Soviet support for the expulsions, as we have seen, Edvard Beneš described to his hosts the prospect that removing the *Sudetendeutsche* would pave the way for the socialization of the Czechoslovak economy as a whole. "Seventy percent of Germans," he told Molotov "are rich people and the transfer of their property would mean not only Czechization, but also the beginning of a large social upheaval."[2]

> The distribution of German property into private hands would create fierce rivalries between people, Beneš indicated; in consequence, the Czechs would be asked to make similar sacrifices as well by accepting far-reaching nationalization. Answering Molotov's question, whether it would be acceptable to the Czechs, Beneš said that it would be hard to convince them, but that the transfer of German property would signal the beginning of general nationalization.[3]

In reality Beneš had no intention of creating a Soviet-style command economy in postwar Czechoslovakia; his intimations in Moscow that he was contemplating something of the kind were as deliberately misleading as his assurances to the Western Allies that only "fascists" and "collaborators" in the Sudetenland were being targeted for removal. There is no question, though, that he desired to move the country far to the left after the war, extending state control of the economy in the process. His reason for doing so was not only to facilitate a close relationship with the USSR, in his view a sine qua non of Czechoslovakia's future security, but to solidify his political standing at home. A "progressive" redistribution of national wealth, Beneš believed, would at once weaken the social classes on which the National Socialist and Peasant parties relied for their support, and reduce the appeal of communism, leaving the president of the Republic, standing above politics, in a position to dictate the national agenda. In the event, Beneš would greatly overestimate both his ability to carry off this act of political triangulation, in a milieu in which the influence of the Red Army and of the National Committees would substantially outweigh that of the Prague government, and his own indispensability to Czechoslovak public life. The Czechoslovak Communist Party, for its part, had its own contrasting ambition: "to make the [border] region both a model and a laboratory for the building of socialism."[4] To the extent that the president was willing to help prepare the way toward this objective, it was happy to proceed in harness with him; once his usefulness was exhausted, it would take the lead on its own.

Equally grandiose visions of turning the borderlands into a Socialist showcase were entertained by the new Polish government also. At a week-long celebration in Wrocław and Jelenia Góra "to welcome the Potsdam territories back into the Polish State," the Communist Minister of Industry, Hilary Minc, rejoiced over "the acquisition of a completely equipped territory with a certain residue of German population which we have every moral and international right to liquidate at a time and by methods which we consider appropriate." He added a warning: "The greatest danger in our western territories is the danger of having small-minded men with a small perspective."[5] Certainly no one could accuse Minc himself or his ministerial colleagues of such a shortcoming. To the contrary, the set of objectives announced by the Polish government for the Recovered Territories seemed ambitious to the point of having become divorced from reality. In August 1945, for example, it set a target of 500,000 colonists to be settled in Olsztyn province before the onset of winter. Predictably, when a count was taken on January 1, 1946, only about 20 percent of that number were to be found in residence.[6]

A factor that hampered the colonization program was that neither the Czechoslovak nor the Polish governments had drawn up a detailed plan during the war to determine the method by which German property was to be seized and redistributed. Initially, to secure Western support for the expulsions, Edvard Beneš had promised the Allies that no expellees would be expropriated without compensation, unless their property had been obtained illegally. The government in exile, though, had no intention of making good on his commitment, which would have imposed an unsustainable economic burden on the postwar state. In an elegant reconciliation of these competing demands, Herbert Ripka revealed in October 1944 the formula upon which Prague would rely when he announced that all *Sudetendeutsche* with a record of collaborationist activities or "Pan-German sentiments and mentalities" would forfeit their property to the Czechoslovak state, and that any compensation due them would be paid by "appropriately adjusting the financial and economic claims which Czechoslovakia will have against Germany."[7] According to Ripka, expellees would be issued with a receipt by the Czechoslovak government stating the value of the possessions taken from them. Czechoslovakia's demand for reparations from Germany would be reduced by an equivalent sum; the expellees could then use the receipts to claim compensation from the postwar German government. This was, though, little more than a propaganda gesture, which had the further advantage of deflecting attention from the precise scale of the country's wartime material losses. In fact, though this could hardly be considered adequate recompense for the systematic terror to which its people had been subjected as a result of the German occupation, economically Czechoslovakia had had a "good" war. According to Jaroslav Krejčí's calculations, real income rose around 20 percent for working-class men, and almost 30 percent for women, between 1939 and 1945.[8] Czechoslovakia also emerged from the war with a larger capital stock than in 1939, thanks to the Germans' decision to locate many industries there where they would be beyond the reach of most Allied bombing. The eventual figure assigned by the Paris Reparations Conference for Czechoslovak war damage, at 347.5 billion crowns ($69.5 million), took no account of this German investment; not coincidentally, however, it did roughly approximate to an initial Czechoslovak estimate—itself an unrealistically low figure—of the value of seized *Sudetendeutsch* property.[9] In any event, no receipts were ever provided to expelled Sudeten Germans, while at the Paris Conference the Prague government, by a second performance of sleight of hand, successfully argued that the proceeds of the expulsions should not be counted against Czechoslovak claims upon postwar Germany inasmuch as the *Sudetendeutsche* in 1938 had been not German but Czechoslovak citizens, thereby rendering the link between expropriation and reparations moot. The Hungarians in 1946 announced their intention to follow the Czechoslovak example; in the event, the fact that the Allies found that Hungary was not entitled to reparations from Germany meant that no compensation, even in the form of valueless receipts, would ever be proposed for expellees.[10] Neither the Polish government in exile nor its Stalinist competitor in Lublin, on the other hand, thought any similar justification necessary: for them it was axiomatic that as the Germans should leave, their property should remain. No question of "compensating" the expellees, even as a theoretical exercise, arose in Warsaw. Had it ever done so, the colossal material damage sustained by Poland under German occupation—of which its devastated capital city stood as a stark illustration—would have enabled the Polish state to make a far more persuasive case than its Czechoslovak counterpart.

The lack of advance planning, though, was to create enormous practical difficulties. Noting the Germans' experience of confiscating and redistributing the goods of national minorities during the war, the *Economist* presciently warned the governments in exile in 1944 that a wild scramble for wealth on the part of the local populations on the ground was likely to be the outcome. "In very many cases," it pointed out, those who had entered into possession of the seized assets had been "not only—and not even mainly—Germans. Croats took possession of the property of Serbs who had been expelled from Croatia. Hungarians enriched themselves at the expense of Roumanians in Transylvania. While Germans grabbed the estates of Poles, Poles inherited the houses and shops of slaughtered or deported Jews." There was no reason to suppose that the Polish or Czechoslovak postwar experience would be very different. Extensive confiscations might even impede the process of economic and social reform, by creating "new and powerful vested interests" that would stand in the way of a more general redistribution of wealth.[11]

These cautions were to be amply borne out by events. As the Wehrmacht retreated north and west in the spring of 1945, the first expropriation decrees were issued by the Polish and Czechoslovak governments. An edict of the Lublin Poles of February 28, 1945, on the "exclusion of elements hostile to the Polish people" from national life, provided for the forfeiture to the state of all property owned by those enrolled on the *Deutsche Volksliste*. This decree caused instant consternation. Almost 3 million inhabitants of the Incorporated Eastern Territories, at least two-thirds of them ethnic Poles, had allowed themselves to be registered as Germans during the war. In hundreds of thousands of cases they had done so as the only alternative to deportation to the *Generalgouvernement*; in Upper Silesia, only fifty thousand of a population of nearly 1.4 million had not done so; and both the London government in exile and local churchmen like Bishop Stanisław Adamski of Wrocław had even urged the population on numerous occasions to sign as a means of avoiding persecution.[12] Some Poles, Adamski reminded his more judgmental compatriots after the war, had been "promoted" to the second category of the *Volksliste* on the basis of their economic importance to the occupiers rather than any professed support for Nazism.[13] Not until more than two months later was a second version issued, in an attempt to check the excesses unleashed by the first. This set up a "verification" process, whereby persons in the third and fourth categories who had been included on the *Volksliste* "against their will or under coercion" and who "proved their adhesion to the Polish nation" would be able to recover their property once they had given satisfactory proofs of their Polishness.

In Czechoslovakia the government's expropriation order, Presidential Decree no. 12, was published still later, on June 21, 1945. Under its terms all land held by Germans, Hungarians, and "traitors and enemies of the Republic" was to be taken over by the state. A National Land Fund under the Ministry of Agriculture (headed by the Communist Julius Ďuriš) would take the land in trust and oversee its redistribution, in tracts of twelve hectares (30 acres), to Czech and Slovak settlers. For commercial enterprises that were too large to be run by a single owner-operator, "national administrators" were appointed by District and Local National Committees. The task of these persons was to assume trusteeship over the businesses and maintain them, where possible, as going concerns until their eventual fate could be decided by the authorities. Offering many opportunities for peculation and personal enrichment, the position of national administrator constituted an important form of patronage and vote buying. Although members of the Communist Party were especially likely to be granted these plum appointments, often the offer of a national administratorship and membership of the party were made simultaneously. Hence confiscated German property became in effect a virtually inexhaustible political slush fund, enabling the Communists to gain the support of persons who would have never been attracted to them for ideological reasons. It was no coincidence that in the May 1946 election, the Communist Party obtained up to 75 percent of the vote in the Sudetenland, approximately double the share it gained in the remainder of the country.[14] The same was true of Poland, where Władysław Gomułka, the future supervisor of the resettlement program, frankly admitted to a Communist Party congress early in 1945 that "the western territories are one of the reasons the government has the support of the people."[15]

An unexpected difficulty for Poland was finding a sufficient number of people to colonize the newly cleared areas. Contrary to the constant declarations of government ministers that Germans had to be removed as quickly as possible to make room for the settlement of Poles displaced by Stalin from the annexed areas east of the River Bug, it soon became clear that the Recovered Territories were in fact facing an acute population shortage. Only about 1.7 million "repatriates" from the east—a figure that includes ethnic Poles expelled from the Ukrainian and Byelorussian Soviet Socialist Republics, the Baltic states absorbed into the Soviet Union, and survivors of Stalin's 1939 clearances of eastern Poland to Siberia—were transferred to postwar Poland, ostensibly to take the place of up to 8 million Germans evicted from the Recovered Territories. A surprisingly low proportion of these eastern "repatriates" found their way to the new western lands, and fewer still stayed there. Many traveled no further than the central provinces, preferring to take up residence in a part of the country they could feel confident would remain Polish rather than face the risks of a pioneer life in another unstable borderland region from which, if the great powers so decided, they might once again have to depart. Still, even if every "repatriate" and all displaced persons of Polish nationality had gone to the Recovered Territories, the numbers simply did not add up. As the Foreign Office in London calculated in 1945, well over a third of the settled population in postwar Poland would have to migrate to the new borderlands if these were to be resettled immediately. To populate them using the natural increase of the rest of the country, on the other hand, would mean that the task would not be completed until 1977.[16]

As a result, the immediate impression taken away by visitors to the Recovered Territories in the early postwar years was of the uncanny emptiness of the landscape. Radio Lublin scarcely exaggerated when, in a call for colonists to populate the region, it announced at the end of May 1945 that "East Prussia is empty."[17] A British commercial attaché, Leonard Holliday, found much the same to be the case when he toured the area in September. Visiting East Prussia, he wrote, was

> indeed an excursion into the wasteland. Field after field lay shoulder-high in a tangle of weeds, indicating clearly that for at least a year they had not been touched. The towns of Deutsch Eylau [Iława], Freistadt [Gdańsk] and to a lesser extent Marienwerder [Kwidzyn], as well as the smaller villages, are not only devastated but also almost empty. These are ruins in the raw, untouched and untidied, looking like horses disembowelled in a bull-ring. The Polish population in this area is still minute. In each town or village there is a post of the Citizens' Militia, manned by fierce-looking characters who might have stepped straight out of some tale of frontier days in the Wild West of Buffalo Bill.[18]

Pomerania was almost as sparsely populated. When Holliday visited there in mid-1946, he traveled "miles of road between Szczecin and the old border where the fields had not been touched, the general average of cultivated land being perhaps 10%.... Even worse was the area south of Lignica which was reverting to moorland."[19] Even in 1947, by which time more than 360,000 farmsteads had been assigned by the government to settlers, a pair of British officials who traversed the Recovered Territories from south to north encountered many completely deserted villages and observed that "All along the route there are large stretches of land with the remnants of the 1945 harvest still standing."[20] This abandonment of productive farmland led to some curious environmental consequences. Jerzy Morzycki, Chief Commissioner for the Control of Epidemics, revealed in September 1946 that the Recovered Territories, and especially East Prussia, "are smitten with a plague of mice. This is due to the fact that last year owing to the ... lack of Polish population, the wheat which had been sown by Germans could not be harvested.... this plague is assuming serious dimensions and the authorities are very anxious to obtain a bacteria [sic] which will produce a pestilence amongst these mice and bring about their death."[21]

Though the spectacle of ghost towns and deserted farmsteads was much less in evidence in Czechoslovakia, here too entire districts could be found entirely bereft of people. Godfrey Lias, the *Times* correspondent in Prague who toured the Sudetenland in the summer of 1947, reported that "Not only are there many empty houses in both town and country but there are even whole villages without an inhabitant. . . . it is only necessary to go a short distance off the beaten track to find large fields of last year's potatoes still unlifted and acres of grain unharvested."[22] This was less the result of any shortage of settlers—by the end of 1945, the population of the borderlands was slightly higher than its prewar figure—as of the fact that as in Poland, the new arrivals displayed a marked preference for congregating in the cities and towns rather than remote rural areas, where communications were poor and amenities few. The rate of agricultural turnover was also extremely high, with almost a third of ex-German farmsteads being abandoned by their new owners after a few years.[23] Making a virtue out of necessity, therefore, the Prague government elected to abandon the cultivation of a considerable amount of arable land and give it over instead to afforestation, justifying the change on the ground that a physical barrier of woodlands was required to stand in the way of a future German invasion.[24] Thus of twenty-nine villages in the neighborhood of Sušice on the edge of the Šumava national park, only seven were chosen for partial colonization in September 1946, the remainder being allowed to fall derelict.[25]

Where stable communities were absent, so too was law and order. This was especially characteristic of the Recovered Territories, where each new group of settlers soon had lurid stories to tell about the Hobbesean dystopias into which many districts had degenerated in the immediate postwar period. The first advance parties to arrive in Wrocław at the beginning of May 1945 found Soviet troops engaging in full-scale shootouts with each other while disputing the possession of ex-German booty: a particularly fierce firefight between two Red Army units vying for control of the food shops on Sienkiewicz Street lasted for two days.[26] "Theft, assault, rape and murder were the (dis)order of the day" among Red Army units in Wielkopolska, where the Polish population was treated by their nominal allies as though they, not the Germans, were the vanquished nation.[27] But Polish security forces too were generally perceived as being the cause rather than the cure for rampant criminality. In Bytów near Gdańsk, gang warfare was being conducted by rival groups of the *Urząd Bezpieczeństwa* (UB), or secret police, two factions of which were enthusiastically beating each other up.[28] British observers correctly noted that a great deal of "the lawlessness attributed to the Poles" could be attributed to "the loutish youths, armed to the teeth, that constitute the 'Militia.'"[29] The Polish authorities' view of the militia was identical. Resettlement officers noted that "there were not enough of them to prevent the looting—or they were too busy doing it themselves."[30] The mayor of the village of Michałkowa was so intimidated by the Mafia-like behavior of the militia unit theoretically under his authority that when he was assigned to be escort of a transport of Germans to the British zone under Operation Swallow, he concealed himself among the expellees in the baggage car and was not discovered until the train reached Marienthal.[31] While countless reports of the militiamen's criminal behavior were received, a Polish observer who conducted a tour of the area between Poznań and Szczecin in August 1945 expressed sympathy for their difficulties, noting that they had little option but to live off the countryside as best they could. "The problem of food supply is as a rule left to the ingenuity of the militiamen themselves. Most of them are young boys.... At best they are armed with rifles, for which in very many cases they have no ammunition.... Hence the role of the militiamen, the upholders of order and protectors of the settlers' property, is reduced to the passive observation of those cases of armed robbery that take place."[32]

In Czechoslovakia, too, the borderlands quickly acquired an unsavory reputation as places where people ventured at their peril. While the crime wave that occurred there during the second half of 1945 and into early 1946 was on nothing like the scale seen in the Recovered Territories, bandits, organized and unorganized criminals, and ne'er-do-wells proliferated to a degree unprecedented in Czechoslovakia's history as an independent state. As in Poland, those wearing uniform, to which they may or may not have been entitled, were if anything more likely than the general population to prey on their fellow citizens. While it was universally acknowledged that Red Army soldiers recognized no distinctions between Czechoslovaks and Germans when it came to robbery, rape, or vandalism, neither did many members of the police, SNB, or Revolutionary Guards. The Czechoslovak Army was blamed for a great deal of the lawlessness, with units like the First Czechoslovak Division that contained a high proportion of Slovaks, Ukrainians, and Volhynians being perceived as especially prone to criminality when deployed in the Czech lands. Frequently, positions of authority were occupied by individuals whose previous record did not bear scrutiny. The head of the so-called "Office for Germans in Svitavy," K. Haas, was a man with a lengthy criminal record. B. Kovář, a partisan "lieutenant" and self-appointed commissioner in Miroslav, south of Moravský Krumlov, was found at the time of his arrest in June 1945 on fraud charges to have had seven previous convictions. Š. Gába from Olomouc, whose principal duty was the arrest of "hostile" persons and confiscation of their property (and who also had a shadowy partisan background), surpassed him with eleven.[33]

An especially vivid example of the freewheeling atmosphere that prevailed in the early postwar days, as well as of the fluidity of the line separating criminals from law enforcers, can be found in the border town of Česká Kamenice, near

Děčín. As David Gerlach describes, at the end of May 1945 a Local National Committee was established which, in accordance with regulations, proceeded to confiscate German property; distribute the clothes, household goods, and other everyday items to the local Czech population; and remit the valuables to Prague. However, the dutiful chairman of the committee, Karel Caidler, quickly fell foul of the head of the local Defense Intelligence detachment which, with the aid of another "partisan" leader of dubious antecedents, Adolf Charous, "engaged in massive expropriation" of the ex-German goods, displaying a particular affinity for "collecting motor vehicles." After Caidler refused to fall in with their money-making schemes, they arrested him and several other committee members on charges of being involved in Werewolf activity; tortured him in an improvised dungeon in the basement of the town's district court; and elevated Charous to the post of town commissar. The latter proceeded to stalk the streets of Česká Kamenice, whip in hand, confiscating German businesses and passing them on to his cronies. "As one former policeman in the town reported, the looting got so out of control that the police did not have time to supervise Germans. They were too busy trying to control the influx of settlers."[34]

Although potential settlers were easier to come by in Czechoslovakia than in Poland, recruiting the right kind of colonist was another matter. The government's expectation that a significant number of emigrants would return from abroad was to be disappointed. By the time the state formally invited expatriate Czechs and Slovaks to return home, on July 31, 1945, most of the best properties had already been officially or unofficially appropriated by others. A central office to oversee the settlement of repatriants was not opened until 1947. As a result, the number of reemigrants remained low. The largest contingent — almost 72,000 — came from Hungary, with more than 35,000 from Volhynia in western Ukraine and 21,000 from Romania also arriving. A considerable proportion had been born abroad; many of those from Hungary spoke neither Czech nor Slovak, and were resented by the native-born population as foreigners and interlopers who were intensifying the competition for confiscated property. While more than Kčs 570 million was spent on Czech-language classes, providing moving grants, and setting up social programs for the incomers, the effort proved a failure. Before long, numbers of the repatriants, complaining of discrimination, were applying to be allowed to return to their countries of origin.[35]

More success was achieved in inducing Czech and Slovak residents of the Sudetenland who had fled to the interior upon the advent of the Nazis in 1938 to return to their ancestral homes. In most cases, these "old settlers" simply came back on their own initiative. Some municipalities also engaged in expulsion as a tool of social engineering, petitioning the authorities to give priority to the removal of their *Sudetendeutsche* "mainly in order to make towns more attractive to potential settlers, who did not wish to have German neighbors."[36] Indeed, indicating just how far the notion of expulsion as a cure-all for social problems had permeated the national consciousness, the Rýmařov Local National Committee demanded in September 1946 that "unreliable inhabitants, hoodlums, gamblers, notorious alcoholics, and gypsies" be expelled alongside the Germans.[37] But state functionaries as well as the local population in the Czech lands complained no less loudly about the influx of "undesirable" elements among the colonists. Class and generational differences underlay some of these antagonisms: as Andreas Wiedemann confirms, the perception that settlers in the borderlands were disproportionately young and working-class was, on the whole, accurate.[38] The number of those who came to seek a new life in the "cleansed" areas was nonetheless impressive. By 1950, one in four of the entire Czech population had moved to the borderlands, although the rate of return migration was also high.[39]

Notwithstanding the departure of the Germans, ethnic tensions, ironically, remained much in evidence. Philip Nichols reported at the end of 1946 that of the considerable number of Slovaks who had come to try their luck in the Sudetenland, "a fair proportion of these colonists had not proved good settlers and have, after looting a certain amount of property, returned to their original homes."[40] Roma families also arrived, giving rise to much local chauvinism. After the Prague government failed to persuade the Allies to agree to an expulsion of Czechoslovakia's ethnic Hungarian population along with the Germans, plans were set in train to move 250,000 of them in a forced internal migration to the northern borderlands. In the end, only 42,000 were transferred, most of whom decamped to their homes in southern Slovakia as soon as they were permitted to do so.

In Poland as well as Czechoslovakia, some efforts were made at the local level to police the migration process and weed out unsuitable or unwanted colonists. An especially robust stance was taken by the Polish resettlement authorities at Miastko, where "work-shy" colonists were permitted to take ten kilograms of personal effects with them and were then frog-marched by the militia to the nearest railway station, to be returned whence they came.[41] The Czech police in the northern Bohemian town of Rychnov dealt likewise with newly arrived Roma from Slovakia, who were suspected of having come to trade with Germans or to steal rather than settle down as genuine migrants.[42] Nevertheless, the perception in both countries that the borderlands were being used as a dumping ground for social or ethnic undesirables did little to encourage would-be colonists from the interior to follow in their wake.

Two obstacles above all stood in the way of an orderly colonization process in all three of the Potsdam countries: the locust cloud of "gold diggers," "gleaners," or "prospectors" who descended on the cleared areas, either to seize the most desirable houses and businesses or simply to loot vacated premises and carry the goods away for use or resale; and the presence of the Red Army. Of the two, the first seemed initially to be the greater menace. In Hungary the government was "considerably disturbed at the possibility of any vacated Swabian properties remaining uninhabited for even twenty-four hours because of the likelihood of looting."[43] While Budapest's task was made somewhat easier by the relatively small scale of the population transfer, in both Poland and Czechoslovakia the central governments lost control of the process of redistributing confiscated German properties from the very outset, and never fully regained it.

It is not too much to say that "gold digging" permeated the whole of Czechoslovak and Polish society, from the very bottom to the highest echelons. After returning to Prague from his wartime exile in London, for example, Herbert Ripka, newly appointed as minister for foreign trade, helped himself to "a large 17-room villa that had originally belonged to German owners who had been deported." (The building is today the Venezuelan Embassy.) The minister "soon outfitted the house with top-quality furniture" obtained from the same source.[44] For some eager pioneers, however, "gold digging" was no more than a continuation of a pattern of profiteering established during the Holocaust. As the *Economist* disdainfully noted in July 1946, in central Europe "a new *Lumpenbourgeoisie* has grown up mushroom-like during the war by looting the property first of murdered Jews and then of expelled Germans."[45]

"Gold digging" even extended to the Christian churches, which enthusiastically embraced the opportunity both to acquire property and to eliminate the local influence of competing sects. Since the nineteenth century at least, Protestantism had been elevated by Czech nationalists as constituting almost as strong a marker of true national identity as was Catholicism in Poland—paradoxically, in a country in which Catholics outnumbered Protestants by about five to one— and "patriotic" clergymen in both countries gave strong practical and theological backing to their governments' efforts to remove those perceived as alien in both religion and race. As Władysław Bartoszewski, the future Polish foreign minister, has recalled, "the Catholic Church took a major part in the Polonization of the Oder-Neisse region. It immediately sent hundreds of priests to the former German territories. The new settlers, almost all of whom were Catholics, said to themselves: The pastor is already there, after all, so everything must somehow be in order."[46] *Głos Katolicki*, the principal Wielkopolska Catholic paper, "openly supported the régime's ethnic cleansing of Poland, and rejoiced that it would result in an ethnoreligious cleansing as well . . ."[47] Of some 3,020 Protestant churches in the Recovered Territories, 2,895 had been transferred to Catholic administration by 1948. Karol Milik, the temporary apostolic administrator who assumed episcopal functions over part of Lower Silesia after the removal of the German bishop there, denied to a visiting British diplomat that any mistreatment of Germans had taken place in the course of the expulsions and accused some of his own German priests of building up "a resistance organization under the skirts of the Church" while awaiting their deportation.[48] Anti-German sentiment in Church circles was not monolithic, and the British Embassy noted one case in which the Catholic diocese of Wrocław "lodged a strong protest against ... manifestations of intolerance" toward Lutheran clergy. A Catholic priest who "refused to celebrate Mass in a Protestant church taken over by the Poles which had been assigned to him" was himself punished by being expelled. By and large, however, the Polish Catholic Church welcomed the removal both of Protestant clergymen and of its own ethnic German priests and religious and lent every assistance to the secular authorities in carrying that agenda out, while vigorously pressing its claims to the temporalities of the dispossessed Protestant sects.[49]

A mirror image of this situation existed in Czechoslovakia where the Catholic clergy, as Emilia Hrabovec says, "dared not risk any sort of open confrontation" with the state for fear of "losing its considerable assets to nationalization ... or the perilous consequences of being labelled regressive and unpatriotic by an increasingly leftist and radicalized society."[50] There was indeed a genuine basis for these anxieties. In the land of Jan Hus the departure of the predominantly Catholic *Sudetendeutsche* was widely hailed by Protestant clergymen in particular as an expression of God's providential design. The Evangelical theologian František Bednář argued in a published defense of the expulsions that the *Sudetendeutsche* had, in effect, been afflicted with a double dose of original sin. Their conduct during the period of Nazi occupation "was but the culmination and manifestation of what had been in their hearts for centuries," standing as they did "wholly and consciously for lies, violence, inhumanity and brutality." Their removal was thus, in the view of the Czechoslovak Protestant churches, "with all due respect for Christianity," a practical and moral imperative. "The continued presence of the German population in Czechoslovakia would in the future have endangered the spiritual state of the nation."[51] This expression of the divine will, needless to say, dovetailed nicely with the temporal aspirations of Czech ecclesiastics. Because the German Lutheran Church had "no longer any legal existence," its property was taken over by the Protestant Church of Czech Brethren. A visiting Scottish divine, however, noted disapprovingly the pressure exerted by "unscrupulous people in other churches" who were advancing their own claims to a share-out of the wealth. Even in this sphere, he remarked, the lure of easy money was becoming "a moral temptation, and the scramble for German property has been not unlike a Californian gold rush, or the distribution of the spoils which followed Henry VIII's dissolution of the monasteries."[52] In the long run, though, mainstream Christian churches in both countries would have cause to regret the uprooting of long-settled communities with their vibrant religious traditions and practices. These proved to be far easier to destroy than to recreate. Especially in Czechoslovakia, religious observance among the settlers was much less visible than had been the case with the displaced populations; in the years to come, shrines and monuments were often valued by their new parishioners chiefly as convenient sources of building materials.[53]

At a more profane level, a Radio Warsaw broadcast alerted listeners in September 1945 to the spread of an alarming new "social disease." Why, the announcer inquired rhetorically, was it so difficult for honest Polish citizens to find a seat in any westbound train? At first glance, the reason seemed obvious. The trains were crowded with colonists on their way to build a new life in the Recovered Territories. Each of these pioneers had been provided with a free travel pass and a state-sponsored grant to meet immediate expenses until they could provide for themselves. The same honest citizens, however, were bemused to observe that the settlers, to all appearances, were bringing practically no possessions with them on their westward journey. Their surprise was still greater when they saw "the same trains coming back packed ten times worse, not only with passengers but with bundles, suitcases, parcels, rucksacks, typewriters, sewing machines, wireless sets, etc." The explanation was obvious: "The 'settlers' are coming back as 'gleaners' loaded with all kinds of goods, acquired more or less illegally."

> The first journey was profitable; let's try it again! When one locality is denuded by the "settlers" they go to another one: from Silesia to Pomerania, from Pomerania to Masuria, and from there back to Silesia. . . . Some people would say that the gleaners are filling our needs in clothing, linen and other commodities; that the impoverished inhabitants of Warsaw also want to sleep on pillows, cover themselves with blankets, and have a clean shirt and a decent suit. The Germans have looted the whole of Poland, so Poland should profit in getting these things at reasonable prices. . . . All this is true; but why cannot social organizations or trade unions do this work and divide them among the people? . . .
>
> Meantime the professional gleaners are (1) stealing from the State by traveling free; (2) overcrowding the trains; (3) causing false statistics in the settlement movement to the West, because the most expert statistician could not guess which are the real and which are the false settlers; (4) denuding the area so completely that the real settlers find emptiness. It is a disease, an epidemic, and as such must be combated with vigor.[54]

That bona fide colonists were being cut out by "gold diggers" and "wild resettlers" who helped themselves to houses, farms, and moveable property without legal authority was undoubtedly true. Bolesław Drobner, the city president of Wrocław, estimated that 60 percent of the newcomers who appeared there in 1945 came for the express purpose of looting; the proportion in Szczecin and other large towns may have been on a similar scale.[55] Civic leaders made frequent complaints to the government in Warsaw over its failure adequately to screen would-be colonists, including a formal protest "after a train pulled in from Cracow carrying a huge consignment of Cracovian 'undesirables'—convicts, speculators, and habitual alcoholics."[56]

The predations of the Red Army, however, probably drove more genuine settlers away than even the most rapacious of "gold diggers." Innumerable reports testified that Soviet troops invariably adhered to "the principle that all that remained when the Germans withdrew is their 'war booty,' machinery and livestock, crops, factory equipment etc."[57] Even "such primitive articles as axes, harrows, scythes etc. have been taken off to Russia."[58] Ironically, the "wild expulsions" of the summer of 1945 had played into their hands: there being no potential settlers to take their places, all that the clearance of the German population achieved, as the Gorzów branch of the State Repatriation Office in Wielkopolska ruefully noted in retrospect, was to result in "all moveable German property in Gorzów becoming booty for Soviet soldiers," as well as leaving the harvest of East Brandenburg to rot in the fields.[59] Likewise, a disillusioned local branch secretary of the Communist Party complained that as soon as incoming Poles succeeded in licking an ex-German farm into shape the Red Army would turn up and expropriate it.

As in Czechoslovakia, then, an even greater challenge than recruiting settlers to the Recovered Territories was inducing them to remain. While Warsaw's preferred agricultural "pioneer" was from east of the Bug, because he knew how to farm and usually brought equipment and stock, "he, however, is not always as glad to come as the Government is to have him. At Kalisz Nowy [Kalisz Pomorski], according to our communist informant, there were eight railway carriages full of new settlers who had sent one of their number to spy out the land and on hearing his report had staged a sit-down strike. A farmer from Tarnopol asked if we would take him with us 'anywhere back in Poland.'"[60] As another exhausted settler told Leonard Holliday, he and his fellow repatriates had "had enough of sleeping by their horses, gun in hand."[61] In many cases, colonists were so short of food that they were obliged to eat their seed grain to enable them to survive the first winter in their new homes.[62] The small size of the holdings allocated to them—typically between seven and fifteen hectares, depending on the quality of the land—also provided little margin for error, at least in the first difficult years. It was no wonder, then, that in the village of Grodków in Silesia, the town clerk confessed to Holliday that the hungry settlers "had to be prevented by force from returning to the east."[63]

Conditions faced by the eastern repatriates were indeed pitiable, especially when the hardship they had already undergone before arriving in their new "homes" is borne in mind. Hundreds of thousands had experiences similar to those of Michał Sobków, who was forced by the Soviets to leave his farm at Koropiec in eastern Galicia in 1945. Upon being displaced, he and his family had waited for two months in a tent city at Pyszkowice for transport to the Recovered Territories. At last they were ordered to move at two hours' notice, cramming themselves and their farm animals into the wagons before the train abruptly departed. When it did, half the wagons were left behind. Sobków and his family had practically no supplies for the journey; the animals started dying from lack of food and water; and people too died and were buried beside the railway line. After a hellish journey lasting more than a month, the Sobków family was set down at Brochów near Wrocław, only to find that previous arrivals had already helped themselves to all the ex-German properties worth having.[64]

The predictable result was disillusionment and anger at the misleading picture being painted by government ministries of life in the new western lands. A visiting British journalist remarked upon the profusion of posters bearing the legend "Come to Poland's New Paradise" blanketing the walls of towns in the central provinces. "'Make your fortune in the West,' say the newspapers. 'Land and Work for All,' proclaims the radio, in broadcast after broadcast."[65] Radio Lublin depicted an especially rosy scene, advising would-be colonists in June 1945 that "All farms in western Pomerania are in good order; there are good buildings and enough equipment, great stores of potatoes and corn. The possibilities for settlement in towns are also good; there are still a number of empty furnished flats, as well as a number of workshops."[66] With no less assurance, *Trybuna Związkowca* promised settlers that in the Recovered Territories "Safety conditions are the very best."[67]

The reality for most was very different. Ambassador Cavendish-Bentinck reported the experience of an acquaintance from Poznań who had traveled with his niece to Szczecin in August 1945 to try their luck. "The prospects seemed alluring—the Government propaganda promised unheard of opportunities for every kind of prospective settler. The overcrowded train with the steps and roofs of the cars covered by adventurous immigrants proved the faith of the Polish public in these promises." The pair found, however, that about 70 percent of the town was "a mass of ruins" thanks to RAF bombing, and that the Red Army had already commandeered most of the surviving houses. A virtual state of war was going on between bands of Soviet soldiers, often under the influence of drink, who preyed indiscriminately on the civilian population, the Polish police and militia, and each other. After two days the would-be settlers returned home. "The train was overcrowded by returning disgusted 'prospectors' and no words were strong enough to express their opinion of the Russian 'goldatesca' and the 'Powers that Be' in Poland at present who tolerate this state of things and take their orders from Moscow."[68] Robin Hankey and Michael Winch, too, found that most of the repatriates to whom they spoke in Lower Silesia "were very discontented . . . complain[ing] that they were frequently robbed by the Russians and some said they would give anything to go anywhere else if they knew where to go."[69] Paradoxically, in the urban parts of the Recovered Territories the crime rate actually rose sharply after the first mad scramble for German property had concluded. The explanation for this phenomenon offered by the British vice consul in Szczecin was that "empty houses and [the] promise of loot attracted a considerable number of adventurers who for a time made a very lucrative existence disposing of their ill-gotten goods in Warsaw and other towns or even selling them to bona fide settlers . . ." Once the supply of easy pickings from German sources ran out, however, this artificially swollen criminal population had had to revert to a life of conventional felony, and the number of killings, muggings, and burglaries skyrocketed as a result.[70]

But if repatriates and colonists from the central provinces had every reason for disillusionment, the ethnic Polish population of the Recovered Territories who had remained there throughout the war felt no less hard done by. An official of the Resettlement Committee in Bydgoszcz discovered as much when he toured the area in July and August 1945. As soon as the Wehrmacht had withdrawn, the Polish cultivators and agricultural laborers of the vicinity had rushed to seize German farms for themselves. Only 25 percent of the land, however, had been allocated by the ministry for locals, the remaining 75 percent being reserved to accommodate settlers from the lost eastern territories and from Central Poland. The indigenes bitterly resented the presence of these newcomers, considering that the labor they themselves had been required to perform on the farms by the Germans during the war gave them a prior claim. Adopting the slogan "Pomerania for the Pomeranians," they refused to make way for the colonists. To make matters worse, the squatters were "devastating" the holdings, selling off livestock and allowing agricultural machinery to break down through neglect. A similar situation prevailed in the town of Bydgoszcz itself, where would-be colonists to whom houses, businesses, and workshops had been assigned turned up only to find local residents already firmly established.[71] While the law undoubtedly favored the official settlers from outside the region, it was far from clear that they possessed a better moral claim.

Occasionally, Poles found the Red Army standing in the way of their efforts to dispossess the original German owners, either because some Soviets made no secret of their Polonophobia or because the Germans were performing useful services for them. In January 1946, the newly appointed minister for the Recovered Territories, Władysław Gomułka, protested to Marshal Zhukov, the local Soviet military commander Konstantin Rokossovsky, and the ambassador to Warsaw Viktor Lebedev, over the undisguised pro-Germanism of some senior Red Army officers and suggested that private billeting of Red Army soldiers in the Recovered Territories be prohibited to prevent their "fraternization with the Germans and favoring them as against the Polish population."[72] There was undoubtedly some basis for such complaints,[73] though cases of this kind were probably not as frequent as is often alleged. In many more instances, Germans had been driven out of their homes by low-ranking Polish officials, "but after a short time they could always come back and then found that though their homes had been looted they could still fix them up after a fashion." As a result, the Germans had become adept at concealing their valuables in the expectation of being able to return for them later. This, though, exposed them to great danger, with predatory elements not hesitating to use torture to force them to reveal the whereabouts of their possessions. After a resident of Lower Silesia was arrested by the Polish secret police in February 1946, for example, he was "beaten by four Poles with rubber truncheons until I gave way and revealed some of the secret hiding places of my cousin's chemist shop."[74] Those who did not have hidden property to disclose sometimes lost their lives under such interrogations.

Because of the level of uncertainty, insecurity, and material hardship, and the skyrocketing prices—the cost of living in the Recovered Territories was more than twice as high as in central Poland, a differential for which the payment by the state of a "Western bonus" to wage earners did not come close to compensating—the rate of return migration was high. By early 1946, one in four new residents of Wrocław had returned home or moved on to a different location where life might be easier. But others remained, determined to stick it out. By no means were all the newcomers carpet-baggers in search of a quick killing. In the same way that millions of Soviet citizens had flocked to half-built cities east of the Urals during the period of the first Five Year Plan in the late 1920s, filled with enthusiasm at the prospect of "building socialism" in their lifetimes, many Poles were excited by the possibilities for adventure and innovation that life in a pioneer society offered. One of them was Jakub Egit, a Jewish activist from Galicia who had served in the Red Army during the war and nearly all of whose family had been exterminated by the Germans in Belzec. After being coopted onto the Central Committee of Polish Jews in the summer of 1945, Egit traveled to Lower Silesia with the idea of setting up a Yiddish-speaking *yishuv*, or Jewish settlement, for concentration camp survivors and their families using confiscated German property. His eye fell on the town of Dzierżoniów (Reichenbach) where, with a view to poetic justice, a local ordinance stipulated that "a German meeting a Jew on the sidewalk must step aside."[75] In the end, though, Egit's experimental community, which had promising beginnings, was suppressed as a Zionist deviation by the Communist authorities and he himself was forced to flee to Canada.

Polish officials often argued that a serious impediment to the colonization of the Recovered Territories was the Western Allies' refusal to confirm that the "provisional administration" of the area that had been assigned to Warsaw by the Potsdam Conference was indeed a permanent and irrevocable fact. Until settlers were given a firm assurance that they would never be required to leave by a decision of the great powers, they would not be willing to take the risk of starting a new life in the borderlands. Certainly the United States was not above seeking to stir up uncertainty about the future of the Recovered Territories for its own purposes. In a speech at Stuttgart in September 1946, Secretary of State James Byrnes caused a brief sensation by reminding his audience that the Potsdam Conference had not given de jure approval of the transfer of "Silesia and other eastern German areas" to Poland, and that "the extent of the area to be ceded to Poland must be determined when the final [peace] settlement is agreed upon." The address was seized upon by Polish Communists as evidence that the West planned to restore Germany to its prewar boundaries as part of an anti-Soviet scheme, and gave a glimmer of hope to expellees that they might after all be able to return home. In reality, the speech had been no more than a political maneuver on Byrnes's part. He was under no illusions that the Recovered Territories would ever be vacated by either the Poles or the Soviets. His intention was rather to force the Soviet Union publicly to defend the existing boundary between Poland and Germany so as to take the wind out of the sails of the German Communist Party in the forthcoming elections in the Soviet occupation zone. The speech had the desired effect, eliciting a public declaration from Molotov that like the other powers at Potsdam, the USSR fully endorsed the population transfers and had "never envisaged any revision of this decision in the future." Though the Soviet foreign minister was rarely in a position to give lectures on morality to anyone, there was nonetheless some force behind his charge that Byrnes, by causing anxiety to the colonists and fruitlessly raising the hopes of the expellees, was guilty of "cruelty . . . both towards the Poles and the Germans themselves."[76] The Stuttgart address was, in Cavendish-Bentinck's words, "a godsend to the Polish Ministry of Propaganda," and was made the pretext for a nationwide campaign of officially inspired "spontaneous" demonstrations, many of which, tellingly, targeted the premises of Stanisław Mikołajczyk's Polish Peasant Party.[77] Among the colonists themselves, however, Byrnes's comments were seen for what they were. Francis Bourdillon of the Foreign Office Research Department, who was touring the Recovered Territories when the speech was made, found that the settlers were largely ignoring it. Their general belief, he reported, was that "'the Russians will not agree to change the frontiers, the Allies will never use force to turn us out, and we shall not yield to anything else.'"[78]

The single largest problem confronting the Polish authorities was what to do about the 2 million ethnic Polish residents of the former Incorporated Eastern Territories who had signed the *Volksliste* during the war, and thus rendered themselves liable to expulsion to the very country that had terrorized and exploited many of them. The basic rule, according to an ordinance of May 6, 1945, "on the exclusion of hostile elements from the Polish national community," was that *Volksdeutsche* possessing Polish citizenship before the war and those whose names appeared under any category of the *Volksliste* were to be deprived of Polish nationality and forfeit their property rights. Because so many persons of Polish ethnicity had signed the *Volksliste* under duress, however, to apply this regulation rigorously would have led to the deportation of hundreds of thousands of Poles who had already suffered grievously at the Germans' hands. There was also the vexed problem of the so-called "autochthon" population—German speakers of Slav descent, most of them Masurians or Kashubians—many of whom preferred to go to Germany with their co-linguists but who were regarded by the government as "Germanized" Poles who needed to be "rehabilitated" for the nation. The law thus provided two paths by which signatories of the *Volksliste* might now regularize their situation.

Ironically, in deciding to restore Polish citizenship to those who had lost it under previous decrees, the government found itself following in the footsteps of Nazi nationality policy. Just as during the war the criteria for inclusion of ethnic Poles on the *Volksliste* had become so permissive as in many cases to be meaningless, so the authorities in Warsaw, for the same reason, felt obliged to ensure that verification committees did not depopulate the new western lands still further by inquiring too meticulously into *Volksliste* signatories' wartime records.[79] Once the "rehabilitation" process had been put in place, therefore, the criteria laid down for recovery of Polish nationality were few and easily satisfied. Under the "administrative rehabilitation" procedure, those who had "a fixed abode in the Recovered Territories before 1st January, 1945," had never been Nazi Party members, stood no higher than Category III in the *Volksliste*, and were willing to make a formal declaration of loyalty to the state before a "verification commission" would normally qualify for restoration of their nationality, initially in the form of a temporary citizenship certificate valid for six months that might in due course be made permanent. Category II *Volksdeutsche* who could not satisfy these requirements but "for other deserving reasons can be considered for Polish citizenship" could instead obtain "judicial rehabilitation" by proving to the satisfaction of a court that they had acted under duress in subscribing to the *Volksliste* and had never voluntarily renounced their Polish national identity. As for the Masurians and other "autochthons," the great majority were not given a choice, but were compelled to take out Polish nationality. (Once emigration became a possibility in the mid-1950s, however, virtually the whole of the Masurian population would decamp to West Germany.)[80]

The State Repatriation Office (PUR) generally encouraged a permissive interpretation of these policies. At Miastko in Pomerania, Pawel Grzeszczak, the local resettlement officer, reported that the slogan guiding verification decisions in the region was "Not a drop of Polish blood beyond the Oder."[81] The peripatetic Leonard Holliday on one of his visits to Upper Silesia also found that the verification commissions there had been told that persons who spoke Polish and had not voluntarily joined German associations were entitled to stay. Even for the minority whose applications were rejected, a second avenue of appeal remained. "Twice I was told that those who fail to pass this test (some of whom were, in fact, pro-Polish) appeal to the Russian authorities who, in a number of cases, have reinstalled them in their houses or farms, driving out the new settlers placed there by the Polish Repatriation Commission."[82]

When it came to returning the property of the "rehabilitates," though, a different attitude normally prevailed. In theory, this should have been held in trust by the PUR or the State Liquidation Office until verification procedures had been concluded. Only in a minority of cases, however, did this happen. Verification commissions lacked guidance as to the criteria to be employed or the means of enforcing their decisions, and while the process was under way, the property had in innumerable cases been "redistributed" or simply stolen while the owner languished in an internment camp for "Germans." Quite apart from the fate of the German expellees, therefore, this regulation left masses of ethnic Poles vulnerable to the whims of local authorities or the depredations of predatory neighbors. The commandant of the Złotów camp, for example, routinely ignored the findings of the local verification commission, keeping "rehabilitated" Poles behind barbed wire while he helped himself to the contents of their houses.[83] Verification commissions were themselves well placed to profit from their official functions, either by taking bribes from applicants to ensure a favorable verdict—

in Poznań, a filing fee of 6,000 zlotys ($110) was demanded of persons seeking to submit a declaration of loyalty—or by denying justified claims so as to enable members to take over the applicants' property.[84] Mirosław Dybowski, a verification inspector in Gdańsk Voivodeship, reported on the "scandalous proceedings" of the commission there, which had turned down every one of the thirty-seven applications it heard on a single day. Not coincidentally, the farms and goods of the rejected applicants were soon in the hands of the commission's cronies in the local branch of the UB. In one especially egregious case revealed by Dybowski, a UB employee named Słysk had taken a shine to the farm owned by a neighboring family, the Regenbrechts, who qualified for verification. Although the family's wartime record was unimpeachable, Słysk had arranged for the father to be imprisoned in the UB lockup in Kwidzyn and the mother and her three children to be sent to a forced labor camp. He then entered into possession of the farm. When Dybowski uncovered one episode of this kind too many, his investigations were abruptly terminated by an official of the County Office for the Rural Areas who notified him that he would be permitted to carry out no further inspections in Kwidzyn.[85]

Beyond these deliberate abuses of power, much of the difficulty stemmed from the fact that the legal situation relating to *Volksdeutsch* property in Poland was anarchic from the outset, with nearly a dozen ambiguous and sometimes mutually contradictory decrees on the subject having been issued by Warsaw between 1944 and 1948. Under the decree of May 6, 1945, only those members of the third and fourth categories of the *Volksliste* who had "voluntarily" identified themselves as German during the war were to suffer confiscation. In practice, it had proven impossible for hard-pressed Resettlement Officers on the ground to make such distinctions, and almost all "Germans," regardless of category, had been expropriated during the first months of peace. Eastern repatriates and settlers from the central provinces were assigned most of these properties, and although they usually lacked legal title to them, so many had invested time and money in them since taking possession that to move these people out again in favor of the "rehabilitated" owners would have been both disruptive and highly unpopular.

On no fewer than three separate occasions the government attempted to rectify this potentially explosive situation. An October 30, 1945 amendment of the resettlement law provided that "rehabilitated" persons whose land had been confiscated and reassigned were entitled to compensation in kind elsewhere.[86] For many reasons, not least a shortage of suitable properties, this proposed resolution of the difficulty was found to be impracticable, as was a similar measure contained in the land reform legislation of the following month. Finally a decree of June 1946 attempted to cut the Gordian knot by repealing all previous statutes. It too, though, had two fatal flaws. It only applied to confiscations that had been carried out according to the earlier laws in force, and was silent about those accomplished entirely without color of law. It was also so poorly drafted that it did not make clear whether persons appearing in any category of the *Volksliste* were now still subject to confiscation—leading to the paradox that unquestioned "Germans" or even "Nazis" who had already been deported might still have a legal claim to their property.[87]

As an official of the legal department of the Liquidation Office in Łódź pointed out, even when the law spoke clearly, it was not being applied by the courts themselves. Despite the government's insistence that the invidious category of "provisional Polishness" be eliminated, public opinion and judges alike often continued to view signatories of the *Volksliste*, coerced or not, as people who had failed to remain true to Poland during the time of the nation's greatest need. That they should be placed on the same legal standing as those who had suffered persecution at the Nazis' hands for refusing to betray their Polishness, even under pressure, was unacceptable to them.[88] The chief of the Polish Repatriation Mission in the British zone spoke for many when he asserted in his official capacity that these persons "were in principle all German collaborationists of various degrees," and must be treated as such. Partly as a result, whereas by July 31, 1946, no fewer than 223,331 rehabilitation applications had been received by the courts, only a third had been resolved a year later. The number entitled to submit petitions who had not done so was still greater. In consequence, as the Łódź Liquidation Office accurately put it, an atmosphere of *"chacun pour soi et Dieu pour tous"* prevailed on the ground, while the courts were routinely handing down judgments relating to the expropriation of property that would not stand up to legal scrutiny.[89]

Though the non-Potsdam countries of expulsion had fewer structural problems with which to contend, the number of deported *Volksdeutsche* being considerably fewer than in Czechoslovakia or Poland, there is evidence to show that the general picture of a poorly managed colonization process holds good in those districts also. An officer of the Allied Military Mission who toured the Romanian countryside around Brașov, Făgăraș, and Sibiu from which the German population had been deported found "large areas of valuable agricultural land . . . just lying idle. Glasshouses producing tomatoes, lettuces and other crops were likewise in a state of abandonment and in some cases would need quite a fair amount of capital to renew and repair the damages caused by the winter frosts."[90] His impression was confirmed by a Reuters journalist who interviewed the ethnic Romanians of the region in 1946. "[A]ll said that they sympathized with the Saxons [*Volksdeutsche*] and were sorry that they had their land property confiscated under agrarian reform, since this land had been given to gypsies to purchase support for the Government, and the gipsies were very lazy and left the land uncultivated."[91] Similarly in Yugoslavia, the minister for colonization, Sreten Vukosavljević, revealed at the end of 1945 that the resettlement program in the Vojvodina had not gone to plan. The terms under which 390,000 hectares of confiscated German lands had been offered to Yugoslav citizens were highly unattractive, with a family of five being entitled to a plot of a mere two hectares in size. Recipients were obliged to wait twenty years before they could sell the holdings. It was hardly surprising, then, that of the forty-five thousand families scheduled for resettlement in the Vojvodina, with the largest proportion coming from Bosnia-Herzegovina, only five thousand had arrived by the end of 1945. Even these were "not accustomed to intensive farming. . . . There will therefore be in the first years after colonisation a definite falling off in production."[92] This turned out to be a considerable understatement. By 1950, a state of rebellion existed in the Vojvodina, as the 230,000 peasants, most of them Serbs, who had been settled on former German farms often violently resisted the exactions of a Yugoslav state that had come to regard them as "kulaks" and "saboteurs."[93]

Economic disruption would undoubtedly prove to be the leading consequence of the expulsions, in both the short and long terms. The governments of the expelling countries had faced this situation with their eyes open, and insisted that a temporary interruption of normal economic activity was a price worth paying. In one of many speeches by Czechoslovak leaders insisting that no loss of production would ever divert the government from its course, Interior Minister Václav Nosek declared in July 1946 that if appeals for exemptions of skilled German workers were granted, "any material advantages that might result from such a course would be neutralized by the cost of the security measures that would be necessary."[94] A frustrated manager at the Poldina chemical works, however, drew attention to the real-world consequences of this policy when he pointed out that his factory "had 9,000 workmen waiting to start but they were held up because the firm could not find replacements for 270 German . . . chemists who had been ejected."[95] In the countryside, too, by the summer of 1946 it had proven necessary to import 6,000 Bulgarian agricultural workers to Bohemia to relieve labor shortages brought about by the deportation of Germans. Similar examples could be cited almost ad infinitum, in Poland as well as Czechoslovakia. Although, according to official Polish figures which were themselves likely to err considerably on the side of optimism, around 4 million colonists had been settled in the Recovered Territories by the end of 1946, industrial production was at a virtual standstill in large part because of the transfer of vital workers. Only 7,000 people were at work in the chemical industry, compared to 180,000 before the war; just five of the fifty-four cotton mills were in operation; and the mechanical engineering sector was in even worse straits.[96]

In each of the expelling countries, governments, residents, and ecclesiastical authorities struggled mightily to eradicate all indications that Germans had ever been present. As Edvard Beneš urged his compatriots, "We must de-Germanize our republic . . . names, regions, towns, customs—everything that can possibly be de-Germanized must go."[97] Place names were changed overnight, often by direct translation into the new language (e.g., the substitution of "Zielona Góra" for "Grünberg"); statues and memorials demolished; and fanciful local histories composed that airbrushed into oblivion centuries of German presence.[98] "In Wrocław the government had special teams that roved for years painting over and chiseling out German inscriptions. Derelict German cemeteries were converted into parks, and headstones were used to line ditches and sewers."[99] The most ambitious—and unrealistic—attempt to accomplish this objective was an order by Commandant Srević of the Banat military region in Yugoslavia that all German signs on buildings be removed within twelve hours, on pain of the immediate execution of the German occupants.[100] Nor was this a passing phase. As late as 1989, applications for visitors' visas to Poland from Germans born in the Recovered Territories were routinely rejected if the applicant used the former German place name when stating his or her place of birth.[101] The de-Germanization effort extended not only to penalizing the use of the German language, but to putting pressure on residents to abandon German-sounding personal names. The success of the campaign, however, was mixed. Cultural and sometimes physical clashes ensued between settler Poles and many of the indigenes of the Recovered Territories, who had absorbed over the years a high degree of Germanization. New place names could also be rejected by the local population, who sometimes "boycotted new names and even broke road signs that identified the new name. . . . For them, place name changes on the lands in which they had been living were never the processes of *re*-Polonisation, but rather Polonisation against their will."[102]

Consigning evidence of German settlements to George Orwell's "memory hole" was one thing; putting self-sustaining communities in their place entirely another. Norman Davies and Roger Moorhouse argue that the repatriates from eastern Poland who came to settle in the Recovered Territories never succeeded in achieving the second of these objectives.

> [U]ntil 1970 at least, they believed their Silesian sojourn to be temporary. . . . They drank excessively. They let drains and heating systems collapse, then suffered in their damp rooms from high rates of rheumatism. They watched in in-

difference as heaps of discarded farm machinery rusted away in their leaking barns. . . . Whenever possible, they told their children to leave for central Poland. Objectively speaking, their fate was just as tragic as that of the German expellees, whose land and property they had so reluctantly inherited. It can only be summarised by the terms apathy, alcoholism and alienation.[103]

While this bleak picture might have been truer of the first generation of settlers than of their descendants, indices of social deprivation and distress remained stubbornly high in the colonized borderlands of all the expelling countries. Despite the vigorous efforts of the Czechoslovak government, alcoholism took a heavy toll of the rural colonists in the Sudetenland.[104] Unbalanced migration patterns—in particular, a reluctance on the part of middle-class professionals to take up residence in the cleared regions—left communities lacking vital amenities and social services. In the district surrounding the western Bohemian town of Tachov, for example, there was only a single doctor for seventeen thousand inhabitants in the early 1950s. A persistent shortage of schoolteachers proved an especially intractable problem, and, together with the lack of cultural infrastructure such as cinemas and libraries, was one of the factors that drove settlers from the rural areas back into the cities. By the mid-1950s this had become a definite pattern; despite energetic state efforts to counter rural depopulation it would continue until the end of the twentieth century. In 1985, the population of the Czech borderlands, natural increase notwithstanding, still had not recovered to the levels recorded in 1930, far less 1945.[105]

Other commentators found that the true impact upon their respective societies became evident only decades after the expulsion operation had been completed. Edvard Kardelj, Tito's vice premier, later ruefully observed to Milovan Djilas that in expelling the *Volksdeutsche*, Yugoslavia had deprived itself of "our most productive inhabitants."[106] Czechoslovakia too never made good the economic ground lost in the second half of the 1940s. Although the proceeds of the confiscation and redistribution of German property were supposed to have been applied to a "Fund of National Renewal" of Kčs 80 billion, a figure that was a small fraction of its true value; only Kčs 34 billion was ever realized by the Czechoslovak state.[107] The author Petr Příhoda, a prolific commentator on public affairs, has argued that beyond this squandering and misappropriation of resources, the expulsions did permanent damage to Czechoslovakia that cannot be measured in monetary terms alone.[108] The attempt to replace organic communities that had evolved over centuries with successors constructed at breakneck speed, and with mobile and fluctuating populations that were heavily dependent on the largesse of a Communist state, hollowed out Czechoslovak society and gravely weakened its political immune system. Nor was the harm confined to the borderlands. The departure of so many people from the central districts to the periphery in such a short time also established unnatural patterns of internal migration which sapped the vitality of the areas abandoned by the settlers no less than the regions into which they were arriving. While not attributing quite so many deleterious consequences to the expulsions, in comparison with the decades of Communist mismanagement that followed them, Eagle Glassheim points out in a study of the northern districts of the former Sudetenland that from the moment the expulsions were first set in train, "central officials never stopped thinking of north Bohemia as a laboratory."[109] The transfer of the Germans, he argues, thus became a template for—and catalyst of—the kind of ill-conceived experiments in top-down Communist utopia building that wreaked havoc upon Czechoslovakia and the other countries in the region during the four decades that followed.

However these long-term ramifications are assessed, it remains the case that the districts that were cleared of Germans in the 1940s cannot be considered advertisements for the positive impact of population transfers. Part of the reason for this was the respective governments' anxiety to declare by fiat that their full integration had already occurred, and prematurely to discontinue the assistance provided by central government. A grandiose Exhibition of the Recovered Territories was held in Wrocław at the end of July 1948 to proclaim "the total integration of the Western and Northern Territories with the rest of the country."[110] Four months later, the government resolved to dissolve the Ministry for the Recovered Territories, on the ground that the need for such an organization no longer existed, and to downgrade the PUR, which was placed under the authority of the Ministry of Public Administration. As one parliamentarian crowed in January 1949, "the problem of the Recovered Territories as a distinct question in People's Poland has ceased to exist."[111] The reality was far different. Though by 1950 some 5 million hectares of former German land in the Recovered Territories had been distributed to 700,000 families and the region had once again become self-sufficient in food, a drift of settlers away from the countryside soon commenced and was accelerated by the government's increasingly coercive agricultural collectivization program.[112] Because only 5 percent of the landholders of ex-German farms ever received full legal titles to their properties, hundreds of thousands of settlers in the Recovered Territories found themselves the victim of a state-sponsored bait-and-switch scheme after just a few years' residence in the area.[113] The majority of the areas of western Poland from which the Germans were removed remain to the present day among the most sparsely settled and economically backward areas of the country. In the cities, for many years, as noted above, a "western bonus" had to be paid to Polish workers to induce them to face the rigors of life in the borderlands. Similar efforts to entice certain categories of residents to parts of the former Sudetenland would continue until the end of the 1980s. In the Czech lands, as Caitlin Murdock points out, even after the fall of Communism "the legacies of postwar and Communist-era population and economic policies continued to set the borderlands apart, earning them an international reputation for poverty and industrial decay, rather than recognition as distinctly Czech national space."[114]

Thus while the postwar resettlements unquestionably provided opportunities for upward social mobility to some, especially those who were already well connected, for most people the promises of a rich share of the former German bounty never materialized. Instead, the material proceeds of the expulsions would in the long run benefit those who came to take the expellees' place little more than those who had been forced to depart.

10

The International Reaction

Johannes Kostka, a German prisoner of war in a British camp in Egypt, wrote to the U.S. Office of Military Government in Frankfurt at the end of 1947 to express his anxiety about his young wife Gertrud, a resident of the southwestern Polish town of Bielsko-Biała (Bielitz). Born in 1921, Gertrud Kostka had barely missed becoming a citizen of the Austro-Hungarian Empire. Although the region was largely inhabited by German speakers, it had been turned over to Poland after the Great War. The question of timing would prove critical in her case. After the invasion of Poland in 1939, instead of being categorized as Austrian she was placed in the second class of the *Volksliste*, for undisputed though politically indifferent Germans; her husband, an engineer from the "old Reich," was called up for military service shortly afterwards. Their daughter Barbara ("Bärbel") was born in October 1944, but died the following spring, like hundreds of thousands of others, in the chaos surrounding the Red Army's advance across Poland. After nearly four years of separation, Johannes Kostka finally received a letter from his wife, which he forwarded to the U.S. authorities.

> After our last meeting you again went to the front line battling for your life. Our life struggle only began after the surrender. Look, I never wrote to you about it, for the need, the hunger and despair cannot be described or told about. But today I have to tell you something. I had to battle for the child, for my mother and myself. I was known as the wife of a *Reichsdeutscher*. That may be sufficient to you to explain my situation. Four times I was separated from Bärbel to be displaced to Siberia with many others; four times a man was able to save me from the fate in store for me. When my child was dying and there was no doctor to help, I broke down. I tried to follow my child. But I was

prevented and the struggle went on. From the first hour of my distress a man helped me, treating me always as a mother and the wife of another man. But now, after almost three years, he took his reward.

I can't offer any oaths in this letter, because I feel void and dead. But just as honest as our mutual life has been, may these last lines be. I have no guilt to confess. I have no tears to shed. I have only this belief that the Lord will help you to trust my words. After a short pain you will find happiness again. For me there will be bleak despair and the hope that the Lord won't leave me and will call me to Him in my dark hour, uniting me with my child. Trusting upon His help I take farewell from you, and my life. I cannot write any more. I can only beg you, please, believe me, I am without blame.

Farewell, Hans.

Johannes Kostka appealed to U.S. officials to ask the Polish government to give priority to the expulsion of his wife — who had become pregnant as a result of her rape — before she carried out her intention of killing herself.[1] Because the United States concerned itself only with expulsions from Czechoslovakia and Hungary, the letter was passed on to the British embassy in Warsaw, with a request for further action. Four months later, the embassy replied to the Foreign Office in London about the matter. Johannes Kostka, it acknowledged, was undoubtedly in a "most trying predicament." Nevertheless,

> any representations we might make to the Polish Government on behalf of a German subject only provide the authorities here with material to use in propaganda against us. In addition, if these representations have any effect at all, it is one of making the situation more difficult for the person in Poland who is concerned.
>
> Moreover, it is firmly held by the Polish authorities that the deportation of Germans is solely an internal Polish matter in which we have no right to interfere. Unless therefore you feel very strongly about this case, we propose that it should be dropped.

The Foreign Office did not; and consequently it was.[2]

The Kostka case encapsulates the official Western response to the manifest failure of the expulsion project to live up to the "orderly and humane" standards stipulated by the Potsdam Agreement. As in almost every other instance in which the question of ameliorating the sufferings of the expellees arose, the first and overriding consideration was the national interests of the Western powers. The second was a fatalistic prediction that any such action was bound either to fail or to have a positively harmful effect — usually, as in this case, advanced in the teeth both of logic and of the facts of the situation. Lastly, although the expulsions were taking place in accordance with the expressed policy of the Anglo-Americans and required their willing participation and collaboration, the Western democracies disavowed any responsibility for the suffering that resulted, which was, they asserted, entirely the concern of the expelling states or of the Germans themselves.

Against this governmental consensus, those individuals and nongovernmental organizations that sought, if not to put an end to the transfer of the Germans, at least to mitigate its ill effects, could make little headway. The greatest obstacle in their path was the victorious Allies' insistence that the *Volksdeutsche* be excluded from any form of international protection or assistance. This did more than simply deny food, clothing, and accommodation to them. So long as the rule prevailed, there existed no organization that was authorized to make representations either to the expelling states or to the Allied military governments in Germany on their behalf. As a result, humanitarian bodies like the Red Cross could be—and in practice frequently were—barred from extending even the minimal amounts of assistance they were in a position to provide. Nor was there any agency, national or international, to which *Volksdeutsche* subjected to inhumane treatment might appeal. Paradoxically, the women and children who made up most of the expellee population occupied a legal status far lower than that of members of the SS, who, as former servicemen of the German armed forces, were protected by the Geneva Convention. Because of this, advocates for the expellees could do little more than try to raise public awareness. While they enjoyed limited success in this regard, it was never enough to make a difference to the way in which the transfers were conducted. This is in itself a remarkable fact. Although the expulsions and their consequences neither could be, nor were, hidden from sight, few Europeans outside the countries immediately concerned, and fewer Americans, noticed that they were taking place. With the exception of the foothold obtained for the Red Cross in Czechoslovakia by Richard Stokes's revelations of October 1946, none of the expelling or receiving governments was at any time compelled by the pressure of public opinion to abandon or modify a policy on which it had previously decided. Outside the communist world, there is probably no undertaking in modern history on a comparable scale in which those who carried it out were able to do so with such a degree of freedom from external scrutiny.

Part of the blindness, it is true, was conscious and willful. Since 1943, when it became increasingly clear that an Allied victory was probable if not certain, a great deal of attention had been devoted in the West to the question of German collective guilt for Nazism and its crimes. By the end of the war, the debate had largely been settled. Opinion polls in Britain showed that large majorities recognized no difference between "ordinary Germans" and "Nazis"; similar surveys in the United States found that Americans thought that Germany was not being treated sufficiently harshly; and a poll in France revealed that 59 percent of respondents favored the expulsion of at least some Germans.[3] While many Westerners may not have subscribed to the Polish and Czechoslovak argument that the *Volksdeutsche* were even more guilty than the people of the "old Reich" by virtue of having added treachery to barbarity, they nonetheless broadly shared Hubert Ripka's belief that "Nazism has been only a modern form and a culminating point of brutal pan-Germanism, with which the minds and hearts of the German people have been thoroughly imbued."[4] And some carried that perception so far forward as to argue that it was appropriate even that children pay the price for Nazi misdeeds. When the London-based National Peace Council issued a call in September 1945 for Britons to accept reduced food rations so that expellee women and children might be fed, a correspondent to the *Daily Herald* condemned those among his countrymen who still harbored "tender feelings towards this race of murderous white savages." A letter signed by sixty war workers was still more outspoken, demanding that the German people be starved as a matter of policy as were "the men, women and children of Greece and Russia during the Nazi occupation . . ."[5] Even some officers attached to Allied Military Government in Germany, like Goronwy Rees, held that mass deaths among expellees were, if not a positive Allied war aim, at any rate a matter of no great significance when set against the overriding objective of avoiding giving unnecessary offence to the Soviet Union:

> It is inevitable that millions of Germans must die in the coming winter. It is inevitable that millions of the nomads who wander aimlessly in all directions across Germany should find no resting place but the grave. . . . These facts could only be altered, if at all, by a universal effort of philanthropy which would reverse the result of the war. . . .
>
> The real danger of Germany at the moment is not that millions of Germans must starve, freeze and die during the winter; it is that out of their misery the Germans should create an opportunity for destroying the unity of the Allies who defeated them.[6]

Views like these, while far from unusual, were still not in the majority. If Westerners considered that all Germans, with the possible exception of children below the age of reason, shared at least some measure of responsibility for the war and deserved punishment for it, they did not agree that any and all forms of punishment were justified. Though a London *Daily Express* report argued that the "wild expulsions" were having a salutary effect, teaching the *Volksdeutsche* that "war does not pay," the rash of stories appearing in the newspapers in the late summer of 1945 on the state in which expellees were arriving in Berlin provoked a short-lived but sharp response in Britain. A protest to Ernest Bevin from the Coventry branch of the Peace Pledge Union, denouncing the expulsions as "absolute stupidity," was described by the Foreign Office as "one of innumerable letters we receive on this question"; by the end of September so many were arriving that Jack Troutbeck drafted a form response to be sent to all future correspondents.[7] Two deputations—the first, organized by George Bell, Anglican bishop of Chichester, representing the Christian churches, and the second a cross-party group headed by Sir William Beveridge—visited Clement Attlee in September and October to ask that all possible steps be taken to relieve the expellees and, at the least, to suspend further evictions during the coming winter. Though the prime minister initially dealt somewhat brusquely with the clergymen, suggesting that those affected by the transfers were "paying the penalty" for their part in the war and asserting that "the particular problem of German refugees from Eastern Europe was not one for which the Government was in any way responsible," the markedly more emollient tone of his response to the second group, to whom he "expressed great sympathy with the objects of the deputation," showed that British policymakers realized there was a risk of the question becoming a cause célèbre.[8]

For a brief period, it seemed that it might indeed do so. The shambles into which the "wild expulsions" were descending caused those opinion formers who had already expressed their opposition to the scheme to remind the public that they had told them so. That these gruesome stories were emerging from central Europe at the same time that the trials of the surviving war criminals were opening at Nuremberg added to public disquiet. In a letter to the *Times*, the philosopher Bertrand Russell drew attention to the fact that one of the charges leveled against the Nazi defendants was their involvement in "deportation, and other inhumane acts committed against any civilian population."

> In eastern Europe now mass deportations are being carried out by our allies on an unprecedented scale.... This is not done as an act of war, but as part of a deliberate policy of "peace."
>
> ... Are mass deportations crimes when committed by our enemies during war and justifiable measures of social adjustment when carried out by our allies in time of peace? Is it more humane to turn out old women and children to die at a distance than to asphyxiate Jews in gas chambers? Can those responsible for the deaths of those who die after expulsion be regarded as less guilty because they do not see or hear the agonies of their victims? Are the future

laws of war to justify the killing of enemy nationals after enemy resistance has ceased?"[9]

Other critics pointed out that the doctrine of "collective responsibility" cut both ways. The publisher Victor Gollancz, himself of Jewish heritage, argued that "if every German was indeed responsible for what happened at Belsen, then we, as members of a democratic country and not of a fascist one with no free Press or parliament, were responsible individually as well as collectively" for what was being done to German women and children in Britain's name.[10] During the following two months, Gollancz organized several successful protest meetings, the largest of which overflowed the Albert Hall.[11] Inspired by Bishops Bell of Canterbury and Garbett of York, a convocation of the Church of England unanimously denounced the expulsions as "a violation of the principles of humanity that the Allies are pledged to uphold."[12] Almost as quickly as it had arisen, however, the wave of popular concern dissipated. The hastily thrown-together organization Save Europe Now, launched by Gollancz in September 1945, made a serious tactical error by appealing to Britons to signify their agreement to a voluntary reduction in food rations so that expellees and other starving Europeans could be fed. Although about sixty thousand people, many of them connected to religious or peace groups, did so, the idea proved generally unpopular.[13] After six years of wartime privation, the British people were highly resistant to any suggestion that their standards of living be cut further, especially to benefit former enemies.[14] Air Chief Marshal Philip Joubert de la Ferté, writing in the *Observer*, probably expressed the mood of his compatriots a great deal more accurately than did Save Europe Now. "I would sooner that my children, brought up in freedom and goodwill towards men, should enjoy full vigour than the Germans, who may be using their strength to make war on the world again in another generation."[15] Save Europe Now also quickly succumbed to "mission creep," turning its attention away from the problem of malnourished expellees to questions ranging from the provision of books and newspapers in Germany to the early release of prisoners of war in Allied custody. Lastly, the announcement at the end of November 1945 that "wild expulsions" would give way to "organized" ones encouraged the belief that the expellees' problems were being effectively addressed. Despite participants' good intentions, then, Save Europe Now and similar groups did more to assuage the moral discomfort of Britons than the physical distress of the *Volksdeutsche*. In Matthew Frank's pardonably cynical, but nonetheless accurate, summation, "The expulsions and the German refugee crisis allowed the British to hold a mirror up to themselves and, on the whole, the British liked what they saw."[16]

By no means, moreover, was the perception that the expulsions were being conducted in an inhumane manner universally shared. Between the wars, the Czechoslovak government had invested heavily in spin-doctoring and overseas news management, in which it had enjoyed much success. The hub of this effort was the Third Section of the Ministry of Foreign Affairs, which directed a massive and well-funded foreign information and propaganda service. In addition to cultivating relations with dignitaries and opinion formers from abroad, the Third Section "served as the government's semiofficial publishing house, crafting newspapers, pamphlets, and other publicity materials in all the major European languages."[17] It controlled the Geneva-based Central European Radio network. It directed, from behind the scenes, the Orbis publishing empire, which not only flooded the European market with disguised "pro-Czechoslovak propaganda texts of all kinds," down to the level of tourist guidebooks, but also kept in print works by friendly foreign writers like Robert Seton-Watson and Lewis Namier that otherwise would have been commercially unviable. It subsidized no fewer than twenty-six French newspapers, radio stations, and press agencies; bankrolled friendly British writers; and secured favorable coverage by buying advertising in international periodicals. And it carried out research for, suggested story ideas to, and paid the traveling expenses of the large number of foreign journalists and authors who came to visit the only post-Versailles state to retain a parliamentary system. During Edvard Beneš's tenure as foreign minister the Third Section justifiably claimed that it "had had a hand in almost every book published outside Czechoslovakia on Czech topics . . ."[18] Hugely expensive though this effort was for a small and only partly developed country, the money was well spent. Between the wars, Czechoslovakia's cultural diplomacy program was by far the most successful and sophisticated in Europe. It was largely due to its efforts that the image of Czechoslovakia as a model Western-style democracy persisted so long—even after the government, following the passage in 1933 of an Enabling Act, increasingly sidelined Parliament by ruling via emergency decrees in a manner in some respects reminiscent of the latter days of the Weimar Republic.

After the war, ex-members of the Third Section resumed the task of forging an image of Czechoslovakia that reflected what Westerners wanted to see in it, and in themselves. This objective was assisted by the fact that in Britain especially, a great many influential media figures were deeply ashamed of the manner in which their country had sold Czechoslovakia down the river in 1938. With ordinary Britons anxious to project their own inglorious record at that time onto a despised class of upper-crust appeasers, "Munich" had become as dirty a word in London as in Prague. Czechoslovakia's obvious postwar orientation toward the

USSR, seemingly matched by the election of a democratic socialist government in Britain, also won the country many new friends in left-wing circles. Even though the restored Beneš government was no longer able to cultivate and entertain foreign journalists on as lavish a scale as in the past, the pro-Czechoslovak bias in the British press was as marked, during the crucial years of 1945–46, as it had been before the war.

Officials in Prague, nonetheless, left as little as possible to chance. Detailed dossiers were compiled by the Ministry of Foreign Affairs and the political intelligence section of the Ministry of the Interior on leading Western journalists, noting their political and ideological backgrounds and associations, and their prior attitudes to Czechoslovak policy. Jon Kimche, correspondent for the Reuters news agency, was described as "competent," but not known for his favorable coverage of the Czechoslovak Republic. Michael Foot, former editor of the London *Evening Standard* and now a Labour Party MP, was said to be responsible for the uncomfortably close attention paid by the *Daily Herald*, the Labour-affiliated newspaper, to the seamier side of Czechoslovak affairs. "There have been warnings," an appreciation of his career recorded, "about Foot's activities in connection with Jaksch."[19]

On the whole, though, the authorities in Prague had few grounds for complaint. Ralph Parker, the London *Times*'s correspondent there in the summer of 1945, was a former Foreign Office specialist on Czechoslovak affairs and a crypto-Communist who would later take up a position as Moscow bureau chief of the *Daily Worker*.[20] In a letter to the *Times* editor, Robin Barrington-Ward, in July 1945, he emphasized the importance of Britain not appearing "unsympathetic to national aspirations" in Central Europe by standing in the way of expulsions, and hoped that at Potsdam the Big Three would put their weight behind the project.[21] Parker's successor, Godfrey Lias, had written a hagiographical biography of Beneš in 1940 and would later translate the president's memoirs for an English-speaking readership. Maurice Hindus, the Prague-based *New York Herald Tribune* correspondent, also had a record of adulatory pro-Czechoslovak publications, including a book hailing the country as a "citadel of humanitarianism" that was virtually a compendium of Third Section talking points.[22] Some journalists, like George Bilainkin of the London *Daily Mail*, thought it their duty when writing of the expulsions to go beyond friendly reportage to frank advocacy. In an interview with Beneš in November 1945, Bilainkin asked the president what "I can do to help you most . . ." Beneš asked him to "make people understand" the imperative need for the removal of the Germans. Bilainkin promised to do so, considering it "the least debt I owe to Czechoslovakia, longest martyr in modern history."[23]

The willing cooperation of foreign assets like these was instrumental in the Czechoslovak government's efforts to deflect international attention from the more disturbing aspects of the expulsions. After Eric Gedye's exposé of conditions in Hagibor camp appeared, for example, Tom Williamson, a British Labour MP and member of the party's National Executive Committee, visited Prague ten days later and delivered a public speech assuring his hosts that "the comments of the British press should not be taken too seriously and that the British Labour Party was convinced of the necessity for transfer of the Germans." Senator Claude Pepper (Democrat of Florida), also passing through Czechoslovakia, expressed himself in similar terms at a press conference shortly afterward.[24] A Potemkin tour was quickly arranged for Sheila Grant Duff, wartime head of the BBC's Czech section, an intimate of Hubert Ripka's, and author of a best-selling and highly sympathetic Penguin Special book on the Munich crisis, so that she could contradict Gedye's charges in the *New Statesman* and other publications on the basis of what she represented to readers as first-hand information.[25] George Bilainkin had already been taken to one of the same showcase camps at Liberec, where he found "pleasant cut flowers" in the room of one of the internees, and admired the "splendid soup" and "new and tasty" bread provided to them.[26] Guy Bettany, Reuters' special correspondent in Prague, inaccurately reassured his readers that "Representatives of the International Red Cross are now given the fullest facilities to inspect [the camps] and to make suggestions, and in the main they have been satisfied with what they have seen."[27] Dennis Bardens of the *Sunday Dispatch*, formerly a liaison officer to the Czechoslovak government in exile in London, was also roped into the exculpation campaign and duly supplied a clean bill of health to the camps he was shown.[28] Even those journalists who were less heavily invested in defending the Beneš government from any criticism habitually "accentuated the positive and wanted to give the Czechs ... the benefit of the doubt. When criticism was levelled, care was taken to exonerate central government of any responsibility and lay the blame on local, invariably Communist, authorities."[29]

The Czechoslovak media, contrariwise, was virtually unanimous in perceiving the malign influence of Germans, and above all that of Wenzel Jaksch, in every adverse comment that appeared in the foreign press. As Evžen Klingler rhetorically inquired in *Svobodné noviny*, the country's leading journal of opinion:

> What does the average reader in Britain know of the fact that the foreign political editor of the "most English of journals," as the *Manchester Guardian* is frequently called, is a journalist of German origin? ... How is the average Englishman to ascertain that most of the foreign political articles in the *Ob-*

server are written by a journalist of German-Polish origin? How can he verify the fact that the *Tribune* is supplied with reports from people in the entourage of Wenzel Jaksch?[30]

Klingler's choice of examples of closet pan-Germans reverting to type was particularly infelicitous, inasmuch as the first, Frederick Voigt of the *Guardian*, had been probably the most outspoken anti-Nazi and antiappeasement member of the European press corps during the 1930s; while the second, Sebastian Haffner of the *Observer*, had fled Germany not only because of his vocal opposition to Hitler but because his marriage to his Jewish wife rendered him liable to a lengthy prison sentence under the Nuremberg Laws.[31] Such niceties, however, were lost on furious Czechoslovak proponents of the expulsions, who continued to attribute all foreign criticism to "Jacksch and others who nowadays promote Sudeten autonomy and the amalgamation of what was formerly called the Sudetenland with Bavaria."[32]

Poland's amateurish attempts at news management were far less successful. Few members of the postwar government were known to Western journalists; almost none, with the exception of Stanisław Mikołajczyk, had any prior relationships with them. Rather than attempt to cultivate the foreign press, then, Polish political and media figures contented themselves either with abusing it for failing to appreciate the necessity of treating the Germans harshly or with fabricating stories intended to show that no harsh treatment was occurring. In the first category was an article in *Dziennik polski*, organ of the London Poles, that paradoxically offered a Marxist analysis of British criticism of the "wild expulsions" from the Recovered Territories. "England's future German customers, future consumers of English goods, have in the light of prospective high profits already become as it were England's favorites. How, otherwise, are English press statements deploring the wrongs suffered by the Germans at the hands of the Poles to be interpreted?"[33] In the second category was a pair of interviews purporting to have been given to Polish journalists by members of the British liaison teams at Kaławsk and Szczecin, who had allegedly said that "movement of expellees could not be better organized . . . health of expellees is excellent and conditions of movement humane . . . expellees leave Poland contented" and that reports in the British press to the contrary were "a downright lie." Both of these statements were disavowed by their supposed authors.[34]

Arguably, no very sophisticated information management apparatus was necessary, in view of the general indifference of public opinion to the question. In the United States, the efforts of human rights activists and their supporters in the press had even less impact than Save Europe Now in Britain. In many respects, the history of the two campaigns ran along similar paths. As in Britain, concern about the expulsions arose as a result of press coverage from Germany, especially the first-person reportage of Anne O'Hare McCormick in the *New York Times*. The leading female foreign correspondent of the day, McCormick had been the first woman to win a Pulitzer Prize for journalism in 1937. After the war, she returned to Europe where she made the reconstruction of the continent her major theme. Some of her harshest criticisms of the Allies' record in this area were reserved for the expulsion program which, in her view, was a contradiction of the ideals for which the war had been fought. "The scale of this resettlement," she wrote in October 1946, "and the conditions in which it takes place are without precedent in history. No one seeing its horrors first-hand can doubt that it is a crime against humanity for which history will exact a terrible retribution."[35] Her colleague, the syndicated columnist Dorothy Thompson (who was herself married to a Czech national) went one step further. In collaboration with a broadcaster of internationalist and Republican leanings, Christopher Emmet, together with other leading public intellectuals from both the left and right wings of American politics like John Dewey, Sidney Hook, A. Philip Randolph, Norman Thomas, and Oswald Garrison Villard, she assisted in the foundation of a Committee Against Mass Expulsions (CAME) based in New York. The committee attempted to arouse public opinion in the United States by holding meetings and publishing pamphlets based largely on eyewitness testimonies by Western journalists and military officers that described, with a good deal of accuracy, the human consequences of the clearances of Czechoslovakia and Poland. Ten thousand copies of the first pamphlet, *The Land of the Dead*, were sold in 1947. Free samples of the second, *Men Without the Rights of Man*, were provided the following year to all members of Congress and of the British House of Commons, the libraries of all universities and colleges in the United States and Canada, and the editorial writers of fifteen hundred newspapers.[36] "By pursuing the will-of-the-wisp of racially pure European States," it argued, "we only aggravate the nationalisms which have bred Europe's wars in the past."[37] Moreover, the lesson of the expulsion pointed inescapably to the fact that mass population transfers could not be accomplished without massive abuse of human rights, something for which the Allies as well as the expelling countries bore a full share of responsibility.

CAME was opposed, however, by the staunchly Germanophobic Society for the Prevention of World War III, headed by the novelist Rex Stout and including Eleanor Roosevelt, the CBS broadcaster William Shirer (future author of the bestselling *Rise and Fall of the Third Reich*), and Senator Harley Kilgore (Democrat of West Virginia) among its collaborators.[38] The committee also came under the fire of the American Friends of Czechoslovakia, of which Beneš himself was honorary chairman and which could boast an even more impressive retinue of well-connected members, among them Nicholas Murray Butler, president of Columbia University, and James T. Shotwell, State Department adviser and president of the Carnegie Endowment for International Peace. This body launched a fierce counterattack against CAME's revelations, insisting that during the first phase of expulsions from Czechoslovakia "most of those . . . driven out of the country were members of the Gestapo, S.S., *Reich* officials or *Reich* refugees."[39] Though the Friends of Czechoslovakia never succeeded in discrediting CAME's claims, the dispute between the rival groups soon began to take on the appearance of a private fight about a faraway land about which most Americans knew nothing. But the principal factor stultifying CAME's propaganda campaign was that it did not begin to hit its stride until the organized expulsions had already been largely completed. In consequence, inasmuch as the committee did not advocate that the expellees be allowed to return home, it remained unclear precisely what it wanted policymakers to do.

The publicity given by leading media figures like Anne McCormick and Dorothy Thompson and pressure groups like CAME to the abuses associated with the expulsions did at least have the effect of causing politicians and others who had been outspoken in their support of population transfers to begin to distance themselves from their own records. Winston Churchill, whose political antennae were more sensitive than most, was among the first to recognize that being identified as one of the authors of mass population transfers was unlikely to enhance his reputation before the bar of history. In a Commons speech of August 1945, he indulged in a typically Churchillian display of crocodile tears over the consequences of his own policy.

> I am particularly concerned, at this moment, with the reports reaching us of the conditions under which the expulsion and exodus of Germans from the new Poland are being carried out. Between 8,000,000 and 9,000,000 persons dwelt in those regions before the war. . . . Sparse and guarded accounts of what has happened and is happening have filtered through, but it is not impossible that tragedy on a prodigious scale is unfolding itself behind the iron curtain which at the moment divides Europe in twain. I should welcome any statement which the Prime Minister can make which would relieve or at least inform us upon this very anxious and grievous matter.[40]

Remarkably, with the exception of the MP-journalist Michael Foot, no one publicly challenged this exercise in self-exculpation.[41] But the perceived need to ensure that the Western democracies would not be held responsible for the actions they had taken underlay a still more extraordinary and self-serving exercise by the U.S. House of Representatives in 1949 and 1950. Sponsored by the House Judiciary Committee, a subcommittee headed by Rep. Francis E. Walter (Democrat of Pennsylvania) conducted a three-week fact-finding tour in Germany and Austria in September 1949, with the mission of demonstrating "the fallacy of the theory of American coresponsibility for the uprooting of German expellees and refugees." The subcommittee duly arrived at this ingenious conclusion by persuading itself that "a very large proportion of the Germans had already been expelled from Eastern Europe" before the Potsdam Conference; that "a large and spontaneous exodus of German nationals" had reduced their numbers further, and that so far as the remainder was concerned, the United States had "agreed to the wording of article XIII [of the Potsdam Agreement] solely because it wanted (1) to make more orderly and humane the inevitable expulsion of those Germans who still remained in eastern Europe, and (2) to open occupied Germany to those who were faced with deportation to remote sub-Arctic territories of Soviet Russia, an equivalent to annihilation. The records of the Potsdam Conference make these facts plain."[42] Specious and transparent though the Walter subcommittee's claims were, they nonetheless signaled a change in attitudes toward the expellees. Previously they had typically been regarded as the sole authors of their own misfortunes. Even a source as far removed from the scene as the *Mercury* of Hobart in Tasmania had applauded their expulsion as just punishment for their having constituted themselves as "traitors within the gates" and "a vast cohesive fifth column" that had waited patiently throughout the 1930s for orders from Berlin to betray their respective countries to the Hitlerite invaders.[43] Partly for that reason, expellees had been explicitly ruled ineligible for aid from any international humanitarian body, including the United Nations Relief and Rehabilitation Agency and the International Refugee Organization.[44] Even the International Committee of the Red Cross as a matter of policy "refrained from expressing their opinion regarding the actual decision of expulsion, since this was a political question for which Governments concerned are solely responsible," and from the end of 1946 decided to withdraw altogether from relief activities aimed at civilians.[45] Thereafter, the CICR had confined itself to raising the question of conditions for expellees with the governments to which its delegations were attached, and to distributing resources confided to it by others. Only three small states that had been neutral during the war—Switzerland, Ireland, and Sweden—did not exclude *Volksdeutsche* from the relief funds they donated to the CICR to assist the continent's needy. Valuable though their assistance had been, even more from the psychological than the physical standpoint, it did not come close to meeting the need: in 1949, the World Council of Churches noted that religious charities in Germany itself had provided more material aid to the expellees than all other agencies, domestic and foreign, put together.[46]

So far as the Christian churches were concerned, indeed, small-scale assistance supplied out of existing funds was all they were prepared to give. To mount a larger appeal to benefit the *Volksdeutsche* would have required at the least a public announcement on their behalf, and this was something that none of them was prepared to make. Although the majority of expellees were Catholic in religion, the Vatican conspicuously refrained from taking a stand against the mass deportations. That Pope Pius XII strenuously opposed them, in theory and in practice, is not in question. In a private meeting with a trio of U.S. congressmen, the pontiff said that "the plight of millions who now must answer to the hideous appellation of 'expellee' was no longer simply a matter for humiliation and regret" and that he was "doggedly determined to see this giant specter of human dereliction forever banished from the conscience of mankind."[47] The pope was also greatly distressed by the way in which wartime antagonisms had divided the institutional Church in the postwar years. According to Michael Phayer, "When Pius learned that Cardinal Hlond banned the use of German after the war in liturgical services in Poland where Volksdeutsch Catholics still lived, he wept."[48] But personal anguish was not matched by public advocacy—except by the elliptical means of the Holy See's appointment of apostolic administrators rather than bishops for the Recovered Territories until June 1972.[49] While the Catholic Church has been justly criticized for the modesty of its response to the persecution of the Jews during the war, it took no more active a stance in support of the expellees afterwards. It may well be that the two were connected, and that the Church hesitated in the postwar years to expose itself to criticism that it was more solicitous of the German people than of those who had experienced near-annihilation at their hands. But although individual priests and bishops, in the United States and central Europe, vigorously condemned mass expulsions as inconsistent with the laws of God, the Holy See never did so. Nor, it is only fair to note, did the governing body of any other Christian denomination.

By the late 1940s, policymakers and commentators—among them General Lucius Clay, Sir Brian Robertson, and Congressman Walter's subcommittee—were coming to the conclusion that the expellee problem was insoluble except by large-scale German emigration.[50] The French government, in particular, feared the consequences of having a larger German population than in prewar years concentrated in a country that in land area was nearly a quarter less. From the perspective of Paris, it was only a matter of time before fresh demands for

Lebensraum disrupted the peace of Europe. Notwithstanding the intensity and longevity of the Franco-German antagonism, then, Georges Bidault's postwar government began exploring the possibility of admitting a significant number of ethnic German expellees as immigrants, both to replace French wartime losses and to encourage other countries to open their doors also. As early as October 1945, the French ambassador in Prague began to indicate his government's interest in accepting up to half a million *Sudetendeutsche* within metropolitan France itself or in the French colonies. Paris, he said, "had found that the Germans were easily assimilated and made good citizens. In this respect they were better potential French citizens than were either the Poles or the Italians."[51] At the Conference of Foreign Ministers meeting in March 1947, Bidault formally stated his readiness to begin ethnic German immigration. So marked, indeed, was the French government's preference for *Volksdeutsch* immigrants specifically that it spurned energetic British efforts to persuade it to accept the largely Polish occupants of Allied displaced persons camps in exchange. The Poles, it advised London, "should remain in Germany to add a peaceful Slavonic leaven to the Teutonic strain, while Germans should emigrate to France in order to become Gallicised and civilised."[52]

Nor was the French the only government to do so. As postwar labor shortages, especially in key industries, began to bite, other countries cast an acquisitive eye on what seemed to be an especially valuable pool of skilled workers. The Swedish government submitted an informal request for two thousand *Sudetendeutsche* in the summer of 1947, helpfully specifying that those desired should be well-qualified persons in engineering, ironworks, glassmaking, the textile industry, and match manufacturing, as well as trained cattlemen. They were to be aged between twenty and forty-five, and to be politically uncompromised.[53] Norway asked the U.S. zonal authorities to supply 150 plate workers, instrument mechanics, toolmakers, and spinners.[54] Industrialists in Britain demanded "Sudeten single women" from the same source "in order to obtain additional labour for our undermanned industries, chiefly textiles."[55] Even in the faraway southern United States, ethnic Germans were actively recruited as a low-wage substitute for Southern black farm laborers who had migrated to the cities of the north and west during the Second World War.[56]

To long-standing opponents of the expulsions, news that the countries that had carried them out intended to solve the social and economic problems they had created by reseeding German minority settlements outside the country's borders seemed little more than a sick joke. Anne McCormick castigated the Bidault proposal, pointing out that France, which to that point had offered no humanitarian objections to what had been a "horrifying operation in wholesale human dumping," now was declaring "in effect, that the surgical operation that made millions of human beings homeless in the name of peace now threatens the peace of France."[57] German leaders expressed their staunch hostility to the idea. That the country should now be deprived of the relatively few skilled workers among the expellee population it had received, leaving it only with the unproductive and unemployable to support from its own meager resources, was so obviously contrary to German economic interests that it could not be entertained.[58]

In the event, surprisingly few Germans, both native-born and expellee, left the country when the Allied ban on emigration was finally lifted in 1949. By then, signs of economic recovery at home meant that the "push" factors that might have caused them to do so were less exigent. The expellee population, among whom women with family ties were a majority, was among the demographic cohort that in nearly all countries and historical eras has been least drawn to emigration. Having already weathered one traumatic displacement to a new and unfamiliar land, moreover, it is understandable that few expellees were keen immediately to face another. For these and other reasons, a remarkably low number of Germans—only 780,000, or less than 2 percent of the population—left the country to live abroad between 1945 and 1961. The proportion of expellees among them was less than half.[59]

That the Allied countries were perfectly willing to accept them, however, indicates that a sea change in perceptions of the *Volksdeutsche* had occurred by the end of the 1940s. A great part of the change was the result of the Cold War, which had seen the Soviet Union replace Nazi Germany as the leading symbol of political depravity. A revealing example of the new narrative that was to take the place of the old was the speech made by John Gibson, head of the U.S. Displaced Persons Commission, to the first group of 500 *Volksdeutsch* immigrants to the United States upon their arrival in October 1951. "Those dates that many of you have told me about—the day your family was ordered to get out of your home, and your homeland—the day an arrest was made—the day that a long term in a prison camp began—the day that you realized that you were no longer free, but the oppressed victims of a Godless dictatorship. These are the dates that this day will erase."[60] In Western discourses, the very term "expellee" would henceforth disappear; ethnic Germans would instead be elevated to the status of "political refugees"—the victims of communism rather than Allied policy. It was a subterfuge with which for the moment most of them were happy to go along, being obviously preferable to that of "fifth columnist" or "Hitler's first converts." By the end of the twentieth century, though, many of them as they approached the end of their lives would feel less comfortable sustaining this polite fiction. Following the collapse of communism, they would become increasingly assertive in shaping their own narratives, and in seeking—or if necessary demanding—their acknowledgment by others.

11

The Resettlement

The attention of historians is naturally drawn to the most dramatic events and critical turning points of the past. Because of this, it is all too easy to overlook the importance of what G. M. Trevelyan describes as those turning points at which "history failed to turn"—moments when a development that might be expected to happen did not, after all, take place.[1] Among these unnoticed near misses of history, the successful resettlement and assimilation of more than twelve million German expellees, up to a tenth of whom did not even speak German, is a particular case in point. According to all rational considerations, the depositing of this vast, impoverished, and traumatized population upon a blitzed country that did not want them and in which no preparations had been made to receive them was a recipe for disaster. In 1919 the Allies had fastened a harsh peace treaty upon Germany at Versailles; the result, fourteen years and an economic depression later, was the rise to power of Adolf Hitler. From every measurable standpoint, the situation in 1945 boded far worse. Germany had lost nearly twice as much of her land area as in 1919, and was no longer able to feed herself. The postwar population of this truncated and divided country, paradoxically, was larger than in 1939, the influx of expellees more than making up for any wartime losses. Economic life was at a virtual standstill, and the ill-advised Allied policy of dismantling all German industry above a certain level for fear that it might be used for possible future war production meant that even the few viable sources of employment that existed were often willfully destroyed.[2] The housing shortage was so critical that some military government officials in the winter of 1945 were basing their assumptions upon the outbreak of an epidemic among the expellees the massive death toll from which would reduce the population to manageable numbers, and without which they could hardly imagine where the newcomers were to be accommodated. As for the new arrivals themselves, relegated to the bottom of the social pyramid and lacking any stake in the status quo, it seemed inconceivable that they would not become the mainstay of some new radical or revanchist movement, of either the extreme Left or the extreme Right, dedicated to obtaining revenge for their recent sufferings and regaining their lost homelands. Almost miraculously, this did not come to pass. Within an incredibly few years, the expellees had become effectively—if not quite completely—integrated into the larger society in both West and East Germany. This should not, though, be seen as any kind of retrospective vindication of Allied policy. Even with the benefit of hindsight their actions appear reckless to an astonishing degree. That Germany and Europe have not suffered the worst consequences that might be expected to proceed from them is due above all to the industry and good sense of many Germans themselves—accompanied by the kind of luck that comes along, at most, once in a lifetime.

In the same way that the Allies had made no plans of any kind during the war to accomplish the removal of the expellees to Germany, they displayed a similar insouciance when questions arose as to how they were to be accommodated and integrated upon arrival. Insofar as anything in the nature of a definite policy existed, it was summed up in the popular maxim, "Make the Germans do it."[3] According to this principle, it was the role of Allied military government "to control German affairs by indirect rule: i.e. they issue instructions to local German authorities and supervise their execution, but wherever possible refrain from taking actual executive action themselves."[4] In itself this was not an unsound notion. But it ran up against two countervailing trends. The first was that the Allies were simultaneously purging the ranks of those Germans who would be directed to "do it," seeking to remove those who were tainted with Nazism from the exercise of all public functions. In the course of a clumsily executed denazification effort, the Anglo-Americans arguably got the worst of both worlds. The weeding-out process was neither rigorous enough to punish all seriously compromised Nazis, nor light-handed enough to leave in office a core of administrators who, whatever their political records, were at least efficient. (The Soviets and their local German assistants, less fastidious—or with fewer illusions—than their Western counterparts generally followed the latter policy, quickly rebranding mid-ranking Nazis who were prepared to serve their new masters obediently as "anti-fascists.")[5] The second problem with making the Germans responsible for carrying out Allied requirements was that they were given no tools with which to do so. As one British administrator, attempting to explain the rationale behind such a seemingly counterproductive stance, put it, "when nearly all the world is suffering from acute shortages of goods . . . it is difficult to arrange, or to defend, that Germany should come anything but last."[6] The human cost of this understandable but, in the long run, arguably self-defeating policy was quickly evident. By August 1945 the daily death rate in Berlin had risen from a prewar level of 150 to 4,000, although its population was now significantly smaller. In the U.S. sector of the city, of every twenty infants born in the summer of 1945, only one would survive.[7] Two months later, the extent of hunger in the city was such that women could be seen "straining the waste water from the kitchen sink of a house where there was an Allied mess, to save from the drain small scraps of grease which could be used again in their own homes."[8]

This was the environment into which, not counting the displaced Germans from the east who were already present in the country, the Allies proposed to inject another 7–8 million human beings. To judge from their subsequent actions, it is difficult to avoid the conclusion that they had not even prepared themselves psychologically, far less administratively, for the consequences of the decisions they had taken more than two years previously. At all events, within weeks of V-E Day Allied military administrators were overwhelmed by the tidal wave of humanity bearing down upon them from the east and south. For the moment, all they could do was to lodge the new arrivals for a night or two anywhere they could be accommodated, and to force the remainder to move on to another place where they might become somebody else's problem. By September, forty-five makeshift reception camps had been set up in Berlin, employing ex-Wehrmacht barracks, schools, and any other building not already being used for other purposes. A typical establishment from this period was the Kruppstrasse camp in the Tiergarten district. A former barracks, all of whose buildings were damaged, this contained 400 bunks but had a population of 3,000 expellees; an overflow of 600 slept "amongst the rubble in the damaged stables." Mothers, children, and the elderly made up more than 80 percent of the inhabitants. Most had arrived on foot from the Stettiner or Lehrter railway stations after their deportation from the Recovered Territories; a quarter were suffering from dysentery. They received a single daily meal of 200 grams of bread and 750 milliliters of soup. After being allowed to spend a night at the camp, they were evicted so that another 3,000 incomers could take their place.[9]

The number seeking admission to the camps greatly exceeded the spaces available. In an effort to induce expellees to bypass Berlin, a policy decision was taken to offer only "the minimum facilities short of inducing disease" and, after October 1, 1945, to withhold ration cards to all new arrivals into the city. All this accomplished, however, was to decant the overflow onto the streets.[10] Thousands never left the station at which they had arrived, sleeping on the platforms or in freight wagons standing in sidings, for weeks or months at a stretch. Others set up improvised tent villages in city parks or woods on the outskirts. As the weather turned colder, many began to die of hypothermia, and the sight of corpses of persons who had spent their last night in doorways, streets, and ditches became an unexceptional early morning spectacle during the first peacetime winter in Germany.

From the morbid but understandable point of view of some Allied officials, however, the number of dead was, if anything, not quite up to expectations. As the *Economist* remarked in November 1945, "There is perhaps a trifle too much fatalism in the forecasts, now so often made, that 'masses of Germans will die by the roadsides in the winter.'"[11] While it would certainly not be correct to say that military governors were positively hoping for a widespread famine or pandemic, the popular belief that the course of nature would solve at least some of the problems of resettlement as soon as the cold weather set in did induce in some quarters a modicum of complacency, in the face of the fresh challenges the "organized expulsions" of the following year could be expected to bring. In the event, though, the winter of 1945 was much milder than normal, and what Hector McNeil had feared might "prove . . . a catastrophe which has not been paralleled in centuries" failed to materialize.[12]

The realization, though, that expellees would not after all die off in the numbers that had been predicted led the occupation authorities bitterly to regret their political masters' mistake in failing to set up a Transfer Commission in Germany with executive powers. Part of the reason for the lack of urgency in trying to create suitable administrative machinery, even at this late hour, to cope with the numbers who would soon arrive was the refusal on the part of the Allied governments to provide their officials on the ground—most of them mid-ranking military officers with no experience of civil administration—with the most rudimentary information as to the nature and scale of the task before them. Colonel John Fye, responsible for liaising between the U.S. military authorities and the Czechoslovaks, recalled that "As late as November 1945 none of the details" of the four-power deal concerning the timing and scope of expulsions had been revealed to his military superiors in Plzeň. "Word came that such an agreement had been made. That was all."[13] Not until January 1946 were the contents of the report of the Inter-Departmental Committee on the Transfer of German Populations of 1944 divulged to the heads of the British Military Government in Germany. Had they seen it earlier, an irate official pointed out, it might have been possible to have had some of its recommendations implemented in the ACC agreement of November 20, 1945. But "at this stage there is no prospect whatever of our obtaining quadripartite agreement to the acceptance of the report or its recommendations." To attempt to do so would only cause the expelling countries to conclude that the Allies intended to go back on their word, and to resume "wild" expulsions in response.[14]

Nonetheless, planning lapses alone cannot explain the lack of cooperation, or even of basic exchanges of information, between the authorities responsible for resettlement in the Allied occupation zones. The indifferent attitude of the French, whose occupation zone in southwest Germany had suffered the least war damage of all and was arguably best placed to accommodate newcomers, is perhaps most easily understood. The government in Paris disapproved of the entire idea of mass expulsions, less on humanitarian grounds than because of its anxiety that the introduction of millions of Germans into a truncated country that could not feed them would give rise on France's western border to the same situation—an overcrowded Germany seeking *Lebensraum* for its surplus people— as had contributed to the rise of Hitler in the 1930s. Although the French had undertaken in the ACC agreement of November 1945 to accept 150,000 Germans temporarily resident in Austria into their zone, they quickly reneged on this commitment. Claiming that they understood this obligation to be to admit up to 150,000 German citizens from the old Reich, rather than *Volksdeutsche*, from Austria, the French accepted into their zone everyone who fell into this category—a mere 4,500—and then promptly closed their doors, declaring their quota as having been fulfilled. As relations between East and West began to sour, it is also, perhaps, not very surprising that few exchanges on expellee problems took place between the Soviet and Anglo-American authorities. But British and American officials also did not communicate with each other on expellee matters, and continued this isolationist stance even after the two countries decided to combine their respective occupation zones into a single entity, facetiously named "Bizonia," in January 1947. Not until the following December, nearly a year after the founding of the Bizone, did the British and U.S. expulsion staffs confer for the first time. It is clear from the minutes of subsequent meetings that not only had the two steered clear of any kind of cooperation until then, but that each possessed astonishingly little knowledge of what was transpiring in the other's zone, and what policies and procedures existed there.[15] It appears, then, that the military governors guarded their independence jealously, possibly out of concern that interzonal exchanges and discussions might lead to unwelcome public scrutiny of their individual resettlement practices.

Still, it is remarkable how closely the methods evolved independently by the three occupying authorities soon came to develop along parallel lines. Though the Soviets had not worked out a defined policy of indirect rule like the other occupying powers, they too were forced to "make the Germans do it" by the sheer magnitude of the avalanche of humanity that descended upon them from the north, east, and south in the summer of 1945. Chaos abounded in the Soviet zone to an extent that was unmatched even in the devastated West. In sheer despair at the number of people with whom they had to deal, Philipp Ther recalls, "the authorities in Saxony had several thousand refugees put on rafts, leaving them to drift down the Elbe . . ."[16] According to the town *Oberbürgermeister,* Frankfurt an der Oder, one of the principal entry points for incomers from the Recovered Territories, recorded some twelve thousand hunger-related deaths between V-E Day and December 1, 1945.[17] At the Kaisersteinbruch reception camp in Austria, which like Germany had similarly been divided into four occupation zones, the Soviet authorities ran out of food for the more than five thousand *Sudetendeutsch* inmates in October and evicted them all, telling them to make their own way to Vienna on foot and fend for themselves there.[18] When a radio broadcast in the Soviet zone the following month announced that all Germans who had ever lived in the Western zones had to leave the state of Brandenburg by November 5 to make room for expellees, vast columns of "homeless, starved old people, children, and Wehrmacht cripples" began filing toward the British zone. Within twenty-four hours of the broadcast, British newspapers reported that "along the 70-mile stretch of road between Weimar and the tripartite frontier junction at Friedland at least half a million people are estimated to be lying in the highways, paths and in ditches."[19] Vociferous Anglo-American protests caused the Soviets to rescind this order, which they blamed on a "translator's error," though some suspicious Westerners remained unconvinced that it was not a deliberate stratagem aimed at influencing the negotiations on the ACC agreement, then in progress, by showing what would happen if the Soviet authorities should ever decide to become uncooperative.[20] The fact that this directive had been preceded by a similarly short-lived one issued by the Saxony authorities at the end of August, requiring 4 million expellees to leave the state within forty-eight hours, suggests, however, that local officials and commanders, overwhelmed by the impossible task confronting them, were simply trying anything that might relieve the pressure upon them and had neither time nor thought to devote to the consequences.[21]

Carrying in the early days the heaviest burden of all as both a zone of resettlement and a zone of transit—between 2 million and 2.5 million transferred people had arrived in the summer of 1945 alone—it was not surprising that eastern Germany should have seen the appearance of the first purely German organization for expellee assimilation. The Central Agency for German Resettlers was launched in September 1945 to oversee the reception and registration of expellees; their distribution between the various *Länder* (states) of the Soviet zone; their accommodation and reequipment; and their integration and assimilation into east German society. The Central Agency received its orders from and reported to the Soviet military authorities, a chain of command that at least had the merit of being short and easily understood. In the Western zones, the administrative apparatus of expellee resettlement that began to evolve in late 1945 and 1946 was more complicated. Most of the day-to-day tasks were carried out by German local government officials at municipal and county (*Kreis*) level. Their activities were supervised by "refugee commissions" in the U.S. zone, and "zonal advisory councils" in the British, some of whose members were to be expellees themselves, subject to the overriding direction of the occupying power. From 1946 on, though, *Land* governments assumed a greater role in the administration of their respective states, and some, beginning with Bavaria, appointed commissioners for expellee and refugee affairs—again on the basis of higher policy directives laid down by the Allied military government concerned. The Anglo-American model, which reflected the importance the Western Allies attached to ensuring that postwar Germany emerged with a decentralized form of government, thus involved a great deal of overlapping spheres of responsibility, with the inevitable confusion and frustration that followed from such a system. What it lacked in efficiency, though, it made up for by bringing a much broader cross-section of German administrative talent to bear on the problems at hand, mitigating to some extent the deficiencies inherent in a regime of government from the top down.

In any event, as already noted, notwithstanding their structural differences the zonal authorities wound up pursuing surprisingly similar policies in dealing with the expellee crisis. Of the challenges they had to face, two short-term and two long-term ones stood out. The immediate priorities were to disperse the incomers between the *Länder*, and somehow find accommodation for them all. Once this had been achieved the more difficult task of integrating them into the German economy, and bridging the gap between expellees and indigenes, would need to be addressed. In fact, these objectives proved to be complementary, inasmuch as the manner in which the first pair of aims was dealt with would have a major impact on the success, or otherwise, of the second.

Overcoming the housing crisis was by far the most urgent task—inasmuch as food supplies could be imported but houses could not, an even more challenging one than dealing with the problem of rationing. With the equivalent of the population of a medium-sized town arriving in Germany every day during 1945 and 1946, the authorities had no choice but to squeeze as many bodies as could possibly be accommodated into every possible space. There was little enough of this. In Düsseldorf, one of the most heavily bombed cities, 93 percent of houses and apartments were uninhabitable at the end of the war. Throughout the country, before the expulsions had begun, "ten Germans were living where only four had lived in 1939 even though some of the cellars and shelters in use hardly deserved the title of housing."[22] One of the very few Allied decisions taken at four-power level, the ACC's Housing Law of March 1946, authorized the requisitioning of surplus dwelling space, even down to the level of vacant rooms in individual houses, to accommodate expellees. Because most undamaged dwellings were in isolated country districts, that was where around 85 percent of the new arrivals were sent.[23] Almost overnight, consequently, rural overpopulation soared to astronomical levels. The small village of Bakede west of Hildesheim, with a normal population of seven hundred, had four hundred additional expellees billeted upon it in April 1946.[24] At Flensburg on the German-Danish border, the *Landrat* was accommodating seventeen expellees in his own house. "Another farmer has given a roof to 70 people, while there are many instances where others have put all their cattle into one byre so that the remaining building can be used by the homeless."[25]

The housing problem was unequally distributed among the three zones in which expellees were admitted. Overall, the Western zones which contained the highest concentration of urban centers and were easiest to reach by Allied bombers were in the worst straits. In 1950, even after five years of reconstruction, the population density per unit of housing stock was twice as high as before the war.[26] Hardest hit of all was the British zone. In July 1946 the rural *Land* of Schleswig-Holstein, whose population had increased by two-thirds due to the influx of expellees, had to be declared a "black" area incapable of absorbing any more newcomers; the Ruhr and Hamburg would soon be placed in the same category. In contrast the Soviet zone, with the exception of large cities like Berlin and Dresden, had come through the war with much less damage; the principal difficulty was that inasmuch as eastern Germany was a predominantly rural region, the quantity of housing was relatively small to begin with. The fact that so many people, both expellees and natives, continuously removed themselves via the "green frontier" from the Soviet to the Western zones, on the other hand, provided a safety valve, however insufficient, that was denied to the hard-pressed British and U.S. authorities.[27]

As the population pressure rose to extreme levels, resettlement authorities adopted more creative—or desperate—solutions. Although they possessed neither natural light nor, in many cases, even the most rudimentary sanitary facilities, air raid bunkers became a favorite option. Seven hundred and fifty expellees occupied one such facility in Hanover; 945 more were in others at Frankfurt am Main; and another 644 in Höchst. Even these, however, soon became unavailable, as Allied theater commanders insisted that they be blown up because of their potential for use in war.[28] At the suggestion of Walter Mann, State

Commissioner for Refugees in Greater Hesse, part of Adolf Hitler's complex at Berchtesgaden was used to provide housing for *Sudetendeutsche*.[29] Despite expedients like these, though, there proved to be no alternative to accommodating expellees for long periods of time in a variety of camps. By the end of 1945, the Central Agency for Resettlers in eastern Germany was overseeing 625 camps of various kinds—former concentration camps, Labor Front barracks, and abandoned POW facilities—with a total population of more than 480,000.[30] The number of camps in the Western zones ran into the thousands.[31]

Authorities in all three zones were exceedingly reluctant to pursue this course. Initially, it had been hoped to maintain the newcomers in reception camps for a few days or at most, where a disease risk was thought to exist and a period of quarantine was indicated, for two or three weeks. Longer stays risked permanently segregating and ghettoizing the expellee population, whereas military government in all three zones was "anxious to do everything possible to get the Germans to accept persons coming from the East as their own people, and not to regard them as foreigners foisted upon them."[32] A great deal of official concern was expressed about the demoralizing effects of extended sojourns in camp environments, which the *Frankfurter Allgemeine Zeitung* feared would lead to the appearance of a pathological sociological subtype, *Homo barackensis*: "*Homo barackensis* has taught humankind in the twentieth century a dreadful truth: progress, humanity, and self-esteem exist only in the context of an unbroken world. When law and order disintegrate, the camp arises—that most gruesome and cruel expression of human capabilities—and with it rises a breeding ground of nihilism."[33]

Unquestionably many examples could be found of expellees who had become deeply demoralized as a result of prolonged stays in isolated camps, where they appeared to have been forgotten by the world. Frau Klug, a resident of Burlagsberg camp some forty miles north of Osnabrück who had been rehoused there in 1945 after fleeing the Recovered Territories, provided a description of the downward spiral that occurred in the course of her seven years' residence there that was true of many other such establishments. In the beginning she had been very pleased to receive any kind of accommodation at all, but the community atmosphere in the camp, positive at the outset, quickly took a turn for the worse.

> At first the barracks stood right in the wood, thus receiving valuable protection from the surrounding trees, but owing to the need for fuel especially in 1946/47 many trees were cut down, thus leaving the barracks standing in an open sandy plain, exposed to wind and bad weather. The drabness of the barracks was also thus exposed, as the buildings were very ramshackle with addi-

tional bits of iron and board tacked on here and there. . . . Soon . . . the community spirit crumbled away and the individual inhabitant lived his own life.

After the currency reform the financial situation became worse and worse, as unemployment increased (at present about 90 percent of the able-bodied men get unemployment pay). When husbands and sons returned from war imprisonment the problem of living space became a catastrophe. . . .

Most of the barracks are in a very bad condition, as the Löningen Municipality had not made any repairs except the roofs having been tarred. All kinds of misery together with an uncertain future made the people grow bitter, as they did not see an end, and so much had been promised but nothing done.[34]

Conditions in innumerable other camps were equally grim. The records of the occupying authorities and humanitarian bodies like the CICR, the Catholic *Caritas* organization, the Protestant *Evangelisches Hilfswerke* and the American Friends Service Committee are replete with descriptions of overcrowded, unheated, disease-ridden, and even roofless facilities in which expellees languished for months or years. Phrases like "reminiscent of a London tube station in the early days of the Blitz"; "dwellings some of which make the impression as if the devil himself had created them"; and "more miserable than the worst POW camps we have ever come across" frequently appear in inspection reports.[35] In Bavaria, the transit camps (*Dulags*) were "still surrounded by walls and/or barbed wire, and refugees who were caught outside without passes were forcibly returned by the police, so that it was difficult not to conceive of the Dulags as detention centres."[36]

But despite fears that camp life was breeding an entire generation of unemployables and sociopaths, concerns of this kind turned out to be overdrawn. Demoralization and despair turned out to be a function not of camp residence as such, but of lengthy stays in remote establishments like Burlagsberg where there were no prospects of employment or self-improvement. In more centrally located facilities, the problem with which the authorities frequently had to deal was not apathy and fatalism on the part of camp populations, but militancy and anger. The former Dachau concentration camp, for example, which was converted to a temporary housing facility for about two thousand *Sudetendeutsche* in 1948, soon became a hotbed of expellee activism. In August 1948, inspired by the example of protesters at Dachau, seventy-two thousand Bavarian camp dwellers began a seven-day hunger strike for better food and conditions. It was not until 1953, however, that a residents' building cooperative managed to construct enough dwelling units to enable most of the original camp cohort to leave. Their places were taken by more recent arrivals from Czechoslovakia, the remnants of the German minority allowed to stay in 1948 by the Prague government, so the final closure of Dachau as an ethnic German housing facility took place only in 1965.

But the same picture was not to be seen everywhere. Meryn McLaren notes that the better refugee camps played an important transitional role in the task of expellee integration: "they gave residents the chance to get used to their situation, and accept that there was no going back, in a supportive and self-contained environment where they could form relationships and assert their cultural identity away from the hostility of the locals."[37] Elsewhere, as at Nuremberg, communal bonds among camp dwellers grew so strong that residents actively resisted efforts to move them into permanent accommodation, leading one official to advise that "police force might be necessary to remove them."[38] This was especially the case if paid work was available for a reasonable proportion of the camp population. Notwithstanding any other deficiencies that might exist the results were usually plain to see even in the physical appearance of the premises. Treffling, a facility west of Klagenfurt in Austria accommodating three thousand *Volksdeutsche* many of whom obtained employment as agricultural laborers with local farmers, impressed a British inspector by the "superior cleanliness and organisation in this camp, for which the inmates are themselves mainly responsible."[39] Even in less well-run places, the availability of jobs proved the key to keeping the amount of time that needed to be spent in insalubrious surroundings as brief as possible.

Matching expellees with employment, however, was an uphill struggle. The paramount necessity between 1945 and 1947 of sending fresh arrivals wherever accommodation could be found for them left the majority stranded in isolated parts of the countryside, where there was no possible use for their skills. This bore especially heavily on the *Sudetendeutsche*, who had made their living disproportionately in industry. Some expellees tried to set up their own businesses in their new locations. The most celebrated example were the glass blowers and jewelry workers of Jablonec nad Nisou (Gablonz) who, after being expelled to the Bavarian municipality of Kaufbeuren, founded a new town—Neu-Gablonz—on its outskirts, restarting production in a disused munitions factory. By 1947 nearly a thousand Gablonzers had reestablished themselves in their traditional occupations, and the products of their industry were contributing to West Germany's export earnings. Despite the attention showered on the Neu-Gablonz experiment, though, this was not a pattern that could be easily replicated elsewhere. Communities had been widely dispersed in the course of the expulsions; few *Sudetendeutsche* possessed skills that could be put to commercial use with quite such ease; and start-up capital was usually unavailable to people whose collateral consisted largely of the clothes they were wearing. Hence even those Gablonzers who wound up in Saxony-Anhalt and Thuringia rather than Bavaria ran into "enormous difficulties" in restarting their enterprises.[40]

Where expellees could find work at all, it tended to be lowly paid if not positively exploitative. This was especially the case in Austria where, in contrast to Germany, *Volksdeutsche* had no legal right to remain. In theory, after responsibility for administering camps for expellees was turned over by the Allied powers to Vienna in 1948, all or most of the *Volksdeutsche* ought to have received permanent resident status. Many, however, did not because of their inability to find an Austrian sponsor who would guarantee that they would not become a public charge. Obliged to renew their residence permit at three- or six-monthly intervals, they were frequently exploited by predatory landlords and employers.[41] A British administrator in the Austrian *Land* of Carinthia complained to the Austrian Chamber of Agriculture in 1947 of local farmers' practice of taking *Volksdeutsch* laborers on for the busy summer period only to dismiss them without notice as soon as the harvest was completed. Expellees were "drawn from the camps and returned to stock when their services are no longer required."[42] The director of an expellees' welfare organization described their employment conditions two years later as analogous to those of "a feudal serf."[43] Not until 1952 did the Austrian Federation of Trade Unions lift labor restrictions on *Volksdeutsche*, enabling them to be hired on terms of equality with Austrian workers in all fields other than the medical profession.

Expellee workers in Germany did not face the same legal obstacles, but neither did they enjoy complete freedom of action. Under the occupation statutes, they could be compelled to fill particular vacancies in the labor market. Some unscrupulous labor offices fell into the habit of descending upon expulsion trains as they arrived at transit camps and dragooning the more productive-looking passengers into hard-to-fill occupations. Thus at Helmstedt in the spring of 1946, the *Arbeitsamt* "selects all the able-bodied men from each convoy as it arrives, separates them from their families and directs them into local industry. Those not fit for work, together with the women & children, are left by the camp for the reception *Kreise*."[44] A slightly different variation on the same theme was practiced by the *Land* authorities in Bavaria who, their counterparts in Württemberg and Greater Hesse protested, practiced a policy of selective admission. Whenever an unauthorized expulsion train from the Sudetenland appeared at the Bebra crossing point, they alleged, the Bavarians admitted it if it carried a high proportion of young adults but invariably turned back those consisting of women and children only. The result was that these *Länder* were saddled with the unemployables, while Bavaria was able to put the productive element immediately to work.⁴⁵ In the Soviet zone, the authorities attempted to overcome the effects of randomly assigning agricultural workers to cities, and white-collar workers to the countryside, by engaging in compulsory intrazonal transfers. On the sole occasion that this was tried, however, the protests of expellees who had already been forcibly displaced once and were unwilling to tolerate another such upheaval were so fierce that the experiment was abandoned as soon as it had begun.

Both in the western and the eastern zones, the new arrivals were frequently confronted with the reality of a "cold homeland." For the settled community, already struggling to survive, the arrival of so many newcomers whose claims to Germanness often seemed to them highly questionable was regarded as too great a burden to bear. The practice of compulsory billeting of expellees did nothing to foster sympathy on the part of the indigenous population, and a rough-and-ready index of the state of relations between the communities could be found in the intensity of resistance to the practice. A Military Government officer remarked that the settled community in the British zone did not hesitate to ignore its legal requirement to accommodate the new arrivals from the east. "At the best they get the minimum prescribed by law and at the worst they have to accept accommodation which is scarcely fit for cattle."⁴⁶ Throughout the whole of Germany, cases of residents openly defying the Housing Law were notorious. Frequently they were abetted in doing so by local German administrators who realized all too well that the settled community possessed votes, whereas expellees typically did not. The case of the *Bürgermeister* of Nieder-Weisel in Hesse who confined thirty-five expellees to two rooms for a two-week period rather than disperse them among the townspeople was far from unusual.⁴⁷ An additional problem was the tendency of those property owners who did comply with the law to treat expellees billeted upon them as unwanted guests or interlopers, who might be denied permission to use bathrooms or kitchens or to enter and leave the premises except at specified times. It is probably true to say that authorities in the western zones were more active in repressing these abuses than their eastern counterparts, and sometimes found creative means of doing so. In 1947, for example, a Frankfurt baker, Wilhelm Rapp, was sentenced along with his wife and two daughters to spend four weeks living in a transit camp as punishment for discriminating against expellees billeted upon them.⁴⁸ The failure to compel the settled community in the Soviet zone to live up to its responsibilities, however, probably owed as much to bureaucratic inefficiencies as to a lackadaisical attitude on the part of the authorities. In Brandenburg alone, an inspection to determine the amount of space available to accommodate expellees had been carried out in only 25,000 of the *Land*'s 600,000 dwellings by 1948.⁴⁹

The Allies' policy was not only to induce the native-born to accept the expellees as fully equal members of the German nation, but to convince expellees themselves that they were "'here to stay' and that irredentist agitation would only work against the interests of a future democratic Germany."[50] Each of these propositions proved to be a hard sell. In both eastern and western Germany, expellees from the Recovered Territories were often referred to derisively as *Wasserpolen* ("watered-down Poles"), "Russians," *Rucksackdeutsche* ("backpack Germans"), and "forty-kilo gypsies" (a reference to the amount of possessions they had supposedly brought with them—though in fact it was usually much less).[51] An American opinion poll in Baden-Württemberg in November 1946 found that only half of the settled community regarded expellees as fellow citizens; the same proportion believed that they would one day go home. More surprisingly, almost as many expellees—some 40 percent—disavowed German identity, describing themselves as Czechoslovaks, Hungarians, or members of other nationalities. Approximately the same number complained that the indigenous population "considered them as human beings of inferior value, as foreigners or as beggars."[52] In some parts of the country, Allied military governors considered that the expellees were looked upon with "hatred"; and that they, for their part, "consider[ed] the natives and not the occupation power their oppressors."[53] Austrians sometimes responded to the strangers in their midst with even greater hostility, although many differentiated between their *Sudetendeutsch* neighbors and the more culturally alien *Volksdeutsche* from Yugoslavia and Romania. *Landesrat* Oberzaucher of Styria, for example, informed the British authorities in 1947 that the typical citizen of his *Land* was unable to understand why "he draws a starvation ration, just because to a large extent the available food is consumed by the numerous foreigners."[54] Ironically, some members of the settled communities in both countries, particularly the less-educated cohorts, concurred with the assessment of the Czechoslovak and Polish governments in blaming the expellees for having "started the war" and brought misery and ruin on the Reich. The decline in mutual understanding was starkly illustrated by a pair of nationwide surveys carried out in Germany in March 1946 and September 1947. On the earlier date, 7 percent of expellees expressed dissatisfaction with the way they had been treated by the indigenous population. On the later, 45 percent did so.[55]

But relations were by no means everywhere so hostile. Sometimes, indigenes and expellees could be drawn together by their mutual disdain for still more despised out-groups, like Polish displaced persons.[56] Others had relatives already living in Germany or Austria who could assist them, or at the least ease the culture shock of starting their lives anew in an unfamiliar environment. And even when relations between the two communities were most strained, a majority of Germans—albeit a bare majority, in which the educated middle class and former

Nazi Party members were disproportionately represented—acknowledged a responsibility to assist the newcomers in their hour of need.

All the same, most expellees had immense difficulties in reconciling themselves to their fate. A sensitive psychological profile drawn up by OMGUS in February 1947 warned that the typical deportee remained unreconciled to

> the prospects of living the rest of his life in a foreign community where the natives are unfriendly and resentful, whose habits are strange, and where everything already belongs to someone else.
>
> The expellee is ready to listen to all reports and rumors of opportunities of going "home," and he will sign any and all petitions placed in front of him by unscrupulous provocateurs to bring this about. He will send chain letters to all his friends as long as he can delude himself with the idea that there is a chance for return. As he looks about himself, it appears to him that he alone lost most in the war since the native Germans, who were not expelled, retained their homes, land and cattle. The expellee will have to own things in his new country before he can be expected to take an interest in it, or develop a sense of "belonging."[57]

Opinion polls confirmed this intense sense of longing for "home." In spite of the ill-treatment that so many had suffered, 85 percent of expellees questioned in the U.S. zone in September 1947 said that they would return to their places of origin if given the opportunity.[58] Although some observers wryly noted that the expellees' nostalgic evocations of their happy former lives in Czechoslovakia or Yugoslavia contrasted dramatically with how these same people had depicted their status as members of "oppressed" minorities in the 1930s, both the scale and the consistency of this response in repeated surveys caused great concern to Allied officials, who saw in it the potential for the rise of a new "revisionist" movement, feeding upon expellees' social and economic marginalization and sense of grievance. This population, a senior U.S. official warned in April 1949, constituted "the most overtly nationalistic faction in post war Germany."[59] Unless their integration could be quickly accomplished, a dangerous situation was likely to arise.

Initially, the occupation forces in all three zones clamped down vigorously on any hint of political mobilization by expellees as such, in contrast to participation in the activities of the legal political parties. While some U.S. officials saw no objection to expellee organizations, considering them "no different from a farmers' party looking after the interests of farmers," General Lucius Clay in June 1946 specifically forbade any such formations. To allow them, he declared, would be the equivalent of suggesting that "each large group of migrants would have been justified in forming political parties. Nothing could have been more injurious to their cause—or to democracy."[60] The British had already taken similar action the previous month. By 1947–48, however, both the British and the U.S. military governments tacitly accepted the emergence of expellee heritage preservation and friendly societies, the so-called Homeland Societies or *Landsmannschaften*. In truth, the distinction between "nonpolitical" and "political" activity was sometimes wafer-thin, and eventually came to be regarded as more trouble than it was worth to try to preserve. After the foundation of the German Federal Republic in May 1949, Konrad Adenauer's government quickly yielded to the inevitable, permitting expellees to form political movements on terms of equality with the other legally recognized parties. By January 1950, the Expellees' and Disenfranchised People's Bloc (*Block der Heimatvertriebenen und Entrechteten*) had been launched with Waldemar Kraft, a former SS captain with a dubious wartime record, as its leader.

The emergence of the expellee lobby as a political force was both a vital element of their integration and a moment of considerable danger for the infant Federal Republic. Nothing was to be gained by trying to repress expellee political mobilization, other than to drive it further to the margins of German society. On the other hand, the possibility of a compact bloc embracing up to a quarter of the electorate, embittered by its recent experiences, and eager to reverse the territorial changes of the postwar years, exercising undue influence within a new and untested democratic regime gave obvious cause for concern.

That the expellees did not become a disruptive element was due to three factors: the moderation of most of their leaders, the growth of the economy, and the surefootedness of Germany's first postwar chancellor, Konrad Adenauer. Contrary to expectations, expellees were not drawn in disproportionate numbers to radical movements. Because most laid the blame for their exile upon the communist regimes governing their homelands, the chances of any substantial number gravitating toward the extreme Left which, in Germany and elsewhere, continued to defend the transfers as an act of political wisdom were always fairly small. But with the exception of a noisy lunatic fringe, expellees largely avoided drifting into the ranks of the "revisionist" Right also. Conscious of the need to reassure fellow Germans as well as international public opinion of their good intentions, the *Landsmannschaften* at a gathering at Stuttgart in August 1950—the fifth anniversary of the Potsdam Conference—adopted a "Charter of the German Expellees." This disavowed "all thought of revenge and retaliation" and called for the promotion of European unity as the only permanent solution to the continent's minority problems. While asserting that "the right to one's homeland is a God-given fundamental right," the charter set out an immediate program consisting entirely of measures to ameliorate expellees' conditions of life within German society. These included equal rights in law and in fact with the settled community; the integration of professional groupings; and a "just and sensible distribution of the burdens of the last war among the whole German people."[61]

The idea of an "equalization of burdens" had already become a mantra among the expellee community, after the Allied authorities directed West Germany's leaders to address the problem in 1948. It received valuable international support early in 1951 from a high-level commission of the Economic Cooperation Administration, the supervisory body of the Marshall Plan, consisting mainly of prominent U.S. and West German academics, including the Harvard economist John Kenneth Galbraith. The commission's report, presented to Adenauer in March 1951, described the problem of the expellees as "basically the problem of Germany herself," and recommended an ambitious program of public spending, costing about DM 12.5 billion ($3 billion), to provide houses, job training, and public works for them over the following six years. This would involve a quadrupling of existing federal expenditure, which would be paid for by borrowing and with receipts from an Equalization of Burdens (*Lastenausgleich*) tax.[62]

While all three of the Federal Republic's major parties had already committed themselves to radical economic measures to deal with the expellees' social and economic problems, Konrad Adenauer's Christian Democratic Union did most to place the issue at the forefront of its program. A crotchety, autocratic, and sometimes devious politician who had served as mayor of Cologne on the ticket of the Catholic Center Party until dismissed by the Nazis in 1933, Adenauer possessed a more finely tuned (though by no means infallible) sense of what was politically feasible than his rivals. He was particularly impressed by what appeared to be a decisive breakthrough by Kraft's Expellees' Bloc in July 1950, when it won nearly a quarter of the seats in the Schleswig-Holstein *Land* elections and followed it up with solid showings in Bavaria and Lower Saxony some months later. In fact there was less to this success than met the eye—in none of the three *Länder* did the Bloc's vote even match the expellees' proportion of the local population—but to Adenauer, who had been chancellor for little more than a year, it underscored the necessity of defusing the threat it posed to the Federal Republic's political future, and not incidentally his own.

Fortunately for him and for Germany, the expellee movement had many points of vulnerability. Its political wing was arguably less important than the *Landsmannschaften*, of which there were twenty with a combined membership of about 1.3 million in the mid-1950s.[63] Based as they were upon geographical groupings, however, they differed on numerous points. The East Prussian *Lands-*

mannschaft, for example, had relatively little in common with its Balkan counterpart, the Homeland Society of Germans from Yugoslavia. The Expellees' Bloc itself was a fractious and argumentative body that never garnered the support of more than a minority of the people it supposedly represented and was prone to splits, mostly on its right. It also included prominent members who were even less savory than its leader Kraft, among them people like Wilhelm Stuckart, the co-author of the Nuremberg Laws who could count himself lucky not to have been hanged for his part in the infamous Wannsee Conference of 1942. Lastly, although expellees were the most marginalized section of the postwar German population, they were by no means the only one seeking the state's attention. Those who had been rendered homeless by Allied bombing (the *Ausgebombt*), disabled war veterans, and other groups with well-organized lobbies all had claims to the government's attention and largesse, and were not willing to play second fiddle to the Bloc.

For as wily a political practitioner as was Adenauer, then, there was much to work upon. His strategy for neutralizing the Expellees' Bloc was simple but effective: to coopt its leaders and persuade its voters that he and the Christian Democrats represented their interests more effectively than their own sectional party could do. The first step was to see the *Lastenausgleich* and other expellee-friendly laws through Parliament before the next federal elections, thereby depriving the Bloc of its most potent cause. This law, adopted in August 1952, created an off-budget fund financed by a 50 percent levy on all capital assets declared by German taxpayers during the "base year" of 1948. Draconian as that appeared, so many exemptions were provided that the tax burden on the settled community was considerably lighter than expected. The levy was not taken up instantly, but could be paid by those affected by it over a thirty-year span. Moreover, as Aidan Crawley observes, "the fact that in the base year the value of property was at its lowest meant that, with the sudden boom in incomes and values due to the [economic] recovery, most people could pay their installments without difficulty."[64] The *Lastenausgleich* was thus a more modest and a longer-lived program than the one envisaged by the Economic Cooperation Administration's report, costing a relatively affordable DM 1.5 billion per annum—or a little over 5 percent of all federal, *Land*, and municipal tax revenues—though eventually, by the time the last payment was made in 2001, DM 145 billion would be disbursed under the scheme.[65] Expellees, and other Germans who had suffered material losses as a result of the war, were eligible to receive compensation from the state on a sliding scale, with 100 percent of the smallest claims being allowed and 6.5 percent of the largest. Expellees could also apply for housing loans and assistance with job training. This measure was followed by an Expellee Law in May

1953, which, as recommended by the Federal Ministry for Expellees, Refugees, and War Victims established four years previously, safeguarded the right of the remaining ethnic German minorities outside the country's borders to immigrate to the Federal Republic without unnecessary complications. Lastly, a Refugee Pension Law, passed in the nick of time before the 1953 elections, provided that expellees and refugees would be eligible for social insurance on the same basis as if they had always lived and worked in the Federal Republic.

Adenauer's second front against the Bloc was to steal its clothes in foreign policy. This did not necessarily represent political posturing on his part, or at any rate not an excessive amount of it. With the exception of the Communists, Germans across the spectrum resented the territorial losses the country had incurred in 1945 and, though they were not prepared to disrupt the peace of Europe on that account, supported the restoration of Germany's 1937 frontiers. Adenauer shared these views at least to some degree, though the unwonted trenchancy with which he expressed them in public probably indicated that he was not unmindful of how sentiments of this kind would be received by the Expellees' Bloc's natural constituency. That its verdict on his performance was generally favorable was demonstrated by the federal elections of 1953. The Christian Democrats and their coalition partners won more than 45 percent of the vote, far surpassing the Social Democratic opposition. The Bloc fell away to less than 6 percent, gaining less support from expellees than the victorious Christian Democrats had done, and making no inroads at all among the settled community. "The election," Michael Hughes observes, "was widely seen as a referendum on Adenauer and his policies—and to the degree it was, Adenauer won." Quickly capitalizing on his victory, the chancellor reached out to the deflated Expellees' Bloc, offering Waldemar Kraft and his deputy, Theodor Oberländer, seats in his Cabinet and thereby "tying the party to Adenauer's policies."[66] Two years later, Kraft and Oberländer would abandon their own party for the Christian Democrats, effectively sealing its fate as a political movement.

Konrad Adenauer and his successors have attracted much criticism for the "opportunistic" and "manipulative" stance they took in the 1950s on the expellee question, and in particular their currying favor with the *Landsmannschaften* by cold-shouldering proposals to improve relations with Germany's eastern neighbors. Although the Christian Democratic leadership neither expected nor, arguably, wanted the reacquisition of the lost territories, compensation from the expelling states for the German property confiscated in 1945, or a "right of return" for expellees from Czechoslovakia, Hungary, and elsewhere, they continued to advocate this unattainable program and to foster harmful illusions among the West German electorate for the sake of political advantage. They insisted that the

Munich Pact of 1938 remained valid regardless of the way in which such a position was bound to be regarded abroad. "For far too long," in Pertti Ahonen's view, "the country's political élites indulged in tactical opportunism, telling expellees and other nationalistic audiences what they wanted to hear, with scant regard for existing realities or possible long-term consequences."[67]

There is something to be said for this interpretation, although its proponents arguably overstate the degree of room for maneuver West Germany's leaders possessed in both domestic and foreign policy during these years. Without doubt Adenauer habitually spoke out of both sides of his mouth when addressing the expellees—who, since the mid-1950s, have remained among the Christian Democrats' most stalwart supporters—and the larger German public. Few of the *Landmannschaften*'s aspirations were achievable under any imaginable circumstances in the 1950s, and are no more so today. The frequency with which those organizations elevated to leadership positions a variety of unlovely personalities with checkered wartime pasts, and the chancellor's willingness to embrace them nonetheless, raises legitimate questions about his judgment and prudence. And his emphasis upon, and exploitation of, the expellee question has frequently been juxtaposed with his more muted acknowledgments of the barbarities for which Nazi Germany was responsible, in the absence of which the expulsions themselves would almost certainly never have taken place.

Acknowledging the truth of all these criticisms, it is still difficult to see even with the benefit of hindsight how Adenauer could have dealt with the challenge confronting him in a significantly different way. Simply to dismiss the concerns and aspirations of so large a proportion of the electorate was politically unrealistic; nor would the other parties have been slow to take advantage had he done so. It is sometimes forgotten that leaders of competing groups were little more scrupulous in arousing expellees' expectations: Willy Brandt of the moderate-left Social Democratic Party, for example, hasted to reassure them in 1961 that "Silesia remains, in our consciousness, German land" (*Schlesien bleibt in unserem Bewusstsein deutsches Land*).[68] To be sure, the successful defusing of the expellee crisis depended on luck to an even greater degree than skill. Adenauer came to the chancellorship at a moment when the relationship between expellees and indigenes was perhaps at its lowest ebb. The currency reform that saw the launch of the Deutschmark in 1948, at a highly unfavorable 1:10 exchange rate with the Reichsmark, hit the new arrivals hardest of all. Unlike the settled community they possessed few noncash assets, and the reform effectively wiped out whatever meager savings they had made and returned them once again to the bottom of the socioeconomic ladder. By the end of 1949, the unemployment rate among expellees was twice as high as among the native population; nearly one in three of the recent arrivals was jobless. Less than a month before the establishment of the Federal Republic, an American official warned that in his own view as well as that of the three German refugee commissioners in the U.S. zone, "the situation today is at least as adverse as it was in 1946."[69]

Probably the most important factor in rescuing the country from this deeply unpromising scenario was the revival of the German economy. From mid-1950 unemployment took a decisive turn downward, until by mid-decade it had virtually been eliminated. West Germany began a long export-driven boom at a pace that is unlikely ever to be repeated by any major developed economy, while the willingness of the expellees themselves to accept modestly paying jobs helped to ease inflationary pressures. The establishment of this virtuous economic cycle not only made expensive social programs like the *Lastenausgleich* law affordable, but progressively liberated the Bonn government from having to make hard choices about whether expellees or indigenes should receive the benefit of limited state resources—choices that in a system based on majority rule would almost inevitably have been made in only one way.

West Germany could not, however, either have foreseen or counted on the indefinite continuance of an unprecedented economic expansion. In the event of a sustained downturn such as had occurred in 1923 or 1929, all the dangers associated with the presence of an unassimilated and freshly disillusioned mass of eight million expellees would have presented themselves again with renewed force. Adenauer could not exclude such a possibility, and had to use every lever of influence he possessed to try to insulate his untested republic against its effects. Inasmuch as the surest way to create a self-fulfilling prophesy of a radicalized and alienated minority would have been to treat the expellees and their chosen representatives with suspicion and reserve, or to attempt to make them disavow their unacceptable opinions before being accepted into the German body politic, the chancellor had little choice but to pursue the policies he did. As Ahonen rightly acknowledges, "the oft-stated claim that expellee integration ranks immediately behind the closely related phenomenon of the economic miracle in West Germany's list of triumphs rings substantially true. The Federal Republic has reason to be proud of its record in this area, especially in view of the many potential hazards that had loomed along the way."[70]

What is, perhaps, more surprising is that East Germany too achieved a rough-and-ready resolution of its expellee problem, albeit by very different means. Of course the obstacles and risks it confronted were of a different nature. The East German government had unlimited instruments of coercion at its disposal. Behind the regime, should it show signs of failing, stood the Soviet Union. There was, then, little danger of the expellees becoming a threat to the survival of the state. As a predominantly agrarian region, moreover, the East faced a food situation that was less critical in the immediate postwar era than elsewhere in Germany. Lastly, the economic underperformance of the East at least had the negative merit that the average gap in the standard of living between newcomers and indigenes was less pronounced and, in principle, more easily bridged than in the Federal Republic.

Nevertheless, the Soviet authorities, the Central Agency for Resettlers, and, after 1949, the East Berlin government could not rely upon force alone to achieve their objectives. The chief difficulty they faced was that expellees were little more welcome in the East than the West. A series of "resettler weeks" in 1948, in which the indigenous community was pressured to make charitable donations of clothing and household goods to the newcomers, yielded embarrassingly low results in many areas. In Thuringia, for example, the philanthropic impulses of the local population with respect to the expellees produced only 110 pairs of shoes, 132 cooking pots, and 10 large stoves.[71] Nor could the authorities proceed to more robust methods, in light of the unpopularity of the regime. In the summer of 1947, for example, the Saxony *Land* government expressed the view that "a compulsory requisition [of goods for redistribution to expellees] is not possible. We cannot risk aggravating the mood of the people."[72] In the end, the Soviet military authorities were driven to provide welfare payments out of state funds. A resettlement grant of three hundred Reichsmarks per adult and a hundred Reichsmarks for each child was provided for new arrivals in October 1946. Even though the intent behind this subvention was partly to boost the performance of the Communist-dominated Socialist Unity Party in the elections of that year, the grant anticipated any similar policy in the Western zones. The Soviets also displayed a surprising degree of flexibility in working with church-based welfare organizations and with the Red Cross, encouraging the latter to concentrate its activities on expellee children in particular.[73] Marshals Zhukov and Sokolovsky proved especially cooperative in this regard.

Nonetheless, the Soviets had no intention of allowing the "resettler" question (the term "expellee" was deemed politically incorrect in the East, as implying undue harshness on the part of the removing governments) to hang over their occupation zone indefinitely. The focus instead was on completing the task of resettlement and assimilation—or at any rate declaring it completed—within a measurable period. Accordingly, great emphasis was placed on moving expellees out of, and then closing, the camps, a task that was largely completed by 1950. Some statistical sleight of hand was necessary to achieve this impressive result; in some places "camps" were officially redesignated "apartment complexes" for the purpose of fulfilling the plan.[74] But the East's record was nonetheless significant, when it is considered that West Germany still had a camp population of 324,000 in 1951 and that the last facility was not finally closed until twenty years later.

The concept of "burden-sharing" gained little purchase in East Germany. As Philipp Ther notes, the perception that the expellees had constituted a Nazi "fifth column," vigorously promoted by the "socialist fraternal countries," implied that they were no more deserving of assistance—and arguably less so—than the settled population. "A *Lastenausgleich* [law] as in the West was therefore impossible for ideological reasons."[75] Accordingly, the Soviet military authorities decided to kill two birds with one stone by tying expellee resettlement to land redistribution. Because most expellees in East Germany, like their counterparts in the West, had already been placed in the countryside—in Brandenburg, nearly 55 percent of the new arrivals were living in settlements of less than two thousand inhabitants in December 1947—this solution had the further advantage that no substantial internal redistribution of the four-million-strong expellee population would be required.[76] Agricultural estates of more than a hundred hectares and those belonging to "war criminals" were broken up and expellees settled on the new smallholdings in numbers out of proportion to their share of the population. By the conclusion of the program, some 567,000 hectares of land were in expellee hands.[77]

The results, though, generally bore out the prognostications of those British officials who had successfully diverted Ernest Bevin from pursuing a similar will-o'-the-wisp in 1944. The land reform program was an expensive failure. "Even at the end of 1946, three-quarters of the *Neubauern* (new farmers) had to work without horses . . . and only one third of the land reform farmers owned a cow. Only one farmstead in four was equipped with a plough, one in five with iron harrows and only one in fourteen with reapers and threshing machines."[78] Those who received livestock and equipment, moreover, tended to be members of the indigenous population, who profited from their superior connections in the rural communities to those overseeing the redistribution, while "resettlers" were largely overlooked. Lastly, exorbitant and unrealistic state requisitions and quotas, which forced the new farmers to turn over even their seed grain and sowing potatoes to the government, made it impossible for many to generate the minimum required for bare survival. As a result, living standards for the *Neubauern* were, as state inspectors reported in 1950, "almost unimaginably low," while the cost of the program, which by 1953 had reached the alarming figure of 900 million marks, was described by Heinrich Rau, the Minister of Planning, as "a bottomless pit."[79] Rather than acknowledge the failure of the experiment and, as West Germany progressively did, recall the expellees from their initial billets in the countryside to the cities and towns as jobs and houses became available for them, the Soviet military authorities doubled down on their losing investment and announced a large-scale rural housing program in 1947. With practically the entire housing budget of the east going into building farmsteads that the resettlers were rapidly abandoning, reconstruction of war-damaged cities was virtually halted. As one *Neubauer* recorded, "The despair and anger among the settlers know no bounds. . . . Whole groups of settlers leave the settlements at night and have fled to the West . . ."[80] Not until 1950 was this costly scheme discontinued, with very little to show for it.

By then, however, the authorities were ready to declare victory and move on. The Central Agency for Resettlers was dissolved in July 1948 and responsibility for its functions transferred to a small and low-profile section of the Ministry of the Interior. From that point on, even the term "resettler" (*Umsiedler*) became almost as taboo as "expellee" had become: all were to be equal citizens of the new German Democratic Republic, without distinction. This shift was reflected in both domestic and foreign policy. At home, the government cracked down hard on unofficial expellee associations of however innocuous a character; as Philipp Ther observes, "[i]n concrete terms, this meant that even complaints about problems of integration could lead to police investigations."[81] Where external affairs were concerned, if Western expellees' sensibilities arguably were excessively pandered to by the Bonn government, those of their Eastern counterparts were completely ignored. In a Soviet-brokered shotgun marriage, the Communist governments of Poland and East Germany concluded the Treaty of Görlitz in July 1950 that recognized the Oder-Neisse line as the permanent frontier between the two countries. This was a crushing psychological blow to Eastern expellees, many of whom had opted for or chosen to remain in the Soviet zone in the hope that they might soon be able to return to their homes. "Some," Ian Connor notes, "lived so close to the border that they could actually see the house they had been forced to leave behind."[82]

As a final sop to the resettlers before they were sent out to fend for themselves in East German society, the state passed the significantly named Law for the Further Improvement of the Situation of Former Resettlers, under heavy pressure from Soviet military governors, in the autumn of 1950. This provided interest-free loans of up to a thousand marks for the purchase of household goods; credits on the same terms for building purposes; and modest scholarship assistance for "resettler" children. Once again the East Germans' ambitions outran their capabilities. Furniture and houseware manufacturers were unable to keep up with the enormous expansion of demand for their products, and in any event neither the central nor *Land* governments possessed the funds available to provide loans to all applicants. Thus, while the German Democratic Republic devoted a much higher proportion of its scanty resources to resettlement activities than the Federal Republic, the results were far more modest and, just as importantly, caused deep disappointment to the intended beneficiaries.

Nonetheless, by the mid-1950s the worst of the problems associated with expellee resettlement had been overcome in both Germanies. It is true that in the East the ruling party's principal strategy for doing so after 1948 was "to gloss over the integration problem and solve it through denial,"[83] but until the erection of the Berlin Wall in 1961 those who remained dissatisfied with this method had the option of voting with their feet and moving, this time as a welcomed "refugee," to the West. More than 830,000 would ultimately do so.[84] In the Federal Republic, the achievement of full employment and the arrival of a newer and more socially marginal cohort yet, the "guest workers" from Turkey and the Mediterranean, proved to be important agents of integration. Certainly the effects of having arrived with nothing and being compelled to start one's life again were not to be overcome easily; numerous studies have shown that not only expellees alone, but even children of expellees, continue to be overrepresented in the ranks of those afflicted by social deprivation. As Marita Krauss points out, moreover, even within the two Germanies no less than between them, there was no uniform pattern of readjustment, so that it is more correct to speak of "integrations," to greater or lesser degrees and of distinct kinds, rather than a single process.[85] But fears of sectional antagonism, juvenile delinquency, and political radicalism were not borne out by experience, and for all the errors and omissions of which both the Allied and German authorities were guilty, the conventional wisdom that the integration efforts were generally successful has proven resistant to even the most determined revisionist assault.

This does not mean, though, that all tensions were resolved. The expulsions remained a profoundly traumatic and divisive episode in a society that had already undergone too many of them since the beginning of the twentieth century. Both at home and abroad they were processed psychologically by means of the same convenient mechanisms—denial, myth-making, decontextualization, rationalization—with which other uncomfortable aspects of the German past were customarily treated. With the fall of communism, the reunification of the country, and the forced confrontation with its eastern and southern neighbors as a result of the expansion of the European Union, however, these strategies began to lose their ability to surround the unresolved issues of the 1940s with a cocoon of comfortable evasion. How and why the "buried history" of the expulsions came to haunt a Germany and a Europe that seemed to all appearances to have transcended, if not actually confronted, their violent pasts is the subject of the final chapters of this book.

12

The Law

Václav Klaus, the Czech president, startled and angered his fellow European leaders in October 2009 when he unexpectedly demanded that they endorse a statement affirming the legality of Edvard Beneš's 1945 decrees authorizing the denationalization, expropriation, and expulsion of Czechoslovakia's German population. The dispute arose as the ratification process of the Lisbon Treaty on centralization of the European Union was drawing to a close. For the treaty to enter into force, the assent of all twenty-seven members of the EU was required. By the time it reached Klaus's desk, the other twenty-six had already ratified it; both houses of the Czech parliament had approved the treaty by large majorities; and the Constitutional Court had reported positively on its compatibility with fundamental Czech law. Only the president's signature was needed for the treaty to take effect. Klaus, however, objected to the Charter of Fundamental Rights incorporated in the Lisbon pact, two of whose provisions, he argued, would expose the Czech Republic to legal claims by German expellees and their descendants. Article 17 of the charter upheld the right to own property, and declared that takings by the state were "subject to fair compensation being paid in good time . . ." Article 19(1) stated unambiguously: "Collective expulsions are prohibited."[1] To ensure that "the Lisbon Treaty will not lead to the breach of the so-called Beneš Decrees," the president announced in a press conference at the Prague Castle, it was necessary to obtain an "exemption" guaranteeing that European courts could not challenge Czech law on the validity of the decrees.[2] If this opt-out was not granted, he threatened to withhold his signature indefinitely, causing the treaty to collapse.

To many observers, Klaus's action in playing the "expulsion card" was no more than a last-ditch maneuver on the part of the famously Euroskeptic president to derail an accord of which he vociferously disapproved. Regardless of whether this was the case, he was by no means the only Czech politician to be deeply concerned about the possible impact of EU legislation on the Beneš decrees. In April 2002, two years before the Czech Republic became a member of the EU, both houses of Parliament in Prague unanimously passed a joint resolution insisting that the "legal and property relations arising from [the decrees] are unquestionable, inviolable, and unchangeable." Tony Blair, the British prime minister; President Vladimir Putin of Russia; and the U.S. under secretary of state, Marc Grossman, each publicly expressed support for the Czech position after Prime Minister Miloš Zeman reminded them that it was "in the interests" of the Potsdam Agreement signatories as well as the Czech Republic to do so.[3] Whether Klaus's objection to the Lisbon Treaty seven years later was tactical or sincere, however, the result was the same. The following month, the leaders of the other EU states provided the requested "opt-out" in the form of a protocol asserting that the charter conferred no new rights on citizens that were not already recognized by the Czech courts. The president thereupon signed the treaty, which took effect in December 2009.

This controversy over the continuing validity of the Beneš decrees drew fresh attention to the applicability of international law to the postwar expulsions. At a moment when the newly established International Criminal Court at the Hague was formulating charges against defendants from the former Yugoslavia based on a statute that defined "deportation or forcible transfer of population" as a "crime against humanity," the notion that decrees authorizing such actions remain legally valid in Europe seemed especially counterintuitive. Viewed from the perspective of international law, though, the expulsions give rise to three separate questions: whether they were lawful at the time; whether they remain lawful today; and whether a similar population transfer elsewhere might be lawful in the future. The answer to each of these questions is far more ambiguous than might be thought at first sight.

The concept of international human rights is a recent development in the world's history. Until the late nineteenth century, the idea of "rights" applied only to those claims that an individual might have against his or her own government. During the Renaissance era, some authorities had suggested the possibility of establishing a regime of individual protection that would in certain circumstances extend across borders. The seventeenth-century Dutch legal scholar Hugo Grotius, for example, described what is nowadays known as the doctrine of "universal jurisdiction" when he argued that monarchs could legitimately bring offenders to justice "not only on account of injuries committed against themselves or their subjects, but also on account of injuries which do not directly affect them but excessively violate the law of nature or of nations in regard to any person whatsoever."[4] Ideas of this type, though, died stillborn. During Grotius's own lifetime, the trend of international relations proceeded decisively in the opposite direction. The Peace of Westphalia, which brought to an end the immensely destructive Thirty Years' War, laid down as a fundamental norm of international law that there was no power or entity superior to the individual state.

This doctrine of state sovereignty, the cornerstone of what to the present day is known as the Westphalian system, remained unchallenged until the Hague Conference of 1899. Ironically, the conference was convened by Tsar Nicholas II of Russia, a man whose name was a byword for autocracy and ruthlessness, as a means of diverting the world's attention from the unenviable human rights record of his own government. Reinventing himself, however unpersuasively, as an apostle of peace, the tsar invited delegations from twenty-six countries to draw up agreements to prevent armed conflict between states and, in the event of these failing in their purpose, to ensure that any resulting wars were conducted as humanely as possible. Accordingly, a series of Hague Conventions was concluded that laid down rules concerning legitimate and illegitimate methods of warfare and established the first court of international arbitration, the Hague Tribunal, since the papacy abandoned its functions in this regard in the fifteenth century. A second conference, with its accompanying conventions, extended these norms in 1907. The Hague Conventions were by no means perfect. They bound only those countries that were signatories. They contained few protections for civilians—a crucial omission that in the future would hamstring the work of humanitarian agencies like the Red Cross. They were silent in circumstances in which a government maltreated its own citizens, rather than the inhabitants of foreign lands its armies were occupying. They applied only to conflicts in which a state of formal war existed, rather than in "undeclared wars" or in peacetime. They provided no means of individual redress, nor any mechanism for enforcement. Nonetheless, they marked a step forward in international law of immense significance. For the first time, they asserted that at least in principle, states and their leaders were answerable to the international community for abusing human rights. It was largely on the basis of the Hague Conventions, which had been ratified by nearly all states by 1914, that the "Nuremberg principle" invalidating the defense of "obeying superior orders" would be codified.

While the Great War seemed to reverse the progress made by international law, it would paradoxically lead to an even more rapid extension of the legal protection of human rights. At first sight, the war was a disaster for the Hague process. Under the pressure of total war, the leading belligerents—led, in nearly all cases, by Germany—systematically violated the undertakings they had given in the Hague Conventions. Hostage taking, the deliberate destruction of historical sites, the use of chemical weapons and of unrestricted submarine warfare, indiscriminate aerial bombing of cities, and compulsory labor all became routine methods of warfare. If the Hague prohibitions against poisoning wells or charging for postage on food parcels sent to prisoners of war were never breached, it was only because these tactics were not at the time considered militarily useful.

The sheer scale of the atrocities committed during the Great War, however, called into being what had never existed until that time: a widespread recognition among the peoples of all countries that modern war had become so destructive that the international protection of civilians, and especially of vulnerable national, ethnic, or religious minorities, had become an urgent necessity. The first step in this process was taken by the Allied governments in May 1915 when, in response to initial reports of the Armenian genocide, they issued a declaration condemning the actions of the Constantinople regime as *"crimes against humanity and civilisation* for which all members of the Turkish Government will be held responsible together with its agents implicated in the massacres."[5] This was an act of revolutionary significance, the first time that any substantial section of the international community had attempted to hold states responsible for crimes committed against their own citizens. In the same vein, the Treaty of Versailles compelled the German government to recognize "the right of the Allied and Associated Powers to bring before military tribunals persons accused of having committed acts in violation of the laws and customs of war."[6] To be sure, the immediate impact of both provisions was minimal. As in the 1990s, when the Clinton administration emerged as the principal opponent of the creation of an international criminal court,[7] Woodrow Wilson and his secretary of state, Robert Lansing, efficiently torpedoed efforts at Versailles to establish a tribunal to prosecute the perpetrators of wartime atrocities—an idea first advanced by Gustave Moynier, vice president of the CICR, in 1872.[8] In both the Turkish and German cases, consequently, the Allies left to their defeated foes the responsibility of trying war criminals. The results were predictable. Only a few lower-ranking functionaries among those responsible for the Armenian genocide were made to stand trial before the tribunal in Constantinople collapsed; in 1923 the regime of Kemal Atatürk granted a blanket amnesty to all involved. The German process was even more farcical. The *Reichsgericht* in Leipzig between 1921 and 1931 initiated 907 prosecutions of persons named by the Allies as guilty of atrocities. Only seven resulted in convictions, the court either accepting what was later to become notorious as the "Nuremberg defense" or, in the vast majority of instances, finding that there was no case to answer. Gerd Hankel has persuasively argued that in Germany itself the widespread belief that war crimes trials were no more than a form of ritual humiliation imposed upon the defeated countries would have tragic consequences in the Second World War, in which the Germans demonstrated their contempt for any kind of legal restraint.[9] But for all that these prosecutions smacked of "victors' justice"—a perception that was only partially counterbalanced by the virtually automatic acquittal or dismissal of charges against the accused—the implication that individuals had a legitimate claim to protection even in the midst of the most destructive war in history did much in other countries to advance the status and prestige of international human rights law.

For much the same reasons, the establishment of an international system to safeguard minority populations became a fundamental part of the postwar reconstitution of Europe. Having discovered at the peace conference the impossibility of redrawing the borders of central and eastern Europe so as to provide "national self-determination" to the hopelessly intermingled peoples of the region, the authors of the Treaty of Versailles fell back on the idea of charging the League of Nations—an immense dustbin into which all the peace settlement's innumerable unresolved problems were unceremoniously dumped—with the protection of national minorities from the very governments the Allies proceeded to set over them. The need for something of the sort was made clear by the fact that despite strenuous efforts to redraw political boundaries, tens of millions of Europeans had been left on the "wrong" side of the new frontiers. More than a third of Romania's population were members of one or another national minority; nearly half of Poland's were not ethnic Poles. Jewish groups also lobbied hard for League protection, fearing all too correctly that in its absence Jews would receive short shrift from the governments of the succession states. In June 1919, then, the Allies prevailed upon the Polish government to conclude a treaty guaranteeing the rights of linguistic and religious minorities and providing for a nebulously defined League oversight system. Similar arrangements for Austria, Bulgaria, Czechoslovakia, Greece, Hungary, Romania, and Yugoslavia soon followed, and by the mid-1920s no fewer than fourteen states had agreed to League supervision of their minority populations.

Like the Hague Conventions, the Minority Protection Treaties had many deficiencies. In most cases, they asserted that national, linguistic, racial, and religious minorities should enjoy the same rights in law as the majority population, and that they should be allowed to educate their children through the language of their choice. But they nowhere defined the criteria for membership of a minority group, leaving it unclear to whom the League's protection applied. With the exception of the Germans of Polish Silesia, the minorities themselves had no right of appeal to the Council of the League, which could investigate only if a complaint was backed by a member state. Inevitably, this meant that the grievances of the largest and most vocal minorities, supported by the most activist governments whose ethnicity they shared, obtained the most attention, while the rights of smaller and less articulate groups, like the Ukrainians of Poland, the Macedonian Slavs of Greece, or the Austrians of Italy, were violated with impunity. The treaties were bitterly resented by many members of the majority populations: as late as 1984 a Polish scholar alleged (inaccurately) that they were "intended to allow the Great Powers to interfere in the affairs of new states-parties to minority treaties, under the pretext of acting in the interest of minorities residing in those states."[10] Lastly, the protection offered by the minorities treaties was not universal, but extended only to the succession states and some others, like Turkey, that had been pressured to sign them. The British stood firmly against any possible extension that might see their treatment of Catholics in Northern Ireland exposed to international scrutiny; the United States, though not a member of the League, was no more anxious to invite world attention to the condition of black Americans. An even more crucial shortcoming was the failure of the Allies at Versailles to require Germany to submit to the League system. As a result, the League Council found it had no basis for intervention when the Nazis commenced their legal assault upon German Jews with the introduction of the Nuremberg Laws in 1935.

The principal weakness of the minority protection regime between the wars, though, was that in 1919 no less than in 1945, ethnic Germans constituted by far the largest single minority population in central and eastern Europe. The League protection system, therefore, consisted to a considerable degree of the victors in the Great War adjudicating upon the complaints of certain members of the vanquished nation about the personal consequences they were experiencing as a result of that defeat. Already suspicious, with some justification, that many of these protests were aimed at revising the postwar settlement rather than redressing immediate grievances, the "League of Victors" proved reluctant to take them seriously. As Mark Mazower notes,

> the League's foray into minority rights pleased no one. The Great Powers increasingly disliked being required to pass judgment on how Poles, Romanians, or Czechs—their client states—were behaving towards their minorities. As Germany and the USSR regained strength, the British and French lost their appetite for anything which might weaken the east European states they had brought into existence. The latter for their part felt humiliated by the international obligations they alone had been forced to sign, and blamed their minorities for publicizing their grievances abroad and failing to assimilate. And

the minorities themselves, as a result of these factors, gradually lost faith in the protection provided by international law, and their complaints to Geneva dried up.[11]

Even before the Nazis made the condition of the *Volksdeutsche* the occasion of their—interminably repeated—"last territorial demand in Europe," therefore, the minority protection system had all but broken down. A deadly blow was dealt to it by the Polish government, which unilaterally announced in September 1934 that it would no longer tolerate League oversight of its treatment of minorities. This was an immensely short-sighted move on Warsaw's part, for "if the German minority were not allowed to appeal to the [League] Council, it would inevitably appeal to Berlin."[12] By the end of the 1930s, "the influence of the Council in this field diminished and almost disappeared."[13]

The virtually unanimous view that the League's experiment with protecting the human rights of vulnerable people was an unmitigated failure—or, in Edvard Beneš's pungent assessment, "ridiculous nonsense"—is nonetheless due for reexamination.[14] Whatever its deficiencies, it was incomparably more humane in conception than the alternative of mass expulsion. It is a measure of the moral retrogression that marked the twentieth century that the authors of the minority rights regime, in contrast to their successors a quarter-century later, "would have considered it barbarous to uproot whole communities in this way simply to suit their own interests."[15] Nor was it always unsuccessful. One indication that it had come closer to its objectives than generally recognized was the determination of the expelling governments that nothing like it should be reestablished after the war, lest it stand in the way of the removal of the Germans. Outlining the Czechoslovak government in exile's plans for the *Sudetendeutsche*, Hubert Ripka insisted that "we cannot allow these matters to form the object of decisions or joint decisions by any international bodies."[16] In making this demand, of course, the expelling states were pushing at an open door. The Allies were no less anxious that no minority protection regime be reconstituted. "The prospect of such protection," the Foreign Office's Inter-Departmental Committee warned in 1944, would "make the operation of transfer harder to carry out."[17] United States Secretary of State Ed Stettinius also agreed at the San Francisco Conference that established the United Nations in the summer of 1945 that the UN Charter should not include "an enumeration of individual and collective human rights and fundamental freedoms."[18] Instead, with the enthusiastic agreement of the other great powers, President Truman successfully proposed that the drawing up of a "Bill of Human Rights" be deferred until some convenient time in the future. Even this, when it finally materialized in the shape of the Universal Declaration of Human Rights, would be no more than a statement of well-meaning aspirations on the part of signatory states rather than a binding commitment.

At the time the expulsions were conceived, astonishingly little thought appears to have to been given to the question of their legality. To be sure, few statutes or legal precedents existed that might have stood in their way. They were to be carried out in peacetime, thereby sidestepping the 1899 and 1907 Hague Conventions that applied only in time of war. They affected a civilian population, which was not entitled to any of the provisions of the 1929 Geneva Conventions. The CICR had drawn attention in 1934 to the paradoxical fact that soldiers who were capable of defending themselves enjoyed far greater protection in international law than civilians who were not, and drew up a draft convention at Tokyo to rectify this situation. The draft provided that civilian internees were to enjoy the benefit of conditions that should "in no case be inferior" to those provided to prisoners of war; deportations were specifically prohibited "unless they are evacuations intended, on account of the extension of military operations, to ensure the security of the inhabitants."[19] Unhappily, the diplomatic conference scheduled for 1940 at which it was intended that this document would be ratified was never held, due to the outbreak of the Second World War. Not until 1949, with the adoption of the Fourth Geneva Convention, were civilians for the first time provided with an instrument specifically designed for their protection.

Undoubtedly the postwar expulsions were not compatible with the Minority Treaties of the League of Nations, of which all the expelling states were signatories. These bound the governments in question to guarantee that "members of racial, religious or linguistic minorities" would "enjoy the same treatment and security in law and in fact" as those of the majority population. The minority treaties, though, suffered from the lack of any enforcement mechanism, and there was nothing to prevent countries that accepted their obligations from abrogating them later, as Poland had done. Moreover, the United Nations concluded after the war that the treaties were no longer binding—not because any subsequent legal instrument superseded them or released the signatories from their obligations, but simply because "between 1939 and 1947 circumstances as a whole changed to such an extent that, generally speaking, the [minorities protection] system should be considered as having ceased to exist."[20] So too did the legal rights of national minorities as such. So far as international law is concerned, Patrick Thornberry suggests, "the post-war world started, as it were, with a *tabula rasa* in the matter of tolerance and encouragement of minorities. States could act as they pleased in relation to their populations if they were not inhibited by a relevant treaty."[21] Moreover, as the British Foreign Office helpfully pointed out, if the Allies cooperated with the Polish and Czechoslovak government in completing the expulsion program, the national minorities problem would for all intents and purposes no longer exist in Europe and the need for a renewed minority protection regime would not arise.[22]

The only remaining legal obstacles that might have stood in the way of the expulsions were the bills of indictment against Germany composed by the Allies during and immediately after the war. An inter-Allied conference of January 1942 listed "mass expulsions" among the offenses for which German perpetrators would be punished.[23] The Polish government in exile eight months later promised the death penalty for those participating in "transfers of population."[24] Most significant of all was the charter of the International Military Tribunal at Nuremberg, drawn up on August 8, 1945 to list the offenses for which the leaders of Nazi Germany were to be tried. At first sight, the charter's definition of "deportation and other inhumane acts committed against any civilian population" as constituting "crimes against humanity" seemed to apply with equal force to the program the Big Three had endorsed at Potsdam less than a week previously. Anticipating that the charter might be invoked against them, however, the Allies limited its application to "any crime within the jurisdiction of the Tribunal"— that is to say, those committed by the Axis countries between January 30, 1933 and May 8, 1945. When defense counsel for Hans Frank, former head of the *Generalgouvernement*, attempted to justify his client's part in the wartime deportation of Poles and Jews by pointing out that the Allies were engaged in a far more massive forced transfer operation less than seventy miles from where the court was sitting, the bench ruled the intervention inadmissible because postwar matters were beyond its jurisdiction. While it might appear contradictory that the charter criminalized deeds by Germany and its allies while leaving identical deeds, if perpetrated by anyone else, untouched, the applicability of the Nuremberg principles has proven far narrower during the past sixty years than is popularly supposed.[25] In the words of the international law scholar Egon Schwelb, the crime against humanity as set forth in the charter is not "the corner-stone of a system of international criminal law equally applicable in times of war and of peace, protecting the human rights of inhabitants of all countries, 'of any civilian population,' against anybody, including their own states and governments."[26] Rather, it covers only those offenses committed in connection with and as part of the waging of "aggressive war," itself a category that has been successfully invoked only against the losers of the Second World War.[27]

Later human rights instruments did little more to fill the gap. The UN Commission on Human Rights, which convened in January 1947 to draw up a statement of universal principles, proved thoroughly hostile to the idea of protecting minorities. Eleanor Roosevelt, its chairwoman, fought strenuously against the efforts of the UN Sub-Commission on the Prevention of Discrimination and the Protection of Minorities to include such a provision. According to Carol Anderson, Roosevelt was always mindful of the danger that an international body might be empowered to pronounce upon the treatment of black Americans in the southern United States, a region almost entirely controlled by the Democratic Party to which she belonged. She therefore "worked to ensure that neither individuals nor nongovernmental organizations would have any authority to petition the UN for redress of human rights violations."[28] Some of the arguments she deployed to this end were, to say the least, curious—most notably her contention that because not all states possessed ethnic or racial minorities, minority rights by definition were not universal and thus had no place in the commission's deliberations. But in any event, the Universal Declaration of Human Rights which it formulated was not, in the words of the U.S. delegate to the Third Committee of the UN General Assembly, "a treaty or international agreement and did not impose legal obligations..."[29] The Genocide Convention too, which was simultaneously being drafted by the UN's Economic and Social Committee, assisted by a legal team, was watered down in response to U.S. pressure. Its first draft had defined "forced and systematic exile of individuals representing the culture of a group" as a form of genocide. The U.S. delegate strongly opposed this clause, pointing out that it "might be interpreted as embracing forced transfers of minority groups such as have already been carried out by members of the United Nations."[30] The prohibition on expulsions was accordingly deleted from the draft Genocide Convention by a vote of 25 to 16, with four abstentions.[31]

In the following decades, numerous legal scholars have attempted to craft theories according to which forced population transfers might be held to contravene international law. The most popular of these is the argument that mass expulsions violate either the principle of *jus cogens*, or "customary international law." The first of these declares that there are certain "peremptory norms" of international law, like the prohibition on genocide or slavery, that no written treaty or legal instrument can override. The Vienna Convention on the Law of Treaties defines a *jus cogens* principle as one "accepted and recognized by the international community of States as a norm from which no derogation is permitted and which can be modified only by a subsequent norm of general international law having the same character."[32] A Working Group on Mass Expulsions at San Remo contended in 1983 that compulsory population transfers, whether sanctioned by treaties or not, by their nature fall under this category and must therefore be considered illegal in all circumstances. The group's concession that "there are many gaps in conventional law and an insufficiently specific coverage of the problem of mass expulsion in both international and domestic law," however, gravely undermined its contention that a universal consensus on the inadmissibility of these actions already existed.[33] One of the difficulties, indeed, in successfully asserting the principle of *jus cogens* is that it seeks to criminalize only what nobody has ever asserted ought to be lawful.

A less sweeping theory is that a ban on expulsions may be inferred from customary international law. By acting in accordance with certain principles as though they were legally binding, states confer on those principles the status of rules of law by dint of long usage and general acceptance. Thus scholars have contended that the Universal Declaration of Human Rights, the Nuremberg Principles, the European Convention on Human Rights, and other statements of commonly accepted norms, while not peremptory obligations, have nevertheless become expressions of customary international law. According to this interpretation, forced population transfers are indirectly prohibited because in practice they are impossible to carry out without acting arbitrarily or indiscriminately against the minority concerned, thereby contravening the customary norms identified with one of these instruments.[34] The difficulty with such a line of reasoning, however, is that the evidence suggesting that the Universal Declaration, the European Convention, and similar statements are indeed customarily followed is far from overwhelming; as Patrick Thornberry says, "Here, as elsewhere, the wish may be father to the thought."[35] One of many counterexamples may be found in the reaction of the international community when Idi Amin expelled the ethnically South Asian population of Uganda—some forty thousand people—in the autumn of 1972. As Alfred-Maurice de Zayas recalls, "The United Nations General Assembly . . . did not adopt any resolution censuring the expulsions, and a proposal before the Sub-Commission for Prevention of Discrimination and the Protection of Minorities that a telegram be sent to the President of Uganda expressing 'serious concern' at the proposed action was defeated by fourteen votes to one, with six members abstaining."[36] Numerous other expulsion operations of a similar kind—for example, the driving out of ethnic Serbs from Kosovo from 1999 onward—have elicited no more vigorous a response.

Nevertheless, with the collapse of the Soviet Union and the disappearance of communism as a governing ideology in Europe during the early 1990s, a second legal avenue bearing upon the expulsions opened up. The spread of democracy to most of the expelling states and their subsequent ratification of documents like the European Convention on Human Rights suggested that surviving expellees, and possibly their descendants, might be able to obtain redress of their denationalization, expropriation, or expulsion through the civil courts. Several test cases were quickly filed, most of them against what since 1993 had become the Czech Republic. Because Czechoslovakia adopted measures to return to its citizens property nationalized by the communist state, the prospects of obtaining a favorable outcome by appealing to the principle of nondiscrimination were greater than in Poland, where relatively little property had been taken into state ownership during the communist era and the need for a comprehensive restitution law thus did not exist. Though none of these expellee challenges was successful, they raised legal questions of great complexity that remain unresolved today and, if left unaddressed, may produce still greater complications in the future.

The stakes involved were high. Although many expellees had, of course, died by the 1990s, a finding that those still alive had wrongfully been deprived of Czechoslovak nationality would have created overnight a proportionately significant cohort of new—or old—citizens in a country with a population of barely 10 million. Even this, though, would pale into insignificance beside the almost unimaginable dilemmas that would arise as a result of a successful claim for the return of confiscated property. In one case, the lands whose restitution an expellee sought were, at the time of his filing claim, in the possession of four state agencies, a municipal corporation, and several commercial companies as well as numerous private individuals. The extent of the liabilities that might arise from demands for compensation for injuries suffered by former inmates of internment camps, or restitution for the forced labor extorted from them, was likewise extremely difficult, if not impossible, to calculate. But above and beyond the question of how much money might be required to satisfy hundreds of thousands if not millions of expellee claims, the entire question had explosive political implications. Alone among Nazi Germany's victims, the Czech Republic had never received restitution payments of however token a character from the Federal Republic of Germany because of a desire not to prejudice expellees' counterclaims to the property of which they had been deprived in 1945. The possibility that the Czech state might have to pay compensation to individuals who during the war had been Reich citizens and supporters of the Nazi occupation, while Czech citizens went unrecompensed for the murder, misery, and terror they had experienced at Germany's hands, was intolerable to Czech public opinion in the 1990s. The likelihood that they would accept and comply with an adverse verdict, or a whole succession of adverse verdicts, on this question even from the weightiest international courts was effectively nil.

For this reason, indeed, Czech laws on the restitution of property seized by the state during the communist era were framed in the early 1990s in such a way as to leave as few opportunities as possible to former expellees to pursue their claims.

The restitution statute passed by the Czechoslovak parliament in 1991 authorized the return to their former owners of property nationalized by the state between the coup of February 1948 and the collapse of the regime in 1989. The advantage of choosing a starting date of 1948 was that it excluded at a stroke almost all *Sudetendeutsche*, who had been expropriated two and a half years earlier, as well as ethnic Hungarians forced out in the abortive population "exchange" between Slovakia and Hungary in 1946–47.[37] To achieve the same end, the law specified that only those possessing Czechoslovak citizenship and permanently resident in the country would qualify for restitution. As a result, German civil claims against the Czech state pursued two separate tracks. The first proceeded through the Czech courts and either maintained that the Beneš decrees contravened the country's new democratic constitution, or accepted the legitimacy of the decrees but asserted that they had been wrongly applied against "antifascists" who ought not to have been expropriated and expelled. The second was conducted through international tribunals like the European Court of Human Rights and the United Nations Human Rights Committee, and held that the decrees, the Czech restitution statute, or both, were incompatible with international laws binding upon the Czech Republic.

Attempts to gain redress via the first track—the Czech domestic courts—have proven almost completely futile. One of the most important cases was adjudicated by the Czech Constitutional Court in March 1995, when Rudolf Dreithaler, a Czech citizen of German origin, claimed the return of a house he had inherited from a *Sudetendeutsch* relative but that had been confiscated before he could take possession. The court's finding was, to say the least, idiosyncratic. On one hand it reaffirmed that the Beneš expropriation decree had been lawfully issued by the president in 1945 and thus remained valid and dispositive. On the other it maintained that the decree did not contradict international law because it had not been used to expropriate anyone for the previous forty years and there was no possibility of its being so used in the future; hence it had "no constitutive character." Lastly, the court found that the expropriation of "persons of German nationality . . . represents no national revenge, but is simply an appropriate response to the aggression of Nazi Germany," in which the *Sudetendeutsche* were implicated and for which they might legitimately be sanctioned. The "gas chambers, concentration camps, mass murder, oppression, killing and dehumanisation of millions," it maintained, were the responsibility not of the Nazis alone, but of those "who quietly profited from this movement, who carried out their orders, and did not offer resistance."[38] Thus the ruling not only relied upon the notion of collective German responsibility for Nazi crimes as an established fact, but left the decree in a constitutional limbo in which it both existed and did not exist according to whether the frame of reference was domestic or international law.

Expellee petitions before international venues, on the other hand, were even less successful. A typical example was the case of Gerhard Malik, who appealed to the UN Committee on Human Rights in the mid-1990s. Twelve years old at the end of the war, Malik was expelled from Nový Jičín in Moravia to the U.S. zone of Germany in July 1946; the house in which he had been born was confiscated. By arbitrarily depriving him of his Czechoslovak citizenship and by drawing up the Czech restitution law in such a way as to exclude him and other *Sudetendeutsche* from its provisions, he alleged, the Czech Republic was in violation of the International Covenant on Human Rights and its Optional Protocol. In its response to the committee, the Czech government argued that at the time of his expulsion Malik had been provided with a six-month window of opportunity to appeal his denationalization and had failed to do so. Moreover, the Czech Constitutional Court decision of March 1995 on the Beneš expropriation decree had declared that this law "no longer operate[d] as a constitutional regulation" and thus could be challenged in the Czech courts. Here too Malik had not exhausted the domestic remedies open to him. Malik responded that the suggestion that he was at fault in failing to petition for restoration of his Czechoslovak nationality in 1945 was unjustified, inasmuch as inhabitants of internment and forced labor camps were in no position to submit such applications and any attempt to do so often resulted in physical maltreatment at the hands of camp staff. If the Czech Republic contended that the petition process Malik had supposedly spurned was an effective remedy that Germans could readily have used to obtain restoration of their citizenship, "it should provide examples of those who did so successfully." Similarly, to claim that a ruling of the Constitutional Court that explicitly affirmed the validity of the Beneš expropriation decree had somehow made it possible to challenge its constitutionality before the same court was no less unreal. The Human Rights Committee, however, declined to hear the case on two entirely different grounds. The fact that the Czech Constitutional Court had upheld the Beneš expropriation decree (No. 108/1945) in the Dreithaler case did not mean that the denationalization decree (No. 33/1945) to which it was linked had been found to be valid as well. Until Malik, and any other similarly situated petitioner, obtained a ruling from the Czech courts on this matter also, the committee declined to intervene.[39] So far as his property claim was concerned, the committee declared that "not every distinction or differentiation in treatment amounts to discrimination." The fact that the Czech Republic had decided to reimburse Czechoslovak citizens for wrongful takings by the state after 1948 did not impose an obligation upon the state similarly to compensate others for improper confiscations prior to that date.

Although the committee therefore declared the petition inadmissible rather than delivering a verdict on the facts of the case, its ruling in *Malik* was nonetheless problematical in two ways. The first was that its assertion that the Covenant did not oblige the Czech Republic to return property to persons not covered by the restitution law ran dramatically counter to verdicts it had already rendered in the case of Czechoslovak citizens who were similarly situated. In *Adam v. Czech Republic* (1996), for example, the Committee asserted that the law's exclusion of Joseph Adam and other ethnic Czechs and Slovaks who had not maintained their citizenship continuously between 1948 and 1989 was an arbitrary act that violated Article 26—the antidiscrimination provision—of the Covenant. The Czech Republic may not have been under any obligation to return confiscated property to anyone. Once it had decided to do so, however, it could not discriminate between one class of expropriated persons and another without breaching the Covenant's guarantee of equal treatment. Yet the Committee had maintained elsewhere that differential treatment, as in the Malik case, was not discriminatory if "the criteria for such differentiation are reasonable and objective and the aim is to achieve a purpose which is legitimate under the Covenant."[40] István Pogány of the University of Warwick School of Law notes that in its references to the specific facts of this case the committee "offered no basis, in either logic or law, for its conclusion that *some* differences in treatment amount to unlawful discrimination while others do not."[41] Nevertheless, the implication of the Malik finding was that his disqualification from restitution was indeed justified by "reasonable and objective" criteria intended to achieve a "legitimate" purpose. In other words, like the Czech Constitutional Court in March 1995, the committee implicitly suggested that the twelve-year-old Malik, by virtue of his share of responsibility for the Nazis' conduct, was, in contrast to Joseph Adam, "reasonably" and "legitimately" dispossessed by the Czechoslovak state.[42]

The second dubious aspect of the *Malik* finding was the contention that the petitioner had not exhausted the domestic remedies available to him because he had not tested in the Czech courts the constitutionality of the Beneš decree (No. 33/1945) by which he was denationalized. In this context it is relevant to note that whereas a petitioner must have exhausted all possible domestic remedies before taking his or her case before an international tribunal, those remedies must be effective. In other words, it is not necessary to pursue a claim through every conceivable domestic venue if it is clear that there is no reasonable expectation that the petitioner may thus obtain the redress he or she seeks. In light of the fact that the Constitutional Court had already declared that the expropriation decree was valid because of the collective responsibility of the *Sudetendeutsche* for Nazi atrocities—an argument with which the committee apparently concurred—it hardly seemed logical to propose to Malik that the same court applying the same analysis to the denationalization decree might very well yield a different result.

That expellees and their descendants ought not to expect effective remedies through the Czech courts was confirmed in a later case heard by the committee in 2005. Eugen Czernin, a *Sudetendeutsch* who had been denationalized, expropriated, and put out to forced labor, petitioned the District National Committee of Jindřichův Hradec in November 1945 for the restoration of his Czechoslovak citizenship under the terms of Decree No. 33/1945. He succeeded in proving his antifascist credentials to the satisfaction of the District National Committee, but his application was still pending at the Ministry of the Interior when he fled to Austria in 1947 to escape the attentions of the NKVD. In 1995, though Czernin had died in exile, his son submitted a claim for the return of his father's property, a necessary condition of which was the final determination of Eugen Czernin's still-pending application for the restoration of his Czechoslovak citizenship. Although the minister of the interior promised to convene a hearing into the matter in 1996, none was ever held. An order of the Constitutional Court in 1997 instructed the Ministry of the Interior to decide the application speedily. This too was ignored. Instead, the Interior Ministry and the Jindřichův Hradec District Office continued to stall the investigation of Czernin's claim in spite of several orders from Czech courts requiring them to do so over the following years. Ultimately the case came before the Human Rights Committee, which found the Czech Republic was continuing to deny the Czernin family an effective remedy and thus was in breach of its international obligations.[43] Welcome as this decision was to the Czernins, it did not affect the progress of the case any more than previous rulings had done. As of 2011, sixty-six years after his application was first submitted, Eugen Czernin's claim to the restoration of his citizenship still remained unresolved.

In both the domestic and the international spheres, the fate of claims by expellees from the Recovered Territories have followed a similar pattern. In 2001 the Polish parliament adopted a law on "reprivatization" of confiscated property that, like its Czech counterpart, would have excluded expellees from its provisions. The question became moot, however, when the then president, Aleksander Kwaśniewski, vetoed the measure. The European Court of Human Rights ruled in 2008 that "individual acts of violence, expulsion, dispossession and seizure or confiscation of property" carried out by the Polish authorities were "instantaneous acts" that did not produce "a continuing situation of 'deprivation of a right.'" The European Convention on Human Rights did not have retrospective effect, and hence could not be held to apply to any violation committed before Poland's ratification of the Convention in 1991.[44]

Nor, despite Václav Klaus's anxieties, has the accession of most of the expelling states to the European Union materially influenced the legal situation. In 2002 the European Parliament, seeking to anticipate any difficulties that might arise from the Czech Republic's application to join the EU, commissioned a legal opinion from three distinguished scholars on the possible incompatibility of the Beneš decrees with European Union law. Though this study, which was principally the work of the former vice chairman of the European Commission on Human Rights, Dr. Jochen Frowein, had no official status, it was plainly intended to set out the line the EU proposed to take. The Frowein opinion concluded that the Beneš decrees posed few serious problems from the standpoint of EU law. While such practices as depriving entire classes of people of nationality and stripping them of their possessions without due process would clearly be unlawful if carried out in 2002, nothing in EU law required member states to provide redress for wrongful acts committed prior to their accession to the Union. The opinion agreed with the UN's Human Rights Committee's finding in the Malik case that the collective expropriation of Germans and Hungarians was a "reasonable" punishment for their disloyalty to the Czechoslovak state; in any case, the fact that the Czech Republic's restitution program would terminate before the country joined the EU meant that its operations could not be challenged by any European agency. Frowein and his colleagues found only two aspects of the Beneš decrees potentially troubling. The first was a provision that had authorized the Czechoslovak state to try "traitors" and "collaborators" in absentia. Any attempt by the present-day Czech Republic to detain persons convicted in 1945 and 1946 through such proceedings would, the opinion warned, "run counter to the fundamental rights and rule of law guarantees which must be applicable as from the date of accession." The second problematic element — Decree No. 115/1946, which provided immunity from prosecution for Czechoslovak citizens who killed or otherwise mistreated Germans in the course of "just reprisals" during the first six months of peacetime — if taken at face value seemed to suggest that even crimes against humanity were beyond the reach of the law, so long as they were perpetrated against Germans before October 1945. The Frowein opinion concluded, however, that because the German government had not insisted that this decree be repealed, it had in effect waived its right to do so under the doctrine of estoppel. Indeed, in a joint declaration of 1997 with the Czech government, it had declared that it did not propose to "burden their relations with political and legal issues which stem from the past." Moreover, it was unjust that Czechoslovak citizens who had been given legal grounds for believing themselves to be immune from prosecution for more than half a century should suddenly find themselves exposed to the possibility of criminal proceedings.[45]

While fresh restitution cases continue to be brought by expellees and their heirs, sufficient experience has now been gained to suggest that none is likely to succeed. Dieter Blumenwitz of the University of Würzburg was almost certainly right to conclude that "there is nothing to be expected ... from the Czech courts which would suggest that the expropriation decrees of 1945 will be repealed."[46] To judge from the Slovak Parliament's resolution in September 2007 that the Beneš decrees were "unalterable," the same will probably prove true of Slovakia's judicial system as well.[47] Tribunals like the UN Human Rights Committee and the European Court of Human Rights continue to deny the admissibility of petitions brought by individuals, even if they have to rely upon strained and arguably inconsistent legal analyses to do so. In particular, as István Pogány notes, the Human Rights Committee's staunch refusal to specify the criteria it applies in finding discriminatory treatment in the case of German expellees to be legally justified "suggests that we must simply await its decisions in individual cases and assume them to be correct."[48] Likewise, if deliberations by the European Court of Justice, the EU's highest court, are to be guided by the Frowein opinion and the Czech opt-out of 2009, there will be no means by which a case brought by an expellee can surmount the threshold of admissibility and obtain a hearing on its merits.

A divergence of opinion has thus appeared between scholars in the academy, many of whom regard the expulsions and their ongoing consequences as self-evident violations of international law, and the courts, which have taken a consistently minimalist stance on the question. James Wolfe of the University of Southern Mississippi, for example, considers that they were in violation of the Hague Conventions as well as the Nuremberg Principles, inasmuch as the decision to expel was made during wartime and "intent to commit acts contravening the law of war is a punishable delict."[49] Alfred-Maurice de Zayas of the Geneva School of Diplomacy is likewise unpersuaded by the argument frequently put forward by the expelling states that the operation was lawful because it had been ratified by the Big Three at Potsdam. For the Allies to be able "to confer legal authority upon Poland, Czechoslovakia and Hungary to expel German civilians, the Allied Powers themselves necessarily must have had this far-reaching and extraordinary authority." Germany, he points out, clearly did not, inasmuch as "deportations ... committed against any civilian population" constituted one of the "crimes against humanity" of which its leaders were convicted at Nuremberg. Yet the Allies never identified the legal basis that permitted them to carry out similar acts with impunity.[50]

Whether the postwar expulsions were lawful at the time of their occurrence remains a question on which no international tribunal has rendered a definitive verdict. The evident reluctance of these bodies even to indicate whether they or their ongoing effects are consistent with the law as it stands today, but instead to sidestep the substantive issue on grounds of admissibility, has relegated the entire question to a legal limbo from which it is unlikely soon to emerge. Most authorities, though, consider that it is at all events certain that no such expulsions could lawfully be carried out in the future. In the aftermath of the dreadful scenes that attended the collapse of Yugoslavia in the 1990s, a number of international instruments—in particular the Rome Statute of the International Criminal Court—have laid down unambiguously that forced transfer of populations, except for the purpose of temporarily relocating them from a war zone for their own safety, is an offense in international law.[51]

Recently, however, Timothy Waters of Indiana University has raised the possibility that a "Sudeten corollary" now exists in customary international law—that is, the legal precedents created by the pattern of states' everyday practices. The fact that court decisions have narrowed to the vanishing point the possibility of victims of the expulsions obtaining redress of any kind is itself a factor in the evolution of international law—which, in the absence of a global lawmaking body such as a world government, is based to a far greater degree on precedent than on statutes. Likewise, the suggestion by the UN Human Rights Committee in the Malik case, and more explicitly by the Frowein opinion, that the *Sudetendeutsche* were justly and reasonably punished with denationalization and expropriation for what Edvard Beneš in 1942 termed their "passive war crimes," indicates that so far as weighty legal authorities are concerned there exists at least one set of circumstances in which ordinary civilians may legitimately be treated in this fashion.[52] To be sure, this does not mean that the proscriptions of forced population transfers in documents like the Rome Statute are likely to be set aside routinely. But neither are those proscriptions as absolute as they appear.

> On the contrary, the statements and actions of states and European institutions reveal a complex but clear conditionality: such measures are unacceptable *in the absence of exigent challenges to the European order.* Europe and its legal order have not rejected resort to ethnic cleansing under all circumstances; they have reserved this right—and an immunity from restitution after invoking it—in response to grave threats to that order. That is the true shape of the law.[53]

Because, however, mass expulsions are nearly always, at least in the perception of those who carry them out, expedients of last resort in the face of extraordinary circumstances, the general acceptance of even one such episode as a legitimate—or at any rate readily excusable—precedent may, as Waters points out, transpire in the future to be one too many. Human beings under great stress are all too prone to make decisions based on poor historical analogies, and it takes no great feat of the imagination to conceive of circumstances in which the case for displacing a seemingly dangerous ethnic, religious, or racial group which the world already regards unsympathetically may appear as compelling as did the transfer of the ethnic Germans in the 1940s. Without equating practices like waterboarding with the means of obtaining information used by the Gestapo, we have already seen how the taboo against torture in the Western world began to erode in the aftermath of the September 11, 2001 attacks to an extent that would have seemed unimaginable only a few years previously.[54] If the presence of an unwanted minority population should once again be seen as giving rise to a perceived international emergency, the case for invoking the "Sudeten corollary" and exploiting the ambiguities and loopholes that continue to exist in the laws regarding forced population transfers will no doubt seem more persuasive still.

13

Meaning and Memory

Robin Hankey, the Foreign Office Poland specialist and onetime diplomat at the Warsaw embassy, was one of a number of influential Britons to receive an unsolicited letter in the summer of 1947 from his friend and former Foreign Office colleague, Michael Vyvyan. Enclosed with the letter was a report written by a twenty-six-year-old woman who had arrived in Germany six months previously after spending more than eighteen months at the Potulice internment camp in Poland. Detailed, specific, and unemotional, though sometimes wryly humorous (the author noted that the quality of the food perceptibly improved after the camp cook was dispensed with at the end of 1946), the report described the systematic abuse, torture, and malnutrition to which inmates at Potulice and one of its nearby subcamps, Nakło nad Notecią—where she had also briefly been detained—were being subjected. The account carried the ring of truth, and was consistent with many other such testimonies the Western Allies had been receiving about Potulice and similar establishments. In his response to Vyvyan, Hankey did not contest the accuracy of anything he had been told. But neither did he think it especially worthy of notice.

> I agree that the conditions which you describe are horrifying. I should have been much more deeply moved if I had not myself been to the extermination camps at Maidanek and Oswiecim [Auschwitz] and satisfied myself by the evidence available that the Poles are telling the truth when they allege that about 6,000,000 Jews and Poles were exterminated like flies by the Germans. Having seen myself 800,000 pairs of shoes of people who had been murdered (including the shoes of tiny children of two and three) . . . I cannot work up much sympathy for the poor Germans, much as I condemn the way they were treated.[1]

In the immediate postwar era, such a response was typical. What is remarkable is that in the more than sixty years that have passed since the expulsion of the ethnic Germans concluded, it largely remains so. In both popular and scholarly treatments of this episode in European history, the Holocaust has generally provided the context for discussions of the expulsion—or even for deciding, as in Hankey's case, whether it ought to be discussed at all. As a result, it occupies a unique position in contemporary historical and ethical discourse. Among the examples of mass human rights violations of modern times, in no other case has the argument been advanced that acknowledging the fact of its occurrence should be discouraged for fear that doing so might tend to diminish the horror that properly ought to be felt in respect of a still greater crime.

Most certainly, the connection between the expulsions and the Holocaust, as well as to the Hitler regime's numerous other atrocities, is both inescapable and appropriate. To try to separate them would be to run the risk of creating a decontextualized narrative of victimization, in which the suffering of Germans comes to overshadow the still greater sufferings Germans inflicted upon others. But if that is where the discussion must begin, it is far from clear that it must also end there. What Hankey failed to see, like many others since, is that a frame of reference that measures acts of violence and injustice against the supreme atrocity of our time and assesses the former as being unworthy of notice in comparison with the latter makes such violations more rather than less likely to be repeated. Quite apart from the question of what acknowledgment is due to the expellees' painful history, moreover, it makes impossible any discussion of the actions and motivations of the perpetrators, implicitly denying their own full humanity by configuring them as morally and ethically incompetent persons who were incapable of assuming responsibility for their actions. Lastly, it evades the uncomfortable but necessary questions that arise for our own times when we are confronted with the disturbing reality of the starved and beaten men, brutalized women, and terrified children that are necessary components of the psychologically satisfying notions of Old Testament justice, visited upon "enemy" populations, to which we remain instinctively attracted.

How these matters are to be talked about without silencing or rendering invisible any of the protagonists is a problem of great difficulty and sensitivity, and one that few people on either side of the debate addressed or even acknowledged in the half-century following the war. For a brief moment in the late 1990s, it seemed as though it might indeed be overcome. Since then, attitudes have hardened once again, and the current discourse on the question in the spheres of politics and the media has degenerated into a dialogue of the deaf. It is doubtful, however, whether attempts to come to grips with the matter may be safely abandoned for an indefinite time. Forced population transfers are very far from being a thing of the past, and there is a growing number of influential voices who see in them the wave of the future. Whatever may be thought of that prospect, gaining the clearest possible perspective on the most important experiment ever carried out in this field is in any case a matter of considerable importance.

As we have seen, while the transfers were under way a propaganda campaign of considerable scale, if not sophistication, was waged by the expelling countries and their advocates abroad and was countered, though largely ineffectively, by isolated figures in the Western media and in nongovernmental organizations. Once the operation had been completed, however, the urgency of the exchanges diminished. In the United States and Britain, supporters and opponents of the expulsions alike came by the early 1950s to accept them as irreversible faits accomplis. In Czechoslovakia, the Communist government of Klement Gottwald sensibly adopted a policy of inviting as little international attention to the subject as possible, a policy continued by his Stalinist successor, Antonín Novotný. In East Germany, discussion of the expulsions was consigned to the same capacious Orwellian memory hole that accommodated all other aspects of the past the regime found inconvenient. When in 1961 the playwright Heiner Müller, for example, attempted to stage a performance of his *The Resettler Woman, or Life in the Countryside* (*Die Umsiedlerin oder das Leben auf dem Lande*), a tongue-in-cheek depiction of the travails of a pregnant expellee assigned a small farm in the bungled land redistribution scheme of 1945, he and his entire cast were arrested after the opening night. Müller was lucky merely to be expelled from the Writers' Union; his director, B. K. Tragelehn, did not escape so lightly, being "sent to an open-face coal mine for two years to learn about the working class through manual labor."[2]

The West German and Polish states, in contrast, took a considerably more activist and almost wholly destructive stance. In 1952, three years after the establishment of the Federal Ministry for Expellees, Refugees, and War Victims, the Bonn government commissioned the noted University of Cologne historian Theodor Schieder—himself born in East Prussia—to compile a scholarly history of the expulsions, as part of its preelection outreach effort to the *Landsmannschaften*. The appointment was one of those displays of tone-deafness for which the new ministry would later become noted, for the selection of Schieder as lead author could hardly have been a less felicitous choice. Although a talented historian, he had been one of a group of NSDAP members actively engaged in *Ostforschung*, or "Eastern research," during the late 1930s. In this capacity he had collaborated on a research project begun just after the conquest of Poland to "work on the historical preconditions for 'large-scale [German] settlement policy in the

Meaning and Memory

eastern territories.'"[3] Schieder's findings were incorporated into the *Generalplan Ost*, the Nazis' chilling genocidal blueprint for the clearance and resettlement of the conquered lands.[4] Though his part in the drafting of this scheme did not become publicly known until after his death in 1984, that a man who had volunteered his talents to the planning of the ethnic cleansing of Poland should only a few years later be overseeing the production of a history that would be perceived as — and in fact was — an indictment of the very policies in which, on a still more ruthless scale, he himself had been actively involved in devising was, to say the very least, deeply unfortunate.

It was all the more so inasmuch as the work his team produced between 1954 and 1961, the eight-volume *Dokumentation der Vertreibung der Deutschen aus Ost-Mitteleuropa*, was not wholly without historical merit. Some of Germany's most talented young historians, including Martin Brozsat, Hans Mommsen, and Hans-Ulrich Wehler were employed on the project, which was based on the first-person interviews and testimonies collected from eleven thousand expellees from across central Europe. Only seven hundred of these were quoted in the final version, the editors having excluded what they regarded as hostile, unreliable, or biased testimonies. The introductory essays were also, at least for the time, methodologically sophisticated, laying stress on the structural factors underlying the expulsions. Nonetheless, the value of the enterprise was vitiated by a number of shortcomings, of which the morally compromised wartime career of its lead author may not have been the most important. The story it told was not so much factually inaccurate as highly partial, tending to convey a misleading impression by selection and omission. Like the concealment of Schieder's own past, Nazism's black record in the countries of expulsion during the war featured hardly at all. The expulsions were shown through a heavily anticommunist filter, exaggerating the degree to which Soviet initiative and Marxist ideology served as motivating forces in the countries involved. The precise nature of *Volksdeutsch* interactions with the majority populations during the war was elided or ignored altogether. Jews featured as walk-on characters, if they featured at all. Some of the young editors no doubt were themselves unaware of these deficiencies. But for all the horrifying detail the *Dokumentation* provided of the cruelties with which the expulsions were often accomplished, the general accuracy of which there is no reason to doubt, the final result was more a propagandistic exercise than a work of disinterested scholarship.

Within Germany this may not have mattered greatly. The *Dokumentation* was little read at home; sales, as Robert Moeller says, were "dismal."[5] Outside the country, however, the appearance of the work raised the temperature greatly. A condensed version in English was published which, although probably not garnering a significantly larger international readership, was perceived as an attempt to generate foreign support for an actively revisionist German foreign policy. The Polish government responded with a quasi-scholarly counteroffensive of its own. Under the auspices of the Poznań-based Western Press Agency (*Zachodnia Agencja Prasowa*), an avalanche of books and pamphlets in several European languages was released from the mid-1950s onward aimed at discrediting the claims of the *Dokumentation* and similar works; denying that the expulsions from the Recovered Territories had been carried out inhumanely (or, in some versions, that they had even been carried out at all, as opposed to a decision en masse by the German population "of their own accord to flee to the West"); and seeking to show that any questioning of the rightness of the Potsdam Agreement by German commentators was part of a millennium-long *Drang nach Osten*, commencing with the Teutonic Knights and continuing to the present day, that Nazism's defeat had merely temporarily interrupted.[6] It is doubtful whether this polemical literature on what was euphemistically styled the German "repatriation," which was far more successful in poking holes in the *Dokumentation*'s dubious statistical calculations of the number of expellees who had lost their lives during the course of the operation than in providing a convincing defense of the Polish government's record, found many more readers than Schieder's weighty tomes had done.[7] But if they managed to persuade only their respective authors, these dueling histories foreshadowed the rhetorical strategies that would be resorted to by both sides when the question of the expulsions reached a higher level of visibility in the 1990s.

During the 1950s, expulsion-related themes figured commonly, though not prominently, in West German popular culture. In particular the so-called *Heimatfilm* genre offered a means of simultaneously acknowledging and eliding the traumata of the recent past. No less than a fifth of all German cinematic productions in the 1950s, Heide Fehrenbach points out, were *Heimatfilme*.[8] While by no means all of them featured or even referred to the "lost *Heimat*" to the east and south, the symbol of the "homeland" provided a safe, shared terrain on which "Germans" of all varieties, including those most recently arrived, could give expression to their sense of identity and of patriotism without raising taboo political topics.[9] In that respect, the *Heimatfilm* was far more significant for what it omitted than for what was shown. Quasi-documentary scenes of "wild" expulsions, life in a Polish or Czechoslovak internment camp, travel in a crowded goods wagon, rapes, and robberies figured nowhere in these productions. Nor, typically, did expellees who had not been German citizens in 1937. The preferred hero or heroine of the expellee-themed *Heimatfilm* was a native of the old Reich from East Prussia or Pomerania who had fled the advancing Red Army in 1945;

while *Sudetendeutsche* were occasionally favored with minor supporting roles, *Volksdeutsche* from Hungary, Yugoslavia, Romania, or the Baltic states were conspicuous by their absence. So too was the war itself. Rather, the films romanticized and celebrated the process by which refugees from the lost eastern territories, while haunted by their traumatic past, found happiness, love, and material success by reconnecting with the enduring German values of work, community, and attachment to place—albeit a different one from their place of birth.

In a pair of trenchant and highly praised critical analyses of such expressions of German mentalities as the *Heimatfilme*, the Schieder instant histories, the glorification of the surviving prisoners of war who returned from Soviet captivity in the mid-1950s, and the much-read first-person accounts of harrowing expellee ordeals like the Königsberg surgeon Hans von Lehndorff's *Ostpreussisches Tagebuch*, Robert Moeller has argued that the attention paid in West Germany to the plight of expellees during the first postwar decade represented above all the articulation of a "rhetoric of victimization" whose purpose was to craft a "usable past" for a country "peopled with innocents..."[10] A paradoxical element of this self-serving narrative was Germans' insistence that discussion of the expulsions had been a taboo even as the constant reiteration of German suffering caused them to be "incorporated into the founding myths of the Federal Republic..."[11] Other historians have challenged, or at least qualified, this interpretation. Though insisting that "German violence was the cause... for violence against Germans," Frank Biess has pointed out that "narratives of victimization constituted a problematic basis for the reconstruction of male subjectivities and for postwar reconstruction at large."[12] Lacking as they did the possibility of "redemptive resolution," these accounts of "feminized suffering" provided few opportunities for the articulation of a new, shared collective identity—the more so inasmuch as the very Germanness of the incomers from the east and south was so often questioned by indigenes of both postwar Germanies.[13] Svenja Goltermann, too, points out that the recency of the trauma which most Germans had experienced—few, in the 1940s, had not been exposed, whether as soldiers, expellees, or civilians under Allied bombing, to death and the personal risk of dying in particularly unpleasant forms—must be taken into account when drawing conclusions about the nature of German society in the 1950s from what its culture did *not* say.[14] Human psychology does not easily or quickly process profoundly disturbing events; when it does so, it characteristically assigns much greater weight to one's own sufferings than to those of others. While this should not be taken as an excuse for the reluctance of so many Germans to assess critically their individual responsibility for the apocalyptic violence their country had inflicted upon its neighbors, it remains the case that few if any societies have responded to disasters, even (or especially) of their own making, with the kind of immediate self-questioning that Germany's victims, as well as historians today, for entirely understandable reasons would wish to have seen.

Whether kitsch productions like the *Heimatfilme* will bear the weight of interpretation Moeller and others rest upon them, however, there is no question that with the arrival to adulthood in the 1960s of the first generation of Germans to have no personal involvement in the war, the public mood with respect to expellees became distinctly less sympathetic. Even as the war of words between the Bonn and Warsaw governments—and their historian proxies—diminished in intensity in the late 1960s and early 1970s as a result of Willy Brandt's pursuit of *Ostpolitik* with Germany's eastern neighbors and the Federal Republic's de facto recognition of the country's postwar boundaries, discussion of Germans' experience of human rights abuses in the immediate postwar period became more difficult at home. The 1960s generation, increasingly prone to regard its immediate predecessor as "accessories to Nazism," began to ask pointed and highly personalized questions about not just political but moral responsibility for the crimes for which Germans were responsible, and in which the Holocaust for the first time came to assume precedence. The result was a decade-long struggle between what Stefan Berger has called a "victims' discourse" (emphasizing German suffering) and a "perpetrators' discourse" (emphasizing German guilt). It was one that shifted decisively in the latter's favor during the 1970s and 1980s, as historians and intellectuals drawn from this postwar generation "began to investigate ordinary Germans and their everyday support for an inhumane and criminal regime."[15] If the discussion of expulsions was not, as Moeller argues, taboo in the 1950s, certainly twenty years later society in the two Germanies was much less willing to engage in it, or even to listen to it. At best, as Rainer Schulze has perceptively observed, it was "assumed and almost expected that in the course of their successful settling into postwar Germany the refugees and expellees would lose, or 'shed,' not only their old collective identities and mentalities, but also the specific experiences and individual memories they had brought with them from the east and would thus become like the natives."[16] If they did so, some aspects of their history might be acknowledged by the public and the state. But this did not mean that society was interested in or ready to listen to those parts of their story that disrupted the national narrative, especially as the formation of the "Grand Coalition" between the CDU and the Social Democrats in 1966 led to a marked shift in Bonn's policy vis-à-vis Germany's eastern neighbors. An early portent of the changing mood was the coalition's decision in 1967 to abandon publication of a new edition of the *Dokumentation der Vertreibung* and to cancel the public release of thousands of new testimonies held at the Federal Archives in Koblenz, so as not to prejudice the possibility of warmer relations with Warsaw and Prague.[17] According to Eric Langenbacher, this marked the beginning of a wider cultural, as well as political, separation between "progressive" forces in West Germany and the expellee population.

> The Social Democrats and Left abandoned and soon demonized expellee groups, the price to be paid for reconciliation and normalization with Eastern Europe. . . . The [Brandt] government disbanded the expellee ministry, cut funding for expellee activities, and refused to publish a report in 1974 on crimes committed against Germans in the course of the expulsion. The SPD newspaper opined that publication "would only help the Nazis here." Henceforth, leftists equated expellees with revanchist, radical-right, neo-Nazis.[18]

In the English-speaking world, dominant narratives about the nature and meaning of the Second World War and its aftermath left even less space for public acknowledgment, far less discussion, of the episode. The new postwar generation retained no memory whatever of the expulsions, which featured almost nowhere in historical or media treatments of the war. Nor was it anxious to form such memories. Martha Kent, the former child detainee in Potulice, found while a postgraduate student of psychology at the University of Michigan in the early 1960s that even in a cosmopolitan academic environment, the image of wartime Germans in any other category than as perpetrators caused intense discomfiture to her American hosts. Sometimes the anxiety and embarrassment this generated was displaced through inappropriate stereotyping, as when one of her professors "greeted me with a mocking *Sieg Heil!*" More typically, though, she discovered that any reference in the United States to her own experiences would be interpreted by her hearers only as an attempted delegitimization of the sufferings of the true victims of the war. "I could hardly mention my childhood in captivity. On rare occasions when the subject came up, people said that Potulice was 'nothing.' The mere mention of my captivity called forth statements of distress and grief over the atrocities of the Nazi era. That was the harm I should have experienced, some people said. . . . Indeed, I [had] got off lightly." As a result of the rigor with which her silence was socially policed in her new homeland, Kent succumbed to a psychological syndrome not uncommon among those who undergo severe trauma as children, especially when the experience is repressed or denied in adulthood. "By 1985 I found that I had lost all language for myself. I couldn't speak or write anything about myself."[19]

Back in Germany, expellee children were subjected to the same pressure to maintain their lifelong "duty" of silence. While a great deal of sociological angst was expressed in the immediate postwar years about the possible rise of an alienated, "asocial," and conscienceless generation of juvenile delinquents, early postwar studies found that according to most measurable psychological indices, expellee children were almost indistinguishable from their counterparts within the indigenous population. Some authorities, notably Karl Valentin Müller, an anthropologist who had himself been evicted from his home in Prague after the war, inferred from this seemingly extraordinary resilience a Darwinian mechanism at work, in which the "fittest" had emerged from the "struggle for existence." By the 1950s, as a result, expellee children were almost entirely passed over as objects of study or concern, while both Germanies congratulated themselves on the striking success of their integrational capabilities. The symptoms of what later would be recognized as "post-traumatic stress disorder" thus went unrecognized, and by the time some of the children had grown to adulthood and were capable of processing the memories they had almost uniformly repressed—usually so as not to increase the burdens borne by their equally damaged parents or carers— they discovered a society more determined than ever not to hear them. In the words of Volker Ackermann, "from the perspective of '1968' the expulsions were a deserved punishment for '1933.'"[20] These youngest victims' continued silence, therefore, was demanded in a variety of subtle and unsubtle ways in the interest of avoiding a different, but equally unsettling, set of questions about the past that a new generation of Germans desired strongly not to ask.

Almost entirely overlooked at the time, though, was that a similar process of national self-questioning was also taking place in Czechoslovakia and Poland, that from analogous premises began pointing in a different direction. After the crushing of the "Prague Spring" of 1968 and the final dashing of hopes that "Socialism with a human face" was possible within the Soviet empire, young Czechoslovak intellectuals and historians, many of whom would be associated with the Charter 77 dissident movement, set out to address the question of how their country had fallen prey with such ease to the depredations of a second foreign totalitarian domination so soon after having emerged from the clutches of the first. A notable and provocative contribution to this debate was a set of "Theses on the Resettlement of the Czechoslovak Germans," published in samizdat form by the Slovak historian Jan Mlynárik under the pseudonym of "Danubius" in 1977. For Mlynárik, the expulsions had less to do with Czechoslovakia's security or national integrity than with the Czechoslovak government's and people's anxiety not to confront their own ignominious record from Munich until V-E Day. In this interpretation, the "senseless" postwar assault upon the *Sudetendeutsche* was explicable in terms of the population's desire "to compensate for their own [wartime] inactivity, if not collaboration, by identifying themselves with the victors and by their ex post 'heroic feat' directed against the defenseless . . ."[21] This, Mlynárik suggested, was the original sin of the Third Republic that had left it so psychologically vulnerable to Communist and Soviet supremacy. It was also a moral challenge to the current generation of dissidents, who could hardly consistently demand from their own government the unconditional respect for the rights of the individual that the expellees had been denied in 1945 and 1946.

> The call to "liquidate" the Germans was an invitation to carry out a patriotic duty: public executions, burning people as human torches, shooting Germans in broad daylight on the streets of Bohemian and Moravian towns, and, ultimately, inhumane expulsion of people from their homes in the years to follow: all this was a massive, practical, everyday training in contempt for the notion of the human person, his dignity, and his rights as the world's highest value. . . . [A] nation that behaves brutally towards others will itself succumb to the poison of these crimes.[22]

Mlynárik's revisionist theses touched off a furor in Czechoslovakia, and by seeking to acquit the *Sudetendeutsche* of collective guilt provided an ironic counterpoint to those contemporaries of his in West Germany who at precisely the same time were insisting upon it.[23] But his bombshell was only the starting point for a broader onslaught against the moral collapse that he and his followers perceived as following from this negation of the ideals of Masaryk's republic. Communism, an economic system that had systematically expropriated and impoverished the people, was not solely a foreign imposition by the Soviet Union, but the logical consequence of the abdication of fundamental values by the Czechoslovak people in the expulsion-generated "gold rush" of 1945. "The expulsion with its consequences taught the nation no longer to respect either material values, or the principle of property, a value built up over generations. It . . . taught [the nation] to steal on a colossal scale. . . . [T]he theft of property . . . has its root and its origin not only in the introduction of socialism, but, already present here, in the unprecedented despoliation and plundering of the three million Germans."[24]

In Poland, similar though much less influential critiques were also offered, the most notable being the dissident intellectual and future senator Jan Józef Lipski's 1981 essay, the main thrust of which is indicated by its title: "Two Fatherlands—Two Patriotisms: Thoughts on the National Megalomania and Xenophobia of the Poles."[25] As Norman Naimark observes, however, "For most Poles, like the Germans, the immediate postwar period was dedicated to forgetting their own culpability for the horrors of the immediate past. . . . The utter brutality of the wartime period, the petty collaboration, Polish complicity in the occupation, and the indifference among the majority to the murder of the Jews—the many instances when survival trumped morality—were wartime phantoms that were pushed into a deep psychological freezer."[26] It was not entirely surprising, then, that the initiative in Poland to move beyond the defensive national-mythological narratives of the past should have come not, as in Czechoslovakia, from intellectuals, but from the Church. Responding in part to a conciliatory statement on the expulsions and the Polish-German frontier by the German Evangelical Church, the Catholic bishops of Poland, influenced among others by Karol Wojtyła of Kraków, the future Pope John Paul II, addressed a letter to the German episcopate in 1965 that referred obliquely to the expulsions with the words: "We forgive and ask for forgiveness."[27] Although the bishops were accused at home of "nonpatriotic behavior and of acting against Poland's interests,"[28] their acknowledgment of mistakes made did not signify any second thoughts on the part of its authors about the justifiability of the Oder-Neisse line. Bishop Wojtyła himself was in the habit of referring to the western borderlands as the "Recovered Territories"—as, significantly, did Pope John XXIII for the first time in 1962.[29] This is not to deny that the bishops' gesture of reconciliation was important, and that it contributed to the partial thaw that made Brandt's *Ostpolitik* possible. Even so, as Pawel Lutomski reminds us, in Poland "the ideological freeze on any open discussion of the status and manner of the expulsion of the Germans and the Poles [in the east] lasted practically until the changes of 1989."[30] It was not until the unification of Germany and the conclusion of "final status" agreements with its neighbors the following year that psychological space was created for fresh explorations of previously taboo topics. Helmut Kohl's explicit declaration of his desire for "the Poles to live in secure borders" and his assurance that "[t]here will be no Fourth Reich" contributed powerfully to that sentiment. A noteworthy product of the new atmosphere was the undertaking in the 1990s of joint research projects into the causes and consequences of expulsions by teams of German historians working alongside their Polish and Czech counterparts.

By the end of the twentieth century, therefore, the ice floes appeared finally to be melting. In a March 1990 resolution, the Hungarian Parliament described the expulsion of the *Volksdeutsche* from that country as an "unjust action." Though cynics saw in this initiative an attempt by Hungary to revive its own claims against its Czech and Slovak neighbors in respect of the displacement of Hungarians in 1946, the resolution did much to mend bridges between Budapest and Berlin.[31] An address the same month by Václav Havel in one of his first acts as Czechoslovakia's first postcommunist president was even more significant, being widely perceived as a breakthrough in relations with Germany. Critically evaluating the manner in which ethnic Germans had been treated in 1945, Havel acknowledged in terms strikingly similar to those of his erstwhile Charter 77 comrade Ján Mlynárik that "Instead of judging those who had betrayed their nation, we hunted them out of the country, passing a sentence unknown to our jurisprudence. That was no punishment, that was revenge." Havel's statement was widely taken to be an official apology to the expellees, and since then has almost invariably been described as such. According to the president himself, though, it neither was, nor was intended to be, any such thing. As he later remarked, "I used far more diplomatic language and did not directly apologize for anything, one reason being that I had no clear mandate to do so."[32] A close reading of the speech supports Havel's contention—most notably his reference to the "justified, but overstated outrage" of the Czechoslovak people, a formula which implied that the fault lay if anything in denying the guilty parties due process before removing them, as well as his insistence that the Nazis had been responsible for injecting the "bacillus of evil" into the Czechoslovak body politic. The misunderstanding was to have long-lasting and unfortunate consequences, however, because it implied to foreign and especially to German observers a change of mind on the part of the Czech and Slovak peoples and their governments that had not in fact taken place.

Thus when after the "Velvet Divorce" of 1993 the new Czech Republic began preliminary discussions about joining the European Union, Helmut Kohl's government was dismayed by what appeared to be a significant retreat on the part of the Czech president, particularly when contrasted with an apparently more generous Polish stance as represented by an address by the Foreign Minister, Władysław Bartoszewski, to a joint session of the German Parliament.[33] A February 1995 speech by Havel, which referred to a "fatal failure of a large part of our ethnic German citizens" as the true reason for their eventual expulsion differed more in tone than content from what he had said five years previously. Followed as it almost immediately was, though, by the Czech Constitutional Court's finding in the Dreithaler case that the Beneš decrees remained in effect, the contretemps brought about a significant and accelerating deterioration in relations between the two countries. A Czech-German declaration of January 1997, in which each state "deplored" the suffering inflicted upon the other during and after the war, attempted to arrest the downward slide by tiptoeing carefully around what had become a political landmine for both sides. While the aspect that captured the headlines was the two governments' mutual expression of "regret" for the sufferings each other's peoples had undergone in the 1930s and 1940s, a narrow reading of the text, which had been drafted to take maximum advantage of creative ambiguity, permitted the interpretation that the Czech government regretted the "excesses" that had occurred as a result of the expulsions, rather than the deportation of the Germans itself. Even this, though, may have been a concession too far for the Czech people, only 49 percent of whom supported the declaration in an opinion poll.[34] The previous year, indeed, 86 percent of respondents in another survey stated that they would "not vote for a party that supported the issuing of an apology to the Sudeten Germans for the expulsions in the post-war period."[35]

What became clear, in fact, as the 1990s drew to a close was that if it could legitimately be said of the German people that they had still not adequately confronted their wartime past, the same held almost equally true of the populations of the expelling countries. Merely because communism had passed away in central Europe, deeply held convictions about responsibility for the war and for the events that succeeded it had not. It is unlikely that in pressing so hard for statements of regret from its neighbors, the Kohl government ever fully appreciated how deeply the narratives of wartime victimization, martyrdom, and justified retribution had entered into the national mythologies that the central European regimes, their Marxism notwithstanding, had successfully constructed. To a still greater degree even than in the Czech Republic or Slovakia, questions in Poland about collective German guilt ran counter to half a century of official promotion of "Western thinking" (*myśl zachodnia*), as well as to a "Polish-national martyrological paradigm" that "offered Poles an identity based in common suffering . . . and at the same time provided a model of national solidarity that could be projected onto the challenges of reconstructing the Polish state and building socialism."[36] The resilience of these concepts, even after the abandonment of the collectivist nostrums that they had been intended to some degree to reinforce, came as an unwelcome surprise to the new Social Democratic administration of Gerhard Schröder, which in 1998 found itself squeezed between what seemed to be a newly militant stance on the part of the governments of both Poland and the Czech Republic—whose gaffe-prone prime minister, Miloš Zeman, escalated tensions still further with a series of intemperate public statements about the *Sudetendeutsche* having been "traitors" and a "German fifth column"—and a Christian Democratic opposition at home that seemed eager to make the unresolved questions of the past into election issues.

Despite Schröder's attempts to lower the rhetorical temperature by assuring Prague in 1999 that his government would neither allow the Sudeten question to stand in the way of the Czech Republic's accession to the EU nor support any claims made by expellees to restitution of or compensation for confiscated property, the controversy continued to escalate. In part this was the result of a renewed sense of Czech vulnerability in the face of a newly unified, self-confident, and increasingly assertive Germany. Czech insecurity, Karl Cordell and Stefan Wolff remind us, "to an extent... can be explained by simply glancing at a map. The Czech Republic is smaller than some German *Länder*."[37] It was also enhanced by a perception that neighboring countries were joining with Germany in "ganging up" on Prague. All too predictably, then, interventions in 2002 by Hungarian politicians, who demanded that the Czech Republic repudiate the Beneš decrees that had legalized the expropriation of Magyar speakers as well as Germans in 1945, and by the obstreperous and irresponsible far-right Austrian governor of Carinthia, Jörg Haider, merely had the effect of provoking the Parliament in Prague into affirming the decrees' inviolability.

The final straw, so far as Czech and Polish opinion was concerned, was the announcement in 2003 by Erika Steinbach, a Christian Democratic member of the Bundestag and leader of the *Bund der Vertriebenen* (Expellee League), that a "Center Against Expulsions" would be opened in Berlin to draw attention to the problem of forced migrations in the modern world. Steinbach had established a foundation for this purpose in 2000, but failed to secure public funding. She now made it clear that the initiative would go ahead regardless, using private money. Once again, the timing was inauspicious. Ever since the controversy over the Beneš decrees in the mid-1990s, German commentators in and out of politics had not troubled to conceal their opinion that the Polish and Czech peoples and governments were some distance behind Germany in their willingness to confront the disturbing aspects of their own recent pasts and now needed to make up the lost ground—advice that the recipients keenly resented.[38] Alarm was added to anger in Poland when an expellee trust organization, the *Preussische Treuhand*, was founded in 2001 to pursue expropriated expellees' restitution claims through the European courts. The appearance of two bestselling books the following year—Günter Grass's novel *Im Krebsgang* (*Crabwalk*), which referred allusively but sympathetically to the expellees, and Jörg Friedrich's *Der Brand* (*The Fire*), an accusatory history of the Allied strategic bombing campaign against German cities in the Second World War—added fuel to the flames. These works betokened, in the view of many foreign observers, a renewed obsession with the image of the innocent and victimized wartime German, and an indifference to the sensibilities of those who had suffered at his or her hands. Steinbach's announcement, and the first intimations that the Center Against Expulsions might be located in close proximity to the Holocaust Memorial in Berlin, seemed to many Poles and Czechs who already considered themselves under a state of psychological siege to be final confirmation that powerful German politicians were intent on using the expulsions as a means to whitewash their own country's disgraceful wartime record as well as to advance financial, and perhaps even territorial, claims against the victims of Nazi Germany.

The response was a firestorm of criticism in both Poland and the Czech Republic directed against the project, Steinbach herself, and the German government. The philosopher Leszek Kołakowski, who as a child had been forcibly displaced and terrorized by German soldiers after the invasion of Poland in 1939, noted acidly that in his country's wartime experience "robbery and deportation were not things that were worthy of commemoration; they were merely the prelude to the occupation."[39] Marek Edelman, the last surviving commander of the Warsaw Ghetto rising in 1943, denounced the Center as a "nationalist and chauvinist" initiative that represented little more than "a thinly disguised return to the idea of *Drang nach Osten*."[40] *Wprost*, a Warsaw newsweekly, featured on its cover a photomontage depicting a uniformed and jackbooted Steinbach, wearing a swastika armband, straddling a submissive Chancellor Schröder.[41] The reverberations of the controversy continued to echo in the years that followed, especially after the conciliatory Polish president, Aleksander Kwaśniewski, who had once been guest of honor at a German expellees' meeting in the town of Elbląg, was succeeded in 2005 by the populist and moderately Germanophobe Lech Kaczyński.[42] In his election campaign, Kaczyński promised to seek reparations in the amount of €54 billion from Germany in respect of Poland's wartime losses; two years later the president's party, *Prawo i Sprawiedliwość* (Law and Justice) sponsored a parliamentary resolution asserting that "Responsibility [for the war] must be borne by the entire German people, the great majority of which supported Hitlerism and accepted Hitler's rule."[43] In Germany itself, Micha Brumlik of the University of Frankfurt pronounced that supporters of the Center Against Expulsions were guilty of "a deliberate historical naïveté that assumes that in the year 1943 and thereafter, proper postwar planning based on human rights would in fact have been possible."[44]

In recent years, the volume of rhetoric over the expulsions has begun to stabilize somewhat, albeit at its current elevated level of hostility and mutual suspicion. The government of Christian Democrat Angela Merkel, which ascended to power in 2005 initially in a coalition arrangement with Gerhard Schröder's Social Democrats, expressed some support for the Center Against Expulsions project. Born in East Germany where reference to the events of the immediate postwar years had indeed been a taboo subject, Merkel was sympathetic to the argument of expellees that their voices had gone unheard for too long. The coalition's manifesto, as a result, declared the two parties' desire to see a "visible sign" of some kind in commemoration of the expulsions appear in Berlin. At the same time, Merkel insisted that the kind of memorial at which the Center aimed was acceptable to her only in circumstances in which "not only German expellees and refugees but others too, of course Polish expellees also, can commemorate their suffering and when one thing in particular is clear: there is to be no reinterpretation of history by Germany."[45] At the end of 2008, the government agreed that the project should be publicly funded and placed under the oversight of the German Historical Museum Foundation—in all likelihood to ensure that Germany's international reputation, which would be implicated in the undertaking in any event, should not be exposed to the risk of injudicious comments or actions by the expellee groups. The Center, it was decided, would be located at the site of the former Anhalter railway station in east-central Berlin, a point of arrival for many thousands of expellees from Poland in 1945.

If there has been one positive result from the polemics of recent years, it has been that the expellees themselves are no longer "viewed by the rest of German society as backward-looking, even crypto-Fascist."[46] There are welcome signs that the expulsions, once regarded as a question of interest only to the Right, may cease to become a political football between the parties. A number of prominent figures on the German left, including Peter Glotz, Daniel Cohn-Bendit, and Helga Hirsch, were outspoken supporters of the Center Against Expulsions, while leading politicians like Otto Schily of the Social Democrats and Antje Vollmar of the Greens have acknowledged that they and their fellow Germans who had "looked away from the crimes of the expulsions" out of discomfort or a sense that the scale of German wartime atrocities made them unmentionable by comparison had failed to do justice either to the expellees themselves or to history.[47] The retirement from active politics in September 2010 of Erika Steinbach—a polarizing figure, if one without whom the Center Against Expulsions would probably never have come into being—may mark the point at which the question of how this episode is to be remembered ceases primarily to be a political one, and begins to be taken up seriously, as it should, by historians and scholars.

As Hans Rothfels—a figure who himself exemplifies the complexity and paradoxicality of the expulsions—put it more than half a century ago, the only context in which the history of this era can be told is "in its horrifying totality." A distinguished historian of Jewish antecedents, Rothfels was forced to flee Germany for his life after his arrest during *Kristallnacht* in 1938; fifteen years later, when he returned from exile, he was to lend his talents to the *Dokumentation der Vertreibung* project. The many commentators, both at home and abroad, who fear that the Center Against Expulsions project might easily degenerate into an exercise in German self-pity or a display of decontextualized atrocity stories have valid concerns that ought not to be dismissed. There are no logical or moral grounds for privileging the history of the postwar expulsions over that of the as yet uncommemorated massive expulsions by Germans of Poles and other *Untermenschen* during the war, far less over the memory of the millions of Jews, Soviets, and others who lost their lives in the course of Germany's demented wartime killing sprees. Rather, the focus of any historical or commemorative treatment of the expulsions, as with the other and greater tragedies of the era, must remain squarely on the human person, which both in 1939–45 and 1945–47 was reduced to an abstract category rather than recognized as an all too vulnerable individual. As Stefan Wolff rightly says, this is "a debate that should essentially be about reconciliation and forgiveness."[48] The closer the debate approaches that ideal, and the more energetically it works to oppose "a culture built around mutual recrimination and one-sided interpretations of the past," the more likely it is to do justice to all those who, during and after the war, were treated by the governments exercising control over them not as persons "born free and equal in dignity and rights," but merely as instruments, representatives, or proxies of the collectivities to which they were declared to belong.[49]

Conclusion

Late in 1947, as the organized expulsions of Germans were coming to an end, the Allied Control Council—Germany's temporary four-power government—invited its Prisoners of War and Displaced Persons Directorate to undertake a study of "the whole question of the transfers of population into Germany," for the purpose of determining how these might better be managed in the future. The response of the U.S. officials who had administered the transfers was not long in coming. On the basis of their experience gained in organizing, supervising, and dealing with the impact of mass expulsions,

> we recommend that the Control Council declare its opposition to all future compulsory population transfers, particularly the forcible removal of persons from places which have been their homes for generations, and that the Control Council refuse, in the future, to accept into Germany any persons so transferred, excepting only repatriated German prisoners of war and persons who were formerly domiciled in Germany.
>
> In formulating this recommendation . . . we have considered the moral and humanitarian aspect of the injustices done to masses of people when an element of a population is forcibly uprooted from long-established homes, has its property expropriated without redress, and is superimposed upon another population already suffering from hunger, insufficient shelter, lack of productive employment and want of social, medical and educational institutions. We have considered that any course of action other than that recommended above would be to invite just condemnation on grounds of economic, social and religious injustices to the persons being transferred, to the present population of Germany and to the populations of nations surrounding Germany.[1]

Their British counterparts had already arrived at a similar conclusion. If any future changes should be made to Germany's frontiers at a peace conference, they declared, a rule should be laid down that "Any territories which may be taken over from Germany . . . [must be] taken over with the whole population living there at the present time."² For the Anglo-Americans, then, enthusiasm for the potentialities of forcible transfer of peoples did not survive its encounter with reality. As the U.S. authorities discovered, this had not lived up to its billing as a quick, clean, and final method of dealing with minority problems. Rather, it turned out that "a tremendous economic and social burden ha[d] been transferred" along with the people, and a job that the expelling governments had finished "is really just beginning for us."³

Subsequent scholarship has borne out the Western Allies' rueful postwar verdict. While the supposed benefits of mass expulsions remained nebulous, the costs were all too apparent. On the most conservative of estimates, hundreds of thousands of expellees—most of whom, if they conformed to the demographic profile of the transferred population as a whole, were women and children—had lost their lives. Millions more were reduced to penury, without the assets they had lost necessarily enriching those who had taken possession of them. The economies of entire regions were disrupted, and two-thirds of a century later the damage done has not yet been repaired. The legacy of bitterness, recrimination, and mutual suspicion between Germany and her neighbors to the east and south has lasted as long, and shows no signs of diminishing in the immediate future.

In light of these facts, it seems extraordinary that the expulsions can still today find scholarly defenders prepared to assert that however inhumane they proved to be, they were nonetheless justified by their results. Three arguments are commonly advanced. In the first, hatred of the *Volksdeutsche* by their non-German neighbors is claimed to have reached such a pitch by 1945 that a radical separation was unavoidable if their wholesale massacre was to be prevented. In the second, their removal is credited with having prevented further European conflicts. And in the third, the ethnic Germans are said to have been properly deported as a just act of punishment for their atrocious conduct prior to and during the war. None of these stands up well in the face of detailed examination.

The "inevitability" thesis is the one most often propounded, probably because it avoids difficult questions about the morality or wisdom of the operation by explaining it as the product of a unique historical situation which can only be judged on its own terms. "It is hard to imagine, in 1945," the historian Włodzimierz Borodziej has recently opined, "any realistic alternatives to the displacement of the Germans."⁴ Why this should have been so was stated baldly by Edward Taborsky, Beneš's legal counselor and later Czechoslovak ambassador to Sweden, in a letter to the *Times* in 1944. The Czechoslovak and Polish peoples, he declared, "simply will not tolerate any longer the presence of any large German minority in their states." For these people to remain would expose them to "extermination" and at best to a period of "prolonged oppression. Thus even on ethical grounds it is better—for the German minorities themselves—to accept the method of the transfer."[5] Beneš himself offered the same justification when he warned a *Times* journalist in March 1945 that "The alternative [to expulsions] would not be humane. It would be a pity if we were penalized for being civilized."[6] The reasoning behind this argument is, to say the least, curious. When, to look no further for an example, Muslims were being driven out of northern and eastern Bosnia in 1992 because of the local Serb majority's resolve no longer to abide their presence, few non-Serb voices could be found to suggest that the operation was defensible on both practical and moral grounds because it would at least prevent their physical annihilation. Michael Ignatieff, who observed a later invocation of the "inevitability thesis" by all sides during the Yugoslav civil wars, explains that its seductiveness and popularity derives precisely from its function as "a moral vocabulary of self-exoneration." Because of the greater crimes of the other side, ethical questions do not arise and "all action is compelled by tragic necessity. . . . Because the other side started it first. Because the other side are beasts and understand no language but violence and reprisal. And so on. Everyone in a nationalist war speaks in the language of fate, compulsion, and moral abdication."[7]

The claim that no power on earth could have compelled the majority populations to acquiesce in the continued presence in their midst of the ethnic Germans has been asserted by its proponents as though it were a self-evident proposition, carrying conviction by mere assertion. This is remarkable inasmuch as the weight of the evidence that exists points in the opposite direction. Contrary to overheated wartime predictions that a bloodbath would ensue in Poland, Czechoslovakia, and elsewhere the moment the tables were turned, the aftermath of V-E Day witnessed practically no spontaneous violence against Germans at all. The only noteworthy exception, the hunting of Germans through the streets of Prague on May 10, 1945, took place in the exceptional context of a bloody popular rising of which the killings of civilians were essentially a continuation. Even these soon came to an end. Only two significant episodes in which the initiative for violence against the Germans came from below occurred thereafter: the Brno "death march" a full three weeks later, and the Ústí nad Labem massacre a month after that. Both occurred, moreover, in circumstances in which soldiers and police not only took no action to preserve law and order, but themselves joined forces with and assisted those who undermined them. While massive violence and terror were part and parcel of the expulsions, they were overwhelmingly the work of agents of the state, acting under orders. Indeed, there is much more documentary evidence, especially in Czechoslovakia, of policemen and soldiers complaining about ordinary citizens' failure to perceive the importance of proceeding ruthlessly and decisively against the Germans than of the need to restrain them. That so little spontaneous violence took place, even after the Czechoslovak people had been exposed to months of radio broadcasts from government ministers in London some of which are uncomfortably reminiscent of the transmissions of Radio Mille Collines in Rwanda half a century later, suggests that central Europeans' powers of self-control were rather greater than they are normally credited with possessing. Furthermore, by 1947, in both Czechoslovakia and Poland, the respective governments moved from an expulsionist to an assimilationist solution for their remaining German minorities, even to the point of forbidding them to leave and fastening local citizenship upon them—in many cases against their will.[8] There is nothing to suggest that these elements of the German population differed from their expelled counterparts in terms of their wartime records; in most cases, the only criterion cited for permitting (or compelling) them to remain was their usefulness to the postwar Czechoslovak or Polish economies. Yet their continued presence failed to generate violence or even significant protest from their immediate neighbors, once again indicating that much of this "uncontrollable" popular hatred on the part of majority populations was in practice more easily contained than is usually alleged.

In addition, the subsequent histories of these countries hardly leads to the conclusion that they had suddenly become ungovernable or unmanageable. In each of them, an unrepresentative and unpopular communist régime was quickly established in the late 1940s without provoking any violent response at all. The notion that central Europeans would not under any circumstances tolerate the presence of Germans but could easily be brought to acquiesce in the elimination of their national sovereignty, the eradication of their human rights and civil liberties, the extinction of their claim to the inviolability of their persons and properties, and their subjection to a quasi-totalitarian foreign overlordship, if true, raises urgent problems of interpretation of the extraordinary workings of these societies that historians have not even begun to address, far less resolve.

The frequently reiterated assertion that the clearance of German populations from Poland, Czechoslovakia, and Hungary has in some way prevented the outbreak of World War III is a proposition so obviously false as hardly to deserve rebuttal. What made for peace in Europe was a lengthy occupation of Germany by both superpowers, which in itself offers a complete explanation of why, so long as it continued, no danger was to be apprehended from that quarter. The successful rehabilitation of the German political system, the inculcation of democratic habits and instincts among the people, and the binding together of postwar Germany within a larger European union are nearly as important factors in the transformation that has taken place in the character of European nation-state interactions since 1945. In these circumstances, the continuing presence of significant ethnic German minorities in Italy, Romania, Hungary, and Russia has not threatened the peace of the continent. There is no reason to suppose that if others had remained in their ancestral homelands a greater menace was to be apprehended.

Lastly, the suggestion that the ethnic Germans were, as presumed fifth columnists before the war or eager Nazi collaborators during it, especially if not uniquely deserving of punishment is no easier to sustain. As we have seen, a rule specifying a minority nationality's unconditional duty of loyalty to a state to which it has been unwillingly attached that can be depended upon to vindicate the Czech or Slovak nation's stance in 1918 and to condemn that of the *Sudetendeutsche* twenty years later is difficult to formulate. As for their wartime record, evidence is scanty that it was any worse than, or different from, that of the German people as a whole. Unquestionably that is quite bad enough, and I should not wish to be interpreted as contending otherwise. But even if all Germans, ethnic or Reich citizens, were equally guilty, not all Germans were equally severely punished. Why the *Volksdeutsche*, who if the worst that can be said about them is true came late to Nazism, should have been imprisoned, expropriated, and deported when the people of the country that originated Nazism and exported it abroad by the most brutal means suffered none of these things is hard to square with notions of strict and impartial justice.

More to the point, it conveniently elides the wartime record of the majority populations, which itself did not always bear close examination. Many Slovaks, for example, bore little less responsibility for the dissolution of Czechoslovakia after the Munich Conference than did the Sudeten Germans. For most of the Second World War, Slovakia was a German client state; Slovak troops took part in the invasion of Poland alongside their German allies in September 1939, and of the Soviet Union in June 1941. With only a single dissenting voice in the Slovak parliament, the great majority of the country's Jewish population was expelled to German-controlled territory, from which only a comparative handful returned alive. Yet few Slovaks were punished after the war for these offenses, and none expelled. Besides, at a more mundane level the postwar meaning of "collaboration" was highly variable, with the same actions—or inactions—attracting either official toleration or condign penalties based on one's ethnicity. During the Great War of 1914–18, J. R. Sanborn points out, some of the inhabitants of central and southeastern Europe "held affinities for one occupying force or another . . . but most people wisely tried to keep their heads down, to stay out of danger when they could, and, when all else failed, to run away. Nothing got you on the end of a rope faster than taking sides in a fluid war with an uncertain outcome."[9] In the Second World War also, this inglorious but time-tested formula for survival was the most popular strategy practiced by ethnic Germans, Czechs, Poles, Hungarians, and most other peoples who were given the opportunity to do so by their Nazi overlords, or, in eastern Poland between 1939 and 1941, their scarcely less vicious Stalinist counterparts.[10] (Tragically, it was an option denied to Jews, Sinti, and Roma.) For only the Germans, though, was it adjudged a "passive war crime" at the end of the conflict.

That such a thing may indeed exist—or at the least, that silence in the face of evil confers a degree of moral culpability—is a suggestion not readily to be dismissed. Christianity is by no means the only creed to speak of "sins of omission" as decisions that must in the end be answered for. But as Victor Gollancz, Dorothy Buxton, and others pointed out, this is a doctrine that cuts both ways. The responsibility of Nazi-era Germans for the actions of their government must not be ignored or forgotten. But between 1945 and 1947, and in some places still later, central Europeans saw their German neighbors—almost all of whom were noncombatants, more than half of whom were female, and many of whom were children—made to wear identifying badges that marked them out for maltreatment; arbitrarily detained in camps and prisons; beaten, raped, or killed with official acquiescence; denied food, medical treatment, and other normal amenities of existence; despoiled; and, in the end, deported. Those who witnessed these scenes had seen them before in the recent past, and knew what they meant. Yet it cannot be said that they were vociferous in their condemnation of such actions, even though they ran few personal risks in doing so. In some parts of Czechoslovakia in the summer of 1945, to be sure, it was an offense, punishable by a fine of up to Kčs 5,000 ($100) or imprisonment for up to two weeks, to intervene on behalf of Germans.[11] But this was not a very draconian punishment, nor was it in force in most places and at most times. No concentration camps awaited those very few Czechoslovaks, like Přemysl Pitter, who found the scenes with which they were confronted on a daily basis incompatible with their consciences. In the event, though, the threat of public condemnation or social ostracism was more than sufficient to persuade doubters to keep their qualms and scruples to themselves.

If this was true of Poles or Czechs, who had at all events the recent memory of German occupation, in all its cruelty and terror, with which to draw comparisons, it was still more true of the Western Allies, whose legal and moral responsibility for what occurred has far too often gone overlooked. One of the most disturbing aspects of the expulsions is how little those Britons and Americans directly involved in their oversight were disturbed by them. The Anglo-Russian journalist Stefan Schimanski, who took second place to no one in his condemnation of Germany and indeed of Germans during the war, was one of the few to go to see for himself the squalid reality of Operation Swallow in progress in the British zone during the spring of 1946. After witnessing the conditions in which the Polish authorities had transported the expellees of the first Swallow train to arrive at Pöppendorf, he recalled, "when I sat in the officers' mess at the camp I could not quite grasp all that had happened. I knew that no S.S. could have outdone such a performance . . . 'What I cannot understand,' I said to the officers sitting at the table, 'is who would have lost if another two carriages had been added to the trains. Or a couple of hundred people taken off the train? Who would have gained one way or the other?'"[12] A few weeks later, Schimanski came across a British soldier "supervising the evacuation of expellees at Travemünde [who] said it was the 'beastliest job' he had ever been asked to do."[13] Such a reaction was exceptional. More typical was the response of Lieutenant Colonel Growse, head of the British Liaison Team at Kalawsk, who upon being relieved in May 1946 wrote of the fond memories he and his soldiers had of the part they had played in the operation. "We shall look back on it as an intensely interesting experience."[14] The thought that they might have taken part in anything morally compromising, far less monstrous, never crossed his mind. The same was not quite true of the chief expulsion officer of the U.S. Army in Czechoslovakia, Colonel John Fye, who wrote that the operation in which he had taken part "could not avoid being cruel in many respects" and drew in "innocent people who had never raised so much as a word of protest against the Czechoslovak people." Women and children, he testified, were routinely "thrown into assembly camps, many of which were little better than the ex-German concentration camps."[15] Yet these stirrings of unease did not prevent Fye from accepting a decoration from the Prague government for his valuable services "in expelling Germans from Czechoslovakia."[16] In the end he, and other bureaucrats and technocrats involved in planning and executing the operation, took refuge in a form of the "instrumental reason" described by Max Horkheimer and Theodor Adorno—coincidentally, at the very moment the expulsions were at their height.[17]

The moral and ethical questions raised by the population transfers are exceptionally complex and difficult, and it is not possible to deal with them exhaustively here. But it is clear that many among the Allied leaderships and peoples derived a degree of vicarious satisfaction from the anguish the expellees were undergoing. They also regarded the deliberately cruel way in which the expulsions were often conducted as not only forgivable but cathartic for the expelling societies themselves—of which Major Denis Healey's lip-smacking anticipation at the 1945 Labour Party Conference of the ordeals the Germans were soon to endure was a typical expression. There is no doubt, as David Curp has said, that the spectacle of "the *Herrenvolk* themselves (or at least their women, children and elderly) being driven from their homes in misery provided a certain grim satisfaction for many Poles who had endured years of racially motivated contempt (punctuated by terror and grief) from their Nazi occupiers."[18] But grievously as these societies had been physically and psychically wounded by their experience of Nazi occupation, the suggestion that they could recover their collective self-esteem only by way of a display of their own capacity for violence and injustice is both psychologically unsound and ethically bankrupt.

If the theory of cathartic cruelty does not hold water logically or morally, still less does it do so legally. Arguably the most objectionable of the legislative instruments handed down at the time of the expulsions was Czechoslovakia's Law No. 115 of 1946, which retroactively legalized "just reprisals for actions of the [German] occupation forces and their accomplices... even when such acts may otherwise be punishable by law." This statute remains in force to the present day; its effect is to block investigation, far less prosecution or punishment, of any of the thousands of murders, tortures, and rapes perpetrated against Germans prior to October 28, 1945. Disturbingly, the Frowein opinion of 2002, while conceding in unusually frank language that Law No. 115 was "a blatant violation of the guaranty of human rights, the rule of law and the obligation of the state to protect all individuals on its territory against violence," went on to argue on the basis of the "cathartic cruelty" principle that whether or not it was repealed, the immunity it offered perpetrators should continue in effect. "It should of course be added immediately," the Frowein opinion said, "that this legislation was adopted after a long period of harsh occupation during which many civilians had been brutally murdered or injured." Most of the German perpetrators had escaped justice for their part in these crimes. Nobody, for example, had ever been prosecuted for the Lidice massacre. To be sure, if one of those responsible were to be identified today, it would be appropriate to prosecute him even at this late date. The Frowein opinion, however, doubted that "people who have committed crimes more than 50 years ago should now stand trial after they have had the confidence throughout their life that they could not be prosecuted for such crimes." Again, it emphasized that what made the two situations different was that abuses directed against Germans "were actions in reaction to what had happened to the Czechoslovak population by Germans between 1938 and 1945. Although most of the victims were innocent it cannot be overlooked that the violence committed against

Germans at that time was in particular a reaction to what had happened during German occupation."[19]

This, however, cannot be correct. In the first place, without in any way understating the immensely traumatic effect of the German occupation, it is far from self-evident that the violent, abusive, and even sadistic behavior of so many Czechoslovaks—and citizens of any of the other expelling states—toward defenseless civilians from 1945 onward was indeed an expression of a completely extraneous impulse that could neither be resisted nor controlled. In the second, the proposition that culpability for gross human rights abuses is reduced or eliminated by the perpetrators' prior experience of victimization would open almost all such episodes to similar pleas in mitigation. The Nazis themselves, indeed, routinely claimed that their atrocities were justified acts of retaliation for previous injuries they had suffered at the hands of their enemies: the continuation of the Allied blockade after the Great War, which had resulted in many civilian deaths; discrimination or persecution of German minorities in neighboring countries between the wars; and so forth. These arguments have rightly been dismissed as self-serving rationalizations. Lastly, to suggest that some grave offenses under international law ought not to be investigated or prosecuted because of one's sympathy for the perpetrators and/or lack of sympathy for the victims is to embark along a very dangerous path. To do so can only lead to a two-tier system of justice, in which crimes against those with whom we identify are sternly punished and similar offenses against those with whom we do not are excused, minimized, or ignored. Such a practice is not in fact a system of justice at all, but its negation.

In this context, attempts by commentators like Elazar Barkan to assign German expellees to what he describes as "the category of less deserving victims, or even undeserving victims" have particularly troubling ramifications.[20] Claims especially by *Sudetendeutsch* expellees for public acknowledgment of their past trauma are in his view "part of a long term effort in Germany to gain parity through suffering, by decontextualising and ahistoricising the victims."[21] To prevent such an outcome from occurring, Barkan raises the possibility of treating "undeserving victims" as groups "whose suffering must be accepted as part of the historical process," and in respect of whose ill-treatment "the obligation of amends or of reparation" ought not to apply.[22] A compelling argument can undoubtedly be made that attempts at this remove in history to reverse the consequences of the expulsions and expropriations would only have the effect of adding new injustices to old ones. And there is every justification for continuing watchfulness to ensure that the history of the expulsions shall not be exploited, now or at any time in the future, for the purpose of minimizing or obscuring the far more horrific atrocities for which Germany in the 1940s bears sole responsibility. But Barkan offers no indication of how his definition of the category of "undeserving victim," who according to this formulation may be abused or killed on the basis of their shared nationality or ethnicity with evildoers without incurring "the obligation of amends or of reparation," is to be reconciled with any meaningful conception of human rights. Even less clear is the means by which this putative two-tiered concept of human worth is to be confined safely to the sphere of the historical past, and not made the basis for equally invidious distinctions between peoples in the present.

That these are not purely academic questions but ones with continuing relevance for our own time is demonstrated by the recent revival of interest in mass population transfers, and the postwar expulsions in particular, as providing a way out of intractable minority problems. The most widely read expression of this school of thought is a 1996 manifesto by a Boston University political scientist, Andrew Bell-Fialkoff, that seeks to prove that whether we like it or not, mass expulsions do provide a permanent solution, particularly in situations where everything else has failed and "'the grim necessity of a population transfer,' in Beneš's words, is the only remaining option." And indeed, for Bell-Fialkoff the removal of Germans from Czechoslovakia stands as the preeminent example of both the practicability and the effectiveness of this method of solving international or intranational disputes: "It goes without saying that the transfer has to be conducted in a humane, well-organized manner, like the transfer of Germans from Czechoslovakia by the Allies in 1945–47."[23]

Unsurprisingly, the bibliography of Bell-Fialkoff's book contains not a single title in the Czech or German languages; his total neglect of these sources no doubt accounts for his ability to sustain this remarkable characterization of what occurred in the Czechoslovak borderlands after the war. But he is far from alone in seeing this episode as providing a model to be followed by others. The Czech prime minister, Miloš Zeman, did so in 2002 when he commended the deportation of the *Sudetendeutsche* to the attention of the Israeli government in its approach to the problem of the West Bank and Gaza.[24] Avigdor Lieberman, the Israeli deputy premier, is already on record as supporting a somewhat milder version of this program, in which Israeli Arabs are to be stripped of their citizenship and transferred to the jurisdiction of the Palestinian Authority against their will in the interest of what is professed to be the greater good. Elsewhere, John Mearsheimer of the University of Chicago has argued the political residue of the former Yugoslavia can only be stabilized by "drawing new borders and transferring populations." The UN, backed by the United States, he contends, should compulsorily relocate about a million Bosniaks, Serbs, and Croats to create "ethnically homogeneous states" in the Balkans. "Wouldn't it make better sense," he asked, "to move populations peacefully rather than at the end of a rifle barrel?"[25] In a similar vein, James Nickel of the University of Miami has attempted to introduce a distinction between "genocidal ethnic cleansing" on the one hand, and forced population transfers that are "motivated by a sincere desire for a stable peace" on the other. The latter, he suggests, can be regarded as "providing the outline of an exception clause in an international norm prohibiting ethnic cleansing," and, notwithstanding the "coercion or force involved," should be considered acceptable "if there were a compelling purpose and no major human rights violations or other major moral obstacles were present."[26] Chaim Kaufmann, Bruce Clark, Daniel Byman, and Michael Mann are other prominent scholars who argue for the continuing relevance of mass expulsions to international conflict resolution, often—as in Kaufmann's case—by sedulously avoiding any mention, far less consideration, of their disastrous record in postwar central Europe.[27] From the other side of the aisle, Stephen Ryan has subjected these proposals for "utopian engineering" to a searching critique. "Far from being a way of avoiding violence, it is difficult not to see 'preventive resettlement' as a violent act in its own right." Nor is it obvious, he cogently observes, that forced population transfers conducted by an international authority must necessarily be more humane or effective than those carried out by individual states.[28]

As the episodes examined in this book show, however, the weightiest objection to population transfers as an instrument of international policy is more fundamental yet. In a nutshell, expulsions are not practicable unless they are carried out quickly; and if they are carried out quickly, they cannot be carried out humanely. Even under the best conditions imaginable, as the British Inter-Departmental Committee report made clear in 1944, mass expulsions are second only to wars in the dislocation, economic upheaval, and social unrest that they produce. Conducting them according to "orderly and humane" criteria is immensely costly and requires many years, if not decades, to accomplish. Once they have been completed, they must be continuously policed for an even longer period to ensure that the displaced population does not seek to return.

These are not, however, the circumstances in which demands for population transfers arise in the real world. Firstly, they are proposed not in an environment of peace and stability but in circumstances of crisis, when the perceived need for rapid and radical solutions is paramount. Secondly, when deciding who must be transferred and who is to be allowed to remain, they invariably involve a search for a scapegoat: "troublesome" minorities are the ones that must leave, not sympathetic ones. Thirdly, national governments and international organizations are rarely interested in diverting the massive amounts of money, logistical facilities, and personnel that are required, for as long as may be required, to succor "troublesome" peoples who are perceived as being at least in part the authors of their own misfortunes. Fourthly, if a transfer is not accomplished quickly, the crisis—and, still more importantly, the hostility toward the targeted population—that gave rise to it is apt to diminish or disappear. This is true of even the bitterest conflicts: it is impossible to conceive of the Western Allies, for example, giving their sanction to a mass clearance of the ethnic Germans if the proposal had been made to them in 1950 rather than 1945. Fifthly, the expelled population is unlikely in all circumstances to acquiesce as tamely in its own removal as did the Germans after the Second World War, or to cease pressing for a "right of return"; indeed, it is arguable that it was only because the experience of living under a totalitarian system had already so grievously weakened the capacity for political organization of the expellees that the operation was made possible in the first place. Finally, as David Curp points out, quite apart from their disruptive economic consequences population transfers are no panacea for the expelling countries themselves. Rather, they are dangerously disruptive expedients whose baleful effects live on in the supposedly "purified" national community, decades after the crisis that gave rise to them has passed.

> The immediate suffering produced by ethnic cleansing is appalling, but is not necessarily its most dangerous effect. An equally, if not more, disturbing aspect of ethnic cleansing is its capacity to generate a self-perpetuating radicalization and popularization of nationally revolutionary politics.
>
> Nationally revolutionary ethnic cleansing . . . led to [the] embrace of xenophobic politics. It also indoctrinated successive generations with extremist nationalism. . . . Ethnic cleansing is a fearfully stabilizing force, capable of sustaining the hatreds and fears that ethnic conflicts generate long after expulsions have been carried out. Instead of being a "clean sweep," ethnic cleansing is a nationally revolutionary force *par excellence* that reinforces the national foundations of ethnic conflicts it appears to destroy.[29]

The most important lesson of the expulsion of the Germans, then, is that if these operations cannot be carried out under circumstances in which brutality, injustice, and needless suffering are inevitable, they cannot be carried out at all. A firm appreciation of this truth, and a determination to be guided by it at all times and in every situation, however enticing the alternative may momentarily seem, is the most appropriate memorial that can be erected to this tragic, unnecessary, and, we must resolve, never to be repeated episode in Europe's and the world's recent history.

NOTES

INTRODUCTION

1. T. Petersen, *Flucht und Vertreibung aus Sicht der deutschen, polnischen und tschechischen Bevölkerung* (Bonn: Stiftung Haus der Geschichte der Bundesrepublik Deutschland, 2005), p. 62.

CHAPTER 1. THE PLANNER

1. *The Times*, October 7, 1938.
2. H. Nicolson, *Peacemaking 1919* (Boston: Houghton Mifflin, 1938), p. 279.
3. Quoted in M. J. Heimann, *Czechoslovakia: The State that Failed* (New Haven, CT: Yale University Press, 2009), p. 47.
4. J. W. Bruegel, *Czechoslovakia Before Munich: The German Minority Problem and British Appeasement Policy* (Cambridge: Cambridge University Press, 1973), p. 65.
5. R. Jakobson, "Problems of Language in Masaryk's Writings," in J. Novák, ed., *On Masaryk: Texts in English and German* (Amsterdam: Rodipi, 1988), pp. 72–3.
6. R. Vansittart, *Manchester Guardian*, April 15, 1944.
7. See J. Bradley, "Czechoslovakia: External Crisis and Internal Compromise," in D. Berg-Schlosser and J. Mitchell, eds., *Conditions of Democracy in Europe, 1919–39: Systematic Case Studies* (Basingstoke, Hampshire: Palgrave Macmillan, 2000), esp. pp. 90–1.
8. T. Zahra, *Kidnapped Souls: National Indifference and the Battle for Children in the Bohemian Lands, 1900–1948* (Ithaca, NY: Cornell University Press, 2008), pp. 107, 121.
9. Z. A. B. Zeman, "Czechoslovakia Between the Wars: Democracy on Trial," in J. Morison, ed., *The Czech and Slovak Experience* (New York: St. Martin's Press, 1992), p. 165.
10. Zahra, *Kidnapped Souls*, p. 112.
11. Quoted in Bruegel, *Czechoslovakia Before Munich*, p. 79.

12. Quoted in L. Rothkirchen, *The Jews of Bohemia and Moravia: Facing the Holocaust* (Lincoln: University of Nebraska Press, 2005), p. 161.
13. For a detailed analysis of the means by which this image was propagated, see A. Orzoff, *Battle for the Castle: The Myth of Czechoslovakia in Europe, 1914–1948* (Oxford: Oxford University Press, 2009).
14. "A German Bohemian Deputy," "National Minorities in Europe: The German Minority in Czechoslovakia," *Slavonic and East European Review* 41 (January 1936): 297–8.
15. Heimann, *Czechoslovakia*, p. 73.
16. U. Völklein, *"Mitleid war von niemand zu erwarten": Das Schicksal der deutschen Vertriebenen* (Munich: Droemer, 2005), p. 10.
17. See, e.g., C. Boyer et al., "Die Sudetendeutsche Heimatfront (Partei), 1933–1938: Zur Bestimmung ihres politisch-ideologischen Standortes," *Bohemia* 38:2 (1997): 357–385; R. M. Smelser, *The Sudeten Problem, 1933–1938: Volkstumspolitik and the Formulation of Nazi Foreign Policy* (Middletown, CT: Wesleyan University Press, 1975).
18. M. Cornwall, "'A Leap into Ice-Cold Water': The Manoeuvres of the Henlein Movement in Czechoslovakia, 1933–1938," in M. Cornwall and R. J. W. Evans, eds., *Czechoslovakia in a Nationalist and Fascist Europe 1918–1948* (Oxford: Oxford University Press, 2007), p. 141.
19. Heimann, *Czechoslovakia*, p. 60.
20. See I. Lukes, "Stalin and Czechoslovakia in 1938–39: An Autopsy of a Myth," in I. Lukes and E. Goldstein, eds., *The Munich Crisis, 1938: Prelude to World War II* (London: Cass, 1999), pp. 13–47.
21. P. Neville, *Hitler and Appeasement: The British Attempt to Prevent the Second World War* (London: Hambledon Continuum, 2006), p. 117; speech by Churchill, *Parliamentary Debates*, Commons, 5th ser., vol. 339, col. 364 (October 5, 1938).
22. *Parliamentary Debates*, Lords, 5th ser., vol. 110, col. 1306 (October 3, 1938).
23. Heimann, *Czechoslovakia*, p. 87.
24. Quoted in Z. A. B. Zeman and A. Klimek, *The Life of Edvard Beneš, 1884–1948: Czechoslovakia in Peace and War* (Oxford: Clarendon Press, 1997), p. 141.
25. M. Hauner, "'We Must Push Eastwards!' The Challenges and Dilemmas of President Beneš after Munich," *Journal of Contemporary History* 44:4 (October 2009): 619–656.
26. E. Beneš, *Odsun Němců: Výbor z pamětí a projevů doplněný edičními přílohami* (Prague: Společnost Edvarda Beneše, 1995), pp. 12–13; E. Táborský, "Politics in Exile, 1939–1945," in V. S. Matamey and R. Luža, eds., *A History of the Czechoslovak Republic 1918–1948* (Princeton, NJ: Princeton University Press, 1973), p. 332.
27. M. Hauner, "Introduction," in E. Beneš, *The Fall and Rise of a Nation: Czechoslovakia 1938–1941*, ed. M. Hauner (Boulder, CO: East European Monographs, 2004), pp. xxiii–xxiv.
28. F. D. Raška, *The Czechoslovak Exile Government in London and the Sudeten German Issue* (Prague: Karolinum Press, 2002), p. 46.
29. Quoted in Zeman and Klimek, *Life of Edvard Beneš*, p. 150.

30. C. Bryant, *Prague in Black: Nazi Rule and Czech Nationalism* (Cambridge, MA: Harvard University Press, 2007), pp. 98, 102.
31. Quoted in Raška, *The Czechoslovak Exile Government in London*, p. 44.
32. Quoted in Bryant, *Prague in Black*, p. 99.
33. D. Reynolds, "Churchill and the British 'Decision' to Fight On in 1940: Right Policy, Wrong Reasons," in R. Langhorne, ed., *Diplomacy and Intelligence During the Second World War: Essays in Honour of F. H. Hinsley* (Cambridge: Cambridge University Press, 1985), pp. 147–167.
34. Raška, *The Czechoslovak Exile Government in London*, p. 40.
35. Ibid., p. 51.
36. Ibid., p. 98.
37. E. Beneš, "The New Order in Europe," *Nineteenth Century and After*, September 1941, 154.
38. E. Beneš, *The War of 1939: Two Addresses of the Czechoslovak President at the Edinburgh and the Glasgow University 5th and 7th November, 1941* (Prague: Společnost Edvarda Beneše, 2005), p. 28.
39. E. Beneš, "The Organization of Postwar Europe," *Foreign Affairs* 20:2 (January 1942): 237–8.
40. Quoted in Zeman and Klimek, *Life of Edvard Beneš*, p. 183. Emphasis in original.
41. Orzoff, *Battle for the Castle*, p. 206.
42. R. J. Crampton, *Eastern Europe in the Twentieth Century and After* (London: Routledge, 1997), pp. 192–3.
43. V. Mastny, *The Czechs under Nazi Rule: The Failure of National Resistance, 1939–1942* (New York: Columbia University Press, 1971), p. 215.
44. See, e.g., J. King, *Budweisers into Czechs and Germans: A Local History of Bohemian Politics, 1848–1948* (Princeton, NJ: Princeton University Press, 2005), pp. 187–8.
45. Quoted in S. A. Garrett, *Conscience and Power: An Examination of Dirty Hands and Political Leadership* (Basingstoke, Hampshire: Palgrave Macmillan, 1996), p. 99.
46. K. Jackson, *Humphrey Jennings* (London: Picador, 2004), pp. 268–9; L. Leff, *Buried by the Times: The Holocaust and America's Most Important Newspaper* (Cambridge: Cambridge University Press, 2005), p. 184.
47. A. J. Kochavi, *Prelude to Nuremberg: Allied War Crimes Policy and the Question of Punishment* (Chapel Hill: University of North Carolina Press, 1998), pp. 22–25.
48. A. F. Noskova, "Migration of the Germans after the Second World War: Political and Psychological Aspects," *Journal of Communist and Transition Politics* 16:1–2 (March–June 2000): 98.
49. Foreign Research and Press Service, "The Transfer of German Populations (with Notes on the Relevant Evidence from Previous Exchanges and Transfers)," February 13, 1942, FO 371/30930, PRO.
50. A. Eden, "Anglo-Czechoslovak Relations," July 2, 1942, quoted in D. Brandes, *Der Weg zur Vertreibung 1938–1945: Pläne und Entscheidungen zum "Transfer" der Deutschen aus der Tschechoslowakei und aus Polen* (Munich: Oldenbourg, 2001), p. 168.
51. Noskova, "Migration of the Germans after the Second World War," 97–8.

52. K. Cordell, *Ethnicity and Democratisation in the New Europe* (London: Routledge, 1999), p. 170.
53. Quoted in A. J. Prażmowska, *Civil War in Poland, 1942–1948* (Basingstoke, Hampshire: Palgrave Macmillan, 2004), p. 169.
54. N. M. Naimark, "Ethnic Cleansing Between War and Peace," in A. Weiner, ed., *Landscaping the Human Garden: Twentieth-Century Population Management in a Comparative Framework* (Palo Alto, CA: Stanford University Press, 2003), p. 230.
55. Memorandum by Council of Ministers of the Polish government in exile, September 27, 1944, in P. Lippóczy and T. Walichnowski, T., eds. *Przesiedlenie ludności niemieckiej z Polski po II wojnie światowej w świetle dokumentów* (Warsaw: Państwowe Wydawnictwo Naukowe, 1982), p. 178.
56. *New York Times*, August 10, 1944.
57. Raška, *The Czechoslovak Exile Government in London*, p. 103.
58. Ibid., p. 107.
59. Minute by Cadogan, January 20, 1925, FO 371/11070, PRO.
60. P. Wilkinson, *Foreign Fields: The Story of an SOE Operative* (London: I. B. Tauris, 1997), p. 58.
61. P. J. Noel-Baker, "Two Years Ago . . . And Now," *London Calling*, July 11, 1940.
62. D. Brandes, "'Otázka transferu . . . Ta je tady Kolumbovo vejce': Českoslovenští komunisté a vyhnání Němců," *Český časopis historický* 103:1 (2005): 89.
63. E. Táborský, *President Edvard Beneš: Between East and West 1938–1948* (Palo Alto, CA: Hoover Institution Press, 1981), p. 161.
64. Quoted in Zeman and Klimek, *Life of Edvard Beneš*, p. 185.
65. Raška, *The Czechoslovak Exile Government in London*, p. 58.
66. Quoted in M. Frank, *Expelling the Germans: British Opinion and Post-1945 Population Transfer in Context* (Oxford: Oxford University Press, 2007), p. 50.
67. Quoted in K. Kersten, "Forced Migration and the Transformation of Polish Society in the Postwar Period," in P. Ther and A. Siljak, eds., *Redrawing Nations: Ethnic Cleansing in East-Central Europe, 1944–1948* (Lanham, MD: Rowman & Littlefield, 2001), p. 78.
68. Address by Welles at Arlington National Cemetery, *Life*, June 15, 1942; S. Welles, *The Time for Decision* (New York: Harper, 1944), p. 355; S. Welles, *Where Are We Heading?* (London: Hutchinson, 1947), p. 108.
69. Quoted in C. Wrigley, *A. J. P. Taylor: Radical Historian of Europe* (London: I. B. Tauris, 2006), p. 141.
70. *Parliamentary Debates*, Lords, 5th ser., vol. 126, cols. 555–6 (March 10, 1943).
71. *Parliamentary Debates*, Lords, 5th ser., vol. 130, col. 1116 (March 8, 1944).
72. See R. M. Douglas, *The Labour Party, Nationalism and Internationalism, 1939–1951* (London: Routledge, 2004), pp. 84–86.
73. Labour Party, National Executive Committee, *The International Post-War Settlement: Report by the National Executive Committee of the Labour Party to be Presented to the Annual Conference to be Held in London from May 29th to June 2nd, 1944* (London: Co-Operative Printing Society, 1944), p. 5.

74. Labour Party, *Report of the Forty-Fourth Annual Conference of the Labour Party* (London: Co-Operative Printing Society, 1945), p. 114.
75. Quoted in D. Brandes, "Edvard Beneš und die Pläne zur Vertreibung/Aussiedlung der Deutschen und Ungarn 1938–1945," in G. Zand and J. Holý, eds., *Transfer–Vertreibung–Aussiedlung im Kontext der tschechischen Literatur* (Brno: Aktion, 2004), pp. 21–2.
76. Labour Party, National Executive Committee, *The International Post-War Settlement*, p. 5.
77. Editorial, "Labour and the Post-War Settlement," *Socialist Commentary*, June 1944.
78. Labour Party, *Report of the Forty-Fourth Annual Conference*, p. 135.
79. *The Economist*, January 17, 1942.
80. Ibid., July 10, 1943.
81. A. G. B. Fisher and D. Mitrany, "Some Notes on the Transfer of Populations," *Political Quarterly* 14:4 (October–December 1943): 370. Emphasis in original in first quote.
82. E. Beneš, *Memoirs of Dr. Eduard Beneš: From Munich to New War and New Victory* (Boston: Houghton Mifflin, 1954), p. 219. Emphasis in original.
83. Ibid., pp. 219, 220.
84. Ibid., pp. 320–334.
85. S. Grant Duff, *The Parting of Ways: A Personal Account of the Thirties* (London: Peter Owen, 1982), p. 135.
86. H. Ripka, *The Future of the Czechoslovak Germans* (London: Czechoslovak-British Friendship Club, 1944), pp. 13–15.
87. *New York Times*, September 10, 1948.
88. Quoted in Ripka, *Future of the Czechoslovak Germans*, p. 16.
89. Jaksch to Beneš, June 22, 1942, quoted in Beneš, *Memoirs of Dr. Eduard Beneš*, p. 307.
90. W. Jaksch, *Can Industrial Peoples Be Transferred? The Future of the Sudeten Population* (London: Sudeten Social Democratic Party, 1943), p. 10.
91. Jaksch to Roberts, February 1, 1945, FO 371/47083.
92. Minute by F. Warner, February 24, 1945, FO 371/47083.
93. Bryant, *Prague in Black*, p. 210.
94. B. Frommer, *National Cleansing: Retribution Against Nazi Collaborators in Postwar Czechoslovakia* (Cambridge: Cambridge University Press, 2005), p. 239.
95. Ripka to R. Schoenfeld, April 20, 1945, U.S. Embassy Czechoslovakia, Classified General Records, 1945–1957, RG 84, Entry 2378A, 350/54/13/03, box 4, NARA.

CHAPTER 2. THE VOLKSDEUTSCHE IN WARTIME

1. J. R. Sanborn, "'Unsettling the Empire': Violent Migrations and Social Disaster in Russia During World War I," *Journal of Modern History* 77:7 (June 2005): 290–304.
2. D. Bloxham, "The Great Unweaving: The Removal of Peoples in Europe, 1875–1949," in R. Bessel and C. B. Haake, eds., *Removing Peoples: Forced Removal in the Modern World* (Oxford: Oxford University Press, 2009), p. 175.
3. S. O'Rourke, "Trial Run: The Deportation of the Terek Cossacks 1920," in Bessel and Haake, *Removing Peoples*, pp. 255–279.

4. T. Martin, "The Origins of Soviet Ethnic Cleansing," *Journal of Modern History* 70:4 (December 1998): 815.
5. J. Burds, "The Soviet War Against 'Fifth Columnists': The Case of Chechnya, 1942–4," *Journal of Contemporary History* 42:2 (April 2007): 272.
6. R. Breitman, *The Architect of Genocide: Himmler and the Final Solution* (New York: Knopf, 1991), p. 46.
7. "Agreement Concluded at Munich, September 29, 1938, between Germany, Great Britain, France and Italy," art. 7, in M. Curtis, ed., *Documents on International Affairs 1938*, vol. 2 (London: Oxford University Press, 1943), pp. 289–291.
8. J. B. Schechtman, *European Population Transfers 1939–1945* (New York: Oxford University Press, 1946), p. 57.
9. See G. Aly and S. Heim, *Vordenker der Vernichtung: Auschwitz und die deutschen Pläne für eine neue europäische Ordnung* (Hamburg: Hoffmann und Campe, 1991), pp. 394–440.
10. Quoted in A. B. Rossino, *Hitler Strikes Poland: Blitzkrieg, Ideology, and Atrocity* (Lawrence: University Press of Kansas, 2003), p. 196.
11. C. Jansen and A. Weckberger, *Der "Volksdeutsche Selbstschutz" in Polen 1939/40* (Munich: Oldenbourg, 1992), p. 25.
12. V. O. Lumans, *Himmler's Auxiliaries: The Volksdeutsche Mittelstelle and the German National Minorities of Europe, 1933–1945* (Chapel Hill: University of North Carolina Press, 1993), p. 95; F. P. Walters, *A History of the League of Nations* (Oxford: Oxford University Press, 1967), pp. 616–7.
13. G. Jérome, "Les milices d'autoprotection de la communauté allemande de Pomérélie, Posnanie et Silésie polonaise (1939–1940)," *Guerres mondiales et conflits contemporains* 41:163 (1991): 58.
14. A. Hitler, *Hitler's Second Book: The Unpublished Sequel to Mein Kampf*, ed. G. L. Weinberg (New York: Enigma, 2003), p. 53.
15. As Michael Burleigh points out, in contrast to the stock image in the democratic countries of Nazi Germany as a totalitarian state running with robotic efficiency, its "government was characterised by multi-centred incoherence, with a war of all against all, bordering on chaos." M. Burleigh, *The Third Reich: A New History* (Basingstoke, Hampshire: Macmillan, 2000), p. 156.
16. L. de Jong, *The German Fifth Column in the Second World War* (London: Routledge & Kegan Paul, 1956), pp. 39–47.
17. See T. Chinciński, "Niemiecka dywersja na Pomorzu w 1939 roku," in T. Chinciński and P. Machcewicz, eds., *Bydgoszcz 3–4 września 1939: Studia i dokumenty* (Warsaw: Instytut Pamięci Narodowej, 2008): 170–204.
18. Jansen and Weckbecker, *Der "Volksdeutsche Selbstschutz" in Polen*, pp. 19, 26–7.
19. M. Phayer, "Pius XII and the Genocides of Polish Catholics and Polish Jews During the Second World War," *Kirchliche Zeitgeschichte* 15:1 (January 2002): 250.
20. Most Western historians put the number of German victims at around four hundred, and express doubt as to whether the precipitating factor was anything other than panic among the understandably jittery Polish troops. In all significant respects, the Bydgoszcz episode conforms closely to the pattern of similar panics leading to massacres

Notes to Pages 44–53   381

by German forces advancing into Belgium and France in the first days of the Great War. See J. Horne and A. Kramer, *German Atrocities 1914: A History of Denial* (New Haven, CT: Yale University Press, pp. 10–78). For a compilation of the most recent Polish scholarship on the episode, which considers German saboteurs and "diversionists" to have played a significant role, see Chinciński and Machcewicz, *Bydgoszcz 3–4 września 1939*.

21. Rossino, *Hitler Strikes Poland*, p. 203.
22. See A. V. Prusin, *The Lands Between: Conflict in the East European Borderlands, 1870–1992* (Oxford: Oxford University Press, 2010), pp. 128–9.
23. Jérome, "Les milices d'autoprotection," 58.
24. Jansen and Weckbecker, *Der "Volksdeutsche Selbstschutz" in Polen*, p. 28.
25. Rossino, *Hitler Strikes Poland*, pp. 68–72.
26. P. R. Black, "Rehearsal for "Reinhard"? Odilo Globocnik and the Lublin *Selbstschutz*," *Central European History* 25:2 (Spring 1992): 204–226.
27. Jérome, "Les milices d'autoprotection," 65–6.
28. See N. S. Lebedeva, "The Deportation of the Polish Population to the USSR, 1939–41," *Journal of Communist and Transition Politics* 16:1–2 (March 2000): 28–45.
29. See D. Crowe, "Germany and the Baltic Question in Latvia 1939–1940," *East European Quarterly* 26:3 (Autumn 1992): 371–389.
30. Schechtman, *European Population Transfers 1939–1945*, p. 125.
31. G. E. Schafft, *From Racism to Genocide: Anthropology in the Third Reich* (Urbana: University of Illinois Press, 2004), p. 135.
32. Schechtman, *European Population Transfers 1939–1945*, p. 161.
33. H. Sommer, *Völkerwanderung im 20. Jahrhundert: Die grosse Heimkehr der Volksdeutschen ins Reich* (Berlin: Wilhelm Limpert-Verlag, 1940), pp. 3–4.
34. A. C. Bramwell, "The Re-Settlement of Ethnic Germans, 1939–41," in A. C. Bramwell, ed., *Refugees in the Age of Total War* (London: Unwin Hyman, 1988), p. 122.
35. Quoted in H. S. Levine, "Local Authority and the SS State: The Conflict over Population Policy in Danzig–West Prussia, 1939–1945," *Central European History* 2:4 (December 1969): 345–6.
36. See P. Łossowski, "The Resettlements of Germans from Lithuania During World War II," *Acta Poloniae historica* 93 (2006): 121–142.
37. See G. Aly, *"Final Solution": Nazi Population Policy and the Murder of the European Jews* (London: Arnold, 1999), pp. 97–8, 108–9.
38. C. Epstein, *Model Nazi: Arthur Greiser and the Occupation of Western Poland* (Oxford: Oxford University Press, 2010), p. 172.
39. Quoted in Aly, *"Final Solution,"* p. 62.
40. C. R. Browning with J. Matthäus, *The Origins of the Final Solution: The Evolution of Nazi Jewish Policy, September 1939–March 1942* (Lincoln: University of Nebraska Press, 2004), p. 66.
41. Quoted in E. Harvey, *Women and the Nazi East: Agents and Witnesses of Germanization* (New York: Columbia University Press, 2005), p. 155.
42. M. Maschmann, *Fazit: Kein Rechtfertigungsversuch* (Stuttgart: Deutsche Verlagsanstalt, 1964), pp. 121–125.

43. Browning, *Origins of the Final Solution*, pp. 93–4.
44. Quoted in L. Rees, *The Nazis: A Warning from History* (London: BBC Books, 1997), p. 138.
45. S. Bannister, *I Lived Under Hitler: An Englishwoman's Story* (London: Rockliff, 1957), p. 92.
46. N. J. W. Goda, "Black Marks: Hitler's Bribery of his Senior Officers During World War II," *Journal of Modern History* 72 (2002): 447.
47. Harvey, *Women and the Nazi East*, p. 165.
48. P. Fritzsche, *Life and Death in the Third Reich* (Cambridge, MA: Belknap Press of Harvard University Press, 2008), p. 171.
49. Harvey, *Women and the Nazi East*, p. 157.
50. Bramwell, "The Re-Settlement of Ethnic Germans," pp. 126–7.
51. D. L. Bergen, "The 'Volksdeutschen' of Eastern Europe, World War II, and the Holocaust: Constructed Ethnicity, Real Genocide," *Yearbook of European Studies* 13 (1999): 70–93. See also M. Gilbert, *The Boys: The Story of 732 Young Concentration Camp Survivors* (New York: Holt, 1998), p. 64.
52. See below, pp. 69–70.
53. Bergen, "The 'Volksdeutschen' of Eastern Europe," p. 73.
54. C. Bryant, "Either German or Czech: Fixing Nationality in Bohemia and Moravia, 1939–1946," *Slavic Review* 61:4 (Winter 2002), p. 691.
55. Bergen, "The 'Volksdeutschen' of Eastern Europe," p. 74.
56. L. Olejnik, *Zdrajcy narodu? Losy volksdeutschów w Polsce po II wojnie światowej* (Warsaw: Trio, 2006), pp. 120–121, 146; J. Grabowski and Z. R. Grabowski, "Germans in the Eyes of the Germans: The Ciechanów District, 1939–1945," *Contemporary European History* 13:1 (February 2004): 28.
57. Bramwell, "The Re-Settlement of Ethnic Germans," p. 129.
58. Z. Klukowski, *Diary from the Years of Occupation* (Urbana: University of Illinois Press, 1993), pp. 239–40 (entry of January 28, 1943).
59. M. J. Chodakiewicz, *Between Nazis and Soviets: Occupation Politics in Poland, 1939–1947* (Lanham, MD: Lexington Press, 2004), p. 162 n. 30.
60. Klukowski, *Diary from the Years of Occupation*, pp. 230–1 (entries of December 10 and 13, 1942).
61. Bryant, "Either German or Czech," p. 689.
62. Quoted in I. Heinemann, "'Another Type of Perpetrator': The SS Racial Experts and Forced Population Movements in the Occupied Regions," *Holocaust and Genocide Studies* 15:3 (Winter 2001): 394.
63. Quoted in Schafft, *From Racism to Genocide*, p. 135.
64. Bergen, "The 'Volksdeutschen' of Eastern Europe," p. 82.
65. Rees, *The Nazis*, p. 142.
66. Harvey, *Women and the Nazi East*, p. 151.
67. D. L. Bergen, "The *Volksdeutsche* of Eastern Europe and the Collapse of the Nazi Empire, 1944–1945," in A. E. Steinweis and D. E. Rogers, eds., *The Impact of Nazism: New Perspectives on the Third Reich and Its Legacy* (Lincoln: University of Nebraska Press, 2003), p. 106.

68. Grabowski and Grabowski, "Germans in the Eyes of the Germans," p. 33.
69. Harvey, *Women and the Nazi East*, pp. 173, 164.
70. Bryant, "Fixing Nationality in Bohemia and Moravia," p. 695.
71. W. Lower, "Hitler's 'Garden of Eden' in Ukraine: Nazi Colonialism, *Volksdeutsche*, and the Holocaust, 1941–1944," in J. Petropoulos and J. K. Roth, eds., *Gray Zones: Ambiguity and Compromise in the Holocaust and Its Aftermath* (Oxford: Berghahn, 2006), p. 194.
72. M. Hastings, *Armageddon: The Battle for Germany, 1944–1945* (New York: Knopf, 2004), p. 408.
73. See, e.g., N. G. Papp, "The German Minority Between the Two World Wars: Loyal Subjects or Suppressed Citizens?" *East European Quarterly* 22:4 (Winter 1988): 495–514.
74. Fritzsche, *Life and Death in the Third Reich*, p. 171.
75. Aly, "Final Solution," p. 126.
76. V. O. Lumans, "A Reassessment of the Presumed Fifth Column Role of the German National Minorities of Europe," in J. K. Burton and C. W. White, eds., *Essays in European History: 1988–89*, vol. 2 (Lanham, MD: University Press of America, 1996), p. 201.
77. Quoted in Bergen, "The 'Volksdeutschen' of Eastern Europe," p. 82.
78. Bramwell, "The Re-Settlement of Ethnic Germans, 1939–41," p. 126.
79. Klukowski, *Diary from the Years of Occupation*, pp. 302, 333 (entries of February 15 and June 8, 1944).
80. E. Schmaltz, "The 'Long Trek': The SS Population Transfer of Ukrainian Germans to the Polish Warthegau and Its Consequences, 1943–1944," *Journal of the American Historical Society of Germans from Russia* 31:3 (Autumn 2008): 1–23.
81. For a representative example, see "W sprawie 'Volksdeutschów,'" *Gazeta Lubelska*, October 10, 1944, quoted in Olejnik, *Zdrajcy narodu?* pp. 69–70.

CHAPTER 3. THE SCHEME

1. Estimates of the number of people displaced during the partition of the Indian subcontinent in 1947, once thought to exceed 20 million, have now been revised downward to approximately half that figure. See S. Wolpert, *Shameful Flight: The Last Years of the British Empire in India* (Oxford: Oxford University Press, 2006), p. 1; Y. Khan, *The Great Partition: The Making of India and Pakistan* (New Haven, CT: Yale University Press, 2007), p. 6.
2. J. M. Scott, "Exile and the Self-Understanding of Diaspora Jews in the Greco-Roman Period," in J. M. Scott, ed., *Exile: Old Testament, Jewish, and Christian Conceptions* (Leiden: E. J. Brill, 1997), p. 202.
3. M. Tanner, *Ireland's Holy Wars: The Struggle for a Nation's Soul, 1500–2000* (New Haven, CT: Yale University Press, 2001), p. 145.
4. P. Lovejoy, "The Slave Trade as Enforced Migration in the Central Sudan of West Africa," in R. Bessel and C. B. Haake, eds., *Removing Peoples: Forced Removal in the Modern World* (Oxford: Oxford University Press, 2009), p. 156.

5. P. C. Perdue, *China Marches West: The Qing Conquest of Central Eurasia* (Cambridge, MA: Belknap Press of Harvard University Press, 2005), p. 333.
6. Bessel and Haake, *Removing People*, p. 3.
7. C. Carmichael, *Genocide Before the Holocaust* (New Haven, CT: Yale University Press, 2009), pp. 24–26.
8. D. Bloxham, "The Great Unweaving: The Removal of Peoples in Europe, 1875–1949," in Bessel and Haake, *Removing Peoples*, pp. 192–3.
9. M. Mazower, *Hitler's Empire: How the Nazis Ruled Europe* (New York: Penguin, 2008), p. 39.
10. C. Grohmann, "From Lothringen to Lorraine: Expulsion and Voluntary Repatriation," *Diplomacy and Statecraft* 16:3 (Autumn 2005): 571–587.
11. G. Jenkins, *Political Islam in Turkey: Running West, Heading East?* (Basingstoke, Hampshire: Palgrave Macmillan, 2008), p. 92.
12. E. Kontogiorgi, "Economic Consequences Following Refugee Settlement in Greek Macedonia, 1923–1932," in R. Hirschon, ed., *Crossing the Aegean: An Appraisal of the 1923 Compulsory Population Exchange Between Greece and Turkey* (New York: Berghahn, 2003), p. 74.
13. R. Hirschon, "The Consequences of the Lausanne Conference: An Overview," in Hirschon, *Crossing the Aegean*, p. 17.
14. Quoted in E. Kontogiorgi, *Population Exchange in Greek Macedonia: The Rural Settlement of Refugees 1922–1930* (Oxford: Oxford University Press, 2006), p. 65.
15. *New English Weekly*, January 18, 1945.
16. M. Frank, *Expelling the Germans: British Opinion and Post-1945 Population Transfer in Context* (Oxford: Oxford University Press, 2007), pp. 25–29.
17. Henderson to William Strang, August 25, 1939, FO 371/23027.
18. Quoted in C. Ponting, *Churchill* (London: Sinclair-Stevenson, 1994), p. 652.
19. M. Kramer, "Introduction," in P. Ther and A. Siljak, eds., *Redrawing Nations: Ethnic Cleansing in East-Central Europe, 1944–1948* (Lanham, MD: Rowman & Littlefield, 2001), p. 6.
20. Foreign Research and Press Service, "The Transfer of German Populations (With Notes on the Relevant Evidence from Previous Exchanges and Transfers)," February 13, 1942, FO 371/30930.
21. F. J. Harbutt, *Yalta 1945: Europe and America at the Crossroads* (Cambridge: Cambridge University Press, 2010), p. 144.
22. "Report of the Inter-Departmental Committee on the Transfer of German Populations," p. 8, A.P.W. (44) 34, May 12, 1945, CAB 121/85.
23. Ibid., pp. 2–3.
24. Minute by Sargent, October 28, 1943, quoted in D. Brandes, *Der Weg zur Vertreibung: Pläne und Entscheidungen zum "Transfer" der Deutschen aus der Tschechoslowakei und aus Polen* (Munich: Oldenbourg, 2001), pp. 262–3; "Report of the Inter-Departmental Committee," p. 4.
25. "Report of the Inter-Departmental Committee," p. 22.
26. Ibid., p. 3.
27. Ibid., p. 19.

28. Ibid., p. 4.
29. Ibid., p. 27.
30. Ibid., p. 30.
31. Armistice and Post-War Committee minutes, 10th meeting, July 20, 1944, CAB 121/85.
32. R. Law, "Food Production, Land Settlement and Large Estates in Germany, and the Problem of the Transferred Populations," December 15, 1944, A.P.W. (44) 125, CAB 87/68; Armistice and Post-War Committee minutes, 1st meeting, January 4, 1945, CAB 121/85.
33. C. R. Attlee, "Post-War Settlement—Policy in Respect of Germany," July 19, 1943, W.P. 42 (322), CAB 66/39.
34. Minute by Troutbeck, September 8, 1945, FO 371/46812.
35. Minute by Toynbee, January 30, 1945, FO 371/46811.
36. "PWE/OSS Daily Intelligence Summary for Germany and Austria" no. 139, January 30, 1945, FO 371/46810.
37. Minute by O'Neill for T. H. Marshall, Foreign Office Research Department, January 31, 1945, FO 371/46810.
38. See Brandes, *Der Weg zur Vertreibung*, pp. 286–290.
39. R. C. Raack, "Stalin Fixes the Oder-Neisse Line," *Journal of Contemporary History* 25:4 (October 1990): 474.
40. Quoted in G. Strauchold, *Myśl zachodnia i jej realizacja w Polsce Ludowej w latach 1945–1957* (Toruń: Wydawnictwo Adam Marszałek, 2003), pp. 85–6.
41. P. E. Mosely, assistant chief of the Division of Political Studies, "Poland—Germany: Territorial Problems: Polish-German Frontier from Silesia to the Baltic Sea," H-27, August 18, 1943, in *FRUS: The Conferences at Washington and Quebec, 1943* (Washington, DC: Government Printing Office, 1970), p. 734.
42. Brandes, *Der Weg zur Vertreibung*, p. 280.
43. Churchill to Roosevelt, October 18, 1944, *FRUS*, vol. 1: *Diplomatic Papers 1944: General* (Washington, DC: Government Printing Office, 1966), p. 1327.
44. Quoted in D. J. Allen, *The Oder-Neisse Line: The United States, Poland, and Germany in the Cold War* (Westport, CT: Praeger 2003), p. 15.
45. R. E. Schoenfeld to Cordell Hull, December 21, 1944, *FRUS*, vol. 3: *Diplomatic Papers 1944: The British Commonwealth and Europe* (Washington, DC: Government Printing Office, 1965), p. 1350.
46. See questions by G. Strauss (Lab., Lambeth North), *Parliamentary Debates*, Commons, 5th ser., vol. 402, col. 1521 (August 2, 1944); R. R. Stokes (Lab., Ipswich), ibid., c. 1539; A. Eden, ibid., c. 1549.
47. *Parliamentary Debates*, Commons, 5th ser., vol. 406, cols. 1483–4 (December 15, 1944).
48. Maurice Petherick (Con., Penryn & Falmouth), ibid., col. 1540 (December 15, 1944).
49. Ibid., col. 1484 (December 15, 1944).
50. Ibid., c. 1562 (December 15, 1944).
51. *Manchester Guardian*, December 16, 1944.
52. G. Orwell, "As I Please," *Tribune*, February 2, 1945.
53. *Chicago Tribune*, December 18, 1944. See also S. Jankowiak, *Wysiedlenie i emigracja*

ludności Niemieckiej w polityce władz Polskich w latach 1945-1970 (Warsaw: Instytut Pamięci Narodowej, 2005), pp. 28-9.
54. D. Reynolds, *In Command of History: Churchill Fighting and Writing the Second World War* (New York: Random House, 2005), pp. 274, 326-7, 418-19, 466.
55. D. Brandes, "National and International Planning of the 'Transfer' of Germans from Czechoslovakia and Poland," in Bessel and Haake, *Removing Peoples*, pp. 289-90.
56. E. Stettinius, 'Memorandum of Suggested Action Items for the President,' n.d. (c. February 4, 1945), in *FRUS, Diplomatic Papers, 1945: The Conferences at Malta and Yalta* (Washington, DC: Government Printing Office, 1955), p. 568.
57. Quoted in J. Fenby, *Alliance: The Inside Story of How Roosevelt, Stalin and Churchill Won One War and Began Another* (London: Simon & Schuster, 2006), p. 366.
58. Verbatim transcript by H. Freeman Matthews, director of the Office of European Affairs, Department of State, of fourth plenary session, Yalta Conference, February 7, 1945, *FRUS: The Conferences at Malta and Yalta* (Washington, DC: Government Printing Office, 1955), p. 720.
59. "Report of the Crimea Conference," February 11, 1945, ibid., p. 974.
60. Minute by Harvey, March 30, 1945, FO 371/47085.
61. Minute by Attlee, April 17, 1945, FO 371/46810.
62. Minutes of Fifth "Terminal" Meeting, Potsdam, July 21, 1945, FO 934/3.
63. F. Taylor, *Dresden, Tuesday, February 13, 1945* (London: HarperCollins, 2004), p. 185.
64. Ibid., p. 376.
65. *FRUS: Diplomatic Papers: The Conference of Berlin (The Potsdam Conference), 1945*, vol. 2 (Washington, DC: Government Printing Office, 1960), p. 1511.
66. Minutes of Sixth "Terminal" Meeting, Potsdam, July 22, 1945, FO 934/3.
67. J. Hynd, "The Problem of the German Refugee Populations in the British Zone," O.R.C. (46) 74, July 27, 1946, FO 945/67.

CHAPTER 4. THE "WILD EXPULSIONS"

1. See P. M. Majewski, "Czechosłowaccy wojskowi wobec problemu wysiedlenia mniejszości niemieckiej i powojennych granic państwa, 1939-1945," *Przegląd historyczny* 90:2 (1999): 169-183.
2. P. Demetz, *Prague in Danger: The Years of German Occupation, 1939-45* (New York: Farrar, Straus and Giroux, 2008), p. 235.
3. H. Perkins to P. Boughey, May 21, 1945, HS 4/51.
4. Postal censorship transcript of letter, June 12, 1945, FO 371/47091.
5. T. Staněk, *Verfolgung 1945: Die Stellung der Deutschen in Böhmen, Mähren und Schlesien (außerhalb der Lager und Gefängnisse)* (Vienna: Böhlau, 2002), p. 115 n. 148.
6. D. Kováč, "Die Evakuierung und Vertreibung der Deutschen aus der Slowakei," in R. G. Plaschka, H. Haselsteiner, et al., eds., *Nationale Frage und Vertreibung in der Tschechoslowakei und Ungarn 1938-1948: Aktuelle Forschungen* (Vienna: Verlag der Österreichischen Akademie der Wissenschaften, 1997), pp. 113-114.
7. Staněk, *Verfolgung 1945*, pp. 106-116, 142.

8. B. Frommer, *National Cleansing: Retribution Against Nazi Collaborators in Postwar Czechoslovakia* (Cambridge: Cambridge University Press, 2005), p. 50.
9. F. A. Voigt, "Orderly and Humane," *Nineteenth Century and After*, November 1945, p. 201.
10. T. Staněk and A. von Arburg, "Organizované divoké odsuny? Úloha ústředních státních orgánů při provádění "evakuace" německého obyvatelstva (květen až září 1945)," part 3: "Snaha vlády a civilních úradu o řízení 'Divokého Odsunu,'" *Soudobé dějiny* 13:3–4 (January 2006): 321–2.
11. Staněk, *Verfolgung 1945*, p. 74.
12. Transcript of Beneš broadcast, October 14, 1945, FO 371/46814. See also Majewski, "Czechosłowaccy wojskowi wobec problemu wysiedlenia mniejszości niemieckiej," 175.
13. Staněk, *Verfolgung 1945*, pp. 115–121; V. Žampach, "Vysídlení německého obyvatelstva z Brna ve dnech 30. a 31. května 1945 a nouzový ubytovací tábor v Pohořelicích, 1.6.–7.7. 1945," *Jižní Morava* 32 (1997): 173–239.
14. Transcript of broadcast, "Marie Ranzenhoferová: A Survivor of the 1945 Brno Death March," Radio Praha, May 12, 2010, http://www.radio.cz/en/article/127839.
15. E. Glassheim, "National Mythologies and Ethnic Cleansing: The Expulsion of Czechoslovak Germans in 1945," *Central European History* 33:4 (2000): 478.
16. Staněk and von Arburg, "Organizované divoké odsuny?" part 2: "Československá armáda vytváří 'hotové skutečnosti,' vláda je před cizinou legitimizuje," *Soudobé dějiny* 13:1–2 (January 2006): 27.
17. Ministry of National Defense, Jablonec nad Nisou, to Ministry of the Interior, July 20, 1945, MV-NR, box 7445, item B 221.
18. Ibid., 26.
19. Staněk and von Arburg, "Organizované divoké odsuny?" part 2, pp. 26–27.
20. D. M. Crowe, *Oskar Schindler* (Boulder, CO: Westview, 2004), pp. 466–471, 473–475.
21. British Embassy, Prague, to German Department, Foreign Office, September 5, 1945; Lance-Bombardier Arnold Gardiner, ex-POW, Stalag IV C, to the under-secretary of state, Foreign Office, November 10, 1945, FO 371/46812; D. Gerlach, "For Nation and Gain: Economy, Ethnicity and Politics in the Czech Borderlands, 1945–1948" (Ph.D. diss., University of Pittsburgh, 2007), p. 73.
22. *New York Times*, April 20, 1946.
23. *Svobodné noviny*, October 2, 1946.
24. J. King, *Budweisers into Czechs and Germans: A Local History of Bohemian Politics, 1848–1948* (Princeton, NJ: Princeton University Press, 2002), p. 195.
25. *Rudé právo*, April 10, 1946.
26. *Pravda* (Plzeň), November 15, 1945.
27. E. Hrabovec, "Neue Aspekte zur ersten Phase der Vertreibung der Deutschen aus Mähren 1945," in Plaschka, Haselsteiner, et al., *Nationale Frage und Vertreibung*, pp. 131–2.
28. Quoted in K. Kersten, "Forced Migration and the Transformation of Polish Society in the Postwar Period," in P. Ther and A. Siljak, eds., *Redrawing Nations: Ethnic*

Cleansing in East-Central Europe, 1944–1948 (Lanham, MD: Rowman & Littlefield, 2001), p. 79.
29. František Havel, chief, Main Division, Ministry of National Defense, "Transfer of Germans: Report of Proceedings," July 16, 1945, MNO 1151/951 (1945).
30. Minutes of meeting of the Main Division, Ministry of National Defense, July 28, 1945, MNO 3292/776.
31. *Svobodné noviny*, August 30, 1946; *Severočeská Mladá fronta*, December 16, 1945; *Rudé právo*, May 16, 1946.
32. G. Lange, "My Experiences at the End of the War and Thereafter," in U. Lange, ed., *East Germany: What Happened to the Silesians in 1945* (Lewes, Sussex: Book Guild, 2000), p. 80.
33. B. Nitschke, "Wysiedlenia Niemców w czerwcu i lipcu 1945 roku," *Zeszyty Historyczne* 118 (1996): 156.
34. *News Chronicle*, January 31, 1946.
35. Undated (c. May 1945) account of E. Melina, Office of Military Government for Germany, Prisoners of War and Displaced Persons Branch, box 133, "Refugee Reports" file, RG 260/390/42/24–25/7–1, NARA.
36. Memorandum by Maj. O. Fischer, November 27, 1945, MNO 238/14266 (1946).
37. Memorandum by Ministry of Recovered Territories Zgorzelec office, May 5, 1947, MZO, 196/541c/B-7415.
38. Hradec Králové National Security Office to Ministry of the Interior, June 18, 1945, MNO 9/4/1/76 (1945).
39. *Severočeská Mladá fronta*, December 16, 1945.
40. See Staněk, *Verfolgung 1945*, p. 161.
41. Moravská Třebová Regional National Committee, "Report on the Question of Germans in Svitavy Region between May 12, 1945 and August 23, 1945," August 24, 1945, MV-NR, box 7446, item B 596.
42. Staněk, *Verfolgung 1945*, p. 72.
43. *Washington Post*, June 17, 1945.
44. Maj.-Gen. E. N. Harmon, C.O., XXII Corps, to Steinhardt, October 23, 1945, State Department papers RG 84, Entry 2378A, 350/54/13/03. U.S. Embassy Czechoslovakia. Classified General Records, 1945–1957, box 3, file 711.9, NARA.
45. Staněk and von Arburg, "Organizované divoké odsuny?" part 2, p. 28.
46. Quoted in R. Bessel, *Germany 1945: From War to Peace* (London: Simon & Schuster, 2009), p. 215.
47. Nitschke, "Wysiedlenia Niemców w czerwcu i lipcu 1945 roku," p. 161.
48. Undated statement of Johanna Janisch, Leimnitz bei Schwiebus, FO 371/46815.
49. B. George, *Les russes arrivent: La plus grande migration des temps modernes* (Paris: Éditions de la Table Ronde, 1966), pp. 229–231.
50. Telegram from R. S. S. Stevenson, British ambassador, Belgrade, to Foreign Office, January 21, 1946, FO 945/360; "Aide-mémoire" by Ministry of Foreign Affairs, Belgrade, January 16, 1946, FO 371/55391.
51. Lt.-Gen. I. Avshich, Yugoslav Military Mission, Berlin, to the Control Commission for Germany (British Element), March 1, 1946, FO 1032/2284.

52. J. M. Troutbeck to Sir A. Street, February 11, 1946, FO 371/55390.
53. Minute by C. O'Neill, January 26, 1946, FO 371/55390.
54. Foreign Office Research Department, "The German Minority in Yugoslavia," February 2, 1946, FO 371/55390.
55. Memorandum by Allied Control Authority Co-ordinating Committee, "Transfer into Germany of German Minorities from Countries not Referred to in the Potsdam Agreement," March 22, 1946; minute by A. A. E. Franklin, Foreign Office, August 12, 1946, FO 371/55525.
56. M. Portmann, "Politik der Vernichtung? Die deutschsprachige Bevölkerung in der Vojvodina 1944–1952: Ein Forschungsbericht auf Grundlage jugoslawischer Archivdokumente," in *Danubiana carpathica: Jahrbuch für Geschichte und Kultur in den deutschen Siedlungsgebieten Südosteuropas* (Munich: Oldenbourg, 2007), pp. 332–3.
57. Note by government of Romania to Gen. V. Vinogradov, acting president, Allied Control Council for Romania, January 13, 1945, FO 371/48536.
58. Minute by Sargent, January 12, 1945, FO 371/48535.
59. Minute by Churchill (with "check" of approval by Stalin), n.d. (October 9, 1944), PREM 3/66/7.
60. Prime Minister's Personal Minutes to Eden, January 18 and 19, 1945, FO 371/48536.
61. Personal and private telegram from Stevenson to Sir A. Cadogan, January 17, 1945, FO 371/48536. For additional eyewitness reports of roundups, see Lieut. P. A. Clifton and Lt.-Col. A. C. Kendall, "Report on Visit to Brasov, Sibiu and Cluj, Jan. 8th to Jan. 11th, 1945," n.d., FO 371/48590.
62. H. G. Beckh, CICR, "Résumé d'un entretien entre M. [J. A.] Graf [CICR adjunct delegate, Bucharest] et le soussigné le 3.9.46," G. 97/IV, box 1165, CICR.
63. Allied Control Authority, Prisoners of War and Displaced Persons Division, "The Return to Germany of German Minorities Now Residing in Austria," August 5, 1946, FO 1005/840; M. Ritter, Catholic Committee for Relief Abroad, "Report on *Volksdeutsch* in Austria," October 21, 1947, FO 1020/2519.
64. A recent history that argued otherwise arrived at its conclusions by taking contemporary newspaper accounts and similarly unverified stories at face value; its findings, however, are contradicted by materials in the Polish and Czech archives, which its author had not consulted. See A. P. Biddiscombe, *Werwolf! The History of the National Socialist Guerrilla Movement 1944–1946* (Toronto: University of Toronto Press, 1998).
65. Staněk, *Verfolgung 1945*, p. 127.
66. V. Mastny, *The Czechs under Nazi Rule: The Failure of National Resistance, 1939–1942* (New York: Columbia University Press, 1971), p. 178.
67. Staněk, *Verfolgung 1945*, pp. 130, 135–7, 164.
68. See, e.g., *News Chronicle*, August 2, 1945; *The Times*, July 28, August 7, 1945; *Severočeská Mladá fronta*, September 6, 1945.
69. Sudeten German Social Democratic Party, *Deportation Drama in Czecho-Slovakia: The Case of a Dying People* (London: Der Sozialdemokrat, 1945), p. 10.
70. Telegram from Nichols to Foreign Office, August 13, 1945, FO 371/47091.
71. Quoted in T. Staněk, *Poválečné "excesy" v českých zemích v roce 1945 a jejich vyšetřování* (Prague: Ústav pro soudobé dějiny, 2005), p. 72.

72. Staněk, *Verfolgung 1945*, p. 181.
73. Ibid., p. 180.
74. Ibid., p. 130.
75. Ibid., p. 181.
76. *Severočeská Mladá fronta*, September 23, 1945.
77. B. Nitschke, "Wysiedlenia Niemców w czerwcu i lipcu 1945 roku," 161–2.
78. Unsigned "Beobachtungen und Eindrücke von einer Reise Poznań-Szczecin-Poznań," August 27, 1945, in W. Borodziej and H. Lemberg, eds., *Die Deutschen östlich von Oder und Neiße 1945–1950: Dokumente aus polnischen Archiven*, vol. 3: *Wojewodschaft Posen, Wojewodschaft Stettin (Hinterpommern)* (Marburg: Verlag Herder-Institut, 2004), p. 378.
79. J. Chumiński and E. Kaszuba, "The Breslau Germans under Polish Rule 1945–1946: Conditions of Life, Political Attitudes, Expulsion," *Studia Historiae Oeconomicae* 22 (1997): 94.
80. C. Kraft, "Who Is a Pole, and Who Is a German? The Province of Olsztyn in 1945," in Ther and Siljak, *Redrawing Nations*, p. 112.
81. M. Djilas, *Wartime* (New York: Harcourt Brace Jovanovich, 1977), p. 423.
82. K. Mulaj, "A Recurrent Tragedy: Ethnic Cleansing as a Tool of State Building in the Yugoslav Multinational Setting," *Nationalities Papers* 34:1 (March 2006): 33.
83. Minute by Murray, British Embassy, to Czechoslovak government in exile, March 8, 1945, FO 371/47085.
84. Minutes of meeting with Deputy Chief of Main Division, Ministry of National Defense, July 28, 1945, MNO 3292/776 (1945).
85. *News Chronicle*, August 24, 1945.
86. *Daily Herald*, August 24, 1945.
87. *The Times*, September 10, 1945.
88. Maj. S. Terrell, "Berlin Survey," August 22, 1945, FO 371/46934.
89. Memorandum by Capt. A. C. Kanaar, September 11, 1945, FO 371/46815.
90. Quoted in M. Frank, *Expelling the Germans: British Opinion and Mass Population Transfers in Context* (Oxford: Oxford University Press, 2007). p. 137.
91. G. Gardiner, "Migration of Death," *Spectator*, October 26, 1945.
92. R. D. Murphy to H. F. Matthews, October 12, 1945, RG 84, 250/57/18/01–02. Office of the U.S. Political Advisor to Germany, Berlin [Robert D. Murphy]. Classified General Correspondence of the Political Advisor, 1944–49, box 1, "October 1945" file, NARA.
93. Undated and unsigned "Memorandum" by Murphy (c. October 12, 1945), ibid.
94. Squadron Leader F. W. Whittick, Displaced Persons Section, British Military Government, "Report on Refugee Situation in Berlin as at 21 Aug 45," August 22, 1945, FO 371/46990.
95. Lieutenant Mora, Liberec, to Ministry of National Defense, Prague, June 19, 1945, ÚPV-T, 217/2, box 308.
96. Staněk and von Arburg, "Organizované divoké odsuny?" part 2, pp. 26–27.
97. Staněk, *Verfolgung 1945*, p. 149.
98. Ibid., p. 163.
99. Voluntary emigration to the U.S. zone was sanctioned by the American military au-

thorities only after October 31, 1945. Unsigned minute, November 2, 1945, Ministerstvo Vnitra records, fond 686 II, file B 300/1253/1945.
100. Staněk, *Verfolgung 1945*, p. 54.
101. Memorandum by 1st Lieut. Jack E. Blaylock, September 1, 1945; memorandum by Maj. Harold E. Graham, October 18, 1945; Col. Y. D. Vesely, "Lack of Co-Operation in Controlling Shipments of Germans by Stribro District National Committee," October 20, 1945, RG 84, Entry 2378A, 350/54/13/03. U.S. Embassy Czechoslovakia. Classified General Records, 1945–1957, 711.9, box 3, NARA.
102. First Military District HQ, "Transfer of Germans from Žitava [Zittau] to Hrádek nad Nisou," October 17, 1945, MNO 9/4/1/40 (1945); unsigned memorandum, "Transfer of Svitavy German Nationals from Žitava to Hrádek nad Nisou—Results of Investigation," October 22, 1945, MNO 9/4/1/41 (1945); SNB, Jablonec nad Nisou, to Ministry of the Interior, October 18, 1945, MV-NR, box 7448, item B 951.
103. Dr. Janoušek, First Military District, Ministry of National Defense, to Ministry of the Interior, December 15, 1945, MNO 9/4/1/64; memorandum by Gen. Heliodor Pika, November 9, 1945, MNO 1151/951.
104. *News Chronicle*, October 15, 1945.
105. Statement by Neumarktl expellees, covered by letter from Political Division, Allied Commission for Austria (British Element) to the Southern Department, Foreign Office, February 14, 1946, FO 945/430.
106. J. Pfeiffer, "Situation à la ligne de démarcation Russe-Tchécoslovaque-U.S.A.," March 21, 1946, G 97/IV, box 1161, CICR.
107. Intelligence Branch, H.Q. British Troops, Berlin, "Conditions in Poland, Polish Occupied Germany and Russian Occupied Germany," September 22, 1945, FO 371/46690.
108. Ibid.
109. R. M. A. Hankey and M. B. Winch, "Tour of Upper and Lower Silesia—September 1945," FO 371/47651.
110. *Parliamentary Debates*, Lords, 5th ser., vol. 139, col. 85 (January 30, 1946).
111. Aide-mémoire by the French Embassy, London, October 6, 1945, FO 371/46813.
112. Allied Control Council, "Plan for the Transfer of German Populations to be Moved from Austria, Czechoslovakia, Hungary, and Poland into the Four Occupied Zones of Germany: Note by the Allied Secretariat," CONL/P (45) 57, November 17, 1945, FO 945/68; Foreign Office to British Embassy, Warsaw, December 1, 1945, FO 371/46815.
113. *New York Times*, December 16, 1945.
114. D. W. C. Harris to D. R. Heath, Director, Office of Political Affairs, October 13, 1945, Office of the U.S. Political Advisor to Germany, Berlin. Classified General Correspondence of the Political Advisor, 1944–49, RG 84, 250/57/18/01–02, box 1, "October 1945" file, NARA.
115. B. V. Cohen to Matthews, November 6, 1946, RG 59, Records of the Department of State Relating to the Problems of Relief and Refugees in Europe Arising from World War II, M 1284, 840.48, reel 59, NARA. See also W. Lasser, *Benjamin V. Cohen: Architect of the New Deal* (New Haven, CT: Yale University Press, 2002), chap. 15.
116. Draft telegram from State Department to U.S. Embassy, Warsaw, November 16, 1945, B. V. Cohen to Matthews, November 6, 1946, RG 59, Records of the Department of

State Relating to the Problems of Relief and Refugees in Europe Arising from World War II, M 1284, 840.48, reel 59, NARA.
117. *Dziennik Polski*, October 18, 1945. See also A. B. Lane, *I Saw Poland Betrayed: An American Ambassador Reports to the American People* (Indianapolis: Bobbs-Merrill, 1948), pp. 182–3, for another account of the same incident.
118. Unsigned and undated minute to J. F. Riddleberger, chief, Division of Central European Affairs, State Department, RG 59, Records of the Department of State Relating to the Problems of Relief and Refugees in Europe Arising from World War II, M 1284, 840.48, reel 59, NARA.
119. J. F. Byrnes to A. B. Lane, U.S. ambassador, Warsaw, November 30, 1945, RG 84, Entry 2378A, 350/54/13/03. U.S. Embassy Czechoslovakia. Classified General Records, 1945–1957, 711.9, box 3, NARA.
120. A. B. Lane to Byrnes, December 4, 1945, *FRUS: Diplomatic Papers, 1945: General: Political and Economic Matters*, vol. 2 (Washington, DC: Government Printing Office, 1967), pp. 1321–2.
121. Hrabčík to Ministry of National Defense, December 21, 1945, MNO 1151/951 (1945).
122. Staněk and von Arburg, "Organizované divoké odsuny?" part 3, p. 372.

CHAPTER 5. THE CAMPS

1. See, e.g., statement of Jan Jungwirt, February 1, 1954, Records of the U.S. High Commissioner for Germany, OMGUS/HICOG Criminal Court Case Files, Berlin, 1945–1955, RG 466/250/84/32/04, box 52, NARA.
2. Statement of Siegfried Oskar Pomper, camp physician, n.d. (c. March 1952), RG 466/250/84/32/04, box 50, NARA.
3. Statement of Wenzel Kneissl, March 23, 1952; statement of Rudolf Kroiher, April 27, 1952, Records of the High Commissioner for Germany: Clemency Board Prisoner Case Files 1945–1955, "H" to "K," RG 466, 250/68/22/5, box 6, "Hrnecek, Wenzel" file, NARA.
4. Statement of Johann Dolezel, July 31, 1952, RG 466/250/84/32/04, box 53, NARA.
5. E. Kogon, *The Theory and Practice of Hell: The German Concentration Camps and the System Behind Them*, 1st rev. ed. (New York: Farrar, Straus and Giroux, 2006), p. 106; statement of W. Hrneček, July 17, 1952, RG 466/250/84/32/04, box 50, NARA.
6. Statement of Mgr. J. Neubauer, July 30, 1952, RG 466/250/84/32/04, box 53, NARA. Prohibitions against pastoral activity in camps were common in Poland as well as Czechoslovakia. See B. Nitschke, *Wysiedlenie ludności niemieckiej z Polski w latach 1945–1949* (Zielona Góra: Wyższa Szkoła Pedagogiczna, 1999), p. 99.
7. Statement of Hrneček, July 18, 1952, RG 466/250/84/32/04, box 50, NARA.
8. Statement of Hrneček, July 16, 1952, RG 466/250/84/32/04, box 50, NARA.
9. Statement of Hrneček, July 25, 1952, RG 466/250/84/32/04, box 50, NARA.
10. Otto Lasch to CICR, March 3, 1946; G 97/1165, CICR; F. E. Kaplan, "Bericht über die Lage der deutsch-sprechenden Menschen in Jugoslawien," April 1, 1946, G 97/1164, CICR.

11. S. Jankowiak, *Wysiedlenie i emigracja ludności Niemieckiej w polityce władz Polskich w latach 1945–1970* (Warsaw: Instytut Pamięci Narodowej, 2005), p. 44.
12. Bogusław Kopka, who has compiled the most detailed database to date of the Polish forced-labor camp system, lists 206 establishments in operation between 1944 and 1950, though the existence of "wild" camps set up by local authorities continues to complicate any definitive count. Joël Kotek and Pierre Rigoulot estimate that in Czechoslovakia, some six hundred places of detention for *Sudetendeutsche* were to be found in Bohemia alone. B. Kopka, *Obozy pracy w Polsce 1944–1950: Przewodnik encyklopedyczny* (Warsaw: Karta, 2002); J. Kotek and P. Rigoulot, *Le siècle des camps: Détention, concentration, extermination* (Paris: Lattès, 2000), p. 534.
13. Letter from Chief Commissioner, MZO Szczecin branch, March 14, 1947; A. Chorzewski, head of the Settlement Unit of the Szczecin Voivodeship Office, to Chief Commissioner, MZO, April 24, 1947, in W. Borodziej and H. Lemberg, eds., *Die Deutschen östlich von Oder und Neiße 1945–1950: Dokumente aus polnischen Archiven*, vol. 3: *Wojewodschaft Posen, Wojewodschaft Stettin (Hinterpommern)* (Marburg: Verlag Herder-Institut, 2004), pp. 513, 526 n. 1.
14. T. Staněk, *Tábory v českých zemích 1945–1948* (Opava: Slezský ústav Slezského zemského muzea, 1996), p. 99. See also the directive by the Ministry of the Interior ordering the closure of "improvised internment camps" for "Germans, sometimes even with members of their families," and requiring the conveyance of their inmates to duly authorized camps, *Predvoj*, August 29, 1945.
15. W. Menzel to CICR Geneva, February 12, 1946, G 97/1161, CICR.
16. L. Olejnik, *Zdrajcy narodu? Losy volksdeutschów w Polsce po II wojnie światowej* (Warsaw: Trio, 2006), p. 75.
17. See, e.g., Office of the Pomeranian Voivodeship to the Świece *powiat* administration, September 14, 1945, directing that "all Germans" were "to be interned in camps and put out to labor without pay." Quoted in Borodziej and Lemberg, *Die Deutschen östlich von Oder und Neiße*, vol. 4: *Wojewodschaften Pommerellen und Danzig, Wojewodschaft Breslau* (Marburg: Verlag Herder-Institut, 2004), p. 126.
18. Olejnik, *Zdrajcy narodu?* p. 133.
19. T. Staněk and A. von Arburg, "Organizované divoké odsuny? Úloha ústředních státních orgánů při provádění "evakuace" německého obyvatelstva (květen až září 1945)," part 2: "Československá armáda vytváří 'hotové skutečnosti,' vláda je před cizinou legitimizuje," *Soudobé dějiny* 13:1–2 (January 2006): 22.
20. Staněk, *Tábory v českých zemích*, p. 23.
21. S. Gabzdilová and M. Olejnik, "Proces internácie nemeckého obyvateľstva na Slovensku v rokoch 1945–1946," *Historický časopis* 50:3 (2002): 425.
22. Staněk, *Tábory v českých zemích*, pp. 105–6.
23. Maj. W. Bradbury, Combined Repatriation Executive, to Gen. S. R. Mickelsen, chief, Prisoners of War and Displaced Persons Division, January 19, 1946, Office of Military Government for Germany, Records of the Civil Administration Division: The Combined Repatriation Executive, U.S. Elements: Records re Interzonal Population Transfers, 1945–49," RG 260/390/42/26–27/6-1, box 227, "Movement of Sudeten-Germans (Vol. I)" file, NARA.

24. Unsigned memorandum, "Les camps de concentration du gouvernement Tito dans le Batchka," dated July 1947, unsigned and undated (c. August 1947) "Liste de camps ou lieux de confinement de personnes appartenant à la minorité éthnique allemande en Yougoslavie (civils)," G 97/1164, CICR.
25. V. Geiger, "Josip Broz Tito i sudbina jugoslavenskih Nijemaca," *Časopis za suvremenu povijest* 40:3 (September 2008): 57; Z. Janjetović, "The Disappearance of the Germans from Yugoslavia: Expulsion or Emigration?" *Revue des études sud-est européennes* 40:1 (2002): 227; M. Portmann, "Repression und Widerstand auf dem Land: Die kommunistische Landwirtschaftspolitik in der jugoslawischen Vojvodina (1944 bis 1953)," *Südost-Forschungen* 65/66 (2006/2007): 349.
26. H. G. Beckh, International Committee of the Red Cross, "Rapport de la mission de M. Beckh en Bavière (Furth i[m]/W[ald] et Munich) du 16 au 23.3.50," n.d., G 97/1158, CICR; J.-L. Muller, *L'expulsion des allemands de Hongrie: Politique internationale et destin méconnu d'une minorité* (Paris: L'Harmattan, 2001), p. 67.
27. H. F. A. Schoenfeld, U.S. Representative in Hungary, to E. Stettinius, June 27, 1945. *FRUS: Diplomatic Papers, 1945: General: Political and Economic Matters*, vol. 2 (Washington, DC: Government Printing Office, 1967), p. 1259.
28. H. G. Beckh, "Compte-rendu d'un entretien du 9.4.46 entre MM. Kolb et de Steiger, délégués, et M. Beckh concernant les minorités en Roumanie," April 11, 1946, G 97/1165, CICR; *Osservatore Romano*, September 30, 1944.
29. R. W. Zweig, "Feeding the Camps: Allied Blockade Policy and the Relief of Concentration Camps in Germany, 1944–1945," *Historical Journal* 41:3 (1998): 826.
30. See J. Caplan, "Political Detention and the Origin of the Concentration Camps in Nazi Germany, 1933–1935/6," in N. Gregor, ed., *Nazism, War and Genocide: Essays in Honour of Jeremy Noakes* (Exeter: University of Exeter Press, 2005), pp. 22–41.
31. B. Kopka, "Polski Gułag," *Wprost*, March 24, 2002; E. Nowak, *Lager im Oppelner Schlesien im System der Nachkriegslager in Polen (1945–1950): Geschichte und Implikationen* (Opole: Zentrales Kriegsgefangenenmuseum Lambinowice-Opole, 2003), p. 57.
32. W. Menzel, head of CICR delegation, Prague, to P. Kuhne, January 28, 1946, G 97/1161, CICR.
33. Georges Dunand, "Camp d'internés civils de Patronka (Bratislava)," July 25, 1945, G 97/1160, CICR.
34. Jean Duchosal, secretary general, CICR, "Internment Camps in Slovakia," January 4, 1946, G 97/1161, CICR. The French-speaking Duchosal was writing in English, and by "cave" he no doubt meant "cellar" (*cave* in French).
35. Report of inspection by Dr. Josef Markowicz, March 31, 1947, MZO 196/541b, AAN.
36. Unsigned memorandum, "Les Camps de Concentration du Gouvernment Tito dans le Batchka," dated July 1947, G 97/1164, CICR.
37. *New York Times*, April 20 and 29, 1946; extract from report of CICR Prague delegation, quoted in E. de Ribaupierre to Mme Dainow, October 2, 1946, G 97/1161, CICR; D. Gerlach, "Beyond Expulsion: The Emergence of 'Unwanted Elements' in the Postwar Czech Borderlands, 1945–1950," *East European Politics and Societies* 24:2 (May 2010): 278; E. Hrabovec, "Neue Aspekte zur ersten Phase der Vertreibung der Deutschen aus Mähren 1945," in R. G. Plaschka, H. Haselsteiner, et al., eds., *Na-*

tionale Frage und Vertreibung in der Tschechoslowakei und Ungarn 1938–1948: Aktuelle Forschungen (Vienna: Verlag der Österreichischen Akademie der Wissenschaften, 1997), p. 122.

38. *Neue Zürcher Zeitung*, May 6, 2002. See also the statement by the Czechoslovak ambassador to the United States, V. S. Hurban, *Washington Post*, September 26, 1945.
39. Beckh to G. Dunand, June 12, 1946; unsigned memorandum, "Les Camps de Concentration du Gouvernement Tito dans le Batchka," dated July 1947, G 97/1164, CICR.
40. See, e.g., Lt.-Col. W. Alkan, RAMC, to the Allied Control Commission for Austria, June 21, 1946, FO 1020/2470.
41. Memorandum by F/O A. Reitzner, RAF, n.d. (c. September 1945), FO 371/46901.
42. Staněk, *Tábory v českých zemích*, p. 25.
43. A. Dziurok and A. Majcher, "Salomon Morel and the camp at Świętochłowice-Zgoda," http://www.ipn.gov.pl/portal/en/2/71. The prisoner, Eric van Calsteren, was one of at least forty-two foreigners, of thirteen different nationalities, known to have been interned at Świętochłowice.
44. Statement of a twenty-six-year-old female Potulice detainee, n.d., covered by letter from O. P. Brennscheidt (the author's cousin) to the CICR, June 15, 1947, G 97/1159, CICR.
45. Herr Lang, Government Commissioner for Refugee Organisation, Regensburg, to the State Secretariat for Refugee Organisation, Munich, August 17, 1948, covering testimony of Walter Hacker and Herbert Loges, fifteen-year-old escapees from Bunzlau, G 97/1156, CICR.
46. Unsigned "Constatations que nos délégués ont faites au cours du mois de juillet 1947 sur la situation des civils internés en Tchécoslovaquie," August 27, 1947, G 97/1162, CICR.
47. T. Staněk, *Poválečné "excesy" v českých zemích v roce 1945 a jejich vyšetřování* (Prague: Ústav pro soudobé dějiny, 2005), p. 79. For official categorizations of Polish camps, see W. Stankowski, *Lager für Deutsche in Polen am Beispiel Pommerellen/Westpreußen (1945–1990): Durchsicht und Analyse der polnischen Archivalien* (Bonn: Kulturstiftung der deutschen Vertriebenen, 2001), pp. 37–9.
48. See, e.g., interview with Prime Minister Zdeněk Fierlinger, *Bulletin of the Ministry of Information, 1st Department*, Prague, September 8, 1945; Gabzdilová and Olejnik, "Proces internácie nemeckého obyvateľstva," 432.
49. See, e.g., circular letter from Dr. Novák, Czechoslovak Ministry of the Interior, November 17, 1945, MV-NR, box 7450, file B 1469.
50. See circular letter of Ministry of the Interior to all Regional National Councils, November 17, 1945, MV-NR, box 7450, file B 1478.
51. Unsigned minute, c. August 20, 1945, Mirošov camp records, fond 534, box 1, file 18, SOA, Plzeň.
52. P. Nichols to Sir O. Sargent, August 11, 1945, FO 371/47154.
53. Nitschke, *Wysiedlenie ludności niemieckiej z Polski*, p. 98.
54. A. Dziurok, *Obóz pracy w Świętochłowicach w 1945 roku: Dokumenty, zeznania, relacje, listy* (Warsaw: Instytut Pamięci Narodowej, 2002).

55. W. Borodziej, "Einleitung," in Borodziej and Lemberg, eds., *Die Deutschen östlich von Oder und Neiße*, vol. 1: *Zentrale Behörden, Wojewodschaft Allenstein* (Marburg: Verlag Herder-Institut, 2000), p. 94; W. R. Dubiański, *Obóz Pracy w Mysłowicach w latach 1945–1946* (Katowice: Instytut Pamięci Narodowej, 2004), pp. 77, 80.
56. Letter from Officer Krenc, Bydgoszcz Civil Registry Office, to the Pomeranian Provincial Voivodship, December 4, 1945, in Borodziej and Lemberg, *Die Deutschen östlich von Oder und Neiße*, vol. 4, p. 167; see also Kopka, "Polski Gułag."
57. Nitschke, *Wysiedlenie ludności niemieckiej z Polski*, pp. 97–98.
58. An exception to this generalization was the incidence of sexual assault or coercion of prisoners by other inmates. Birgit Beck has also pointed out that members of the German armed forces stationed in occupied countries observed no such restraint with respect to the unincarcerated civilian population. See J. G. Morrison, *Ravensbrück: Everyday Life in a Women's Concentration Camp 1939–45* (Princeton, NJ: Markus Wiener, 2000), p. 229; B. Beck, "Sexual Violence and Its Prosecution by Courts Martial of the *Wehrmacht*," in R. Chickering, S. Förster, and B. Greiner, eds., *A World at Total War: Global Conflict and the Politics of Destruction, 1937–1945* (Cambridge: Cambridge University Press, 2005), pp. 317–331.
59. Thus Přemysl Pitter recorded the 1945 case of a German woman in a Prague camp who had been raped 120 times over the course of several weeks. Staněk, *Tábory v českych zemích*, p. 85.
60. Unsigned "Extrait d'un rapport de camp fait par un observateur étranger," August 1945; second report, same title and date, G 97/1160, CICR.
61. J. Duchosal, "Internment Camps in Slovakia," January 4, 1946, G 97/1161, CICR.
62. G. Dunand, "Camp d'internés civils de Patronka (Bratislava)," July 25, 1945, G 97/1160, CICR.
63. Copy of Royal Artillery, "W" Assembly Centre, Leibnitz, report, n.d. (c. September 1946); Capt. R. Camidge to Central Civil Affairs Office, Control Commission for Austria (British Element), September 19, 1946, FO 1020/2470.
64. Report by Antoni Białecki, Deputy Director, Division IV, Katowice Voivodeship Office for Public Security, May 16, 1945; report by staff of the 8th Self-Defense Battalion of the Internal Security Corps, August 8, 1945, in Borodziej and Lemberg, *Die Deutschen östlich von Oder und Neiße*, vol. 2: *Zentralpolen, Wojewodschaft Schlesien (Oberschlesien)* (Marburg: Verlag Herder-Institut, 2003), pp. 83, 101.
65. Statement of twenty-six-year-old Potulice detainee, G 97/1159, CICR.
66. Statement by Wilhelm Lubberich to the Hamburg Red Cross, February 2, 1949, ibid.
67. Quoted in Staněk, *Tábory v českych zemích*, p. 80.
68. Captain Dix, 313 Field Security Section, Frontier Control, to Styria District Security Office, March 24, 1947, FO 1020/2471.
69. Captain of Police Václav Heřmanov, regulations for employment of Mirošov detainees, June 3, 1945, Mirošov camp records, fond 534, box 2, file 15, SOA, Plzeň.
70. Staněk, *Tábory v českych zemích*, p. 113.
71. See, e.g., the complaint of the Velkostatek Liblín-Libštejn-Zikov firm, Liblín, to the District National Committee, Rokycany, September 6, 1945, Mirošov camp records, fond 534, box 2, file 13, SOA, Plzeň.

72. *Strážmistr* Grédl, SNB, to the Terešov SNB, August 16, 1945, Mirošov camp records, fond 534, box 1, file 10, SOA, Plzeň.
73. Report by I. Cedrowski on sanitary conditions in Pomerania Voivodeship prisons and camps for the period January 1, 1946–March 1, 1947, April 11, 1947, in Borodziej and Lemberg, *Die Deutschen östlich von Oder und Neiße*, vol. 4, p. 263.
74. See, e.g., M. Schenk-Sopher, "Note on Conditions in 'Rupa' Internment Camp," July 17, 1945, ÚPV-T, box 11, item 488.
75. Gabzdilová and Olejnik, "Proces internácie nemeckého obyvateľstva," 433.
76. P. W. Mock, "Camp d'internés civils de Petržalka (Bratislava)," November 6, 1945; same, "Camp d'internés civils de Trnavská Cesta, Bratislava," November 15, 1945, G 97/1160, CICR.
77. Dr. B. Nohel, "Bericht über Besuch des Spitals 'Selmovska,'" n.d. (c. May 1946), G 97/1161, CICR.
78. Report by A. Białecki, May 16, 1945, in Borodziej and Lemberg, *Die Deutschen östlich von Oder und Neiße*, vol. 2, p. 82.
79. Quoted in Olejnik, *Zdrajcy narodu*, p. 153.
80. British Embassy, Belgrade, to Southern Department, Foreign Office, July 18, 1946, FO 371/55525.
81. See, e.g., memorandum by Dr. Haas, Czechoslovak Ministry of the Interior, for the Office of the Prime Minister, November 30, 1946, ÚPV, box 1163, file 1424/4.
82. See, e.g., telegram from Nichols to Foreign Office, June 19, 1945, FO 371/47088; same, "Weekly Information Summary for week of July 31–August 6, 1945," August 6, 1945, FO 371/47091; same, "Weekly Information Summary for week of August 17–22, 1946," August 23, 1946, FO 371/56004; report by Major E. M. Tobin, Kaławsk, n.d. (c. April 1946), FO 1052/324; Lt.-Col. F. L. Carroll, "German Expellee Movement from Poland—Tour of Lt.-Col. F. L. Carroll, in Company with Cmdr. T. Konarski, Polish Representative, Combined Repatriation Executive," March 1, 1946, FO 1052/470; J. H. Marton, "A Forgotten People," *Contemporary Review*, January 1947.
83. Minute by Major P. B. Monahan, Directorate of Civil Affairs (Displaced Persons), February 4, 1946, FO 938/241.
84. The CICR delivered another 2.5 tonnes of food to the Ruzyně camp near Prague at the same time, but was unable to determine what had happened to it. Menzel to Paul Kuhne, January 28, 1946, G 97/1161, CICR.
85. Menzel to Max Huber, president of the CICR, September 14, 1945, G 97/1160, CICR; inspection report by Menzel on visits to Modřany, Ruzyně, Hradištko, and Štěchovice camps, n.d. (c. October 21, 1945), G 97/1160, CICR.
86. Death certificates for Mirošov camp, May 11–October 18, 1945, Mirošov camp records, fond 534, box 2, file 15, SOA, Plzeň; inspection report by Menzel on visits to Modřany, Ruzyně, Hradištko, and Štěchovice camps, n.d. (c. October 21, 1945), G 97/1160, CICR.
87. Unsigned memorandum, "Les Camps de Concentration du Gouvernement Tito dans le Batchka," dated July 1947, G 97/1164, CICR.
88. Minute by J. Colville, August 15, 1946, FO 371/55525.
89. Quoted in B. Soukupová, "Německá menšina v českém veřejném mínění po druhé

světové válce: Několik poznámek k etnickému klimatu v postevropském čase," *Historica* [Ostrava] 16 (2009): 284.

90. Draft telegram from Nichols to C. F. A. Warner, Foreign Office, June 25, 1945, FO 817/14.

91. Col. J. H. Fye, "Final Report—Transfer of German Populations from Czechoslovakia to U.S. Zone, Germany," November 30, 1946, p. 7, Margaret Eleanor Fait papers, accession no. 84040–9.02, box 4, file 16, Hoover Institution Archives, Stanford University.

92. Letter from Kežmarok District National Committee to the Slovak National Council, July 27, 1945, quoted in Gabzdilová and Olejník, "Proces internácie nemeckého obyvateľstva," 427.

93. As a result of *Obzory*'s revelations, the Ministry of Information suppressed the journal and initiated criminal proceedings against its editors and publishers in December 1945. These were eventually dropped and the paper reappeared after receiving an official censure, only to be banned once again, this time permanently, following the 1948 coup. See M. Drápala, "Na ztracené vartě západu: Poznámky k české politické publicistice nesocialistického zaměření v letech 1945–48," *Soudobé dějiny* 5:1 (January 1998): 16–24.

94. *Obzory* 1:12 (November 20, 1945): 177–8.

95. Ibid., 1:14 (December 8, 1945): 210.

96. Letter from František Jilek, ibid., 220.

97. Letter from Hanuš Wollner, ibid., 220–1.

98. Letter from Dr. Bedřich Bobek, ibid., 219.

99. Olejnik, *Zdrajcy narodu?* p. 169.

100. Gedye had gained access to Hagibor by posing as a Red Cross official. *Daily Herald*, October 9, 1945; *Yorkshire Post*, June 11, 1945; *Daily Mail*, October 4, 1945.

101. Steinhardt to James F. Byrnes, October 3, 1945, U.S. Embassy, Czechoslovakia, Classified General Records, 1945–1957, Department of State records RG 84, 350/54/13/03, box 1, NARA.

102. Nichols to C. F. A. Warner, Foreign Office, July 30, 1945; Sir O. Sargent to Nichols, August 24, 1945, FO 371/47154.

103. Memorandum by H. Krajewski, State Repatriation Office, Szczecin, October 29, 1946, MZO 196/541b.

104. P. Kuhne to Otto Lasch, German Red Cross, April 15, 1946, G 97/1165, CICR.

105. G. Dunand, "Conversations et audiences à Prague," May 25, 1945, G 97/1165, CICR. Two days previously, Václav Nosek had warned the Czechoslovak cabinet about the level of scrutiny exercised by the CICR. See Staněk and von Arburg, "Organizované divoké odsuny?" part 3: "Snaha vlády a civilních úřadu o řízení 'Divokého Odsunu,'" *Soudobé dějiny* 13:3–4 (January 2006): 322.

106. Olga Milošević, Secretary General, Yugoslav Red Cross, to CICR Geneva, G 94/1164, CICR.

107. Beckh, "Compte-rendu d'entretiens que le soussigné a eux [sic] avec M. Ehrenhold le 2.2.1949," February 2, 1949; "Compte-rendu d'un entretien avec M. Boesch le 27.5.1946," n.d., G 97/1159, CICR.

108. A. Kędzia, "Działalność opiekuńcza i lecznicza Polskiego Czerwonego Krzyśa w akcji repatriacyjnej i przesiedleńczej na Pomorzu Zachodnim," *Archiwum historii i filozofii medycyny* 64:2–3 (2001): 175–188.
109. See A.-L. Sans, "'Aussi humainement que possible': Le Comité International de la Croix-Rouge et l'expulsion des minorités allemandes d'Europe de l'Est 1945–1950 (Pologne-Tchécoslovaquie)," M.A. thesis, University of Geneva, 2003.
110. Menzel to CICR Geneva, February 18, 1946, G 97/1161, CICR.
111. See J.-C. Favez, *Une mission impossible? Le CICR, les déportations et les camps de concentration nazis* (Lausanne: Payot, 1988).
112. Beckh to F. Siordet and E. de Weck, November 9, 1949, G 97/1164, CICR. See also telegram from British Embassy, Belgrade, to Foreign Office, September 1, 1946, FO 371/55525.
113. British Embassy, Belgrade, to Southern Department, Foreign Office, December 14, 1945; telegram from German Department, Foreign Office, to British Embassy, Belgrade, March 14, 1946, FO 371/55525.
114. Foreign Office to Belgrade Embassy, November 15, 1946, FO 371/55525.
115. Telegram from Belgrade Embassy to Foreign Office, August 19, 1946, FO 371/55525.
116. Telegram from Belgrade Embassy to Foreign Office, September 1, 1946, FO 371/55525.
117. *Daily Herald*, March 11, 1946. At a speech in Sheffield the previous spring, John Hynd noted that the lowest standard of nutrition provided to inmates at Belsen during the war had been 800 calories a day.
118. *Manchester Guardian*, October 10, 1946.
119. Dr. Haas to Office of the Prime Minister, October 30, 1945, ÚPV, box 1163, file 1424/4; *Manchester Guardian*, November 20, 1946.
120. CICR Prague delegation to Division des Prisonniers, Internés et Civils (PIC), CICR Geneva, November 21, 1948, G 97/1161, CICR.
121. O. Lehner, Prague delegation, CICR, to PIC Division, January 30, 1947, G 97/1162, CICR.
122. Statement of J. Dolezel, July 31, 1952, U.S. High Commissioner for Germany, OMGUS/HICOG Criminal Court Case Files, Berlin, 1945–1955, Department of State records RG 466/250/84/32/04, box 53, NARA.
123. Beckh, "Exposé sur l'activité que le CICR a déployé dans le domaine des "Volksdeutsche" et Allemands de l'Est—Problèmes encore à resoudre," May 10, 1949, G 97/1158, CICR; A. C. White, Control Commission for Germany (British Element), report of interrogation of Gerda Schreinert, ex-detainee of Jaworzno camp, March 12, 1949, FO 1110/172.
124. J. A. Graf, adjunct delegate, CICR Bucharest delegation, to CICR Geneva, June 12, 1946, G 97/1165, CICR.
125. C. Reichard, CICR delegation, Prague, to P. Colombo, CICR Geneva, July 14, 1947, G 97/1162, CICR.
126. The *Volksdeutsche* internment facility at the former Auschwitz main camp (Auschwitz I) had a capacity of fifteen hundred. After the release or transfer to other camps of the last ethnic Germans in April 1947, it was briefly used as a detention center for members of Poland's Ukrainian minority arrested under a later ethnic cleansing

scheme, Operation "Wisła" (Vistula), before being converted into a permanent memorial site in 1948. Kopka, *Obozy pracy w Polsce*, pp. 147–8.
127. Note for the Minister of Public Administration concerning the Interministerial Commission for *Volksdeutsch* Labor Camp Affairs, January 31, 1949, in Borodziej and Lemberg, *Die Deutschen östlich von Oder und Neiße*, vol. 1, p. 394.
128. At the then prevailing rates of exchange, approximately fifteen dollars, or three weeks' wages for an ordinary laborer.
129. Intelligence Organisation, Allied Council for Austria (British Element), "Movement of Volksdeutsche into the British Zone of Austria," June 13, 1947. FO 1020/2748.
130. Prague Embassy to Northern Department, Foreign Office, March 4, 1949, FO 1110/171.
131. G. MacDonogh, *After the Reich: From the Liberation of Vienna to the Berlin Airlift* (London: John Murray, 2007), p. 157; *Der Spiegel*, November 4, 1951.
132. T. Staněk, *Verfolgung 1945: Die Stellung der Deutschen in Böhmen, Mähren und Schlesien (außerhalb der Lager und Gefängnisse)* (Vienna: Böhlau, 2002), p. 156.
133. *Jewish Daily Forward*, July 29, 2005.
134. In 2008 Tadeusz Skowyra, then eighty-four years of age, was charged in Katowice with offenses carrying a maximum three-year sentence, in respect of his tenure as commandant of Mysłowice camp in Upper Silesia. As of the date of publication of this book, the trial—probably the last of its kind to be held in Poland—had not taken place. *Die Welt*, May 19, 2008.
135. Deutsche National-Zeitung, *Verbrecher-Album der Sieger: Die 100 furchtbarsten Schreibtischtäter und Vollstrecker des Vernichtungskrieges gegen Deutschland* (Munich: FZ-Verlag, 1997).
136. M. H. Tenz, *The Innocent Must Pay: Memoirs of a Danube German Girl in a Yugoslavian Death Camp 1944–1948* (Bismarck, ND: University of Mary Press, 1991).

CHAPTER 6. THE "ORGANIZED EXPULSIONS"

1. Maj. F. A. C. Boothby, No. 1 Liaison Team, Kaławsk, to Lt.-Col. B. I. James, Refugees Branch, Military Government, Hanover, "Report on Train No. 165," May 18, 1946, FO 1049/515.
2. Memorandum by Maj. E. Nelsen Exton, Chief Protective Officer, UNRRA HQ, British Army of the Rhine, July 2, 1946; Capt. F. Garner, "Report on Train No. 165 (Jewish)," n.d., FO 1049/515.
3. Maj.-Gen. G. W. E. J. Erskine, Office of the Deputy Military Governor, Control Commission for Germany (British Element) (CCG [BE]) to the Control Office for Germany and Austria (COGA), July 23, 1946, FO 1032/836.
4. Unsigned and undated "Extract from a Report by an Officer of PW & DP [Prisoners of War and Displaced Persons] Division Visiting Marienthal Transit Camp on 6/7th July 46."; memorandum by Erskine, July 23, 1946, FO 1049/515.
5. CRX's permanent staff consisted of two officers appointed by each of the four occupying powers and a representative of UNRRA. Additional experts were appointed by the occupying powers as required. Lt.-Gen. F. E. Morgan, Chief of Operations,

UNRRA German Mission, Field Informational Letter no. 12, October 22, 1945, Series S-0527, box 0090, UNRRA Subject Files 1943–1949, "Repatriation—Conditions Affecting Poland" file, vol. 1, UNRRA records, United Nations Archive, New York City.
6. N. Davies and R. Moorhouse, *Microcosm: Portrait of a Central European City* (London: Jonathan Cape, 2002), p. 437.
7. Kenchington to Col. A. C. Todd, Deputy Chief, Prisoners of War and Displaced Persons Division, CCG (BE), January 5, 1946; Advanced Headquarters, CCG (BE), Berlin, to Main HQ, CCG (BE), Lübbecke, January 29, 1946, FO 1052/470.
8. Statement of Lord Jowitt, *Parliamentary Debates*, Lords, 5th ser., vol. 139, col. 82 (January 30, 1946).
9. Advanced Headquarters, CCG (BE), Berlin, to Main HQ, CCG (BE), Lübbecke, February 13, 1946, FO 1052/470.
10. Maj. A. K. Jones, PW & DP Division, CCG (BE), n.d. (c. February 1947), FO 1052/472.
11. Agreement between Lt.-Col. F. L. Carroll, British Representative, Combined Repatriation Executive, Berlin, and Lt.-Cmdr. T. Konarski, Polish Representative, February 14, 1945, FO 945/560.
12. Agreement between M. Trunov, Director General and Representative of the Delegation of the Soviet Occupation Zone in Germany, and Dr. A. Kučera, Counsellor of the Ministry of Internal Affairs and Representative for the Evacuation of Germans from the Czechoslovak Republic, June 1, 1946, FO 1052/471; agreement between Lt.-Col. Maslennikov, Soviet Representative, Combined Repatriation Executive, and Konarski, May 5, 1946, in P. Lippóczy and T. Walichnowski, eds., *Przesiedlenie ludności niemieckiej z Polski po II wojnie światowej w świetle dokumentów* (Warsaw: Państwowe Wydawnictwo Naukowe, 1982), pp. 68–9.
13. Red Cross memorandum, January 9, 1946; Walter Menzel to CICR Geneva, March 4, 1946, Archives Générales 1918–1950, B 97/IV, box 1161, CICR.
14. Col. J. H. Fye, "Final Report—Transfer of German Populations from Czechoslovakia to U.S. Zone, Germany," November 30, 1946, pp. 7, 10, 15, Margaret Eleanor Fait papers, accession no. 84040-9.02, box 4, file 16, Hoover Institution Archives, Stanford University.
15. "Summary of minutes of a meeting held on 8th and 9th January [1946] between Czechoslovak and United States authorities regarding arrangements for the transfer of Czechoslovak Germans to the American zone of occupation in Germany," n.d., FO 1049/297; undated and unsigned CRX memorandum, c. winter 1946, Office of the Military Government for Germany, Prisoners of War and Displaced Persons Branch, RG 260/390/42/24–25/7–1, box 128, NARA.
16. Memorandum by W. Barker, First Secretary, British Embassy, Prague, December 18, 1945, FO 817/14.
17. Fye, "Final Report," p. 16.
18. Telegram from W. Mitchell Carse, British Political Mission, Budapest, to Foreign Office, December 13, 1945, FO 371/55390; telegram from CRX to CCG (BE), December 22, 1945, FO 1032/2284.
19. Footage from the film, preserved in the Steven Spielberg Film and Video Archive at the

United States Holocaust Memorial Museum, may be seen online at http://resources.ushmm.org/film/display/main.php?search=simple&dquery=Tape+Number%3A+920&cache_file=uia_dtfAHp&total_recs=2&page_len=25&page=1&rec=2&file_num=1475.
20. O. Bamborough, British Consul, Karlovy Vary, to P. Nichols, British Ambassador, Prague, January 26, 1946, FO 945/432.
21. A. L. Lloyd, "A People Moves Out," *Picture Post*, August 17, 1946.
22. Reuter's news agency report, February 13, 1946, FO 371/55391; Capt. D. Bloodworth, "Report on Visits to Budaors on 30 and 31 Jan 46 to Inspect Arrangements for Deportation of Schwabians," February 1, 1946, ibid.; telegram from Maj.-Gen. W. S. Key, U.S. representative, ACC (H), to the commanding officer, United States Forces Austria (Rear), Salzburg, January 20, 1946, FO 1032/2284; Lt.-Col. H. G. Reeder II, PW & DP Division, to General S. R. Mickelsen, chief, PW & DP Division, January 30, 1946, Office of Military Government for Germany, Records of the Civil Administration Division: The Combined Repatriation Executive, U.S. Elements: Records re Interzonal Population Transfers, 1945–49, RG 260. 390/42/26–27/6-1, box 221. "C.R.X. Memos to Polish Representative" file, NARA.
23. Monsignor P. Ramatschi, Wrocław archdiocese, "Report on the First Red-Cross Train which Brought Sick, Old, Care-Needing and Bed-Ridden Persons from Breslau to Aurich," July 1, 1946, FO 1049/515.
24. *Manchester Guardian*, March 10, 1946.
25. Report by Dr. Busekirt, medical adviser to Military Government 508 (R) Detachment, Lübeck, March 8, 1946, FO 1052/323.
26. Report by Lieut. C. M. Weldon, Commandant, Pöppendorf camp, March 7, 1946, FO 1052/470.
27. Lt.-Col. F. C. Davis, Military Government, Westphalia Region, to PW & DP Division, CCG (BE), May 15, 1946, FO 1052/323.
28. Col. R. M. Jerram, PW & DP Division, "Operation Swallow: Extract from Various Reports, Letters and Visits of British Staff Officers," n.d. (c. March 1946), appendix B: statistical table of first 112 Swallow arriving trains, March 19, 1946, FO 1052/323.
29. Memorandum by officer commanding, MilGov, Land Westfalen, March 13, 1946, FO 1052/470.
30. Maj. A. K. Jones, "A Report on SWALLOW and the Visit to 508 R/Det and 626 DP/Det by Majors Barber and Jones of PW and DP Division," April 5, 1946, FO 1052/323. The British cartoonist Frederick Roland Emett ("Rowland Emmett") was renowned for his drawings of comically dilapidated and obsolete trains, many of which resembled the absurdist creations of his American contemporary, Rube Goldberg.
31. 709 (R) Detachment, Military Government, "Second Report on Swallow Trains," n.d. (c. March 25, 1946), FO 1052/470.
32. Jerram, "Operation Swallow: Extract from Various Reports, appendix B: first 112 Swallow arriving trains, March 19, 1946, FO 1052/323; Brigadier A. G. Kenchington, Chief of Prisoners of War and Displaced Persons Division, CCG (BE) to the Deputy Chief of Staff (Policy), British Army of the Rhine, April 30, 1946, FO 1052/471.

33. Extract from report by officer commanding, Military Government Grasleben Detachment, n.d. (c. March 1946), FO 1052/323.
34. Jerram, "Operation Swallow: Extracts from Various Reports."
35. Major Bieostocki [sic], Commandant of the Group of Operations, Kaławsk, to the British Liaison Team, n.d. (c. June 28, 1946), FO 1052/474.
36. Memorandum by Lieut. C. Weldon, Commandant, Pöppendorf Camp, for 8 Corps HQ, Military Government, March 7, 1946, FO 1052/471.
37. Lt.-Col. F. L. Carroll, CRX, to Lt.-Cmdr. T. Konarski, May 20, 1946, FO 1052/324.
38. Memorandum by No. 1 British Liaison Team, Kaławsk, June 4, 1946, FO 1052/324.
39. Telegram from 709 (R) Detachment, Military Government, to CCG (BE) Main HQ, Lübbecke, April 23, 1946, FO 1052/323.
40. Lt.-Col. H. L. V. Beddington, Commanding Officer, No. 2 Liaison Team, Szczecin, to Kenchington, Weekly Report no. 6, June 18, 1946, FO 1052/324.
41. Jerram to Advance HQ, CCG (BE), Berlin, April 26, 1946, FO 1052/474; memorandum by No. 1 British Liaison Team, Kaławsk, June 4, 1946, FO 1052/374.
42. Boothby to Wolski, June 26, 1946, FO 1052/474.
43. Memorandum by Col. Zdzisław Bibrowski, Polish Repatriation Mission, Berlin, March 11, 1946, MZO 196/527a/B-5638.
44. Kazimierz Kuźmicki to Roman Fundowicz, Commissar for German Repatriation Affairs, Wrocław, August 12, 1946, MZO 541b/B-7414.
45. Telegram from CCG (BE), Berlin to CCG (BE), Lübbecke, April 2, 1946, FO 1052/470.
46. Transcript of broadcast by Radio Warsaw, March 27, 1946, FO 371/55393.
47. Troutbeck to Mark Turner, COGA, April 12, 1946, FO 371/55392.
48. Telegram from Foreign Office to Cavendish-Bentinck, April 10, 1946, FO 371/55393.
49. Telegram from Cavendish-Bentinck to Foreign Office, April 13, 1946, FO 371/55393.
50. Telegram from Cavendish-Bentinck to Foreign Office, April 15, 1946, FO 371/55393; F. Savery to R. M. A. Hankey, April 23, 1946, FO 371/55394.
51. Wilberforce to Troutbeck, April 4, 1946, FO 945/67.
52. Minute by A. A. E. Franklin, n.d. (c. April 19, 1946), FO 371/55394.
53. Minute by D. Allen, April 19, 1946, FO 371/55394.
54. Telegram from CCG (BE), Advance HQ, Berlin, to War Office, May 1, 1946, FO 945/67.
55. Telegram from Bevin to Cavendish-Bentinck, May 7, 1946, FO 371/55393.
56. Telegram from Strang to British Embassy, Warsaw, March 28, 1946.
57. Lt.-Col. P. F. A. Growse, "Report by Liaison Team, Kohlfurt, up to 3 May 1946," May 4, 1946, FO 1052/474.
58. Minute by Beddington, April 6, 1946, FO 1052/323.
59. S. Jankowiak, "'Cleansing' Poland of Germans: The Province of Pomerania, 1945–1949," in P. Ther and A. Siljak, eds., *Redrawing Nations: Ethnic Cleansing in East-Central Europe 1944–1948* (Lanham, MD: Rowman & Littlefield, 2001), p. 95.
60. Dr. Ilse Reicke–von Hülsen, "The Situation of the Women during the Polish Occupation," n.d., enclosed with letter from Col. R. Jones, HQ Military Government, Lower Saxony, to Political Division, CCG (BE), Berlin, December 27, 1946, FO 1049/521.

61. MZO instruction notes, n.d. (c. 1946), MZO 541d/B-7416; A. Anatol, "Material do okolnika MZO dot. repatriacji niemców," January 13, 1946, MZO 527a/B-5638.
62. J. Walters, British Vice Consul, Szczecin, May 26, 1946, FO 371/56596.
63. Memorandum by Wacław Majewski, MZO, Warsaw, August 21, 1948, MZO 541h/B-7420.
64. Jankowiac, "'Cleansing' Poland of Germans," p. 100.
65. P. Dudkiewicz, *Starost* of Wolinsky Powiat, to the Settlement Department, Szczecin, August 5, 1947, MZO 541h/B-7420.
66. J. Chumiński and E. Kaszuba, "The Breslau Germans under Polish Rule 1945–1946: Conditions of Life, Political Attitudes, Expulsion," *Studia Historiae Oeconomicae* 22 (1997): 98.
67. Memorandum by Inspector J. Lipiński, PUR, Szczecin, July 16, 1948, MZO 541h/B-7420.
68. Memorandum by L. Lacisz, Inspection Department, MZO, June 2, 1947, MZO 541b/B-7414.
69. Report by Maj. E. M. Tobin, Commanding Officer, Marienthal transit camp, n.d. (c. April 1946), FO 1052/324.
70. Telegram from CCG (BE), Lübbecke, to CCG (BE), Berlin, May 30, 1946, FO 1072/471.
71. Telegram from CCG (BE), Lübbecke, to CCG (BE), Berlin, May 31, 1946, FO 1052/474.
72. Boothby to the Voivode, Lower Silesia, May 17, 1946, MZO 541f/B-7418.
73. Boothby to Lt.-Col. B. I. James, 229 (P) Det Mil Gov, Hanover, May 19, 1946, FO 1052/474.
74. Boothby to James, May 25, 1946, FO 1052/474.
75. See, e.g., manifests of expulsion trains to Soviet zone, December 14–24, 1946 inclusive, MZO 527e/B-7334.
76. Report of the Inspection Department, MZO, on inspection on March 12–13, 1946, of Assembly Camp no. 3 (Szczecin-Gumieńce), April 15, 1946, in W. Borodziej and H. Lemberg, eds., *Die Deutschen östlich von Oder und Neiße 1945–1950: Dokumente aus polnischen Archiven*, vol. 3: *Wojewodschaft Posen, Wojewodschaft Stettin (Hinterpommern)* (Marburg: Verlag Herder-Institut, 2004), p. 454.
77. Extract from report of No. 2 British Liaison Team, Szczecin, in letter from Maj. F. J. Sibley, CRX, to PW & DP Division, Berlin, January 20, 1947, FO 1052/472.
78. Beddington to Kenchington, April 18, 1946, FO 1052/323.
79. Statement by Friedrich Geppert, transport leader of train no. 76, April 7, 1946, FO 1052/474.
80. Cavendish-Bentinck to R. M. A. Hankey, October 16, 1946, FO 1049/515.
81. Capt. F. Garner, commanding officer, no. 2 British liaison team, Szczecin, to Kenchington, February 1, 1947, FO 1052/475.
82. Monthly report for March 1947 by Dr. Władysław Michno, head of the PUR Health Unit, Szczecin, April 5, 1947, in Borodziej and Lemberg, *Die Deutschen östlich von Oder und Neiße*, vol. 3, p. 514.

83. Report by J. Adamkiewicz, head of the PUR Health Unit, Białogard, March 1, 1947, ibid., pp. 508–510.
84. Reports by E. Kinsner, MZO, July 3 and 4, 1946, MZO 541b/B-7414.
85. Report by L. Musial and J. Lipiński, MZO, May 2, 1947, MZO 541b/B-7414.
86. Kazimierz Kuźmicki to Roman Fundowicz, July 28 and August 12, 1946, MZO 541b/B-7414.
87. Kuźmicki to Fundowicz, August 12 and October 6, 1946, MZO 541b/B-7414.
88. Boothby to Aleksander Barchacz, Voivode of Lower Silesia, June 14, 1946, in Borodziej and Lemberg, *Die Deutschen östlich von Oder und Neiße*, vol. 3, p. 580; report of the Inspection Department, MZO, on Assembly Camp no. 3, Szczecin, April 15, 1946, ibid., p. 454.
89. Notes by the commandant, Kaławsk embarkation point, for meeting with Fundowicz, June 28, 1946, in Borodziej and Lemberg, *Die Deutschen östlich von Oder und Neiße*, vol. 3, pp. 580–581; Boothby to Fundowicz, July 11, 1946, ibid., p. 592; Chief Representative for the Repatriation of the German Population, MZO, to Barchacz, August 21, 1946, ibid., p. 598.
90. Kinsner to MZO, November 25, 1946, MZO 541c/B-7415.
91. J. Lipiński, PUR, to Main Delegate, MZO, Szczecin, December 14, 1946, MZO 541h/B-7420.
92. Report by Adam Targosz, PUR, November 8, 1946, MZO 541d/B-7416; I. Zawadzki to MZO, January 7, 1947, MZO 541b/B-7414.
93. Report by Lipiński for the Voivode of Szczecin, September 20, 1946, in Borodziej and Lemberg, eds., *Die Deutschen östlich von Oder und Neiße*, vol. 3, p. 477.
94. Beddington to Kenchington, April 18, 1946, FO 1052/323.
95. Letter from A. Richter, April 7, 1946, FO 1052/324.
96. Statement of Käthe Hoffman, Kaławsk, July 1, 1946; Boothby to the Voivode of Silesia, same date, FO 1052/474.
97. Kuźmicki to Fundowicz, July 18, 1946, MZO 541c/B-7415.
98. M. Langer to PUR headquarters, January 15, 1947, in Borodziej and Lemberg, *Die Deutschen östlich von Oder und Neiße*, vol. 3, p. 493.
99. Statement by Franz Muller, transport leader, train no. 74, April 6, 1946, FO 1052/474.
100. Memorandum by Maj. I. E. Carr, Military Government, Hanover, June 13, 1946, FO 1052/324.
101. Cavendish-Bentinck to C. F. A. Warner, Foreign Office, September 19, 1945, FO 371/47651.
102. See J. T. Gross, *Fear: Anti-Semitism in Poland after Auschwitz. An Essay in Historical Interpretation* (New York: Random House, 2006), pp. 81–117.
103. S. Rolinek, "Jüdische Fluchthilfe im Raum Salzburg: Das Netzwerk von Bricha und Betar 1945 bis 1948," in T. Albrich, ed., *Flucht nach Eretz Israel: Die Bricha und der jüdische Exodus durch Österreich 1945* (Innsbruck: Studien Verlag, 1998), pp. 93–118. See also S. Rolinek, *Jüdische Lebenswelten 1945–1955: Flüchtlinge in der amerikanischen Zone Österreichs* (Innsbruck: Studien Verlag, 2007).
104. A. J. Kochavi, *Post-Holocaust Politics: Britain, the United States, and Jewish Refugees, 1945–1948* (Chapel Hill: University of North Carolina Press, 2001), p. 175.

105. W. H. B. Mack to Troutbeck, December 6, 1945, FO 371/46661.
106. Telegram from Hankey to Foreign Office, January 9, 1946, FO 371/57684.
107. J. Walters, "Stettin General Report No. 3," May 26, 1946, FO 371/56596.
108. Maj. E. M. Tobin to CCG (BE) Main HQ, Hanover, June 12, 1946, FO 1052/324.
109. Boothby to Lt.-Col. B. I. James, 229 (P) Det. Military Government, Hanover, June 15, 1946, FO 1052/474.
110. Boothby to Ford, July 11, 1946, FO 1052/474.
111. Report by Ford for Kenchington, December 27, 1945, FO 1952/470.
112. Maj.-Gen. J. S. Lethbridge, Chief, Intelligence Division, BAOR to Lieut.-Gen. Sir Brian Robertson, Deputy Military Governor, British zone, Germany, dated "Jul 46," FO 1030/331.
113. G. W. Rendel to Hector McNeil, n.d. (c. January 9, 1946), FO 371/57684.
114. Erskine to Sir Gilmour Jenkins, COGA, August 1, 1946, FO 945/68.
115. Lethbridge to Robertson, "Jul 46"; unsigned and undated BAOR memorandum, "Organisation in Prague for the Despatch of Illegal Polish Immigrants to Palestine"; Robertson to Sir Arthur Street, Permanent Secretary, COGA, August 14, 1946, FO 1030/331.
116. T. Staněk and A. von Arburg, "Organizované divoké odsuny? Úloha ústředních státních orgánů při provádění "evakuace" německého obyvatelstva (květen až září 1945)," part 3: "Snaha vlády a civilních úradu o řízení 'Divokého Odsunu,'" *Soudobé dějiny* 13:3–4 (January 2006): 342.
117. See, e.g., unsigned and undated (c. September 1945) "Transport Calculation," MNO 1151/951 (1945).
118. Gen. B. Boček, Chief of Staff, Ministry of National Defense, to Lieut.-Gen. Dratvin, Office of the Prime Minister, May 6, 1946, ÚPV-T, 127/2, box 308, Prague.
119. Memorandum by Gen. P. Bohumil, April 10, 1946, MNO 2617/785 (1946).
120. *Pravda* (Plzeň), July 27, 1946; *Sever*, July 30, 1946; F. Frenzel to the Ministry of the Interior, June 27, 1945, MV-NR, box 7446, file B 458.
121. A. Kučera to Z. Fierlinger, June 9, 1946, ÚPV-T 127/2, box 308.
122. *Rudé právo*, May 16, September 8, 1946.
123. Gen. K. Klapálek, "Observations on the Transfer of Germans into the Soviet Occupation Zone," December 18, 1946, MNO 196/1140 (1946).
124. Unsigned memorandum, "Transfer of Germans in May and June 1946: Negotiations with American Generals in Prague," April 10, 1946, MNO 2617/785 (1946).
125. Second Division to HQ, Military Region 1, January 15, 1946, Vojenská oblast 1 papers, file 52005, VÚA.
126. Gen. K. Klapálek, "Observations on the Transfer of Germans into the Soviet Occupation Zone," December 18, 1946, MNO 196/1140 (1946).
127. Undated and unsigned memorandum on Sudeten expulsions (c. winter 1946), U.S. PW & DP Division, OMGUS RG 260/390/42/24–25/7–1, box 128; Capt. H. W. Lambert, Expulsion Officer, Furth im Wald, "Problems Encountered in Accepting Sudeten German Refugees," March 5, 1947, Office of Military Government for Germany, Records of the Civil Administration Division, Prisoners of War and Displaced

Persons Branch: Records Relating to Expellees in the U.S. Zone, 1945–49, RG 260/390/42/26/1-2, box 189, "Expellees (Czech) 1947" file, NARA.
128. Capt. H. W. Lambert, "Problems Encountered in Accepting Sudeten German Refugees.'
129. Capt. Charles B. Rovin, Chief, Refugee Section, OMGB, to Col. J. H. Fye, Third U.S. Army Liaison Officer to the General Staff, Ministry of National Defense, Prague, August 5, 1946, box 127, RG 260/390/42/24–25/7–1, NARA.
130. Lambert, "Problems Encountered in Accepting Sudeten German Refugees."
131. Fye, "Final Report," p. 22.
132. Lt.-Col. O. Zampach, Czechoslovak Army, to Fye, September 6, 1946, box 127, RG 260/390/42/24–25/7–1, NARA.
133. W. Rudolf to the Fond Národní Obnoby, Liberec, December 14, 1946; C. G. Haucke, shipping agency, Liberec, to Schröder-Barkhausen law firm, Alsfeld (Hesse), November 23, 1946, OMGUS RG 260/390/42/24–25/7–1, box 128, NARA.
134. Lt.-Col. H. S. Messec, PW & DP Division, OMGUS, to the Public Safety Officer, October 2, 1946, OMGUS RG 260/390/42/24–25/7–1, box 128, NARA.
135. Lt.-Col. E. J. Jordan, Chief, Plans and Operations Branch, OMGB, to Messec, May 31, 1946, box 128, OMGUS RG 260/390/42/24–25/7–1, box 128, NARA.
136. Maj. W. T. Bradbury, CRX, to Lt.-Col. Ott, PW & DP Division, OMGUS, November 2, 1945, box 128, OMGUS RG 260/390/42/24–25/7–1, box 128, NARA.
137. State Commission for Refugees, Schwaben and Neuberg, to State Commission for Refugees, Munich, April 16, 1946, box 128, OMGUS RG 260/390/42/24–25/7–1, box 128, NARA.
138. Medical report by Dr. Böhm, Bavarian Red Cross, Wissau, April 13, 1946, box 128, OMGUS RG 260/390/42/24–25/7–1, box 128, NARA.
139. *Manchester Guardian*, September 12, 1946.
140. Staněk and von Arburg, "Organizované divoké odsuny?" part 2: "Československá armáda vytváří 'hotové skutečnosti,' vláda je před cizinou legitimizuje," *Soudobé dějiny* 13:1–2 (January 2006): 32; N. Naimark, *The Russians in Germany: A History of the Soviet Zone of Occupation, 1945–1949* (Cambridge, MA: Belknap Press of Harvard University Press, 1995), p. 148.
141. J. A. Grant, British Consulate, Bratislava, to Nichols, June 26, 1946, FO 371/55395.
142. W. Frąck, Deputy Commissar for Repatriation Affairs, Wrocław, to the Commissar for Repatriation Affairs for Lower Silesia, January 3, 1946, in Lippóczy and Walichnowski, eds., *Przesiedlenie ludności niemieckiej z Polski po II wojnie światowej*, pp. 135–7.
143. Maj.-Gen. G. P. Hays, Deputy Military Governor, OMGUS, Berlin, to Col. F. Dastich, October 22, 1947; Messec to Hays, August 16, 1947, RG 260/390/42/26/1-2, box 189, "Expellees (Czech) 1947" file, NARA.
144. Telegram from Maj. A. E. Levey, OMGUS, to Capt. Haller, U.S. Forces, European Theater, June 8, 1946, RG 260/390/42/26/1-2, box 189, "Expellees" file, NARA.
145. Col. J. H. Fye, "Final Report—Transfer of German Populations from Czechoslovakia to U.S. Zone, Germany," November 30, 1946, p. 45, Margaret Eleanor Fait papers, ac-

cession no. 84040-9.02, box 4, file 16, Hoover Institution Archives, Stanford University; A. Bauerkämper, "Assimilationspolitik und Integrationsdynamik: Vertriebene in der SBZ/DDR in vergleichender Perspektive," in M. Krauss, ed., *Integrationen: Vertriebene in den deutschen Ländern nach 1945* (Göttingen: Vandenhoeck & Ruprecht, 2008), p. 34; Naimark, *The Russians in Germany*, p. 148.
146. Draft memorandum by Thicknesse, n.d. (c. November 23, 1946), FO 1049/492.
147. Unsigned memorandum, "Proposed British Policy with Regard to the Movement of Germans into the British Zone with a View to Permanent Residence," March 1946, FO 1051/497.

CHAPTER 7. THE NUMBERS GAME

1. *Der Spiegel*, January 25, 1947.
2. *Picture Post*, February 15, 1947.
3. Maj. E. M. Tobin, "Report on Train No. 514 carrying Expellees under Operation Swallow," December 27, 1946, FO 1049/739.
4. Ibid.
5. Tobin, "Report on Swallow Train No. 513 ex Kohlfurt," December 18, 1947, FO 1052/323; unsigned and undated "Nominal Roll of Frostbite Cases on Swallow Train no. 513 of 15 Dec. 1946," ibid., unsigned and undated "Brief for the Deputy Military Governor for his Discussion with the Chancellor," FO 1049/739; Dr. Loebell, Marienthal camp physician, "Second Report on Swallow Train no. 513 of 15 Dec 1946," December 17, 1946, FO 1052/472.
6. Telegram from Advanced HQ, CCG (BE), Berlin, to Main HQ, CCG (BE), Lübbecke, January 18, 1947, FO 1052/472.
7. *The Times*, February 1, 1947.
8. B. Nitschke, *Wysiedlenie ludności niemieckiej z Polski w latach 1945-1949* (Zielona Góra: Wyższa Szkoła Pedagogiczna, 1999), n. 278.
9. "Note of the French Delegation on Transport Difficulties Confronting Transfers of Population in Germany," November 30, 1945, FO 1032/2284.
10. Brig. A. C. Kenchington to PW & DP Division, July 6, 1946, FO 1052/471.
11. Memorandum by Col. A. C. Todd, Deputy Chief, PW & DP Division, July 8, 1946, FO 1052/471.
12. Telegram from Main HQ, CCG (BE), Lübbecke, to COGA, June 29, 1946, FO 1052/471.
13. Telegram from Sir William Strang, Political Adviser to the Commander-in-Chief, Germany, to British Embassy, Prague, April 23, 1946; P. B. Nichols, British Ambassador, Prague, to C. R. Attlee, July 31, 1946, FO 945/432.
14. Col. J. H. Fye, "Final Report—Transfer of German Populations from Czechoslovakia to U.S. Zone, Germany," November 30, 1946, pp. 20-21, Margaret Eleanor Fait papers, accession no. 84040-9.02, box 4, file 16, Hoover Institution Archives, Stanford University.
15. J. Hynd, "The Problem of the German Refugee Populations in the British Zone," O.R.C. (46) 74, July 27, 1946, FO 945/67.

16. Nichols to Attlee, July 31, 1946, FO 945/432; minute by the head of the Political Department, Office of the Prime Minister, Prague, on discussions between Ambassador Steinhardt and Dr. F. Ševčík, July 23, 1946, ÚPV-T, 127/2, box 308, Prague; Fye, "Final Report," p. 18.
17. Telegram from Main HQ, CCG (BE), Lübbecke, to CRX Schleswig-Holstein and Hanover regions, July 19, 1946, FO 1052/471.
18. Maj. E. A. L. Ford, CRX, to PW & DP Division, July 26, 1946; telegram from 709 (R) Detachment, Military Government, to Ford, same date, FO 1052/471.
19. Maj. F. A. C. Boothby to Lieut.-Col. B. I. James, 229 (P) Detachment, Military Government, Hanover, July 14, 1946; Kenchington to Headquarters, PW & DP Division, July 25, 1946, FO 1052/471.
20. Telegram from Advanced HQ, CCG (BE), Berlin, to Control Office for Germany and Austria, July 14, 1946, FO 371/55395.
21. Minute by A. A. E. Franklin, July 19, 1946, FO 371/55395.
22. Telegram from Control Office for Germany and Austria to Advanced HQ, CCG (BE), Berlin, August 6, 1946, FO 1049/515; same to same, October 23, 1946, FO 945/673.
23. Minute by Sargent, December 3, 1945, FO 371/46816.
24. Minute by Sargent, December 3, 1945, FO 371/46816; minute by R. M. A. Hankey, July 21, 1946; same to Warner, July 26, 1946, FO 371/55395; A. A. E. Franklin, "Operation Swallow," August 24, 1946, FO 371/55396.
25. Transcript of Radio Warsaw broadcast, July 18, 1946, FO 371/55396; D. Wilson, Foreign Office, to R. S. Crawford, COGA, July 30, 1946, FO 1049/515.
26. Kenchington to Crawford, n.d (c. October 3, 1946), FO 371/55397.
27. Ibid.
28. Table by Lieut.-Col. Ugriumov and Lieut.-Cmdr. T. Konarski, Soviet and Polish Representatives, CRX, showing transfers of Germans from Poland to the Soviet zone, November 30, 1945–June 15, 1946, FO 1052/471.
29. "Report of the Activities of C.R.X.," DPOW/P (46) 50, April 26, 1946, FO 1005/839; same title, DPOW/P (46) 82, July 12, 1946, FO 1005/840; Kenchington to Crawford, n.d (c. October 3, 1946), FO 371/55397.
30. Telegram from Main HQ, CCG (BE), Lübbecke, to Advanced HQ, CCG (BE), Berlin; April 6, 1946, FO 1032/2285; Lt.-Col. E. D. Bevan, Military Government, to CCG (BE), Lübbecke, May 18, 1946, FO 1052/474.
31. Kenchington to Erskine, October 1, 1946, FO 1052/472; "Report of the Activities of C.R.X.," DPOW/P (46) 101, August 26, 1946.
32. Telegram from Advanced HQ, CCG (BE) to COGA, August 19, 1946, FO 371/55396.
33. J. Misztal, "Wysiedlenia i repatriacja obywateli polskich z ZSRR a wysiedlenia i przesiedlenia niemców z Polski—próba bilansu," in H. Orłowski and A. Sakson, eds., *Utracona ojczyzna: Przymusowe wysiedlenia deportacje i przesiedlenia jako wspólne doświadczenie* (Poznań: Instytut Zachodni, 1996), pp. 69–70.
34. Ministry of Foreign Affairs to Ministry of National Defense, March 28, 1946, ÚPV-T 127/2, box 308.
35. Memorandum by Lieut.-Col. G. B. Vaughan-Hughes, PW & DP Division, British

Military Government, Germany, August 10, 1946; minutes of 20th meeting of quadripartite PW & DP Directorate, April 5, 1946, FO 1032/2285.
36. Maj. A. K. Jones, "German Expellees from Poland (Operation "Swallow"), n.d., FO 1052/472; British Consul General, Frankfurt am Main, to C. E. Steel, Political Division, CCG (BE), Berlin, August 27, 1947, FO 945/760.
37. Telegram from CCG (BE), Berlin, to COGA, August 19, 1946, FO 371/55396.
38. Erskine to Col. J. P. Prawin, Polish Military Mission, August 26, 1946, FO 1049/515.
39. Telegram from Cavendish-Bentinck to Foreign Office, September 2, 1946, FO 1049/515.
40. Prawin to the Office of the Deputy Military Governor, CCG (BE), September 3, 1946, FO 1049/515. Emphasis in original.
41. Circular telegram by PW & DP Division, Lemgo, September 11, 1946, FO 1032/2285.
42. Minute by Franklin, September 13, 1946, FO 371/55397.
43. Erskine to Prawin, September 20, 1946, FO 1049/515.
44. Kenchington to Crawford, n.d (c. October 3, 1946), FO 371/55397.
45. Polish Ministry of Foreign Affairs to British Embassy, Warsaw, September 30, 1946; minute by D. Wilson, October 8, 1946, FO 1049/515.
46. L. D. Clay to G. H. Weems, May 19, 1946, *FRUS, 1947: Eastern Europe, the Soviet Union*, vol. 4 (Washington, DC: Government Printing Office, 1972), p. 376 n. 14; "Report of the Activities of C.R.X.," DPOW/P (46) 62, May 24, 1946, FO 1005/840.
47. J.-L. Muller, *L'expulsion des allemands de Hongrie: Politique internationale et destin méconnu d'une minorité* (Paris: L'Harmattan, 2001), p. 31.
48. S. Balogh, "Population Removal and Population Exchange in Hungary After World War II," in F. Glatz, ed., *Études historiques hongroises 1990* (Budapest: Institute of History of the Hungarian Academy of Sciences, 1990), p. 410.
49. Á. Tóth, "Zwang oder Möglichkeit? Die Annahme der Maxime von der Kollektivschuld und die Bestrafung der Deutschen Minderheit in Ungarn," in R. G. Plaschka, H. Haselsteiner, et al., eds., *Nationale Frage und Vertreibung in der Tschechoslowakei und Ungarn 1938–1948* (Vienna: Verlag der Österreichischen Akademie der Wissenschaften, 1997), p. 101.
50. Muller, *L'expulsion des allemands de Hongrie*, pp. 42–44, 48, 154.
51. C. D. Eby, *Hungary at War: Civilians and Soldiers in World War II* (University Park: Pennsylvania State University Press, 1998), p. 292.
52. Telegram from Gascoigne to Foreign Office, May 15, 1945, FO 371/46810; E. Roman, *Hungary and the Victor Powers 1945–1950* (New York: St. Martin's Press, 1996), p. 64. The latter work incorrectly states that "the western powers did not receive a similar request . . ."
53. J. Grew to H. F. Arthur Schoenfeld, U.S. Representative in Hungary, June 14, 1945, *FRUS: Diplomatic Papers, 1945: General: Political and Economic Matters*, vol. 2 (Washington, DC: Government Printing Office, 1967), p. 1254.
54. Telegram from Gascoigne to Churchill, June 26, 1945, FO 371/46810.
55. Muller, *L'expulsion des Allemands de Hongrie*, pp. 85–6.
56. Undated "Report on the Deportation of Germans from Hungary," covered by letter

Notes to Pages 211–15   411

from Marshal K. Y. Voroshilov to Gen. O. P. Edgcumbe, December 8, 1945, FO 371/55390.
57. Maj. A. D. Spottswood, U.S. Forces in Austria, Displaced Persons Division, to Maj. Wiliam Bradbury, CRX, January 16, 1946; same to Col. E. E. Hyde, chief, Displaced Persons Division, January 4, 1946; telegram from Key to Hyde, February 7, 1946; same to Commanding General, U.S. Forces in Austria, March 14, 1946; Maj. J. F. Asselta to ACC (H), May 9, 1946; same to same, same date; telegram from Lt.-Col. J. D. Wilmeth, ACC (H) to PW & DP Branch, OMGUS, July 23, 1945; telegram from Clay to ACC (H), June 2, 1946, Office of Military Government for Germany papers, Records of the Civil Administration Division: The Combined Repatriation Executive, U.S. Elements: Records re Interzonal Population Transfers, 1945–1949, box 226, "Movement of Swabians, vol. I" file, RG 360/390/42/26–27/6-1, NARA.
58. Transcript of Radio Budapest transmission, January 18, 1946, FO 371/55390.
59. G. H. Weems, "Final Report by the United States Military Representative on the Allied Control Commission for Hungary," Annex F, September 15, 1947, *FRUS, 1947: Eastern Europe, the Soviet Union,* vol. 4, p. 376.
60. Minute by O'Neill, March 28, 1946, FO 371/55624.
61. Quoted in A. F. Noskova, "Migration of the Germans after the Second World War: Political and Psychological Aspects," *Journal of Communist Studies and Transition Politics* 16:1–2 (March–June 2000): 106.
62. "Agreement on Conditions Established for the Execution of Swabian Expulsion Program," signed by George Weisz, Executive Officer, Refugee Branch, PW & DP Division, OMGUS, and Dr. Julius Fischer, head of Presidential Section, Ministry of the Interior, Budapest, August 22, 1946, FO 371/55397.
63. Minutes by Franklin, September 14, 1946, FO 371/55397; August 27, 1946, FO 371/55396.
64. Copy of letter from Weems to Lt.-Gen. V. P. Sviridov, November 9, 1946, FO 371/55398.
65. Gyula Fischer, Chief of Presidential Section, Ministry of the Interior, to Weems, December 4, 1946; extract from minutes of ACC (H) meeting, December 6, 1946, FO 371/55398.
66. I. Sayer and D. Botting, *Nazi Gold: The Story of the World's Greatest Robbery—and Its Aftermath* (New York: Congdon & Weed, 1984), p. 187.
67. Gen. O. P. Edgcumbe, "Memorandum on the Deportation of Swabians," November 21, 1946, FO 371/55398.
68. Extract from minutes of ACC (H) meeting, December 6, 1946, FO 371/55398; copy of letter from Nagy to Weems, n.d. (c. March 1947), FO 945/673; Weems to Sviridov, March 27, 1947, ibid.
69. Weems to Clay, summarizing complaint of Hungarian government, April 24, 1947, FO 371/64224.
70. M. Mevius, *Agents of Moscow: The Hungarian Communist Party and the Origins of Socialist Patriotism 1941–1953* (Oxford: Clarendon Press, 2005), p. 137.
71. Muller, *L'expulsion des Allemands de Hongrie,* p. 117.

72. Noskova, "Migration of the Germans after the Second World War," 106.
73. A. K. Helm, British Political Mission, Budapest, to Bevin, July 23, 1947, FO 371/64225; "Report of the Activities of C.R.X.," DPOW/P (47) 60, April 19, 1947, FO 1005/842.
74. Mevius, *Agents of Moscow*, p. 139.
75. Maj. M. Hanley, "Deportation of Swabians," August 28, 1947, FO 371/64225.
76. Report by Corporal C. Sassie, Field Security Service, August 28, 1947, FO 371/64225.
77. Muller, *L'expulsion des allemands de Hongrie*, p. 119.
78. Quoted in Noskova, "Migration of the Germans after the Second World War," 106.
79. Telegram from Sir William Strang to Foreign Office, December 20, 1946, FO 1049/515.
80. Telegram from 508 (R) Detachment, Military Government, Lübeck, to Main HQ, CCG (BE), Lübbecke, January 6, 1947; memorandum by British Liaison Team, Szczecin, January 14, 1947, FO 1052/323.
81. Chief Commissioner, MZO, to the Director of the PUR Voivodeship Department, "January 4, 1947" [recte February 4, 1947], in W. Borodziej and H. Lemberg, eds., *Die Deutschen östlich von Oder und Neiße 1945–1950: Dokumente aus polnischen Archiven*, vol. 3: *Wojewodschaft Posen, Wojewodschaft Stettin (Hinterpommern)* (Marburg: Verlag Herder-Institut, 2004), p. 492.
82. Letter from Polish Red Cross administrative headquarters, Szczecin Voivodeship, April 11, 1947, in Borodziej and Lemberg, *Die Deutschen östlich von Oder und Neiße*, vol. 3, pp. 516–517.
83. MZO note on death rate among the German population of Gdańsk, April 9, 1947, ibid., p. 261.
84. Telegram from PW & DP Division, Lemgo, to PW & DP Division, CCG (BE). Berlin, February 1, 1947, FO 1032/835.
85. *Parliamentary Debates*, Commons, 5th ser., vol. 432, col. 58W (January 22, 1947).
86. Undated minute (c. February 25, 1947) by Vaughan-Hughes, FO 1052/472. Emphasis in original.
87. Col. R. Thicknesse, Deputy Chief, PW & DP Division, to Col. Pulverman, PW & DP Division, CCG (BE), Lemgo, June 9, 1947, FO 1052/472.
88. I. T. M. Pink, Deputy Chief, Political Division, CCG (BE), Berlin, to PW & DP Division, Berlin, February 8, 1947, FO 1052/472.
89. "Report of the Activities of C.R.X.," DPOW/P 46 (132), November 25, 1946, FO 1005/841; Jones, "German Expellees from Poland (Operation 'Swallow')"; untitled COGA memorandum, February 7, 1947, FO 945/673.
90. Prawin to Kenchington, May 8, 1947, FO 1052/472.
91. Kenchington to Thicknesse, March 5, 1947, FO 1052/472.
92. British Embassy, Warsaw, to Foreign Office, April 29, 1947, FO 945/673.
93. Vaughan-Hughes to Main HQ, CCG (BE), Lübbecke, November 1, 1946; telegram from Advanced HQ, CCG (BE), Berlin, to Main HQ, November 4, 1946, FO 1049/515.
94. Allied Control Authority, PW & DP Directorate, "Intention of the British Authorities to Discontinue the Acceptance of Germans to be Transferred from Poland (Point of View of the Soviet Member)" [Major General Yurkin], October 26, 1947, FO 945/673.

95. Vaughan-Hughes to T. Williamson, Manpower Division, CCG (BE), Berlin, October 25, 1947, FO 1052/466.
96. E. E. Swanstrom, *Pilgrims of the Night: A Study of Expelled Peoples* (New York: Sheed & Ward, 1950), pp. 13, 18–19.
97. M. Frank, *Expelling the Germans: British Opinion and Post-1945 Population Transfer in Context* (Oxford: Clarendon Press, 2007), p. 256.
98. The meeting took place on April 12, 1946. Fye, "Final Report," p. 29.
99. "Bi-Monthly Report of the Military Governor, U.S. Zone, on Displaced Persons, Stateless Persons and Refugees for the Period February 1–March 31, 1947," RG 260/390/42/24–25/7–1, Office of the Military Government for Germany (OMGUS) PW & DP Branch, box 128, "Bi-Monthly Reports, 1946 to 1947" file, NARA.
100. British Consul General, Frankfurt am Main, to C. E. Steel, Political Division, CCG (BE), Berlin, August 27, 1947; unsigned and undated "Statement Issued by the United States Authorities," FO 945/760.
101. Maj.-Gen. F. A. Keating to James R. Newman, Director, Office of the Military Governor, Hesse, April 27, 1947, RG 260/390/42/24–25/7-1, OMGUS, PW & DP Branch, box 128, "Expellee General" file, NARA.
102. Chancery, British Embassy, Prague, to Northern Department, Foreign Office, March 4, 1949, FO 1110/171.
103. "Statement Issued by the Czechoslovak Authorities," August 23, 1947, FO 945/760.
104. E. Mayer, CICR delegation, Munich, to D. de Traz, head of the Prisoners, Internees, and Civilians Division, CICR, June 16, 1948, Archives Générales 1918–1950, G. 97/IV, box 1157, CICR.
105. Agreement between Capt. Laskowski, Polish Military Mission, Berlin, and Col. Maslennikov, Soviet Military Administration in Germany, April 12, 1947, in P. Lippóczy and T. Walichnowski, eds., *Przesiedlenie ludności niemieckiej z Polski po II wojnie światowej w świetle dokumentów* (Warsaw: Państwowe Wydawnictwo Naukowe, 1982), pp. 71–73; B. Nitschke, *Vertreibung und Aussiedlung der deutschen Bevölkerung aus Polen 1945 bis 1949* (Munich: Oldenbourg, 2004), p. 235.
106. Head of the Kałavsk transit station to the Director, PUR Wrocław, April 24, 1947, in Borodziej and Lemberg, *Die Deutschen östlich von Oder und Neiße*, vol. 4: *Wojewodschaften Pommerellen und Danzig, Wojewodschaft Breslau* (Marburg: Verlag Herder-Institut, 2004), p. 633.
107. Dr. Ziemplinski, medical officer of the PUR transit station, Kałavsk, to the Chief Physician, PUR, July 1, 1947; in Borodziej and Lemberg, eds., *Die Deutschen östlich von Oder und Neiße*, vol. 1: *Zentrale Behörden, Wojewodschaft Allenstein* (Marburg: Verlag Herder-Institut, 2000), p. 331; telegram from Inspector E. Kinsner to the Main Representative, MZO, May 16, 1947, ibid., vol. 3, p. 531.
108. Report by PUR Kałavsk, June 22, 1947, in Borodziej and Lemberg, *Die Deutschen östlich von Oder und Neiße*, vol. 4, pp. 644–647.
109. F. Ehrenhold, "Rapport sur la visite du Centre de Formation des Trains d'Evacués allemands à KAŁAWSK (anciennement Kohlfurth)," August 21, 1947, Archives Générales 1918–1950, G. 97/IV, box 1158, CICR.
110. K. Uscinewicz to MZO, November 12, 1947, MZO 541b/B-7414.

111. Minute signed "Kurpias," MZO, Tuplice, August 29, 1947; minute by Inspector E. Kinsner, MZO, September 18, 1947, MZO 541g/B-7419.
112. Nitschke, *Vertreibung und Aussiedlung*, p. 250.
113. I. Kostiashov, "Vyselenie nemtsev iz Kaliningradskoi oblasti v poslevoennye gody," *Voprosy istorii* (June 1994): 186–7. See also E. Beckherrn and A. Dubatow, eds., *Die Königsberg-Papiere: Schicksal einer deutschen Stadt. Neue Dokumente aus russischen Archiven* (Munich: Langen Müller, 1994), pp. 199–223.
114. Misztal, "Wysiedlenia i repatriacja obywateli polskich z ZSRR a wysiedlenia i przesiedlenia niemców z Polski—próba bilansu," 59.
115. Ibid., p. 62.
116. Nitschke, *Vertreibung und Aussiedlung*, p. 266.
117. Ibid., p. 258.
118. Minute by Jerzy Szczepanik, PUR, June 21, 1948, MZO 541g/B-7419.
119. L. Olejnik, *Zdrajcy narodu? Losy volksdeutschów w Polsce po II wojnie światowej* (Warsaw: Trio, 2006), p. 196.
120. Wolski to the Plenipotentiary for the Repatriation of the German People, August 18, 1946; minute by MZO Main Delegate for Repatriation Affairs, September 27, 1946; Roman Fundowicz, Commissar, PUR Wrocław, to the MZO Main delegate, MZO 527c/B-7332, AAN.
121. Boothby to James, June 22, 1946, FO 1052/474.
122. Nichols to Attlee, "The Transfer of Germans from Karlovy Vary," November 30, 1946, FO 371/56070.
123. *Rudé právo*, November 12, 1946.
124. Telegram from Nichols to Bevin, December 27, 1946, weekly information summary for December 22–27, 1946, FO 371/56005.

CHAPTER 8. THE CHILDREN

1. W. L. Montandon, "Visite et ravitaillement d'une internée allemande au camp de rassemblement de MODŘANY près Prague," May 1, 1946, G 97/IV, box 1161, CICR.
2. E. E. Swanstrom, *Pilgrims of the Night: A Study of Expelled Peoples* (New York: Sheed & Ward, 1950), p. 48.
3. Ibid., p. 50.
4. Deposition of Anneliese Gerbing, nurse at Szczecin-Gumieńce transit camp, n.d. (c. April 1946), FO 1052/474.
5. I. Heinemann, "'Until The Last Drop of Good Blood': The Kidnapping of 'Racially Valuable' Children and Nazi Racial Policy in Occupied Eastern Europe," in A. D. Moses, ed., *Genocide and Settler Society: Frontier Violence and Stolen Indigenous Children in Australian History* (Oxford: Berghahn Books, 2004), pp. 387–411; R. Hrabar, Z. Tokarz, and J. E. Wilczur, eds., *Kinder im Krieg—Krieg gegen Kinder: Die Geschichte der polnischen Kinder, 1939–1945* (Reinbek bei Hamburg: Rowohlt, 1981), pp. 181–244.
6. I. Heinemann, *Rasse, Siedlung, deutsches Blut: Das Rasse- und Siedlungshauptamt*

der SS und die rassenpolitische Neuordnung Europas (Göttingen: Wallstein, 2003), p. 508 n. 104.
7. N. Davies and R. Moorhouse, *Microcosm: Portrait of a Central European City* (London: Jonathan Cape, 2002), pp. 395–6.
8. Heinemann, "'Until The Last Drop of Good Blood,'" pp. 250–255.
9. T. Zahra, *Kidnapped Souls: National Indifference and the Battle for Children in the Bohemian Lands, 1900–1948* (Ithaca, NY: Cornell University Press, 2008), p. 113.
10. N. Wingfield, *Flag Wars and Stone Saints: How the Bohemian Lands Became Czech* (Cambridge, MA: Harvard University Press, 2007), p. 161.
11. Ibid., p. 131.
12. See C. Bryant, "Either German or Czech: Fixing Nationality in Bohemia and Moravia, 1939–1946," *Slavic Review* 61:4 (Winter 2002): 683–706.
13. See P. Hauser, "The German Minority in Poland in the Years 1918–1939: Reflections on the State of Research and Interpretation. Proposals for Further Research," *Polish Western Affairs* 32:2 (1991): 13–38.
14. G. Jérome, "Les milices d'autoprotection de la communauté allemande de Pomérélie, Posnanie et Silésie polonaise (1939–1940)," *Guerres mondiales et conflits contemporains* 41:163 (1991): 57.
15. British Embassy Weekly Information Summary for week of January 4–10, 1946, FO 371/56003.
16. Undated memorandum by J. W. Taylor, chargé d'affaires, British Embassy, Prague, "Food Rations in Bohemia, Moravia and Silesia for 1 Person for 4 Week's [*sic*] Period (20.8 to 16.9.1945)," c. September 3, 1945, FO 371/47093.
17. Commandant of the Szczecin-Stołczyn Commissariat to the Szczecin City President, December 18, 1945, in W. Borodziej and H. Lemberg, eds., *Die Deutschen östlich von Oder und Neiße 1945–1950: Dokumente aus polnischen Archiven*, vol. 3: *Wojewodschaft Posen, Wojewodschaft Stettin (Hinterpommern)* (Marburg: Verlag Herder-Institut, 2004), p. 424.
18. T. Staněk, *Tábory v českych zemích 1945–1948* (Opava: Slezský ústav Slezkého zemského muzea, 1996), p. 60.
19. V. Geiger, "Josip Broz Tito i sudbina jugoslavenskih Nijemaca," *Časopis za suvremenu povijest* 40:3 (September 2008): 57.
20. T. Staněk and A. von Arburg, "Organizované divoké odsuny? Úloha ústředních státních orgánů při provádění "evakuace" německého obyvatelstva (květen až září 1945)," part 3: "Snaha vlády a civilních úřadu o řízení 'Divokého Odsunu,'" *Soudobé dějiny* 13:3–4 (January 2006): 338.
21. Unpublished memoir by Pitter, quoted in T. Pasák, "Přemysl Pitters Protest: Eine unbekannte Stimme Gegen die Greuel in den Internierungslagern 1945," *Bohemia* 35 (1994): 94–5. Vogl's name is misspelled as "Vogel" in this article.
22. G. Dunand to V. Nosek, July 5, 1945, G 97/IV, box 1160, CICR.
23. Staněk, *Tábory v českych zemích*, p. 90.
24. S. Gabzdilová and M. Olejník, "Proces internácie nemeckého obyvateľstva na Slovensku v rokoch 1945–1946," *Historický časopis* 50:3 (2002): 434.

25. Nichols to Bevin, October 19, 1945, FO 371/46814.
26. Circular letter from G. Dunand to Geneva-based relief organizations, May 28, 1946, G 97/IV, box 1155, CICR.
27. Circular no. 45 of the Ministry of Public Security's Department of Prisons and Camps, April 15, 1945, in Borodziej and Lemberg, eds., *Die Deutschen östlich von Oder und Neiße*, vol. 1: *Zentrale Behörden, Wojewodschaft Allenstein* (Marburg: Verlag Herder-Institut, 2000), p. 148; A. Dziurok, *Obóz Pracy w Świętochłowicach w 1945 Roku: Dokumenty, Zeznania, Relacje, Listy* (Warsaw: Instytut Pamięci Narodowej, 2002), pp. 24–26.
28. Ministry of Labor and Social Welfare to MZO, dated "June 1947," in Borodziej and Lemberg, *Die Deutschen östlich von Oder und Neiße*, vol. 1, p. 339.
29. Note for the Minister of Public Administration concerning the Inter-Ministerial Commission for *Volksdeutsche* Labor Camp Affairs, January 31, 1949, ibid., p. 393; report of the Commission of Inspection for the Camps for Germans at Potulice, Leszno, and Jaworzno, August 16, 1949, ibid., p. 405.
30. Staněk, *Tábory v českých zemích*, p. 60.
31. Register of Mirošov assembly camp, September 13, 1945, Koncentrační tábor Mirošov records, fond 534, box 1, file 18, SOA Plzeň.
32. I. Willoughby, "Czech Police Investigation Names Two Responsible for June 1945 Murder of Sudeten Germans," Radio Prague, June 2, 2009, http://www.radio.cz/en/article/116881.
33. S. H. Roberts, *The House that Hitler Built* (London: Methuen, 1939), p. 205; D. Macardle, *Children of Europe: A Study of the Children of Liberated Countries, their Wartime Experiences, their Reactions, and their Needs* (London: Victor Gollancz, 1951), p. 35. For a more accurate perspective, see N. Stargardt, *Witnesses of War: Children's Lives under the Nazis* (New York: Random House, 2005), p. 35.
34. E. Bártová, "Největší poválečný masakr němců vyřešen: Známe vrahy," June 1, 2009, http://aktualne.centrum.cz/domaci/kauzy/clanek.phtml?id=638627.
35. R. R. Stokes, "Memorandum on visit to Camp at MOST (MATHEUSEN) [sic], USTI and LITOMERICE on 10.9.46," n.d., G 97/IV, box 1161, CICR.
36. Dr. O. Lehner, CICR Head of Delegation, Prague, to the Minister of the Interior, August 6, 1947; unsigned memorandum, "Constatations que nos délégués ont faites au cours du mois de juillet 1947, sur la situation des civils internés en Tchécoslovaquie," August 27, 1947, G 97/IV, box 1162, CICR.
37. Herr Lang, Regierungsbeauftragter für das Flüchtlingswesen, Regensburg, to the Staatssekretariat für das Flüchtlingswesen, Munich, August 17, 1948, G 97/IV, box 1156, CICR.
38. Unsigned memorandum, "Les camps de concentration du gouvernement Tito dans le Batchka," July 1947, G 97/IV, box 1164, CICR.
39. Lt.-Col. A. C. Kendall and Maj. G. B. Shirlaw, "Report on Turnu-Măgurele Internment Camp, Visited on the 17th of September 1945 together with an American and a Russian Delegate," FO 371/48670.
40. Menzel to Nosek, September 4, 1945, G 97/IV, box 1160, CICR.
41. M. Gärtner, K. Gärtner, A. Gimpl, and E. Gimpl, "Tatsachenbericht," n.d., covered by

letter from M. Iconomow, CICR delegate, Salzburg, to CICR Geneva, May 13, 1947, G 97/IV, box 1164, CICR.
42. Unsigned memorandum, covered by letter from O. P. Brennscheidt (the author's cousin) to the CICR, June 15, 1947, G 97/IV, box 1159, CICR.
43. *Daily Herald*, October 9, 1945.
44. W. L. Montandon, "Distribution de marchandises au camp d'internement de Prague-Hagibor et ravitaillement du camp de P[risonniers de] G[uerre] et d'internés civils 'Auto-Park,' à Prague-Smichov," December 23, 1945, G 97/IV, box 1161, CICR.
45. *Obzory*, November 24, 1945.
46. Gabzdilová and Olejník, "Proces internácie nemeckého obyvateľstva na Slovensku," p. 429.
47. P. W. Mock, "Camp d'internés civils de Petržalka (Bratislava)," November 6, 1945, G 97/IV, box 1160, CICR.
48. Memorandum by Menzel on visits to Modřany, Rusyn, Hradišťko, and Stechovice camps, n.d. (c. November 1945), G 97/IV, box 1160. CICR.
49. Mock, "Camp d'internés civils de Trnavská Cesta, Bratislava," November 15, 1945, G 97/IV, box 1160, CICR.
50. Maud Schenk-Sopher, "Report on Conditions in 'Rupa' Internment Camp," July 17, 1945, ÚPV-T, box 11c, item 488.
51. Staněk, *Tábory v českych zemích*, p. 90.
52. *Daily Herald*, October 9, 1945.
53. M. Saschková to the Prague Delegation, CICR, dated "January 1946"; Menzel to CICR Geneva, January 9, 1946; letter from P. Drozd, Veltrusy nad Vltavou, January 5, 1946, G 97/IV, box 1160, CICR.
54. Dr. A. Bedo, Chief, Eligibility Division, Preparatory Commission for the International Refugee Organization, to A. Brownlee, January 13, 1948, Aleta Brownlee papers, accession no. 69059–9.13, box no. 5, "Displaced Persons—Children: Ethnic Germans (*Volksdeutsche*), 1945–1949" folder, Hoover Institution Archives, Stanford University.
55. Macardle, *Children of Europe*, p. 301.
56. M. I. Robinson, Rayner's Lane, London, in *Daily Herald*, September 16, 1945.
57. *Parliamentary Debates*, Commons, 5th ser., vol. 414, col. 366 (October 10, 1945).
58. *Parliamentary Debates*, Lords, 5th ser., vol. 138, col. 388 (December 5, 1945).
59. *Parliamentary Debates*, Lords, 5th ser., vol. 138, col. 390 (December 5, 1945).
60. *Parliamentary Debates*, Commons, 5th ser., vol. 414, col. 2362 (October 26, 1945).
61. *Daily Herald*, October 12, 1945.
62. Pasák, "Přemysl Pitters Protest"; *Obzory*, November 24, 1945.
63. See, e.g., *Rudé právo*, May 8, 1946.
64. H. H. C. Prestige, Aliens Department, Home Office, to C. F. A. Warner, Foreign Office, September 19, 1945; B. A. B. Burrows, Foreign Office, to Prestige, October 9, 1945, FO 817/14.
65. C. O'Neill to J. E. Barrell, Private Secretary to the Chancellor of the Duchy of Lancaster, February 7, 1946, FO 938/241.
66. Minute by Maj. P. B. Monahan, Civil Affairs (Displaced Persons) Division, War Office, February 4, 1946, FO 938/241.

67. Hynd to P. J. Noel-Baker, February 15, 1946, FO 938/241.
68. Nichols to J. M. Troutbeck, Foreign Office, April 1, 1946, FO 938/241.
69. R. M. A. Hankey and M. Winch, "Tour of Upper and Lower Silesia—September 1945," October 8, 1945, FO 371/47651.
70. Lt.-Col. P. F. A. Growse, British Liaison Team, Kaławsk, to the Voivode of Lower Silesia, Wrocław, April 22, 1946, FO 1052/471.
71. Telegram from Archibald Clark Kerr, Moscow Embassy, to Foreign Office, June 13, 1945, FO 371/47087; telegram from Nichols, Prague Embassy, to Foreign Office, June 22, 1945, FO 371/47088.
72. Quoted in Sudeten German Social Democratic Party, *Evidence on the Reign of Racialism in Czechoslovakia* (London: Der Sozialdemokrat, 1945), p. 11.
73. See, e.g., Szczecin City Council to the Szczecin Voivodeship Department of Public Safety, December 20, 1946; same to Szczecin Voivodeship Settlement Department, October 15, 1947, in Borodziej and Lemberg, *Die Deutschen östlich von Oder und Neiße*, vol. 3, pp. 488–9, 565–6.
74. B. Frommer, "Expulsion or Integration: Unmixing Interethnic Marriage in Postwar Czechoslovakia," *East European Politics and Societies* 14:2 (2000): 382.
75. G. E. Schafft, *From Racism to Genocide: Anthropology in the Third Reich* (Urbana: University of Illinois Press, 2004), pp. 127–8; D. Majer, *"Non-Germans" Under the Third Reich: The Nazi Judicial and Administrative System in Germany and Occupied Eastern Europe, with Special Regard to Occupied Poland, 1939–1945* (Baltimore: Johns Hopkins University Press, 2003), pp. 121–7, 246–8.
76. T. Zahra, "'Children Betray Their Father and Mother': Collective Education, Nationalism, and Democracy in the Bohemian Lands, 1900–1948," in D. Schumann, ed., *Raising Citizens in the "Century of the Child": The United States and German Central Europe in Comparative Perspective* (Oxford: Berghahn, 2010), pp. 187, 196–7.
77. A. Warring, "Intimate and Sexual Relations," in R. Gildea, O. Wieviorka, and A. Warring, eds., *Surviving Hitler and Mussolini: Daily Life in Occupied Europe* (Oxford: Berg, 2007), pp. 107–8, 112.
78. Order in Council No. 12250/M.E. (1945), December 22, 1945, FO 371/55390.
79. Polish Red Cross, Wrocław, to the Main Delegate for Repatriation Affairs, MZO, July 3, 1946, MZO 527c/B-7332.
80. Memorandum by S. Jarzyk, Office of the Plenipotentiary for Lower Silesia, February 12, 1946, MZO 323/B-5427.
81. Text of Decree no. 33, August 2, 1945, FO 371/47154.
82. Frommer, "Expulsion or Integration," p. 388.
83. *Nová doba*, August 23, 1946.
84. *Obzory*, November 24, 1945.
85. Quoted in Frommer, "Expulsion or Integration," p. 393.
86. Quoted ibid., pp. 392–3.
87. Quoted ibid., p. 399 n. 64.
88. *Právo lidu*, August 3, 1946.
89. Marriage Law of September 24, 1945, Art. XII, quoted in J. Szułdrzyński, *The Pattern*

of Life in Poland, vol. 6: *The Family* (Paris: Mid-European Research and Planning Centre, 1952), p. 47.
90. E. Roman, *Hungary and the Victor Powers 1945-1950* (New York: St. Martin's Press, 1996), p. 66.
91. Statement of a twenty-six-year-old female Potulice detainee, n.d., covered by letter from O. P. Brennscheidt (the author's cousin) to the CICR, June 15, 1947, G 97/1159, CICR.
92. M. Kent, *Eine Porzellanscherbe im Graben: Eine deutsche Flüchtlingskindheit* (Berne: Scherz, 2003), p. 83.
93. HQ Military Government, Lk Husum & Eiderstedt, CCG (BE) to 312 HQ Military Government, Schleswig-Holstein Region, September 16, 1946, FO 1052/358.
94. Unsigned letter to Landsratsamt, Herford, May 16, 1946, concerning Robert Hauk; same to same, May 15, 1946, concerning Josefa Arndt; unsigned and undated (c. May 1946) statement concerning Ida Hartmann; unsigned and undated (c. May 1946) statement concerning Magdalena Martin; unsigned and undated (c. May 1946) statement concerning Lisbeth Fladda, FO 1052/474.
95. See, e.g., letter from H. J. von Joeden, July 1, 1946, G 97/box 1161, CICR.
96. Chief Secretary, Office of the Deputy Military Governor, to the General Department, Control Office for Germany and Austria, June 14, 1946, FO 1049/515.
97. Statement by M. Runge, April 11, 1946, FO 1052/323.
98. Dr. Mawick, Oberkreisdirektor of Kreis Grafschaft Bentheim, to the Oberpräsident, Regional Youth Office, Hanover, April 16, 1946, FO 1052/474.
99. O. Lehner, head of CICR delegation, Prague, to the Ministry of the Interior, August 6, 1947, G 97/1162, CICR.
100. Davies and Moorhouse, *Microcosm*, p. 445.
101. K. Cordell and S. Wolff, "Ethnic Germans in Poland and the Czech Republic: A Comparative Evaluation," *Nationalities Papers* 33:2 (June 2005): 262, 268.
102. Macardle, *Children of Europe*, p. 285.
103. Unpublished typescript memoir, "Whose Children," box 9, part II, p. 201, Aleta Brownlee papers, Hoover Institution Archives.
104. Circular letter from Brownlee, September 20, 1948, box no. 5, "Displaced Persons—Children: Ethnic Germans (*Volksdeutsche*), 1945–1949" folder, Brownlee papers.
105. W. Byford-Jones, *Berlin Twilight* (London: Hutchinson, 1947), pp. 54–5.
106. Swanstrom, *Pilgrims of the Night*, p. 49.

CHAPTER 9. THE WILD WEST

1. Memorandum by Inspector Jan Slowikowski, MZO, August 18, 1948; statement by Tomasz Dziedzic, Jelenia Góra Municipal Authority in Szklarska Poręba, February 9, 1948; memorandum by Ryszard Pietkiewicz, Wrocław Voivodeship Settlement Department, January 29, 1948; minute by Kazimierz Ociepka, Szklarska Poręba, May 12, 1948; minute by Dziedzic, May 13, 1948, MZO 196/783/B-5903.
2. Quoted in F. D. Raška, *The Czechoslovak Exile Government in London and the Sudeten German Issue* (Prague: Karolinum Press, 2002), p. 66.

3. Z. Zeman and A. Klimek, *The Life of Edvard Beneš 1884–1948: Czechoslovakia in Peace and War* (Oxford: Clarendon Press, 1997), p. 189.
4. Quoted in E. Glassheim, "Ethnic Cleansing, Communism, and Environmental Devastation in Czechoslovakia's Borderlands, 1945–1989," *Journal of Modern History* 78:1 (March 2006): 78.
5. V. F. Cavendish-Bentinck to E. Bevin, September 13, 1945, FO 371/47608.
6. C. Kraft, "Who Is a Pole, and Who Is a German? The Province of Olsztyn in 1945," in P. Ther and A. Siljak, eds., *Redrawing Nations: Ethnic Cleansing in East-Central Europe, 1944–1948* (Lanham, MD: Rowman & Littlefield, 2001), p. 116.
7. *Manchester Guardian*, October 30, 1944.
8. J. Krejčí and P. Machonin, *Czechoslovakia, 1918–92: A Laboratory for Social Change* (New York: St. Martin's Press, 1996), p. 79.
9. A. Suppan, *Austrians, Czechs, and Sudeten Germans as a Community of Conflict in the Twentieth Century* (Minneapolis: Center for Austrian Studies, 2006), p. 34.
10. I. S. Pogány, *Righting Wrongs in Eastern Europe* (Manchester: Manchester University Press, 1997), p. 54.
11. *The Economist*, January 1, 1944.
12. L. Olejnik, *Zdrajcy narodu? Losy volksdeutschów w Polsce po II wojnie światowej* (Warsaw: Trio, 2006), pp. 27–28, 32.
13. W. R. Dubiański, *Obóz pracy w Mysłowicach w latach 1945–1946* (Katowice: Instytut Pamięci Narodowej, 2004), p. 7; A. Ehrlich, "Between Germany and Poland: Ethnic Cleansing and Politicization of Ethnicity in Upper Silesia under National Socialism and Communism, 1939–1950" (Ph.D. diss., Indiana University, 2005), pp. 209, 220.
14. Z. Radvanovský, "The Social and Economic Consequences of Resettling Czechs into Northwestern Bohemia, 1945–1947," in Ther and Siljak, *Redrawing Nations*, p. 251.
15. Quoted in Y. Weiss, "Ethnic Cleansing, Memory and Property—Europe, Israel/Palestine, 1944–1948," in R. Gross and Y. Weiss, eds., *Jüdische Geschichte als allgemeine Geschichte: Festschrift für Dan Diner zum 60. Geburtstag* (Göttingen: Vandenhoeck & Ruprecht, 2006), p. 164.
16. Foreign Office Economic Intelligence Department, "The Polish Settlement and the Population of Germany," August 27, 1945, FO 371/46990.
17. Unsigned memorandum of Polish government in exile, London, "Conditions in Poland (Memorandum no. 5)," n.d. (c. June 1945), FO 371/47649.
18. L. G. Holliday, First Secretary (Commercial), British Embassy, Warsaw, "Report on a Tour of the Baltic Ports," n.d. (c. September 16, 1945), FO 371/47650.
19. Holliday, "Observations on a Tour Made Between May 5th and May 14, 1946 by Mr L. G. Holliday, First Secretary (Commercial) of H.M. Embassy, Warsaw," May 20, 1946, FO 371/36596.
20. P. Ther, *Deutsche und polnische Vertriebenen: Gesellschaft und Vertriebenenpolitik in der SBZ/DDR und in Polen 1945–1956* (Göttingen: Vandenhoeck & Ruprecht, 1998), p. 190; memorandum by Special Reports Branch, H.Q. Intelligence Division, CCG (BE), May 18, 1947, FO 943/321.
21. Cavendish-Bentinck to Hankey, September 24, 1946, FO 371/56691.
22. Untitled memorandum by G. Lias, June 10, 1947, covered by letter from Sir Anthony

Rumbold, British Ambassador, Prague, to G. M. Warr, Northern Department, Foreign Office, August 15, 1947, FO 371/65823.
23. J. Topinka, "Zapomenutý kraj: České pohraničí 1948–1960 a takzvaná akce dosídlení," *Soudobé dějiny* 12:3–4 (2005): 538–9.
24. *Svobodné slovo*, August 2, 1945.
25. *Pravda* (Plzeň), September 26, 1946.
26. N. Davies and R. Moorhouse, *Microcosm: Portrait of a Central European City* (London: Jonathan Cape, 2002), p. 408.
27. T. D. Curp, "The Politics of Ethnic Cleansing: The P.P.R., the P.Z.Z. and Wielkopolska's Nationalist Revolution, 1944–1946," *Nationalities Papers* 29:4 (2001): 585.
28. Jan Czyśew, Starost's Office, Gdańsk, "Situation Report for the Month of April, 1946, from the Area of the Administrative District of Bytow, Gdańsk Voivodeship," n.d., MZO 196/666/B-5777.
29. Report by Maj. E. M. Tobin, n.d. (c. April 1946), FO 1052/324; Lt.-Col. P. F. A. Growse, "Report by Liaison Team, Kohlfurt, up to 3 May 1946," May 4, 1946, FO 1052/474.
30. Kraft, "Who Is a Pole, and Who Is a German?" p. 114.
31. British Army of the Rhine Intelligence Bureau report on interrogation of Filip Stanisław Kornelak, June 22, 1946, FO 371/56596.
32. Unsigned "Beobachtungen und Eindrücke von einer Reise Poznań-Szczecin-Poznań," August 27, 1945, in W. Borodziej and H. Lemberg, eds., *Die Deutschen östlich von Oder und Neiße 1945–1950: Dokumente aus polnischen Archiven*, vol. 3: *Wojewodschaft Posen, Wojewodschaft Stettin (Hinterpommern)* (Marburg: Verlag Herder-Institut, 2004), p. 384.
33. T. Staněk, *Verfolgung 1945: Die Stellung der Deutschen in Böhmen, Mähren und Schlesien (außerhalb der Lager und Gefängnisse)* (Vienna: Böhlau, 2002), p. 85.
34. D. W. Gerlach, "For Nation and Gain: Economy, Ethnicity and Politics in the Czech Borderlands, 1945–1948," (Ph.D. diss., University of Pittsburgh, 2007), pp. 40–45.
35. J. Vaculík, "Reemigrace zahraničnich Čechů a Slováků v letech 1945–1948," *Slezský sborník* 93:1–2 (1995): 53–58.
36. Gerlach, "For Nation and Gain," p. 80.
37. Ibid., p. 94.
38. A. Wiedemann, *"Komm mit uns das Grenzland aufbauen!" Ansiedlung und neue Strukturen in den ehemaligen Sudetengebieten 1945–1952* (Essen: Klartext, 2007), pp. 165–9.
39. A. von Arburg, "Tak či onak: Nucené přesídlení v komplexním pojetí poválecné sídelní politiky v českých zemích," *Soudobé dějiny* 10:3 (2003): 253.
40. P. B. Nichols, "The Transfer of Germans from Karlovy Vary," November 30, 1946, FO 371/56070.
41. Report by Pawel Grzeszczak, Resettlement Officer, Miastko, June 28, 1946, MZO 196/666/B-5777, AAN.
42. D. Gerlach, "Beyond Expulsion: The Emergence of 'Unwanted Elements' in the Postwar Czech Borderlands, 1945–1950," *East European Politics and Societies* 24:2 (May 2010): 280–1.
43. Maj. A. D. Spottswood, Displaced Persons Division, U.S. Forces in Austria, to Col.

E. E. Hyde, December 28, 1945, Office of Military Government for Germany Records of the Civil Administration Division: The Combined Repatriation Executive, U.S. Elements: "Records re Interzonal Population Transfers, 1945–49," "C.R.X. Memos to Polish Representative" file, RG 260, 390/42/26–27/6–1, box 221, NARA.
44. Z. Březina, "The Czechoslovak Democrat: The Life, Writing, and Politics of Hubert Ripka from 1918 to 1945" (Ph.D. diss., Boston University, 2008), pp. 260–1.
45. *The Economist*, July 20, 1946.
46. *Der Spiegel* interview with Bartoszewski, 2002, in S. Auer and S. Burgdorff, eds., *Die Flucht: Über die Vertreibung der Deutschen aus dem Osten* (Stuttgart: Deutsche Verlags-Anstalt, 2002), p. 166.
47. T. D. Curp, *A Clean Sweep? The Politics of Ethnic Cleansing in Western Poland, 1945–1960* (Rochester, NY: University of Rochester Press, 2006), p. 56.
48. Holliday, "Observations on a Tour Made Between May 5th and May 14, 1946 by Mr L. G. Holliday, First Secretary (Commercial) of H.M. Embassy, Warsaw," May 20, 1946, FO 371/56596.
49. See G. Strauchold, *Myśl zachodnia i jej realizacja w Polsce Ludowej w latach 1945–1957* (Toruń: Wydawnictwo Adam Marszałek, 2003), pp. 86–7.
50. E. Hrabovec, "The Catholic Church and Deportation of Ethnic Germans from the Czech Lands," *Journal of Communist Studies and Transition Politics* 16:1–2 (March–June 2000): 66.
51. F. Bednář, *The Transfer of Germans from Czechoslovakia from the Ideological and Ecclesiastical Standpoint* (Prague: Protestant Publishing Company, 1948), pp. 26, 57–8.
52. Rev. Robert Smith, D.D., in *The Scotsman*, November 5, 1946.
53. Topinka, "Zapomenutý kraj," 554.
54. Transcript of Radio Warsaw broadcast, September 10, 1945, FO 371/46990.
55. P. Kenney, *Rebuilding Poland: Workers and Communists, 1945–1950* (Ithaca, NY: Cornell University Press, 1997), p. 140.
56. Davies and Moorhouse, *Microcosm*, p. 438.
57. Unsigned and undated memorandum, "Land Reform" (c. September 1945), FO 371/47651.
58. Cavendish-Bentinck to Sargent, August 26, 1945, FO 371/47650.
59. Curp, *A Clean Sweep?* p. 54.
60. Holliday, "Observations of a Tour Made Between May 5th and May 14, 1946."
61. Ibid.
62. Ther, *Deutsche und polnische Vertriebenen*, p. 167.
63. Holliday, "Report on a Tour in Silesia," August 28, 1945, FO 371/47650.
64. Davies and Moorhouse, *Microcosm*, p. 427.
65. Charles Lambert, in *Daily Herald*, November 7, 1945.
66. Transcript of Radio Lublin broadcast, June 2, 1945, FO 371/46731.
67. Quoted in Kenney, *Rebuilding Poland*, p. 143.
68. Unsigned letter, "A Trip to Stettin," August 15, 1945, covered by letter from Cavendish-Bentinck to Bevin, August 23, 1945, FO 371/47650.

69. R. M. A. Hankey and M. B. Winch, "Tour of Upper and Lower Silesia—September 1945," October 8, 1945, FO 371/47651.
70. J. Walters, British Vice Consul, Szczecin, "Stettin General Report No. 3, May 26, 1946, FO 371/56596.
71. F. Król, Voivodeship Resettlement Committee, Bydgoszcz, September 5, 1945, MZO 665/B-5776.
72. W. Gomułka to G. Zhukov, K. Rokossovsky, and V. Lebedev, January 10, 1946, in Borodziej and Lemberg, eds., *Die Deutschen östlich von Oder und Neiße*, vol. 1: *Zentrale Behörden, Wojewodschaft Allenstein* (Marburg: Verlag Herder-Institut, 2000), p. 205.
73. For a similar pattern in the Soviet occupation zone of Germany, see N. Naimark, *The Russians in Germany: A History of the Soviet Zone of Occupation, 1945–1949* (Cambridge, MA: Belknap Press of Harvard University Press, 1995), pp. 92–3.
74. Deposition of A. Richter, Brackewede bei Bielefeld, April 17, 1946, FO 1052/324.
75. J. Egit, *Grand Illusion* (Toronto: Lugus, 1991).
76. Quoted in D. J. Allen, *The Oder-Neisse Line: The United States, Poland, and Germany in the Cold War* (Westport, CT: Praeger, 2003), p. 52.
77. Cavendish-Bentinck to Bevin, September 21, 1946, FO 371/56598; A. B. Lane, *I Saw Poland Betrayed* (Indianapolis: Bobbs-Merrill, 1948), pp. 262–3.
78. F. B. Bourdillon, "Impressions of Poland," n.d. (c. November 1945), FO 371/56598.
79. D. Gosewinkel and S. Meyer, "Citizenship, Property Rights and Dispossession in Postwar Poland (1918 and 1945)," *European Review of History* 16:4 (August 2009): 587.
80. R. Blanke, "When Germans and Poles Lived Together: From the History of German-Polish Relations," in K. Bullivant, G. Giles, and E. Pape, eds., *Germany and Eastern Europe: Cultural Identities and Cultural Differences* (Yearbook of European Studies, vol. 13) (Amsterdam: Rodopi, 1999), p. 47.
81. Report by Pawel Grzeszczak, Resettlement Officer, Miastko, May 17, 1946, MZO 196, 666/B-5777.
82. L. G. Holliday, "Report on a Tour in Silesia," August 28, 1945, FO 371/47650.
83. Draft report by an officer of the MZO Inspectorate, October 27, 1946, in Borodziej and Lemberg, *Die Deutschen östlich von Oder und Neiße*, vol. 3, p. 481.
84. Olejnik, *Zdrajcy narodu?* p. 105.
85. Report by M. Dybowski, May 24, 1946, in Borodziej and Lemberg, *Die Deutschen östlich von Oder und Neiße*, vol. 3, pp. 217–18.
86. Olejnik, *Zdrajcy narodu?* p. 101.
87. Unsigned and undated MZO memorandum (c. December 1947), "The Question of Returning Property to Persons who during the War of 1939–1945 Derogated from their Nationality/The so-called *Volksdeutsche*," MZO 499/B-5609.
88. Olejnik, *Zdrajcy narodu?* pp. 106–7.
89. A. Malinowski, Main Liquidation Office Legal Department, Łódź, to the Finance Ministry, July 26, 1947, MZO 499/B-5609, AAN.
90. Lt.-Col. C. R. S. Wheeler, "Tour of 1427 Kes by Lt. Col. Wheeler," n.d., FO 371/48590.
91. E. M. Barker, "Notes on a Journey to Transylvania February 21–26 1946," n.d., FO 371/59125.

92. M. Portmann, "Politik der Vernichtung? Die deutschsprachige Bevölkerung in der Vojvodina 1944–1952: Ein Forschungsbericht auf Grundlage jugoslawischer Archivdokumente," in *Danubiana carpathica: Jahrbuch für Geschichte und Kultur in den deutschen Siedlungsgebieten Südosteuropas* (Munich: Oldenbourg, 2007): 335; R. C. S. Stevenson, British Ambassador, Belgrade, to Bevin, November 23, 1945, FO 371/48876.
93. M. Portmann, "Repression und Widerstand auf dem Land: Die kommunistische Landwirtschaftspolitik in der jugoslawischen Vojvodina (1944 bis 1953)," *Südost-Forschungen* 65/66 (2006/2007): 370–393.
94. Speech by Nosek at Liberec, July 14, 1946, quoted in British Embassy Weekly Information Supplement for the week of July 12–18, 1946, FO 371/56004.
95. Memorandum by W. Barker, First Secretary, British Embassy, Prague, June 29, 1945, FO 817/14.
96. L. G. Holliday, "Memorandum," October 28, 1946, FO 371/55831.
97. Quoted in Glassheim, "Ethnic Cleansing, Communism, and Environmental Devastation," 74.
98. Curp, *A Clean Sweep?* p. 84.
99. E. Langenbacher, "Ethical Cleansing? The Expulsion of Germans from Central and Eastern Europe," in N. A. Robins and A. Jones, eds., *Genocides by the Oppressed: Subaltern Genocide in Theory and Practice* (Bloomington: Indiana University Press, 2009), p. 64.
100. Order of October 18, 1944, quoted in Portmann, "Politik der Vernichtung?" 342.
101. T. Urban, *Der Verlust: Die Vertreibung der Deutschen und Polen im 20. Jahrhundert* (Munich: C. H. Beck, 2004), p. 181.
102. J. Yoshioka, "Imagining Their Lands as Ours: Place Name Changes on Ex-German Territories in Poland after World War II," in T. Hayashi, ed., *Regions in Central and Eastern Europe: Past and Present* (Sapporo: Slavic Research Centre, Hokkaido University, 2007), p. 285.
103. Davies and Moorhouse, *Microcosm*, p. 433.
104. Topinka, "Zapomenutý kraj," 552.
105. Wiedemann, *"Komm mit uns das Grenzland aufbauen!"* pp. 411, 427.
106. M. Djilas, *Wartime* (New York: Harcourt Brace Jovanovich, 1977), p. 423.
107. B. F. Abrams, "Morality, Wisdom, and Revision: The Czech Opposition of the 1970s and the Expulsion of the Sudeten Germans," *East European Politics and Societies* 9:2 (Spring 1995): 245–6.
108. "F. Jedermann" [P. Přihoda], *Verlorene Geschichte: Bilder und Texte aus dem heutigen Sudetenland* (Cologne: Bund-Verlag, 1985), pp. 86–125.
109. Glassheim, "Ethnic Cleansing, Communism, and Environmental Devastation," 88.
110. Strauchold, *Myśl zachodnia*, p. 322.
111. L. Dura, quoted ibid., p. 334.
112. H.-Å. Persson, "Viadrina to the Oder-Neisse Line: Historical Evolution and Regional Cooperation," in S. Tägil, ed., *Regions in Central Europe: The Legacy of History* (West Lafayette, IN: Purdue University Press, 1999), p. 242.

113. Ther, *Deutsche und polnische Vertriebene*, p. 225.
114. C. Murdock, *Changing Places: Society, Culture, and Territory in the Saxon-Bohemian Borderlands, 1870–1946* (Ann Arbor: University of Michigan Press, 2010), p. 208.

CHAPTER 10. THE INTERNATIONAL REACTION

1. J. Kostka to OMGUS, Frankfurt am Main, November 27, 1947, box 128, OMGUS RG 260/390/42/24–25/7–1, NARA.
2. Chancery, British Embassy, Warsaw, to Northern Department, Foreign Office, March 9, 1948; Northern Department to Political Division, CCG (BE), April 9, 1948, FO 1049/1514.
3. S. Casey, *Cautious Crusade: Franklin D. Roosevelt, American Public Opinion, and the War against Nazi Germany* (New York: Oxford University Press, 2001), p. 222; G. MacDonogh, *After the Reich: From the Liberation of Vienna to the Berlin Airlift* (London: John Murray, 2007), p. 11. See also A. Capet, "Deux regards antinomiques sur l'Allemagne, 1933–1946," in J.-P. Pichardie, ed., *Contre le nazisme ou contre l'Allemagne: Le débat sur l'anti-germanisme en Grande-Bretagne depuis la Deuxième Guerre mondiale* (Rouen: Centre d'études en littérature et civilisation de langue anglaise, 1998), esp. pp. 7–16.
4. H. Ripka, "Czechoslovakia's Attitude to Germany and Hungary," *Slavonic and East European Review* 23 (1945): 48.
5. *Daily Herald*, September 19 and 20, 1945.
6. G. Rees, "Problems of Germany," *Spectator*, November 2, 1945.
7. A. Jones, Honorary Secretary, Peace Pledge Union, Coventry, to Bevin, September 11, 1945; unsigned minute, September 27, 1945, FO 371/46812; minute by Troutbeck, October 7, 1945, FO 371/48612.
8. Chichester to Attlee, September 4, 1945; minute by Troutbeck, September 8, 1945, FO 371/46812; *Daily Herald*, September 14, 1946; *The Times*, October 26, 1945; M. Frank, *Expelling the Germans: British Opinion and Post-1945 Population Transfer in Context* (Oxford: Oxford University Press, 2007), pp. 157–8.
9. *The Times*, October 23, 1946.
10. V. Gollancz, *In Darkest Germany* (Hinsdale, IL: Regnery, 1947), p. 19.
11. *Daily Herald*, November 27, 1945.
12. Church of England, Synod of York, *The York Journal of Convocation, Containing the Acts and Debates of the Convocation of the Province of York in the Sessions of 11th and 12th October, 1945* (York: W. H. Smith, 1945), p. 54.
13. *The Times*, January 3, 1946.
14. J. Farquharson, "'Emotional but Influential': Victor Gollancz, Richard Stokes, and the British Zone of Germany, 1945–9," *Journal of Contemporary History* 22:3 (July 1987): 505–6, 511.
15. *Observer*, January 13, 1946.
16. M. Frank, "The New Morality—Victor Gollancz, 'Save Europe Now' and the German Refugee Crisis, 1945–46," *Twentieth Century British History* 17:2 (2006): 255.

17. A. Orzoff, *Battle for the Castle: The Myth of Czechoslovakia in Europe, 1914–1948* (Oxford: Oxford University Press, 2009), p. 71.
18. Ibid., p. 74.
19. Circular letter from Gen. Josef Bartík, Ministry of the Interior, October 13, 1945, ÚPV-T, box 11, item 782; Interior Ministry to Zdeněk Fierlinger, September 19, 1945, ÚPV-T, box 11, item 831; same to same, November 30, 1945, ÚPV-T, box 11, file 1064. A useful overview of the Czechoslovak intelligence services during this period can be found in I. Lukes, "The Czechoslovak Special Services and Their American Adversary During the Cold War," *Journal of Cold War Studies* 9:1 (Winter 2007): 3–28.
20. P. Knightley, *The First Casualty: From the Crimea to Vietnam—The War Correspondent as Hero, Propagandist, and Myth Maker* (New York: Harcourt Brace Jovanovich, 1975), pp. 251–2, 266.
21. Postal censorship transcript of letter from Parker to Barrington-Ward, July 9, 1945, FO 371/47090.
22. M. G. Hindus, *We Shall Live Again* (New York: Doubleday, Doran, 1939).
23. G. Bilainkin, *Second Diary of a Diplomatic Correspondent* (London: Sampson Low Marston, 1947), p. 380 (entry of November 16, 1945).
24. L. Steinhardt to J. Byrnes, November 3, 1945; same to same, December 6, 1945, Records of the U.S. Department of State Relating to the Internal Affairs of Czechoslovakia 1945–1949, RG 59, LM 84, 860F.00, reel 1, NARA.
25. See, e.g., *New Statesman and Nation*, October 27, 1945.
26. Bilainkin, *Second Diary of a Diplomatic Correspondent*, pp. 263–4 (entry of September 28, 1945).
27. Quoted in J. B. Schechtman, *Postwar Population Transfers in Europe 1945–1955* (Philadelphia: University of Pennsylvania Press, 1962), p. 69.
28. Frank, *Expelling the Germans*, pp. 188–9.
29. Ibid., p. 189.
30. *Svobodné noviný*, October 17, 1945.
31. For particulars of Haffner's attitude to "pan-Germanism," see his prewar (but posthumously published) memoir, *Geschichte eines Deutschen: Die Erinnerungen 1914–1933* (Stuttgart: Deutsche Verlags-Anstalt, 2000).
32. J. Bartl, "Internační tábory: Lživá propaganda o týraní Němců," *Pravda* (Plzeň), December 28, 1945.
33. *Dziennik polski*, October 18, 1945.
34. See text of alleged interview with Lt.-Col. P. F. A. Growse in P. Lippóczy and T. Walichnowski, eds., *Przesiedlenie ludności Niemieckiej z Polski po II Wojnie Światowej w świetle dokumentów* (Warsaw: Państwowe Wydawnictwo Naukowe, 1982), p. 203; telegram from CCG (BE), Berlin to 508 (R) Detachment, Military Government, April 20, 1946, concerning statements allegedly made by Capt. Thomson, Szczecin, to the *Kurier Szczeciński*; same to 709 (R) Detachment, April 22, 1946, concerning statements attributed to Growse, Kaławsk, telegram from 508 (R) Detachment to CCG (BE), May 9, 1946; CCG (BE) to War Office, May 11, 1946, FO 1052/323.
35. *New York Times*, October 23, 1946.

36. Circular letter from C. T. Emmet, June 30, 1947; Dr. Alexander Boeker to Prof. Ferdinand A. Hermens, Notre Dame University, November 24, 1947, Christopher T. Emmet papers, acc. 74105 8M.47/48, box 19, Hoover Institution Archives, Stanford University, Palo Alto, California.
37. Committee Against Mass Expulsions, *Men Without the Rights of Man: A Report on the Expulsion and Extermination of German Speaking Minority Groups in the Balkans and Prewar Poland* (New York: The Committee, 1948), p. 3.
38. See S. Casey, "The Campaign to Sell a Harsh Peace for Germany to the American Public, 1944–1948," *History* 90:1 (January 2005): 62–92.
39. Wm. Jay Schieffelin and Brackett Lewis, American Friends of Czechoslovakia, to Oswald Garrison Villard, March 22, 1946, Emmet papers, acc. 74105 8M.47/48, box 19.
40. *Parliamentary Debates*, Commons, 5th ser., vol. 413, cols. 83–4 (August 13, 1945).
41. *Daily Herald*, March 6, 1946.
42. United States, Congress, House of Representatives, *Expellees and Refugees of German Ethnic Origin: Report of a Special Subcommittee of the Committee on the Judiciary, House of Representatives, Pursuant to H. Res. 238, A Resolution to Authorize the Committee on the Judiciary to Undertake a Study of Immigration and Nationality Problems* (Report No. 1841) (Washington, DC: Government Printing Office, 1950), p. 6.
43. *Mercury* (Hobart), October 16, 1945.
44. See *Constitution of the International Refugee Organization*, January 14, 1947. Annex I, part II: "Persons Who Will Not Be the Concern of the Organization."
45. Dr. H. G. Beckh to G. W. von Fleckenstein, German-American League, Montrose, CA, March 10, 1947; Dr. R. Voegeli, chief, Division des Délégations, CICR, Geneva, to Dr. K. Laupper, Linz bureau, September 20, 1946, Archives Générales 1918–1950, G. 97/IV, box 1155, CICR.
46. See letters of thanks from German expellees for Irish aid, Department of External Affairs records 419/4/22, 419/4/22/2A, National Archives of Ireland, Dublin; Beckh to Roger Gallopin, director-delegate, CICR, May 18, 1949, Archives Générales 1918–1950, G. 97/IV, box 1156, CICR.
47. U.S. Congress, *Displaced Persons in Europe and their Resettlement in the United States*.
48. M. Phayer, "Pius XII and the Genocides of Polish Catholics and Polish Jews During the Second World War," *Kirchliche Zeitgeschichte* 15:1 (January 2002): 261–2.
49. See J. Pietrzak, "Działalność kard. Augusta Hlonda jako wysłannika papieskiego na Ziemiach Odzyskanych w 1945 r.," *Nasza Przeszłość* 42 (1974): 195–249; V. C. Chrypinski, "Church and Nationality in Postwar Poland," in S. P. Ramet, ed., *Religion and Nationalism in Soviet and East European Politics* (Durham, NC: Duke University Press, 1988), pp. 244–6.
50. See, e.g., *The Economist*, March 22, 1947.
51. Memorandum by P. B. Nichols, October 10, 1945, FO 817/14.
52. Minute by A. W. H. Wilkinson, November 29, 1947, FO 371/64225.
53. "Memorandum Concerning an Immigration to Sweden of Displaced Persons from

Austria, Written in Consequence of Lieutenant General J. Balmer's Letter to Sweden's Chargé d'Affaires in Vienna, Malling, June 17, 1947," FO 371/66754.
54. Maj. H. Jacobsen, Norwegian Military Mission, to W. W. Schott, Chief, Allied Liaison and Protocol Section (U.S. Element), Berlin, July 19, 1947, Office of Military Government for Germany, Records of the Civil Administration Division, Prisoners of War and Displaced Persons Branch: Records Relating to Expellees in the U.S. Zone, 1945–49, RG 260/390/42/26/1-2, box 189, "Expellees (Czech) 1947" file, NARA.
55. W. B. Bradshaw, Ministry of Labour and National Service, to T. J. Bligh, Treasury, October 18, 1948, LAB 9/193.
56. Memorandum by the Committee for Christian Action, n.d. (c. January 1951), Displaced Persons Commission, Legal Division General Records, Subject File, RG 278/350/C/48/02, box 63, "German Ethnic" file, NARA.
57. *New York Times*, March 17, 1947.
58. G. E. C. Ball, Ministry of Labour and National Service, to W. B. Bradshaw, December 16, 1948, LAB 9/13.
59. C. Lieb, "Moving West: German-Speaking Immigration to British Columbia, 1945–1961" (Ph.D. diss., University of Victoria, 2008), p. 106.
60. Speech by Gibson, October 1, 1951, Records of the Displaced Persons Commission, Legal Division General Records, Subject File, RG 278/350/C/48/02, box 63, "German Ethnic" file, NARA.

CHAPTER 11. THE RESETTLEMENT

1. G. M. Trevelyan, *British History in the Nineteenth Century (1782–1901)* (London: Longmans, Green, 1922), p. 292.
2. See S. J. Wiesen, *West German Industry and the Challenge of the Nazi Past, 1945–1955* (Chapel Hill: University of North Carolina Press, 2003), pp. 60–64.
3. S. Schraut, *Flüchtlingsaufnahme in Württemberg-Baden 1945–1949: Amerikanische Besatzungsziele und demokratischer Wiederaufbau im Konflikt* (Munich: Oldenbourg, 1995), p. 45.
4. "Outline Sketch of British Military Government in Germany," n.d. (c. May 1945), FO 371/46974.
5. See, e.g., T. R. Vogt, *Denazification in Soviet-Occupied Germany: Brandenburg, 1945–1948* (Cambridge, MA: Harvard University Press, 2000).
6. Quoted in J. Farquharson, "'Emotional but Influential': Victor Gollancz, Richard Stokes, and the British Zone of Germany, 1945–9," *Journal of Contemporary History* 22:3 (July 1987): 511.
7. M. Balfour and J. Mair, *Four-Power Control in Germany and Austria 1945–1946* (Oxford: Oxford University Press, 1956), p. 76.
8. *Manchester Guardian*, October 15, 1945.
9. R. R. Plimmer, Manpower Division, Military Government, "Report on Visits to German Refugee Camp, Krupp Strasse, Tiergarten, 17th and 18th Sept. 1945," September 20, 1945; Plummer, "Refugees: The Position As It Affects Berlin," September 22, 1945, FO 1049/205.

10. Brig. W. R. N. Hinde, Deputy Military Governor, British Troops, Berlin, to Main HQ, CCG (BE), Lübbecke, November 7, 1945, FO 1032/2298.
11. *The Economist*, November 16, 1945.
12. *Parliamentary Debates*, Commons, 5th ser., vol. 414, col. 370 (October 26, 1945).
13. Col. J. H. Fye, "Final Report—Transport of German Populations from Czechoslovakia to U.S. Zone, Germany," November 30, 1946, p. 7, Margaret Eleanor Fait papers, accession no. 84040–9.02, box 4, file 16, Hoover Institution Archives, Stanford University.
14. I. T. M. Pink, Political Division, CCG (BE) to Kenchington, February 4, 1946; Robertson to Street, February 23, 1946, FO 1049/492.
15. Lt.-Col. H. S. Messec, PW & DP Division, OMGUS, to Brig. A. C. Kenchington, PW & DP Division, CCG (BE), January 9, 1948; "Minutes of Second Meeting of U.S. and British Military Government Representatives on Expellees and Dislodged Germans," February 6, 1948, Office of the Military Government for Germany, Prisoners of War and Displaced Persons Branch, RG 260/390/42/24–25/7–1, box 131, "Meetings General" file, NARA.
16. P. Ther, "Expellee Policy in the Soviet-Occupied Zone and the GDR: 1945–1953," in D. Rock and S. Wolff, eds., *Coming Home to Germany? The Integration of Ethnic Germans from Central and Eastern Europe in the Federal Republic* (Oxford: Berghahn, 2002), p. 60.
17. *News Chronicle*, January 31, 1946.
18. *Manchester Guardian*, October 19, 1945.
19. Ibid., November 5, 1945.
20. *The Economist*, November 10, 1945.
21. *News Chronicle*, August 30, 1945.
22. Balfour and Mair, *Four-Power Control in Germany and Austria*, pp. 7–8.
23. Text of address by Werner Middelmann, Assistant Director, Bundesministerium für Vertriebene, Bonn, at the Conference of the Red Cross Societies, Hanover, April 9–14, 1951, United Nations High Commission for Refugees papers, series 1, Classified Subject Files 1951–1970, fond 11: Records of the Central Registry, box 265, File 15/4/1 (part I), UNHCR.
24. Letter from A. Richter, April 17, 1946, FO 1052/324.
25. *British Zone Review* 1:17 (May 11, 1946).
26. H. Lukaschek, Federal Expellee Minister, "Die Bedeutung der Heimatvertriebenen in der Deutschen Bundesrepublik (Westdeutschland), n.d. (c. April 1950), Bundeskanzleramt papers B 136/805, Bundesarchiv, Koblenz (BAK).
27. I. Connor, *Refugees and Expellees in Post-War Germany* (Manchester: Manchester University Press, 2007), p. 206.
28. Frau Oehler, German Red Cross, Hanover, "Report on the Inspection of Refugee Accommodation," November 8, 1946, FO 1032/2293; Maj. S. L. Hatch, Chief, Public Welfare and Displaced Persons Division, OMGUS, Hesse, "Weekly Summary Report of Public Welfare and Displaced Persons Division of Week 14–20 September 1946," September 21, 1946; same title, week of January 5–11, 1947, January 13, 1947, Office of Military Government, Hesse, Civil Administration Division: Correspondence re.

Public Welfare Branch Activities, 1945–48, RG 260/390/49/26–27/4–5, box 1113, "Weekly Summaries" file, NARA.
29. Office of Military Government for Greater Hesse, "Report on Länderrat Meeting, Evacuee Committee, held on 28 May 1946, 1000 hrs, at Stuttgart, Villa Reitzenstein," May 30, 1946, OMGUS RG 260/390/42/24-25/7-1, Box 130, NARA.
30. M. Völklein, *"Mitleid war von niemand zu erwarten": Das Schicksal der deutschen Vertriebenen* (Munich, Droemer, 2005), p. 56.
31. S. Wolff, *The German Question since 1919* (Westport, CT: Praeger, 2003), p. 79.
32. Richard Wilberforce, Control Office for Germany and Austria, London, to P. Dean, Foreign Office, August 9, 1946, FO 371/55913.
33. Quoted in M. Krauss, "Die Integration Vertriebener am Beispiel Bayerns—Konflikte und Erfolge," in D. Hoffmann and M. Schwartz, eds., *Geglückte Integration? Spezifika und Vergleichbarkeiten der Vertriebenen-Eingliederung in der SBZ/DDR* (Munich: Oldenbourg, 1999), p. 50. See also V. Ackermann, "Homo barackensis: Westdeutsche Flüchtlingslager in den 1950er Jahren," in V. Ackermann, B.-A. Rusinek, and F. Wiesemann, eds., *Anknüpfungen: Kulturgeschichte–Landesgeschichte–Zeitgeschichte: Gedenkschrift für Peter Hüttenberger* (Essen: Klartext, 1995), pp. 330–346.
34. M. Klug, "Report on Burlagsberg Refugee Camp near Löningen i[m] O[ldenburger Münsterland]," n.d. (c. October 1952), Bundesministerium für Vertriebene, Flüchtlinge und Kriegsgeschädigte papers, B 150/569, folder 1, BAK.
35. E. C. Wilkinson, Minister of Education, "Visit to Germany, 2nd-6th October, 1945," October 10, 1945, FO 371/46935; HQ, Company D, 3rd Mil Govt Regiment, Welfare-Refugee Section, U.S. Army, weekly report for week ending August 16, 1947, Office of the Military Government for Germany, PW & DP Branch. box 127, "Chronological File of Outgoing Correspondence" file, RG 260/ 390/42/24–25/7–1, NARA; D. Favre, Baden-Baden delegation, CICR, "Camp de Refugiés de Giessen," February 8, 1950, Archives Générales 1918–1950, G. 97/IV, box 1157, CICR.
36. H. Marcuse, *Legacies of Dachau: The Uses and Abuses of a Concentration Camp, 1933–2001* (Cambridge: Cambridge University Press, 2001), p. 162.
37. M. McLaren, "'Out of the Huts Emerged a Settled People': Community-Building in West German Refugee Camps," *German History* 28:1 (March 2010): 41.
38. N. Gregor, *Haunted City: Nuremberg and the Nazi Past* (New Haven, CT: Yale University Press, 2008), p. 45.
39. M. F. Cullis, "Report on Visit to Displaced Persons' Camps in British Zone of Austria," n.d. (c. August 1946), FO 1020/36.
40. Connor, *Refugees and Expellees in Post-War Germany*, p. 207.
41. Dr. J. Richter, Director, *Volksdeutscheberatungstelle*, "Report on the Present Situation of the *Volksdeutsche* in Austria," September 1950, FO 1020/2519.
42. D. A. Griffin, Assistant to the Chief Civil Affairs Officer, *Land* Kärnten, to the Secretary of the Chamber of Agriculture, Klagenfurt, September 8, 1947, FO 1020/2748.
43. Richter, "Report on the Present Situation of the Volksdeutsche in Austria."
44. Authorised Representative of the *Regierungspräsident* for the Transit Camps of Siegen to British Military Government, March 24, 1946, FO 1051/498.

45. Office of Military Government for Greater Hesse, "Report on Länderrat Meeting, Evacuee Committee, held on 26 Apr 46 1000 hrs, at Stuttgart, Villa Reitzenstein," April 27, 1946, OMG, PW & DP Branch, RG 260/390/42/24–25/7–1, box 130, NARA.
46. Maj.-Gen. W. C. D. Knapton, DCOS (Executive), CCG (BE), Lübbecke, to the deputy regional commissioners of the *Länder* in the British zone, January 9, 1948, FO 1032/2525.
47. Hatch, "Weekly Summary Report of Public Welfare and Displaced Persons Division of Week 7–13 September 1946," September 17, 1946, OMG, Hesse, Civil Administration Division: Correspondence re. Public Welfare Branch Activities, 1945–48, RG 260/390/49/26–27/4–5, box 1113, "Weekly Summaries" file.
48. *Chicago Tribune*, September 25, 1947.
49. Connor, *Refugees and Expellees in Post-War Germany*, p. 204.
50. George Weisz, Chief, Refugee Branch, Civil Administration Division, OMGUS, to Mrs. H. Doerr, Democratization Branch, April 7, 1949, OMG, PW & DP Branch, RG 260/390/42/24–25/7–1, box 127, "Chronological File of Outgoing Correspondence" file, NARA.
51. A. Kossert, *Kalte Heimat: Die Geschichte der deutschen Vertriebenen nach 1945* (Berlin: Siedler, 2008), p. 41.
52. "An Investigation to Determine Any Changes in Attitudes of Native Germans Toward the Expellees in Württemberg-Baden," November 14, 1946, Office of Military Government for Germany, OMGUS Surveys Branch, Information Control Division, RG 260/390/42/24–25/7–1, box 128, NARA.
53. Capt. Walter Schoenstedt, HQ Company D, 3rd Mil Govt Regiment, Welfare-Refugee Section, OMG Bavaria, "Weekly Report for Week Ending 30 August 1947," August 30, 1947, OMG, PW & DP Branch, RG 260/390/42/24–25/7–1, box 130; memorandum by Alfred J. Bach, Intelligence Detachment Heilbronn, OMG Württemberg-Baden, to Chief, Information Control Division, OMG Württemberg, December 3, 1946, OMG, Records of the Civil Administration Division, PW & DP Branch: Records Relating to Expellees in the U.S. Zone, 1945–49, RG 260/390/42/26/1-2, box 187, "Psychological conditions–Buchen (Expellees)" file, NARA.
54. *Landesrat* Oberzaucher, Graz, to Major E. J. Taylor, H.Q. *Land* Steiermark, Displaced Persons Section, n.d. (c. March 1947), FO 1020/2748.
55. Information Control Division report no. 81, "German Reactions to Expellees and DPs," December 3, 1947, OMG, Records of the Civil Administration Division, PW & DP Branch: Records Relating to Expellees in the U.S. Zone, 1945–49, RG 260/390/42/26/1-2, box 187, "Military Surveys (Expellees)" file, NARA.
56. For an example, see A. R. Seipp, "Refugee Town: Germans, Americans, and the Uprooted in Rural West Germany, 1945–52," *Journal of Contemporary History* 44:4 (October 2007): 675–695.
57. OMGUS draft memorandum, "Expellees," February 8, 1947, OMG, OMGUS Surveys Branch, Information Control Division, RG 260/390/42/24–25/7–1, box 128, NARA.
58. Information Control Division report no. 81, "German Reactions to Expellees and

DPs," December 3, 1947, OMG, Records of the Civil Administration Division, PW & DP Branch: Records Relating to Expellees in the U.S. Zone, 1945–49, RG 260/390/42/26/1-2, box 187, "Military Surveys (Expellees)" file, NARA.

59. G. Weisz, to Director, Civil Administration Division, April 28, 1949, OMG, PW & DP Branch, RG 260/390/42/24–25/7–1, box 127, "Chronological File of Outgoing Correspondence" file, NARA.

60. Memorandum by H. Parkman, Director, Civil Administration Division, June 25, 1946; Clay to Parkman, June 27, 1946, OMG, Records of the Civil Administration Division, PW & DP Branch: Records Relating to Expellees in the U.S. Zone, 1945–49, RG 260./390/42/26/1-2, box 190, "Expellees Political Activity" file, NARA.

61. Text of "Charta der deutschen Heimatvertriebenen," August 5, 1950, Bundeskanzleramt records, B 136/9087, BAK.

62. Economic Cooperation Administration, *The Integration of Refugees into German Life: A Report of the ECA Technical Assistance Commission on the Integration of the Refugees in the German Republic Submitted to the Chancellor of the Federal Republic of Germany, March 21, 1951* (Bonn, n.p., n.d., 1951).

63. P. Ahonen, *After the Expulsion: West Germany and Eastern Europe 1945–1990* (Oxford: Oxford University Press, 2003), p. 30.

64. A. Crawley, *The Spoils of War: The Rise of Western Germany 1945–1972* (New York: Bobbs-Merrill, 1973), p. 190.

65. Kossert, *Kalte Heimat*, p. 100.

66. M. L. Hughes, *Shouldering the Burdens of Defeat: West Germany and the Reconstruction of Social Justice* (Chapel Hill: University of North Carolina Press, 1999), p. 179.

67. Ahonen, *After the Expulsion*, p. 278.

68. Quoted in Kossert, *Kalte Heimat*, p. 172.

69. G. Weisz, to Director, Civil Administration Division, April 28, 1949, OMG, PW & DP Branch, RG 260/390/42/24–25/7–1, box 127, "Chronological File of Outgoing Correspondence" file, NARA.

70. Ahonen, *After the Expulsion*, pp. 273–4.

71. P. Ther, *Deutsche und polnische Vertriebene: Gesellschaft und Vertriebenenpolitik in der SBZ/DDR und in Polen 1945–1956* (Göttingen: Vandenhoeck & Ruprecht, 1998), p. 162.

72. Quoted in Völklein, "*Mitleid war von niemand zu erwarten*," p. 61.

73. Sir W. Strang to J. Troutbeck, November 15, 1945; same to same, November 27, 1945, FO 371/46978; same to same, March 6, 1946; same to same, April 18, 1946, FO 1049/508.

74. Connor, *Refugees and Expellees in Post-War Germany*, p. 205.

75. Ther, *Deutsche und Polnische Vertriebene*, p. 212. See also M. Schwartz, "Lastenausgleich: Ein Problem der Vertriebenenpolitik im doppelten Deutschland," in M. Krauss, ed., *Integrationen: Vertriebene in den deutschen Ländern nach 1945* (Göttingen: Vandenhoeck & Ruprecht, 2008), pp. 167–193.

76. A. Bauerkämper, "Assimilationspolitik und Integrationsdynamik: Vertriebene in der SBZ/DDR in vergleichender Perspektive," ibid., pp. 27–8.

77. N. Naimark, *The Russians in Germany: A History of the Soviet Zone of Occupation, 1945–1949* (Cambridge, MA: Belknap Press of Harvard University Press, 1995), p. 157.
78. Ther, "Expellee Policy in the Soviet-Occupied Zone and the GDR," pp. 64–5.
79. M. Schwartz, "Staatsfeind 'Umsiedler,'" in S. Auer and S. Burgdorff, eds., *Die Flucht: Über die Vertreibung der Deutschen aus dem Osten* (Stuttgart: Deutsche Verlags-Anstalt, 2002), p. 211.
80. Quoted in Naimark, *The Russians in Germany*, p. 159.
81. Ther, "Expellee Policy in the Soviet-Occupied Zone and the GDR," p. 71.
82. I. Connor, "German Expellees in the SBZ/GDR and the 'Peace Border,'" in A. Goodbody, P. Ó Dochartaigh, et al., eds., *Dislocation and Reorientation: Exile, Division and the End of Communism in German Culture and Politics* (Amsterdam: Rodopi, 2009), p. 169.
83. Ther, "Expellee Policy in the Soviet-Occupied Zone and the GDR," p. 62.
84. Kossert, *Kalte Heimat*, p. 223.
85. Krauss, "Integrationen: Fragen, Thesen, Perspektiven zu einer vergleichenden Vertriebenenforschung," in Krauss, *Integrationen*, 11.

CHAPTER 12. THE LAW

1. European Parliament, "Charter of Fundamental Rights of the European Union," 2007/C 303/01, *Official Journal of the European Union*, December 14, 2007, http://eur-lex.europa.eu/LexUriServ/LexUriServ.do?uri=OJ:C:2007:303:0001:0016:EN:PDF.
2. "Statement of President Václav Klaus on the Ratification of the Lisbon Treaty," October 9, 2009, http://www.hrad.cz/en/president-of-the-cr/current-president-of-the-cr-vaclav-klaus/selected-speeches-and-interviews/96.shtml.
3. T. W. Waters, "Remembering Sudetenland: On the Legal Construction of Ethnic Cleansing," *Virginia Journal of International Law* 47:1 (Autumn 2006): 105; J. Rupnik, "Joining Europe Together or Separately? The Implications of the Czecho-Slovak Divorce for EU Enlargement," in J. Rupnik and J. Zielonka, eds., *The Road to the European Union*, vol. 1: *The Czech and Slovak Republics* (Manchester: Manchester University Press, 2003), p. 48 n. 61.
4. H. Grotius, *De Jure Belli ac Pacis*, book II, chap. 20.
5. Quoted in S. L. Goldenberg, "Crimes Against Humanity—1945–1970: A Study in the Making and Unmaking of International Criminal Law," *Western Ontario Law Review* 10:1 (1971): 5. Emphasis in original.
6. *The Treaty of Peace between the Allied and Associated Powers and Germany, the Protocol Annexed Thereto . . . Signed at Versailles, June 28th, 1919* (London: HMSO, 1919), art. 228.
7. S. Power, *"A Problem from Hell": America and the Age of Genocide* (New York: Basic Books, 2002), p. 491.
8. D. M. Segesser, "'Unlawful Warfare Is Uncivilised': The International Debate on the Punishment of War Crimes, 1872–1918," *European Review of History* 14:2 (June 2007): 216.

9. See G. Hankel, *Die Leipziger Prozesse: Deutsche Kriegsverbrechen und ihre strafrechtliche Verfolgung nach dem Ersten Weltkrieg* (Hamburg: HIS Verlag, 2003).
10. W. Czapliński, "The Protection of Minorities under International Law (Comments on the Alleged Existence of a German Minority in Poland)," *Polish Western Affairs* 25:1 (1984): 126.
11. M. Mazower, "The Strange Triumph of Human Rights, 1933–1950," *Historical Journal* 47:2 (June 2004): 382–383.
12. F. P. Walters, *A History of the League of Nations* (Oxford: Oxford University Press, 1967), p. 616.
13. Ibid., p. 410.
14. E. Beneš, *Odsun Němců: Výbor z pamětí a projevů doplněný edičními přílohami* (Prague: Společnost Edvarda Beneše, 1995), p. 22. See also, e.g., S. Sierpowski, "Les dilemmes à la Société des Nations au sujet des minorités," *Polish Western Affairs* 25:2 (1984): 187–210; J. Zarnowski, "Le système de protection des minorités et la Pologne," *Acta Poloniae Historica* 52:1 (1985): 105–124.
15. P. B. Finney, "'An Evil for All Concerned': Great Britain and Minority Protection After 1919," *Journal of Contemporary History* 30:3 (July 1995): 542.
16. H. Ripka, *The Future of the Czechoslovak Germans* (London: Czechoslovak-British Friendship Club, 1944), p. 18.
17. "Report of the Inter-Departmental Committee on the Transfer of German Populations," May 12, 1944, A.P.W. (44) 34, CAB 121/85.
18. Telegram from British delegation, San Francisco Conference on International Organisation, to Foreign Office, May 16, 1945, FO 371/50843.
19. CICR, "Draft International Convention on the Condition and Protection of Civilians of Enemy Nationality who are on Territory Belonging to or Occupied by a Belligerent," 1934, http://www.icrc.org/ihl.nsf/FULL/320?OpenDocument.
20. P. Thornberry, *International Law and the Rights of Minorities* (Oxford: Clarendon Press, 1991), p. 72.
21. Ibid., p. 113.
22. Minute by J. D. Mabbott, Foreign Office Research Department, June 8, 1945, FO 371/50843.
23. *The Times*, January 14, 1942.
24. Ibid., October 20, 1942.
25. Goldenberg, "Crimes Against Humanity–1945–1970," pp. 5–9.
26. E. Schwelb, "Crimes Against Humanity," *British Yearbook of International Law* 23 (1946): 206.
27. Whether crimes against humanity exist in law independently of international armed conflict remains disputed. For a discussion of this question, see W. A. Schabas, *An Introduction to the International Criminal Court*, 3d ed. (Cambridge: Cambridge University Press, 2007), pp. 98–103.
28. C. Anderson, *Eyes Off the Prize: The United Nations and the African American Struggle for Human Rights, 1945–1955* (Cambridge: Cambridge University Press, 2003), p. 133.
29. Quoted in Thornberry, *International Law and the Rights of Minorities*, pp. 231–2.

30. Quoted ibid., p. 72. See also J. Cooper, *Raphael Lemkin and the Struggle for the Genocide Convention* (Basingstoke, Hampshire: Palgrave Macmillan, 2008).
31. W. A. Schabas, "'Ethnic Cleansing' and Genocide: Similarities and Distinctions," in *European Yearbook of Minority Issues*, vol. 3 (Leiden: Brill, 2005), pp. 118–120.
32. International Institute of Humanitarian Law, *Report of the Working Group on Mass Expulsion* (San Remo, International Institute of Humanitarian Law, 1983), p. 5.
33. Quoted in A. Aust, *Handbook of International Law*, 2d ed. (Cambridge: Cambridge University Press, 2010), p. 10.
34. See J.-M. Henckaerts, *Mass Expulsion in Modern International Law and Practice* (The Hague: Martinus Nijhoff, 1995), esp. pp. 8–45.
35. Thornberry, *International Law and the Rights of Minorities*, p. 240.
36. A.-M. de Zayas, "An Historical Survey of Twentieth Century Expulsions," in A. C. Bramwell, ed., *Refugees in the Age of Total War* (London: Unwin Hyman, 1988), p. 32.
37. E. Barkan, *The Guilt of Nations: Restitution and Negotiating Historical Injustices* (Baltimore: Johns Hopkins University Press, 2001), p. 135.
38. Quoted in T. W. Ryback, "Dateline Sudetenland: Hostages to History," *Foreign Policy* 105 (Winter 1996–97): 173.
39. *Malik v. Czech Republic*, Communication No. 669/1995, U. N. Doc. CCPR/C/64/D/669/1995 (November 3, 1998).
40. United Nations, Office of the High Commissioner for Human Rights. "General Comment No. 18: Non-Discrimination," October 11, 1989, http://www.unhchr.ch/tbs/doc.nsf/0/3888b0541f8501c9c12563ed004b8d0e?Opendocument.
41. I. S. Pogány, "International Human Rights Law, Reparatory Justice and the Re-Ordering of Memory in Central and Eastern Europe," *Human Rights Law Review* 10:3 (2010): 422. Emphasis in original.
42. P. Macklem, "Rybná 9, Praha 1: Restitution and Memory in International Human Rights Law," *European Journal of International Law* 16:1 (February 2005): 18.
43. United Nations, Human Rights Committee, *Selected Decisions of the Human Rights Committee under the Optional Protocol, International Covenant on Civil and Political Rights*, vol. 8 (New York: United Nations Publications, 2007), pp. 78–84.
44. European Court of Human Rights, Fourth Section, "Decision as to the Admissibility of Application no. 47550/06 by *Preussische Treuhand GmbH & Co., KG A. A.* against Poland," October 7, 2008, http://cmiskp.echr.coe.int/tkp197/view.asp?action=html&documentId=841872&portal=hbkm&source=externalbydocnumber&table=F69A27FD8FB86142BF01C1166DEA398649.
45. European Parliament, Directorate-General for Research, *Legal Opinion on the Beneš-Decrees and Accession of the Czech Republic to the European Union*, PE 323.934 (October 2002), http://www.europarl.europa.eu/activities/committees/studies/download.do?language=en&file=26119#search=%20%20%22legal%20opinion%20on%20the%20benes-decrees%22%20.
46. D. Blumenwitz, "Standards for the Political Handling of Dealings Concerning Property after World War II," in G. Loibi, ed., *Austrian Review of International and European Law 2001*, vol. 6 (The Hague: Martinus Nijhoff, 2003), p. 189.
47. S. Auer, "Slovakia: From Marginalization of Ethnic Minorities to Political Participa-

tion (and Back?)," in B. Rechel, ed., *Minority Rights in Central and Eastern Europe* (Abingdon, Oxfordshire: Routledge, 2009), p. 201.
48. Pogány, "International Human Rights Law," 422.
49. J. H. Wolfe, "International Law and Diplomatic Bargaining: A Commentary on the Sudeten German Question," *Bohemia* 14 (1973): 384.
50. A.-M. de Zayas, "The Legality of Mass Population Transfers: The German Experience 1945–48," *East European Quarterly* 12:1 (Spring 1978): 15.
51. See Schabas, *An Introduction to the International Criminal Court*, p. 105.
52. See above, p. 33.
53. Waters, "Remembering Sudetenland," 127. Emphasis in original.
54. P. Maguire, *Law and War: International Law and American History*, rev. ed. (New York: Columbia University Press, 2010), pp. 213–4.

CHAPTER 13. MEANING AND MEMORY

1. R. M. A. Hankey to M. Vyvyan, Trinity College, Cambridge, July 11, 1947, FO 371/66217.
2. J. L. Guntner and A. M. McLean, eds., *Literary Theory and Theater Practice in the German Democratic Republic* (Cranbury, NJ: Associated University Presses, 1998), p. 11; J. Kalb, *The Theater of Heiner Müller* (Cambridge: Cambridge University Press, 1998), pp. 78–86.
3. M. Burleigh, *Germany Turns Eastwards: A Study of Ostforschung in the Third Reich* (Cambridge: Cambridge University Press, 1988), p. 165.
4. D. L. Bergen, *War and Genocide: A Concise History of the Holocaust* (Lanham, MD: Rowman & Littlefield, 2009), p. 168.
5. R. G. Moeller, *War Stories: The Search for a Usable Past in the Federal Republic of Germany* (Berkeley: University of California Press, 2001), p. 84.
6. Zachodnia Agencja Prasowa, *1939–1950: Population Movements Between the Oder and Bug Rivers* (Poznań: Wydawnictwo Zachodnie, 1961), pp. 8, 10.
7. See I. Haar, "Die deutschen 'Vertreibungsverluste': Zur Entstehungsgeschichte der Dokumentation der Vertreibung," *Tel Aviver Jahrbuch für deutsche Geschichte* 35 (2007): 251–272.
8. H. Fehrenbach, *Cinema in Democratizing Germany: Reconstructing National Identity after Hitler* (Chapel Hill: University of North Carolina Press, 1995), p. 146.
9. See J. von Moltke, *No Place Like Home: Locations of Heimat in German Cinema* (Berkeley: University of California Press, 2005), pp. 135–142.
10. R. G. Moeller, "War Stories: The Search for a Usable Past in the Federal Republic of Germany," *American Historical Review* 101:4 (October 1996): 1013, 1026.
11. Moeller, *War Stories*, p. 174.
12. F. Biess, *Homecomings: Returning POWs and the Legacies of Defeat in Postwar Germany* (Princeton, NJ: Princeton University Press, 2006), pp. 6, 15.
13. See, e.g., S. Spülbeck, "Ethnography of an Encounter: Reactions to Refugees in Postwar Germany and Russian Migrants after the Reunification—Context, Analogies and

Changes," in A. J. Rieber, ed., *Forced Migration in Central and Eastern Europe, 1939–1950* (London: Frank Cass, 2000), p. 179.

14. S. Goltermann, "The Imagination of Disaster: Death and Survival in Postwar West Germany," in A. Confino, P. Betts, and D. Schumann, eds., *Between Mass Death and Individual Loss: The Place of the Dead in Twentieth-Century Germany* (Oxford: Berghahn, 2008), pp. 261–274.
15. S. Berger, "On Taboos, Traumas and Other Myths: Why the Debate About German Victims During the Second World War Is Not a Historians' Controversy," in B. Niven, ed., *Germans as Victims: Remembering the Past in Contemporary Germany* (Basingstoke, Hampshire: Palgrave Macmillan, 2006), p. 217.
16. R. Schulze, "The Politics of Memory: Flight and Expulsion of German Populations after the Second World War and German Collective Memory," *National Identities* 8:4 (December 2006): 369.
17. A. Kossert, *Kalte Heimat: Die Geschichte der deutschen Vertriebenen nach 1945* (Berlin: Siedler, 2008), p. 189.
18. E. Langenbacher, "Ethical Cleansing? The Expulsion of Germans from Central and Eastern Europe," in N. A. Robins and A. Jones, eds., *Genocides By the Oppressed: Subaltern Genocide in Theory and Practice* (Bloomington: Indiana University Press, 2009), p. 69.
19. M. Kent, "Exceptional Bonds: Revenge and Reconciliation in Potulice [Potulitz], Poland, 1945 and 1998," in S. B. Várdy and T. H. Tooley, eds., *Ethnic Cleansing in Twentieth-Century Europe* (Boulder, CO: Social Science Monographs, 2003), pp. 623–4.
20. V. Ackermann, "Das Schweigen der Flüchtlingskinder: Psychische Folgen von Krieg, Flucht und Vertreibung bei den Deutschen nach 1945," *Geschichte und Gesellschaft* 30:3 (2004): 461. See also A. Lehmann, *Im Fremden ungewollt zuhaus: Flüchtlinge und Vertriebene in Westdeutschland 1945–1990* (Munich: C. H. Beck, 1991).
21. J. Mlynárik, *Thesen zur Aussiedlung der Deutschen aus der Tschechoslowakei, 1945–1947* (Munich: Danubius, 1985), p. 24.
22. Ibid., p. 42.
23. See B. F. Abrams, "Morality, Wisdom, and Revision: The Czech Opposition of the 1970s and the Expulsion of the Sudeten Germans," *East European Politics and Societies* 9:2 (Spring 1995): 234–255.
24. Mlynárik, *Thesen zur Aussiedlung der Deutschen aus der Tschechoslowakei*, pp. 48–9.
25. T. Urban, *Der Verlust: Die Vertreibung der Deutschen und Polen im 20. Jahrhundert* (Munich: C. H. Beck, 2004), pp. 188–9.
26. N. M. Naimark, "The Persistence of the 'Postwar': Germany and Poland," in F. Biess and R. G. Moeller, eds., *Histories of the Aftermath: The Legacies of the Second World War in Europe* (Oxford: Berghahn, 2010), p. 23.
27. G. Weigel, *Witness to Hope: The Biography of Pope John Paul II* (New York: HarperCollins, 1999), pp. 178–180.
28. M. Zaborowski, *Germany, Poland and Europe: Cooperation and Europeanisation* (Manchester: Manchester University Press, 2005), p. 69.

29. E. Moszyński, "The Church on the Western Territories," *Polish Perspectives* 16:2 (February 1973): 20.
30. P. Lutomski, "The Polish Expulsion of the German Population in the Aftermath of World War II," in A. M. Kacowicz and P. Lutomski, eds., *Population Resettlement in International Conflicts: A Comparative Study* (Lanham, MD: Lexington, 2007), p. 103.
31. Kossert, *Kalte Heimat*, p. 305.
32. V. Havel, *To the Castle and Back* (New York: Random House, 2008), p. 140.
33. P. Lutomski, "Acknowledging Each Other as Victims: An Unmet Challenge in the Process of Polish-German Reconciliation," in L. Cohen-Pfister and D. Wienröder-Skinner, eds., *Victims and Perpetrators, 1933–1945: (Re-)Presenting the Past in Post-Unification Culture* (Berlin: De Gruyter, 2006), p. 246.
34. *New York Times*, January 22, 1997.
35. K. Cordell and S. Wolff, "Ethnic Germans in Poland and the Czech Republic: A Comparative Evaluation," *Nationalities Papers* 33:2 (June 2005): 261.
36. J. Huener, *Auschwitz, Poland, and the Politics of Commemoration, 1945–1979* (Athens: Ohio University Press, 2003), pp. 52–3. See also D. Matelski, "Polityka narodowościowa PRL wobec mniejszości niemieckiej (1944–1989)," *Przegląd historyczny* 88:3–4 (1997): 487–497.
37. K. Cordell and S. Wolff, *Germany's Foreign Policy Towards Poland and the Czech Republic: Ostpolitik Revisited* (Abingdon, Oxfordshire: Routledge, 2005), p. 59.
38. See, e.g., M. Alexander, "Die tschechische Diskussion über die Vertreibung der Deutschen und deren Folgen," *Bohemia* 34:2 (1993): 407–8.
39. *Die Zeit*, September 18, 2003.
40. *Tygodnik Powszechny*, August 17, 2003.
41. *Wprost*, September 21, 2003; P. Lutomski, "The Debate about a Center against Expulsions: An Unexpected Crisis in German-Polish Relations?" *German Studies Review* 27:3 (October 2004): 449.
42. S. Crawshaw, *Easier Fatherland: Germany and the Twenty-first Century* (London: Continuum, 2004), p. 157.
43. Langenbacher, "Ethical Cleansing," p. 63.
44. M. Brumlik, *Wer Sturm sät: Die Vertreibung der Deutschen* (Berlin: Aufbau, 2005), p. 88.
45. Quoted in R. Wittlinger, "The Merkel Government's Politics of the Past," *German Politics and Society* 26:4 (Winter 2008):
46. N. Davies and R. Moorhouse, *Microcosm: Portrait of a Central European City* (London: Jonathan Cape, 2002), p. 483.
47. Crawshaw, *Easier Fatherland*, p. 159.
48. S. Wolff, *The German Question since 1919* (Westport, CT: Praeger, 2003), p. 168.
49. Cordell and Wolff, *Germany's Foreign Policy towards Poland and the Czech Republic*, p. 78; "Universal Declaration of Human Rights" (1948), art. 1.

CONCLUSION

1. "Draft Report to the Coordinating Committee Concerning the Question of Population Transfers," submitted by the U.S. Representative, October 23, 1947, DPOW/P (47) 74, RG 260/390/50/32/06, OMG, PW & DP Directorate: General Records, 1945–1948, box 382, file 13, NARA.
2. PW & DP Directorate, "Section VII–Population Transfers," February 5, 1947, FO 371/64222.
3. PW & DP Branch, "Memorandum to Major General Keating—Subject: Sudeten Transfers," December 13, 1946, OMG, Records of the Civil Administration Division, PW & DP Branch: Records Relating to Expellees in the U.S. Zone, 1945–49, RG 260/390/42/26/1-2, box 187, "Agreements Expellees" file, NARA.
4. W. Borodziej, "Ucieczka—Wypędzenie—Wysiedlenie Przymusowe," in A. Lawaty and H. Orłowski, eds., *Polacy i niemcy: Historia—kultura—polityka* (Poznań: Wydawnictwo Poznańskie, 2003), p. 104.
5. *The Times*, February 18, 1944.
6. Quoted in M. Frank, *Expelling the Germans: British Opinion and Post-1945 Population Transfer in Context* (Oxford: Oxford University Press, 2007), p. 95.
7. M. Ignatieff, *Blood and Belonging: Journeys into the New Nationalism* (London: BBC Books, 1993), p. 45.
8. K. Cordell and S. Wolff, "Ethnic Germans in Poland and the Czech Republic: A Comparative Evaluation," *Nationalities Papers* 33:2 (June 2005): 258, 263, 265.
9. J. R. Sanborn, "'Unsettling the Empire': Violent Migrations and Social Disaster in Russia During World War I," *Journal of Modern History* 77:2 (June 2005): 303.
10. For particulars of collaborationist activities in support of the Soviet invaders, see A. V. Prusin, *The Lands Between: Conflict in the East European Borderlands, 1870–1992* (Oxford: Oxford University Press, 2010), pp. 136–148.
11. T. Staněk, *Verfolgung 1945: Die Stellung der Deutschen in Böhmen, Mähren und Schlesien (außerhalb der Lager und Gefängnisse)* (Vienna: Böhlau, 2002), p. 184.
12. S. Schimanski, *Vain Victory* (London: Victor Gollancz, 1946), p. 115.
13. Ibid., p. 116.
14. Lt.-Col. P. F. A. Growse, "Report by Liaison Team, Kohlfurt, up to 3 May 1946," May 4, 1946, FO 1052/474.
15. Col. J. H. Fye, "Final Report—Transport of German Populations from Czechoslovakia to U.S. Zone, Germany," November 30, 1946, p. 45, p. 6, Margaret Eleanor Fait papers, accession no. 84040–9.02, box 4, file 16, Hoover Institution Archives, Stanford University.
16. *Rudé právo*, November 12, 1946.
17. M. Horkheimer and T. W. Adorno, *Dialectic of Enlightenment* (London: Allen Lane, 1973).
18. T. D. Curp, "The Politics of Ethnic Cleansing: The P.P.R., the P.Z.Z. and Wielkopolska's Nationalist Revolution, 1944–1946," *Nationalities Papers* 29:4 (2001): 594–5.
19. European Parliament, Directorate-General for Research, "Legal Opinion on the

Beneš-Decrees and the Accession of the Czech Republic to the European Union," October 2002, paras. 45–52.
20. E. Barkan, "Deserving and Undeserving Victims: Political Context and Legal Framework of Hard Cases of Reparation," in K. de Feyter, S. Parmentier, et al., eds., *Out of the Ashes: Reparation for Victims of Gross and Systematic Human Rights Violations* (Antwerp: Intersentia, 2005), p. 88.
21. Ibid., p. 93.
22. Ibid., pp. 102, 103.
23. A. Bell-Fialkoff, *Ethnic Cleansing* (New York: St. Martin's Press, 1996), pp. 230, 220.
24. *Ha'aretz*, February 18, 2002.
25. *New York Times*, March 31, 1993.
26. J. W. Nickel, "What's Wrong with Ethnic Cleansing?," *Journal of Social Philosophy* 26:1 (Spring 1995): 12–13.
27. See C. D. Kaufmann, "When All Else Fails: Ethnic Population Transfers and Partitions in the Twentieth Century," *International Security* 23:2 (Autumn 1998): 120–156; B. Clark, *Twice a Stranger: The Mass Expulsions that Forged Modern Greece and Turkey* (Cambridge, MA: Harvard University Press, 2006); D. L. Byman, *Keeping the Peace: Lasting Solutions to Ethnic Conflicts* (Baltimore: Johns Hopkins University Press, 2002); M. Mann, *The Dark Side of Democracy: Explaining Ethnic Cleansing* (Cambridge: Cambridge University Press, 2004).
28. S. Ryan, *The Transformation of Violent Intercommunal Conflict* (Aldershot, Hampshire: Ashgate, 2007), p. 67.
29. T. D. Curp, *A Clean Sweep? The Politics of Ethnic Cleansing in Western Poland, 1945–1960* (Rochester, NY: University of Rochester Press, 2006), p. 193.

Bibliography

ARCHIVAL AND UNPUBLISHED SOURCES

Archives du Comité International de la Croix Rouge, Geneva
Comité International de la Croix Rouge et du Croissant Rouge records.
Archiwum Akt Nowych (Central Archives of Modern Records), Warsaw
Ministerstwo Ziem Odzyskanych (Ministry for the Recovered Territories) records.
Archives of the United Nations High Commission for Refugees, Geneva
UNHCR records.
Bundesarchiv, Koblenz
Bundeskanzleramt records.
Bundesministerium für Vertriebene, Flüchtlinge und Kriegsgeschädigte records.
Hoover Institution Archives, Palo Alto, California
Aleta Brownlee papers.
Christopher Emmet papers.
Margaret Fait papers.
Národní archiv České republiky (National Archives of the Czech Republic), Prague
Ministerstvo vnitra (Ministry of the Interior) records.
Úrad předsedníctva vlády (Office of the Prime Minister) records.
National Archives of Ireland, Dublin
Department of External Affairs records.
National Archives and Records Administration, College Park, Maryland
Department of State records.
Displaced Persons Commission records.
Office of Military Government for Germany records.
Supreme Headquarters Allied Expeditionary Forces records.
U.S. High Commission for Germany records.
Public Record Office, Kew, UK
Cabinet Office records.
Foreign Office records.

Ministry of Labour records.
Státní oblastní archiv (State District Archives), Plzeň
Stod Internment Camp records.
Mirošov Concentration Camp records.
United Nations Archive, New York City
UN Relief and Rehabilitation Administration records.
Vojenský ústřední archiv (Military Central Archives), Prague
Ministra národní obrany (Ministry of National Defense) records.

PRINTED PRIMARY SOURCES

American Friends Service Committee. *Reports on Conditions in Central Europe*. Philadelphia: The Committee, 1946.
Bannister, S. *I Lived Under Hitler: An Englishwoman's Story*. London: Rockliff, 1957.
Barton, B. *The Problem of 12 Million German Refugees in Today's Germany*. Philadelphia: American Friends Service Committee, 1949.
Beckherrn, E. and A. Dubatow, eds. *Die Königsberg-Papiere: Schicksal einer deutschen Stadt. Neue Dokumente aus russischen Archiven*. Munich: Langen Müller, 1994.
Bednář, F. *The Transfer of Germans from Czechoslovakia from the Ideological and Ecclesiastical Standpoint*. Prague: Protestant Publishing Company, 1948.
Beneš, E. *Memoirs of Dr. Eduard Beneš: From Munich to New War and New Victory*. Boston: Houghton Mifflin, 1954.
———. *Odsun Němců: Výbor z pamětí a projevů doplněný edičními přílohami*. Prague: Společnost Edvarda Beneše, 1995.
———. *The Fall and Rise of a Nation: Czechoslovakia 1938–1941*, ed. M. Hauner. Boulder, CO: East European Monographs, 2004.
———. *The War of 1939: Two Addresses of the Czechoslovak President at the Edinburgh and the Glasgow University 5th and 7th November, 1941*. Prague: Společnost Edvarda Beneše, 2005.
Bilainkin, G. *Second Diary of a Diplomatic Correspondent*. London: Sampson Low Marston, 1947.
Borodziej, W. and H. Lemberg, eds. *Die Deutschen östlich von Oder und Neiße 1945–1950: Dokumente aus polnischen Archiven* (4 vols.). Marburg: Verlag Herder-Institut, 2000–2004.
Byford-Jones, W. *Berlin Twilight*. London: Hutchinson, 1947.
Church of England. Synod of York. *The York Journal of Convocation, Containing the Acts and Debates of the Convocation of the Province of York in the Sessions of 11th and 12th October, 1945*. York: W. H. Smith, 1945.
Committee Against Mass Expulsions. *The Land of the Dead: Study of the Deportations from Eastern Germany*. New York: The Committee, 1947.
———. *Men Without the Rights of Man: A Report on the Expulsion and Extermination of German Speaking Minority Groups in the Balkans and Prewar Poland*. New York: The Committee, 1948.

Cseh, B. G. *Documents of the Meetings of the Allied Control Commission for Hungary 1945–1947.* Budapest: MTA Jelenkor-kutató Bizottság, 2000.

Curtis, M., ed. *Documents on International Affairs 1938,* vol. 2. London: Oxford University Press, 1943.

Czechoslovakia. Ministry of Information. *Programme of the Czechoslovak Government of the National Front of Czechs and Slovaks, Agreed to at the First Government Meeting in Košice on April 5th 1945.* Prague: The Ministry, 1945.

———. *Bulletin of the Ministry of Information, 1st Department.* Prague: The Ministry, 1945–47.

Czechoslovak Information Service. *President Benes on War and Peace: Statements by Dr. Edvard Benes, President of the Czechoslovak Republic, during his Visit to the United States and Canada in May and June 1943.* New York: The Service, 1943.

Czechoslovak Provisional Government. *The New Czechoslovakia: Program of the Provisional Czechoslovak Government.* Pittsburgh: Ludovy Dennik, n.d. (c. 1945).

Dickens, A. G. *Lübeck Diary.* London: Victor Gollancz, 1947.

Djilas, M. *Wartime.* New York: Harcourt Brace Jovanovich, 1977.

Economic Cooperation Administration. *The Integration of Refugees into German Life: A Report of the ECA Technical Assistance Commission on the Integration of the Refugees in the German Republic Submitted to the Chancellor of the Federal Republic of Germany, March 21, 1951.* Bonn, n.p., n.d., 1951.

Fetter, J. *The Sudetens–A Moral Question.* New York: William-Frederick Press, 1947.

Fisher, A. G. B. and D. Mitrany, "Some Notes on the Transfer of Populations," *Political Quarterly* 14:4 (October–December 1943): 363–371.

Galbraith, J. K. *Recovery in Europe: An International Committee Report.* Washington, DC: National Planning Association, 1946.

"German Bohemian Deputy, A." "National Minorities in Europe: The German Minority in Czechoslovakia," *Slavonic and East European Review* 41 (January 1936): 295–300.

Gollancz, V. *In Darkest Germany.* Hinsdale, IL: Regnery, 1947.

———. *Our Threatened Values.* Hinsdale, IL: Regnery, 1948.

Grant Duff, S. *German and Czech: A Threat to European Peace.* London: Victor Gollancz, 1937.

———. *The Parting of Ways: A Personal Account of the Thirties.* London: Peter Owen, 1982.

Great Britain. Parliament. *Parliamentary Debates,* 5th series.

Haffner, S. *Geschichte eines Deutschen: Die Erinnerungen 1914–1933.* Stuttgart: Deutsche Verlags-Anstalt, 2000.

Havel, V. *To the Castle and Back.* New York: Random House, 2008.

Hindus, M. G. *We Shall Live Again.* New York: Doubleday, Doran, 1939.

———. *The Bright Passage.* New York: Doubleday, 1947.

Hitler, A. *Hitler's Second Book: The Unpublished Sequel to Mein Kampf,* ed. G. L. Weinberg. New York: Enigma, 2003.

International Institute of Humanitarian Law. *Report of the Working Group on Mass Expulsion.* San Remo, International Institute of Humanitarian Law, 1983.

Jaksch, W. *Can Industrial Peoples Be Transferred? The Future of the Sudeten Population.* London: Sudeten German Social Democratic Party, 1943.

Kent, M. *Eine Porzellanscherbe im Graben: Eine deutsche Flüchtlingskindheit.* Bern: Scherz, 2003.

Kovály, H. M. *Under a Cruel Star: A Life in Prague 1941–1968.* Cambridge, MA: Plunkett Lake Press, 1986.

Klukowski, Z. *Diary from the Years of Occupation.* Urbana: University of Illinois Press, 1993.

Labour Party (Great Britain). *The International Post-War Settlement: Report by the National Executive Committee of the Labour Party to be Presented to the Annual Conference to be Held in London from May 29th to June 2nd, 1944.* London: Co-Operative Printing Society, 1944.

———. *Report of the Forty-Fourth Annual Conference of the Labour Party.* London: Co-Operative Printing Society, 1945.

Lane, A. B. *I Saw Poland Betrayed: An American Ambassador Reports to the American People.* Indianapolis: Bobbs-Merrill, 1948.

Lippóczy, P. and T. Walichnowski, eds. *Przesiedlenie ludności niemieckiej z Polski po II wojnie światowej w świetle dokumentów.* Warsaw: Państwowe Wydawnictwo Naukowe, 1982.

Lockhart, R. H. B. *The Diaries of Sir Robert Bruce Lockhart,* vol. 2: 1939–1965, ed. K. Young. London: Macmillan, 1980.

Mackenzie, C. *Dr Beneš.* London: Harrap, 1946.

Maschmann, M. *Fazit: Kein Rechtfertigungsversuch.* Stuttgart: Deutsche Verlagsanstalt, 1964.

Merritt, A. J. and R. L. Merritt, eds. *Public Opinion in Occupied Germany: The OMGUS Surveys, 1945–1949.* Urbana: University of Illinois Press, 1970.

Mlynárik, J. *Thesen zur Aussiedlung der Deutschen aus der Tschechoslowakei, 1945–1947.* Munich: Danubius, 1985.

Neary, B. U. and H. Schneider-Ricks, eds. *Voices of Loss and Courage: German Women Recount Their Expulsion from East Central Europe 1944–1950.* Rockport, ME: Picton, 2002.

Nicolson, H. *Peacemaking 1919.* Boston: Houghton Mifflin, 1938.

Office of Military Government for Germany. Prisoners of War and Displaced Persons Division. *Report on Refugees and Expellees.* Berlin: OMGUS, 1947.

Ripka, H. *The Future of the Czechoslovak Germans.* London: Czechoslovak-British Friendship Club, 1944.

———. "Czechoslovakia's Attitude to Germany and Hungary," *Slavonic and East European Review* 23 (1945): 47–54.

Roberts, S. H. *The House That Hitler Built.* London: Methuen, 1939.

Schieder, T., et al., eds. *Dokumentation der Vertreibung der Deutschen aus Ost-Mitteleuropa,* 5 vols. Bonn: Bundesministerium für Vertriebene, Flüchtlinge und Kriegsgeschädigte, 1953–61.

Schimanski, S. *Vain Victory.* London: Victor Gollancz, 1946.

Sommer, H. *Völkerwanderung im 20. Jahrhundert: Die grosse Heimkehr der Volksdeutschen ins Reich.* Berlin: Wilhelm Limpert-Verlag, 1940.

Sudeten German Social Democratic Party. *Deportation Drama in Czecho-Slovakia: The Case of a Dying People*. London: Der Sozialdemokrat, 1945.

———. *Evidence on the Reign of Racialism in Czechoslovakia*. London: Der Sozialdemokrat, 1945.

Swanstrom, E. E. *Pilgrims of the Night: A Study of Expelled Peoples*. New York: Sheed & Ward, 1950.

United Nations. Human Rights Committee. *Selected Decisions of the Human Rights Committee under the Optional Protocol, International Covenant on Civil and Political Rights*, vol. 8. New York: United Nations Publications, 2007.

United States. Congress. House of Representatives. *Hearings Before Subcommittee No. 1 of the Committee on the Judiciary, House of Representatives, Eighty-First Congress, First Session, on H.R. 1344: A Bill to Amend the Displaced Persons Act of 1948, March 2, 4, and 9, 1949*. Washington, DC: Government Printing Office, 1949.

———. *Expellees and Refugees of German Ethnic Origin: Report of a Special Subcommittee of the Committee on the Judiciary, House of Representatives, Pursuant to H. Res. 238, A Resolution to Authorize the Committee on the Judiciary to Undertake a Study of Immigration and Nationality Problems* (Report No. 1841). Washington, DC: Government Printing Office, 1950.

United States. Department of State. *Foreign Relations of the United States*. Washington, DC: Government Printing Office, 1955–1971.

Welles. S. *The Time for Decision*. New York: Harper, 1944.

———. *Where Are We Heading?* London: Hutchinson, 1947.

Zachodnia Agencja Prasowa. *1939–1950: Population Movements Between the Oder and Bug Rivers*. Poznań: Wydawnictwo Zachodnie, 1961.

BOOKS, ARTICLES, AND DISSERTATIONS

Ackermann, V. *Der "echte" Flüchtling: Deutsche Vertriebene und Flüchtlinge aus der DDR 1945–1961*. Osnabrück: Universitätsverlag Rasch, 1995.

Ahonen, P. *After the Expulsion: West Germany and Eastern Europe 1945–1990*. Oxford: Oxford University Press, 2003.

Ahonen, P., Corni, G., et al. *People on the Move: Forced Population Movements in Europe in the Second World War and its Aftermath*. Oxford: Berg, 2008.

Allen, D. J. *The Oder-Neisse Line: The United States, Poland, and Germany in the Cold War*. Westport, CT: Praeger, 2003.

Aly, G. *"Final Solution": Nazi Population Policy and the Murder of the European Jews*. London: Arnold, 1999.

Aly, G. and C. B. Haake, eds. *Removing Peoples: Forced Removal in the Modern World*. Oxford: Oxford University Press, 2009.

Aly, G. and S. Heim. *Vordenker der Vernichtung: Auschwitz und die deutschen Pläne für eine neue europäische Ordnung*. Hamburg: Hoffmann & Campe, 1991.

Anderson, C. *Eyes Off the Prize: The United Nations and the African American Struggle for Human Rights, 1945–1955*. Cambridge: Cambridge University Press, 2003.

Annan, N. *Changing Enemies: The Defeat and Regeneration of Germany.* London: Harper-Collins, 1995.
Auer, S. and S. Burgdorff, eds. *Die Flucht: Über die Vertreibung der Deutschen aus dem Osten.* Stuttgart: Deutsche Verlags-Anstalt, 2002.
Aust, A. *Handbook of International Law,* 2d ed. Cambridge: Cambridge University Press, 2010.
Bacque, J. *Crimes and Mercies: The Fate of German Civilians under Allied Occupation 1944–1950.* London: Little, Brown, 1997.
Balfour, M. and J. Mair. *Four-Power Control in Germany and Austria, 1945–1946.* Oxford: Oxford University Press, 1956.
Barkan, E. *The Guilt of Nations: Restitution and Negotiating Historical Injustices.* Baltimore: Johns Hopkins University Press, 2001.
Bass, G. J. *Stay the Hand of Vengeance: The Politics of War Crimes Tribunals.* Princeton, NJ: Princeton University Press, 2000.
Bell-Fialkoff, A. *Ethnic Cleansing.* London: St. Martin's Press, 1996.
Benz, W., ed. *Die Vertreibung der Deutschen aus dem Osten: Ursachen, Ereignisse, Folgen.* Frankfurt am Main: Fischer, 1985.
Bergen, D. L. *War and Genocide: A Concise History of the Holocaust.* Lanham, MD: Rowman & Littlefield, 2009.
Bessel, R. *Germany 1945: From War to Peace.* London: Simon & Schuster, 2009.
Bessel, R. and C. B. Haake, eds. *Removing Peoples: Forced Removal in the Modern World.* Oxford: Oxford University Press, 2009.
Biddiscombe, A. P. *Werwolf! The History of the National Socialist Guerrilla Movement 1944–1946.* Toronto: University of Toronto Press, 1998.
Biess, F. *Homecomings: Returning POWs and the Legacies of Defeat in Postwar Germany.* Princeton, NJ: Princeton University Press, 2006.
Bramwell, A. C., ed. *Refugees in the Age of Total War.* London: Unwin Hyman, 1988.
Brandes, D. *Der Weg zur Vertreibung: Pläne und Entscheidungen zum "Transfer" der Deutschen aus der Tschechoslowakei und aus Polen.* Munich: Oldenbourg, 2001.
Brandes, D., Ivaničková, E., and Pešek, J., eds. *Erzwungene Trennung: Vertreibungen und Aussiedlungen in und aus der Tschechoslowakei 1938–1947 im Vergleich mit Polen, Ungarn und Jugoslawien.* Essen: Klartext, 1999.
Breitman, R. *The Architect of Genocide: Himmler and the Final Solution.* New York: Knopf, 1991.
Brown, M. D. *Dealing with Democrats: The British Foreign Office and the Czechoslovak Émigrés in Great Britain, 1939 to 1945.* Frankfurt am Main: Peter Lang, 2006.
Browning, C. R. with Matthäus, J. *The Origins of the Final Solution: The Evolution of Nazi Jewish Policy, September 1939–March 1942.* Lincoln: University of Nebraska Press, 2004.
Bruegel, J. W. *Czechoslovakia Before Munich: The German Minority Problem and British Appeasement Policy.* Cambridge: Cambridge University Press, 1973.
Brumlik, M. *Wer Sturm sät: Die Vertreibung der Deutschen.* Berlin: Aufbau, 2005.
Bryant, C. *Prague in Black: Nazi Rule and Czech Nationalism.* Cambridge, MA: Harvard University Press, 2007.
Bullivant, K., Giles, G., and Pape, E., eds., *Germany and Eastern Europe: Cultural Iden-*

tities and Cultural Differences (Yearbook of European Studies, vol. 13). Amsterdam: Rodopi, 1999.

Burleigh, M. *Germany Turns Eastwards: A Study of Ostforschung in the Third Reich*. Cambridge: Cambridge University Press, 1988.

———. *The Third Reich: A New History*. Basingstoke, Hampshire: Macmillan, 2000.

Byman, D. L. *Keeping the Peace: Lasting Solutions to Ethnic Conflicts*. Baltimore: Johns Hopkins University Press, 2002.

Carmichael, C. *Genocide Before the Holocaust*. New Haven, CT: Yale University Press, 2009.

Casey, S. *Cautious Crusade: Franklin D. Roosevelt, American Public Opinion, and the War against Nazi Germany*. New York: Oxford University Press, 2001.

Chinciński, T. and P. Machcewicz, eds. *Bydgoszcz 3–4 września 1939: Studia i dokumenty*. Warsaw: Instytut Pamięci Narodowej, 2008.

Chodakiewicz, M. J. *Between Nazis and Soviets: Occupation Politics in Poland, 1939–1947*. Lanham, MD: Lexington Press, 2004.

Clark, B. *Twice a Stranger: The Mass Expulsions That Forged Modern Greece and Turkey*. Cambridge, MA: Harvard University Press, 2006.

Connor, I. *Refugees and Expellees in Post-War Germany*. Manchester: Manchester University Press, 2007.

Cooper, J. *Raphael Lemkin and the Struggle for the Genocide Convention*. Basingstoke, Hampshire: Palgrave Macmillan, 2008.

Cordell, K. *Ethnicity and Democratisation in the New Europe*. London: Routledge, 1999.

Cordell, K. and S. Wolff. *Germany's Foreign Policy towards Poland and the Czech Republic: Ostpolitik Revisited*. Abingdon, Oxfordshire: Routledge, 2005.

Crampton, R. J. *Eastern Europe in the Twentieth Century and After*. London: Routledge, 1997.

Crawley, A. *The Spoils of War: The Rise of Western Germany 1945–1972*. New York: Bobbs-Merrill, 1973.

Crawshaw, S. *Easier Fatherland: Germany and the Twenty-first Century*. London: Continuum, 2004.

Crowe, D. *Oskar Schindler*. Boulder, CO: Westview, 2004.

Curp, T. D. *A Clean Sweep? The Politics of Ethnic Cleansing in Western Poland, 1945–1960*. Rochester, NY: University of Rochester Press, 2006.

Davies, N. *God's Playground: A History of Poland, 1795 to the Present*, 2 vols. Oxford: Clarendon Press, 1981.

Davies, N. and R. Moorhouse. *Microcosm: Portrait of a Central European City*. London: Jonathan Cape, 2002.

De Jong, L. *The German Fifth Column in the Second World War*. London: Routledge & Kegan Paul, 1956.

Demetz, P. *Prague in Danger: The Years of German Occupation, 1939–1945*. New York: Farrar, Straus and Giroux, 2008.

Deutsche National-Zeitung. *Verbrecher-Album der Sieger: Die 100 furchtbarsten Schreibtischtäter und Vollstrecker des Vernichtungskrieges gegen Deutschland*. Munich: FZ-Verlag, 1997.

De Zayas, A.-M. *Nemesis at Potsdam: The Anglo-Americans and the Expulsion of the Germans—Background, Execution, Consequences*. London: Routledge & Kegan Paul, 1979.

———. *A Terrible Revenge: The Ethnic Cleansing of the East European Germans, 1944–1950*. New York: St. Martin's Press, 1994.

Douglas, R. M. *The Labour Party, Nationalism and Internationalism, 1939–1951*. London: Routledge, 2004.

Dow, J. E. *The German Nation: Displacement and Resettlement*. New York: American Press, 1968.

Dubiański, W. R. *Obóz pracy w Mysłowicach w latach 1945–1946*. Katowice: Instytut Pamięci Narodowej, 2004.

Dziurok, A. *Obóz pracy w Świętochłowicach w 1945 roku: Dokumenty, zeznania, relacje, listy*. Warsaw: Instytut Pamięci Narodowej, 2002.

Eby, C. D. *Hungary at War: Civilians and Soldiers in World War II*. University Park: Pennsylvania State University Press, 1998.

Egit, J. *Grand Illusion*. Toronto: Lugus, 1991.

Epstein, C. *Model Nazi: Arthur Greiser and the Occupation of Western Poland*. Oxford: Oxford University Press, 2010.

Esser, H. *Die Hölle von Lamsdorf: Dokumentation über ein polnisches Vernichtungslager*. Münster: Vienerius, 1971.

Faulenbach, B. and A. Helle, eds., *Zwangsmigration in Europa: Zur wissenschaflichen und politischen Auseinandersetzung um die Vertreibung der Deutschen aus dem Osten*. Essen: Klartext, 2005.

Favez, J.-C. *Une mission impossible? Le CICR, les déportations et les camps de concentration nazis*. Lausanne: Payot, 1988.

Fehrenbach, H. *Cinema in Democratizing Germany: Reconstructing National Identity after Hitler*. Chapel Hill: University of North Carolina Press, 1995.

Fenby, J. *Alliance: The Inside Story of How Roosevelt, Stalin and Churchill Won One War and Began Another*. London: Simon & Schuster, 2006.

Frank, M. *Expelling the Germans: British Opinion and Mass Population Transfer in Context*. Oxford: Oxford University Press, 2007.

Fritzsche, P. *Life and Death in the Third Reich*. Cambridge, MA: Belknap Press of Harvard University Press, 2008.

Frommer, B. *National Cleansing: Retribution against Nazi Collaborators in Postwar Czechoslovakia*. Cambridge: Cambridge University Press, 2005.

Garrett, S. A. *Conscience and Power: An Examination of Dirty Hands and Political Leadership*. Basingstoke, Hampshire: Palgrave Macmillan, 1996.

George, B. *Les Russes arrivent: La plus grande migration des temps modernes*. Paris: Éditions de la Table Ronde, 1966.

Gilbert, M. *The Boys: The Story of 732 Young Concentration Camp Survivors*. New York: Holt, 1998.

Grass, G. *Im Krebsgang*. Göttingen: Steidl, 2002.

Gregor, N. *Haunted City: Nuremberg and the Nazi Past*. New Haven, CT: Yale University Press, 2008.

Gross, J. T. *Polish Society under German Occupation: The Generalgouvernement, 1939–1944*. Princeton, NJ: Princeton University Press, 1979.

———. *Fear: Anti-Semitism in Poland After Auschwitz—An Essay in Historical Interpretation*. New York: Random House, 2006.

Guntner, J. L. and A. M. McLean, eds., *Literary Theory and Theater Practice in the German Democratic Republic*. Cranbury, NJ: Associated University Presses, 1998.

Hahn, E. and H. H. Hahn. *Die Vertreibung im deutschen Erinnern: Legenden, Mythos, Geschichte*. Paderborn: Schöningh, 2010.

Hankel, G. *Die Leipziger Prozesse: Deutsche Kriegsverbrechen und ihre strafrechtliche Verfolgung nach dem Ersten Weltkrieg*. Hamburg: HIS Verlag, 2003.

Harbutt, F. J. *Yalta 1945: Europe and America at the Crossroads*. Cambridge: Cambridge University Press, 2010.

Harvey, E. *Women and the Nazi East: Agents and Witnesses of Germanization*. New York: Columbia University Press, 2005.

Hastings, M. *Armageddon: The Battle for Germany, 1944–1945*. New York: Knopf, 2004.

Heimann, M. J. *Czechoslovakia: The State That Failed*. New Haven, CT: Yale University Press, 2009.

Heinemann, I. *Rasse, Siedlung, deutsches Blut: Das Rasse- und Siedlungshauptamt der SS und die rassenpolitische Neuordnung Europas*. Göttingen: Wallstein, 2003.

Henckaerts, J.-M. *Mass Expulsion in Modern International Law and Practice*. The Hague: Martinus Nijhoff, 1995.

Hirschon, R., ed. *Crossing the Aegean: An Appraisal of the 1923 Compulsory Population Exchange Between Greece and Turkey*. Oxford: Berghahn, 2003.

Hofmann, A. R. *Die Nachkriegszeit in Schlesien: Gesellschafts- und Bevölkerungspolitik in den polnischen Siedlungsgebieten 1945–1948*. Cologne: Böhlau, 2000.

Horne, J. and A. Kramer. *German Atrocities 1914: A History of Denial*. New Haven, CT: Yale University Press, 2001.

Hrabar, R., Z. Tokarz, and J. E. Wilczur, eds., *Kinder im Krieg—Krieg gegen Kinder: Die Geschichte der polnischen Kinder, 1939–1945*. Reinbek bei Hamburg: Rowohlt, 1981.

Huener, J. *Auschwitz, Poland, and the Politics of Commemoration, 1945–1979*. Athens: Ohio University Press, 2003.

Hughes, M. L. *Shouldering the Burdens of Defeat: West Germany and the Reconstruction of Social Justice*. Chapel Hill: University of North Carolina Press, 1999.

Ignatieff, M. *Blood and Belonging: Journeys Into the New Nationalism*. London: BBC Books, 1993.

Jackson, K. *Humphrey Jennings*. London: Picador, 2004.

Jaksch, W. *Europe's Road to Potsdam*, ed. K. Glaser. New York: Praeger, 1963.

Jankowiak, S. *Wysiedlenie i emigracja ludności Niemieckiej w polityce władz Polskich w latach 1945–1970*. Warsaw: Instytut Pamięci Narodowej, 2005.

Jansen, C. and A. Weckbecker. *Der "Volksdeutsche Selbstschutz" in Polen 1939/40*. Munich: Oldenbourg, 1992.

"Jedermann, F." [P. Příhoda]. *Verlorene Geschichte: Bilder und Texte aus dem heutigen Sudetenland*. Cologne: Bund-Verlag, 1985.

Jenkins, G. *Political Islam in Turkey: Running West, Heading East?* Basingstoke, Hampshire: Palgrave Macmillan, 2008.

Kacowicz, A. M. and P. Lutomski, eds. *Population Resettlement in International Conflicts: A Comparative Study*. Lanham, MD: Lexington, 2007.

Kalb, J. *The Theater of Heiner Müller*. Cambridge: Cambridge University Press, 1998.

Kenney, P. *Rebuilding Poland: Workers and Communists 1945–1950*. Ithaca, NY: Cornell University Press, 1997.

Khan, Y. *The Great Partition: The Making of India and Pakistan*. New Haven, CT: Yale University Press, 2007.

King, J. *Budweisers into Czechs and Germans: A Local History of Bohemian Politics, 1848–1948*. Princeton, NJ: Princeton University Press, 2002.

Kittel, M. *Vertreibung der Vertriebenen? Der historische deutsche Osten in der Erinnerungskultur der Bundesrepublik (1961–1982)*. Munich: Oldenbourg, 2007.

Knightley, P. *The First Casualty: From the Crimea to Vietnam—The War Correspondent as Hero, Propagandist, and Myth Maker*. New York: Harcourt Brace Jovanovich, 1975.

Kochavi, A. J. *Prelude to Nuremberg: Allied War Crimes Policy and the Question of Punishment*. Chapel Hill: University of North Carolina Press, 1998.

———. *Post-Holocaust Politics: Britain, the United States, and Jewish Refugees, 1945–1948*. Chapel Hill: University of North Carolina Press, 2001.

Koehl, R. *RKFDV: German Resettlement and Population Policy, 1939–1945. A History of the Reich Commission for the Strengthening of Germandom*. Cambridge, MA: Harvard University Press, 1957.

Kogon, E. *The Theory and Practice of Hell: The German Concentration Camps and the System Behind Them*, 1st rev. ed. New York: Farrar, Straus and Giroux, 2006.

Kontogiorgi, E. *Population Exchange in Greek Macedonia: The Rural Settlement of Refugees 1922–1930*. Oxford: Oxford University Press, 2006.

Kopka, B. *Obozy pracy w Polsce 1944–1950: Przewodnik encyklopedyczny*. Warsaw: Karta, 2002.

Kossert, A. *Kalte Heimat: Die Geschichte der deutschen Vertriebenen nach 1945*. Berlin: Siedler, 2008.

Kotek, J. and P. Rigoulot. *Le siècle des camps: Détention, concentration, extermination*. Paris: Lattès, 2000.

Krauss, M., ed. *Integrationen: Vertriebene in den deutschen Ländern nach 1945*. Göttingen: Vandenhoeck & Ruprecht, 2008.

Krejčí, J. and P. Machonin. *Czechoslovakia, 1918–92: A Laboratory for Social Change*. New York: St. Martin's Press, 1996.

Kulischer, E. M. *The Displacement of Population in Europe*. Montreal: International Labour Office, 1943.

Lasser, W. *Benjamin V. Cohen: Architect of the New Deal*. New Haven, CT: Yale University Press, 2002.

Lattimore, B. G. *The Assimilation of German Expellees into the West German Polity and Society since 1945: A Case Study of Eutin, Schleswig-Holstein*. The Hague: Martinus Nijhoff, 1974.

Leff, L. *Buried by the Times: The Holocaust and America's Most Important Newspaper.* Cambridge: Cambridge University Press, 2005.

Lehmann, A. *Im Fremden ungewollt zuhaus: Flüchtlinge und Vertriebene in Westdeutschland 1945–1990.* Munich: C. H. Beck, 1991.

Lenarcik, M. *A Community in Transition: Jewish Welfare in Breslau-Wrocław.* Opladen: Verlag Barbara Budrich, 2010.

Lieberman, B. *Terrible Fate: Ethnic Cleansing in the Making of Modern Europe.* Chicago: I. R. Dee, 2006.

Linek, B. *Polityka antyniemiecka na Górnym Śląsku w latach 1945–1950.* Opole: Stowarzyszenie Instytut Slaski, 2000.

Lumans, V. O. *Himmler's Auxiliaries: The* Volksdeutsche Mittelstelle *and the German National Minorities of Europe, 1933–1945.* Chapel Hill: University of North Carolina Press, 1993.

Luža, R. *The Transfer of the Sudeten Germans: A Study of Czech-German Relations, 1933–1962.* New York: New York University Press, 1964.

Macardle, D. *Children of Europe: A Study of the Children of Liberated Countries, Their War-time Experiences, Their Reactions, and Their Needs.* London: Victor Gollancz, 1951.

MacDonogh, G. *After the Reich: From the Liberation of Vienna to the Berlin Airlift.* London: John Murray, 2007.

Maguire, P. *Law and War: International Law and American Justice,* rev. ed. New York: Columbia University Press, 2010.

Majer, D. *"Non-Germans" Under the Third Reich: The Nazi Judicial and Administrative System in Germany and Occupied Eastern Europe, with Special Regard to Occupied Poland, 1939–1945.* Baltimore: Johns Hopkins University Press, 2003.

Mann, M. *The Dark Side of Democracy: Explaining Ethnic Cleansing.* Cambridge: Cambridge University Press, 2004.

Marcuse, H. *Legacies of Dachau: The Uses and Abuses of a Concentration Camp 1933–2001.* Cambridge: Cambridge University Press, 2001.

Mastny, V. *The Czechs under Nazi Rule: The Failure of National Resistance, 1939–1942.* New York: Columbia University Press, 1971.

Mazower, M. *Hitler's Empire: How the Nazis Ruled Europe.* New York: Penguin, 2008.

Meehan, P. *A Strange Enemy People: Germans under the British, 1945–1950.* London: Peter Owen, 2001.

Mevius, M. *Agents of Moscow: The Hungarian Communist Party and the Origins of Socialist Patriotism 1941–1953.* Oxford: Clarendon Press, 2005.

Moeller, R. G. *War Stories: The Search for a Usable Past in the Federal Republic of Germany.* Berkeley: University of California Press, 2001.

Moltke, J. von. *No Place Like Home: Locations of* Heimat *in German Cinema.* Berkeley: University of California Press, 2005.

Morrison, J. G. *Ravensbrück: Everyday Life in a Women's Concentration Camp 1939–45.* Princeton, NJ: Markus Wiener, 2000.

Muller, J.-L. *L'expulsion des allemands de Hongrie: Politique internationale et destin méconnu d'une minorité.* Paris: L'Harmattan, 2001.

Murdock, C. *Changing Places: Society, Culture, and Territory in the Saxon-Bohemian Borderlands, 1870–1946*. Ann Arbor: University of Michigan Press, 2010.

Naimark, N. M. *The Russians in Germany: A History of the Soviet Zone of Occupation, 1945–1949*. Cambridge, MA: Belknap Press of Harvard University Press, 1995.

———. *Fires of Hatred: Ethnic Cleansing in Twentieth-Century Europe*. Cambridge, MA: Harvard University Press, 2001.

Neville, P. *Hitler and Appeasement: The British Attempt to Prevent the Second World War*. London: Hambledon Continuum, 2006.

Nicholas, L. H. *Cruel World: The Children of Europe in the Nazi Web*. New York: Knopf, 2005.

Nitschke, B. *Vertreibung und Aussiedlung der deutschen Bevölkerung aus Polen 1945 bis 1949*. Munich: Oldenbourg, 2004.

Nowak, E. *Lager im Oppelner Schlesien im System der Nachkriegslager in Polen (1945–1950): Geschichte und Implikationen*. Opole: Zentrales Kriegsgefangenenmuseum Lambinowice-Opole, 2003.

Olejnik, L. *Polityka narodowościowa Polski w latach 1944–1960*. Łódź: Wydawnictwo Uniwersytetu Łódźkiego, 2003.

———. *Zdrajcy narodu? Losy volksdeutschów w Polsce po II wojnie światowej*. Warsaw: Trio, 2006.

Orłowski, H. and A. Sakson, eds. *Utracona ojczyzna: Przymusowe wysiedlenia deportacje i przesiedlenia jako wspólne doświadczenie*. Poznań: Instytut Zachodni, 1996.

Orzoff, A. *Battle for the Castle: The Myth of Czechoslovakia in Europe, 1914–1948*. Oxford: Oxford University Press, 2009.

Paikert, G. C. *The German Exodus: A Selective Study on the Post–World War II Expulsion of German Populations and Its Effects*. The Hague: Martinus Nijhoff, 1962.

———. *The Danube Swabians: German Populations in Hungary, Rumania and Yugoslavia and Hitler's Impact on their Patterns*. The Hague: Martinus Nijhoff, 1967.

Perdue, P. C. *China Marches West: The Qing Conquest of Central Eurasia*. Cambridge, MA: Belknap Press of Harvard University Press, 2005.

Persson, H.-Å. *Rhetorik und Realpolitik: Großbritannien, die Oder-Neiße-Grenze und die Vertreibung der Deutschen nach dem Zweiten Weltkrieg*. Potsdam: Verlag für Berlin-Brandenburg, 1997.

Perzi, N. *Die Beneš-Dekrete: Eine europäische Tragödie*. St. Pölten: Niederösterreichisches Pressehaus, 2003.

Petersen, T. *Flucht und Vertreibung aus Sicht der deutschen, polnischen und tschechischen Bevölkerung*. Bonn: Stiftung Haus der Geschichte der Bundesrepublik Deutschland, 2005.

Plaschka, R. G., H. Haselsteiner, et al., eds. *Nationale Frage und Vertreibung in der Tschechoslowakei und Ungarn 1938–1948: Aktuelle Forschungen*. Vienna: Verlag der Österreichischen Akademie der Wissenschaften, 1997.

Pogány, I. S. *Righting Wrongs in Eastern Europe*. Manchester: Manchester University Press, 1997.

Pohl, D. *Von der "Judenpolitik" zum Judenmord: Der Distrikt Lublin des Generalgouvernements 1933–1944*. Frankfurt am Main: Peter Lang, 1993.

Ponting, C. *Churchill*. London: Sinclair-Stevenson, 1994.
Power, S. *"A Problem from Hell": America and the Age of Genocide*. New York: Basic Books, 2002.
Prażmowska, A. J. *Civil War in Poland, 1942–1948*. Basingstoke, Hampshire: Palgrave Macmillan, 2004.
Proudfoot, M. J. *European Refugees 1939–52: A Study in Forced Population Movement*. Evanston, IL: Northwestern University Press, 1956.
Prusin, A. V. *The Lands Between: Conflict in the East European Borderlands, 1870–1992*. Oxford: Oxford University Press, 2010.
Raška, F. D. *The Czechoslovak Exile Government in London and the Sudeten German Issue*. Prague: Karolinum Press, 2002.
Rees, L. *The Nazis: A Warning from History*. London: BBC Books, 1997.
Reynolds, D. *In Command of History: Churchill Fighting and Writing the Second World War*. New York: Random House, 2005.
Rey-Schyrr, C. *Histoire du Comité international de la Croix-Rouge*, vol. 3: *De Yalta à Dien Bien Phu, 1945–1955*. Geneva: Georg Éditeur, 2007.
Rolinek, S. *Jüdische Lebenswelten 1945–1955: Flüchtlinge in der amerikanischen Zone Österreichs*. Innsbruck: Studien Verlag, 2007.
Roman, E. *Hungary and the Victor Powers, 1945–1950*. New York: St. Martin's Press, 1996.
Rossino, A. B. *Hitler Strikes Poland: Blitzkrieg, Ideology, and Atrocity*. Lawrence: University Press of Kansas, 2003.
Rothkirchen, L. *The Jews of Bohemia and Moravia: Facing the Holocaust*. Lincoln: University of Nebraska Press, 2005.
Rummel, R. J. *Death by Government*. New Brunswick, NJ: Transaction, 1994.
Ryan, S. *The Transformation of Violent Intercommunal Conflict*. Aldershot, Hampshire: Ashgate, 2007.
Rystad, G., ed. *The Uprooted: Forced Migration as an International Problem in the Post-War Era*. Lund: Lund University Press, 1990.
Sayer, I. and D. Botting. *Nazi Gold: The Story of the World's Greatest Robbery—and Its Aftermath*. New York: Congdon & Weed, 1984.
Schabas, W. A. *An Introduction to the International Criminal Court*, 3d ed. Cambridge: Cambridge University Press, 2007.
Schafft, G. E. *From Racism to Genocide: Anthropology in the Third Reich*. Urbana: University of Illinois Press, 2004.
Schechtman, J. B. *European Population Transfers 1939–1945*. New York: Oxford University Press, 1946.
———. *Postwar Population Transfers in Europe 1945–1955*. Philadelphia: University of Pennsylvania Press, 1962.
Schraut, S. *Flüchtlingsaufnahme in Württemberg-Baden 1945–1949: Amerikanische Besatzungsziele und demokratischer Wiederaufbau im Konflikt*. Munich: Oldenbourg, 1995.
Shephard, B. *The Long Road Home: The Aftermath of the Second World War*. London: Bodley Head, 2010.
Smelser, R. M. *The Sudeten Problem, 1933–1938: Volkstumspolitik and the Formulation of Nazi Foreign Policy*. Middletown, CT: Wesleyan University Press, 1975.

Snyder, T. *Bloodlands: Europe Between Hitler and Stalin*. New York: Basic Books. 2010.
Solonari, V. *Purifying the Nation: Population Exchange and Ethnic Cleansing in Nazi-Allied Romania*. Washington, DC: Woodrow Wilson Center Press, 2010.
Staněk, T. *Tábory v českých zemích 1945–1948*. Opava: Slezský ústav Slezského zemského muzea, 1996.
———. *Verfolgung 1945: Die Stellung der Deutschen in Böhmen, Mähren und Schlesien (außerhalb der Lager und Gefängnisse)*. Vienna: Böhlau, 2002.
———. *Poválečné "excesy" v českych zemích v roce 1945 a jejich vyšetřování*. Prague: Ústav pro soudobé dějiny, 2005.
Stankowski, W. *Lager für Deutsche in Polen am Beispiel Pommerellen/Westpreußen (1945–1990): Durchsicht und Analyse der polnischen Archivalien*. Bonn: Kulturstiftung der deutschen Vertriebenen, 2001.
Stargardt, N. *Witnesses of War: Children's Lives under the Nazis*. New York: Random House, 2005.
Stern, F. *Five Germanys I Have Known*. New York: Farrar, Strauss and Giroux, 2006.
Strauchold, G. *Myśl zachodnia i jej realizacja w Polsce Ludowej w latach 1945–1957*. Toruń: Wydawnictwo Adam Marszałek, 2003.
Suppan, A. *Austrians, Czechs, and Sudeten Germans as a Community of Conflict in the Twentieth Century*. Minneapolis: Center for Austrian Studies, 2006.
Szułdrzyński, J. *The Pattern of Life in Poland*, vol. 6: *The Family*. Paris: Mid-European Research and Planning Centre, 1952.
Táborský, E. *President Edvard Beneš: Between East and West, 1938–1948*. Palo Alto, CA: Hoover Institution Press, 1981.
Tanner, M. *Ireland's Holy Wars: The Struggle for a Nation's Soul, 1500–2000*. New Haven, CT: Yale University Press, 2001.
Taylor, F. *Dresden, Tuesday, February 13, 1945*. London: HarperCollins, 2004.
Tenz, M. H. *The Innocent Must Pay: Memoirs of a Danube German Girl in a Yugoslavian Death Camp 1944–1948*. Bismarck, ND: University of Mary Press, 1991.
Ther, P. *Deutsche und polnische Vertriebene: Gesellschaft und Vertriebenenpolitik in der SBZ/DDR und in Polen 1945–1956*. Göttingen: Vandenhoeck & Ruprecht, 1998.
Ther, P. and A. Siljak, eds. *Redrawing Nations: Ethnic Cleansing in East-Central Europe, 1944–1948*. Lanham, MD: Rowman & Littlefield, 2001.
Thornberry, P. *International Law and the Rights of Minorities*. Oxford: Clarendon Press, 1991.
Trevelyan, G. M. *British History in the Nineteenth Century (1782–1901)*. London: Longmans, Green, 1922.
Urban, T. *Der Verlust: Die Vertreibung der Deutschen und Polen im 20. Jahrhundert*. Munich: C. H. Beck, 2004.
Várdy, S. B. and T. H. Tooley, eds. *Ethnic Cleansing in Twentieth-Century Europe*. Boulder, CO: Social Science Monographs, 2003.
Vernant, J. *The Refugee in the Post-War World*. New Haven, CT: Yale University Press, 1953.
Völklein, U. *"Mitleid war von niemand zu erwarten": Das Schicksal der deutschen Vertriebenen*. Munich: Droemer, 2005.

Vogt, T. R. *Denazification in Soviet-Occupied Germany: Brandenburg, 1945–1948.* Cambridge, MA: Harvard University Press, 2000.
Walters, F. P. *A History of the League of Nations.* Oxford: Oxford University Press, 1967.
Weigel, G. *Witness to Hope: The Biography of Pope John Paul II.* New York: HarperCollins, 1999.
Wiedemann, A. "Komm mit uns das Grenzland aufbauen!" *Ansiedlung und neue Strukturen in den ehemaligen Sudetengebieten 1945–1952.* Essen: Klartext, 2007.
Wiesen, S. J. *West German Industry and the Challenge of the Nazi Past, 1945–1955.* Chapel Hill: University of North Carolina Press, 2003.
Wilkinson, P. *Foreign Fields: The Story of an SOE Operative.* London: I. B. Tauris, 1997.
Wingfield, N. M. *Minority Politics in a Multinational State: The German Social Democrats in Czechoslovakia, 1918–1938.* Boulder, CO: East European Monographs, 1989.
———. *Flag Wars and Stone Saints: How the Bohemian Lands Became Czech.* Cambridge, MA: Harvard University Press, 2007.
Wiskemann, E. *Czechs and Germans: A Study of the Struggle in the Historic Provinces of Bohemia and Moravia.* London: Oxford University Press, 1938.
———. *Germany's Eastern Neighbours: Problems Relating to the Oder-Neisse Line and the Czech Frontier Regions.* London: Oxford University Press, 1956.
Wolff, S. *The German Question since 1919.* Westport, CT: Praeger, 2003.
Wolpert, S. *Shameful Flight: The Last Years of the British Empire in India.* Oxford: Oxford University Press, 2006.
Wrigley, C. A. *J. P. Taylor: Radical Historian of Europe.* London: I. B. Tauris, 2006.
Yildirim, O. *Diplomacy and Displacement: Reconsidering the Turco-Greek Exchange of Populations, 1922–1934.* New York: Routledge, 2006.
Zaborowski, M. *Germany, Poland and Europe: Cooperation and Europeanisation.* Manchester: Manchester University Press, 2005.
Zahra, T. *Kidnapped Souls: National Indifference and the Battle for Children in the Bohemian Lands, 1900–1948.* Ithaca, NY: Cornell University Press, 2008.
Zand, G. and J. Holý, eds. *Transfer–Vertreibung–Aussiedlung im Kontext der tschechischen Literatur.* Brno: Aktion, 2004.
Zeman, Z. A. B. and A. Klimek. *The Life of Edvard Beneš 1884–1948: Czechoslovakia in Peace and War.* Oxford: Clarendon Press, 1997.

Abrams, B. F. "Morality, Wisdom, and Revision: The Czech Opposition of the 1970s and the Expulsion of the Sudeten Germans," *East European Politics and Societies* 9:2 (Spring 1995): 234–255.
Ackermann, V. "Homo barackensis: Westdeutsche Flüchtlingslager in den 1950er Jahren." In V. Ackermann, B.-A. Rusinek, and F. Wiesemann, eds., *Anknüpfungen: Kulturgeschichte—Landesgeschichte—Zeitgeschichte: Gedenkschrift für Peter Hüttenberger.* Essen: Klartext, 1995: 330–346.
———. "Das Schweigen der Flüchtlingskinder: Psychische Folgen von Krieg, Flucht und Vertreibung bei den Deutschen nach 1945," *Geschichte und Gesellschaft* 30:3 (2004): 434–464.

Alexander, M. "Die tschechische Diskussion über die Vertreibung der Deutschen und deren Folgen," *Bohemia* 34:2 (1993): 390–409.
Arburg, A. von. "Tak či onak: Nucené přesídlení v komplexním pojetí poválecné sídelní politiky v českých zemích," *Soudobé dějiny* 10:3 (2003): 253–271.
Auer, S. "Slovakia: From Marginalization of Ethnic Minorities to Political Participation (And Back?)." In B. Rechel, ed., *Minority Rights in Central and Eastern Europe*. Abingdon, Oxfordshire: Routledge, 2009: 195–209.
Balogh, S. "Population Removal and Population Exchange in Hungary After World War II." In F. Glatz, ed., *Études historiques hongroises 1990*. Budapest: Institute of History of the Hungarian Academy of Sciences, 1990: 407–432.
Barkan, E. "Deserving and Undeserving Victims: Political Context and Legal Framework of Hard Cases of Reparation." In K. de Feyter, S. Parmentier, et al., eds., *Out of the Ashes: Reparation for Victims of Gross and Systematic Human Rights Violations*. Antwerp: Intersentia, 2005: 83–104.
Bártová, E. "Největší poválečný masakr němců vyřešen: Známe vrahy," June 1, 2009, http://aktualne.centrum.cz/domaci/kauzy/clanek.phtml?id=638627.
Bauerkämper, A. "Assimilationspolitik und Integrationsdynamik: Vertriebene in der SBZ/ DDR in vergleichender Perspektive." In Krauss, *Integrationen*: 22–35.
Beck, B. "Sexual Violence and Its Prosecution by Courts Martial of the Wehrmacht." In R. Chickering, S. Förster, and B. Greiner, eds., *A World at Total War: Global Conflict and the Politics of Destruction, 1937–1945*. Cambridge: Cambridge University Press, 2005: 317–331.
Bergen, D. L. "The 'Volksdeutschen' of Eastern Europe, World War II, and the Holocaust: Constructed Ethnicity, Real Genocide," *Yearbook of European Studies* 13 (1999): 70–93.
———. "The *Volksdeutsche* of Eastern Europe and the Collapse of the Nazi Empire, 1944–1945." In A. E. Steinweis and D. E. Rogers, eds., *The Impact of Nazism: New Perspectives on the Third Reich and Its Legacy*. Lincoln: University of Nebraska Press, 2003: 101–128.
Berger, S. "On Taboos, Traumas and Other Myths: Why the Debate about German Victims During the Second World War Is Not a Historians' Controversy." In W. J. Niven, ed., *Germans as Victims: Remembering the Past in Contemporary Germany*. Basingstoke, Hampshire: Palgrave Macmillan, 2006: 210–224.
Black, P. R. "Rehearsal for 'Reinhard'? Odilo Globocnik and the Lublin *Selbstschutz*," *Central European History* 25:2 (Spring 1992): 204–226.
Blanke, R. "When Germans and Poles Lived Together: From the History of German-Polish Relations." In K. Bullivant, G. Giles, and E. Pape, eds., *Germany and Eastern Europe: Cultural Identities and Cultural Differences* (Yearbook of European Studies, vol. 13). Amsterdam: Rodopi, 1999: 37–55.
Bloxham, D. "The Great Unweaving: The Removal of Peoples in Europe, 1875–1949." In Bessel and Haake, *Removing Peoples*: 167–208.
Blumenwitz, D. "Standards for the Political Handling of Dealings Concerning Property after World War II." In G. Loibi, ed., *Austrian Review of International and European Law 2001*, vol. 6. The Hague: Martinus Nijhoff, 2003: 183–204.
Bookbinder, P. "A Bloody Tradition: Ethnic Cleansing in World War II Yugoslavia," *New England Journal of Public Policy* 19:2 (Winter 2005): 99–109.

Borák, M. "Fenomén tzv. vojenskych táborů nucené práce v Československu a jeho mezinárodni souvislosti," *Slezský sborník* 98:1–2 (2000): 78–92.

Borodziej, W. "Ucieczka—Wypędzenie—Wysiedlenie Przymusowe." In A. Lawaty and H. Orłowski, eds., *Polacy i niemcy: Historia—kultura—polityka*. Poznań: Wydawnictwo Poznańskie, 2003: 98–106.

Boyer, C., et al. "Die Sudetendeutsche Heimatfront (Partei), 1933–1938: Zur Bestimmung ihres politisch-ideologischen Standortes," *Bohemia* 38:2 (1997): 357–385.

Bradley, J. "Czechoslovakia: External Crisis and Internal Compromise." In D. Berg-Schlosser and J. Mitchell, eds., *Conditions of Democracy in Europe, 1919–39: Systematic Case Studies*. Basingstoke, Hampshire: Palgrave Macmillan, 2000: 85–105.

Bramwell, A. C. "The Re-Settlement of Ethnic Germans, 1939–41." In Bramwell, *Refugees in the Age of Total War*: 112–132.

Brandes, D. "Edvard Beneš und die Pläne zur Vertreibung/Aussiedlung der Deutschen und Ungarn 1938–1945." In Zand and Holý, *Transfer–Vertreibung–Aussiedlung*: 11–28.

Brandes, D. "'Otázka transferu . . . Ta je tady Kolumbovo vejce': Českoslovenští komunisté a vyhnání Němců," *Český časopis historický* 103:1 (2005): 87–114.

Brown, M. "The Diplomacy of Bitterness: Genesis of the Potsdam Decision to Expel Germans from Czechoslovakia," *Western Political Quarterly* 11:3 (September 1958): 607–626.

Bryant, C. "Either German or Czech: Fixing Nationality in Bohemia and Moravia, 1939–1946," *Slavic Review* 61:4 (Winter 2002): 683–706.

Burds, J. "The Soviet War Against 'Fifth Columnists': The Case of Chechnya, 1942–4," *Journal of Contemporary History* 42:2 (April, 2007): 267–314.

Capet, A. "Deux regards antinomiques sur l'Allemagne, 1933–1946." In J.-P. Pichardie, ed., *Contre le nazisme ou contre l'Allemagne? Le débat sur l'anti-germanisme en Grande-Bretagne depuis la deuxième guerre mondiale*. Rouen: Centre d'études en littérature et civilisation de langue anglaise, 1998: 7–32.

Caplan, J. "Political Detention and the Origin of the Concentration Camps in Nazi Germany, 1933–1935/6." In N. Gregor, ed., *Nazism, War and Genocide: Essays in Honour of Jeremy Noakes*. Exeter: University of Exeter Press, 2005: 22–41.

Casey, S. "The Campaign to Sell a Harsh Peace for Germany to the American Public," *History* 90:1 (January 2005): 62–92.

Cattaruzza, M. "Espulsioni di massa di popolazioni nell'Europa del XX secolo," *Rivista storica italiana* 113:1 (2001): 66–85.

Cesarini, D. "Camps de la mort, camps de concentration et camps d'internement dans la mémoire collective britannique," *Vingtième siècle* 54 (April–June 1997): 13–23.

Chinciński, T. "Niemiecka dywersja na Pomorzu w 1939 roku." In Chinciński and Machcewicz, *Bydgoszcz 3–4 września 1939*: 170–204.

Chrypinski, V. C. "Church and Nationality in Postwar Poland." In S. P. Ramet, ed., *Religion and Nationalism in Soviet and East European Politics*. Durham, NC: Duke University Press, 1988: 241–263.

Chumiński, J. and E. Kaszuba. "The Breslau Germans under Polish Rule 1945–1946: Conditions of Life, Political Attitudes, Expulsion," *Studia Historiae Oeconomicae* 22 (1997): 87–101.

Connor, I. "The Radicalization That Never Was? Refugees in the German Federal Republic." In F. Biess, M. Roseman, and H. Schissler, eds., *Conflict, Catastrophe and Continuity: Essays on Modern German History*. Oxford: Berghahn, 2007: 221–236.

———. "German Expellees in the SBZ/GDR and the 'Peace Border.'" In A. Goodbody, P. Ó Dochartaigh, et al., eds., *Dislocation and Reorientation: Exile, Division and the End of Communism in German Culture and Politics*. Amsterdam: Rodopi, 2009: 167–196.

Cordell, K. and S. Wolff. "Ethnic Germans in Poland and the Czech Republic: A Comparative Evaluation," *Nationalities Papers* 33:2 (June 2005): 255–276.

Cornwall, M. "'A Leap into Ice-Cold Water': The Manoeuvres of the Henlein Movement in Czechoslovakia, 1933–1938." In M. Cornwall and R. J. W. Evans, eds., *Czechoslovakia in a Nationalist and Fascist Europe 1918–1948*. Oxford: Oxford University Press, 2007: 123–142.

Crowe, D. "Germany and the Baltic Question in Latvia 1939–1940," *East European Quarterly* 26:3 (Autumn 1992): 371–389.

Curp, T. D. "The Politics of Ethnic Cleansing: The P.P.R., the P.Z.Z. and Wielkopolska's Nationalist Revolution, 1944–1946," *Nationalities Papers* 29:4 (2001): 575–603.

Czapliński, W. "The Protection of Minorities under International Law (Comments on the Alleged Existence of a German Minority in Poland)," *Polish Western Affairs* 25:1 (1984): 121–136.

Demshuk, A. "Citizens in Name Only: The National Status of German Expellees, 1945–53," *Ethnopolitics* 5:4 (November 2006): 383–397.

De Zayas, A.-M. "The Legality of Mass Population Transfers: The German Experience 1945–48," *East European Quarterly* 12:1 (Spring 1978): 1–23.

———. "An Historical Survey of Twentieth Century Expulsions." In Bramwell, *Refugees in the Age of Total War*: 15–37.

Drápala, M. "Na ztracené vartě západu: Poznámky k české politické publicistice nesocialistického zaměření v letech 1945–48," *Soudobé dějiny* 5:1 (1998): 16–24.

Farquharson, J. "'Emotional but Influential': Victor Gollancz, Richard Stokes, and the British Zone of Germany, 1945–9," *Journal of Contemporary History* 22:3 (July 1987): 501–519.

Finney, P. B. "'An Evil for All Concerned': Great Britain and Minority Protection after 1919," *Journal of Contemporary History* 30:3 (July 1995): 533–551.

Frank, M. "The New Morality—Victor Gollancz, 'Save Europe Now' and the German Refugee Crisis, 1945–46," *Twentieth Century British History* 17:2 (2006): 230–256.

Frommer, B. "Expulsion or Integration: Unmixing Interethnic Marriage in Postwar Czechoslovakia," *East European Politics and Societies* 14:2 (2000): 381–410.

Gabzdilová, S. "Nemecká menšina na Slovensku koncom druhej svetovej vojny," *Moderní dějiny* 10 (2002): 111–136.

Gabzdilová, S. and M. Olejnik. "Proces internácie nemeckého obyvateľstva na Slovensku v rokoch 1945–1946," *Historický časopis* 50:3 (2002): 423–438.

Geiger, V. "Logori za folksdojčere u Hrvatskoj nakon Drugoga svjetskog rata 1945–1947," *Časopis za suvremenu povijest* 38:3 (September 2006): 1081–1100.

———. "Epidemija tifusa u logorima za folksdojčere u Slavoniji 1945./1946. i posljedice," *Časopis za suvremenu povijest* 39:2 (October 2007): 367–383.

———. "Josip Broz Tito i sudbina jugoslavenskih Nijemaca," *Časopis za suvremenu povijest* 40:3 (September 2008): 801–818.
Genizi, H. "Interfaith Cooperation in America on Behalf of the D.P. Acts, 1948–1950," *Holocaust and Genocide Studies* 8:1 (Spring 1994): 75–93.
Gerlach, D. "Beyond Expulsion: The Emergence of 'Unwanted Elements' in the Postwar Czech Borderlands, 1945–1950," *East European Politics and Societies* 24:2 (May 2010): 269–293.
Glassheim, E. "National Mythologies and Ethnic Cleansing: The Expulsion of Czechoslovak Germans in 1945," *Central European History* 33:4 (December 2000): 463–486.
———. "Ethnic Cleansing, Communism, and Environmental Devastation in Czechoslovakia's Borderlands, 1945–1989," *Journal of Modern History* 78:1 (March 2006): 65–92.
Goda, N. J. W. "Black Marks: Hitler's Bribery of His Senior Officers During World War II," *Journal of Modern History* 72:2 (June 2002): 413–452.
Goldenberg, S. L. "Crimes Against Humanity—1945–1970: A Study in the Making and Unmaking of International Criminal Law," *Western Ontario Law Review* 10:1 (1971): 1–55.
Goltermann, S. "The Imagination of Disaster: Death and Survival in Postwar West Germany." In A. Confino, P. Betts, and D. Schumann, eds., *Between Mass Death and Individual Loss: The Place of the Dead in Twentieth-Century Germany.* Oxford: Berghahn, 2008: 261–274.
Gosewinkel, D. and S. Meyer. "Citizenship, Property Rights and Dispossession in Postwar Poland (1918 and 1945)," *European Review of History* 16:4 (August 2009): 575–595.
Grabowski, J. and Z. R. Grabowski, "Germans in the Eyes of the Germans: The Ciechanów District, 1939–1945," *Contemporary European History* 13:1 (February 2004): 21–43.
Grohmann, C. "From Lothringen to Lorraine: Expulsion and Voluntary Repatriation," *Diplomacy and Statecraft* 16:3 (Autumn 2005): 571–587.
Haar, I. "Die deutschen 'Vertreibungsverluste': Zur Entstehungsgeschichte der *Dokumentation der Vertreibung,*" *Tel Aviver Jahrbuch für deutsche Geschichte* 35 (2007): 251–272.
Hauner, M. "Aux sources de la question allemande chez le jeune Edvard Beneš," *Revue des études slaves* 70:4 (1998): 932–942.
———. "'We Must Push Eastwards!' The Challenges and Dilemmas of President Beneš after Munich," *Journal of Contemporary History* 44:4 (October 2009): 619–656.
Hauser, P. "The German Minority in Poland in the Years 1918–1939: Reflections on the State of Research and Interpretation. Proposals for Further Research," *Polish Western Affairs* 32:2 (1991): 13–38.
Hayden, R. M. "Schindler's Fate: Genocide, Ethnic Cleansing, and Population Transfers," *Slavic Review* 55:4 (Winter 1996): 727–748.
Heinemann, I. "'Another Type of Perpetrator': The SS Racial Experts and Forced Population Movements in the Occupied Regions," *Holocaust and Genocide Studies* 15:3 (Winter 2001): 387–411.
———. "'Ethnic Resettlement' and Inter-Agency Co-operation in the Occupied Eastern Territories." In G. D. Feldman and W. Seibel, eds., *Networks of Nazi Persecution: Bureaucracy, Business and the Organization of the Holocaust.* Oxford: Berghahn, 2004: 213–235.
———. "'Until The Last Drop of Good Blood': The Kidnapping of 'Racially Valuable' Children and Nazi Racial Policy in Occupied Eastern Europe." In A. D. Moses, ed.,

Genocide and Settler Society: Frontier Violence and Stolen Indigenous Children in Australian History. Oxford: Berghahn, 2004: 244–266.

Hirschon, R. "The Consequences of the Lausanne Conference: An Overview." In Hirschon, *Crossing the Aegean*: 13–22.

Hrabovec, E. "Neue Aspekte zur ersten Phase der Vertreibung der Deutschen aus Mähren 1945." In Plaschka, Haselsteiner, et al., *Nationale Frage und Vertreibung in der Tschechoslowakei und Ungarn 1938–1948*: 117–140.

———. "The Catholic Church and Deportations of Ethnic Germans from the Czech Lands," *Journal of Communist Studies and Transition Politics* 16:1–2 (March–June 2000): 64–82.

Huebner, T. "The Internment Camp at Terezín, 1919," *Austrian History Yearbook* 27 (1996): 199–211.

Jacques, C. "Le 'Centre Contre les Expulsions' de Berlin: Un débat centre-européen autour de la 'culture mémorielle,'" *Revue d'Allemagne et des Pays de langue allemande* 40:3 (2008): 421–436.

Jakobson, R. "Problems of Language in Masaryk's Writings." In J. Novák, ed., *On Masaryk: Texts in English and German*. Amsterdam: Rodopi, 1988: 55–80.

Janák, D. "Politické a legislativní aspekty táborů nucené práce," *Slezský sborník* 98:1–2 (2000): 93–109.

Janjetović, Z. "The Disappearance of the Germans from Yugoslavia: Expulsion or Emigration?" *Revue des études sud-est européennes* 40:1 (2002): 215–231.

Jankowiak, S. "'Cleansing' Poland of Germans: The Province of Pomerania, 1945–1949." In Ther and A. Siljak, *Redrawing Nations*: 87–106.

Jenne, E. K. "Ethnic Partition under the League of Nations: The Cases of Population Exchange in the Western Balkans." In E. Chenoweth and A. Lawrence, eds., *Rethinking Violence: States and Non-State Actors in Conflict*. Cambridge, MA: MIT Press, 2010: 117–140.

Jérome, G. "Les milices d'autoprotection de la communauté allemande de Pomérélie, Posnanie et Silésie polonaise (1939–1940)," *Guerres mondiales et conflits contemporains* 41:163 (1991): 51–74.

Kaufmann, C. D. "When All Else Fails: Ethnic Population Transfers and Partitions in the Twentieth Century," *International Security* 23:2 (Autumn 1998): 120–156.

Kędzia, A. "Działalność opiekuńcza i lecznicza Polskiego Czerwonego Krzyża w akcji repatriacyjnej i przesiedleńczej na Pomorzu Zachodnim," *Archiwum historii i filozofii medycyny* 64:2–3 (2001): 175–188.

Kent, M. "Exceptional Bonds: Revenge and Reconciliation in Potulice [Potulitz], Poland, 1945 and 1998." In Várdy and Tooley, *Ethnic Cleansing in Twentieth-Century Europe*: 617–630.

Kersten, K. "Forced Migration and the Transformation of Polish Society in the Postwar Period." In Ther and Siljak, *Redrawing Nations*: 75–86.

Komska, Y. "Border Looking: The Cold War Visuality of the Sudeten German Expellees and Its Afterlife," *German Life and Letters* 57:4 (October 2004): 401–426.

Kontogiorgi, E. "Economic Consequences Following Refugee Settlement in Greek Macedonia, 1923–1932." In Hirschon, *Crossing the Aegean*: 63–78.

Kostiashov, I. V. "Vyselenie nemtsev iz Kaliningradskoi oblasti v poslevoennye gody," *Voprosy istorii* (June 1994): 186–188.

Kováč, D. "Die Evakuierung und Vertreibung der Deutschen aus der Slowakei." In Plaschka, Haselsteiner, et al., *Nationale Frage und Vertreibung in der Tschechoslowakei und Ungarn 1938–1948*: 111–116.

———. "Organizovaný odsun nemcov zo Slovenska roku 1946," *Historický časopis* 49:2 (2001): 237–254.

Kraft, C. "Who Is a Pole, and Who Is a German? The Province of Olsztyn in 1945." In Ther and Siljak, *Redrawing Nations*: 107–120.

Kramer, M. "Introduction." In Ther and Siljak, *Redrawing Nations*: 1–41.

Krauss, M. "Die Integration Vertriebener am Beispiel Bayerns—Konflikte und Erfolge." In D. Hoffmann and M. Schwartz, eds., *Geglückte Integration? Spezifika und Vergleichbarkeiten der Vertriebenen-Eingliederung in der SBZ/DDR*. Munich: Oldenbourg, 1999: 47–56.

———. "Integrationen: Fragen, Thesen, Perspektiven zu einer vergleichenden Vertriebenenforschung." In Krauss, *Integrationen*: 9–21.

Lange, G. "My Experiences at the End of the War and Thereafter." In U. Lange, ed., *East Germany: What Happened to the Silesians in 1945*. Lewes, Sussex: Book Guild, 2000: 72–85.

Langenbacher, E. "Ethical Cleansing? The Expulsion of Germans from Central and Eastern Europe." In N. A. Robins and A. Jones, eds., *Genocides by the Oppressed: Subaltern Genocide in Theory and Practice*. Bloomington: Indiana University Press, 2009: 58–83.

Lebedeva, N. S. "The Deportation of the Polish Population to the USSR, 1939–41," *Journal of Communist and Transition Politics* 16:1–2 (March 2000): 28–45.

Levine, H. S. "Local Authority and the SS State: The Conflict over Population Policy in Danzig–West Prussia, 1939–1945," *Central European History* 2:4 (December 1969): 331–355.

Linek, B. "Recent Debates on the Fate of the German Population in Upper Silesia 1945–1950," *German History* 22:3 (Autumn 2004): 372–405.

Łossowski, P. "The Resettlements of Germans from Lithuania During World War II," *Acta Poloniae historica* 93 (2006): 121–142.

Lovejoy, P. "The Slave Trade as Enforced Migration in the Central Sudan of West Africa." In Bessel and Haake, *Removing Peoples*: 149–166.

Lower, W. "Hitler's 'Garden of Eden' in Ukraine: Nazi Colonialism, *Volksdeutsche*, and the Holocaust, 1941–1944." In J. Petropoulos and J. K. Roth, eds., *Gray Zones: Ambiguity and Compromise in the Holocaust and Its Aftermath*. Oxford: Berghahn, 2006: 185–204.

Lukes, I. "Stalin and Czechoslovakia in 1938–39: An Autopsy of a Myth." In I. Lukes and E. Goldstein, eds., *The Munich Crisis, 1938: Prelude to World War II*. London: Cass, 1999: 13–47.

———. "The Czechoslovak Special Services and Their American Adversary During the Cold War," *Journal of Cold War Studies* 9:1 (Winter 2007): 3–28.

Lumans, V. O. "A Reassessment of the Presumed Fifth Column Role of the German National Minorities of Europe." In J. K. Burton and C. W. White, eds., *Essays in European History: 1988-89*, vol. 2. Lanham, MD: University Press of America, 1996: 191–212.

Lutomski, P. "The Debate about a Center against Expulsions: An Unexpected Crisis in German-Polish Relations?" *German Studies Review* 27:3 (October 2004): 449–468.

———. "Acknowledging Each Other as Victims: An Unmet Challenge in the Process of Polish-German Reconciliation." In L. Cohen-Pfister and D. Wienröder-Skinner, eds., *Victims and Perpetrators, 1933–1945: (Re-)Presenting the Past in Post-Unification Culture*. Berlin: De Gruyter, 2006: 241–261.

———. "The Polish Expulsion of the German Population in the Aftermath of World War II." In A. M. Kacowicz and P. Lutomski, eds., *Population Resettlement in International Conflicts: A Comparative Study*. Lanham, MD: Lexington, 2007: 99–114.

Lylloff, K. "Kan lægeløftet gradbøjes? Dødsfald blandt og lægehjælp til de tyske flygtninge i Danmark 1945," *Historisk Tidsskrift* 99:1 (June 1999): 33–67.

Macklem, P. "Rybná 9, Praha 1: Restitution and Memory in International Human Rights Law," *European Journal of International Law* 16:1 (February 2005): 1–23.

Majewski, P. M. "Czechosłowaccy wojskowi wobec problemu wysiedlenia mniejszości niemieckiej i powojennych granic państwa, 1939–1945," *Przegląd historyczny* 90:2 (1999): 169–183.

Makino, U. "Final Solutions, Crimes Against Mankind: On the Genesis and Criticism of the Concept of Genocide," *Journal of Genocide Research* 3:1 (2001): 49–73.

Martin, T. "The Origins of Soviet Ethnic Cleansing," *Journal of Modern History* 70:4 (December 1998): 815–861.

Matelski, D. "Polityka narodowościowa PRL wobec mniejszości niemieckiej (1944–1989)," *Przegląd historyczny* 88:3–4 (1997): 487–497.

Mazower, M. "Minorities and the League of Nations in Interwar Europe," *Daedalus* 126:2 (Spring 1997): 47–63.

———. "The Strange Triumph of Human Rights, 1933–1950," *Historical Journal* 47:2 (June 2004): 379–398.

Mazur, Z. "Poland's Western Frontier in the State Department's Concepts During World War II," *Polish Western Studies* 21:2 (1980): 274–296.

McLaren, M. "'Out of the Huts Emerged a Settled People': Community-Building in West German Refugee Camps," *German History* 28:1 (March 2010): 21–43.

Misztal, J. "Wysiedlenia i repatriacja obywateli polskich z ZSRR a wysiedlenia i przesiedlenia niemców z Polski—próba bilansu," in Orłowski and Sakson, *Utracona ojczyzna*.

Moeller, R. G. "War Stories: The Search for a Usable Past in the Federal Republic of Germany," *American Historical Review* 101:4 (October 1996): 1008–1048.

Moszyński, E. "The Church on the Western Territories," *Polish Perspectives* 16:2 (February 1973): 19–23.

Müller, R. D. "The Results of the War." In R. D. Müller and G. R. Ueberschär, eds., *Hitler's War in the East: A Critical Assessment*, 3d ed. Oxford: Berghahn, 2009: 345–366.

Mulaj, K. "A Recurrent Tragedy: Ethnic Cleansing as a Tool of State Building in the Yugoslav Multinational Setting," *Nationalities Papers* 34:1 (March 2006): 21–50.

Musekamp, J. "Brno/Brünn 1938–1948: Eine Stadt in einem Jahrzehnt erzwungener Wanderungen," *Zeitschrift für Ostmitteleuropa-Forschung* 53 (2004): 1–44.

Naimark, N. M. "Ethnic Cleansing Between War and Peace." In A. Weiner, ed., *Landscaping the Human Garden: Twentieth-Century Population Management in a Comparative Framework*. Palo Alto, CA: Stanford University Press, 2003: 218–235.

———. "The Persistence of the 'Postwar': Germany and Poland." In F. Biess and R. G. Moeller, eds., *Histories of the Aftermath: The Legacies of the Second World War in Europe*. Oxford: Berghahn, 2010: 13–29.

Nickel, J. W. "What's Wrong with Ethnic Cleansing?" *Journal of Social Philosophy* 26:1 (Spring 1995): 5–15.

Nitschke, B. "Wysiedlenia Niemców w czerwcu i lipcu 1945 roku," *Zeszyty Historyczne* 118 (1996): 155–171.

———. "Polacy wobec Niemców: Odpowiedzialność Niemców za zbrodnie wojenne," *Zeszyty Historyczne* 123:2 (1998): 3–24.

Noskova, A. F. "Migration of the Germans after the Second World War: Political and Psychological Aspects," *Journal of Communist Studies and Transition Politics* 16:1–2 (March–June 2000): 96–114.

Papp, N. G. "The German Minority Between the Two World Wars: Loyal Subjects or Suppressed Citizens?" *East European Quarterly* 22:4 (Winter 1988): 495–514.

Pasák, T. "Přemysl Pitters Protest: Eine unbekannte Stimme gegen die Greuel in den Internierungslagern 1945," *Bohemia* 35 (1994): 90–104.

Persson, H.-Å. "Viadrina to the Oder-Neisse Line: Historical Evolution and Regional Cooperation." In S. Tägil, ed., *Regions in Central Europe: The Legacy of History*. West Lafayette, IN: Purdue University Press, 1999: 211–258.

Pešek, J. "Nemci na Slovensku po ukončení povojnového hromadného odsunu (1947–1953)," *Historický časopis* 46:2 (1998): 261–280.

Phayer, M. "Pius XII and the Genocides of Polish Catholics and Polish Jews during the Second World War," *Kirchliche Zeitgeschichte* 15:1 (January 2002): 238–262.

Pietrzak, J. "Działalność kard. Augusta Hlonda jako wysłannika papieskiego na Ziemiach Odzyskanych w 1945 r," *Nasza Przeszłość* 42 (1974): 195–249.

Pisorski, J. M. "Polish *Myśl Zachodnia* and German *Ostforschung:* An Attempt at a Comparison." In I. Haar and M. Fahlbusch, eds., *German Scholars and Ethnic Cleansing, 1919–1945*. Oxford: Berghahn, 1995: 260–271.

Pogány, I. S. "International Human Rights Law, Reparatory Justice and the Re-Ordering of Memory in Central and Eastern Europe," *Human Rights Law Review* 10:3 (2010): 397–428.

Portmann, M. "Repression und Widerstand auf dem Land: Die kommunistische Landwirtschaftspolitik in der jugoslawischen Vojvodina (1944 bis 1953)," *Südost-Forschungen* 65/66 (2006/2007): 370–393.

———. "Politik der Vernichtung? Die deutschsprachige Bevölkerung in der Vojvodina 1944–1952: Ein Forschungsbericht auf Grundlage jugoslawischer Archivdokumente." In *Danubiana carpathica: Jahrbuch für Geschichte und Kultur in den deutschen Siedlungsgebieten Südosteuropas*. Munich: Oldenbourg, 2007: 321–360.

Raack, R. C. "Stalin Fixes the Oder-Neisse Line," *Journal of Contemporary History* 25:4 (October 1990): 467–488.

Radvanovský, Z. "The Social and Economic Consequences of Resettling Czechs into Northwestern Bohemia, 1945–1947." In Ther and Siljak, *Redrawing Nations*: 241–260.

Reynolds, D. "Churchill and the British 'Decision' to Fight On in 1940: Right Policy, Wrong Reasons." In R. Langhorne, ed., *Diplomacy and Intelligence During the Second World War: Essays in Honour of F. H. Hinsley*. Cambridge: Cambridge University Press, 1985: 147–167.

Rolinek, S. "Jüdische Fluchthilfe im Raum Salzburg: Das Netzwerk von Bricha und Betar 1945 bis 1948." In T. Albrich, ed., *Flucht nach Eretz Israel: Die Bricha und der jüdische Exodus durch Österreich 1945*. Innsbruck: Studien Verlag, 1998: 93–118.

Rothfels, H. "Zehn Jahre danach," *Vierteljahrshefte für Zeitgeschichte* 3:3 (July 1955): 227–239.

Rupnik, J. "Joining Europe Together or Separately? The Implications of the Czecho-Slovak Divorce for EU Enlargement." In J. Rupnik and J. Zielonka, eds., *The Road to the European Union*, vol. 1: *The Czech and Slovak Republics*. Manchester: Manchester University Press, 2003: 16–50.

Ryback, T. W. "Dateline Sudetenland: Hostages to History," *Foreign Policy* 105 (Winter 1996–97): 162–178.

Sanborn, J. R. "'Unsettling the Empire': Violent Migrations and Social Disaster in Russia During World War I," *Journal of Modern History* 77:2 (June 2005): 290–324.

Schabas, W. A. "'Ethnic Cleansing' and Genocide: Similarities and Distinctions." In *European Yearbook of Minority Issues*, vol. 3. Leiden: Brill, 2005: 109–128.

Schechla, J. "Ideological Roots of Population Transfer," *Third World Quarterly* 14:2 (June 1993): 239–275.

Schmaltz, E. "The 'Long Trek': The SS Population Transfer of Ukrainian Germans to the Polish Warthegau and Its Consequences, 1943–1944," *Journal of the American Historical Society of Germans from Russia* 31:3 (Autumn 2008): 1–23.

Schulze, R. "The Politics of Memory: Flight and Expulsion of German Populations after the Second World War and German Collective Memories," *National Identities* 8:4 (December 2006): 367–382.

Schwartz, M. "Staatsfeind 'Umsiedler.'" In Auer and Burgdorff, *Die Flucht*: 205–215.

———. "Lastenausgleich: Ein Problem der Vertriebenenpolitik im doppelten Deutschland." In Krauss, *Integrationen*: 167–193.

Schwelb, E. "Crimes Against Humanity," *British Yearbook of International Law* 23 (1946): 178–226.

Scott, J. M. "Exile and the Self-Understanding of Diaspora Jews in the Greco-Roman Period." In J. M. Scott, ed., *Exile: Old Testament, Jewish, and Christian Conceptions*. Leiden: E. J. Brill, 1997: 173–220.

Segesser, D. M. "'Unlawful Warfare Is Uncivilised': The International Debate on the Punishment of War Crimes, 1872–1918," *European Review of History* 14:2 (June 2007): 215–234.

Seipp, A. R. "Refugee Town: Germans, Americans, and the Uprooted in Rural West Germany, 1945–52," *Journal of Contemporary History* 44:4 (October 2007): 675–695.

Shik, N. "Sexual Abuse of Jewish Women in Auschwitz-Birkenau." In D. Herzog, ed., *Bru-

tality and Desire: War and Sexuality in Europe's Twentieth Century. Basingstoke, Hampshire: Palgrave Macmillan, 2009: 221–246.

Sierpowski, S. "Les dilemmes à la Société des Nations au sujet des minorités," *Polish Western Affairs* 25:2 (1984): 187–210.

Soukupová, B. "Německá menšina v českém veřejném mínění po druhé světové válce: Několik poznámek k etnickému klimatu v postevropském čase," *Historica* [Ostrava] 16 (2009): 277–294.

Spülbeck, S. "Ethnography of an Encounter: Reactions to Refugees in Post-war Germany and Russian Migrants after the Reunification—Context, Analogies and Changes." In A. J. Rieber, ed., *Forced Migration in Central and Eastern Europe, 1939–1950*. London: Cass, 2000: 175–190.

Staněk, T. and A. von Arburg. "Organizované divoké odsuny? Úloha ústředních státních orgánů při provádění 'evakuace' německého obyvatelstva (květen až září 1945)," part 1: Předpoklady a vývoj do konce května 1945," *Soudobé dějiny* 12:3–4 (2005): 465–533.

———. "Organizované divoké odsuny? Úloha ústředních státních orgánů při provádění 'evakuace' německého obyvatelstva (květen až září 1945)," part 2: Československá armáda vytváří 'hotové skutečnosti' vládaje před cizinou legitimizuje," *Soudobé dějiny* 13:1–2 (2006): 13–49.

———. "Organizované divoké odsuny? Úloha ústředních státních orgánů při provádění 'evakuace' německého obyvatelstva (květen až září 1945)," part 3: Snaha vlády a civilních úřadů o řízení 'divokého odsunu,'" *Soudobé dějiny* 13:3–4 (2006): 321–376.

Stola, D. "Pologne 1944–1948: Vers un état 'purement Polonais,'" *Revue d'Europe centrale* 2:2 (1994): 191–199.

Suppan, A. "Éviction et déportation de masse des allemands hors de Tchécoslovaquie, de Hongrie et de Yougoslavie 1945–1948." In F.-D. Lichtenhan, *Europe 1946: Entre le deuil et l'espoir*. Paris: Éditions Complexe, 1996: 77–85.

Táborský, E. "Politics in Exile, 1939–1945." In V. S. Matamey and R. Luža, eds., *A History of the Czechoslovak Republic 1918–1948*. Princeton, NJ: Princeton University Press, 1973: 322–342.

Ther, P. "Expellee Policy in the Soviet-Occupied Zone and the GDR: 1945–1953." In D. Rock and S. Wolff, eds., *Coming Home to Germany? The Integration of Ethnic Germans from Central and Eastern Europe in the Federal Republic*. Oxford: Berghahn, 2002: 56–76.

Topinka, J. "Zapomenutý kraj: České pohraničí 1948–1960 a takzvaná akce dosídlení," *Soudobé dějiny* 12:3–4 (2005): 534–585.

Tóth, Á. "Zwang oder Möglichkeit? Die Annahme der Maxime von der Kollektivschuld und die Bestrafung der Deutschen Minderheit in Ungarn." In Plaschka, Haselsteiner, et al., *Nationale Frage und Vertreibung in der Tschechoslowakei und Ungarn 1938–1948*: 89–130.

Trapp, G. and P. Heumos. "Antibarbaros: Johannes Urzidils publizistische Tätigkeit in Medien der tschechoslowakischen Exilregierung 1940–1945," *Bohemia* 40:2 (1999): 417–435.

Vaculík, J. "Reemigrace zahraničnich Čechů a Slováků v letech 1945–1948," *Slezský sborník* 93:1–2 (1995): 53–58.

Vaško, V. "Kardinál Beran a jeho zápas s totalitou: Portrét osobnosti," *Soudobé dějiny* 8:2–3 (2001): 384–408.
Wallace, W. V. "From Czechs and Slovaks to Czechoslovakia, and from Czechoslovakia to Czechs and Slovaks." In S. Dunn and T. G. Fraser, eds., *Europe and Ethnicity: The First World War and Contemporary Ethnic Conflict*. London: Routledge, 1996: 47–66.
Warring, A. "Intimate and Sexual Relations." In R. Gildea, O. Wieviorka, and A. Warring, eds., *Surviving Hitler and Mussolini: Daily Life in Occupied Europe*. Oxford: Berg, 2007: 88–128.
Waters, T. W. "Remembering Sudetenland: On the Legal Construction of Ethnic Cleansing," *Virginia Journal of International Law* 47:1 (Autumn 2006): 63–148.
Weiss, Y. "Ethnic Cleansing, Memory and Property—Europe, Israel/Palestine, 1944–1948." In R. Gross and Y. Weiss, eds., *Jüdische Geschichte als allgemeine Geschichte: Festschrift für Dan Diner zum 60. Geburtstag*. Göttingen: Vandenhoeck & Ruprecht, 2006: 158–185.
Wetzel, F. "Missverständnisse von klein auf? Die Vertreibung der Deutschen in tschechischen und deutschen Schulbüchern," *Zeitschrift für Geschichtswissenschaft* 53:10 (2005): 955–968.
Wittlinger, R. "The Merkel Government's Politics of the Past," *German Politics and Society* 26:4 (Winter 2008): 9–27.
Wolfe, J. H. "International Law and Diplomatic Bargaining: A Commentary on the Sudeten German Question," *Bohemia* 14 (1973): 372–385.
Wolff, S. "Can Forced Population Transfers Resolve Self-Determination Conflicts? A European Perspective," *Journal of Contemporary European Studies* 12:1 (April 2004): 11–29.
Yoshioka, J. "Imagining Their Lands as Ours: Place Name Changes on Ex-German Territories in Poland after World War II." In T. Hayashi, ed., *Regions in Central and Eastern Europe: Past and Present*. Sapporo: Slavic Research Centre, Hokkaido University, 2007: 273–287.
Zahra, T. "'Children Betray Their Father and Mother': Collective Education, Nationalism, and Democracy in the Bohemian Lands, 1900–1948." In D. Schumann, ed., *Raising Citizens in the 'Century of the Child': The United States and German Central Europe in Comparative Perspective*. Oxford: Berghahn, 2010: 186–205.
Žampach, V. "Vysídlení německého obyvatelstva z Brna ve dnech 30. a 31. května 1945 a nouzový ubytovací tábor v Pohořelicích, 1.6.–7.7. 1945," *Jižní Morava* 32 (1997): 173–239.
Zarnowski, J. "Le système de protection des minorités et la Pologne," *Acta Poloniae Historica* 52:1 (1985): 105–124.
Zeman, Z. A. B. "Czechoslovakia Between the Wars: Democracy on Trial." In J. Morison, ed., *The Czech and Slovak Experience*. New York: St. Martin's Press, 1992: 163–166.
Zettl, A. "Dachau/Buchenwald/Gakowa: Reminiscences of a World War II Survivor," *Journal of Political and Military Sociology* 33:2 (Winter 2005): 267–276.
Zweig, R. W. "Feeding the Camps: Allied Blockade Policy and the Relief of Concentration Camps in Germany, 1944–1945," *Historical Journal* 41:3 (1998): 825–851.

Alrich, A. A. "Germans Displaced from the East: Crossing Actual and Imagined Central European Borders, 1944–1955." Ph.D. diss., Ohio State University, 2007.

Březina, Z. "The Czechoslovak Democrat: The Life, Writing, and Politics of Hubert Ripka from 1918 to 1945." Ph.D. diss., Boston University, 2008.
Egupova, E. "The Issue of Private Property Restitution in the [sic] Interstate Relations: The Sudeten German Case." M.A. thesis, Central European University, 2008.
Ehrlich, A. "Between Germany and Poland: Ethnic Cleansing and Politicization of Ethnicity in Upper Silesia under National Socialism and Communism 1939–1950." Ph.D. diss., Indiana University, 2005.
Gerlach, D. "For Nation and Gain: Economy, Ethnicity and Politics in the Czech Borderlands, 1945–1948." Ph.D. diss., University of Pittsburgh, 2007.
Lieb, C. "Moving West: German-Speaking Immigration to British Columbia, 1945–1961." Ph.D. diss., University of Victoria, 2008.
Lyon, P. W. "After Empire: Ethnic Germans and Minority Nationalism in Interwar Yugoslavia." Ph.D. diss., University of Maryland, College Park, 2008.
Sans, A.-L. "'Aussi Humainement que Possible': Le Comité International de la Croix-Rouge et l'expulsion des minorités allemandes d'Europe de l'Est 1945–1950 (Pologne-Tchécoslovaquie)." M.A. thesis, University of Geneva, 2003.

PERIODICALS

British Zone Review
Chicago Tribune
Contemporary Review
Daily Express
Daily Herald
Daily Mail
Daily Telegraph
Dziennik Polski
The Economist
Foreign Affairs
Gazeta Ludowa
Ha'aretz
Der Heimatbote
Jewish Daily Forward
Kurier Szczeciński
Life
London Calling
Manchester Guardian
The Mercury (Hobart, Tasmania)
Naše pravda
Neue Zürcher Zeitung
New English Weekly
News Chronicle
New Statesman and Nation
New York Daily News
New York Herald Tribune
New York Times
Nineteenth Century and After
Nová doba
Observer
Obzory
Osservatore Romano
Picture Post
Political Quarterly
Pravda (Plzeň)
Právo lidu
Predvoj
Reynolds' News
Rudé právo
Scotsman
Sever
Severočeská Mladá fronta
Slavonic and East European Review
Socialist Commentary
Spectator
Der Spiegel
Sudetendeutsche Zeitung
Svobodné noviný

The Times
Tribune
Tygodnik Powszechny
Wall Street Journal
Washington Post

Die Welt
Wprost
Yorkshire Post
Die Zeit

Index

ACC agreement, 124–28, 243; Housing Law, 308; and Hungary [ACC(H)], 166–68, 207, 209, 210, 212–14; and numbers, 198, 201–6, 207, 209, 210, 212–14, 220–22; and "organized expulsions," 125, 160, 162, 164, 166–68; and resettlements, 304, 305, 306, 308
Ackermann, Volker, 354
Adam, Joseph, 340
Adamski, Bishop Stanisław, 109, 260
Adam v. Czech Republic, 340
Adenauer, Konrad, 316–21
Adorno, Theodor, 369
Africa, forced migration in, 67, 336
Ahonen, Pertti, 320
Alexander II, tsar of Russia, 39
Alexander the Great, 67
Allen, Denis, 173
Allied Control Council, 111, 124, 363; and ACC agreement, *see* ACC agreement
Alversdorf transit camp, 170, 177
Aly, Götz, 52
Amin, Idi, 336
Anderson, Carol, 335
Angly, Edward, 107
Arburg, Adrian von, 128
Arciszewski, Tomasz, 86
Armenians: forced migration of, 68; genocide of, 70, 329

Armstrong, Hamilton Fish, 17, 21
Arndt, Josefa, 250
Asia, forced migration in, 67, 68
Atatürk (Kemal Mustafa), 70, 329
Atlantic Charter (1941), 86
Attlee, Clement, 80, 88–89, 151, 288
Auschwitz concentration camp, 1, 127, 134, 138, 144, 145, 235
Austria: and *Anschluss*, 13, 14, 41; deportations to, 76, 99, 113, 117, 122–23; and ethnic Germans, 46, 125, 312; expellees repulsed at border, 99, 107, 123; and League of Nations, 330; occupation zones of, 306
Austro-Hungarian Empire, 8, 9, 12, 68, 130, 284; ethnic cleansing in, 39, 232

Babylonian Captivity, 67
Bački Jarak internment camp, 146, 153, 156
Balabán, Josef, 19
Baltic states: ethnic expulsions from, 46, 47–49, 51; fifth column fears in, 59–60; Soviet control of, 41, 46, 48, 51; *Volksdeutsche* in, 38, 41–42, 61
Bamborough, Oswald, 166, 167
Bannister, Sylvia, 53
Bardens, Dennis, 292
Barkan, Elazar, 371–72
Barrington-Ward, Robin, 291

Barthélemy, Joseph, 14
Bartoszewski, Władysław, 267, 357
Bauer, Gerd, 249
Bavaria: selective admission to, 312–13; transit camps in, 310
Bednář, František, 268
Belgium: fifth column fears in, 43; and World War I, 68
Bell, Bishop George, 288, 289
Bell-Fialkoff, Andrew, 371
Beneš, Edvard, 6, 7–9, 11–12, 13, 75, 332, 344; assassination ordered by, 21–23; comeback of, 15–18, 36; decrees issued by, 98, 101, 246, 326–27, 338, 339, 340–41, 342–43, 357, 359; exile of, 8, 14–15, 16, 19–23, 26, 27–28, 34–35, 36; mass expulsions supported by, 16, 18–25, 27–28, 30, 32, 33–34, 36–38, 76, 78, 83, 124, 149, 210, 222, 227, 257–58, 280, 365; and propaganda, 290, 291, 292, 295
Bergen, Doris, 56, 59
Berger, Stefan, 352
Berlin crisis, 154
Berlin Wall (1961), 325
Bessel, Richard, 68
Bettany, Guy, 292
Beveridge, Sir William, 288
Bevin, Ernest, 80, 172, 173, 182, 220, 236, 288, 323
Bidault, Georges, 298
Biess, Frank, 351
Bilainkin, George, 291, 292
Bismarck, Otto von, 69
Blair, Tony, 327
Bloxham, Donald, 68
Blum, Léon, 14
Blumenwitz, Dieter, 343
Boček, Bohumil, 97
Bohemia: ethnic Germans in, 58, 136; German occupation of, 15, 19, 22; provisional government, 8; recolonization of, 281
Bolesławiec (Bunzlau) children's camp, 139, 237

Bonyhád internment camp, 136
Boothby, Frederick, 158, 170, 173, 177, 183, 199
Borodziej, Włodzimierz, 364
Bourdillon, Francis, 275
Bramwell, Anna, 57
Brandt, Willy, 320, 352, 353, 356
Bray, Charles, 117
Breitinger, Fr. Hilarius, 44
Britain: and ACC agreement, 124–25, 198, 201–6, 220–22, 304; and Atlantic Charter, 86; complicity of, 3, 23–33, 37, 73, 74–76, 81, 85–87, 92, 93; Czech government in exile in, 17–18, 19–21, 23, 26, 35–36; Czechoslovakia abandoned by, 7, 14–15, 290; and Dunkirk, 19; fifth column fears in, 43, 150; Inter-Departmental Committee report, 74–77, 83, 89, 372; and Munich, 7–8, 14–15, 17, 18, 26, 290; occupation zone, see Germany: British zone; Operation Swallow, 168–74, 183, 184–85, 196–206, 212, 217–22, 264, 369; and "organized expulsions," 124–25, 161, 162–64, 168–70, 173–75, 177, 180, 192; and population transfers, 72–80, 85, 94; and postwar expectations, 87; Special Operations Executive, 26; Transfer Commission, 89; and "wild expulsions," 102, 112, 118, 287–88; and World War II, 17, 18, 19, 23, 80, 84, 87, 289
Brno: "Death March," 98–100, 105, 365; ethnic manipulation in, 10; Kaunitz College camp in, 96, 155
Brno-Jundrov internment camp, 237
Brownlee, Aleta, 252
Brozsat, Martin, 349
Brumlik, Micha, 360
Bryant, Chad, 37, 56
Buchenwald concentration camp, 118, 192
Bulgaria, 111, 330
Burlagsberg refugee camp, 309–10
Butler, Nicholas Murray, 295
Buxton, Dorothy, 368

Bydgoszcz (Bromberg), Poland, massacre in, 44, 45
Byford-Jones, Wilfred, 252
Byman, Daniel, 372
Byrnes, James F., 126–28, 274–75

Cadogan, Alexander, 26
Caidler, Karel, 265
Catholic Church War Relief Services, 221, 230
Caucasus, forced migration in, 68
Cavendish-Bentinck, Victor, 149, 172–73, 178, 182, 204–5, 220, 271, 274
Cecil, Lord Robert, 29
Cedrowski, Ignacy, 143–44, 156
Central Agency for Resettlers, 309, 322–24
Černý, Vojtěch, 236–37
České Křídlovice children's camp, 139, 237
Chamberlain, Neville, 14, 18
Charous, Adolf, 265
Cherokee nation, Trail of Tears, 67
children, 229–53; abuse of, 238, 242, 251; adoption of, 231, 250, 251, 252; assimilation of, 354; deaths of, 230, 235, 236–37, 238–40, 242, 243, 252; as forced labor, 230, 233, 234, 237, 250; Hitler Youth, 236–37, 245; in internment camps, 137, 138–39, 151, 230–31, 233–40, 247, 249–50; of mixed marriages, 231–32, 244–48; national identity of, 231–32, 236–37, 241–48, 251; in orphanages, 243–44; repressed memories of, 354; separated from families, 229–30, 235, 237, 244, 249–53; starving, 233–34, 235, 238, 239–40, 252; undesirable ethnicity of, 231–33, 239–41, 245–49
China, forced migrations in, 67
Chomutov massacre, 96–97
Churchill, Winston, 14, 17, 19, 27, 72, 75, 81, 82, 84, 85–88, 89–90, 91, 94, 112, 295
CICR (International Committee of the Red Cross), 14, 97, 112, 191, 218, 223, 224, 229, 235, 236, 237–39, 240, 242, 253, 286, 292, 296, 310, 322, 328, 329

Clark, Bruce, 372
Clark, Norman, 117
Clay, Lucius D., 185, 206–7, 211, 214, 222, 297, 315
Clinton administration, 329
Cohen, Benjamin, 126
Cohn-Bendit, Daniel, 361
Cold War: and concentration camps, 150–51, 154; and mass expulsions, 305; and public opinion, 299–300; "stolen children" in, 251
Colville, John, 146
Committee Against Mass Expulsions (CAME), 294–95
communism, fall of, 325, 358
concentration camps, 130–57; categories of, 139–40; children in, 137, 138–39, 151, 234, 239; citizens' committees on, 136–37; closure of, 153–54; and Cold War propaganda, 150–51, 154; deaths in, 133, 134, 137, 139, 140–41, 145, 146, 153, 155, 157, 195–96; disease in, 134, 137, 139, 140, 145, 155; downward spiral in conditions of, 309–10; ethnic Germans sent to, 15, 45, 74, 135, 156, 309–11; food in, 144–46, 147, 151–52, 346; forced labor, 15, 134, 135, 137, 139, 140, 142–44, 152, 153, 154, 234, 337; inmate categories, 138–39; Jews in, 22, 35, 137–38, 140, 156; map, 131; Nazi models for, 98, 132, 136, 137, 138, 139, 146, 148, 151–52, 156; "organized expulsions" to (transit camps), 163, 165, 168, 170, 173–74, 175, 176, 178–81, 186, 190, 192–93, 303–6; as payback for the war, 132, 146–48, 289; POWs in, 138; "protective custody" in, 59; and public opinion, 146–49, 151–52, 157; and Red Cross, 135, 136, 141, 144–46, 149–50, 152–53; torture in, 132–33, 140; trials for abuses in, 154–56; unclear data on, 134, 135–36, 145–46; violent treatment in, 132–33, 134, 137, 140, 141–42, 156; "wild expulsions" to (internment camps), 96, 99, 104, 106–7, 112, 117–18, 122, 123, 127,

concentration camps (continued) 136–37, 176; women in, 22, 134, 137, 138, 141–42, 151, 235; "young thugs" in charge of, 138, 140, 147, 170
Connor, Ian, 324
Cordell, Karl, 251, 359
Cornwall, Mark, 13
Crawley, Aidan, 318
Crimes against humanity, 328–30, 345
Cromwell, Oliver, 67
Curp, David, 370, 373
Curtin, John, 72, 84
Curzon, George Nathaniel, 70, 72
Cyprus, Turkish invasion of, 72
Czechoslovakia, 7–38; Beneš decrees, see Beneš, Edvard; borders of, 21, 36; breakup of, 7, 34, 367; Charter 77 movement, 354, 357; citizenship, 101, 246, 338, 339–41, 366; Communist Party in, 14, 26–27, 30, 98, 100, 102–3, 115, 149, 154, 256–58, 261, 281–82, 348, 355, 366; constitution of, 9; Czech-German declaration (1997), 357–58; District National Committees, 97–98, 100, 101, 102–3, 105–7, 120–22, 134–35, 187–89, 244, 246–48, 257, 266; ethnic cleansing in, 15, 36, 96–99, 231–36, 359, 365–66; ethnic manipulation in, 10; fifth column fears in, 102, 113–16, 323, 358; formation of, 9; Germanization in, 59; German occupation of, 15, 16, 95, 98, 208, 232, 245, 248, 259, 337, 370–71; government in exile, 17–22, 23, 26, 27, 34–36, 94, 332; "Great Decree" in, 37; Hrádek incident, 114; Law No. 115 (1946), 370; and League of Nations, 330; liberation of, 37, 257; "May days," 96, 102; memory and forgetting, 354–62; and Munich, 7–9, 11, 14–18, 26, 27, 35, 40, 61, 117, 290, 292, 367; National Assembly, 101; National Council, 17; nationalism within, 9, 10, 18; National Land Fund, 260–61; National Security Force (SNB), 100, 136, 138, 147, 190, 198; and Population Transfer Commission, 77–79; population transfers from, 1, 2, 23–24, 29, 32, 36, 73, 76, 78–81, 85, 89, 90, 91, 93, 94–103, 105–8, 112, 116–17, 128, 185–92, 198, 203, 206, 210, 222–23, 226–27, 248, 293, 326–27, 357, 371; postwar economy of, 143, 281–83; postwar planning for, 20, 257–58; and Potsdam, 101, 111, 115; "Prague Spring" (1968), 354; propaganda of, 290–93, 295, 348; property confiscated in, 255, 256, 257–59, 260–61, 265, 281, 337–38, 355; resistance movement (ÚVOD) in, 19, 20, 22, 95, 102–3, 113; Second Republic, 15, 16, 355; Secret Study Group, 94; and Soviet Union, 14, 16, 17, 24, 27, 34, 37, 257, 291; Sudetendeutsche in, 8–15, 17–38, 76, 79, 96–99, 102–3, 107, 113–15, 117, 125, 268, 338, 366–67; territory lost to Germany, 7–8, 36; Vlasov Army, 95; war damage in, 259
Czechoslovak Legion, 12
Czech Republic, 2; EU membership of, 327, 342, 357, 358; legal claims against, 326–27, 337–43; see also Czechoslovakia
Czernin, Eugen, 341

Dachau concentration camp, 118, 130, 151, 310–11
Daladier, Edouard, 14
"Danubius" (Mylnárik), 354–55, 357
Danzig, 45, 46, 76, 77, 108
Danzig–West Prussia, 46, 50–51
Darfur, 68
Dastich, František, 103, 186
Davies, Norman, 161, 280
Debrecen internment camp, 136
Deutsche Volksliste, 55–57, 59, 61, 135, 245, 260, 275, 277–78
Deutsche Volksunion, 156
Deutschstämmige, 56
Dewey, John, 294
Djilas, Milovan, 116, 281
Dmowski, Roman, 24
Dobrzyńska, Marta, 218

Dragojlović, Jana, 156
Dreithaler, Rudolf, 338, 339, 357
Drobner, Bolesław, 270
Drozda, V., 107
Drtina, Prokop, 22
Dubiański, Wacław, 140
Duchosal, Jean, 141
Duda, Emma, 229, 249
Duda, Teodor, 155
Duff, Sheila Grant, 292
Duriš, Julius, 260
Dyborski, Mirosław, 277
Dymek, Walenty, 44

East Prussia, 77; and Poland, 24, 76, 82, 86, 88; resettlement of, 262; *Volksdeutsche* from, 200, 225
Economic Cooperation Administration, 317, 318
Edelman, Marek, 360
Eden, Anthony, 21, 23, 24–25, 28, 74, 83, 85, 87, 88, 112
Edgcumbe, Oliver, 213, 214
Eggers, Paul, 191
Egit, Jakub, 273–74
Eichmann, Adolf, 50, 51, 161
Eigi, Irma, 53
Einsatzgruppen, 45
Eisenhower, Dwight D., 128, 156
Emmet, Christopher, 294
Erdei, Ferenc, 208
Erskine, G. W. E. J. "Bobby," 159, 205–6
Europe, postwar, redrawing the map of, 66–67, 74
European Convention on Human Rights, 336, 338, 341–42
European Union: Charter of Fundamental Rights, 326; Lisbon Treaty, 326; membership in, 327, 342, 357, 358, 367
European unity, 316–17, 325
Expellee League (*Bund der Vertriebenen*), 359
Expellees' and Disenfranchised People's Bloc, 316, 317–19

Fehrenbach, Heide, 350–51
Fenyö, Miksa, 211
Fierlinger, Zdeněk, 97, 119, 152, 235
Filipovo internment camp, 146, 153
Fischer, Gyula, 213
Fischer, Otakar, 104
Fisher, Allan, 32, 33
Fladda, Lisbeth, 250
Foot, Michael, 241, 291, 295
Forster, Albert, 50–51
France: and ACC agreement, 124, 125, 198, 305; and Alsace-Lorraine, 69–70, 85; classification scheme in, 69–70; Czechoslovakia abandoned by, 7, 11, 14; fifth column fears in, 43; German population in, 297–99; and Munich, 7, 11, 14, 15, 17; and occupation zone, 125, 305; and World War I, 68; and World War II, 17
Franco-Prussian War (1870), 69
Frank, Hans, 334
Frank, Karl Hermann, 13, 27, 35, 95
Frank, Matthew, 289
Franklin, Andrew, 200, 201, 205
Friedrich, Jörg, *Der Brand (The Fire)*, 359
Frommer, Benjamin, 37, 244, 246
Frowein, Jochen, 342, 343, 344, 370
Frydruch, Josef, 248
Fulbrook, Mary, *History of Germany 1918–2008*, 2
Fye, John H., 147, 164–65, 186, 189, 192, 198, 222, 227, 304, 369

Gabzdilová, Soňa, 4
Gakowa internment camp, 137, 146, 237
Galbraith, John Kenneth, 317
Garbett, Cyril, Archbishop of York, 289
Gardiner, Gerald, 118
Gascoigne, A. D. F., 209
Gęborski, Czesław, 141, 155, 156
Gedye, G.E.G. (Eric), 148, 238, 240, 292
Geiger, Vladimir, 4
Geneva Conventions, 138, 149, 286, 333
genocide, 68, 70, 329, 335

Gerlach, David, 265
German Democratic Republic: borders of, 324; formation of, 324–25
German Federal Republic: economic growth of, 321; formation of, 62, 154, 316, 321, 351; and *Landsmannschaften*, 316–20, 348; *Lastenaugsleich* in, 318–19, 321, 323; *see also* Germany
German Historical Museum Foundation, 361
Germanness, determination of, 49, 56–58, 60, 61, 65, 78, 231–33, 244–46, 351
Germany: Allied Control Council, 111, 124, 363; *see also* ACC agreement; and *Anschluss*, 13, 14, 41; Berlin Wall (1961), 325; borders of, 74, 82–83, 87, 227, 274, 319, 352, 364; British zone, 125, 161, 162–64, 168–70, 173–75, 177, 180, 192, 197–206, 209, 217–22, 307–8; Center Against Expulsions, 359–62; Communist Party (KPD) in, 123–24, 274, 319, 322; concentration camps in, 74, 89, 127, 130–57, 323; cost of resettlement borne by, 78; Criminal Police investigation (1940), 44; Czech-German declaration (1997), 357–58; denazification in, 302; deportations to, 15, 18–21, 23–24, 46–52, 66, 70, 76–77, 85, 89, 90, 91, 150, 192–93, 303; *see also* "organized expulsions"; "wild expulsions"; duty of silence in, 353–54; East, *see* German Democratic Republic; ethnic cleansing within, 39, 40, 41, 228; euthanasia program "T-4" in, 49; evacuations to, 63, 112, 119–20; expellees assimilated in, 302, 307–9, 311–25; expellees repulsed at borders, 100–101; financial claims of, 360; French zone, 125, 305; *Generalplan Ost*, 41, 60, 349; *Heimatfilme*, 350–51, 352; *Heim ins Reich*, 46–52, 60, 124; *Kristallnacht* (1938), 361; and *Lebensraum*, 43; memory and forgetting, 349–52, 357–58; Nazi atrocities in, 116, 320, 347, 353, 371; Nazi Party in, 13, 228, 315; Nazi Reich in, 3, 7, 32, 73, 78, 94, 232, 275, 286, 332, 337–38, 349, 350, 368; Nazi-Soviet Pact, 27, 39, 41, 45, 48, 52, 81, 256; occupation statutes in, 312–13; and *Ostpolitik*, 352–53, 356; payback for war, 66, 80, 90, 92, 95–98, 132, 146–48, 240–42, 286–89, 296, 314, 340, 342, 344, 347, 351–52, 357, 360, 364, 367–68, 369–71; postwar economy of, 78, 89, 150–51, 193, 209, 299, 301–3, 307–8, 310, 317, 321–25; postwar generation in, 352–54; reparations payments from, 77, 259, 337–38, 371; reunification of, 325, 356; Soviet zone, 125, 128, 161–62, 163, 164, 169, 170–71, 175, 177, 186–88, 192, 200–203, 215–17, 221, 223–26, 306–7, 308, 321–25; SS protected in, 286; Supreme Allied Authority in, 77; territorial losses of, 11, 319, 364; territories absorbed by, 7–8, 14, 41, 43; U.S. zone, 125, 159, 164–66, 182, 186, 187, 189–90, 192, 198–99, 206–7, 208, 211–14, 217, 219, 222–23, 226, 303, 307; West, *see* German Federal Republic; and World War I, 11, 68, 70, 301, 328–29; and World War II, 90, 95, 207, 330, 334
Gibson, John, 299
Glassheim, Eagle, 99, 282
Glotz, Peter, 361
Glubczyce assembly camp, 181, 226
Goebbels, Joseph, 7, 19, 42, 43, 44
Goering, Hermann, 49
Gollancz, Victor, 241, 289, 368
Goltermann, Svenja, 351
Gomułka, Władysław, 83, 155, 261, 273
Gorochov, S. N., 186
Gottwald, Klement, 30, 182, 348
Grass, Günter, *Im Krebsgang (Crabwalk)*, 359
Great Britain, *see* Britain
Great Depression, 12
Great War, *see* World War I
Greece: Communist Party of, 72; and League of Nations, 330; Macedonian

Slavs in, 331; Nazi occupation of, 287; temporary camps in, 74; and Turkey, 18, 31, 47, 70–72, 73, 76, 85
Greiser, Arthur, 50–51, 55, 59
Grew, Joseph, 209
Grigg, Sir James, 79–80
Gronowo internment camp, 236
Grossman, Marc, 327
Grotius, Hugo, 327, 328
Growse, Lieutenant Colonel P. F. A., 173, 369
Grzeszczak, Pawel, 276
Guderian, Heinz, 54
Gyöngyösi, János, 208, 209
Gypsies: persecution of, 15, 39; property of, 112

Haake, Claudia, 68
Hácha, Emil, 15, 16
Haffner, Sebastian, 293
Hagibor internment camp, 146, 151–52, 238, 240, 292
Hague Conventions, 328–29, 330, 333, 343
Haider, Jörg, 359
Halifax, Lord Edward, 15
Hankel, Gerd, 329
Hankey, Robin, 182–83, 201, 272, 346–47
Hanley, M., 216
Hapsburg Empire, 12
Harmon, Ernie, 107
Harriman, Averell, 83–84
Harris, Sir Arthur, 156
Harris, David, 126
Hartmann, Ida, 250
Harvey, Oliver, 88
Hauk, Lydia, 249–50
Havel, František, 103
Havel, Václav, 356–57
Healey, Denis, 30, 370
Heimann, Mary, 15
Heim ins Reich, 46–52, 60, 124
Henderson, Sir Nevile, 72
Henlein, Konrad, 12–13, 25, 26, 27, 34, 35
Henry VIII, king of England, 269

Herrenvolk, 63
Heydrich, Reinhard, 21–23, 50, 51, 56, 59
Hilberg, Raul, 59
Himmler, Heinrich, 21, 41, 45, 47, 48–49, 50, 52, 54, 55, 56, 60, 69, 230, 231
Hindenburg, Paul von, 39
Hindus, Maurice, 291
Hirsch, Helga, 361
Hitler, Adolf, 309, 360; anti-Semitism of, 183; and Czechoslovakia, 7, 13, 14, 18, 25, 34, 208; and *Heim ins Reich*, 46–52; *Mein Kampf*, 42; opposition to, 26, 35, 293; and Poland, 45, 46–47, 82, 233; and population transfers, 21, 31, 32, 39, 40–43, 46, 49, 64, 65, 72, 73, 94, 156, 160; rise to power, 12, 13, 17, 301, 305; "second book" of, 42; and World War II, 19, 33, 42, 87, 296
Hitler Youth, 236–37, 245
Hohne (Bergen-Belsen) displaced persons camp, 185
Holliday, Leonard, 262, 270–71, 276–77
Holocaust, 159, 161, 267, 347; and final solution, 39; revisionists, 3–4, 156; survivors, 182, 185, 199, 234–35, 274
Holocaust Memorial, Berlin, 359
Hook, Sidney, 294
Hoover, Herbert, 28
Horkheimer, Max, 369
Hrabáček, Josef, 96
Hrabčík, František, 119
Hrabovec, Emilia, 268
Hradišt'ko internment camp, 146, 239
Hrdlička, Josef, 120–21
Hrneček, Wenzel, 130, 132–34, 139, 154–55
Hughes, Michael, 319
Hull, Cordell, 83
humanitarian agencies, 94, 221–22; and payback to Germans for war, 296; Red Cross, *see* CICR
Hungary: and ACC(H), 166–68, 207, 209, 210, 212–14; Communist Party of, 208, 210, 215–16; fifth column fears in, 61, 323; and League of Nations, 330; as Nazi

Hungary (continued)
  client state, 51, 207, 209; and population transfers, 1, 63, 90, 192, 198, 206, 208–17, 223, 338, 356, 366; and Potsdam, 111, 207, 209; property confiscated in, 207–10, 215, 216, 255, 260; *Volksdeutsche* in, 38, 61, 91, 125, 207–10; and war reparations, 259
Hus, Jan, 268
Hynd, John, 199, 219, 243

Ignatieff, Michael, 365
Industrial Revolution, 67
International Covenant on Human Rights and its Optional Protocol, 339–40
International Criminal Court, the Hague, 327, 344
International Declaration on the Rights of the Child, 240
International Refugee Organization (IRO), 240–41, 252, 296
International Transfer Commission, 89, 91
Iran, ethnic Germans in, 111
Iraq, forced migration in, 68
Ireland: and Act of Resettlement, 67; neutrality of, 296; Northern, Catholics in, 331
Israel: Ministry of Justice, 156; West Bank and Gaza, 371
Italy, 41, 48, 331

Jaksch, Wenzel, 13, 15, 20, 21, 25–26, 33–36, 37–38, 114, 117, 291, 292–93
Janisch, Johanna, 109
Janjetović, Zoran, 4
Janko, V., 113
Jaworzno internment camp, 138–39, 141, 145, 154, 250
Jenkins, Gareth, 71
Jews: and anti-Semitism, 24, 32, 182; in concentration camps, 22, 35, 156, 274; and ethnic cleansing, 39, 49, 50, 51, 60; forced migration of, 68, 101, 211, 334, 367; and Holocaust, *see* Holocaust; identification of, 45; *Kristallnacht*, 361; and League of Nations, 330; massacres of, 45, 58, 60, 182, 199, 267, 356, 362; in mixed marriages, 248; and "organized expulsions," 158–59, 181–85; persecution of, 15, 40, 243, 255, 297; property confiscated, 49, 52, 53, 255, 260, 267; and written history, 349
John Paul II, Pope (Karol Wojtyła), 356
John XXIII, Pope, 356
Jordan, Edgar, 190
Joubert de la Ferté, Sir Philip, 289
Jowitt, Lord William, 124
Junkers, 80

Kaczyński, Lech, 360
Kaisersteinbruch reception camp, 306
Kaławsk assembly camp, 175, 177, 180, 218, 219, 223, 224, 226, 293
Kanaar, Adrian, 117–18
Kapoun, Josef, 98
Kardelj, Edvard, 281
Karp, William, 214
Katyń Forest massacre, 87, 256
Kaufmann, Chaim, 372
Keating, Frank, 222
Kemal, Mustafa "Atatürk," 70, 329
Kenchington, Arthur G., 202
Kent, Martha, 249, 353
Key, William, 213
Kielce, pogrom in, 182, 199
Kilgore, Harley, 294
Kimche, Jon, 291
Kinsner, Edmund, 179, 180
Klapálek, Karel, 188
Klaus, Václav, 2, 326–27, 342
Kleist, Ludwika von, 60
Klingler, Evžen, 292–93
Klug, Frau, 309
Klukowski, Zygmunt, 57, 58, 61, 62
Kohl, Helmut, 356, 357, 358
Kołakowski, Leszek, 360
Konev, Ivan, 63

Koppe, Wilhelm, 52–53
Kopřiva, Ladislav, 242
Kostka, Gertrud, 284–85
Kostka, Johannes, 284–85
Koszalin internment camp, 137, 176
Kovács, Imre, 207–8
Kraft, Claudia, 116
Kraft, Waldemar, 316, 317–19
Kraków, pogrom in, 182
Krauss, Marita, 325
Krejčí, Jaroslav, 259
Kreysa, Miroslav, 186
Kristallnacht, 361
Kruppstrasse camp (Berlin), 303
Kruševlje internment camp, 137, 145, 237, 238
Krut, Aleksy, 140
Kučera, Antonín, 185, 187
Kundt, Ernst, 35
Kunert, H. and J., 101–2
Kuźmicki, Kazimierz, 179
Kvashnin, Aleksandr Petrovich, 202–3
Kwaśniewski, Aleksander, 341, 360

Lambert, H. W., 188, 189
Łambinowice detention camp, 134, 141, 155
Landrock, Kurt, 155
Landsmannschaften (Homeland Societies), 316–20, 348
Lane, Arthur Bliss, 126–28
Laner, Anna, 189
Lange, Gunter, 103
Langenbacher, Eric, 353
Lansing, Robert, 329
Lanškroun, "People's Tribunal" in, 96
Laski, Harold, 29
Lausanne, Treaty of, 18, 70–72, 73, 74, 78
law: bills of indictment, postwar, 334; and crimes against humanity, 327, 329–30, 334; Czech law No. 115 (1946), 370; doctrine of estoppel, 342–43; doctrine of universal jurisdiction, 327–28; grounds of admissibility, 344; Hague Conventions, 328–29, 330, 333, 343; and humanitarian agencies, 328, 333; international human rights, 327–33, 344, 371; and *jus cogens* ("customary international law"), 335–36; legal claims for restitution, 326, 336–43, 360; and Lisbon Treaty, 326–27; Minority Protection Treaties, 330–32, 333; and precedent, 344–45; Rome Statute of ICC, 344; and September 11 attacks, 345; and state sovereignty, 328; "Sudeten corollary," 344–45; takings by the state, 326, 337–38, 340; two-tier justice system, 371–72; Universal Declaration of Human Rights, 332–33, 334–35, 336; and warfare, 328–30, 334, 343
League of Nations, 14, 26, 29, 42, 71, 72, 88, 182, 330–33; Minority Protection Treaties, 330–32, 333
Lebedev, Viktor, 273
Lehndorff, Hans von, 351
Leipzig, *Reichsbericht* in, 329
Ležáky massacre, 22, 23
Lias, Godfrey, 262–63, 291
Liberec detention center, 190–91
Lidice massacre, 22–23, 231, 370
Lieberman, Avigdor, 371
Linek, Bernard, 4
Linzervorstadt concentration camp, 132–34, 139, 152, 154
Lipiński, Józef, 180, 181
Lipski, Jan Józef, 355
Lisbon Treaty (2009), 2, 326–27
Lithuania: German occupation of, 41; Soviet control of, 46, 51; *Volksdeutsche* in, 40–41; and World War I, 68
Litoměřice children's camp, 237
Llewellin, J. J., 1st Baron, 241
Lloyd George, David, 8
Loch, Doctor, 194–96
Łoziński, Kazimierz, 58
Lublin, Polish government in, 81–83, 87, 88, 259, 260
Lutomski, Paweł, 356

Mabbott, John, 73–74
Macardle, Dorothy, 251
Macartney, C. A., 28
Magyars, 8, 9, 10, 14
Majdanek detention camp, 134
Malik, Gerhard, 339–41, 342, 344
Mann, Michael, 372
Mann, Walter, 308–9
Manstein, Erich von, 54
Marek, Bohuslav, 236
Mareš, Michael, 95
Marienthal transit camp, 158–59, 177, 194–97, 217–18
Marshall Plan, 317
Martin, Magdalena, 250
Martin, Terry, 40
Masaryk, Jan, 27, 150, 182, 242–43
Masaryk, Tomáš Garrigue, 7–8, 9, 10, 11, 17, 18, 147, 355
Maschmann, Melita, 52–53
Matthews, Harrison Freeman "Doc," 118
Mauthausen concentration camp, 22, 211, 235
Mayer, Eric, 223
Mayhew, Christopher, 154
Mazower, Mark, 69, 331
McCormick, Anne O'Hare, 294, 295, 298–99
McLaren, Meryn, 311
McNeil, Hector, 241–42
Mearsheimer, John, 371
Melina, Emilie, 103–4
Menzel, Walter, 150
Merkel, Angela, 360–61
Mevius, Michael, 216
Meziměstí assembly camp, 188
Miklós, Béla, 166, 208, 214
Mikołajczyk, Stanisław, 81, 84, 86, 87, 102, 275, 293
Milik, Karol, 268
Minc, Hilary, 258
Mindszenty, Jószef Cardinal, 211, 249
Mirošov detention camp, 139–41, 143, 146
Mitrany, David, 32–33

Mlynárik, Jan "Danubius," 354–55, 357
Mock, Pierre W., 144–45
Modřany internment camp, 229
Modzelewski, Zygmunt, 220
Moeller, Robert, 349, 351, 352
Molotov, Vyacheslav, 215, 217, 257, 274
Mommsen, Hans, 349
Montandon, Willy, 229
Moorhouse, Roger, 161, 280
Moravia: deportations into, 15; German occupation of, 15, 19, 22; provisional government, 8; *Sudetendeutsche* in, 58
Morel, Salomon, 140, 155–56
Morzycki, Jerzy, 262
Moscow Conference (1944), 83, 84, 112
Mountevans, E. E., 1st Baron, 241
Moynier, Gustave, 329
Mulaj, Klejda, 116
Müller, Heiner, *The Resettler Woman*, 348
Muller, Jean-Léon, 209
Müller, Karl Valentin, 354
Munich Conference (1938), 7–9, 11, 14–18, 26, 27, 35, 40, 61, 117, 290, 292, 320, 367
Murdock, Caitlin, 283
Murphy, Robert, 118, 126, 127
Mussolini, Benito, 41, 48
Mydlovary labor colony, 134

Nagy, Ferenc, 208, 214
Nagy, Imre, 210
Naimark, Norman, 355
Namier, Lewis, 290
National Peace Council, 287
Nationalsozialistische Arbeitsbewegung, 43
nation-state, rise of, 67
"nations" vs. "states," 30–31
Nazi-Soviet Pact, 27, 39, 41, 45, 48, 52, 81, 256
neo-Nazis, 353
Netherlands: fifth column fears in, 43, 60; Free Netherlands forces, 60
Neubauer, Mgr. Josef, 133
Neu-Gablonz (new town), 311–12
Nicholas II, tsar of Russia, 39, 328

Nichols, Philip, 18, 21, 34, 115, 147, 149, 235, 243, 266
Nickel, James, 373
Nicolson, Harold, 8
Nigeria, slavery in, 67
Nitschke, Bernadetta, 4, 108, 128, 224
Noel-Baker, Philip, 26, 29
Norway, 245, 298
Nosek, Václav, 97, 98–99, 138, 223, 235, 238, 279
Novák, Zdeněk, 147
Nováky internment camp, 144–45, 239
Novotný, Antonín, 348
Nuremberg, refugee camps in, 311
"Nuremberg defense," 329–30
Nuremberg Laws, 293, 318, 336, 343
Nuremberg trials, 288–89, 329–30, 334, 343

Oberländer, Theodor, 319
observation camps, 60
Old Testament, 67
Olejnik, Leszek, 148
Olejník, Milan, 4
O'Neill, Con, 81, 201, 211
Operation Barbarossa, 51
Operation Honeybee, 125
Operation Swallow, 168–74, 183, 184–85, 196–206, 212, 217–22, 264, 369
Ordzhonikidze, Sergo, 40
"organized expulsions," 158–93; and ACC agreement, 125, 160, 162, 164, 166–68; of aged and "undesirables," 168–69, 171, 172–76, 188–90, 200, 226; of antifascists, 191–92, 338; to British zone, 161, 162–64, 168–70, 173–75, 177, 180, 192; chaos in, 159–61, 171, 173–76, 178, 180, 181, 187, 210–11; Combined Repatriation Executive (CRX), 160–63, 172–74, 177, 192; and deaths, 160, 165, 168, 169, 178–79, 180, 187, 190–91, 394; and disease, 174, 177, 179, 188, 303; end of, 187, 192–93, 217, 226–28; and food, 166, 167, 168, 169–70, 171, 173, 177, 178, 210; hazards in, 178–81, 188, 224; media observers of, 166–67, 171; negotiations for, 161–66; Operation Swallow, 168–74, 183, 184–85, 196–206, 212, 217–22, 264, 369; "out of turn," 176–77, 178; poor treatment in, 168–69, 170, 173, 190; procedures in, 175, 186, 188; and Red Cross, 165, 184, 191; rejections of, 166, 177, 225; and resettlement, 160–61, 165, 186, 254–83; scams in, 159, 177, 179, 181, 189–90, 200–201, 276–77; to Soviet zone, 161–62, 163, 164, 169, 170–71, 175, 177, 186–88, 192, 223–26; start dates for, 161–63, 165, 187; to transit camps, 163, 165, 168, 170, 173–74, 175, 176, 178–81, 186, 190, 192–93, 303–6; transport in, 158–59, 160–64, 167, 169, 172, 174, 175, 177–78, 180, 187–88, 190, 191–92; to U.S. zone, 159, 164–66, 182, 186, 187, 189–90, 192; "young thugs" involved in, 170; and Zionists, 158–59, 181–85
Orwell, George, 86, 280
Osóbka-Morawki, Edward, 183
Ottoman Empire, 68, 70

Palestine: Arabs and Jews in, 72; destination for bogus expellees, 159, 181–85
Paris Peace Conference, 7, 8, 9, 13–14, 18, 31
Paris Reparations Conference, 259
Parker, John, 29
Parker, Ralph, 291
Parragi, György, 211
Patrónka internment camp, 137, 141
Patton, George S., 37, 63
Pazúr, Karol, 155
Peace of Westphalia, 328
Peace Pledge Union, 288
Pearl Harbor, 59, 73
Pechman, Bohumil, 143
Peel Commission (1936), 72
Pepper, Claude, 292
Perkins, Harold, 96
Pethick-Lawrence, Frederick, 86

Petržalka internment camp, 144, 239
Pfeiffer, Jean, 123
Phayer, Michael, 44, 297
Philip II of Macedonia, 67
Piłsudski, Józef, 42
Pitter, Přemysl, 234–35, 242–43, 244, 368
Pius XII, Pope, 297
Pogány, István, 340, 343
Pohořelice, internment camps, 99
Poland: borders of, 24, 74, 82–83, 86, 88, 90, 274, 356; Church in, 267–68, 297, 356; Communist Party in, 83, 244, 261, 270, 274, 324, 366; and Curzon Line, 72, 87; ethnic cleansing in, 267–68, 349; euthanasia in, 49; fifth column fears in, 43–44, 59–60, 323; *Generalgouvernement*, 46, 51, 57–58, 63, 82, 135, 260, 334; German invasion of, 35, 42–44, 45, 360, 367; German occupation of, 45, 46, 108, 230, 259, 268, 275, 370; government in exile, 24, 25, 75, 81, 84, 87, 259, 334; Incorporated Eastern Territories, 46, 49–50, 52–55, 57, 61, 63, 233, 260, 275; memory and forgetting, 355–56, 358–60; minority populations in, 330–32; National Security Office, 104–5; and Oder-Neisse line, 24, 81, 82, 89, 91, 128, 267, 324, 356; People's Militia, 136, 224; Population Transfer Commission, 77–79; population transfers from, 1, 2, 23–25, 32, 45–47, 49–50, 52, 62–63, 74–75, 78–85, 86, 87, 90, 93, 94, 103–5, 108–10, 112, 116–17, 123–24, 126–28, 167–82, 192, 198, 203, 206, 217–21, 224–26, 369; population transfers to, 44, 47, 258; and postwar planning, 258, 259; and Potsdam, 111; and propaganda, 293, 348, 350; property confiscated in, 49–50, 52, 255, 258, 259–60, 275–78, 282, 337; PUR agency, 174–76, 179, 181, 224, 226, 276, 278, 282; Recovered Territories, *see* Recovered Territories; revenge against, 45; *Selbstschutz* militias in, 58; "September Campaign" in, 43–44; and Soviet Union, 24, 41, 45–46, 48, 75, 81–83, 87, 225–26, 256; territories ceded to, 11, 23, 25, 74–75, 81, 84, 85, 87, 88, 89, 90, 93; underground in, 60; *Volksdeutsche* in, 38, 41, 42–45, 47, 48, 49, 69, 73, 91, 125, 135, 366; Warsaw Ghetto rising (1943), 360; Warsaw Uprising (1944), 256

Pomerania: interim camps in, 51, 144; as Polish territory, 93

Popovice (Pfaffendorf) internment camp, 137

Pöppendorf transit camp, 163, 168, 170, 369

population transfers, 1–6; aftershocks of, 225–28; Allied complicity in, 23–25, 27–33, 36, 64, 65, 66–67, 73, 78–79, 88, 125, 127, 193, 286, 296, 302, 332, 333–34, 343, 363, 368–69, 373; chaos of, 66, 89, 198, 303, 305–6; and cultural identity, 316; death toll in, 1–2, 44, 62, 195–97, 218, 225, 306; *Dokumentation* of, 348–50, 352, 361; economic effects of, 77, 78, 101, 193, 227, 279–83, 301–3, 364, 372–73; as ethnic cleansing, 39–41, 68–69, 96–99, 227–28, 230–31, 267–68, 373; failures of program, 60, 186–87, 364; and food, 89, 195, 204; and forced labor, 54, 111, 112, 120–21, 180, 181, 193, 208, 277, 337; future probability of, 348; *Heim ins Reich*, 46–52; human rights abuses in, 227–28, 368, 373; human suffering in, 63, 94, 116, 194–97, 211, 224, 373; and incoming colonists, 39, 41, 43, 47, 48, 49, 53–55, 60, 88, 313–15; inefficiency of, 49, 50–52, 304; "inevitability" thesis, 364–66; international reaction to, 284–300; to internment camps, 96, 99, 104, 106–7, 112, 117–18, 122, 123, 127, 130–57; and jobs, 66, 311–13, 320–21; lack of preparation for, 65–66, 74, 94, 302–5; and the law, *see* law; memory and forgetting, 350–62; and mixed marriages, 48, 231–32, 244–48; and moral issues, 118–19, 127, 289, 294, 352, 365, 368–70; numbers of, 195, 201–4, 217,

219–23, 225–26; opposition to, 32–33, 46–47, 288, 294–95, 359–62, 372–73; "orderly and humane," 90, 91, 93, 129, 204–6, 211, 219, 226, 285, 296, 372; overlooked in history, 2–6, 62, 325, 352–54; and political mobilization, 315–20; and property confiscation, 30, 47–48, 49–50, 52–55, 65, 78, 98, 101, 105–6, 112, 148, 161, 186, 248, 254–61, 319, 337–38, 364; and resettlement, 66, 160–61, 165, 186, 254–83, 301–25; rewriting history, 371–72; and right of return, 319, 373; the scheme, 65–92; scholarly defense of, 364; solving minority problems via, 371–72; statistics unreliable on, 63, 65, 99, 201–4, 209–10, 219–20; transport for, 66, 74, 78, 89, 198, 223–24; and vigilante violence, 59–60, 95–96, 104, 105; in wartime, 47, 62; *see also* "organized expulsions"; "wild expulsions"

Postoloprty internment camp, 96, 236–37

Potsdam Conference (1945), 89–92, 188, 223, 350; and Czechoslovakia, 101, 111, 115; fifth anniversary of, 316–17; and Hungary, 111, 207, 209; and the law, 327, 334, 343; "orderly and humane" transfers under, 90, 91, 93, 129, 204–6, 211, 219, 226, 285, 296, 372; and resettlement, 274; and "wild expulsions," 107, 115, 116, 117, 119, 123–24, 126, 127

Potulice internment camp, 138, 141–42, 143–44, 238, 240, 249, 346, 353

"Prague Spring" (1968), 354

Prášil, Karel, 96

Prawin, Jakub, 205, 220–21, 223

Přerov massacre, 155

Příhoda, Petr, 281

Putin, Vladimir, 327

Qing Empire, China, 67
Quinn, Marjorie, 96

Raack, R. C., 82
racial purity, 32–33, 41, 43, 45, 47

Rădescu, Nicolae, 111, 112
Radio Warsaw, 201
Rákosi, Mátyas, 211, 215, 217
Randolph, A. Philip, 294
Ranzenhoferová, Marie, 99
Rapp, Wilhelm, 313
Raška, Francis, 25
Rau, Heinrich, 323
Recovered Territories, Poland: children in, 234; and Czechoslovakia, 107; denial of expulsions in, 350; expellees' claims in, 341; German occupation of, 108; and internment camps, 135, 150; and numbers, 192, 202–4, 219, 258, 261–62, 279; and "organized expulsions," 159, 161, 164, 167–68, 169, 170–71, 174, 178, 192, 199, 200; and "wild expulsions," 104–5, 109, 117, 119, 124, 126, 128, 293; and "Wild West," 254, 258, 263, 269, 271–75, 279, 280–81, 282

Red Army: civilian flight from, 1, 61, 62, 75, 79, 81, 88, 103, 350; Czechoslovakia liberated by, 37, 257; in Hungary, 208; and internment camps, 135, 141, 226; and Katyń Forest massacre, 87, 256; and "organized expulsions," 169, 171, 175, 178, 187, 188, 225; and Warsaw Uprising (1944), 256; and "wild expulsions," 105, 107–9, 111, 119, 121, 128, 270; and "Wild West," 264, 267, 270, 271–74

Red Army Faction, 2
Red Cross, *see* CICR
Rees, Goronwy, 287
Reich citizenship, 61
Reich Commissariat for the Strengthening of Germandom (RKFDV), 47, 49, 50, 56
Reichsdeutsche, 54, 55, 57–58, 61–62
religion, as mark of identity, 71
Renaissance, 327
Rendel, Sir George, 184
Ribbentrop, Joachim von, 41
Riđica labor camp, 141, 145
Ripka, Hubert, 14, 18, 25, 26, 34, 37, 258, 287, 292, 332

Roberts, Frank, 25, 35
Robertson, Sir Brian, 185, 205, 297
Rokossovsky, Konstantin, 273
Roman Empire, end of, 49
Romania: citizenship in, 112; Communist Party in, 112; evacuations from, 63; fifth column fears in, 59–60, 61; forcible removals from, 1, 93, 110, 111; land lying idle in, 278–79; and League of Nations, 330; minority populations in, 330; Soviet control of, 41; territory ceded by, 51–52; *Volksdeutsche* in, 61, 111–13, 153
Roosevelt, Eleanor, 294, 334–35
Roosevelt, Franklin D., 17, 24, 27–28, 75, 83, 84, 86, 87, 88, 94
Rosenberg, Alfred, 41
Rothfels, Hans, 361
Rothschild, Joseph, 2
Rudolfsgnad (Kničanin) internment camp, 137, 154, 156
Runge, Max, 250
Rupa (Prague) internment camp, 239
Russell, Bertrand, 288–89
Russian Revolution, 40
Ruthenia, 8, 36, 208
Rwanda, Radio Mille Collines, 366
Ryan, Stephen, 372

Salem witch trials, 115
Salzgitter concentration camp, 222
Samokhvalov, Nikita S., 104
Sargent, Sir Orme, 76, 111, 149, 200
Sassie, C., 216–17
Save Europe Now, 289, 293
Savery, Frank, 172
Saxony, interim camps in, 51
Scandinavia, German invasion of, 245
Schechtman, Joseph, 48
Schieder, Theodor, 348–50, 351
Schily, Otto, 361
Schimanski, Stefan, 369
Schindler, Oskar, 101
Schoenfeld, Rudolf, 84
Schröder, Gerhard, 358, 360

Schulze, Rainer, 352
Schwelb, Egon, 334
Schwiebus, expulsions from, 109
Second Vienna Award, 51
Sekič (Lovčenac) internment camp, 146, 153
September 11 attacks, 345
Seton-Watson, Robert, 290
Sèvres, Treaty of, 70
Shirer, William, 294
Shotwell, James T., 295
Sicherheitsdienst, 43
Sikawa internment camp, 250
Sikorski, Władysław, 24
Silesia, 24, 88, 93, 124, 226, 274, 330
Skerniewice prison, 250
Skowyra, Tadeusz, 140
slavery, and international law, 335
Slavs, ethnic cleansing of, 39
Slovakia: anti-Czech stance of, 15, 35; anti-fascists in, 191; fifth column fears in, 61; as German client state, 232, 367; internment camps in, 236; judicial system of, 343; minority populations in, 8, 14, 137; and Munich, 15, 367; and population transfers, 338, 357; Republic of, 15; *Sudetendeutsche* in, 61, 136
Slovenia, evacuations from, 63
Smutný, Jaromír, 11
Smyrna, sack of, 70, 73
Sobków, Michał, 271
social engineering, 30, 231, 257, 265–66, 372
Society for the Prevention of World War III, 294–95
Sokolovsky, Vasily, 111, 322
Soviet Union: and ACC agreement, 124, 125, 201–3, 305–6; Bolshevik Revolution, 40; Communism in, 17, 355; and Czechoslovakia, 14, 16, 17, 24, 27, 34, 37, 257, 291; ethnic cleansing in, 39–40, 42, 46, 68; expansionism of, 36, 41; Five Year Plans, 273; German invasion of, 35, 287, 367; labor forces in, 76, 111, 112, 135,

208; and Munich, 14; Nazi-Soviet Pact, 27, 39, 41, 45, 48, 52, 81, 256; occupation zone, *see* Germany: Soviet zone; and "organized expulsions," 124–25, 161–62, 163, 164, 169, 170–71, 175, 177, 186–88, 192, 206; and Poland, 24, 41, 45–46, 48, 75, 81–83, 87, 225–26, 256; postwar expectations, 87, 88; Red Army, *see* Red Army; support for expulsion, 26, 27, 29, 73, 74, 90, 92, 93, 111–12; and "wild expulsions," 100, 104–6, 107–8, 111–12, 119–24, 128; and World War II, 20, 73, 87
Spina, Franz, 11
Spottswood, A. D., 210
Spychalski, Marian, 182
Stalag IV C (Wistritz), 101
Stalin, Joseph, 39, 45; and Baltic states, 48–49; and Churchill, 75, 81, 88, 112; and ethnic Germans, 29, 40, 42, 65, 72, 76; and population transfers, 23, 27, 29, 40, 81–84, 90, 261; at Potsdam, 206; and territorial expansion, 24, 36, 41–42, 46, 51; and World War II, 14, 87; at Yalta, 89
Stalingrad, Battle of, 59, 207
Staněk, Tomáš, 4, 115, 128, 239
Steinbach, Erika, 359, 360, 361
Steinberg, Elan, 156
Steinhardt, Laurence, 149, 166
Sternberg, Günther, 158–59
Stettinius, Ed, 86, 88, 332
Stokes, Richard, 151–52, 237, 286
Stout, Rex, 294
Strahovský internment camp, 137
Strang, Sir William, 217
Strauss, George, 32
Stresemann, Gustav, 11
Stuckart, Wilhelm, 318
Suchdol nad Odrou camp, 235, 239–40
Sudetendeutsche, 8–15, 17–38; activists among, 10–11, 12–13; anti-Nazi, 15, 33, 35–36; craftsmen, 135; evacuations of, 63, 76, 117; expulsion of, 15, 18–33, 46, 76, 99–103, 105, 107, 113–15, 199, 332, 338, 354–55; in internment camps, 132–34; jobs for, 311–13; murders of, 96–97, 113; as passive war criminals, 33, 34, 38, 367; Reich citizenship of, 61, 232; women and children, 247–48
Sudetenland: and Czechoslovakia, 8–15, 18, 25; ethnic manipulation in, 10, 40; German takeover of, 7–8, 130; interim camps in, 51; recolonization of, 186, 263, 265–66, 281, 282, 283; and Transfer Commission, 77
Svidník internment camp, 137
Sviridov, Vladimir Petrovich, 213
Svoboda, Ludvík, 98, 102
Svoboda, V., 120
Swanstrom, Msgr. Edward, 221, 230, 252
Sweden: neutrality of, 296; skilled workers imported to, 298
Świdwin assembly camp, 179
Świerczewski, Karol, 108, 109
Świętochłowice-Zgoda concentration camp, 138, 140, 155–56
Switzerland, neutrality of, 296
Szczecin-Gumience assembly camp, 168, 172, 173–74, 175, 178, 179, 197, 218, 219, 234, 293
Szczepanik, Jerzy, 226

Taborsky, Edward, 364
Tanner, Marcus, 67
Targosz, Adam, 181
Târgu Jiu detention camp, 134, 136
Taylor, A. J. P., 28
Tehran Conference (1943), 75
Tenz, Maria, 156
Terrell, Stephen, 117
Teutonic Knights, 350
Ther, Philipp, 306, 323, 324
Theresienstadt concentration camp, 130, 134, 155
Thicknesse, Ralph, 185, 192
Thirty Years' War, 328
Thomas, Norman, 294
Thompson, Dorothy, 294, 295

Thornberry, Patrick, 333, 336
Tito (Josef Broz), 110–11, 116, 122, 136, 151
Tobin, E. M., 195, 196
torture, taboo against, 345
Toynbee, Arnold, 80–81
Tragelehn, B. K., 348
Treffling refugee camp, 311
Trevelyan, G. M., 301
Troutbeck, Jack, 74, 80, 172, 288
Truman, Harry S., 90, 94, 332
Trzciński, Kazimierz, 254–55, 256
Tuplice (Lubusz) assembly camp, 175, 223, 226
Turkey: and Armenian genocide, 70, 329; and Cyprus, 72; ethnic Germans in, 111; and Greece, 18, 31, 47, 70–72, 73, 76, 85; "guest workers" in Germany from, 325; and Soviet Union, 39
Turnu Măgurele camp, 237

Uganda, expulsions from, 336
Ukraine, evacuations from, 63
Ukrainians, Aryanized, 41
United Nations, 77, 88; Charter of, 332; Commission on Human Rights, 334–35, 338, 341, 342, 344; establishment of (1945), 332; Genocide Convention, 335; Relief and Rehabilitation Administration (UNRRA), 78, 182, 184–85, 187, 229, 240, 243, 296; UNICEF, 241; Universal Declaration of Human Rights, 332–33, 334–35, 336
United States: and ACC agreement, 124–28, 164–66, 198, 203–4, 214, 222; and Atlantic Charter, 86; black Americans in, 331, 335; complicity of, 3, 27–28, 32, 73, 74, 81, 83, 84, 86, 92, 93, 94, 296; immigrants assimilated in, 73, 125, 299; and international law, 329, 334–35; Japanese incarcerated in, 73; and Munich, 8, 15, 17; and Native Americans, 67, 73; neutrality of, 17; occupation zone, see Germany: U.S zone; OMGUS, 198, 206–7, 211–12, 222–23; and "organized expulsions," 124–25, 159, 164–66, 182, 186, 187, 189–90, 192, 206–7, 211; and postwar expectations, 87; public opinion in, 293–98; and "wild expulsions," 106, 107, 118, 120–21, 126–28; and World War II, 20, 73, 87
Upper Silesia, 76, 77–78, 88
Ústí nad Labem massacre, 114–16, 365

Vansittart, Lord Robert, 29
Vatican: as court of international arbitration, 328; and expulsions, 297
Veltrusy children's camp, 240
Versailles, Treaty of, 11, 13, 15, 70, 301, 329, 330, 331
Veselý, Alois, 132
Vienna Convention on the Law of Treaties, 335
Villard, Oswald Garrison, 294
Vinogradov, Vladislav, 111, 112
Vogl, E., 235
Voigt, Frederick A., 97, 293
Volksbund, 209
Volksdeutsche, 3, 38, 40–64, 79, 91, 110–11, 150–51, 207, 286, 349, 364
Volksdeutsche Mittelstelle (VoMi), 47
Vollmar, Antje, 361
Voroshilov, Kliment, 166
Vukosavljević, Sreten, 279
Vyvyan, Michael, 346

Walter, Francis E., 296, 297
Wanderbund, 43
Wannsee Conference (1942), 318
war crimes, 3–4, 92; changing definitions of, 73, 329–30; Nuremberg trials, 288–89, 329–30, 334, 343; passive, 33, 34, 38, 60
Warthegau district, 46, 50, 51, 52, 53, 62–63, 81
waterboarding, 345
Waters, Timothy, 344, 345
Weems, George "Pappy," 213–14
Wehler, Hans-Ulrich, 349

Weimar Republic, 11
Welles, Sumner, 28
Wells, H. G., 14
Werewolves, 113–16, 265
Westphalian system, and state sovereignty, 328
Wiedemann, Andreas, 266
Wiesenthal, Simon, 182
"wild expulsions," 91, 93–128, 176, 193; and ACC agreement, 124–28, 202; Allied backlash, 117–19, 126–27; and antifascists, 101–2, 105, 106; arbitrary selections for, 101–3; attempts to return home, 103–4, 128; at border crossings, 104, 107–8, 119, 120–23; "Brno Death March," 98–100, 105, 365; chaos of, 103, 104–6, 111, 112–13, 288, 305; compared to Nazi atrocities, 96–97, 98, 108, 116, 117–19, 126–27, 228, 369; deaths in, 96, 99, 101, 109–10, 117, 120, 122, 129; difficulties of, 99, 100, 104–5, 107–8, 119–23; and disease, 99, 106, 110, 117; humanitarian crisis in, 119–20; to internment camps, 96, 99, 104, 106–7, 112, 117–18, 122, 123, 127, 136–37, 176; and journalists, 117–18, 348; local initiatives in, 104–5; and loss of citizenship, 101, 112–13; myth of, 94–95; and "organized expulsions," 125, 173, 176; pace of, 116–17, 125; passivity of victims in, 113, 115–16, 373; by police and military, 94, 96–97, 100, 105, 106, 107–9, 111, 112, 113, 116, 119–20, 124; and property confiscation, 101, 105–6, 112, 270; and public opinion, 125, 288, 293; and revenge-seeking, 95–96, 287–88; transport for, 109–10, 117–20, 121–24, 125; unclear data on, 96, 99, 128; violence of, 94–98, 104, 105–7, 108, 114–16; and Werewolves, 113–16
"Wild West": churches in, 267–69; economic disruption in, 279–83; gold diggers in, 267, 269–70, 355; lawlessness in, 263–65, 266–67, 270, 277–78; name of, 256–57; population shortages in, 261–66, 278–79, 282; returnees to, 265, 273, 274, 276;
Williamson, Tom, 292
Wilson, Duncan, 206
Wilson, Woodrow, 8, 88, 329
Wilsonianism, 14, 29, 63
Winch, Michael, 272
Wingfield, Nancy, 2
Witte, Eugen de, 33
Wojtyła, Karol (Pope John Paul II), 356
Wolfe, James, 343
Wolff, Stefan, 251, 359, 362
Wolski, Władysław, 161–62, 170, 179, 204, 206, 223, 225
World Council of Churches, 297
World Jewish Congress (WJC), 156
World War I: aims of Allies in, 13, 18; Czechoslovak Legion in, 12; forced migrations of, 68–69; passive civilians in, 367–68; postwar shifts in boundaries, 30–31, 70; and Versailles, 11, 13, 15, 70, 301, 329, 330, 331; and war crimes, 328–29
World War II: Allies in, 17–18, 287; and appeasement, 87; and bills of indictment, 334; and border disputes, 18; destruction in, 90, 259, 359; Dunkirk in, 19; duration of, 37, 95; ethnic cleansing in, 39–41; expansion of, 20; fifth column fears in, 43–44; narratives of, 353–54; onset of, 16, 42, 333; passive civilians in, 368; Peace Conference, 116; population exchanges in, 71, 160; postwar flux, 93–94; reparations for, 77, 259, 337–38, 371; "September Campaign" (1939), 43–44; Stalingrad, 59, 207; V-E Day, 95, 103; and war crimes, 330, 334, 343
World War III, prevention of, 294–95, 366–67
Wrocław assembly camps, 179, 180, 181

Yalta Conference (1945), 81, 87–88, 89
Yugoslavia: ethnic cleansing in, 2, 60, 344, 365; Extraordinary Review Com-

Yugoslavia (continued)
   missions, 136; fifth column fears in, 61, 110; forcible removals from, 1, 63, 68, 93, 110–11, 116, 122–23, 281, 327, 344; German invasion of, 61; lands confiscated in, 279; and League of Nations, 330; *Prinz Eugen* division in, 60; state dissolved, 61; *Volksdeutsche* in, 38, 61, 63, 91, 93, 110–11, 116, 136, 150–51, 200

Ząbkowice Śląskie (Frankenstein) camp, 179

Zahra, Tara, 10, 231
Zámostí internment camp, 134
Zayas, Alfred-Maurice de, 336, 343
Zeman, Miloš, 327, 358, 371
Zeman, Zbyněk, 10
Zhukov, Georgy, 119, 120, 162, 273, 322
Zimne Wody (Kaltwasser) camp, 141
Zionist organizations, 158–59, 181–85, 274, 137
Zipsers, 137
Złotów internment camp, 276
Zorin, Valerian, 119